# NEBRASKA SIGN-POSTS

*Robert Henri's Years on the Great Plains*

ALSO BY PETER OSBORNE

*Images of the Five Mile Woods*
*The Five Mile Woods: A History*
*The Trains of Our Memory: A History of the Railroad Museum of Pennsylvania 1965-2015*
*No Spot in This Far Land Is More Immortalized: A History of Pennsylvania's Washington Crossing Historic Park*
*Where Washington Once Led: A History of New Jersey's Washington Crossing State Park*
*So Many Brave Men: The Battle at Minisink Ford*
- With Mark Hendrickson and Jon Inners -
*Lewis and Clark and Me*
*For Always, Memories of Janis*
*Our Town: Historic Port Jervis 1907-2007*
-With Dan Dwyer -
*Vigilance & Perseverance: The History of the Old Decker Stone House*
*Hail Matamoras: Matamoras, Pennsylvania 1905-2005*
- Compiled and designed –
*Put The Dog on The Phone! The Collected Newspaper Columns of Janis Osborne*
- Compiled and designed –
*The Delaware River Heritage Trail Guide*
*Images of America: Promised Land State Park*
*Images of America: Hacklebarney & Voorhees State Parks, New Jersey*
*Images of America: High Point State Park and the Civilian Conservation Corps*
*We Can Take It! The Roosevelt Tree Army at New Jersey's High Point State Park 1933-1941*

# NEBRASKA SIGN-POSTS

*Robert Henri's Years on the Great Plains*

Peter Osborne

NEBRASKA SIGN-POSTS
Robert Henri's Years on the Great Plains
By Peter Osborne

Published by
The Robert Henri Museum and Art Gallery
Cozad, Nebraska


ISBN 979-8-218-10019-3 (soft cover)
Library of Congress Control Number: 2022920636

BIOGRAPHY & AUTOBIOGRAPHY / Artists, Architects,
ART / Individual Artists
HISTORY / United States / State & Local / Midwest (IA, IL, IN, KS, MI, MN, MO, ND, NE, OH, SD, WI)

Cover and book design by Peter Osborne and The Wild Horse Creek Company
First Edition
10 9 8 7 6 5 4 3 2 1
Printed in the United States of America

Dedicated To

*The visionaries who created*
*The Robert Henri Museum and Historical Walkway*
*and*
*those who have continued with its mission.*

*We go eastward to realize history and study the works of art and literature. Retracing the steps of the race. We go westward as into the future, with a spirit of enterprise and adventure.*[1]

Henry David Thoreau
Henry David Thoreau: A Life of the Mind

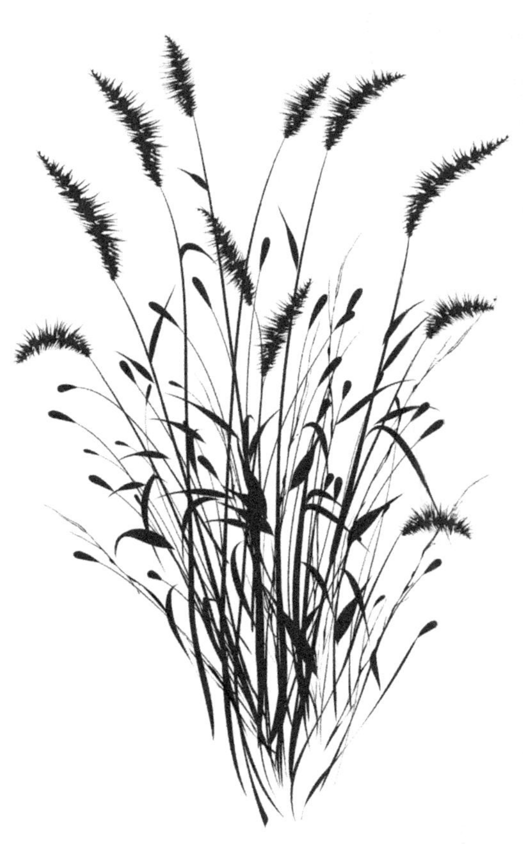

# Contents



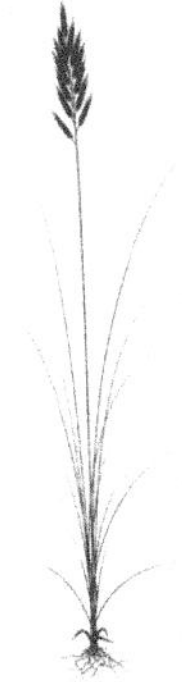

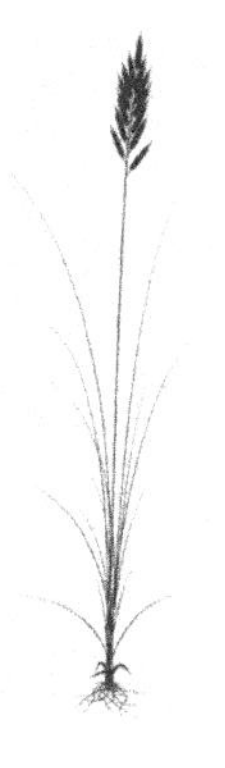

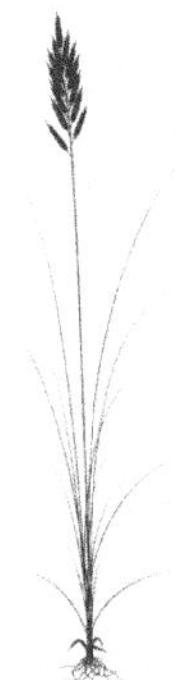

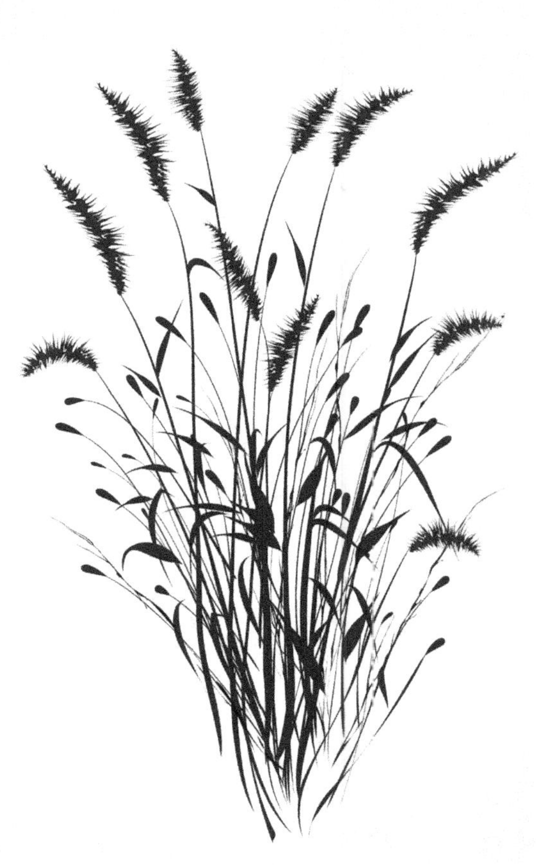

# Foreword

*There are moments in our lives, there are moments in a day, when we seem to see beyond the usual. Such are the moments of our greatest happiness. Such are the moments of our greatest wisdom. If one could but recall his vision by some sort of sign. It was in this hope that the arts were invented. Sign-posts on the way to what may be. Sign-posts toward greater knowledge.*[1]

Robert Henri
The Art Spirit
1923

JUST RIGHT ARE THE TWO WORDS THAT reflect this important time in our museum's history as this book becomes available. As you open it and begin to turn the pages, please sit back to enjoy days of reading, and perhaps be surprised when least expected.

Nestled in the rich Great Platte River Valley is the boyhood home of the internationally acclaimed artist Robert Henri, then known as *Bob Cozad.* One may walk along the river, knowing that Robert left his footprints on either side of the banks. It was to this river that Robert rode his horse Darby and talked to the locals about the beautiful seasons in Cozad, Nebraska. I invite you to travel with me, taking a journey by reading *Nebraska Sign-Posts: Robert Henri's Years on the Great Plains* by Peter Osborne, which navigates you not only along the Platte River, but to the main street of our town of Cozad.

As I write this, I am sitting in the dining room of John and Theresa Cozad where they dined with their sons Johnny and Robert Cozad. I also have the honor to serve as President of the Board of Directors for the Robert Henri Museum and Art Gallery. I am surrounded by those fellow members who are visionaries and can share ideas that come to fruition. It is interesting to hear someone say . . . what if, or do you think it is possible, or wouldn't that be ideal. I find that there is no limit to what comes forth.

This book is one of the projects that came from those various discussions because it has been needed for many years. When Peter asked me to write the foreword for this book, I unquestionably felt honored to have been chosen to express my thoughts on paper.

Sitting at the Cozad dining room table, I lean back to comment on a particular section of the book. But how can one choose any one part? This history reveals so much scholarly research, again, reflective of world travels. So many historical pieces have been found here. In your library, you are now embracing an historic jewel.

I must share, briefly, my personal love for beauty and art. My adventures span the globe, traveling to museums and admiring sculptures, enhanced by architecture. I admired the work of Robert Henri and visited museums all across

the country looking for his work. Yet, being a native Nebraskan, I believe the time he spent here was transformative and stayed with him for the rest of his life. While his biographers have briefly explored the Nebraska chapter, we believe his experience here was a unique one and must have impacted his philosophies and art.

NEBRASKA SIGN-POSTS

Searching for a new director for the museum in 2018 we placed an advertisement on the Nebraska Museum Association's job website. Within a short time, I received a packet in the mail from Peter Osborne with a job resume and list of references, seeking the position. On behalf of the board, I contacted Peter to have an opportunity to meet with him. A date was set up to have him meet with the board members at the museum. Great interview, one board member said to me: *Don't let him get away.*

We offered him the job, and he accepted. Peter was a perfect fit for us with his years of experience as a museum director, historian, writer and lecturer. He is a dependable, dedicated, and effective leader, and brought organizational, communication and interpersonal skills to the Robert Henri Museum and Art Gallery. Peter started the next week after our interview with him, taking on the mission of moving the museum into the next chapter of its storied history.

He is now a Robert Henri historian regarding the Nebraska chapter of the artist's life! And right away in his new job he could not help but think that there is a book (or several books) to be written about Henri, his family and history that would include people who have been involved with bringing the museum to where it is.

Without Peter Osborne there would not have been this book. Through his research as a historian, he unearthed a number of significant finds in personal letters, primary documents, and decades old newspaper articles stored in boxes throughout the museum.

Finally, we owe a debt of gratitude to the original board of directors who had the foresight to make this, the former home and hotel of John Jackson Cozad into the Robert Henri Museum. We owe that same debt of gratitude to museum staff and volunteers for their years of passion and dedication to this museum. Each has played a critical role in making the Robert Henri Museum and Art Gallery what it is today.

Share your findings with those you love, the brush is dipped in rich colors and the *Legacy* belongs to you.

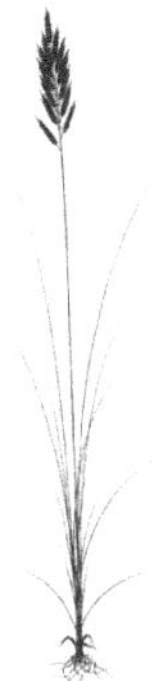

Marlene Jensen Geiger
President
Robert Henri Museum and Art Gallery

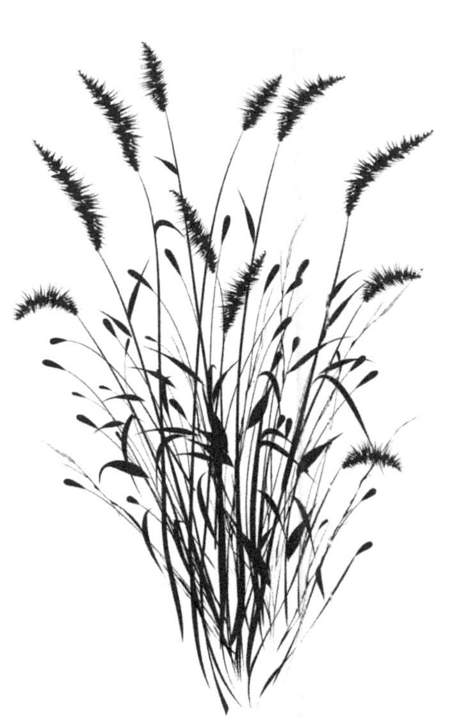

# Introduction

*When we started the entire project, we didn't have any idea it would grow into such a large undertaking. But one thing always leads to something else so you can't just pass that by. It gets included to improve the project.*[1]

Shirley Paulsen

Leader of the Effort to Restore the Robert Henri Boyhood Home

On July 12, 1929, in a hospital bed in New York City, Robert Henri, the well-known American artist and teacher, died. With his passing a remarkable career ended although his influence would continue in the art world decades into the future and remains to this day.

Only a few people close to him – family and several friends – knew the actual story of his formative years and the sign-posts of his youth on the Great Plains. That remarkable story would not be revealed to the public until more than twenty-five years later. Tradition has it that when he left Cozad, Nebraska for the last time, in 1884, Robert Cozad (*later Robert Henri*) (1865-1929) never returned to the town that his father, John Jackson Cozad (1830-1906), had established along the main line of the Union Pacific Rail Road.[2]

Over the last sixty-five years, much has been written about the Nebraska legacy of Robert Henri. Unfortunately, what has attracted the most attention and press was the shooting of a deputy sheriff and area rancher, Alf Pearson, by John Cozad and the Cozad family's disappearance after that. Yet, there is so much more to the story.

The seminal work on the topic is, and has been, the 1960 publication entitled *Son of the Gamblin' Man* and written by Mari Sandoz. It is a fictional account of Robert Henri's youth in Nebraska. She would state that her book was based on facts, a result of her extensive research, but that parts of the book and dialogue were fictional.[3]

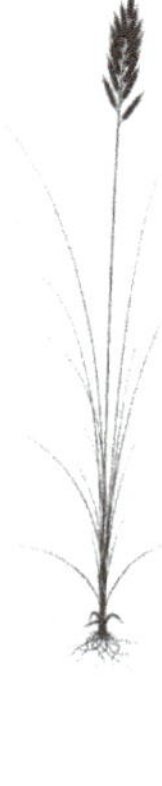

Since then, there has not been an effort to look anew at all the information that resides not only in our museum's collection but also in other area archives that did not exist at the time. Robert Henri's two biographers, William Homer (1929-2012), author of *Robert Henri and His Circle* (1988), and Bennard Perlman (1928-2016), author of *Robert Henri: His Life and Art* (1991), both described the Cozad family's time in Nebraska but did not tell the story in detail. Both focused on Henri's remarkable artistic and teaching career.

Still, there have been several works that made major contributions to the telling of the larger Cozad story including *Battle of the Bridges* (1992) by Rex German and Russ Czaplewski and *Early History of the Cozad Community and*

*Pioneer Families 1873-1998* (1998) by Charles E. Allen, Frank Johnson, and Glenda France. In addition, there have been shorter works, for example Betty Menke's *The Rebirth of the Cozad Revelation* (1985), and the various research papers (1980s) undertaken by Kieth (sic) Buss who was associated with the Cozad Historical Society.

These books and papers are the foundation on which this current effort rests. This manuscript fills in many of the details of the Cozad story and reveals new information that has since come to light. Altogether, these resources and this effort provide a truer understanding of the *Nebraska Sign-posts* of Robert Henri. We are probably as close as we will ever be to knowing about the events of those days of long ago until new primary sources surface.

When my tenure as the executive director of the Robert Henri Museum and Art Gallery began in the late fall of 2018, I started reviewing the museum's literature, reading about the Cozads, the community's history, various reports about the museum building, efforts to create a museum in the 1980s, and listening to our guides interpreting the museum and gallery for visitors. One of the things that struck me was the various interpretations of the legacy of the Cozads that were being presented. Every museum, art gallery and historic site faces this challenge when they interpret an important site to the general public.

As the months went by, I explored boxes tucked away in closets and opened files in various cabinets to determine what resources the museum had. It became clear that there was a great deal of archival material that needed to be collated, organized, researched and evaluated. Found within the boxes and cabinets was a treasure trove of documents that came from a variety of sources and included some of the Cozad family's personal files, notebooks and scrapbooks. Digging deeper and reviewing many of those documents also led me to question the interpretation that we were offering visitors, including my own.

In 2019, a new strategic plan was developed for the museum that called for undertaking a new effort to interpret the Cozad family's history in Cozad, looking at the influence of Nebraska on Robert Henry Cozad (*later Robert Henri*), studying the architectural history of the building and revealing the institutional history of the museum. From that plan came two major new exhibitions, a national conference and this book.

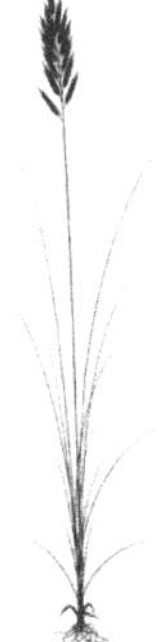

The exhibition space in the Art Gallery was redesigned in the summer of 2019 and during the course of the planning it was clear that we needed to start over and begin anew as there was so much conflicting information and layers upon layers of traditions and stories that had been cobbled together over the decades. The result of that effort was a new exhibition called *Through My Own Language: Robert Henri and His Portraits, Landscapes and Sketches.*

In late 2021 another component of the strategic plan was fulfilled when a national conference focused on Robert Henri was held in Cozad. Hosted by the museum, the author made two presentations that revealed to participants his findings on this Nebraska legacy. For the first time Henri's association with the Cornhusker State was discussed in detail along with various aspects of his artistic and teaching career.

A third project was completed in late 2022 and was the first comprehensive exhibition that looked at the Cozads and their time here in Nebraska, the history of the building, and the institutional history of the museum. Entitled *Robert Henri: From the 100th Meridian to International Fame,* this introductory exhibit was designed for visitors who did not have any knowledge of the Cozad story and were looking for a brief overview when visiting our site. Much of the material used in both exhibitions was the result of the research being conducted for this book.

## A Broader Lens

There has long been a need for a new look at this Nebraska legacy and the fascinating mosaic of the Cozad story for Henri scholars, aficionados, visitors and museum staff. This book evaluates the known data and attempts to bring some order to it but also reveals so much more than has been previously known. Like Shirley Paulsen's observation that began the Introduction, this project found that one source led to another and to another, and one question led to another.

When one tells the history of the Cozad family's role in the community, the Henri legacy in Nebraska, and the story of the museum, it must be told through a broader lens than it traditionally has. In many ways, this saga represents in microcosm the history of our nation, the state of Nebraska, and the development of Dawson County.

This is the story of the region's indigenous peoples, the Pawnees, and the early homesteaders and settlers with their ties to the Eastern states and former homelands in Europe. The region's transportation network played a crucial role in the creation of the Cozad community and its subsequent development. *The Great Platte River Road*, which followed ancient pathways along one of America's most important inland rivers, allowed for the creation of the Oregon, California and Mormon trails, or as they were collectively known, the *Overland Trails*. While all three had seen their most significant use before John Cozad's settlement was established in 1873, an occasional wagon or wagon train following their routes continued to pass by until the 1890s.

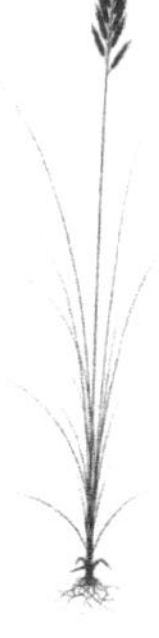

The Union Pacific Rail Road, which had transported John J. Cozad through Nebraska in 1872, and many times after that, had arrived at what is present-day Cozad in the fall of 1866. A large delegation of important government leaders, financiers and supporters had come to this location to celebrate the company having reached the 100th Meridian. This was a significant benchmark that the national government had established for the railroads to achieve in order to receive federal funding and free land as they proceeded west. The Union Pacific's role in this story is a significant one, as is John Cozad's ties to one of the most powerful corporations of its time.

It is also the story of the establishment of a community in a harsh landscape under difficult odds and then regularly facing natural calamities. There were conflicts between ranchers, homesteaders, and land developers like John Cozad, and finally there was a wild, wild West atmosphere that is often depicted in movies.

The handsome and aloof Cozad was a fascinating person who defies a simple characterization and seemed to be in conflict wherever he went and lived. He was a strong-willed and determined man with a wide range of visions that were always forward looking. His shooting of Alf Pearson in 1882 ended the family's role in the community and bookended his arrival a decade earlier that had begun with such great hopes.

And, most importantly, in the small central Nebraska town that bears the name of his father, Robert Henri, or *Bob Cozad,* as he was known when living here, was becoming an aspiring writer and budding artist. We believe that the Nebraska experience had an important influence on his career and the values as expressed in his artwork and his seminal book, *The Art Spirit.*

## A Remarkable Journey

As part of our mission, we want to provide a source of information that helps our visitors, volunteers and members better understand this history. We also hope that it will also provide readers with a better accounting of the Ohio, Nebraska and Colorado legacies in the Midwest and Mountain West chapters of Robert Henri's life and how they shaped the artist's future. These connections played an important role in the development of Henri's philosophies and artistic talents.

Today, the Robert Henri Museum and Art Gallery is moving forward with the goal of becoming a national center for preserving Robert Henri's legacy. One can only wonder what Robert Henri might have thought of all of this. Also, one must wonder what Theresa and John Cozad would have thought about the honor of their home being restored and used as a museum. Or, that pictures of their portraits painted by Robert Henri have a place of honor in their former dining room.

This book is divided into four parts. The first reveals the Cozad story in its entirety and the second part reveals the unraveling of mysteries of that story, the third part tells about the family's private residence and hotel and its subsequent history. A fourth section includes an essay by the author. It explores all these topics and more. It is the first edition of this fascinating story and there will certainly be future revisions as more information comes to light.

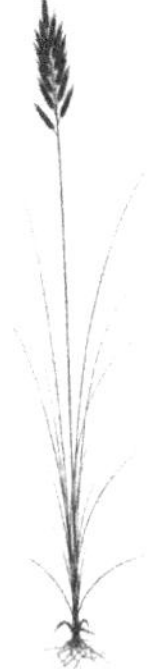

Peter Osborne
Red Cloud, Nebraska

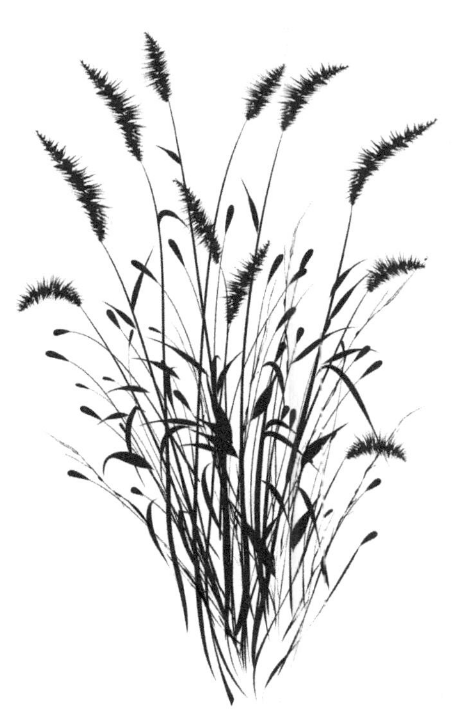

# Part I

# The Cozad Story

*This story is . . . a most unusual one and yearns for a Romantic Pen.*[1]
Richard Lee (John J. Cozad) to Jules Sandoz, 1903

*How satisfying it was to have the mystery solved at last.* [2]
The Riggs Family in America
Marjorie Nelson

# *Chapter 1*

# Setting the Stage

*Westward The Star of Empire Takes Its Way.* [3]
From a Poster Encouraging Homesteaders to come to Cozad, Nebraska

*Go West Young Man.* [4]
Believed to have been said by
Horace Greeley, Editor and Supporter of Westward Expansion

LONG BEFORE HOMESTEADERS AND IMMIGRANTS BEGAN TO pass through and settle in central Nebraska in the nineteenth century, the region had been peopled by Native Americans. Indigenous peoples have inhabited what is now Nebraska for thousands of years. During the last two millenniums, the Pawnees lived here and occupied a wide swath of territory that included parts of present-day Nebraska, Kansas and South Dakota.

South-central Nebraska has also been the location of significant transportation arteries with its rivers, trails, railroads and later roadways crossing it. The *Great Platte River Road*, as it has been called, was *the grand corridor of America's westward expansion* and followed the route of the Platte River beginning at the Missouri River, at the eastern end of Nebraska, to the western end and then continuing into the states of Colorado and Wyoming.[5]

The word *Platte* has two possible origins. The first is from French explorers and means *broad expanse* or *broadwater* because of its mile-wide width in places. Another interpretation is that the Otoe and Missourias named the river two Otoe-Missouria words *Ni Brathge* which means water flat.[6] There are two branches, the North Platte and South Platte, which meet in North Platte, Nebraska. The northern branch of the river begins in northern Colorado, winds through Wyoming and then flows into Nebraska. The southern branch begins near Pike's Peak in Colorado. The river can be raging in the spring with the melting snow coming down from the mountains to the west and then run dry in the summer exposing miles of pure sand. It was said to be *too thick to drink and too thin to plow.*[7]

This river route became the basis for the creation of the Overland Trails including the Mormon, Oregon and the California trails which were most heavily used between 1841 and 1869. Part of the Pony Express route in use from 1860-1861 also passed near the Platte River in Nebraska.

The use of those trails was followed by the construction of the Union Pacific Railroad which arrived in the place that later became Cozad in 1866. It proceeded westward until it met the Central Pacific Railroad at Promontory Summit, Utah, in 1869. For the first time a transcontinental railroad was in operation. Then, less than five decades later, the newly designated *Lincoln Highway* was dedicated, the first automobile road to cross America. It was succeeded by U.S. Route 30.

Ironically, as the reader will soon find out, the modern version of the highway begins in Atlantic City, New Jersey and continues westward. Just a little over one mile to the southeast of the starting point of today's Route 30 is Texas Avenue, the location where John J. Cozad built his next real estate empire after leaving Cozad, Nebraska.

The modern Atlantic City Expressway, the main roadway from the New Jersey shore to Philadelphia to the west, also ends just blocks from Texas Avenue. Philadelphia was an important place in the lives of the Cozad boys, John A. (*later Frank Southrn*) and Robert (*later Robert Henri*). John went to Jefferson Medical College (now Thomas Jefferson University) and Robert attended the Pennsylvania Academy of Fine Arts.[8] And, in another interesting coincidence, Route 30 now passes just two blocks to the south of the Robert Henri Museum and Art Gallery. At one time, the original Lincoln Highway passed directly in front of the museum on East 8th Street.

Finally, there is Interstate Route 80 which begins just west of New York City and ends in San Francisco, California. The termination of the interstate in the east is a relatively short distance from where Robert Henri's home was in Gramercy Park in New York. The highway is located just one mile south of the museum and its route was surely a place where Robert Cozad played as a boy along the Platte River and where his father owned many acres of pasture.

## The First Peoples

There have been indigenous peoples in what is now Nebraska for thousands of years. They are grouped by category into several broad eras – the Paleo-Indian Period, the Archaic Period, the Plains-Woodland Period, and the Historic (or Contact) Period. Evidence of the peoples from all these eras can be found in the state.

An important Paleo archaeological site was found in Frontier County along the shore of the Medicine Creek Reservoir. It is located less than sixty miles southwest of Cozad. These peoples (c. 40,000 BC – c. 14,000 BC) are believed to have been roaming and hunting mammoths on the plains of Nebraska for a very long time. At the La Sena Mammoth site along the reservoir, the remains of a mammoth that was butchered by humans, were uncovered by archaeologists. The remains date from twenty-one to twenty-two thousand years ago.[9]

There are two other Paleo sites nearby including the Jensen Mammoth site which is northeast of Cozad along Buffalo Creek. There, a mammoth was found that also exhibited signs of butchering and dates to about twenty-three thousand years ago. A third site is located at Lake McConaughy and dates to about thirty thousand years.[10]

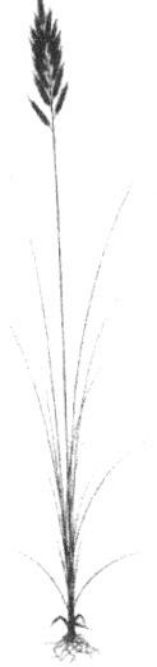

The Paleo-Indians were a nomadic hunting culture, and their main quarry

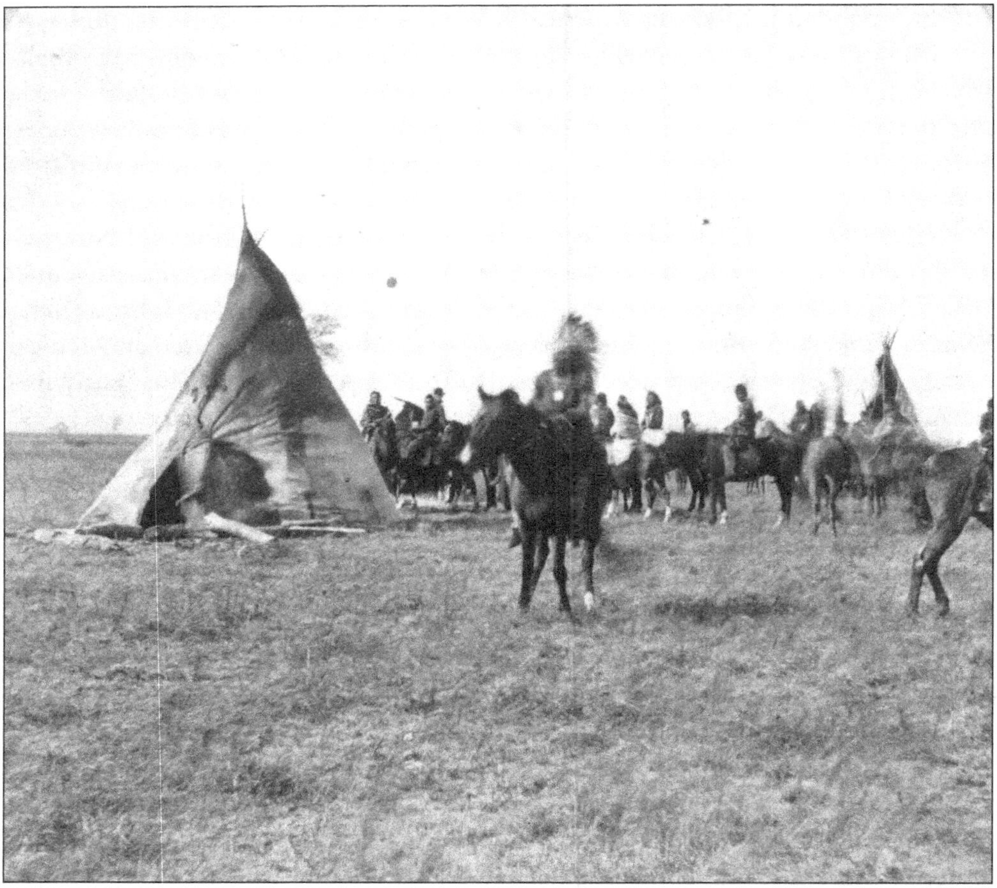

*Courtesy Library of Congress (Control Number 2005675917)*

*When settlers arrived in the Platte River Valley, Pawnee Indians could still be seen. Within three decades they would be gone from the region. This photograph comes from the Union Pacific Railroad archives and is dated 1866.*

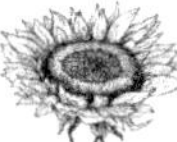

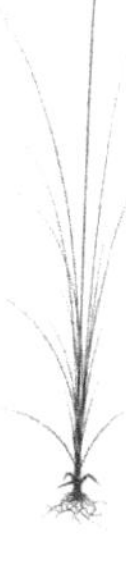

were woolly mammoths and mastodons. Some have suggested that they may have hunted this large elephant-like animal into extinction. They also hunted giant bison, and fish and birds were included in their diet. The most notable artifact associated with the Paleo-Indians are the Clovis spear points which were an effective hunting tool along with knives, drills and choppers. Late Paleo sites have been found in western Nebraska.[11]

Between 8,000 BC and 1,000 BC, an era described as the Archaic Period, there developed a more diversified culture. They were hunters and gatherers, eating meat and fish and collecting plants to eat. Typically, the kinds of artifacts found representing this era include spear points, knives, axes, drills, scrapers, and choppers along with pottery. Archaic sites have been found along the Medicine Creek in Frontier County.[12]

The next era, the Plains-Woodland Period, began about 1 AD and lasted until approximately 1,000 AD as these people spread all across Nebraska and the Great Plains. They too were hunters and gatherers who lived in small communities or camps and were the first Native Americans to use bows and arrows. These people used clay pottery, amulets, pecking stones, pestles, axes, knives, scrapers, projectile points which are still found in farm fields, along with sinkers that were used for fishing. They were succeeded by a grouping called the *Village Farmers* as they created villages that were unfortified which they returned to after hunting forays.[13]

Finally, there is the Historic or Contact Period when the protohistoric Pawnees began to succeed the previous culture. By the time the expeditions of Coronado, which passed through Nebraska in the mid-1500s, the Pawnees, the tribe most familiar to Nebraskans, were spread across south and central Nebraska. In 1673, the Pawnee Indians are noted on a map produced by Father Jacques Marquette, a French missionary explorer.[14]

The Pawnees were an agricultural people, living in large villages, and sharing communal earthen lodges. During the summer they left their villages on hunting expeditions and lived in tipis. Most notably they were corn growers, and today the state is known as the Cornhusker State because of the perfect environment for growing corn. They also grew beans, pumpkins, and squash. The bison was a major source of food as well. A major change in the Pawnee culture came with the introduction of the horse, and by 1800, horses were very much a part of their lives. This development also caused a weakening of traditional Pawnee culture.[15]

It is thought that in 1838 there were ten thousand Pawnee Indians in Nebraska. Other Indian tribes in Nebraska included the Cheyenne, Arapaho, Lakota, Ponca, Omaha and Otoe-Missouria-Winnebago-Iowan peoples.[16]

When the migrations of Europeans and Americans across the Great Plains began, with the creation and use of the Oregon, California and Mormon trails, the population of Pawnees began to decline as a direct result of the introduction of diseases such as cholera. Attacks by the Lakota Sioux also added to the decline. In 1857, they relinquished their land to the federal government, except for a small reservation. By 1861, there were less than thirty-five hundred Pawnees left. They agreed to move to the Indian Territory in 1874, just after John Cozad had arrived.[17]

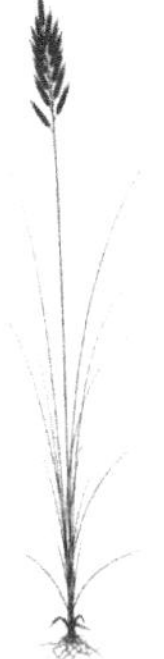

The most well-known of the skirmishes between the native peoples and settlers in the region occurred on August 7, 1864, when raids by the Cheyenne and Sioux in Plum Creek killed a number of travelers in their wagons. This was known as the Plum Creek Massacre. Three years later the Cheyenne damaged a section of railroad track west of Plum Creek, and as a result, a train wreck occurred with several deaths to railroad employees. It came to be known as the Turkey Leg Raid. Then, on April 29, 1868, a third encounter, called the Tobin Indian Raid, occurred when three railroad employees were killed.[18]

When a Union Pacific Railroad celebratory excursion arrived in late October 1866 at what is now Cozad, Pawnee Indians were photographed nearby with tipis as part of a reenactment program for the supporters of the railroad from all over the country.

In 1876, just three years after settlers began moving into the Cozad area, the Battle of the Little Big Horn, also commonly known as Custer's Last Stand, took place in southeastern Montana. It was the most decisive Indian victory over the United States military in the nation's history, but it also marked the beginning of the final destruction of the Native American life on the Great Plains.

## The Overland Trails

*The Great Platte River Road*, an ancient pathway and transportation corridor, followed the route of the Platte River. The muddy, shallow river had been seen by numerous European explorers prior to 1800, and of course the indigenous peoples for millennia. The Spanish had known about the Great Plains for more than two hundred years, and at least fifty years before the English had arrived at Jamestown in Virginia. The French had also arrived early on and had been involved with trading with the Indians.[19]

For Americans, the importance of the Great Platte River Road grew with the completion and findings of the Lewis and Clark Expedition in 1806. It became an important link in the nineteenth century trails that crossed the country from the Missouri River to the California and the Oregon territories. The Oregon Territory then included a wide swath of land including the present states of Oregon, Washington, Idaho, and sections of Wyoming and Montana.[20]

In 1812, just six years after the return of the *Voyage of Northwestern Discovery*, Robert Stuart, who was employed at the recently created Astoria trading post at the mouth of the Columbia River in Oregon, began a trek eastward. He was carrying reports for John Jacob Astor, the great fur magnate, and led a group of men who created a new trail that crossed the Continental Divide near the South Pass in Wyoming. It provided an easier passage over the Rocky Mountains than the Lewis and Clark Expedition had used much farther north. Then they traveled down the Platte to the Missouri River, and to the East.[21]

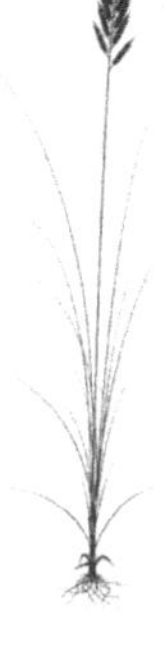

Using wagons for the first time, a group of fur traders used the route that became the Oregon Trail, passing along the Platte River in 1830.[22] In 1836, a two-wheeled cart arrived in Idaho, and two years later another two-wheeled cart made it all the way to Oregon, an important development for one of the future overland trails. Then, in 1841, the first group of settlers with wagons, passed along the Platte River, arrived at Soda Springs in Idaho and divided. A portion of

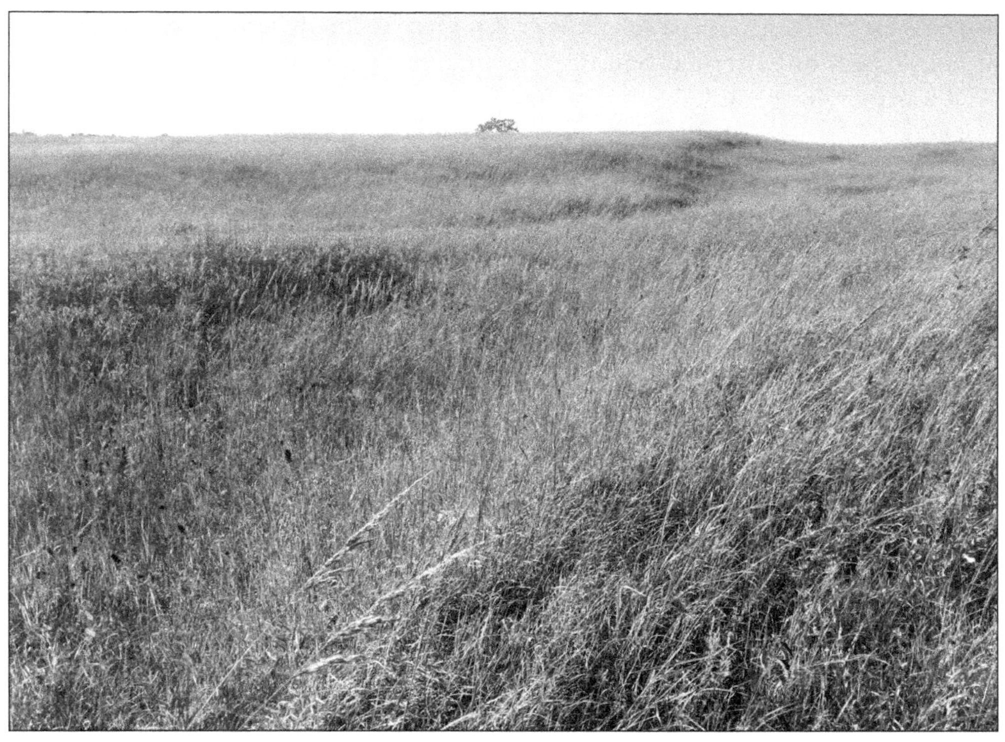

Courtesy Peter Osborne

*Some remnants of the Oregon, California and Mormon trails remain in Nebraska, although in most cases there are just swales left that show the route where thousands of Conestoga wagons passed. In many cases even the swales have disappeared in time because the land where they passed has been farmed. This is a long section of the Oregon Trail in Rock Creek Station State Historical Park in Fairbury, Nebraska. The Oregon and California trails passed on the south side of the Platte River, and the Mormon Trail passed on the north side along present day U.S. Route 30.*

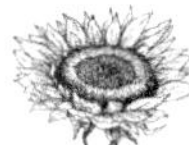

the group went to California and the remainder to Oregon.[23] The following year John Fremont explored the Missouri River-South Pass route and wrote a report that was widely disseminated and promoted the Platte River route as the best one to get to the West.[24]

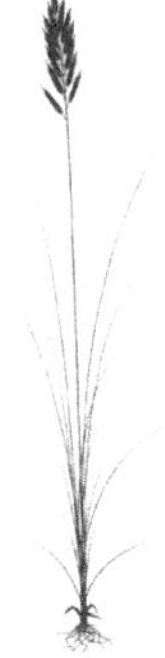

Beginning in 1843, overland migrations began in earnest and during the next two decades about five hundred thousand emigrants passed over what collectively became known as the *Overland Trails* and included the main routes of the Oregon and California trails and several years later, the Mormon Trail.[25] The destinations for the first two trails were the California Territory and the Oregon Territory. Neither had been admitted as states into the Union yet but both became a part of the United States in 1850 and 1859 respectively. Shortly after the Oregon and California trails came into use the third overland trail was established in 1847 by the Mormons, a religious group more formally known as the Church of Jesus Christ of Latter-day Saints.[26] The final termination point of the Mormon Trail was the Great Salt Lake in the Utah Territory which also later became a state in 1896.

There were a number of jumping off points for these trails including Kansas City and St. Joseph, in Missouri, Nebraska City and Omaha in Nebraska and Nauvoo in Illinois. Other towns along the Missouri River also hosted those who were willing to set out across the West and sold them supplies to make the trek.

While there is a general consensus of where the routes of the trails were located, there was considerable overlap as can be seen on today's maps recreating the routes. The California trail became a sprawling network of side trails with many extended branches which often paralleled the routes of both the Mormon and Oregon trails. For many miles the routes of the Oregon and California trails were one and the same and included the route of the short-lived Pony Express, particularly in Nebraska and Wyoming.

The trails did not just follow a single route from a beginning to an end point. Various side or feeder trails merged into the main trails, and routes within routes were created over time. For example, there was a side trail that merged into the

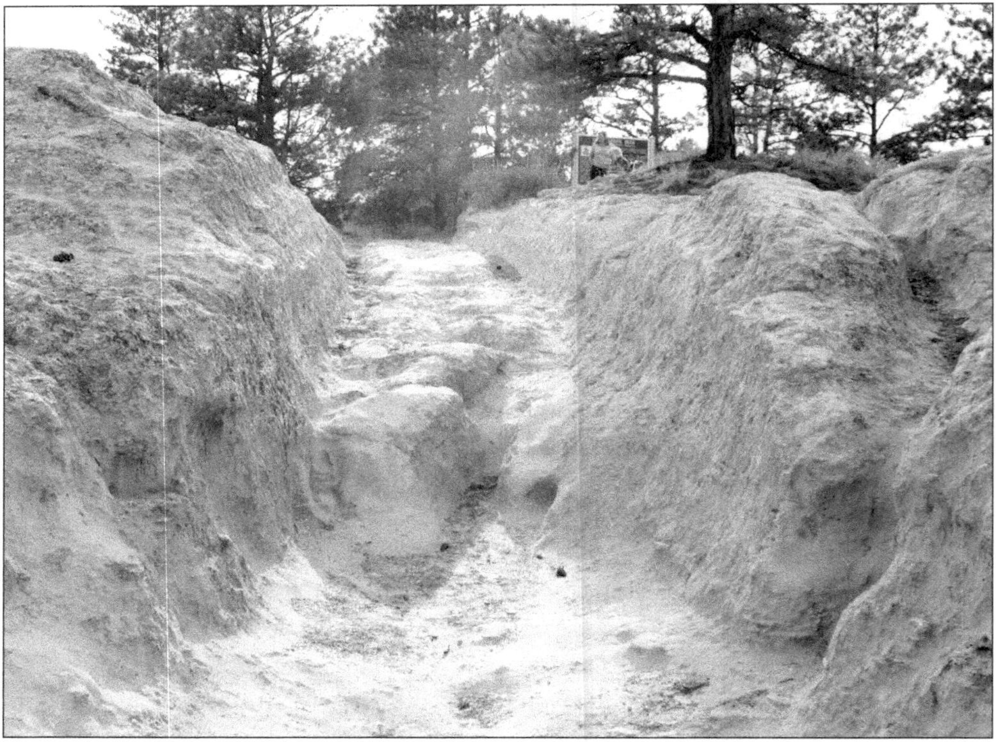

*Courtesy Peter Osborne*

*In some places, like Guernsey, Wyoming, the thousands of Conestoga wagons cut deep ruts into the stone that remain to this day.*

main California and Mormon trails north of David City. It originated in Nebraska City. Today that branch intersects U.S. Route 6 at a location west of Lincoln and is marked with a distinctive red, white and blue pole on a bluff alongside the road. It is not far from the Blue River State Recreation Area.

Beginning east of Fort Kearny, Nebraska, the Oregon, California and Mormon trails paralleled each other or even merged at points into one prairie roadway until they reached Wyoming, where they separated and headed off in different directions. Within several years after they first came into use the Overland Trails became broad and well used roadways described as having the width of as many as ten roads back East.[27]

The travelers and their wagons left an indelible mark on the landscape with the deep ruts cut by the wagon wheels. Once the ruts got too deep or impassable, the emigrants simply created a new roadbed nearby.

### The Latter Day Saints

The Mormon's faith tradition had begun in upstate New York but because of vicious and violent persecution, they kept moving westward to avoid trouble which had been common in the areas where they settled. Some adherents were murdered, their property destroyed, and many were forced to leave their homes which were burned to the ground. Because of their religious beliefs and their desire to be separate, the route that the Mormons followed in Nebraska was generally on the north side of the Platte River, roughly following the present-day U.S. Route 30 until it crossed the river at Laramie, Wyoming.[28]

However, there was also a South Mormon Trail which paralleled the Platte from Columbus, Nebraska, to Wyoming, which would have put the Mormons in contact with those on the other trails especially during the period of the California Gold Rush from 1849-56. After 1856 they returned to the trail on the north side of the Platte. Travelers on the Oregon and California trails were said to hear the voices of Mormons singing hymns and drifting across the river from the main trail. In all, sixty thousand Mormons came across the country in this fashion.[29]

The Murphy wagons or prairie schooners, as they were known, with their sailboat-like appearance, carried the emigrants westward with their teams of oxen and were the most common form of transportation on the trail. However, others traveled lightly, on horseback or walking. One of the unique features of the Mormon Trail was the use of handcarts in 1856 and for several years after in addition to the more common wagons. Handcarts were mainly used by European immigrants going to Salt Lake City. The handcarts allowed for a small carrying capacity for each individual assigned to a team and in total could carry up to four hundred and fifty pounds. It could be pulled by one person. Two excellent reproductions of the wagons and carts can be found at the Archway in Kearney, Nebraska and the Mormon Trail Interpretive Center in Omaha.[30]

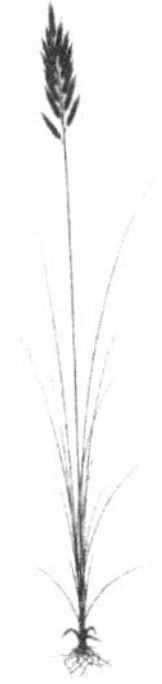

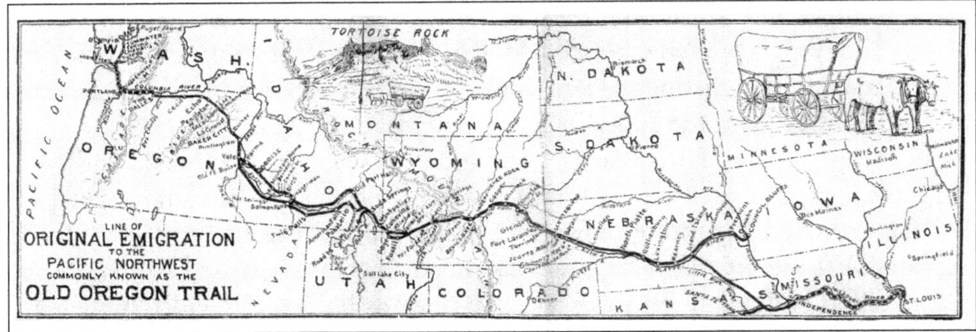


*Robert Henri Museum and Art Gallery Collection*

*The Route of the Oregon Trail*

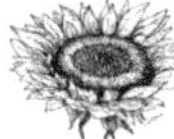

The travelers of the Overland Trails faced a host of numerous difficult trials. Streams and rivers had to be forded in good weather and bad, water was not always safe to drink, and military forts had to be established along the routes to provide protection and safe havens. Cholera, occasional Indian raids, and internal troubles that were faced within the traveling groups all produced challenges. There were wide expanses of prairies where grasslands extended out onto the horizon for miles.

Families often traveled in groups as did parties from specific communities. Women regularly took over a wagon and handled men's chores when they had to. About one in seventeen of the travelers lost their lives, and at the time of the use of the trails small graveyards or individual burials were a common sight along its length.[31] Today, there are graves still preserved along the trail that continue to attract historical interest including Susan Hail's marked grave on a lonely hilltop in Kenesaw, northwest of Hastings, Nebraska.[32]

As the travelers proceeded farther west, family heirlooms were simply left behind and discarded on the vast plains as loads were lightened for the oxen. The movement of the wagon trains was continuous because every day lost to delay meant a possible catastrophic ending of the journey due to the early arrival of winter.

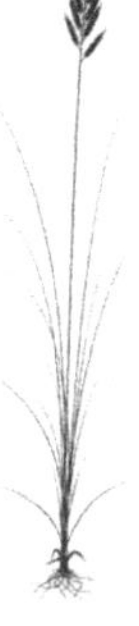

The Oregon, California and Mormon trails continued to be used, although more sporadically, until the 1890s. Between 1841 and 1866 it is estimated that about five hundred thousand people passed along the Platte River valley.[33]By then, rail travel had become common, convenient, less wearisome, and more economically feasible, particularly after 1869 when the transcontinental railroad was completed connecting the continent from the Atlantic to the Pacific. However, for those who still wanted to travel overland to California and Oregon, the trails remained an option.

An important result of the arrival of the railroad, and the developing transportation network, is that the waystations and communities that had once been important stops on those trails and Pony Express disappeared. Some were moved to the north of the Platte River such as Plum Creek, present-day Lexington; others just faded away.[34]

Even after the establishment of Cozad by John Cozad in late 1873, an occasional prairie schooner passed by or crossed his land holdings. The Oregon and California trails, which ran along the south side of the Platte River, traversed lands owned by John J. Cozad. The Mormon Trail, located between the railroad and the north side of the Platte, also ran through properties owned by Cozad near the present city of Cozad, and just a short distance from today's Robert Henri Museum and Art Gallery. Increasingly the land through which the schooners passed was settled, presumably changing the routes of the original trails to some degree as they had to skirt a growing number of farmsteads which were being fenced in.[35]

Most of the remains of the trails in the Dawson County area have long vanished, plowed under and the acreage used for farming, particularly where the land was tillable. This is the case south of Cozad where the trail ran parallel to the river and across flat land. In 1955, when the *Early History of the Cozad Community and Pioneer Families* was published, Harry Allen contributed a short essay that reported that a remnant of the trail could be seen in the late nineteenth century crossing Township 10, Section 24, and Range 24.

Recreated maps of the Oregon Trail show it crossing at the northeastern corner of the section while the historic marker shows it crossing at the southeastern corner. The 1868 survey, created by the state's Surveyor General, of Township 10, Range 24, which is the most accurate and contemporary description, shows it coming into Section 24 from the east midway between the northern and southern boundaries of the section. The survey of Range 23, shows it coming in from the east and paralleling the Platte River.[36] This discrepancy may be explained by realizing that the trail was always in a state of flux, moving as the conditions dictated like reroutes, flooding, streams or other natural challenges or homesteaded land.[37] Unfortunately, there are few, if any, remains of these storied trails near Cozad to be seen anymore. One can still trace the approximate routes by following the national trail system roadside markers.

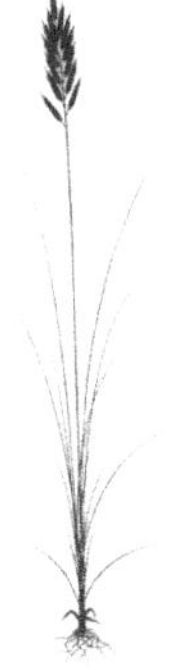

Efforts to preserve the Oregon Trail's history began decades after its use ended. Robert Harvey, Nebraska's first state surveyor, became the first president of the Oregon Trail Memorial Commission in 1911 and the commission located the length of the Oregon Trail in the state in an effort to preserve its route. It worked with a variety of organizations to complete its work.[38] In 1912, the state of Nebraska and the commission marked its route, and those granite markers can still be seen on roadsides, often where the trail crossed a highway. There are monuments in Kearney and Dawson County that still designate the route of the trail.

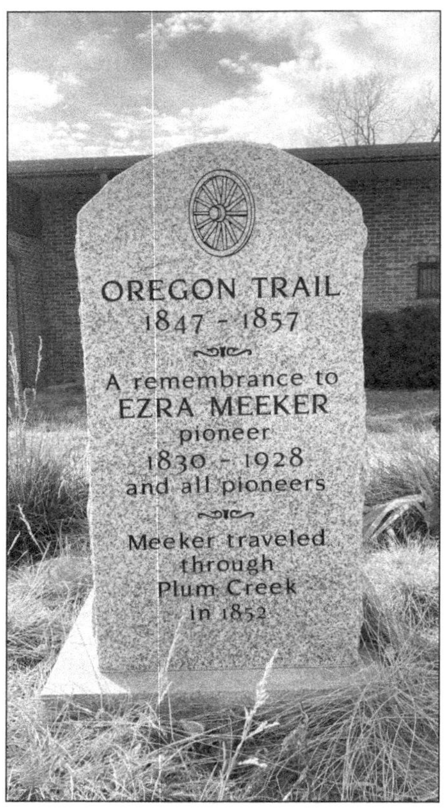


*Courtesy Peter Osborne*

*Ezra Meeker, an early supporter of preserving the Oregon Trail, is memorialized at the Dawson County Historical Museum in Lexington, Nebraska.*

Ezra Meeker, an early pioneer who had traveled west on the trail and passed through today's Lexington in 1852, later returned to Iowa. Then he followed the trail westward again by car. Meeker went on to lead the effort to preserve the trail in its entirety. He founded the Oregon Trail Association in the hopes of achieving that goal.

Today, where possible, the former routes of the trails and their history are preserved by the National Park Service through a national historic trail system. The federal headquarters for the *National Historic Oregon Trail* is located in Baker City, Oregon. The headquarters for the *California National Historic Trail* is located in Santa Fe, New Mexico.

The *Mormon Pioneer National Trail* passes from Nauvoo, Illinois, to Salt Lake City, Utah. The Mormon Trail Center at the Winter Quarters preserves its history and is an excellent museum. It is located in Omaha, the site where the Mormons first wintered in Nebraska. A recreated prairie schooner can be seen there along with a pair of oxen and a handcart.

Today, evidence remains of the Oregon and California trails elsewhere including sections of swales or what appear to be deeply eroded ditches cut into the landscape. A long swale is preserved at the Rock Creek Station State Historical Park in Fairbury, Nebraska. In areas where there were beds of sandstone, the trail ruts remain deeply cut into the stone. An excellent example of this phenomenon survives in Guernsey, Wyoming, at the Oregon Trail Ruts National Monument.

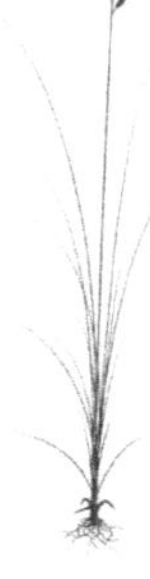

### The Pony Express and the Overland Stage

The first efforts to get mail across the country began in 1849 with the Gold Rush in California. Over the next decade a variety of methods were used, including sea-based venues that included a land crossing and several overland routes that traveled through the Southwest. For a number of years, a stagecoach service delivered the mail semi-monthly. The U.S. Congress debated as to what routes those services should use and the heavy cost involved. By 1859, with the death of a U.S. Postmaster General who had promoted this system, a closing of routes occurred and with that came more debate. For some, like the U.S. Senator from New York, William H. Seward, the postal system was critical. He said:

*I regard the inland postal system as a great instrumentality for maintaining, preserving and extending this Union.*[39]

It was this debate that brought about a short-lived postal delivery system that was called the Pony Express. Organized in early 1860, the mail system and its operations were developed very quickly with a route beginning in St. Joseph, Missouri and ending in Sacramento, California. Using seventy-five ponies and taking ten and half days, riders made use of designated stops every ten to fifteen mile changing horses at each stop. Then, riders were changed every seventy-five miles. The service delivered the mail that was carried in a leather pouch called a *mochila*. To service the riders and transfers of mail there were one hundred and nineteen Pony Express relay stations along the entire route, each with a station keeper. It cost five dollars for a half ounce letter which was later reduced to one dollar. At first a weekly service, it became a semi-weekly service.[40]

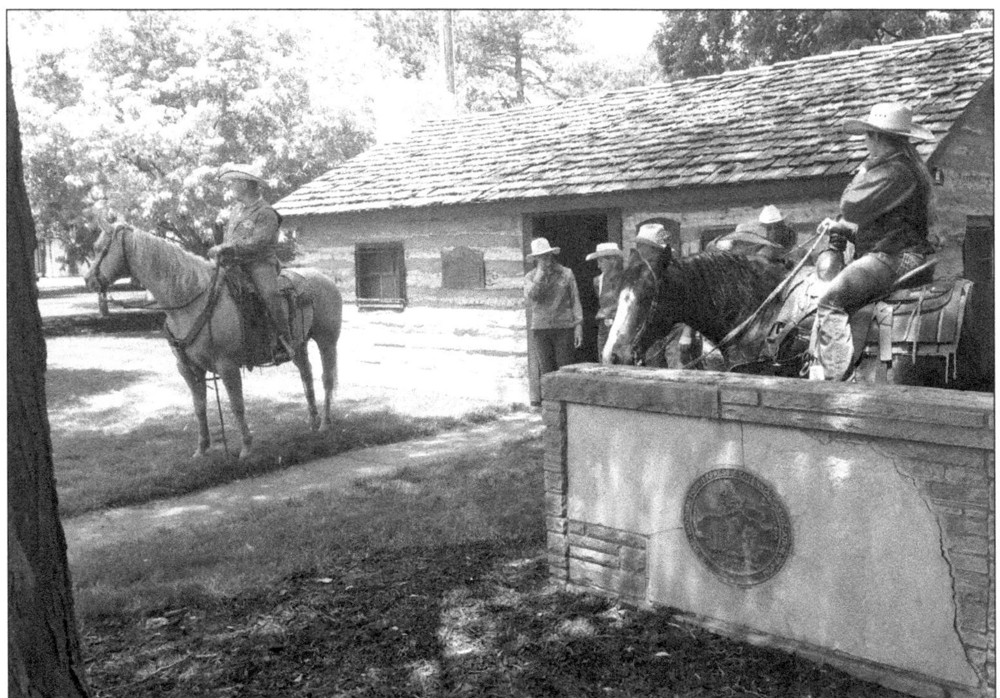

*Courtesy Peter Osborne*

*The Pony Express, while a short-lived enterprise in the mid-nineteenth century, is still remembered every year with the annual Re-ride that goes from Missouri to California and stops for a quick exchange of horses and the mail in Cozad.*

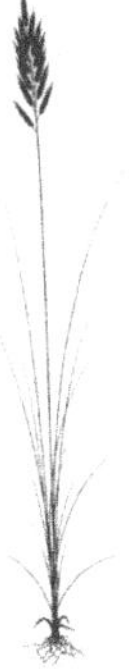

The service only ran for a short time, eighteen months, until October 1861, when a telegraph line along its route was finished and became operational. With the use of the telegraph, the need for the Pony Express ended.[41] While the Pony Express did not have any association with Cozad, its route passed to the south, paralleling the Platte River generally following the route of the California and Oregon trails.[42]

A stagecoach line, the Central Overland California and Pike's Peak Express Company, purchased the assets of the Pony Express company and used its various stations for stagecoach stops. The Central Overland stage line was ultimately sold to Wells Fargo and Company, which consolidated all the stage lines of the West. Their success was short-lived as the company believed that it would take longer for the transcontinental railroads to be built, something that, unfortunately for the company, did not occur. [43]

The Pony Express had long disappeared by the time the Cozads stepped off a Union Pacific train in 1873, and few, if anyone, later living in Cozad would have remembered the riders on fast galloping horses coming through that desolate area. However, the old postal delivery system became a part of the region's heritage along with the regular passage of the stagecoaches.

### The Homestead Act of 1862

Beginning at the conclusion of the Revolutionary War, the federal government began a complicated effort to distribute unclaimed lands that had once belonged to the native peoples west of the Alleghenies. At first it was an unorganized effort but with the passage of the Land Ordinance of 1785 the government introduced a systematic way to distribute this land. Land was divided into six-mile square townships. This was divided into thirty-six sections that measured one square mile or six hundred and forty acres. Initially, potential landowners were required to purchase a full square for $1 an acre, an amount that would come to be too high for most Americans at the time.[44]

Over time, efforts were made to change the Land Ordinance, beginning in the mid-nineteenth century, and at least three times legislation passed the House of Representatives only to be rebuffed by the Senate. In 1860, a new Homestead Bill was passed by both houses only to be vetoed by then President James Buchanan. These efforts had all failed because of what new states might become – slave or free. By 1860-61 with the country deeply fractured, states began to secede from the Union. Finally, in 1862, with the nation in the middle of the Civil War, and with Abraham Lincoln as its president, a bill promoting homesteading finally passed both houses and was signed by the chief executive.[45]

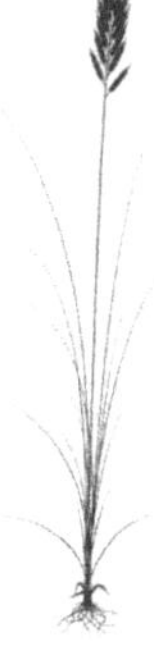

On January 1, 1863, Daniel Freeman filed one of the first claims for land under the new act along with four hundred and seventeen others. The land that Freeman claimed was in eastern Nebraska, near present-day Beatrice.[46] With the rush of people coming onto the Great Plains, the population of the territory of Nebraska, which had been created in 1854, exploded, and it entered the Union on March 1, 1867, as the thirty-seventh state.

As a result of the large land grants made to the railroads, and large numbers of homesteaders who were settling in the state, counties were created. Additionally, small towns were established across the state, usually five or six miles apart from each other, with the more successful and larger ones located along the routes of the various railroads or branch lines. They were often named to honor founders, presidents or in some cases prominent officials such as Gosper County, named for John Gosper, Nebraska's Secretary of State at the time of that county's incorporation. Dawson County was originally established in 1861 by the territorial government but not formally organized until June 20, 1871, by Acting Governor William James. Its first commissioners were elected one month later.[47]

There is some controversy about whom the county is named for, but *History-Nebraska* believes it was named for John L. Dawson, a former Congressman from Pennsylvania who died in 1870 but had been involved with homesteading legislation. There is another body of thought that it was named for Jacob Dawson, the first postmaster of the town of Lancaster, now Lincoln, Nebraska.[48]

### The Union Pacific Rail road

The arrival of the railroad to both Nebraska and what became the City of Cozad was the result of a complicated two-decade effort that involved various sectional interests in the country including the North pitted against the South, the issue of slavery and whether its introduction into the new territories should be allowed. There was also the choice between one of four proposed routes for the railroads to get to the Pacific, and through which region they would travel. There were powerful political interests to be satisfied along with various state's interests. There were other factors too, including the onset of the California and Colorado gold rushes, and the need to transport mail, freight, goods and people across the vast interior in a more economical and efficient manner.[49]

The first discussions to construct a railroad from the East to the Pacific began in 1841. This effort would not conclude until two railroads met at Promontory Point in Utah in 1869. The long struggle witnessed involvement of some of the era's most influential political leaders including United States Congressman and later Senator Stephen Douglas, Senator Thomas Hart Benton, Secretary of War Jefferson Davis, and numerous other politicians from Missouri and Iowa.[50]

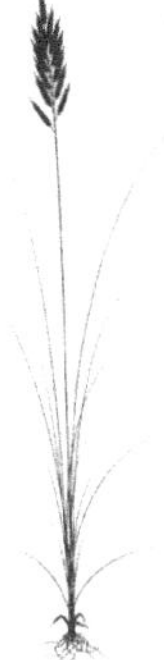

Of the four routes that were considered on which to construct a railroad across the country, the route that followed the Platte River valley had considerable support. The route was already well known by hundreds of thousands of travelers because of the Pony Express, the heavy use of the Overland Trails, and stagecoach lines. However, other routes also had important supporters for different reasons.

Finally, on July 1, 1862, in the midst of the Civil War, and with the Southern states having seceded, the Congress eliminated the possible southern routes and chose the Platte Valley route. It passed the Pacific Railway Act that dictated the terms for the construction of the railroad and the financial benefits that would come to the companies when certain milestones were met. Among the benefits were millions of acres of ground that was to be sold by the railroads.

The Pacific Railway Act specified that the railroads had to complete the building of one hundred miles of track each year, and, if they did not meet those goals, they would forfeit benefits such as land grants and funding. A later act required the completion of the construction of the *Pacific Railroad*, as it was known, by 1876.[51]

In September 1862, the United State Congress chartered the Union Pacific Company to construct the eastern end of a railroad. In addition, the legislative body also agreed to give support to the Central Pacific Company's efforts to build the western end of the transcontinental railroad. On December 2, the entire effort began from the eastern terminus at Omaha with a groundbreaking by Nebraska Territorial Governor Alvin Saunders holding the ceremonial spade. Work was delayed by complications due to the Civil War.[52]

It was a remarkable effort and the kind of transcontinental project that had never been attempted before. First came the surveyors, then several hundred graders who prepared the roadbed. Following them were large teams of construction crew members, supplies and materials, a complicated dance of logistics that required a remarkable effort at coordination. They could lay as much as two miles of track a day.[53]

A significant benchmark for the railroad, and a great advertisement tool, going west was reaching the 100th Meridian, (west of Greenwich, England) a line of longitude which ran from Canada to Mexico. The meridian was simply located on maps and not on the ground with any kind of permanent or substantial marking similar to what were later used to mark townships and sections. A spike may have been driven into the ground to designate the spot but no record of that was ever recorded and it is not found noted on survey maps of the late 1860s.[54]

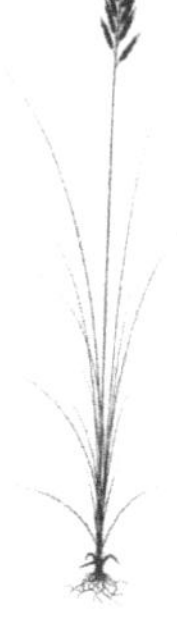

On October 5, 1866, the construction crew which had begun laying track in Omaha earlier that spring arrived at the 100th Meridian, the present-day location of Cozad. They were almost two hundred and fifty miles west of where they began.[55] *Blind Tom*, a horse who was actually blind, and who had been bringing the first wagonloads of rail, spikes and hay westward across Nebraska, may have led the way. Behind him were other wagons, one thousand men and four locomotives with ten cars each bringing supplies forward to a warehouse that quickly was reassembled as the effort moved westward.[56] After passing the 100th Meridian, the whole operation continued its steady march westward towards North Platte.

The Union Pacific Rail Road's vice president, Thomas C. Durant, who saw

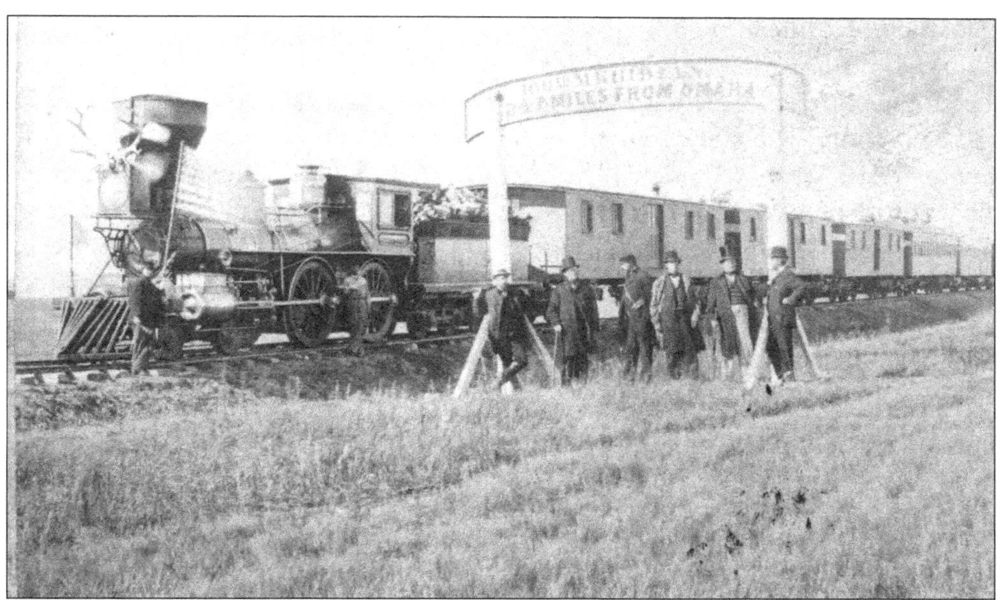

*Courtesy Library of Congress (Control Number 2005682857)*

*When the Union Pacific Railroad arrived at the 100th Meridian in 1866, a major celebration took place, and photographs of the festivities were taken.*

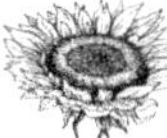

the publicity value and financial potential of the accomplishment had already arranged for an excursion to begin from New York City to the site of the 100th Meridian as the construction crews made their way across Nebraska. Because none of the rival railroads had achieved this goal, it was hoped the celebratory excursion would also bring new capital and support to the transcontinental project.[57]

Durant's excursion train left on October 15, switched across and onto several rail lines and made its way westward picking up other participants and arrived in Omaha to a huge celebration. Then all the guests crossed Nebraska, passing over the 100th Meridian on October 24 and proceeding to North Platte, where it was turned around and began its eastward return.[58] On October 26, the train stopped at the special location. Most of the two hundred and fifty passengers stepped off and onto the prairie grass that only weeks before had been a hub of activity led by Blind Tom. A band played, there were toasts and some of the younger travelers danced.[59]

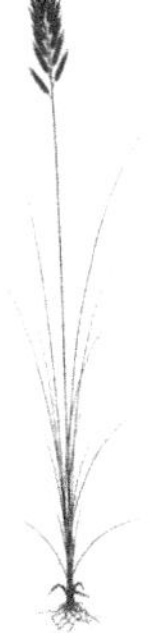

A ceremony was conducted at the site where a wooden sign had been erected that stated:

*100th Meridian*
*247 Miles from Omaha.*[60]

The guest list on the train was a veritable who's who of the era. It included Robert Todd Lincoln, the son of the late President Abraham Lincoln, who had signed the railroad legislation in 1862 and had been assassinated just a year and a half before. Also, George Pullman, the founder of the Pullman Car Company, the senators-elect from Nebraska, J. M. Thayer, T. W. Tipton, and Alvin Saunders, the territorial governor of the soon to be state of Nebraska, other U.S. senators, newspaper editors and reporters, representatives of the Army, and Rutherford B. Hayes, a Congressman from Ohio, and a future president, were all on the train.

The train included two steam locomotives, the Director's car, four new Pullman sleeping coaches for the use of the guests, a mess car, mail car fitted up as a refreshment saloon and a baggage-supply car. In addition, there was the coach that had transported Abraham Lincoln on a trip and purchased from the Federal government. It was now the personal car of Thomas Durant.[61]

After the ceremony, the excursion returned east. The celebration was recorded for posterity in photographs and these images survive today in the archives of the Library of Congress and the Union Pacific. Three years later, the two railroads met in Utah and the transcontinental railroad was complete.[62]

A piece of rail that was used during those first two decades of the railroad's operation in Cozad can still be seen at the Robert Henri Museum. When the rail from a spur that crossed Highway 30 was removed as the roadway was being widened, area resident Arlen Gibbens discovered a small section that was dated 1886. Lloyd Keller, who worked for the city, cleaned the rail up and Gibbens gave it to the museum.

## The 100th Meridian

The 100th Meridian held significance beyond the transcontinental railroad's efforts. The exact location of the meridian on the ground was not always definitive and in the nineteenth century, while surveying in remote areas, it was more difficult for surveyors to establish longitude than latitude. When the railroad was being surveyed and built, the 100th Meridian was simply drawn on an engineer's map and perhaps a metal stake was driven into the ground at the approximate location. There was also no need to pinpoint the meridian with the exacting accuracy that is possible today. Even if it was off by hundreds of feet it made very little difference at a time when it was simply a point along the line of a transcontinental railroad that was almost eighteen hundred miles long.

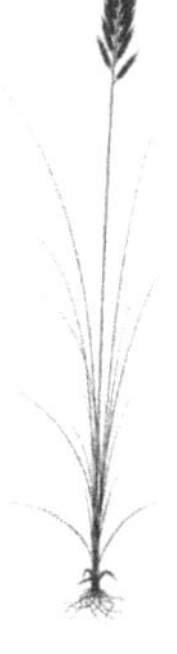

While the 100th Meridian does not appear on any of the early survey maps that were made of the Cozad area, it was placed on survey maps done elsewhere. In 1859, for example, it was located on the ground with a monument and drawn on a map of the Red River region in Texas. The line lays out where the eastern line of the Texas panhandle and the eastern boundary of the Oklahoma panhandle is located.[63]

Only a few other monuments designating a precise longitude were erected elsewhere in Nebraska. A monument was erected in North Platte in 1874 to designate the latitude at 41°04' 39.49" and longitude at 100°45' 33.13". Another monument designating longitude in Omaha, and used for all of the regional surveys after, was placed in the Capital Hill section of the city. A school now stands on the site, and the marker has been covered over and replaced on several occasions as various expansion projects were done at the Omaha Central High School.[64]

This unique line of longitude at the 100th Meridian that had been artificially created on maps had an even greater significance that was noted more than a decade after railroad construction crews passed over it. On April 3, 1878, a railroad surveyor with the United States Army and a geologist with the United States Geographical and Geological Survey of the Rocky Mountain Region, John Wesley Powell, submitted a report to the U.S. Congress. It was entitled *Report on Survey of the Rocky Mountain Region* and proclaimed that:

*In fact, a broad belt (along the 100th Meridian) separates the Arid Region of the west from the Humid Region of the east.*[65]

The state historic marker located at the place where the railroad's 100th Meridian sign stood words it slightly differently when it states:

*The 100th Meridian was the natural demarcation line extending northward from the western shore of the Gulf of Mexico. Evaporation from the gulf waters supplies most of the rainfall east of the Meridian. West of the Meridian precipitation comes largely from the Pacific which is generally insufficient for agricultural needs without irrigation. Here on the Meridian East meets the Arid West.*[66]

It was not until more recent times that efforts were made to pinpoint with greater accuracy where the 100th Meridian lay in Cozad. A number of years ago, P. O. Billing, the former city engineer for Holdrege, Nebraska, took measurements and determined that the 100th Meridian was one hundred and fifty feet from the center of Cozad, or fifty paces east of the center of Avenue G, now called Meridian Avenue.

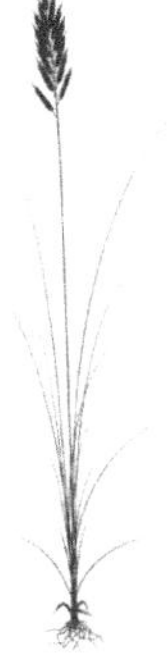

In 1998, it was located using more modern techniques with even greater accuracy, and it was determined to be situated west of the city's downtown. Readings showed that it is four thousand feet from the present Meridian Avenue. A stone marker was erected and designates the actual location of the meridian, not far from the north-south runway of the Cozad Municipal Airport. The monument can be seen on the northern side of the highway.[67]

However, the theoretical and environmentally significant 100th Meridian as originally designated by John Wesley Powell, the transition zone where humid East meets the arid West, is moving eastward. It is now believed to be one hundred and fifty miles from its original designation, and actually much closer to the 98th Meridian. This is because the region is becoming dryer and as a result the practice of using irrigation on farm fields is moving farther east. This phenomenon was first noted by Walter Webb in his book *The Great Plains* in the 1930s.[68]

The 100th Meridian remains a matter of pride for the community and continues to play an important role in the city's identity. For two decades, the wooden sign placed along the railroad track by the railroad in 1866 greeted visitors going in either direction. Sometime in the 1880s, the sign disappeared. A new monument, made of stone native to the area, was erected by the Cozad chapter of the Daughters of the American Revolution in 1933 at approximately the same location, next to the present Union Pacific station.[69]

An approximation of the original sign hangs in the 100th Meridian Museum next to the Robert Henri Museum. A modern sign has also straddled U.S. Highway 30 designating the community as the site of the meridian for decades. Even today, promotional efforts continue to draw attention to that line. The meridian was also immortalized by Wallace Stegner in his 1954 book *Beyond the 100th Meridian.*

## The Colonization Efforts

The two major railroads of Nebraska, the Union Pacific and the Burlington and Missouri River Railroad were given almost eight million acres of land, as part of the federal government's efforts to build a transcontinental railroad. The state also gave more than five hundred thousand acres of land to the smaller rail lines that crossed the state. In those cases, each received tens of thousands of acres, with two of them receiving one hundred thousand acres. All of the land grants amounted to almost seventeen percent of the total acreage of Nebraska.[70]

The Union Pacific Rail Road received almost five million acres of ground which included alternate sections extending outward on either side of the track for twenty miles. It amounted to twenty sections of land for each mile of railroad track laid.[71] After receiving the land, the railroad companies began to patent and locate their holdings and sell it as quickly as possible to generate revenue. Equally important to the railroad companies in the long term, was the development of towns along their routes with active and prosperous farming communities. Those settlements would provide a steady source of income with the shipment of farm goods back East.

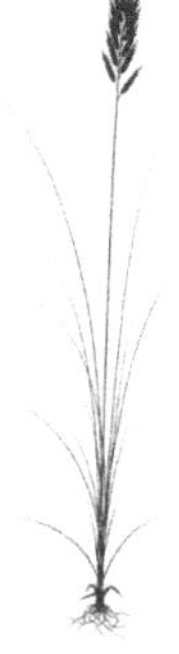

The railroads and various public and private interests promoted their lands back East in a variety of ways, including advertisements, brochures, colonization bulletins, lecturers and even immigration agents in the United States and Europe. The fruits of the labors of Nebraska farmers were advertised all across the eastern

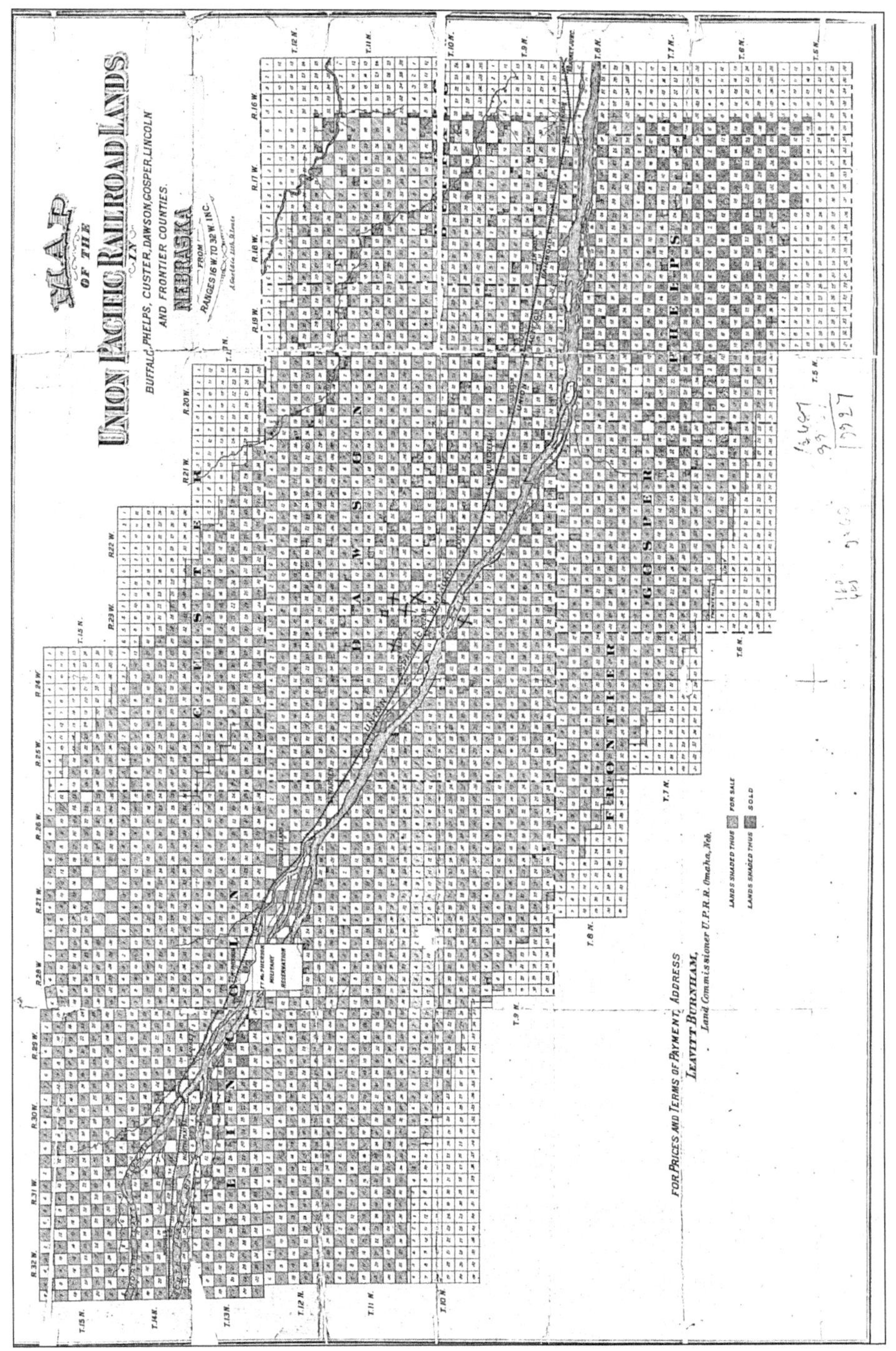


*Robert Henri Museum and Art Gallery Collection*

*This land map of the Union Pacific Railroad shows how the land was initially divided between the federal government and the railroad, creating a checkerboard effect on a map.*

part of the country, and the state's various agencies partnered with the railroads in their promotional efforts. This major effort was also done to counter the theory that had been held for several decades that the Great Plains were simply a *Great American Desert.*[72]

Homesteaders could acquire eighty acres at the minimum price of $2.50 per acre. On average, the Union Pacific sold its land for $4.27 per acre between 1871 and 1883. Equally importantly, the railroad provided long-term credit for buyers, including John J. Cozad, an Ohio investor and land speculator.[73]

The companies encouraged groups of people to come, including various ethnic groups such as the Swedes, Russo-Germans, or settlers from Nova Scotia, for example. In addition, religious groups and their movements to Nebraska were coordinated by the religious leaders of a particular church.[74] The Union Pacific pushed its colonization efforts westward along the Platte River Valley and by 1873 there were more than two thousand families and forty groups to the east of Buffalo County (which includes present-day Kearney) and a large Swedish contingent in Phelps and Kearney counties.

In late 1872, a smartly dressed Easterner, passing through the Platte River Valley on a Union Pacific train, stopped at Willow Island to evaluate the advantages of the country and began to formulate a vision to create a town at the 100th Meridian. The colonization efforts of the Union Pacific Rail Road had attracted John J. Cozad's attention. And so begins the story of Cozad, Nebraska and Robert Henri's roots to the state. However, before that auspicious occasion, the journey of the Cozads to Nebraska began several centuries before in France where John's ancestors were from, to New Amsterdam, which would later become New York City, to central and northeastern New Jersey, to Virginia, and then to Ohio.

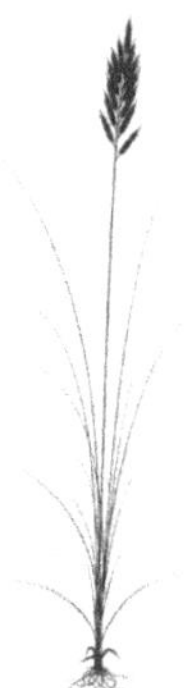

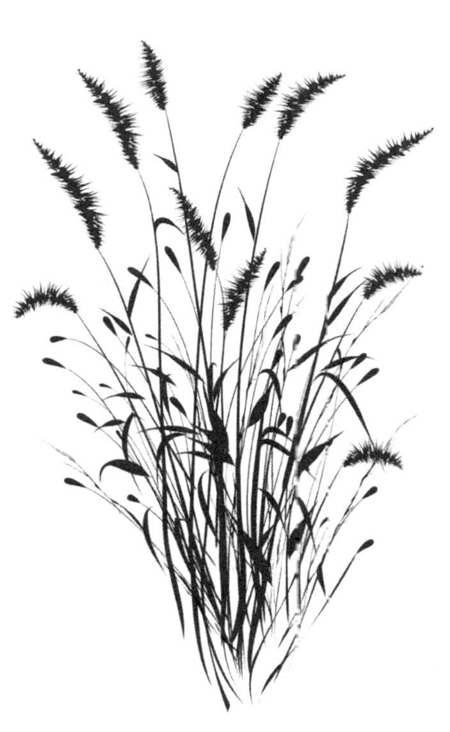

## *Chapter 2*

# Arrival of the Gamblin' Man

*Mr. Cozad spent money very liberally in putting up buildings and improvements in the place (Cozad-dale), hoping to make a permanent manufacturing town, but his views were not realized as evidenced by the many tenantless houses.*[1]

History of Warren County, Ohio

*The grain fields of Europe are mere garden patches beside the green oceans which roll across the Great Plains.*[2]

Correspondent
Cincinnati Gazette

JOHN COZAD'S DECISION TO CREATE A COMMUNITY in the Platte River Valley was the result of a number of influences including a family history of emigrating, land acquisition, speculation, developing new communities and finally, his own ambitious nature and the desire to succeed.

Cozad's ancestors on his father's side originated in Leyden, Holland, and then emigrated to New York, then known as New Amsterdam. The surname was then spelled *Cossart* although it would later be changed to Cozad. It was known to have twenty different varieties of spellings.[3]

After leaving New York, members of the family went to central and northwestern New Jersey and moved to Upshur County in the central part of present-day West Virginia, then in western Virginia. Cozad's grandfather, Job Cozad (1769- c. 1825?), married Catherine Fink (c.1770-c.1830) in 1791, and by this marriage there were nine children. They initially settled on the Hews River, near Buchanan, in the western part of Virginia and then moved to Ohio, settling near Hallsville, east of Cincinnati and south of Columbus. Job and two of his sons, Henry (1792-1861) and Daniel (1793-1815) served in the War of 1812 and both Job and Henry were Methodist ministers.[4] Henry (1792-1861) was married four times – to Jane Law (c. 1797 -1831), Margaret Clark (1802-1834), Mary Gregg (1802-1856) and Sythey Darby (1812-1869).[5]

Henry Cozad established Allensville in 1837 in Richmond Township. It was initially located in Ross County, and then incorporated into Jackson County. Because of a series of changes in various county boundaries Richmond Township ultimately was located in the newly established Vinton County in 1850. This small settlement was about six miles south of Hallsville and named for William Allen. Allen was a congressman for whom Henry had voted, and who served as a United States Senator from 1837-49 and was then governor of the state from 1874-76. Henry Cozad would also serve as the town's first merchant and postmaster. It was about one hundred twenty miles to the west of the ancestral home of his father, Job.[6]

One of three sons born of the marriage of Henry and his second wife, Margaret, was John Jackson Cozad, who was born on November 9, 1830, in Allensville. His mother died just three years after his birth, and John had a difficult relationship with Henry's third wife Mary, his stepmother. He left the family farm at the age of twelve to begin a life of adventure in 1842. He was later described as *a wanderer on the face of the earth.*[7]

John Cozad would ultimately continue his family's tradition of land development by creating a vast real estate empire that would ultimately spread across four states – Ohio, Nebraska and Colorado and lastly, New Jersey. There has also been a belief that Cozad even created a town in South America, although that has never been confirmed. It was a far more ambitious vision than any of his ancestors had ever dreamed of.[8]

To begin what became his purchase of far-flung real estate holdings, he acquired a farm in Vinton County, followed by several properties in Cincinnati, and established the town of Cozaddale, Ohio, about thirty miles northeast of Cincinnati. He then moved on to creating another community in Nebraska - Cozad. Creating communities, and developing real estate was something in the family's blood and a dominant theme in John J. Cozad's whole life.

## The Cincinnati Years

John Cozad (1830-1906) arrived in Cincinnati, Ohio, when he left home after falling out with his stepmother, and wanted to make, as he called it, *an easier living*, rather than the more arduous job of being a farmer or a farm hand. One Cozad historian believes that he first went to Circleville, Ohio, before moving onto Cincinnati.[9] In Cincinnati, he found a job as a cabin boy on one of the many river boats that plied the Ohio and Mississippi rivers of the era. By this time thousands of travelers were coming down the Ohio River annually by steamboats.[10]

Working in this setting brought him in contact with gamblers who played cards while traveling the rivers. From that experience came his career as a professional gambler and as he got older, extensive travels across the United States and even to South American countries, although where he went there is not known.[11]

Cozad went to California during the Gold Rush, even hiring bodyguards to protect him after he proved to be such a successful gambler. One of his gambling partners is said to have later been elected governor of that state. This may have been John McDougal (c. 1818-1866). He was also badly injured in several blackjacking incidents.[12]

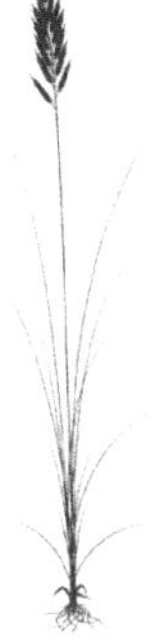

He became known as the *King of Gamblers* and was a master at the game of Faro and in fact was so successful at cards that he was barred from some gambling establishments. Cozad's ability to name the last card in a typical game was remarkable and infallible as one person recalled. Faro was then much more popular than poker and was the game of choice in the era.[13] Eugene Young and Samuel Schooley, two early Cozad settlers, would later recall that it was straight poker that was his favorite game and not Faro.[14]

While it has often been assumed that the profession was considered a tawdry one in that period it was not so.[15] In fact, as John Sloan, Robert Henri's (*Robert Henry Cozad*) best friend, would later say:

*Back in the sixties and seventies this kind of gambling was an honorable profession and regarded as a gentleman's prerogative.*[16]

He was physically described as:

*. . . courtly, with a commanding aspect and distinguished in appearance.*[17]

It was during one of his travels that Cozad met Theresa Gatewood (1837-1923), whose parents, Robert Burke Gatewood (1807-1884) and Julia Ann Jones (1813-1909), owned the Gatewood Hotel in Malden, Virginia (present-day West Virginia).[18]

They married on June 13, 1857, in Kanawha, Virginia (present-day West Virginia) along the Kanawha River, just as her parents had done.[19] They honeymooned in White Sulphur Springs, then a summer destination for wealthy Virginians and for three U.S. presidents. They stayed in Richmond, Virginia for a short time and then the Cozads proceeded on to Cincinnati, Ohio, not far from the real estate projects of his ancestors and about two hundred miles northwest of Malden. At the time John was twenty-seven and Theresa was nineteen. Cozad had been associated with the city for perhaps as many as fifteen years.[20]

## THE OHIO COUNTRY

Hector St. John de Crevecoeur, the writer who so poignantly described the American character in his *Letters from an American Farmer* in 1782, described Ohio, ten years before it was to become a state, when he wrote:

*It is without doubt the most fertile country, with the most varied soil, the best watered, and that which offers to agriculture and commerce, the most abundant and easy resources, of those which Europeans have ever discovered . . .*[21]

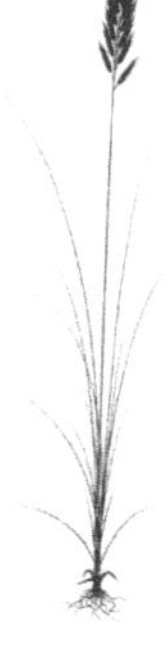

When the newlyweds arrived in Cincinnati, it was a bustling and rising city on the banks of the Ohio River with a six-mile shared shoreline with Kentucky directly to the south. The city was the region's commercial center and goods were shipped up and down the major waterway. Known at the time as *The Queen City, The Queen of the West* or the *City of Seven Hills*, the city was also a transportation nexus for five railroads, one of the most important manufacturing cities in the country, and the center of population in the United States. It was a major hog processing center too as hundreds of thousands of hogs were butchered there annually. The city was also home to breweries, distilleries, boat works, soap plants, shoe factories and beet processing plants. The metropolis was rapidly expanding, three hundred and thirty-six buildings were built in 1861 and it was the fastest growing city in America as immigrants poured in from Ireland and Germany. The population of the state grew from more than forty-two thousand people in 1800 to almost two hundred and thirty-one thousand by 1810. Soon, thousands were coming down the Ohio River annually by steamship.[22]

A major new opera house opened just after the Cozads arrived, and there was a major fine art gallery owned by William Wiswell that the family presumably frequented. Also, there was a large collection of public and private schools.[23]

One writer said about Cincinnati:

*I consider Cincinnati at the present time one of the most representative and fairly average of the great cities of the States . . . Observing this I saw that in Cincinnati I could study the present position and future prospects of the American republic better than in most other cities.*[24]

## The Civil War Arrives

The Civil War had a significant impact on the city, and before its outset Abraham Lincoln passed through on his way to his inauguration. Because it bordered a slave state, attacks were threatened by the Confederacy, and small raids were made on Cincinnati itself in 1862 along with a siege.[25] In 1863, after the Battle of Gettysburg, Confederate Brigadier General John Morgan crossed the Ohio River from the south and into Indiana, and then came into Ohio, not far from Cincinnati, plundering everything in his path. The governor called out the militia as Morgan proceeded eastward and came within twenty miles of Allensville. After the defeat of Morgan and his Confederate forces, the city remained a major important center for the military and a leading weapons storehouse for the Union Army.[26]

It is believed that John J. Cozad did not serve in the Union Army during the Civil War, which suggests he may have purchased the services of a soldier as so many wealthier citizens of the era were able to do. A John Cozad, aged 33, and living in Richland Township in Vinton County, is listed as married and his occupation shown as a farmer. He is included in the *Consolidate List Of Persons Class 1* who were subject to military duty compiled in June 1863. He was thirty at the beginning of the war and was listed as living in the same state of his birth. No records have been found indicating any service in the Union Army or why he may have even been exempted from service or if someone else served in his stead. There is another John J. Cozad who served in an Iowa regiment.[27]

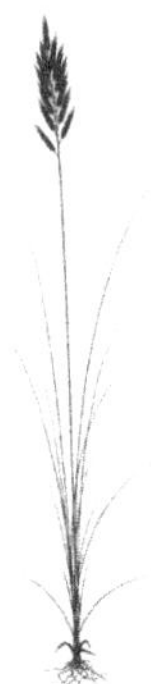

One speculation is that John J. Cozad may have been a Confederate or a supporter of the Southern cause. Neither of the major biographies of Robert Henri suggest that, nor is there any information that the author could find to support this. It is known that Cozad was related to Thomas Jonathan "Stonewall" Jackson (1824-1863), a general in the Confederate States Army, who died at the Battle of Chancellorsville in 1863 after being mistakenly shot by one of his own forces. He was related distantly to the Cozads by the marriage of Elizabeth Cozad (1779-1845) to John Jackson Jr. (1760-1821).[28]

Another possibility is that Theresa Gatewood Cozad, who was a member of the Gatewood family, may have been a Southern sympathizer although there is no evidence of that. The Gatewoods had been in Virginia for more than two centuries and the pull of that state may have been a strong one for her when she was in Ohio. Possibly she influenced Cozad to refrain from entering the conflict. And as will be seen later, John Cozad changed his name to honor a Southern signer of the Declaration of Independence, Richard Lee. However, there are no family traditions that have come down about Civil War service in any of the biographies that have been written about Robert Henri and if there had been, certainly there would have been some acknowledgement of service. More research needs to be done on this subject.

While it is not known what happened to the Cozads during the war, perhaps John and Theresa Cozad left Cincinnati as the war pushed northward and across the river from the city. They might have gone back to Vinton County which was farther away from the Ohio River although General Morgan's forces came within twenty miles to the south of Allensville. They may have even gone elsewhere.

After the war's conclusion, normal life resumed and Cincinnati continued its march toward progress. For example, the Cincinnati-Covington Bridge, an engineering triumph, opened and created a new thoroughfare to the South. By 1868, the city was known as the largest and wealthiest inland city in America. The city was regularly annexing land to provide for its future. The 1870 Federal Census revealed that there were 216,239 people living in the city with almost twenty-five thousand residences.[29]

## Life in the Queen City

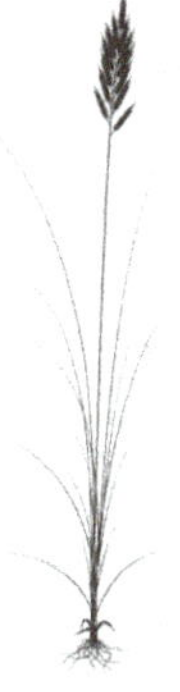

The Cozad lived in several places in Cincinnati although the record is incomplete. The first citation of John Cozad living in the city shows him at 192 Bar Street in 1859 and 1860. Then, an 1861 reference shows him as a real estate agent at 325 Longworth. A year later there is no mention of him or in 1863. The same is true for 1866. By1867 he was boarding at 182 Plum Street.[30]

The Cozads came to live at Plum and 5th Streets, which was in the center of the city, about six city blocks north from the Ohio River.[31] They later moved to 44 Hathaway Street which is where it is known they lived in 1879. Theresa described their house as *the finest on the street* and John Cozad also owned three other houses

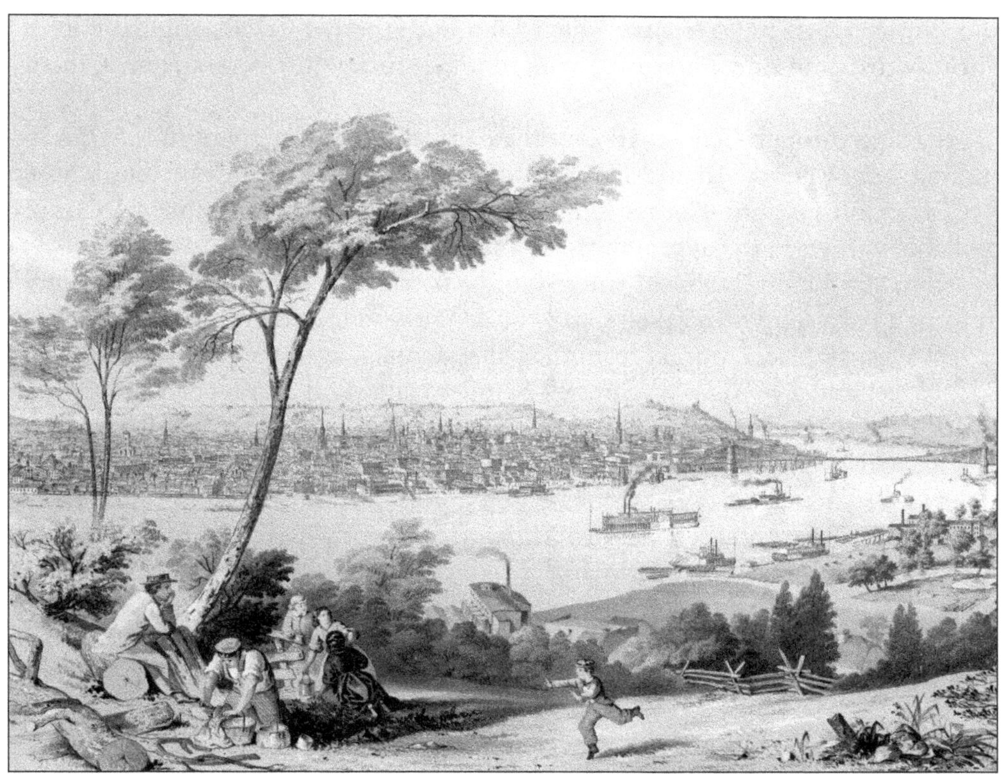

*Courtesy Library of Congress (Control Number 2003654043)*
*Cincinnati, Ohio*
*1868*

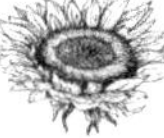

on the same street in addition to other properties around Cincinnati.[32]

Julia and Robert Gatewood and other family members followed the Cozads to Cincinnati during the Civil War. The 1860 U.S. Census shows them living in Kanawha Salines in Virginia in 1860. By 1863 they were residing in Cincinnati as evidenced by a lawsuit that Julia Gatewood was involved with and the fact that they are listed in a city directory.[33]

Another piece of history that may be relevant is the move may have occurred because of the controversial creation of the state of West Virginia, which had separated from the Confederate state of Virginia in 1863. The Gatewoods had previoulsy been living in what became the new state. Like the Cozads, this chapter of the family history is somewhat unclear[34]

The Gatewoods lived at, and ran, the Kanawha House, a boarding establishment, which also housed sons Traber Gatewood, and Samuel Early Gatewood, along with another son, James Gatewood. The boarding house was located at 5th

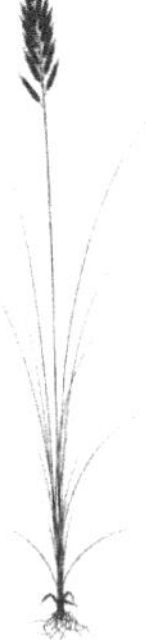

and Plum streets, the street on which John and Theresa Cozad originally lived. They owned a second hotel in Covington, Kentucky, just across from Cincinnati.[35]

Passing through Cincinnati over the decades were a variety of luminaries including John Quincy Adams, Harriet Beecher Stowe, Abraham Lincoln, Ulysses S. Grant, and numerous other Union officials. The Gatewoods and the Cozads probably witnessed the appearances of some of them.[36]

By 1868 John Cozad had entered into a partnership with Samuel Gatewood to form a real estate firm called Cozad and Gatewood. Their offices were located at 229 West 5th Street, not far from their first home. Cozad also had offices at 183 Race Street and 116 West 6th Street.[37] Samuel Gatewood also owned the *Central Dining Saloon*, catering as its advertisement said - *for Ladies and Gentlemen* - that was located at 173 Elm Street which was also near the family's home. Traber Gatewood, Theresa Cozad's brother, entered into an apprenticeship to become a dentist in the city and then went to Missouri and worked as a dentist. Sometime afterward he returned to Cincinnati.[38]

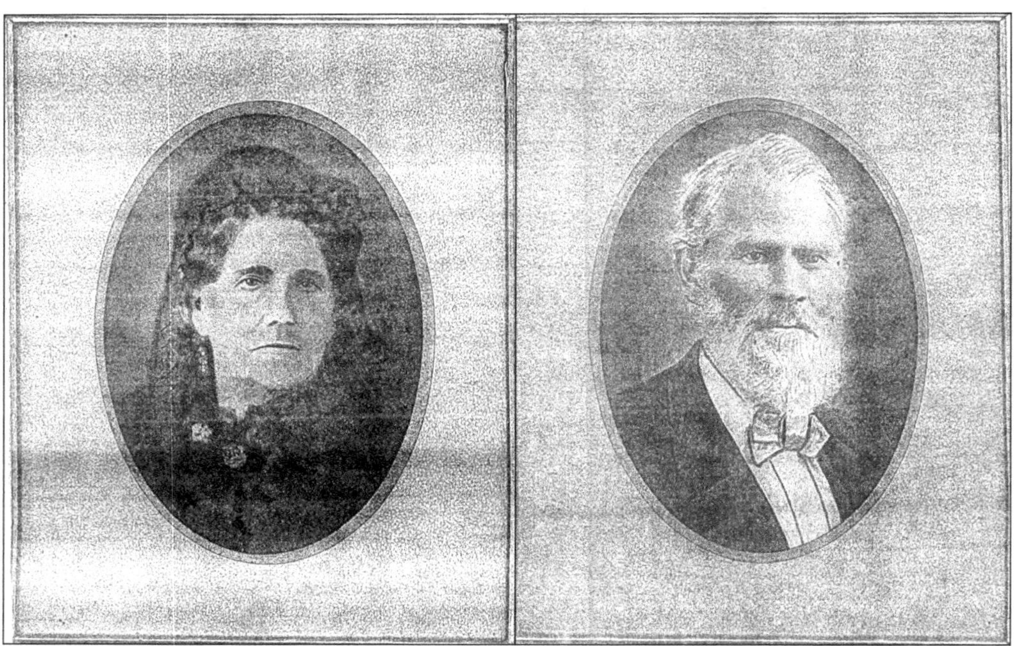

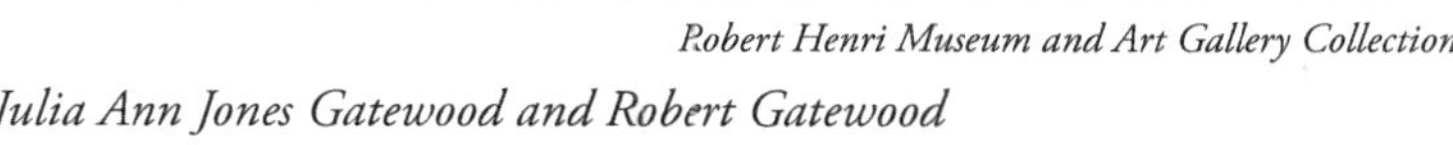

*Robert Henri Museum and Art Gallery Collection*

*Julia Ann Jones Gatewood and Robert Gatewood*

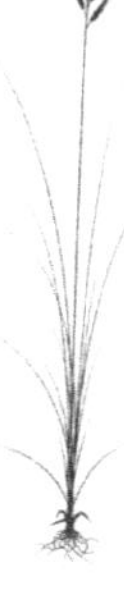

## The Cozad Boys Are Born to be Great Men

Both of the oldest Cozad sons were born in the city, John (Johnny) Anthony, on November 29, 1862, and Robert Henry on June 24, 1865, the same day that the final conclusion of the Civil War was marked by the surrender of Galveston, Texas. John was named for his father, and Robert was named for both of his grandfathers.[39]

John and Robert were, in the parlance of today, homeschooled, in their formative years. As part of their education Theresa instilled great hopes in her boys as she believed they would become *great men*, a hope that ultimately did come to fruition.[40]

Like his brother Johnny, Robert attended the Chickering Classical and Scientific Institute, a private school in Cincinnati. Founded in 1855 by J. B. Chickering it was originally known as Chickering's Academy. One curious connection, and perhaps the reason the boys were sent there, was because one of the instructors was William Venable (1836-1920). Venable had a long teaching career and the Cozads might have known that because his family had lived in Waynesville, in the same county in which Cozaddale would later be created. Near the end of Robert's time at the school, or just after he finished, Venable became the principal and proprietor of the school.[41]

By the time Robert Cozad began at the venerable institution, there were more than two hundred students attending classes. Many of the graduates went onto college or scientific schools.[42] Cozad had above average grades in most of the courses he studied, and his general average was 80 or above. He took courses like arithmetic, geography, geology, declamation (dramatic oration), composition, Greek, Latin, German. He had trouble with spelling, a trait that would remain apparent in his letters and notebooks for decades to come, as well as Latin and German. In the spring of 1879, he was late seven times, but in 1878 and 1879 was not absent at all. He was described as being *remarkably bright*. Both John and Theresa Cozad signed his report cards. Today the Robert Henri Museum and Art Gallery owns three of his report cards from his years at Chickering.[43]

Theresa Cozad's philosophy, and one that can be seen reflected in the adult lives of her boys was:

*Each day – must get books – learning to talk, to think – to read – about common things, Right and Wrong.*[44]

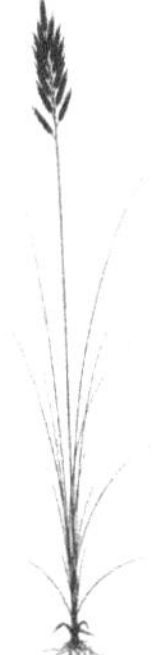

The goals for her life were written in a notebook, and these too would be echoed in the lives of her boys:

*Love nature and books: seek them and you will be happy; for virtuous friendship, love and knowledge of mankind must inevitably accompany these, all things thus re-*

*peating their influence in due season.*[45]

In the years to come Theresa would write to her son Johnny:

*Of course, our greatest interest has been for our boys . . .* [46]

The Cozads would have been exposed to the rich cultural events in the city including its art galleries. Theresa Cozad also took her two young boys, Johnny (1862-1933) and Robert (1865-1929), to concerts, operas, theater presentations, the library and to attend services at St. John's Methodist Episcopal Church as they got older. In the matter of politics, the family members were Democrats.[47]

Mari Sandoz believed that Robert's mother exposed him to Cincinnati's most well-known artist, Frank Duvenek, who painted *The Whistling Boy* in 1872. Curiously, Duvenek was inspired by seventeenth-century masters Diego Velázquez and Frans Hals, two artists who would come to inspire Robert in his artistic career. The Cincinnati Art Museum, one of the Midwest's most important art museums would not be constructed until 1886, long after the Cozads were gone although the Cincinnati Museum Association, an organization created to build an art museum was organized in 1881.[48]

One of the most significant events that the Cozads must have attended was the Cincinnati Industrial Exposition which was held annually in Cincinnati between 1870 and 1888 to showcase the products of Cincinnati business owners. The expositions also promoted the economic development of the city, and thousands of people from all over the country came to attend.[49]

Interestingly, there is no mention of either John or Theresa Cozad in the late nineteenth century histories written about Cincinnati. Given that it was a town of two hundred thousand, that may be explained by his simply being a resident who had not yet earned the reputation as the wealthy businessman and community developer he became in the next decade. Neither must have been active in the affairs of the community, or at least in such a way that it would have garnered notice. John is listed in the real estate and business listings in the city directories. At the time, there were more than forty real estate agents working in the city.[50]

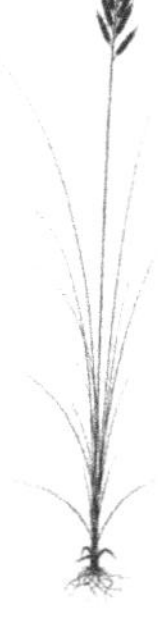

## The Birth of Cozaddale

It is not known when or why John Cozad developed the vision to create a new community that would be called Cozaddale. However, it is known that his first land purchases in the southern end of Warren County, Ohio began in 1867. Warren County was adjacent to the northeast corner of Hamilton County, where Cincinnati was located. It was midway between Cincinnati and Allensville. Prior to Cozad's purchases, a small settlement called Spence's Station had been located there, founded by John W. Spence. For at least thirty years, Spence was the gen-

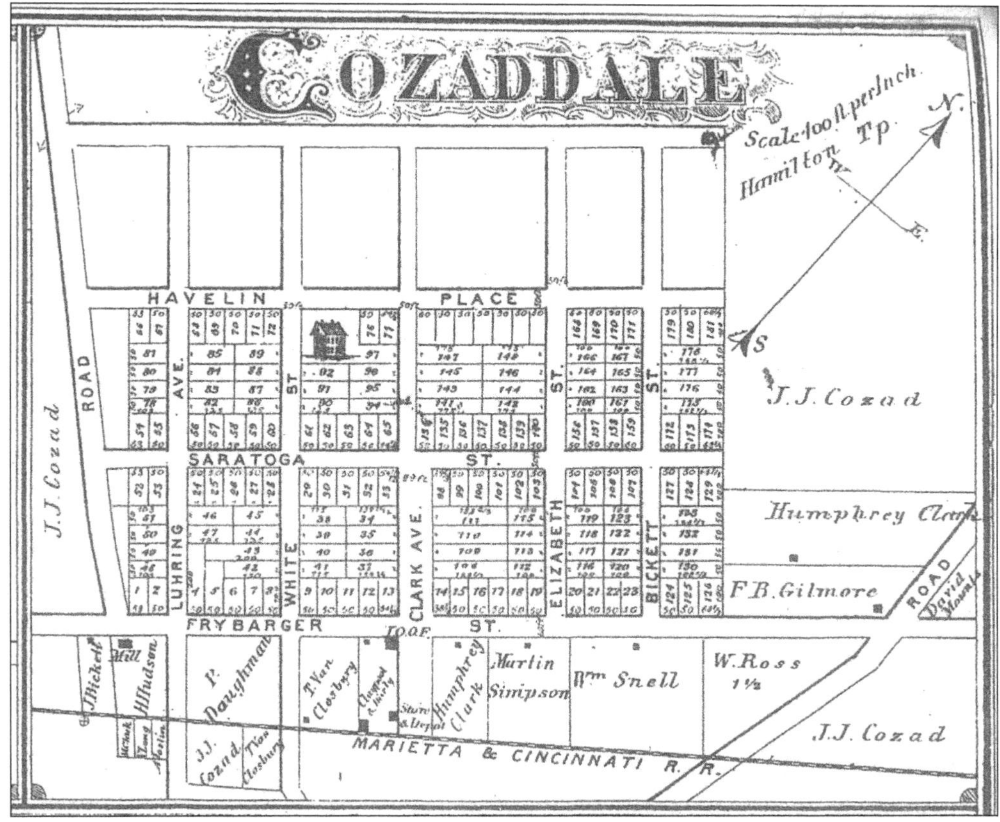


*Robert Henri Museum and Art Gallery Collection*

*This 1870s atlas map of Cozaddale shows the large footprint of John Cozad's holdings in the small Ohio town. Just as he would do in Nebraska, he owned large lots, including one along the railroad, and he probably had owned at one point many of the smaller numbered lots in the town.*

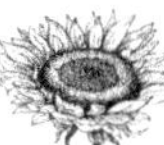

eral store owner, postmaster and railroad agent. By 1868, John Cozad is listed in the Cincinnati business directories as residing in Spence's Station.[51]

It is believed by one of Henri's biographers that John had a vision for a manufacturing community that would be a magnet for Union Army veterans. There may have been a variety of factors at work. Was it because he had seen the expositions where manufacturing was featured along with the arts? Perhaps it was because he saw the city annexing land and growing rapidly and that it would ultimately expand out toward the north and east to where he was thinking about building a new community? Perhaps the theme of developing communities by previous generations of family members was his inspiration. Or was it a desire to find a less urban environment? After all, hundreds of thousands of hogs were being processed every year, and the population was growing quickly in Cincinnati.

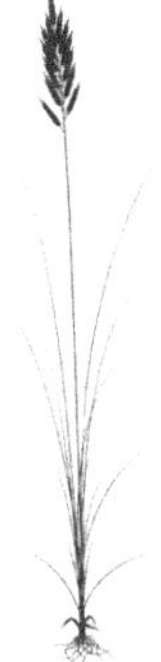

Their home was in the middle of a congested part of town. Hazel Phillips in her publication entitled *Invincible Gambler*, speculated that John earned a great deal of winnings on an Ohio-Mississippi riverboat and with those funds had decided to build a new community. Or was it the restlessness that is one of the defining features of John J. Cozad's life.[52]

Implementing his vision, Cozad purchased more than three hundred acres over the course of several years in the area surrounding what became Cozaddale. He acquired the land from Daniel Snell. [53] After those earlier land purchases, the Cozads moved to Hamilton Township near the southern boundary of the county and lived in a farmhouse that he renovated.[54]

The 1870 Federal Census of Warren County lists John J. and Theresa along with their sons, as living in the township. John Sr.'s occupation was shown to be in *Dry Goods Dealer, Ret(itred?);* Theresa was listed as *keeping house;* two of their boys, John and Robert, *attending school;* and a third son, Plunet (1870), identified later as Plunkett, was at home. The Cozads had two domestic servants – Caroline Rash (30) and Sara Caddis (41), along with one farm laborer, George Kebler (30).[55] At the time of this major change in their lives, John was forty-one and Theresa was thirty-four.

Cozad then platted Cozaddale which became an unincorporated village in Hamilton Township in 1871.[56] The new town was about one hundred miles west of the town his father had founded in Vinton County. A new post office was established at the same time the town was established, and John J. Cozad was named its first postmaster on June 2, 1871. He served until 1873. A post office had previously been located in Dallasburgh, one mile to the west of Cozaddale, having been established in 1848.[57]

Most importantly, the town was located along the Marietta and Cincinnati Railroad, a vital transportation artery which had opened in 1857, the same time the Cozads married and arrived in Cincinnati.[58] Because the city was only a short trip by rail, the Cozads maintained ties to Cincinnati and visited it regularly.

Cozad's effort is said to have been the *first development project* in Warren County. Cozad divided his community into two hundred lots crisscrossed by eight streets. He invested heavily in the community, organizing a building association, constructing several homes and a three story building, establishing businesses for potential residents to live in and work at, and creating a manufacturing town. In the 1870 Census, he was reported to have real estate valued at fifteen thousand dollars and personal real estate worth fifteen hundred dollars. Later, there were stores, a creamery, mill, saloon, dance hall, and a blacksmith shop established.[59]

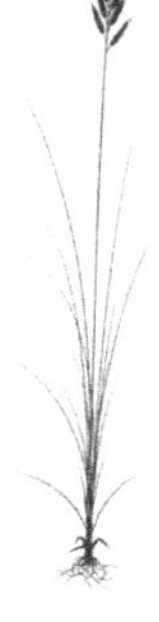

He may have even donated the property and the costs of building the Methodist Church there. He was even a member of the Independent Order of Odd Fellows that was established there.[60]

It was during these years that John Cozad traveled to Washington, D.C., to have a portrait made by the famed photographer, Mathew Brady at his studio at 352 Pennsylvania Avenue.[61] Brady was known for his photographs of the famous and well known and had a gallery in which the photos were displayed.[62] In the photograph he stands proud, looking out to the future as it would appear. Another photograph, a headshot, was taken but it is not known when. Some have suggested that it was his wedding photograph.

## The House on the Hill

Another major investment in the community that he made was the construction of a beautiful two-story Italianate styled brick house that was attached to a smaller farmhouse that had been refurbished and which the family had lived in since either 1867 or 1868.[63]

The side-gabled brick structure was built in the fashion of home construction that was used from 1840-1885 and described as being *High Victorian Italianate.* The house was built using the more decorative features of the style including the imposing tall brick construction, wide overhanging eaves with numerous decorative brackets, heavy lintels over each window, floor to ceiling windows on the first floor, and two-over-two windows on the second floor.[64]

One of the most distinctive features of the house was the handsome three-story tower on the front side that included a large dome on top. Only about fifteen percent of Italianate buildings have towers and an even fewer have domes

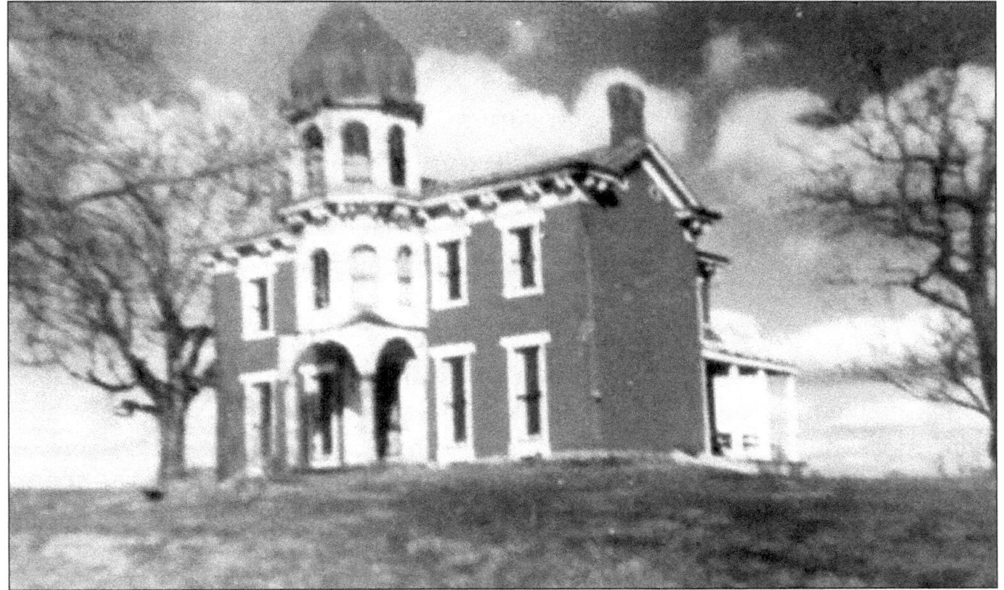

*Robert Henri Museum and Art Gallery Collection*

*The home that John Cozad built for his family in Cozaddale, Ohio, is similar in style to the hotel and residence that he built in Cozad. It was constructed of brick, but the museum's design does not include an elaborate tower in the front or bracketing along the roof line.*

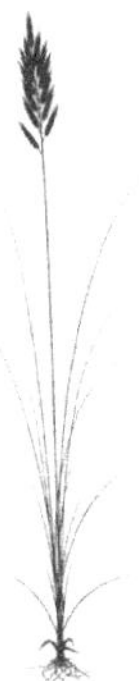

at the top as most of the towers are square. It created an imposing entrance to the building.[65]

After the Cozad's left Cozaddale the residential building was purchased by Decatur Wylie who was known to be the owner in 1877. The next owner was Frank Wylie and the building was remodeled by him in 1893.[66]

### A Sad Chapter

Altogether the Cozads had six children. Tragically, four did not survive including William Early (1867?-1870), who was born in Warren County, and was a little more than three years old when he died in Cozaddale.[67] Plunkett, identified previously as Plunet (1869-1870), was born in Cozaddale, and died from cholera.[68] A fifth child, Alexander (1871-1873), was born in Cozaddale which is also where he died.[69] An infant girl (1873), the last of the children born to John and Theresa, lived for just one day, and was born in Cozaddale also.

It is believed that all four of these children were buried in Lot No. 24, Section 28 in the Cemetery of Spring Grove in Cincinnati as the family owned a plot there. Today a small circular marble marker remains there indicating the location.[70]

Robert was very sickly during his first year living in Cozaddale. For Theresa Cozad, the memories of the Cozaddale experience must have reflected a deep sadness as four of her children died there. It may have also been a factor in why the Cozads left their town behind. From that point forward Theresa focused her attention on the two surviving boys.[71]

### Westward Ho

John J.'s efforts to create a prosperous town in Ohio were not successful and apparently, by 1872, he was already investigating real estate in Nebraska. The Union Pacific Rail Road was selling millions of acres along its right of way and the federal government was awarding land to homesteaders willing to make a commitment.[72]

There were probably several factors that brought this project to a close, the first of which may have been its location and the proximity to the larger metropolis of Cincinnati.[73] Another source states that there was controversy between him and the local building association. Bennard Perlman, a Henri biographer, believes that the building association Cozad had created was dissolved and that a suit was brought against Cozad by an unidentified party claiming that Cozad owed him thirteen hundred dollars. The plaintiff won his case.[74]

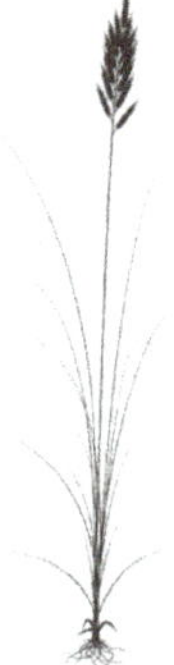

It has also been speculated by one Ohio author that Cozad won a large sum in a card game there and that he was accused of cheating. According to this source he left Cozaddale immediately afterwards. Mari Sandoz believed that there had been an argument, although she does not describe what it was over. In addition, the death of four of their children there may also have been a contributing factor.[75]

Yet another tradition is that he had abdominal troubles, which he believed was cancer, and he thought that Nebraska might be a place to restore his health. Another theory is that he had tuberculosis.[76] At the end of the day, it does not matter the cause, the Cozads left and moved on to Nebraska.

As to John Cozad's time associated with Cozaddale, for the first time he becomes a part of the larger historical record as his real estate efforts are remembered in *The History of Warren County,* which was published in 1882. Prior to that he is listed in city directories and land records. He is also remembered in a much later history of Cozaddale, entitled *Invincible Gambler*, which states that he left his Ohio community sometime in 1873, and which coincides with what is known of his new interests in Nebraska. Another history of the community, *Warren County Local History* by Dallas Bogan also looks at the Cozad connection to his town. Perhaps the stories about the various other controversies are true. Or, perhaps he quickly lost interest in his Ohio investment for something that was more promising financially. Or, maybe he wrote it off as an unsuccessful venture given what was happening as a national financial crisis began that year which was described as the *Panic of 1873*. But given the rather short time that he had invested in it before he moved on to the next project, one can only speculate until more definitive evidence is found. He retained ownership of the platted Ohio lands until the 1880s.[77]

No matter the reason, Cozad and his family left that community development effort behind permanently after 1873. By 1880, nine years after he had platted the town, there were only one hundred and forty-three people living there, along with two stores and a shoe shop. Today, it is a small hamlet at a crossroads.[78] And, while the Cozads continued to maintain ties to Cincinnati, John Cozad's name last appears in the Cincinnati city directories in 1879.[79]

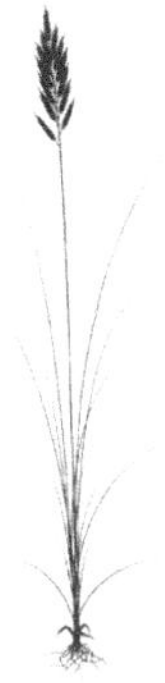

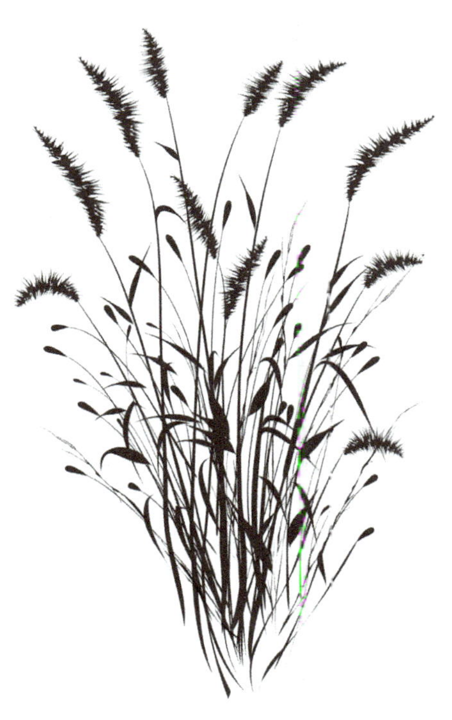

## *Chapter 3*

# The Valley of the Platte

*My parents, Mr. and Mrs. John Cusack lived in Darr, then called Coyote, 1872-1881. And father was the section boss at that time. I have heard him tell about meeting Mr. Cozad. It seems Mr. Cozad always wore a high, black silk hat and carried a cane, and while at work father saw him walking along the railroad track and asked him what he was looking for. He replied he was looking for a location for a town. My father suggested why not locate a town at the 100th Meridian and showed him where it was located and told him it was halfway between Coyote and Willow Island, and he did.*[1]

Recollection of Mrs. C. P. Hord, July 23,1952
daughter of John Cusack
Section Boss of the Union Pacific Railroad

*He (John Cozad) found a country that suited him in every respect, and that he intended to bring and invest near this point, every cent of his extensive fortune.*[2]

Edwin W. Sandison
Agent, Union Pacific Rail Road, Willow Island, Nebraska
1873

*Mr. Cozad and friends have a large and grand field of labor before them, and as they have within their reach all the necessaries required to build up a large, wealthy and prosperous city, I cannot help picturing this grand enterprise crowned with a brilliant future. May success and prosperity forever accompany such noble undertakings.*[3]

Edwin W. Sandison
Agent, Union Pacific Rail Road, Willow Island, Nebraska
1873

MARI SANDOZ BEGINS HER BOOK, *Son of the Gamblin' Man*, with the story of a tall, handsomely dressed man walking westward along the main line of the Union Pacific from Coyote (*present-day Darr*), to an unnamed place in the summer of 1872. It is believed that her account is based on the recollections of Mrs. C. P. Hord, the daughter of John Cusack. He was the section boss of the portion of the Union Pacific Rail Road that included Coyote and present-day Cozad. Traveling westward from Coyote on a handcart he saw Cozad walking toward him. After looking a potential town site over, Cusack and Cozad headed west to Willow Island.[4]

Another version of this story comes from a family genealogy entitled *The Riggs Family in America*. In this account, also set in the summer of 1872, the nattily dressed man got off a westbound train at Willow Island, halfway between present-day Gothenburg and Cozad.[5]

Richard Costin, along with several other men, took this stranger back eastward on a rail hand car to the place where the Union Pacific's sign stood to mark the 100th Meridian. It was there that the man in the swallow-tail suit decided to build a community.[6]

Yet another source, the Union Pacific's land agent in Willow Island, Edwin Sandison, said in 1873 that the distinguished and well-dressed man had made a short visit to the area in the fall of 1873. The land agent had taken him out on a trip to show him the countryside.[7] It was also in 1873 that John Cozad apparently tried to negotiate a land purchase with area resident Josiah Huffman for a town site in Willow Island to no avail.[8]

One version of the story comes from Robert Gatewood, a nephew to Theresa, and Robert Cozad's cousin, who wrote an essay entitled *Who Was Robert Henri?* in 1932. He said that John Cozad took the railroad to Kearney, was able to get a horse, and rode out to Fort McPherson on the north side of the Platte River and then back forty miles on the south side of the river to approximately the location of the 100th Meridian. Because Robert Gatewood and John J. Cozad discussed his time in Nebraska one must wonder if in fact this story may be the correct one. In a 1964 letter to a Henri biographer, Gatewood suggested that

John Cozad had come west to explore the region in 1868 and came back in 1873 to create his town.[9]

Another Cozad researcher has a slightly different version of this story in that he states that John Cozad left Ohio and came west on a wagon train bound for the West Coast. He then departed at Omaha, buying a horse and proceeding westward along the Platte River.[10]

However, in the end, perhaps all the versions of this story are true, or that some combination of those events did indeed happen, but the mists of time have made that impossible to resolve with certainty. In the end it is known that the man's first encounter with the area that would become home to him occurred in either 1872 or 1873.

That man was John J. Cozad (1830-1906), a professional gambler, real estate developer and land speculator from Cincinnati, Ohio. Cozad's arrival that summer, just one year after Dawson County was legally created, came with much ambition and possibility but was ultimately bookended with tragedy, disappointment, and legal peril a decade later.

Much has been written over the last half century about John Cozad, the founder of the town that bore his name, builder of the substantial brick structure that served as his family's private residence and a hotel, and the shooting of a rancher. And yet even as his legacy still casts a long shadow over that small city, his time in Nebraska was short-lived as he also spent time in Denver, Colorado, and elsewhere in that state, and back in Ohio where he had established Cozaddale.

## The Soil is Rich

There were a number of factors that drew John J. Cozad to Nebraska. Just fifty years before, in 1820, the vast interior of the United States had been described as the *Great American Desert* by U. S. Army Major Stephen Long, leader of the first scientific exploration up the Platte. He served as a military explorer, topographical engineer, and later a railway engineer.[11]

The population of the territory, then state, increased dramatically after the passage of the Kansas-Nebraska Act in 1854. At the time of the act's signing by the president, the population of Nebraska stood at 2,732, almost all of it in the eastern part along the Missouri River. At the time it came into the Union in 1867, there were about fifty thousand residents. By 1870 there were almost one hundred and twenty-three thousand residents, and by 1880 there were more than four hundred fifty thousand. Those arriving came from Ohio, New York, Pennsylvania, Illinois, Iowa, Indiana and Missouri. The flow of population into Nebraska continued at a strong pace over the two decades after the Civil War and was due largely to the construction of the railroads across the state and the federal government homesteading policies.[12]

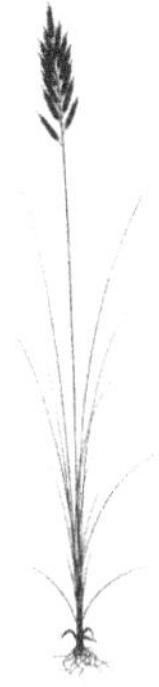

By 1860, farming in the Nebraska Territory was becoming increasingly profitable, as both corn and wheat were successfully being grown and sent to market. In that year more than one million bushels of corn had been harvested along with almost one hundred and fifty thousand bushels of wheat. Media accounts promoted the richness of the soil and the success of the farmers. Agriculture revenue dwarfed that of the few manufacturers in the territory.[13]

An article in the *Cincinnati Gazette*, a newspaper John J. Cozad might have read, said:

*The soil is very rich, and the mind falters in its attempt to estimate the future of such a valley, or its immense capabilities.*[14]

In 1865, just one year before the railroad arrived at present-day Cozad, Samuel Bowles, the editor of a Massachusetts publication, rode westward on a stagecoach and described the Platte River valley in his book *Across the Continent* :

*The valley of the Platte, through these Plains, is the natural highway across the continent. Other valleys and routes have similar advantages, but in minor degree: this unites the most; for it is central – it is on a line of our great cities and our great industries, East and West, and it is the longest, most continuous. A smooth, hard stage road is made by simply driving over it; a railroad awaits only sleepers and rails.*[15]

Whether John Cozad saw Bowles' book is not known but there were other publications with similar descriptions, and which could often be found in the nation's newspapers. As Bowles pointed out, the Platte River Road was part of a longer corridor of communities that, even then, were seen to become important and rising cities including San Francisco, Denver, Salt Lake City, Omaha, Chicago and the smaller cities in between. That observation remains true to this day and curiously the Robert Henri Museum's visitors today continue to come from California, Denver, Omaha, Lincoln, Chicago and New York, that very same transcontinental corridor that so attracted Cozad to Nebraska.

Mari Sandoz described how the river valley looked when John Cozad first saw it:

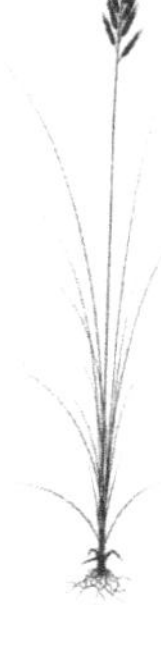

*. . . As he looked to the northern horizon, edged by hazy bluffs cut into folds that must be brush and scrub timber tucked into breaks and canyons. A mile or so south of him a low line of brushy trees marked by the Platte River, and farther on a hazier line of bluffs, even and flat topped as a great mesa, stretched along the horizon. Between these two bluff lines lay the fertile valley of the Platte, fifteen to twenty miles wide and stretching westward from back at the Missouri River out across Nebraska . . .*[16]

The valley was also described as *an immense hay meadow.*[17] There is one direct quote from John J. Cozad that remains in the historical record describing his feelings about Nebraska and in particular the Platte River valley. The Union Pacific's land agent relayed that Cozad said the following on his 1873 trip:

*The locality excels the state of California as far as California surpasses the eastern and southern states.*[18]

When getting back to Cozaddale that fall he told people, probably many of those early colonizers and family members, that:

*He found a country that suited him in every respect, and that he intended to bring and invest near this point, every cent of his extensive fortune.*[19]

The geographic location was also appealing to Cozad as it sat on the imaginary but significant demarcation of the 100th Meridian, even if it was an approximation of where the line actually was. It was also a location that the railroad had wanted to see developed as a town. And what better place where one might someday relocate the nation's capital of the country at its very center as John Cozad is said to have dreamed of doing? How many communities could make such a claim? [20]

The draw of the West to Easterners and Europeans was a powerful influence as evidenced by the importance of the Oregon, California and Mormon trails. New York City newspaper publisher Horace Greeley, who is often mistakenly attributed with printing the quote: *Go West young man,* provided a powerful incentive for people to take up homesteading.[21] In 1872 he had been nominated by the National Liberal Convention for the presidency at their assembly in Cincinnati. Railroads, the territories, states and corporations all advertised the benefits of living in the West and the richness of the land.

While those travelers in Murphy wagons or *prairie schooners* as they were called, were initially headed to the West Coast or Utah, as time went by some simply stopped along the way and began settling in places that later became the states of Iowa, Nebraska, North Dakota, South Dakota, and Kansas. By then railroad travel had made the journey much easier, quicker and cheaper than the months long journey across the Great Plains under difficult conditions. That was certainly the case by the time John J. Cozad stopped in 1872 and brought his first group of homesteaders in 1873.

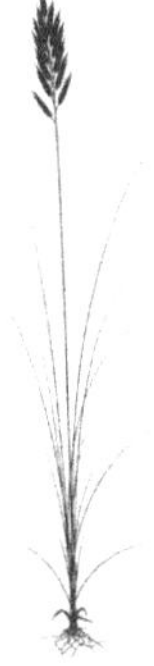

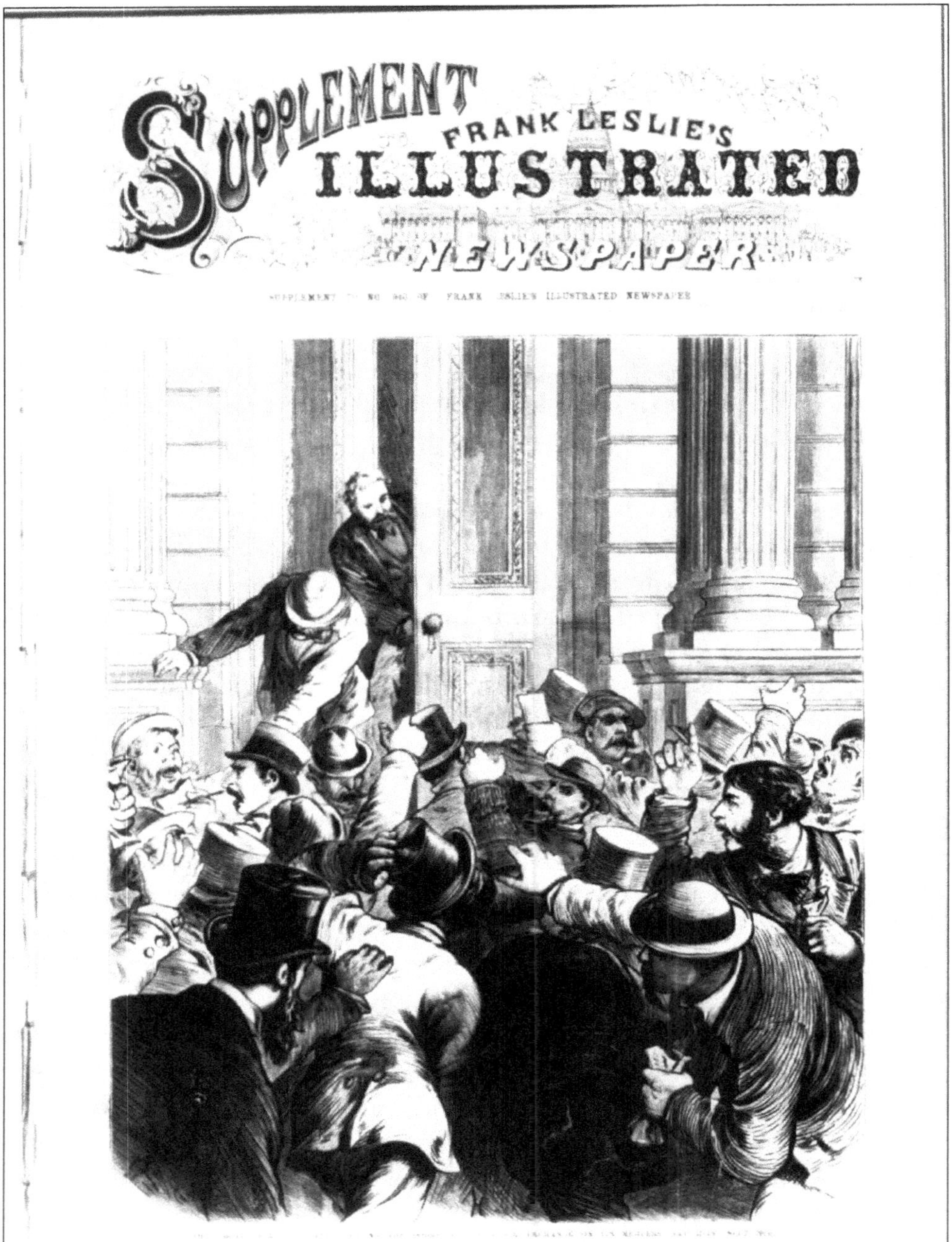

Supplement
Frank Leslie's
Illustrated
Newspaper

Courtesy Library of Congress (Control Number 99614016)

*Panic of 1873*

## The Panic of 1873

The Civil War, fought from 1861-65, was very much in the nation's consciousness and development in the decades that followed. Veterans of the Confederate and Union armies had begun moving to the West to try to begin anew. Both the North and South had paid a terrible price both in human and economic terms as a result of the war. The southern states had been wrecked physically and economically by the war, and major societal changes were underway as well. For the South, the transition from a slave economy was a difficult one. The reconstruction of the South, which began at the war's conclusion, would not end until decades later. The Northern states were growing increasingly industrialized and would take the rest of the nation forward with it. The country was transformed from an agricultural economy to an industrialized one.

Against that backdrop, a final factor that also contributed significantly to the Cozad story but is not often written about was the financial crisis known as the *Panic of 1873*. An economic depression that had begun in Europe spread across the Atlantic and to the United States in the fall of 1873. Its roots were many, including speculative investments in railroads and the damages caused by major fires in Chicago and Boston among others. However, it became a major crisis in September when, Jay Cooke and Company, a firm holding bonds for the Northern Pacific Railway, collapsed in New York City. The financial panic that ensued swept across America and to the agricultural economy in Nebraska.[22]

The country's economy collapsed and fell into a five-year depression that certainly must have figured not only in John Cozad's calculations but those who came to the Cozad Colony with him initially and afterwards. Many who came to Nebraska left dreary and troubled cities, failed banks and a wrecked economy behind to start over. In October of 1873, just weeks after the collapse of the Jay Cooke Company, Cozad took out his first homestead claim in what became Cozad, Nebraska.[23]

And, finally, in the spring of 1873, there was an epidemic of cholera that spread through Cincinnati for six months killing more than two hundred.[24]

## A Nebraska Land Baron

As the railroad construction moved west in the years that followed the 1862 transcontinental railroad legislation, the land was surveyed and divided into townships and then subdivided into sections. Individual surveyors, under contract with the Federal government, were hired to locate, survey and run the township and section lines all across the state. The government and railroad were assigned alternate sections in a forty-mile-wide strip to release for homesteaders or to sell. As a result, there was a checkerboard-like effect shown on period maps and surveys.[25]

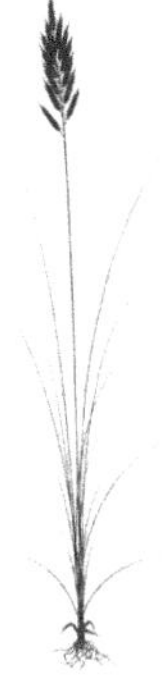

Among those many contracts were surveys for the three townships that would include crucially located real estate near the railroad at the 100th Meridian that Cozad later purchased including Township No. 10 North, Range No. 23 West of the 6th Principal Meridian;, Township No. 10 North, Range No. 24 West of the 6th Principal Meridian; and Township No. 11 North, Range No. 24 West of the 6th Principal Meridian.[26] The land to the south of Cozad, Township No. 10 North, Range No. 24 West of the 6th Principal Meridian, present-day Fairview, was initially surveyed in 1865 by Oliver Short, and then the township lines were surveyed in the summer and fall of 1868-69 by Chancey Wiltse and William Allason. The subdivisions were surveyed in 1869 by Wiltse.[27]

The land that included the town of Cozad (Township No. 10 North, Range No. 23 West) was surveyed by William J. Allason in the late summer and fall of 1868. The last township (Township No. 9 North, Range No. 23 West) was originally surveyed by Oliver Short in 1865 and the township and subdivision lines were marked by William Allason, three years later, and five years before John Cozad arrived on the scene. It is not clear if this Allason is the same surveyor as William J. Allison, a government surveyor and contractor who had been awarded numerous contracts for running lines of latitude, township lines and section lines across the state.[28]

When John Cozad arrived in 1873, the land in the townships nearest the meridian and the route of the Union Pacific Railroad had been surveyed and marked. When he took prospective purchasers out onto the prairie in the years to come, he was looking for those corners of the sections as had been designated and marked with wood posts five years before. Some had probably been obliterated by the harsh weather.

Cozad then began a sustained effort acquiring vast tracts of land through purchases and options. The record regarding John Cozad's landholdings is a complicated one, and there are various accounts about his transactions that have come down from different sources that do not always match. His first interest was in creating a community at the 100th Meridian, but Cozad also continued to think about building his community at Willow Island. In the end, Josiah Huffman and the cattlemen around the area must have given him pause so he focused back on the 100th Meridian. Purchasing survey maps from the land office in North Platte, Cozad began to explore the area and search out various sections for the best land.[29]

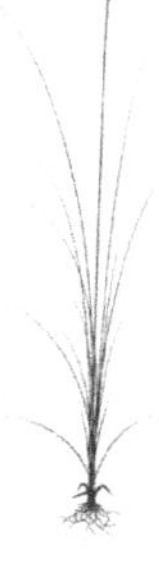

From Federal government records, it is known that John Cozad purchased one hundred and sixty acres, as a tree claim, in the northwest quarter of Township No. 10, Range No. 23 West, Section 8 on October 6, 1873. This parcel, the first that Cozad claimed in Dawson County, was located next to Section 7 on the east. Section 7 later became the city of Cozad. It was also the first claim of land in this section which was owned by the Federal government. By the spring and fall of 1874, others were also buying land in Township No. 10 North, Range No. 24 West of the 6th Principal Meridian.[30]

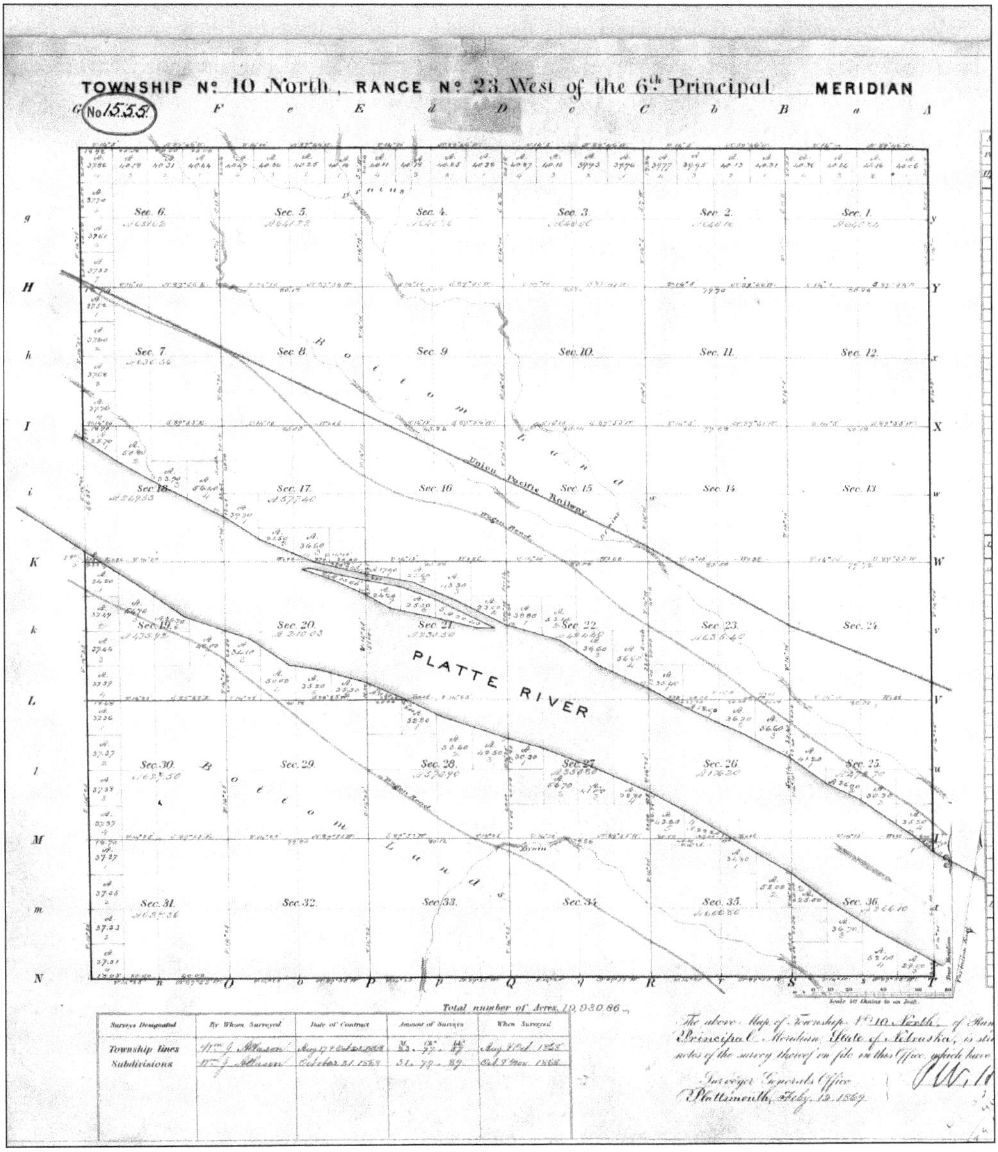

Courtesy Nebraska State Surveyors Office

*This survey map was created by contractor surveyors in 1868 and then certified by the Surveyor General in 1869. Sections 6 and 7 include much of present day Cozad, Nebraska. The Oregon Trail is shown as a wagon trail south of the Platte River, and the Mormon Trail is also shown as a wagon trail to the north of the river.*

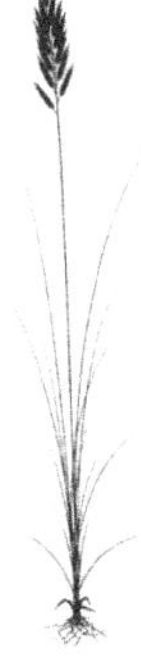

A tree claim was an inducement by the Timber Culture Act of 1873 to encourage homesteaders to plant trees in the hopes that it would change the ecosystems of the West and provide fuel and timber in the future along with windbreaks. If an individual acquired one hundred and sixty acres he was required to plant forty acres of trees. However, because of loopholes in the law, most of those claims were never planted with trees and the law was ultimately repealed in 1891. Cozad did pay ten dollars for the land that was worth two dollars and fifty cents an acre.[31]

According to the *Early History of the Cozad Community and Pioneer Families 1873-1998* and which is confirmed by land records:

*The first homestead taken out in Cozad township was by John J. Cozad himself on October 6, 1873. It, however, was cancelled, as were homesteads taken out by Dan (recorded as Van) B. Gatewood and Humphrey Clark, on December 11 of that year.*[32]

Why those claims were ultimately relinquished is not clear. Van Gatewood's December 11, 1873, purchase of one hundred and seventy-two acres in Section 18, (Township 10 North, Range 23 West) was only half the size of a typical section because much of it was under the Platte River. It too was a tree claim and had been owned by the Federal government. Later, Traber Gatewood, Robert Gatewood, and John Cozad would also buy properties in this section which were near the Platte River and directly south of Section 7. In reality, it was not John Cozad who filed the first claim, but Francis Moore, on September 30, 1873, And, in fact, Richard May, filed for a claim on April 1873 in the Cozad area, but probably in the Grand Island land office although nothing ever came of that claim. The first successful homesteaders were Humphrey Clark, Traber Gatewood and Jefferson Hill who received the first land patents in 1875.[33]

At the same time Cozad met with Union Pacific land officials and negotiated to purchase a series of tracts using the company's favorable credit plan for speculators, thereby undertaking the necessary steps to establish a Nebraska colony but also a larger real estate empire just as he had done in Ohio. On December 6, 1873, the Union Pacific Railroad Company contracted to sell two thousand acres to John Cozad which according to the *Early History of the Cozad Community* included the following:

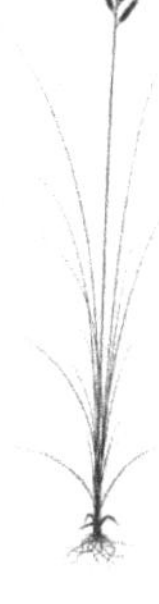

*The original town of Cozad or that portion of the present city which is located south of 8th Street is a part of Section Seven, Township Ten North, Range Twenty-three in Dawson County, Nebraska. On December 6, 1873, the Union Pacific Railroad Company contracted to sell to John J. Cozad the South Half (S1/2) of Section Seven, all of Section Five, the North Half (N1/2) of Section Seventeen in Township Ten, Range Twenty-three; all of Section Thirty-one, Township Eleven, Range Twenty-three:*

*the North Half (N1/2) of the Southwest Quarter (SW1/4 and the West Half (W1/2) of the Southwest Quarter (SW1/4) of Section One, Township Ten, Range Twenty-four for the consideration of $9,554.00.*[34]

All of these sections and partial sections were near or around what became the city of Cozad, although they were not all contiguous. Then, on February 11, 1880, the Union Pacific conveyed to Cozad three hundred and twenty acres which completed his acquisition of all of Section 7. The initial series of land acquisitions were paid off by Cozad in 1880 as he received a conveyance after a significant legal dispute that he settled with the railroad. A second transaction occurred on the same day and Cozad also paid the company off at that time as part of the settlement. This transaction included:

*All the even numbered blocks and fractional portions thereof from 2 to 98, and the balance of the north half of Section Seven for the consideration of $6,030.*[35]

Section 7 included the land where the current grain elevators and other agricultural businesses are situated and lay on both sides of the railroad tracks. However, most of the land that lay on the south side of the tracks was prone to flooding and it is curious that an 1884 Dawson County map shows the larger developed section of the town to the south of the railroad tracks and not to the north, which was where the town's business district and residential areas were ultimately organized.[36]

Section 6, which lays directly to the north of Section 7, and of present-day 8th Street, was not initially owned by Cozad. Three other individuals – Joseph Sharer, Marcus Long and Alonzo Tyler, initially acquired various parts of Section 6 in early 1875, as did Traber Gatewood, but John Cozad would come to purchase those sections from the first three previous owners later that year.[37] This section is where the majority of the residential part of Cozad came to be developed including what is now the property of the Robert Henri Museum. In the years to come, variously named additions were platted in this section.

Cozad now owned all of the sections that became the business center of the present-day Cozad, which gave him an immense influence there just as had happened in Cozaddale.[38]

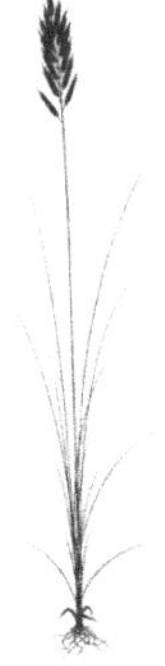

### Forty Thousand Acres

These earliest land transactions led to many others. It has long been believed that Cozad bought about forty thousand acres of land.[39] While some land may have been purchased outright, it is likely that most of those acres were bought on option. Cozad used the Union Pacific's financing tools to create a real estate empire which clearly demonstrates Cozad's land development abilities and financial acumen. In addition, Cozad would serve as a land agent for the railroad during his time in Nebraska.

To this day there remain disagreements as to how much land Cozad acquired and when it was acquired. According to a newspaper story that appeared in the *Omaha Bee* in late December 1873, John Cozad's total land acquisitions, between Willow Island (west of Cozad) and Coyote (east of Cozad), were about eight thousand acres.[40] Cozad also acquired many acres that lay to the south of the Platte.[41] Some of the land, particularly that along the river bottom, would be used for his own hay business, and the remainder he sold to homesteaders.

*The Battle of the Bridges* authors speculate that he may have also had options on thirty-two thousand acres.[42] A friend, T. J. Patterson, bought two thousand five hundred acres adjacent to Cozad's lands and even some in Cozad.[43] Another story that appeared in the *Omaha Republican*, also in late December 1873, said that he had invested fifty thousand dollars in land purchases.[44]

Bennard Perlman states that Cozad purchased twenty sections of land from the railroad. This would total twelve thousand eight hundred acres.[45] Mari Sandoz in her *Son of the Gamblin' Man* believed that he bought forty thousand acres both in and around his settlement at the 100th Meridian.[46] Sandoz also suggests that he initially bought six thousand acres.[47]

Yet another source that suggests how much land John Cozad owned in that first year comes from Theresa Cozad, who kept a small notebook with a variety of entries from different dates and years. Robert would later note that it was her last notebook. The figure cited in this notebook may have been a guess or a vague recollection. It may have also included the Ohio lands, or it could have been failed memories of an older woman. No matter, she wrote:

*Owned in 1873, 20,000 acres.*[48]

Dr. Robert Gatewood, a nephew of Theresa Cozad suggests the that initial purchase was fifty thousand acres.[49] There is a newspaper article that appeared in the *Gallipolis Journal* from Gallipolis, Ohio on April 9, 1874 by a potential settler who states that Cozad at that point owned twenty thousand acres of land.[50] This does confirm Theresa Cozad's recollections.

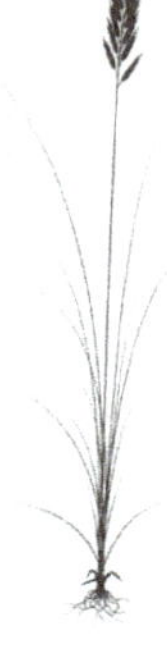

Laura Rody, a Wilson Public Library (Cozad) staff member, has done extensive research on the early land transactions in the Cozad area and has come to the following conclusions which may in fact be closer to the truth than any of the other sources. She wrote to the author:

*Cozad purchased UPRR land likely at peak price in 1873, at an average of $5.55/ac in Nebraska. However, that average price included "bluff" lands far from the river and RR. Bluff lands are assessed at half the value as the valley lands. The price Cozad paid is therefore skewed up. We know from Land Agent Sandison that Cozad purchased 8,000 acres for $50,000. And we know from History Nebraska that land* *speculators were offered different terms than actual settlers. Whereas, actual settlers were offered only 10% down with 10 years credit at 6% interest, no part of principle due for 2 years; land speculators had to put down 20% and had 5 years to pay. Cozad did indeed make a deal for 40,000 acres. At a price of $6.25 / acre. Probably heavily tilted in favor of prime ag land along the river and RR, no bluffs. 40,000 acres at $6.25 equals a $250,000 land deal. 20% of $250,000 is $50,000 - his down payment. He gained title to 20% of his 40,000 acre deal - or 8,000 acres. He bought at peak, then the price collapsed.*

*Taxes are only due on land that is patented. Cozad may be following the lead of the RR by taking the land in chunks, rather than all at once, to avoid the tax bill of 40,000 - not that he paid all his taxes anyway. He's kind of playing the same game as the RR. County Commissioners Meeting Sept 30, 1876 (vol 1, pg 122) - Cozad goes before commissioners and states that his lands in 1875 are not taxable, as the patents were not issued until March 10, 1875. The board orders an investigation. If found true by the treasurer and clerk, his taxes are to be removed for the year.*

*It's also interesting to note, how in some of the early stories of Cozad pioneers, they state they or their parents bought land that was quite close to Cozad from the railroad...<u>not</u> John J. Something is going on there. If he defaulted on his credit terms, and switched to simply being a land agent for the RR, he would have earned a commission without the taxes or as much risk - especially given the drought and grasshoppers.In the letter E Damon wrote home to Gallia, Co, he stated that lands were selling for $7-10/ac. Cozad would have had to sell at that price to not lose his shirt. The dust-up with land Agent Sandison would be because Sandison was offering new arrivals better terms, straight from the RR without a mark-up. How did the RR hold the lands in reserve? What land was Sandison selling?*

*Did Cozad ever make a second payment? Land records would suggest no but that could be because he was selling them so quickly in early - mid 1874. His lawsuit against the UPRR would suggest yes. He sued UPRR for inducing him to buy 16,000 acres. I infer from that statement that he made his 2nd payment of $50,000 and received title to another 8,000 acres and now he wants most of his money back. Then he defaults and the land is "repo'd". If he purchased it in late 1873, he would have had until late 1878 to complete his end of the deal. He doesn't. Maybe he thought he could get an extension from the RR due to grasshoppers and drought, just like the Federal Gov't did for the homesteaders when they passed the Settler's relief bill, but the RR wasn't going to play nice. By 1880-1881 he's down to just over 5000 acres - in his name. However, he rents out 10,000 haying land to the Fillmore County company. It looks like he's trying to make a buck from the land he defaulted on. He probably thinks cutting hay that's going to grow back next year isn't damaging the land. No one will know in a year's time. It'll look like a large herd of cattle or sheep was moved through*

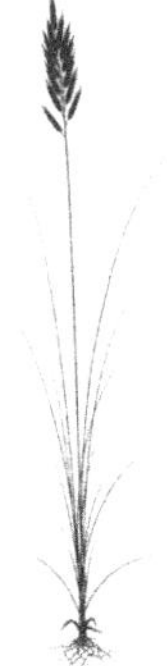

*If everything had gone to plan, he never would have needed anything more than his initial $50,000 investment.. It would have looked like a revolving loan fund now.*

*Cozad would make the initial $50,000, 20% payment, then sell the original 8,000 acres of land at a mark-up. Regaining his initial $50,000 (plus profit), he would use that to make the 2nd payment. Just keep rolling that recouped $50,000 over each payment period. If he had gotten away with it, he would have been brilliant! The gamble would have paid off. Whatever was left over to sell after the last 20% payment would have been pure profit. But the drought, grasshoppers, battles with the Union Pacific, and low price of homesteading got in the way. ($18 for 160 acres of homestead land or pre-empt for $400 per quarter vs 160 acres at $7 equaling $1,120 from Cozad.)* [51]

The more prized land was sold for between seven and ten dollars an acre, the lesser land for two dollars per acre. Cozad sold land to homesteaders and ranchers alike and even offered free rail fare if prospective buyers purchased their land from him as did the railroad. Homesteaders in the region could acquire land for $2.50 an acre. Comparatively, the Union Pacific was selling land, on average for $4.27 an acre. Generally, the railroad sold land between $3 and $5 per acre. As for the federal government, after 1872, it gave away three hundred and twenty acres of land for free to homesteaders who would settle on it after the payment of processing costs. By the spring of 1874 most of the land six miles out from the railroad on either side had been sold.[52]

It is also noteworthy that in the years to come Cozad, probably the county's largest individual and residential landowner, or at least one of the largest, did not pay his property taxes in a timely way. That would come to cause great consternation among his fellow townspeople and county residents as will be shown.[53]

### THE OHIO OR COZAD COLONY

As with the first appearance of John J. Cozad, there are several accounts of when he arrived in central Nebraska to establish his new community. One account has him and his entire family arriving in May 1873 and staying at Willow Island until the early fall of 1873.

Willow Island was then a desolate outpost on the railroad that had recently witnessed prairie fires and the entirety of the community included a station, box car on a siding, several houses, a saloon, and general store. Cowboys regularly passed through the town stopping at the various establishments.[54]

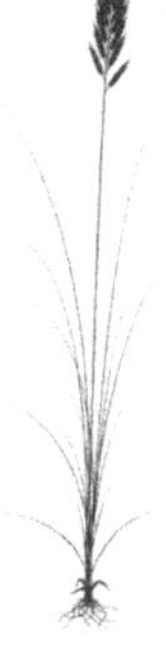

During that visit the Cozads lived with the Costin family in part of the section house normally used for railroad workers near the tracks. The two boys slept outside in a teepee and were given horses on which they traveled all around the area. The head of the Costin family was the same railroad section foreman who had taken Cozad back to the 100th Meridian sign the previous year.[55]

Jerry Costin, the son of the Union Pacific foreman, later recalled that several Pennsylvania railroad company cars were left on a siding at Willow Island, and that the contingent then went to what became Cozad to begin building a new community. Timber was cut and bricks were made, and it is believed that several homes and business structures were built. With the initial land purchases John Cozad had begun the basis for his planned community that was initially called the *Ohio Colony* or the *Cozad Colony*, and years later would be incorporated as the city of Cozad.[56]

According to this account, Robert Gatewood, Theresa's father, sent a hammock to Nebraska which she hung near the Platte River and often used. During that summer, twenty-one-year-old Traber Gatewood, Theresa's younger brother, also came out and stayed with the family.[57] That fall the entire family returned to Cincinnati or Cozaddale to begin planning for the future.

It is generally agreed that the first group of colonists, thirty in number, including Cozad family members, arrived at Willow Island on December 7, 1873. This group included John J. and Theresa Cozad and their sons, John and Robert. Others included Julia and Robert Gatewood, Traber Gatewood, and David Claypool, a nephew of John J's and others.[58]

When the Cozads returned to the Platte River Valley at the end of 1873, little could they have known how difficult it would be to establish a community there. For those intrepid travelers on the Great Plains, at the beginning of winter, the situation must have looked pretty daunting. Upon their arrival, Mr. Costin, dressed in a buffalo robe, brought a cast iron kettle full of beans and buffalo meat. Surely that must have been a welcome meal.[59]

Then, a wagon loaded with supplies made its way eastward to the 100$^{th}$ Meridian where it was unloaded, and the creation of the community began alongside the railroad tracks. An immigrant car, furnished with bunks, and a box car were brought to the newly established settlement and placed on a siding. The box car had the words *Cozad* painted on each end and served as the initial train station. And with that, a place with a name was established. For the early part of that first winter, the colonists lived in sod huts or some kind of primitive housing, but then as lumber arrived, the true building began. By 1874 there were fifteen homes built.[60]

The next group of settlers arrived in February 1874, a little more than one hundred years after the Ohio Company had begun the settlement of the future state along the Ohio River. One must wonder if Cozad fancied himself like those New England settlers who came to Marietta, Ohio, and began a settlement there in 1784. It was just eighty miles to the east of Allensville.[61]

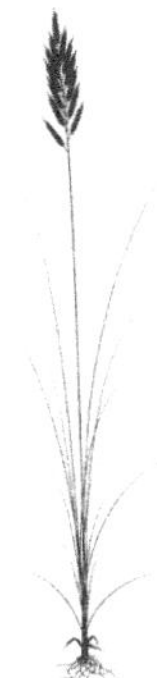

## The Colonizers

The intrepid people who came to the Ohio Colony were a hearty lot and some were determined to do whatever it took to build a new life in Nebraska. They were from Ohio, Indiana, Illinois, Michigan, Virginia, Kentucky, New York

☞ PLEASE HANG THIS UP.

# Ho! for THE Great Platte Valley!

# GRAND EXCURSIONS!

An EXCURSION will leave

## CINCINNATI, OHIO,

The THIRD TUESDAY in September, at 7 o'clock p.m. and EVERY TUESDAY thereafter during the year 1879, for

## COZAD, DAWSON CO., NEB.,

The town of Cozad is situated on the Union Pacific R. R., 247 miles west of Omaha.

### The Ohio or Cozad Colony,

Which five years ago located in Dawson County, is situated almost in the center of the State, and on the line of the famous one-hundredth meridian, and is in the midst of as fine an agricultural region as can be found on the continent, with less waste land than any locality within our knowledge. The soil over this whole region of country is composed of drift and a rich vegetable mould, which ages have decomposed, and is found to consist of the richest elements known to agriculturists, and is from two to eight feet in depth. A great harvest has been gathered this season; as much grain was sown last Spring as in 1878. From [illegible] to 40 bushel of wheat were raised last year to one bushel sown. From 40 to 60 bushels of barley and oats raised from one bushel sown. Fifty bushels of potatoes raised from one bushel of seed, and all other crops in proportion.

### The Colony Represents $1,000,000,

and is composed of some of the best men from Ohio, Indiana, Pennsylvania, Michigan, Virginia, Kentucky, New York and other States, and they are not desperate and wild, as some suppose those to be who live in a new country, but they are staunch supporters of religion and morality. Our schools are excellent, and we employ the best teachers.

### "Westward the Star of Empire takes its Way."

100,000 people located in Nebraska in the year 1878, and it is estimated that at least 175,000 will locate here this year, consequently the State is fast settling up; therefore, take advantage of these Excursions at low rates.

Trains of emigrants with their families are steadily moving into this valley. Men of small means and men whose property is heavily mortgaged, opportunities are here presented to you to escape the usurer or money-lender, and to acquire free homes of your own, of 320 acres of land, free from taxation from five to eight years, in a rich, productive and healthy country.

REMEMBER! that you need not buy land, 320 acres of which every citizen over the age of 21 years, male or female, native or foreign born, are entitled to Free of Cost; but since the late large and continued emigration West, these inducements are being taken advantage of every day and are fast disappearing, so that in a few more years there will be no government land left in this beautiful Platte Valley, which is yet destined to be the center of the wealth and population of this country.

### The Union Pacific Railroad

is the world's thoroughfare, and settlers upon this line enjoy great advantages. The long trains which daily pass over the roads loaded with passengers from every nation will carry a knowledge of this magnificent country to every part of the world. The result must be rapid settlement, enhanced value to property and business prosperity.

### A GREAT STOCK LOCALITY.

Go and see the stock interest that has been paying from 50 to 100 per cent. The fact is substantiated that stock of all kinds subsist the entire winter upon what they gather for themselves. The native buffalo grass cures into hay before the Fall frosts, and is quite as nutritious as when green. Cattle come out in good condition in the Spring without other feed than this. GRAIN GROWING should always be accompanied with the raising of stock; and this country affords facilities for the production of BOTH GRAIN AND LIVE STOCK. For SHEEP RAISING there is no finer country on the globe! Here is a fine opening to the stock man, wool-grower and dairy farmer, with the certainty of realizing immense profits.

**HEALTHFULNESS.**---Among the attractive characteristics of Nebraska is the wonderful salubrity of its climate. The high altitude, the dry and bracing character of the atmosphere, and the universal purity of the water, render this State peculiarly favorable to persons predisposed to pulmonary and rheumatic diseases. Fever and ague are unknown. Winters are short with but little snow. The autumns are like long Indian summers, reaching into the latter part of December. The country is exceedingly well watered and crossed by timber-bordered streams. The PLATTE RIVER AFFORDS SPLENDID MILL SITES. HARD TIMES in the East has caused thousands to emigrate to this State, and the consequence is that times are extremely good and labor of all kinds in demand. THESE EXCURSIONS have been arranged for the purpose of extending facilities to those who desire to visit this great country; so don't take our word for what we set forth in this Circular, but COME AND SEE FOR YOURSELF thousands of acres of the most beautiful land your eyes ever looked upon, within sight of the town of Cozad, and to be had without money and without price.

"THE 100th MERIDIAN" is a Weekly Paper published at Cozad, and makes it a point to give all the News in regard to the Country. Subscription Price $1.00 per annum. Trial Subscription, for 3 months 25 Cts.

**Rates from Cincinnati, O., to Cozad, Nebraska, Straight Tickets, $22.00, Round Trip Tickets, $35.00.**

These tickets are FIRST-CLASS, are good for 40 DAYS, on any train, and will be sold on EXCURSION DAYS by

**Joseph Goldberg & Son, 183 Race St., bet. 4th and 5th, Cincinnati, O.**

David Claypool, Editor of "100th Meridian." Traber Gatewood, Postmaster, Cozad, Dawson Co., Nebraska.

*Robert Henri Museum and Art Gallery Collection*

*John Cozad had posters printed up to promote the Cozad or Ohio Colony and distributed them in Ohio and elsewhere to attract homesteaders and businessmen to his newly formed community. This poster, printed in 1879, promoted cheap railroad tickets to Nebraska, either one way or round trip.*

and Pennsylvania. Some were from Vinton County, Cozaddale and Cincinnati and known to John Cozad previously. Many would live out the remainder of their lives in the community they helped to found while others moved elsewhere in Nebraska.[62] Some were Civil War veterans coming as a result of the passage of the Homestead Act.[63]

Those who stayed were often bound together by familial and marital relationships including the Cozads, Gatewoods, Claypools, Schooleys and McIntyres.[64] The Claypools and McIntyres were cousins. The Schooleys, who were from the area near Cozaddale, had married into the Claypool family. The Gatewoods were of course related to Theresa Gatewood Cozad.[65] But they were also bound together by the extraordinarily difficult challenges that they faced together in those early years.

Others came but were ultimately discouraged by the hard times due to various forces of nature such as hail, drought, locusts and grasshoppers in addition to the disputes with ranchers. They chose to return East from where they had come, and their names are largely forgotten.

*John and Theresa (Gatewood) Cozad*

John J. Cozad has been described in many ways; a visionary, loving, haughty, having a violent temper, arrogant, generous, a leader, professional card player, husband, selfish, cruel, commanding, immaculate dresser, an assassin, killer, loner, and close friend. To his friends and relatives, he was faithful, particularly those who had come west with him to colonize Nebraska. In the records of the Robert Henri Museum and various books that have been written, one can find many stories that display those various aspects of his character and all of them have an element of truth to them.[66]

There are varying accounts of his youth. It has been suggested that Cozad was born in California, although the historical record clearly shows otherwise. He had left home in Ohio at twelve and as a boy became very proficient at card games, both straight poker and faro, ultimately becoming a professional gambler. He traveled extensively gambling on riverboats and trains, going to the California goldfields, and crisscrossing the eastern, southern and western regions of the United States and even going to South America. His nickname, as reported in a Cincinnati newspaper in 1867, was *Panama John* which may be an indication of where Cozad had journeyed during one of his earlier travels during the Gold Rush.[67]

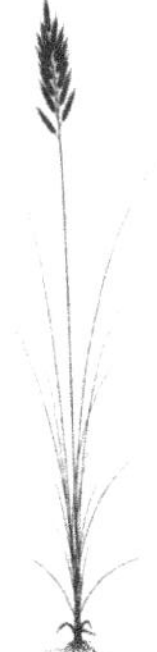

As a professional gambler he was very successful, so much so that his wife once told her friend Clara Riggs that he had won fifty thousand dollars in Omaha during that fateful summer of 1872 as he waited for a train. She also told the same story to a Mrs. Costin at Willow Island.[68] If converted to today's dollars that would amount to one and a quarter million dollars.

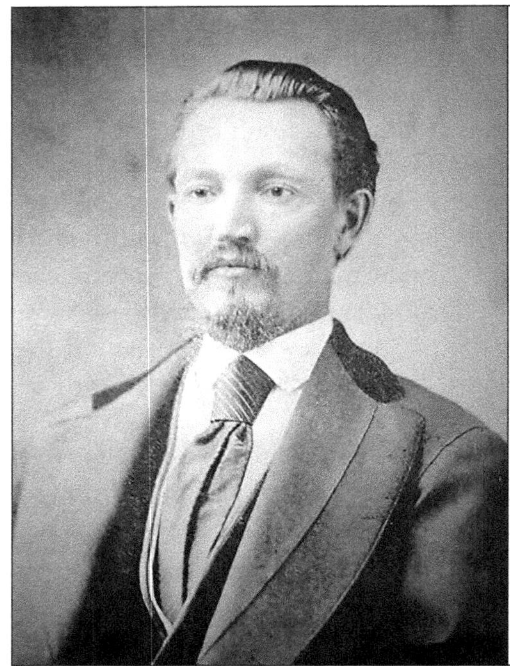

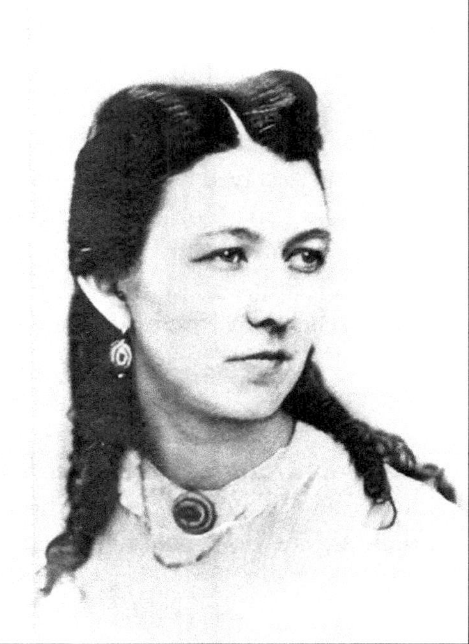

Courtesy Andrew Cozad

*John and Theresa Cozad*

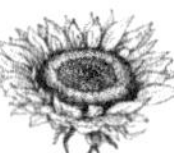

It is also known that John Cozad won nine thousand dollars in three deals of faro in Denver in 1881.[69] These accounts belie the fact that biographers argue that Cozad gave up gambling when his children were born.[70] Yet in one of those ironies Cozad would fight against gambling in the town he created even though much of his wealth was dependent on it. Contemporary accounts of him in newspapers describe him as a very wealthy man.[71]

He was also a man who had been exposed to the seedier side of life during his travels, working the gambling halls and going to saloons. Some of those parts of his life were suggested by Mari Sandoz when she described an episode when a King O'Dell came to Cozad after getting out of prison to settle some scores with John Cozad. Whether that particular story is true or not, the possibilities of having been involved with some shadowy figures seems very likely.[72]

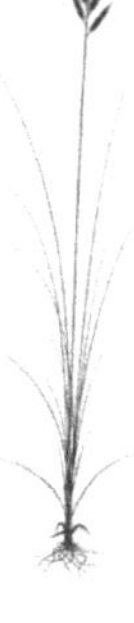

Sam Schooley would later recall that:

*Whenever Mr. Cozad would run short of money, he would leave for Chicago or New York where big gambling parlors were maintained. His favorite game and the one in which he usually indulged was that of straight poker. He would be gone usually for two to three weeks. When he returned, he was well supplied with quantities of green backs . . . He always took some little time to study them (the other players), their actions, their mannerisms in playing a hand. When the stakes were high, meaning several thousand dollars in a pot, usually the other fellow would by some act, movement or statement indicate where he believed he held the winning hand. Apparently Mr. Cozad became more cool and calculating the higher stakes got.*[73]

John J. was also an ambitious man, and those ambitions would drive him to create two communities, Cozaddale, Ohio and Cozad. Cozad even believed, because of his large investments in Nebraska and his connections to the Union Pacific, that he might even become a United States Senator representing the state.[74]

One of his best friends during his time in Cozad, Sam Schooley, would later recall that while he knew him:

*He was about six feet in height and weighed about 185 pounds, neither lean nor fat. He had black hair and piercing black eyes that seem as though they could read your mind. He always appeared to be in vigorous health. He was a meticulous dresser for that day and age, particularly when most of the people in that area wore only ordinary, cheap clothes. He was usually attired in a black suit with vest to match and the coat was usually a Prince Albert type with a split tail. His vest was adorned with a pretentious gold watch and chain and in the necktie he frequently wore a diamond stick pin. He also wore a large diamond ring and when in full attire, with a high silk hat, he carried a gold-headed cane.*[75]

Schooley also relayed that:

*In speech, he had a well-modulated and clear voice, used no more words than were necessary to express what he had to say and was very decisive. In mannerism, he was the aloof type and never permitted people to see anything rather than a cold exterior. Even though it was common practice in the early days and still later to call people by their first names if they had sufficient acquaintance to permit them to do so, no one seems to know of any person who addressed John J. Cozad as other than Mr. Cozad.*[76]

For all that has been written about John J. Cozad, he remains an enigma. Perhaps he is best described by Henri biographer William Homer:

*He was a typical American of a type almost extinct: an individualist, an adventurer, and a speculator. Yet he was also something of an idealist, as his plans for building communities testify. In these activities all reports lead us to believe that Cozad was a model of independent action, fighting fairly but vigorously for his beliefs against seemingly insurmountable obstacles.*[77]

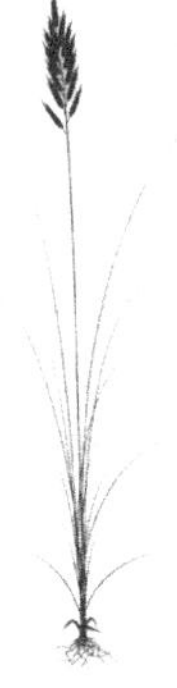

Another view of John Cozad comes from his brother-in-law Traber Gatewood who wrote in a letter to Theresa after John died in 1906:

*His many good deeds will be a monument to his memory. I have seen the workings of his good heart, his charity. And his many kind acts to my father's (Robert Gatewood) family. . . he was charitable and proved it many cases by giving of his money . . . his name will be long remembered after we are all gone and forgotten.*[78]

Theresa Gatewood Cozad, a Virginian to whom John was married, was described in the same account as:

*. . . very much a lady, always beautifully dressed, the daughter of a couple who operated a hotel in Virginia. How crude accommodations must have dismayed her.*[79]

Also, it was said of her that:

*She was a beautiful lady, always decorously dressed and very sensitive to the fine arts.*[80]

The burden of maintaining the family's well-being fell to Theresa as she spent more time in the Cozad Colony than John J. because he was often traveling dealing with various business interests and gambling.

*The Gatewoods*

The patriarchs of the Gatewood family were Robert Burke Gatewood (1807-1884) and Julia Jones Gatewood (1813-1909) who were from Malden, Virginia, and a well-respected family. There are several different accounts of the number of children they had. One source, a Henri biographer believed they had four children - three boys and a daughter. Another source states that there were five children, only three of whom survived to adulthood. Julia's obituary says that she had nine children. The three children who are known to have survived to adulthood are: Van Burke (1836-1903), Theresa (1837-1923), and Alexander Traber (1852-1928).[81]

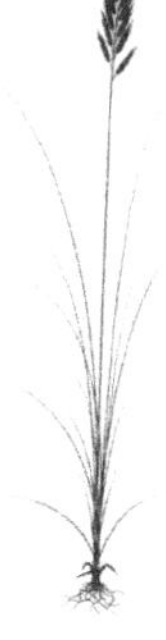

Robert's ancestors had come from England to Virginia in the seventeenth century and had descended from English royalty. Robert, like his future son-in-law, had gone to California during the years of the Gold Rush both as a seeker of wealth, and captain of a wagon train. Robert Cozad later recalled that his grandfather had passed by what was to become the Ohio Colony in 1855. Gatewood's return home found him sailing around Cape Horn and up the East Coast.[82]

Upon his return he went into the salt manufacturing business in the Kanawha Salines area near Malden. The region was rich in salt mines, a resource

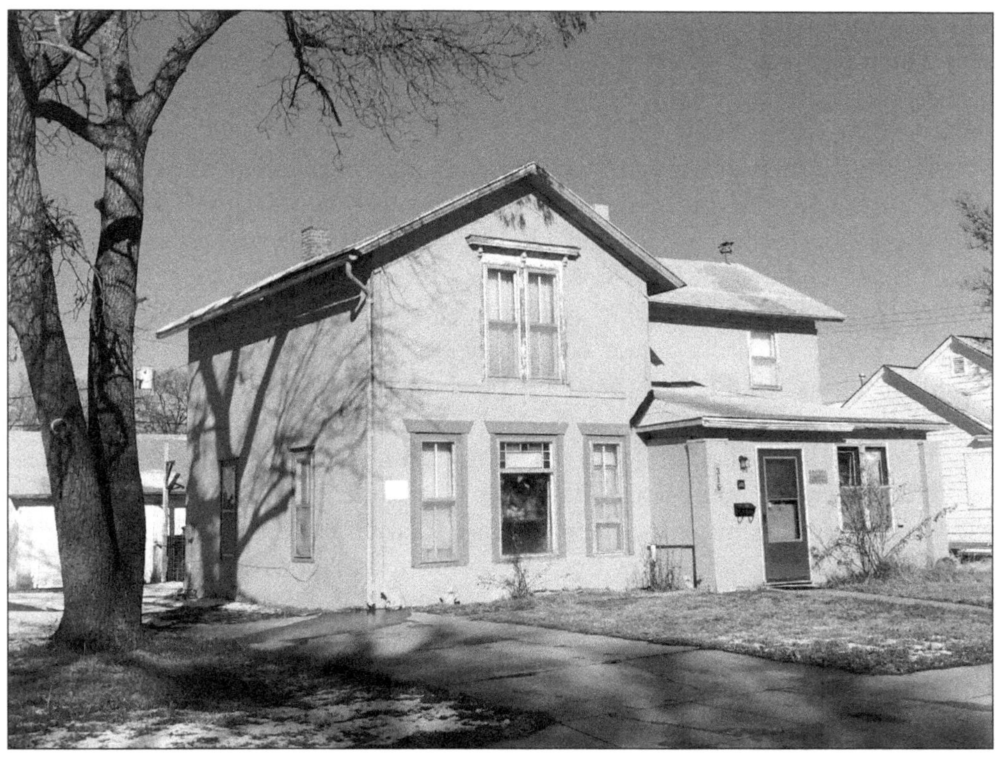

*Courtesy Coco Canas*

*This is believed to be the Robert and Julia Gatewood house that was once located across the street from the Robert Henri Museum. The house was later moved to 311 East 11th Street in Cozad. Additions and changes were subsequently made to the building.*

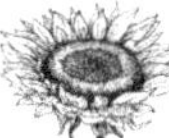

that is still harvested there. It was at one time, in the nineteenth century, the largest salt producing area in the United States. One of his young workers was Booker T. Washington, who later became the famous American educator and advisor to presidents. There, on the Gatewood farm, Washington learned how to read and write. The Gatewoods also owned the Malden House Hotel in Malden, Virginia (*now West Virginia*) and a farm. The Gatewoods also had hotels in Gallipolis, Ohio, and Covington, Kentucky. They were well-connected to a variety of politicos including U.S. senators from West Virginia.[83]

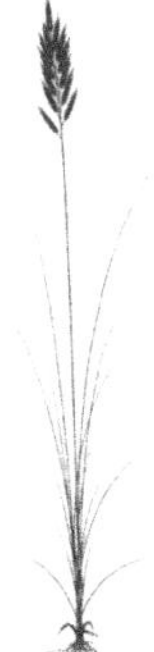

Julia and Robert were among the group of the earliest settlers to come to Nebraska following their daughter and son-in-law just as they had done leaving Virginia and going to Cincinnati. It is believed that they came to the fledgling community in December 1873, although another source says that they did not arrive until February 1874.[84]

Robert opened a grocery business in town and Julia managed a retail establishment, called The Bee Hive Store. The building, located at the northwest corner of Meridian and 8th Streets, would come to serve as a drug and grocery store, and also offered mercantile goods. It also served as a variety store and a boarding house in other times.[85]

Their residence, a two-story wood framed building, said to be built in 1873, was located across the street from today's Robert Henri Museum where the municipal parking lot is now located (2023). Their home was later moved three blocks north and east to 11th Street, just a block south from the Cozad Community Health Center. (*In 2023 it stands in this location and is painted a bright pink.*)[86] Robert and Julia would come to own a number of other properties in Cozad that Julia would retain after his passing in 1884. She also cooked at the Cozad's hotel for the guests.

Two of Julia's children would play significant roles in the community. Theresa and Traber, also known as A.T. Traber Gatewood, came out in the spring of 1873 with the first group of settlers, buying a quarter section within the area now known as Cozad.[87] Both were among the first permanent settlers, arriving on December 7, 1873.[88]

Traber would come to play a major part in the community, serving it in a variety of roles. He would serve as the town's first postmaster, and helped build its first houses including the first sod house, owned by Sam Atkinson.[89] He helped erect the first Cozad hotel which was a wood-framed building, and later the current Robert Henri Museum building using manufactured brick. He also manufactured the brick used in many of the other buildings constructed in the town, and owned a drug store in partnership with another early arrival, Sam Schooley.[90]

Gatewood also helped in the attempts to build a bridge across the Platte River. He helped to legally organize the town and would serve as the second chairman of the town's board and founded the newspaper called *The One Hundredth Meridian*. Gatewood was also a member of the first school board, and board member of the Cozad Building and Loan Association. Traber maintained his dental practice as well as a drug store and was thought to be the only dentist west of Hastings in those early years and one of the state's oldest practicing dentists.[91]

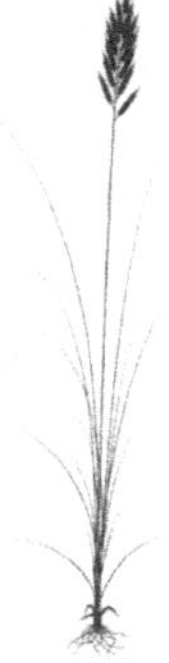

He also ran for state office as a Democrat two different times, once for Congress, another time for State Senate, losing both times and he also ran for Secretary of State, losing in that contest too.[92] Gatewood was considered a personal friend of William Jennings Bryan. He ran for sheriff in Dawson County many times, losing in each election cycle. Aside from John Cozad, he was probably one of the most influential people in the town.[93]

### *The Claypool Families*

Three brothers, David, William and Robert Claypool, were among the founding colonizers. They were all born in Vinton County, Ohio, the same coun-

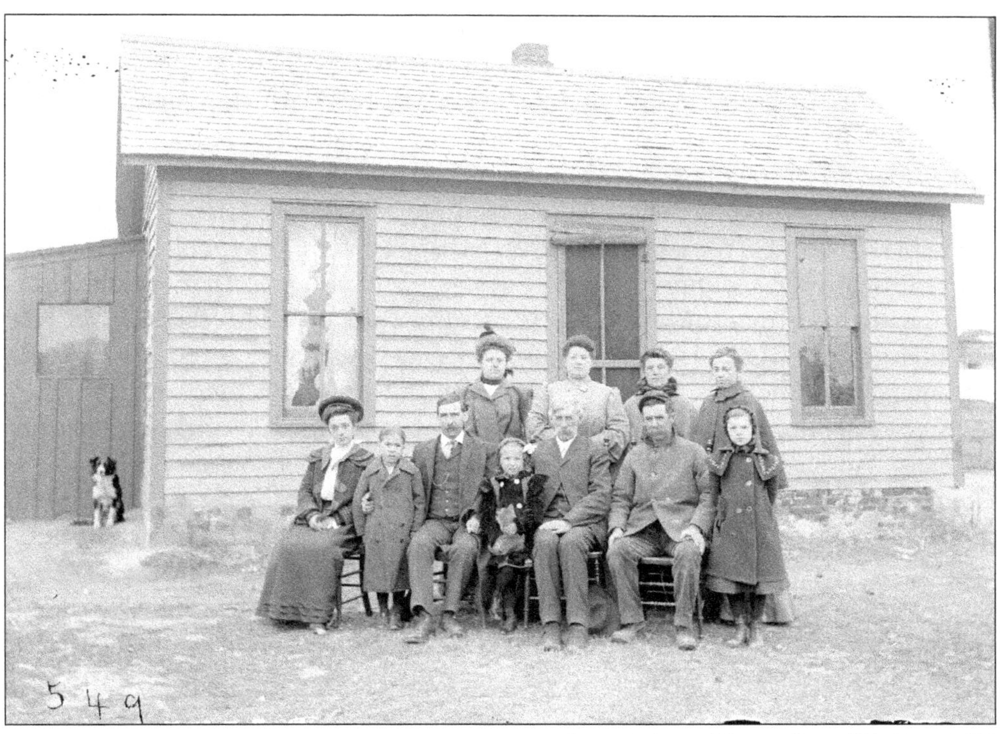


*Courtesy Library of Congress (Digital Id nbhips 13582)*

*David Claypool, seated in the center, was one of the original colonizers of Cozad and is pictured with his family in front of his original home. The photograph was taken by Solomon D. Butcher, the well-known Nebraska photographer, in 1904.*

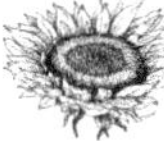

ty where John J. Cozad had been born and in fact they were nephews of Cozad.[94]

David Claypool (1840-1923), the oldest, was living in Cozaddale when he came to Nebraska in April 1873. At the time, as part of a long life of public service, he was then serving on the Hamilton Township Board of Education. His obituary states that he was with Cozad when the latter met John Cusack and showed Cozad where to establish his new town.[95]

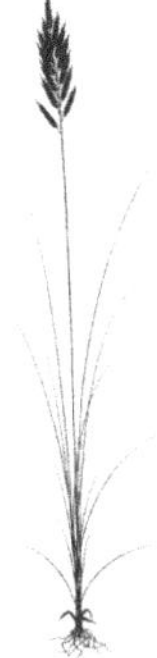

David would come to be an important ally of Cozad and prominent member of the community. He was an editor of *The One Hundredth Meridian* newspaper, the community's second, published initially on July 4, 1876. (The first, *The Colonist*, was published in March 1876, but its run was short-lived.)[96] He went into business with his brother William, owning a farm implement store known as Claypool Brothers and assisted Cozad in building a sod bridge over the Platte River. The oldest brother was also active in real estate development, establishing the Claypool and Colley's Addition (1885) and the Claypool and Dale's Addition (1892) and often assisting Cozad by witnessing legal documents. He also served as a justice of the peace and on the school board.[97]

One project that he was involved with that forever changed the community was the creation of the Cozad Ditch Company in 1895, which built a canal that drew water from the Platte River and forever improved the lives of area farmers and ranchers by providing water to irrigate crops.[98]

David Claypool was married three times – to Mary Clark(1860), Mary Hensel (1876) and Orpha Myers (1894). Mary Clark and Claypool were married in 1860 in Vinton County, Ohio. She died on September 1, 1873, two months after giving birth to a son, Henry. It is presumed she died in Nebraska. Because the first group of colonizers had arrived in May 1873 and stayed through the summer she and her son may have died when the group was preparing to return back East. Area historian Kieth Buss believed that she died in the home that her husband had recently built on East 8th Street. She and her son are buried in the Cozad Cemetery and are the first known burials there. At the time, it was then a private burying ground but was later purchased by the Cozad Cemetery Association.[99]

David and his third wife, Orpha, moved to Kearney where they separated. David returned to Cozad. He died in the town he helped to found on January 10, 1923 and was buried in the Cozad cemetery.[100]

William Claypool (1844-1923) married Sarah Schooley (1848-1936), the sister of Sam Schooley, another important figure in the settling of the town. They had a daughter Margaret (Maggie) (1867-1950), and it is a color photocopy of her autograph book that the museum now owns. While among the early settlers, they later moved to Gering, Nebraska, where they died.[101]

The third, and youngest brother, Robert (1856-1907) also came to Cozad in the early years. He was married to Mattie Darner. Her father, John, helped found the Church of Christ in Cozad.[102]

*The Schooleys*

One of the earliest of the settlers to Cozad was Sam W. Schooley (1852-1941), who arrived in October 1876 with his brother-in-law William Claypool. Schooley's brother, Jake, had also been among those early colonizers. Originally from Vinton County, Ohio, he was born in the same county where Henry Cozad, John J.'s father had created Allensville. His ancestors had been Quakers.[103] At a young age his family had moved to Missouri. In Missouri he suffered from an allergy due to malaria and needed to find a different place to live. From there he traveled through Kansas and then the Platte River valley. Once he arrived in Cozad, just a little over a year after the first immigrants, he became an important figure in the town. The town and precinct's population was then about one hundred souls. Being a good hunter, there were times when his prowess fed everyone in the small community.[104]

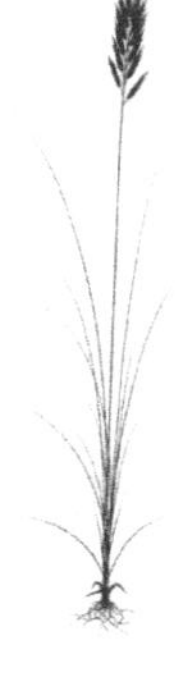

Soon after arriving, he developed a close friendship with John Cozad and Schooley's obituary stated that he knew Cozad better than any other person. Schooley worked for Cozad building the bridge across the Platte River. It was during a break in the project that Schooley and Cozad sat together for a day and Cozad told him his whole life story. He set the type for the *100th Meridian* newspaper for a time, owned a real estate and insurance business called Schooley and Koch, was a partner with Traber Gatewood in a drug business and a lawyer. Schooley served on the local school board, was a police judge and city attorney. He would continue to play a critical role in the life of the Cozad family for the rest of his life.[105]

Married to Ella, who had been previously married, they had no children who survived into maturity. Their home was just one block west of City Park (now Veterans Park) although it was moved three blocks west and stands today at 315 West 9th Street surrounded by a white picket fence. The Schooleys later sold the plot of land in the center of the city to the municipality for a modest fee. This was developed into City Park (now Veterans Park) with a deed restriction that it would always remain a park. Today it remains a beautiful asset to the city.[106]

Ida Claypool, a daughter of David and Mary Claypool, married George Schooley in 1877 in Cozad. George was a brother of Sam Schooley.[107]

### Other Early Colonizers

There were other early colonizers as well including members of the Pearson and Hills, Russells, and Cummings families. William Ross, Dr. Donogh and Samuel Atkinson, all from Ohio, were also part of the original party.[108] Other early pioneers included Jonathan and Benjamin Gardner, Joe Morris, T. A. Taylor, John Handley, and Tom Stevenson. In the decade to come hundreds of others followed the call of the West and Nebraska and settled in the greater Cozad region.[109]

### Ho! For the Great Platte Valley

With a beachhead established, Cozad then began to promote his new settlement back East in earnest by hanging posters and taking out advertisements in Cincinnati and Indianapolis. The first one appeared on March 10, 1874 in a Cincinnati newspaper.[110] During 1874, a new group of immigrants arrived each month and in April, for example, seventy-five families arrived.[111] An 1876 advertisement in the town of Hillsboro, Ohio newspaper stated that:

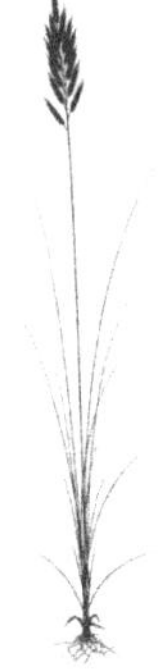

*An opportunity never before presented to obtain a pleasant home, near the greatest railroad in the world, with all the conveniences of an old settlement, including churches, schools, telegraph, etc.*[112]

The Robert Henri Museum owns one of the posters that Cozad printed up and distributed in 1879 to promote his colony. Like so many publications of the time it accentuates only the positive, for example, that the Ohio Colony was located in an agricultural region that was as good as any, and that people were flocking to Nebraska by the thousands. Some of the *best men* from the states of Ohio, Indiana, Pennsylvania, Michigan, Virginia, Kentucky, New York had all found their way westward and to his colony according to the promotional poster. Because of its proximity to the Union Pacific Railroad there would be rapid settlement, wealth, and prosperity. All those claims were true but as will be seen, did not reflect the difficult challenges that faced early homesteaders.[113]

Noting the troubling economic times back East, Cozad offered excursions to visit the colony. The 1879 poster states that tickets were $22 for a one-way ticket and $35 for a round trip ticket.[114] Excursion trains left Cincinnati, Ohio and Indianapolis, Indiana weekly, on Tuesdays, and continued for the duration of the fall. Tickets could be purchased from Joseph Goldberg, an agent who operated out of John Cozad's office in Cincinnati and only on the excursion day.[115]

Edwin Sandison, the agent for the Union Pacific at Willow Island, would say at the beginning of this ambitious effort:

*Mr. Cozad and friends have a large and grand field of labor before them, and as they have within their reach all the necessaries required to build up a large, wealthy and prosperous city, I cannot help picturing this grand enterprise crowned with a brilliant future. May success and prosperity forever accompany such noble undertakings.*[116]

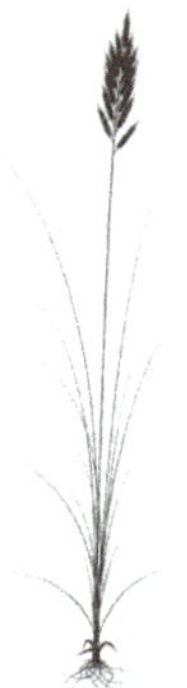

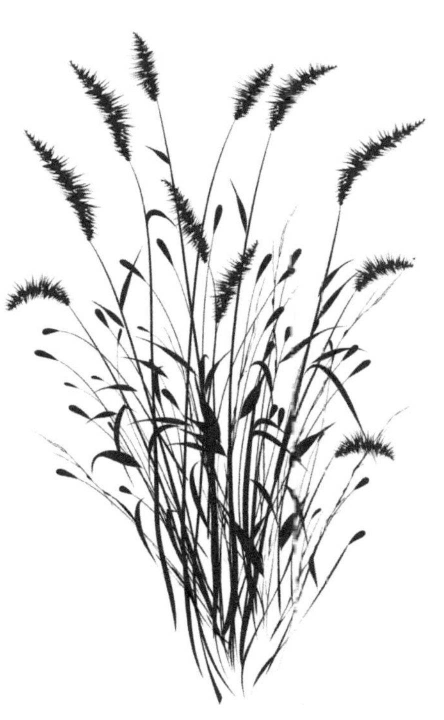

## *Chapter 4*

# Building a Community

*The first sod house we built was 12 x 14, without a floor. The cost in cash was $.75 for two half windows. We had to pull the string latch to get the door open.*[1]

William Walker
Early History of the Cozad Community

*Cozad City, Dawson County, is striding fast toward success. . . Come and see, judge for yourselves, and we assure you that each and all will join with the great American Traveler, Bayard Taylor, in terming the Platte Valley the most beautiful land ever looked upon.*[2]

Omaha Weekly Republican
May 14, 1874

WHEN JOHN COZAD SPOKE WITH JOHN CUSACK during that serendipitous meeting on the railroad line near present-day Cozad, one Cozad historian wrote that he said he would establish a new town at the 100th Meridian with the associated grain elevators, loading pens, cattle yards, factories, mills, churches and schools. And, as the tradition has come down through time, Cozad wanted to create an avenue, located on a north-south line on the 100th Meridian. It would be tree-lined and would be the perfect location for a home for his wife and family. Along that avenue he planned initially for building that white mansion with pillars, although ultimately he came to build a structure that resembled the one he had built in Cozaddale. He saw himself owning a great country estate and the honor that it would bring to him and his wife and his boys.[3]

The actual site of that settlement was not ideal in some ways. It was quickly realized that there would be seepage into the basements of the buildings that were constructed because of the high water table. The wells that those early settlers dug would be tainted. In fact, in the years to come those observations would be correct, as the area directly to the south of the railroad track did indeed flood regularly until Interstate 80 was built creating a kind of levee against the rising water of the Platte. Mari Sandoz wrote that some believed that the town should be moved farther north but that David Claypool argued that they needed to be as near to the railroad as possible.[4]

It has long been believed that John Cozad considered the community as *his town* and that is how it has also been interpreted at the Robert Henri Museum for four decades. Even though John J. Cozad had been, and continued to be a gambler, it is believed that, at least initially, he wanted to create an idyllic utopia with no gambling permitted, no alcohol allowed, no prostitution, no weapons and the influences that they brought. Curiously, they were the kinds of places that he so often frequented. It was to be unlike the many Western towns that were beginning to rise from the prairies at the time.[5]

And while he had initially hoped to create a community in this ideal image, by 1880, just seven years after the community's establishment, Robert Cozad was reporting in his diary about a potential saloon opening in town.[6] John Gatewood, a son of Van Burke Gatewood and brother to Theresa Cozad, who owned a pharmacy in town, noted that in 1882, he sold alcoholic beverages that were drank for medicinal purposes.[7] Soon there were ladies of the night in an establishment that was located in a house just east of town and some gambling was done in the darkness of the evening.[8]

In the early years he wielded enormous influence. In addition, the tightly knit group of relatives owned many of the most critical business establishments. However, as time went by, that influence waned as more settlers moved into the area who had no connection to John Cozad, and centers of power within the community changed.

The first structure in what is now Cozad, if one can describe it as such, was a railroad box car that sat on a railroad siding with the word *Cozad* painted on each end.[9] Temporary structures or sod huts, or *soddies* as they were called, were soon erected to house those early colonizers and the early waves of settlers.[10] The first wood-framed home built in Cozad was that of Sam Atkinson, about a mile and a half north of town. During the construction of this home, local Native Americans who were passing through stopped to look in the house and then ate the food set aside in dinner pails.[11]

Wood was shipped out from Ohio and the first structures were constructed, either in December 1873, or early 1874. Those wood-framed buildings were built near each other along with the Cozad's temporary family home, which also served as a hotel. Two stories tall, and called the *Immigrant Hotel*, its operations were managed by Theresa's parents, Julia and Robert Gatewood. The Cozads did not live in the settlement full-time, at least in the settlement's formative years. By the fall of 1874 there were five residences and the Immigrant Hotel in the fledgling community with as many as six families staying with the Gatewoods.[12] A post office opened in the summer of 1874 and by at least one account there were fifteen homes standing.[13]

The small settlement was located along the Union Pacific Rail Road's line and along the new county road that had been laid out just two years earlier. This road, the creation of which was a result of the passage of a bond issue voted on by a handful of county residents in 1872, ran from the eastern end of the county to the western end. It paralleled the railroad and was near or on the Mormon Trail.[14] It was along this road which was the approximate location of where those first structures were sited and is where the present passenger station stands today along Highway 30.

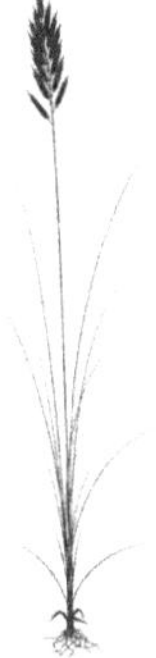

The *Omaha Weekly Republican* provided a particularly upbeat assessment that same year when it wrote:

*Cozad City, Dawson County, is striding fast toward success. . . Come and see, judge for yourselves, and we assure you that each and all will join with the great American Traveler, Bayard Taylor, in terming the Platte Valley the most beautiful land ever looked upon.*[15]

However, less than two and a half years after the construction of that cluster of buildings - the Gatewood's hotel and the buildings along the railroad tracks - a fire consumed all of them on April 29, 1876. With it many of the Cozad's personal belongings, including clothing, jewelry, cash, furniture and his business papers were destroyed.[16]

The origins of the fire were never discovered. The fire killed one man, Jackson O'Neill, who was thought to have been intoxicated. O'Neill was an attorney who had competed with John J. Cozad for real estate transactions in the area. Questions have been raised as to why there is no mention of his pregnant widow and two children and why he was buried in Plum Creek. There was some speculation that the fire was deliberately set by a disgruntled business owner.[17]

Some even suspected that John A. Cozad was the arsonist and Mari Sandoz in her *Son of the Gamblin Man* suggests that the older son had been involved although his father John Cozad did not believe this. It has also been suggested that enemies from Plum Creek may have been the arsonists.[18]

The fire discouraged many of those early settlers, as the focal point of the settlement was gone. Some simply went back to where they had come from and resumed their previous lives.[19] At one point the population in the community dwindled down to just five families in the town and ten families in the surrounding area.[20]

It is not known what the Cozads did between 1876-79 for a residence although they may have stayed with the Gatewoods at a new and quickly rebuilt hotel. At the time they were not living in Nebraska full-time but going back and forth between Cozad and Cincinnati. The details of this period remain murky and unclear even today.

Despite these challenges Cozad continued on, trains arrived bringing new colonists, and John continued to invest heavily in the town. He built a school, three business buildings, and attempted to build a sod bridge across the Platte River. He spent tens of thousands of dollars on the various promotional efforts and construction projects.[21]

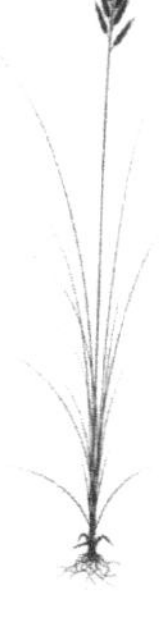

In time a business district was created and grew. A second railroad station was also consumed by fire, and a third one, a wood-framed structure, was built and used until a new station replaced it in 1925. The former station was moved and relocated to 402 East 4th Street in Cozad where it still stands (2022).[22] In 1925, Gilbert Stanley Underwood, the famed Union Pacific architect, designed the present station. In 1990 it was moved to 105 Highway 30 and turned over to a non-profit organization.[23]

A newspaper was established and called *The 100th Meridian* and which initially was published by David Claypool.[24] Copies of the paper were distributed back East in a continued effort to promote the community. F. W. Funk owned a general store and P. S. Gilbert maintained the *Cozad House*, another hotel. Social events became common including one on July 4, 1875, when a baseball game was held between the Cozad team and the Fort McPherson team.[25] Fraternal organizations were formed including the Cozad Lodge No. 55 (Oddfellows) in 1875.[26] A Cozad Coronet Band played at events in the later years of the nineteenth century.

## Hard Times

While in the long term there was steady progress, from the moment they stepped off the Union Pacific passenger cars in the Platte Valley in those early days, there were only hard times for those early settlers, especially during the first decade. Despite the glowing reviews from Omaha newspapers and other press, a number of issues confronted those early settlers immediately. Among the difficulties, at least for the colonizers, in the years that the Cozads were there, were the natural challenges. No descriptions of these challenges had found their way into the posters that John Cozad distributed or the advertisements that the Union Pacific placed all over the country.

The natural calamities that befell those pioneer settlers between 1873 and 1876 included invasions of grasshoppers or locusts, hail, prairie fires, wind, tornadoes, fierce heat, bitter cold, late spring frosts, blizzards, and drought. Just six months after arriving on the Great Plains, beginning on July 20-22, 1874, those early colonizers, were swarmed by locusts in a wave that was more than one hundred miles wide and eighteen hundred miles long, stretching all the way from Canada to Texas. It was the worst infestation of grasshoppers in the history of Nebraska although there had also been other recent years where the grasshoppers had invaded including 1857, 1860, 1865 and 1866. The swarms were even larger when there was no rain, and in 1875 and 1876 the region was again inundated with grasshoppers.[27]

Huge clouds of the insects would come across the horizon, darkening the sky, eating everything in their path as well as covering everything. Eating any vegetation and bark they also ate harnesses, clothing, handles of tools and brooms, and fence posts. Steam locomotives could not operate because the grasshoppers covered the tracks and were like grease.[28] The Rocky Mountain Locusts had passed through the Great Plains with regularity every seven to twelve years and returned again to Nebraska in 1893. One decade later, they were gone completely, as they became extinct.[29]

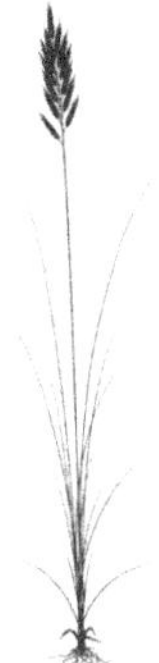

Prairie fires began without any kind of warning and swept across the vast expanses of land. The fires would destroy any structure in their path and would burn thousands of acres of crops and grasslands.[30]

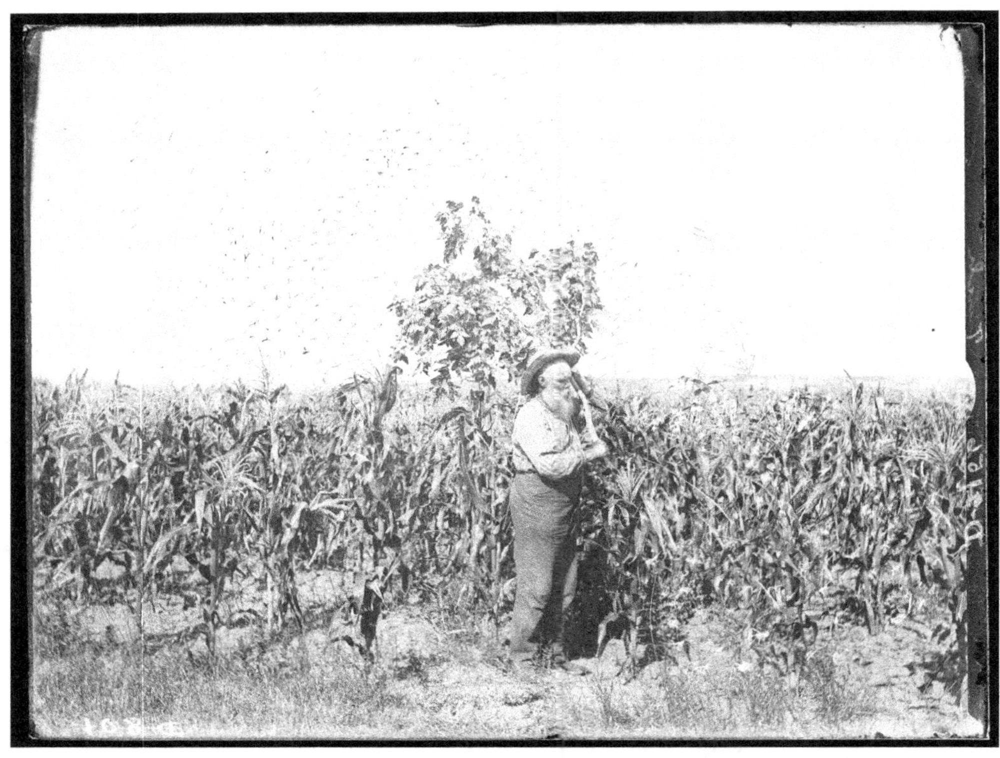

Courtesy Library of Congress (Digital ID Nbhips 12600)

*Here Ephriam Swain Finch demonstrated how he attempted to kill grasshoppers during the plagues of the 1870s.*

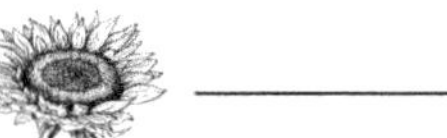

During the four seasons of the year, the settlers were continually exposed to harsh weather that included a wide range of temperatures on any given day. In one particularly difficult winter, Union Pacific trains were refusing to drop off a load of coal so Traber Gatewood stopped a train and took a carload of coal for the immigrants but paid for it as well.[31]

In 1880-81 a terrible winter saw the deaths of thousands of cattle and in fact Traber Gatewood estimateed that ten thousand had died along the Platte and in Cozad. After overgrazing the previous years, the cattle had migrated southward in hopes of finding food. When they came through Cozad, people stayed in their homes, afraid of the starving and desperate longhorns. Cattle were dying by the thousands and wandering through Cozad looking for feed.[32]

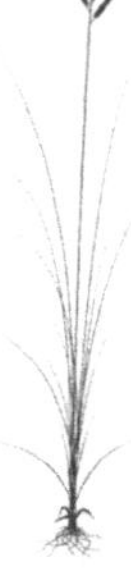

Drought was another calamity that befell those early settlers. Rain was not always forthcoming, and farmers often lost all of their crops in the heat of the summer. It was not until the early 1880s when alfalfa was introduced in Dawson County, a hardy plant that provided feed, and the1890s, when things began to improve for the region's farmers because of the introduction of irrigation, which provided a reliable source of water for their crops.[33]

Cozad was a frontier town and the immigrants had additional challenges that they faced aside from environmental ones. There were violent altercations as some took the law into their own hands and occasional lynchings, or as they were referred to as the rule of *Judge Lynch's law. Mob rule*, or *mob law*, often carried the day.[34] Between 1874 and 1882 there were twelve lynchings in Nebraska.[35] A lynching almost occurred in Cozad except for John Cozad's intercession, according to Mari Sandoz. Jerry Cozad, a cousin, had been shot by John McIntyre after an argument. McIntyre retreated to a house and a mob gathered making threats to hang him. That tragedy was avoided when John Cozad stepped into the fray and broke it up.[36]

A lynching did take place in Plum Creek around the time of the great fire in Cozad in 1876. In this case, Tom Hallowell was hanged by a mob after he shot the deputy sheriff when the officer had broken down his front door with orders to evict him. After being arrested and placed in jail, Hallowell was taken from his cell, and lynched from the second floor of the front of the courthouse in the middle of the night.[37]

These events were the result of land disputes, horse thievery, political fights, violence and probably the most difficult and dangerous one; dealing with the ranchers and cattlemen who used the open space as their own personal free range in the early settlement years.

Among the first cattlemen to arrive in Central Nebraska were the Olive brothers, Print and Ira. They first began to bring cattle up from Texas in 1869 when an original shipment was brought to Fort Kearny. Soon they saw that the lands to the north and west of Kearney were ideal for grazing cattle and that the Nebraska prairies and plains were largely a free and open range with no necessity to pay for the right to use them. In the ensuing years they spread their operations across Custer, Buffalo, Valley and Sherman counties.[38]

Mari Sandoz, an expert on the western life during the nineteenth century wrote:

> *Unfortunately, the Cozads struck the worst region in Nebraska for lawlessness, and outside of the Olive regions of Texas and Johnson County in Wyoming, with the most cattleman violence.*[39]

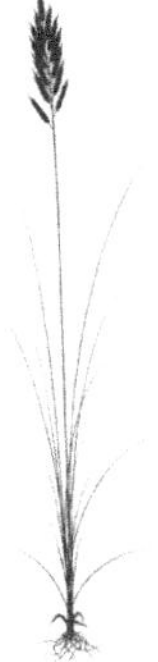

The ever-increasing violence in Texas, where many of them had their operations centered, gave pause to the cattlemen who began to move their herds northward. In 1876, the Olive brothers moved three herds of cattle numbering between fifteen and twenty thousand head northward. One of the main centers of their shipping operations became Plum Creek, although residents of the town were also alarmed by the violence they brought to the growing village.[40]

In time, the cattlemen soon found those open lands increasingly being closed off to grazing as the Herd Law of 1871 required that cattle had to be controlled with fenced-in areas so that their herds did not trample crops and the hard work of the newly arrived homesteaders.[41]

The cattlemen, particularly those north and west of Cozad, were opposed to the homesteaders for a variety of reasons. At the time there was a popular theory that *rain would follow the plow*, an idea that as more land was plowed more rain would fall.[42] The ranchers did not believe this theory was true, and in fact believed that the homesteaders would give up, leaving behind a nightmare of legal challenges with regard to the ownership of the land that would take a great deal of time and effort to undo. They also felt that the government was misguided in its approach to homesteading and would prove to be mistaken. To some degree they were correct as time has borne out.[43]

Homesteaders for their part were building a future and creating farms on lands purchased from the government, railroad, and through agents like Cozad. The whole dynamic between the cattlemen and homesteaders would change in the decades to come as the number of immigrants increased dramatically and began putting up barbed wire fences, blocking water holes, growing crops, needing pasture, and cutting hay for their own animals. Cattlemen with large herds were ultimately forced to change how they managed their operations. In time, most cattle owners became a combination of farmer and rancher with herds numbering under one hundred head.[44]

One of the most horrific confrontations occurred between two homesteaders, Luther Mitchell and Ami Ketchum, and cattleman Print Olive and his violent gang of Texans. Said to be the richest cattleman in Nebraska and owning one half of the cattle in the Custer County area, Print Olive was born Isom Prentice Olive.[45]

There are several versions of the story but one version states that Olive's men drove their cattle through the lands of Ketchum and destroyed his crops, after which the deadly dispute began. Another version is that Mitchell and Ketchum stole some Olive cattle which were discovered in cattle pens in Kearney ready to be shipped. A third version states that the two homesteaders may have killed some of Olive's cattle. When Olive's brother, Bob, also known as Bob Stevens, and recently appointed a deputy sheriff, confronted Mitchell and Ketchum, he was killed in a shootout on November 27, 1878.[46]

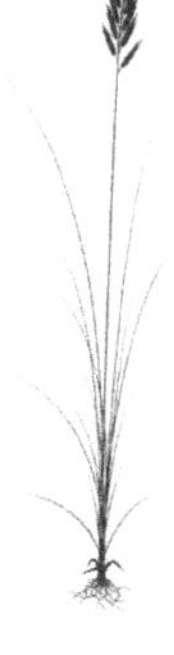

After fleeing, Mitchell and Ketchum were captured and jailed in Kearney. Mitchell and Ketchum were returned to the newly formed Custer County, and enroute Olive's men captured the homesteaders, shot and lynched them. Their burned bodies were later found in a canyon not far from present day Callaway near where they were homesteading. It was a gruesome story that made the state and national newspapers and the perpetrators of the crime were called the *Man Burners*. The whole episode also angered and embarrassed John Cozad because these kinds of incidents made it less likely that homesteaders would come out.[47]

Print Olive, who lived in Oconto, was found guilty, sentenced to life in prison but was released a year later in 1880 after a retrial. Ultimately, he was killed in 1886 by an associate in Colorado. After his removal from the region, troubles between the cattlemen and homesteaders subsided.[48]

Cozad and his sons also had trouble with Print Olive and his gang. Olive was driving cattle up from Texas when the senior Cozad sent his boys to watch their fence lines to be sure that the fields were not trampled on, or hay stolen from them. While the ranchers agreed to keep their cattle off the Cozad land, they also shot at Robert's dog.[49] These kinds of clashes between ranchers and homesteaders were typified by the dispute between a rancher, Alf Pearson, and John J. Cozad, which would mark an important turning point in the community's development and create a tragic disruption of the Cozad family's life with far-reaching effects. Ironically, Cozad had promoted the region as *A Great Stock Locality* for the raising of grain, and livestock including sheep and dairy cows.[50]

### Isolation on the Plains

In addition, other challenges remained for those early homesteaders of Cozad. For example, there was no way to get across the Platte River to transport goods from the areas that were farther south of Cozad and into town. There was, however, a bridge at Plum Creek, later Lexington, that forced farmers and ranchers to go eastward to conduct business rather than northward. Indeed, all of the trade from south of the Platte made its way to Plum Creek.

Even though Union Pacific trains passed through regularly, Cozad like so many Nebraska towns of the era, was a very isolated place. Until Cozad's population grew substantially in the 1890s there were just a small number of businesses and residences located there. It was difficult to get equipment and supplies for residents.[51]

Finally, many who came out to Nebraska from the east were simply unprepared for the challenges or unable to meet them. Farmers from the East found themselves engaged in a different kind of farming or former businessmen who came to farm just found the life so different from what they were used to. Many came to try their hand at farming and business only to find the circumstances and challenges too difficult and left. While the posters that they had seen back East extolled the bounty of the land, only desolation, drought, grasshoppers and conflict had greeted those hearty souls in the early years. For almost ten years there was no meat available except for the wildlife that lived on prairies including deer, buffalo, antelope, elk, cranes, ducks and geese. Charitable contributions of clothing, seed and food stuffs were sent out under the auspices of the Nebraska Aid Society.

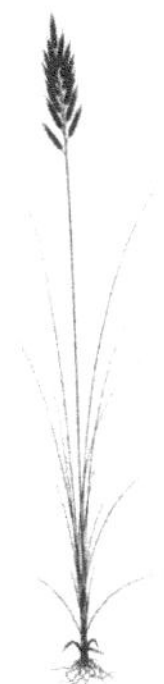

Even Congress was petitioned to send aid to the areas that were depopulating. Various diseases were a plague to many of the settlers, particularly the children.[52]

Initially most homesteaders lived in sod houses, or *soddies* as they were called. Constructed with squares of turf for the walls, and with grass roofs and dirt floors, they only had small windows which allowed little light from the outside. They were drafty and cold in the winter and occasionally snakes would poke their heads out to a surprised family. Cows often wandered and found themselves standing on the roof tops. Soddies were primitive and pictures of those settlers with furniture out in front to show their families and friends back East are common. In time they would come to build wood framed structures.

One description of a soddie comes from William Walker, an early settler to the Cozad area. He wrote:

> *The first sod house we built was 12 x 14, without a floor. The cost in cash was $.75 for two half windows. We had to pull the string latch to get the door open.*[53]

### Investing in the Future

In spite of all of the challenges and hardships, Cozad invested heavily in making the town a flourishing community just as he had tried to accomplish in

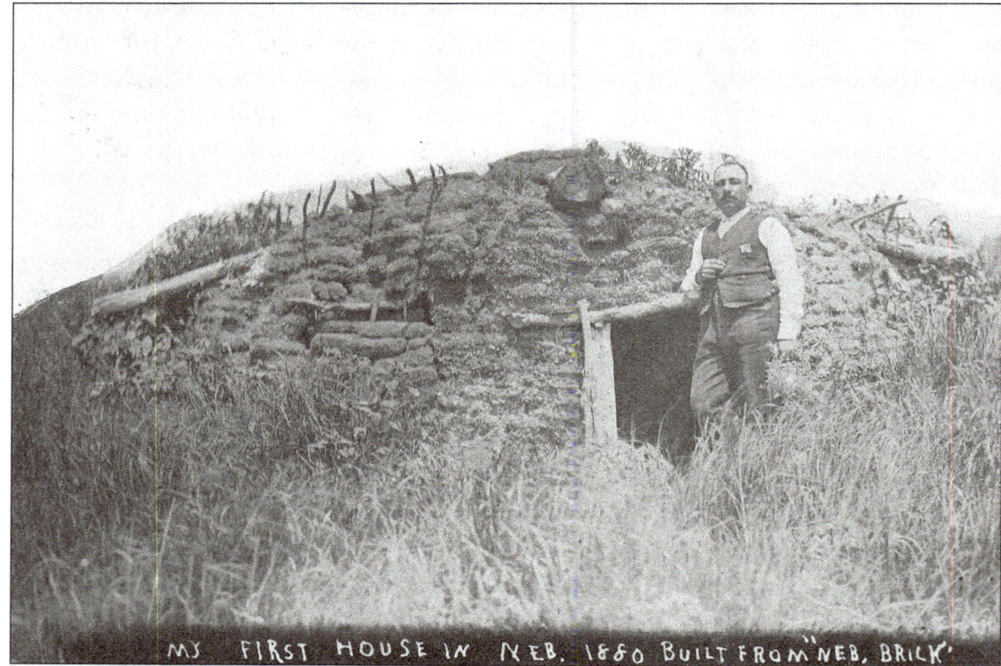


*Courtesy Library of Congress (Digital ID nbhips 10216)*

*This photograph was taken by well-known Nebraska photographer Solomon D. Butcher, in front of his first dugout. He documented the early pioneering history of Nebraska. This type of structure is what the early emigrants would have constructed upon their arrival.*

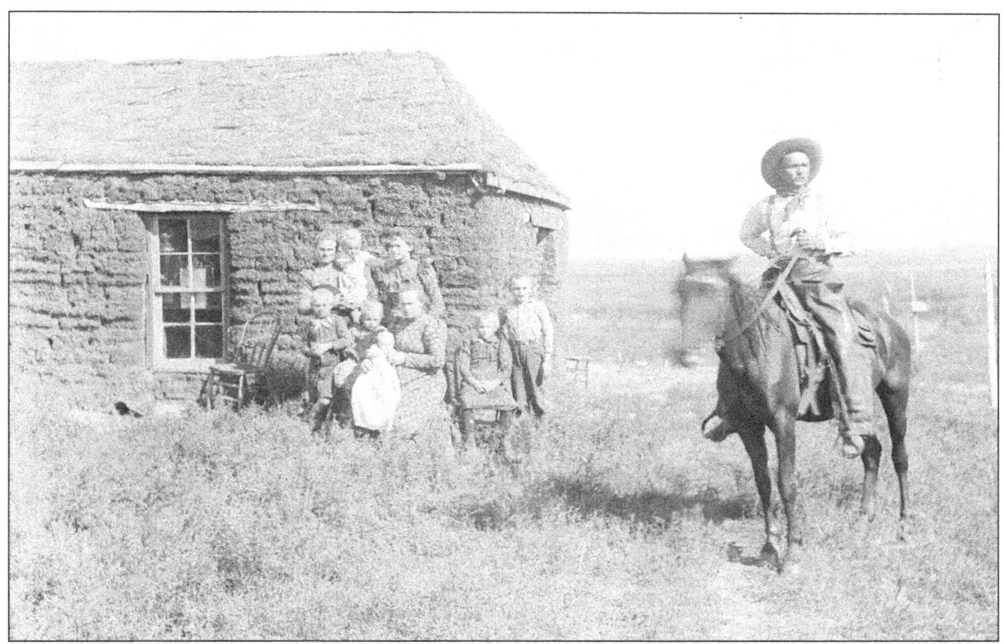

*Courtesy Library of Congress (Digital ID nbhips 10186)*

*This photograph was also taken by Solomon D. Butcher of the J.C. Crum sod house in Loup County, Nebraska. It is typical of the many soddies that dotted the landscape in the last quarter of the nineteenth century.*

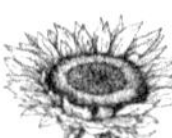

Cozaddale. His efforts also reflect the progressive thoughts of the time. In 1875, a new state constitution was approved and one of its features was that it provided a complete system of public schools. For his part, Cozad built a small two-room brick school in 1874-75 (believed to be worth $5,000). The first floor was used for students, the second floor for church, entertainment, and fraternal organizations.[54]

A new high school was built in 1880 and it is not clear if Cozad built it or if it was a publicly financed project. Cozad constructed three business buildings and set up several businesses and, in the process, hired only local residents to complete the work. It has been suggested that he spent forty thousand dollars in these various endeavors.[55]

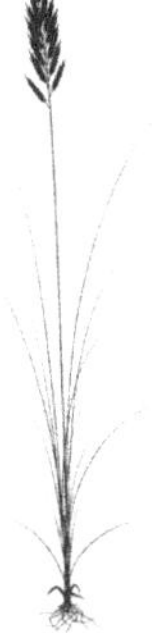

After one particularly difficult year Cozad purchased wheat seed for area farmers to encourage them to try again and keep his community alive.[56] It is worth remembering that if he was unable to retain settlers, the community would have disappeared and would have been a failure, not unlike what had happened in Cozaddale.

It was not uncommon at the time when communities were being created from an empty landscape for the founder, or founding corporation, to make an offer of land for houses of worship. John Cozad followed that custom and on June 19, 1875, made the offer to a number of traveling businessmen that he would donate a block of land in the town, with any representative making the choice of lot, on which they could build a church. This group that he was visiting with were representatives of the Presbyterian Church of the United States and they chose Block 174 on which to locate their church and parsonage. Cozad prepared a deed on that June day for the Presbyterian officials. For some reason, a Presbyterian church was never built on that site. A congregation was not organized until 1892, and a church not built until 1925.[57]

The following passage from the *Testimonial of Appreciation* prepared by members of the Presbyterian Church describe him as:

> *The pioneer here – a gentleman of wealth and culture from Cincinnati, Ohio who generously proposed to donate to any denomination a block of land with the town . . . whereon to erect a church and parsonage, together with the brick to build the same . . .*[58]

## Bridging the Platte River

One of the most notable acts of John J. Cozad's generosity came as a result of the county's inability, but more likely, its unwillingness to build a bridge south of the Cozad Colony. That act came in the form of his constructing a bridge across the Platte River, south of Cozad using his personal funds.

One of the most politically charged issues of the time was the attempt by both Cozad and Willow Island to construct bridges across the Platte. It was clear that the bridge at Plum Creek had been a significant factor in its economic development. Both Cozad and Willow Island made attempts to get the county to bond the construction, and, in both cases, failed.

In 1874, as settlers began arriving in larger numbers into the area, Dr. O. G. Chase, the owner of a new store in the fledgling downtown, decided to find a way to create a crossing to get people from south of the river into town. Because of the difficulty in crossing the river, those early homesteading families were going to Plum Creek instead of doing their business in Cozad.[59]

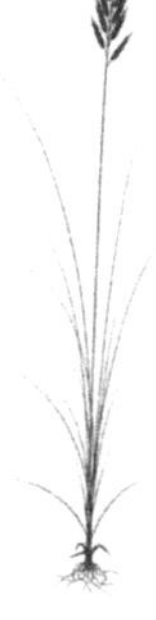

The first bridge to cross the Platte was completed in Plum Creek and opened on July 4, 1873, at that same time that the Cozads spent their first summer in Nebraska. Then, in 1875, Josiah Huffman, the county commissioner pushed through a proposal to build a bridge at Willow Island although in the end it was not built, an injunction was served stopping the work.[60] Four bridges were built over the Platte and Loup rivers and Buffalo Creek by the county, but not one for Cozad.[61]

Cozad continued to try and get the county to finance a bridge and, in the fall of 1876, the voters of the Cozad Precinct voted to approve the bridge bonds. The financing, would come essentially from the Union Pacific, which owned the largest amount of taxable land in the area, was apparently passed by a two-thirds vote. Twenty-four residents voted for the bridge and ten voted against it. However, an injunction was filed and the process ended even though the county commissioners were willing to move forward with the necessary bonds. The railroad blocked a second proposed election. Curiously, the Union Pacific was opposing someone who had been an important ally and customer in John Cozad but was probably more worried about the precedent it would set across its entire line.[62]

Another important opponent of the bonds was Edmund Winchell, who wanted to see a new community created in what became Gothenburg, and who also owned a business in Cozad but had become a Cozad opponent. He was also a county commissioner who represented the far western district in the county.[63]

Fording the shallow river south of Cozad was complicated by the quicksand that was often found along its route and with horses getting mired in it. In some places it was impossible to ford. Dr. Chase acquired a flatboat and created a ferry to get people across the river. However, with the low level of the river in various seasons this method often proved inefficient and ineffective.[64]

Chase discussed this with John Cozad because Cozad also saw the need to connect the settlers south of the Platte with his fledgling community to the north. His largest landholdings were on the south side of the river and were also a source of income because of his land sales. [65]

In fact, he is believed to have even considered creating a new town along the route of the former Pony Express and Oregon Trail at the former Kauffman place. There remains some historical discrepancy about this town because J. Albert Hill and J. J. Douglass laid out a town that they called the One Hundredth Meridian City in January 1875 at the same Kauffman property according to an Omaha newspaper article. They plotted the town and sold between twenty-five and thirty lots to people. Its first street was called Almy Street after a nearby resident.[66]

Because the tax levy on the forty thousand acres that he owned would have amounted to thousands of dollars of revenue to the county, Cozad had hoped that some of the county's tax revenues would be spent building a bridge across the Platte south of the community.[67] Like the other three towns in the county, all needed a bridge over the river to improve their prospects. He also hoped that residents of his town would ultimately be the beneficiary of having Cozad become the county seat, which certainly created problems for him with the residents of Plum Creek.

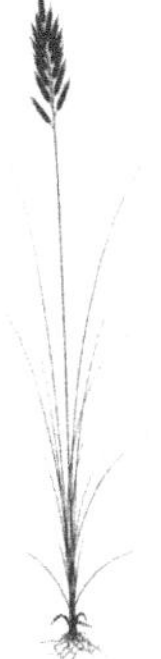

His decision to build a bridge would be of great benefit to those initial homesteaders on several levels. First, they had suffered through devastating natural calamities in those early years along with the natural difficulty of establishing new lives. In undertaking this project, he only hired people from the community in and around Cozad. Among those who worked on the bridge was David Claypool, Sam Schooley and even the Cozad boys. Then after its construction, the population south of the river would have access to the community to the north without having to ride many miles to get to Plum Creek and would be able to conduct their business in Cozad instead.

The design that Cozad settled on in 1874-75 was to narrow the channel of the river, building approaches on both ends made of sod and then a wooden pile bridge spanning the wide but shallow river.[68] He would create three channels for the water to pass through but also narrow the river channels. The basic design is one that has been used on every bridge crossing the Platte in the years since then. With his design he also hoped to make the river navigable all the way to the Missouri River and that his unique design might be adopted by the government. That idea turned out to be an unfulfilled dream.[69]

His vision for a bridge was not the only one. Dr. O. G. Chase had proposed another, on July 4, 1876, as the editor of the *One Hundredth Meridian* newspaper. His design called for the construction of a corduroy bridge of logs that would actually be below the level of the river and would have sand bars naturally created on the upstream side. Chase believed that at most ten inches of water would cover the bridge and that for most of the year just six inches of water would cover the bridge. It would also include a removable walkway for the winter months. Because the bridge structure was beneath the water level it would not rot.[70] In the end the Cozad design prevailed because he was funding it.

Sometime in either 1874 or 1875 the construction of the Cozad sod bridge began.[71] There were many challenges that came to the forefront including seasonal flooding, the funding of it, the hiring of a work crew that consisted of local men and apparently some vandalism by Plum Creek interests. This damage necessitated the posting of men related to the family at the bridge full time to prevent future incidents.[72]

One event came to confirm the locals' image of John J. Cozad. It occurred on the first pay day. Roy Anderson, a son of an early settler, described the scene on the Platte when he wrote:

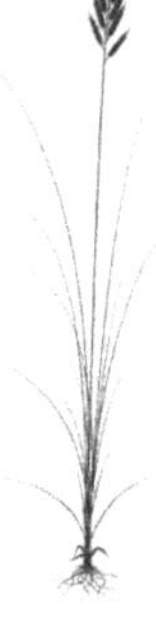

*Cozad come down with a stack of gold and poured it out in a scoop shovel to pay the men. They were working for a dollar a day and it made Pa so dam (sic) mad that he made Cozad put the money back in the sack and keep it mostly out of sight. He told Cozad that it was too much of a temptation for the men in their circumstances.*[73]

Some twenty teams with men worked on the project, and forty acres of sod were stripped off the land as work progressed. Piles were driven into the riverbed to support the superstructure. A fundamental flaw in the design Cozad had chosen was that the sod approaches to the bridge were not strong enough to withstand the spring flooding. Twice, in 1875 and 1876, floods damaged the Cozad bridge.[74] In 1878, flooding erased much of the progress. However, John Cozad continued on with the project as son Robert writes of the work still continuing into the summer of 1880 when he made diary entries about it. It was also a dangerous effort as Johnny almost drowned as he was involved with repairing the bridge after flooding and was caught up in the current and debris.[75]

At some point after 1880, a work stoppage occurred, although it is not clear from the historical records when that exactly happened or why it happened. It is said that there was *an altercation*, and on that day, only Sam Schooley remained on the job. One possible date for the ending of the work is given in *Early History of the Cozad Community and Pioneer Families 1873-1998*. Here the authors suggest the fall of 1882. In this scenario, they suggest that just after the work ended, the fatal dispute about pay between Alf Pearson and John Cozad took place which ended with Cozad shooting him.[76] No matter the cause, the Cozad-led bridge effort was abandoned and never finished. This stoppage more likely occurred between the summer of 1880 and the summer of 1881 when the Cozad family moved to Denver.[77]

Today, all that remains from that effort are perhaps a few of the pilings and some sections of the bridge approaches. Several pilings from the various bridge-building efforts can still be seen in the north branch of the river, just south of Interstate 80. Some of the pilings were cut off by those seeking lumber and others may still be buried in the river channel along with the boat that was used for the operation of the pile driver, which was abandoned along the shoreline. A little island in the middle of the river, part of Cozad's efforts to narrow the channel, remained and Sam Schooley described it later as *Cozad's monument*. It is estimated that Cozad paid between twenty-five and fifty thousand dollars for the construction of the bridge, including wages and materials.[78]

### The Evolution of a Railroad Stop into a Village

Much has been written about the creation of the city and it has long been thought that it was incorporated in late 1873, when the first settlers and immigrants arrived. However, that is not the case. The actual legal incorporation of the city came years later, although it is correct to say that Cozad was established that year.

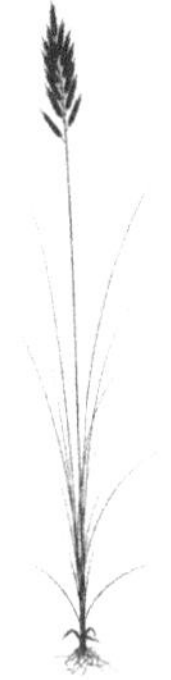

As for the name of the community, an article in the *Omaha Republican* in December 1873 said that the newly established town was to be called *Cozad City*, a name that everyone in that initial group of settlers had desired. This citation from a contemporary source is important, given that it was relayed by the Union Pacific railroad's land agent Edwin Sandison, who knew John Cozad.[79] There is another source, without any attribution, that suggested that Cozad did not want the town named after him, but it was done in his absence on one of his trips back

East.[80]

The first indication that a community had been established was that a railroad stop was designated in 1873 with the placement of a railroad car with *Cozad* painted on each end. A post office for the community was then authorized with the name Cozad, and the first postmaster, Traber Gatewood, was appointed, on June 18, 1874.[81] There has also been a suggestion that Julia Gatewood was the first postmaster, although the postal records state that it was Traber. Perhaps she managed the office or worked as an employee frequently enough that people thought she was the postmaster.

The story of the legal creation of the city is complicated because of what was occurring in the county's political leadership. Dawson County had only been established with its present dimensions in 1871, just two years before Cozad arrived. In addition, because the railroad lay on the north side of the Platte River, the development of the major centers of commerce for the county all would come to lie on that side as well, because no bridges crossed the river.

Initially, after the legal designation of the county's final boundaries, the county was divided into three districts – District One included the Overton area, District Two encompassed the central part of the county including Plum Creek (later Lexington) and then District Three which took in Willow Island and the area that was to become Cozad. The area west of Willow Island (to become the future Gothenburg) was not assigned to a district because there were almost no settlers living there. At the time, the county's entire population was thought to be about forty men and they were the only ones who could vote and thus be counted.[82]

To increase the population located within its boundaries, a County Board of Immigration was established to promote efforts to attract Easterners to Dawson County. They began their efforts in Philadelphia and New York. An *Emigrant House* was built in Plum Creek after the county accepted bids to build a structure that would serve as a kind of welcome center. As settlers began to come westward, they stopped and stayed in Plum Creek. Buildings were erected and crops planted, and Plum Creek quickly developed as a commercial center. By 1874, there were one hundred homes and more than twenty businesses, three churches and a school. Soon twenty-five hundred acres were planted in and around Plum Creek.[83]

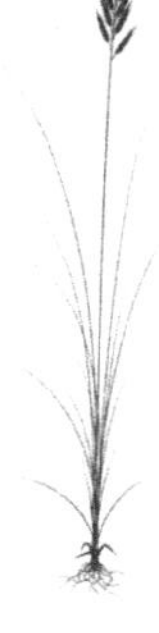

A bridge across the Platte was proposed and subsequently funded by the county to access the important region south of the community that lay along the Republican River. By July 1873, the bridge was complete and Plum Creek now had access to a broad territory of trade. People came from all over the region to conduct business in the town and it quickly became an important trade center.

This is relevant to the Cozad story because by the time that John J. Cozad arrived, both in May and December 1873, Plum Creek was already an important railroad stop having been incorporated on April 25, 1872, and known as a *cow-man economy* given the importance of the cattle industry in the region. At one point the Union Pacific was sending out fifteen hundred cars of beef to the East as it was on the southern end of the extensive cattle range.[84] It was also a place to where supplies were shipped. The town was more advanced in its economic development than any other settlement in the region, and in fact, more than the town of Lancaster, where the state capital would be located, and later called Lincoln.[85]

Several contemporary sources provide interesting insights into what Plum Creek, Cozad and Willow Island were like in 1879. They provide important comparisons and reveal why it is that Plum Creek ultimately became the largest and most important community in the county. A tour guide manual of the route of the Union Pacific and Central Pacific railroads described Plum Creek in this way:

*Plum Creek is the county-seat of Dawson County, has about 500 inhabitants: a fine brick court-house with jail underneath, one church edifice, school-house, two or three hotels, stores, warehouses, etc. It is a point where considerable broom corn is purchased and shipped; has a semi-weekly stage line across the Republican Valley to Norton, in the State of Kansas, and a weekly newspaper. There is a substantial wagon bridge across the Platte River, nearly three-quarters of a mile in length. It is located in the midst of a very fine grazing country, though in favorable seasons crops have done well. With irrigation, perhaps they might be made a certainty. This town also enjoys quite a trade with the upper Republican Valley.*[86]

The *Nebraska Gazetteer and Business Directory* reported in 1879 that:

*Plum Creek is the county seat and is situated on the southeast portion of the county, on the Union Pacific Railroad. It is two miles from the Platte River, and has a population of six hundred. A bridge across the Platte nearly a mile long, and which cost $55,000, gives connection with the southern part of the state, and secures trade even from the Republican Valley. The records of the U.P. office show that during the year ending August 25, 1878, there were 210 cars of stock shipped from this point. The number received, freighted with coal, lumber, and general merchandise, was much larger.*

*The courthouse is a brick structure, built in 1875, and its lower portion is converted into a county jail. The Episcopalians have a very neat church and Baptists, Methodists, and Presbyterians have organized and started services. The Masons and kindred societies have lodges here. The change which a few years has effected this locality are very great. Then it was a favorite spot for Indian attacks upon emigrant and railroad trains, and some of the most fiendish acts were here perpetrated by them, but now peaceful industry and civilization have caused the wilds to glow with pictures of prosperity.*[87]

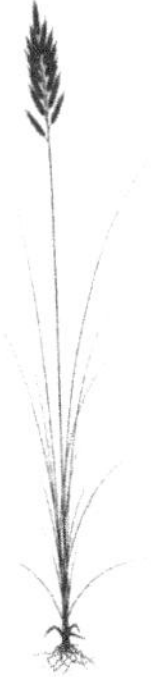

An early contemporary description of Cozad comes from an Army officer's diary. Second Lieutenant J. E. H. Foster was part of an expedition to find a band of Native Americans who were reported in the area and who had caused problems near Brady. His group of men would travel fifty miles east from Fort McPherson in an effort to find them, and an entry on April 30, 1874 can be found in his diary. He wrote:

*100 in the Shade! Passed through the Great Growing City of Cozad which consists now of 17 and ¾ houses and all brand new – Their Hotel Building is really one of the best looking structures that I have seen west of Omaha – The town is not much more than six weeks old and bids fair to amount to something, as its founder is very wealthy and famous as a builder of cities. The greatest institution that they have in town is the 100th Meridian – They have a huge signboard announcing the astonishing fact planted in a prominent position.*[88]

Another description of Cozad that also comes from the *Nebraska Gazetteer and Business Directory in* 1879 described the community thus:

*Cozad, a station and post office on the U.P. railroad, 15 miles west of Plum Creek, the county seat, and near the center of the county. The town was located by John J. Cozad, of Cincinnati, Ohio, in 1874, and has several large brick buildings but at the present are unoccupied. The population is 20.*[89]

From a travel guide of the same year comes the following description of the town:

*Cozad - So named after a gentleman from Cincinnati, Ohio, who purchased about 40,000 acres of land here from the railroad company; laid out the town; built quite a number of houses; induced people to settle here; has resold a good deal of his land, but still has about 15,000 acres in the immediate vicinity. Along the railroad track, west of Plum Creek, the traveler will notice that the buffalo grass has been rooted out by what is called prairie or blue-joint grass. This last is an annual grass and is killed by frost, after which it resembles dark colored brick – a reddish brown appearance. It has but little nutriment after the frost comes, but if cut and cured in July or August, makes an excellent quality of hay. The buffalo grass is just over the divide a little way, but is giving way to that just named. Some men of capital near Cozad, are interesting themselves in sheep raising, and frequently from this place west you will see large herds of cattle. Cozad is 245.1 miles from Omaha, with an elevation of 2,480 feet. It has two or three stores, school-house, hotel, several large dwellings, and with favorable seasons for growing crops in the future, will become quite a town. The Platte Valley at this point is about twenty miles wide.*[90]

Finally, an 1879 article in the *Omaha Weekly Republican* reported that:

*In 1874, John J. Cozad of Cozad Dale, Ohio, bought of the railway company 40,000 acres of land twenty miles west of Plum Creek, on the line of the Union Pacific Railroad, which he projected as the site of the town. The place was named Cozad, in his honor, and he brought out a colony of people. But the majority of them got early discouraged, when the interest flagged, and went away. There is quite a large collection of houses yet remaining there, some of them very substantial, but the majority of them are tenantless. It is an excellent location for a real live body of settlers.*[91]

Another contemporary view of the struggling colony can be found in Robert Cozad's 1878 scrapbook. Contained in its pages is the following humorous poem written by Harry Millie on the fourth anniversary of the arrival of the first colonists to the Cozad Colony on December 7:

*To The West*
*To the West! To the West! to the land of the free*
*Where we shoot the slow elk and make jolly beef tea*
*Where the skunk scents the air, and the rattlesnakes crawl*
*But the land is so plenty there's room for us all*
*We read the Meridian, play Euchre and smoke,*
*The ladies are merry and love a good joke,*
*The times all our own, and we needn't work here,*
*For what is the use when the crops won't appear.*

*To the West, to the West if you love fun like me,*
*Come out and be tickled at the wonders you'll see.*
*Do not stop at Plum Creek, but come on to Cozad,*
*For this is the country for which your (sic) so mad.*

*To the West, to the West, for this is the key,*
*To the Black Hills and Utah to get rich and marry*
*Every man has a wife and some men have more*
*For if you wish it you can get three or four.*
*Quarter sections are plenty and land is so cheap;*
*The water is sparkling, and are our wells not deep;*
*The deer and jack rabbit are what we all eat,*
*And the rats of the Court House for our dogs are good meat.*[92]

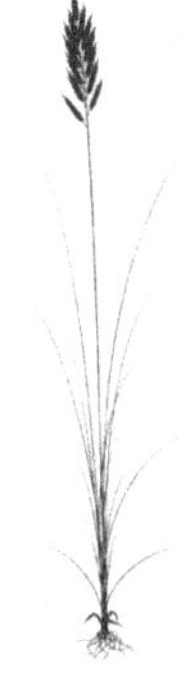

A description of Willow Island comes from the same 1879 tourist guide previously cited:

*Willow Island is the next station; so named from the large number of willow bushes on the island in the river nearby. It is 250.1 miles from the Missouri, and has an elevation of 2,511 feet. The prairie or blue-joint grass still continues along the side of the track, and the bluffs on the south side of the river seem more abrupt. They are full of ravines or "draws," and these sometimes have timber in them. At this station, a large quantity of cedar piles and telegraph poles are delivered. They are hauled some forty miles from the canyons in the South Loup Valley. There is a store at this station and a corral nearby where stock is kept; with a few old log and mud buildings, rapidly going to decay in the vicinity. The glory of this place, if it ever had any, has long since departed, but it may, nevertheless, yet become the pride of stockmen, who shall count their lowing herds by the thousand.*[93]

One of the larger cattle operations in the area was owned by Josiah Huffman, the same Huffman who had refused Cozad's offer of purchasing a town site in Willow Island. Typical of the ranchers of the time, when Huffman became the county commissioner for District Three, he made it clear that he was not interested in promoting emigration into his part of the county.[94] However, by this point Willow Island had a population of one hundred, five times that of Cozad, even though they were not promoting settlement.

### Incorporating the City of Cozad

In September 1874, just three years after the original creation of the county, the county's districts were changed, in part perhaps to counter John J. Cozad, one of the county's largest landowner aside from the railroad. District One, which included Overton, was expanded to the west, almost to Plum Creek. District Two, which included Plum Creek was enlarged, also to the west and now included Cozad. District Three was expanded west to the county line.[95]

Surely one of the intended effects was to box John Cozad out of the halls of power in Dawson County. Because Plum Creek had more residents, a condition that remains to this day, it was believed that a representative from Cozad (or John himself) would never hold the seat in District Two. The district had the largest population in the county which made it the most powerful. This also reflected the competitive rivalry between what became the four main communities of Dawson County. However, this political decision would have far reaching consequences for John Cozad, his community, and the county.[96]

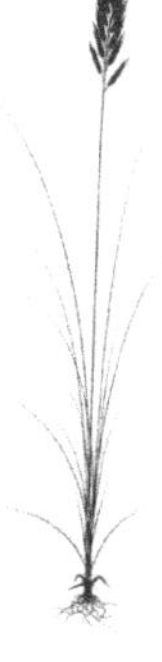

## Scandals and Struggles

Another political development is that John Cozad, very early on, wanted to move the county seat of government from Plum Creek to Cozad. It is not known what factors encouraged him to propose this but in early 1873, just as his community was being created and organized, there were several ongoing controversies that would have attracted his attention. First was the effort started by Dawson County to build a new courthouse. By mid-1873, the effort was approved by the commissioners and the gathering of construction materials began.

The project, however, was halted temporarily when the railroad decided to move its operations one mile west from Plum Creek over a land dispute. It left behind its first depot and other structures on the original Plum Creek site. In April 1874, with the town relocated westward, the county's commissioners approved a new construction contract, and the building was erected.[97] Perhaps Cozad had seen this as an opening because of the challenges that the county was facing with its courthouse project and proposed to move it to Cozad.

The second controversy, having taken place prior to the Plum Creek difficulties, was the state's struggle with its own capital city development project. The creation and location of where the capital should be located was the focus of an intense political battle between various communities across the state as many felt that the capital should be located elsewhere. This fierce fight included deception by all sides.

Consideration was even given to locating the capital outstate, perhaps to Kearney or Plum Creek. Both communities were located adjacent to the railroad, north of the Platte River, and were, unlike Lancaster, the proposed location, in the center of the state. Lancaster was situated in the far eastern end of the state.

In the end, the political forces for the capital being located in Lancaster prevailed. Lancaster's name was changed to Lincoln as part of the entire capital complex negotiations and was chosen to be the site of the state capital complex in 1867. A new capital building was built and opened in late 1868.[98]

A second controversy that occured during the Plum Creek challenges concerned financial irregularities and malfeasance with regard to the capital building construction and land development in the new city of Lincoln. The scandal grew to such proportions that by 1871, Governor David Butler was impeached and removed from office for his part.

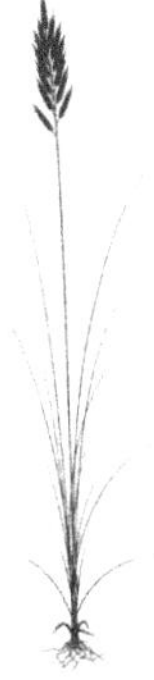

The whole episode continued to reverberate across the state. Delegations across the state, including one from Cozad, arrived at the capital to lobby for the moving of the capital. In the late winter of 1875, a capital company was created in Plum Creek to issue stock to raise funds to move the capital to central Nebraska along with building all the required state buildings. Cozad also proposed raising more than two hundred thousand dollars to build the capital in Cozad City. By this time the state's capital building, which had been poorly constructed, was beginning to deteriorate. These statewide efforts obviously went nowhere as Lincoln remains the state capital today although at the time there was a proposal to cut the state in half and form a new state if the various proposals were stonewalled.[99]

Then, with these controversies going on, Cozad inserted himself into a conversation which even by those days' standards seemed pretty lofty. He, along with many Nebraskans, wanted to see the nation's capital moved to Nebraska and to Cozad in particular which was nearly in the center of the country. He traveled to Washington D.C. to promote this vision along, with a second one. Cozad also proposed building a railroad line from Cozad to the Black Hills in South Dakota in the hopes of capitalizing on the discovery of gold there and managing a major transportation artery into the lands of the Sioux Indians. He also wanted to build yet another city.[100]

For the Cozad settlement's first four years of existence, its governmental obligations and management were overseen by Dawson County. That certainly must have troubled John Cozad given his relationship with the county from the beginning.[101]

Cozad traveled to Lincoln to set about getting Cozad legally established and that was accomplished. In 1877, trustees were appointed to manage the governmental affairs of the community; W. H. Irwin was named the chairman, and D. M. Dale was chosen as the clerk. Little else is known about the arrangement. Whether John Cozad was involved with its actual management is not known although one can surmise that he retained significant influence.[102]

As late as 1879 the area around John J. Cozad's initial settlement was still being called the Ohio Colony, or the Cozad Colony. By that point, a small hamlet had been established and called *Cozad* but the vast area surrounding the village was actually the *Cozad Precinct*.[103]

For a community to become legally incorporated the county commissioners were required to approve it. Sixty-three residents presented their petition to the county, and Cozad was officially incorporated as a village on February 11, 1886. The first trustees were David Claypool, Martin Gering, William Irwin, Traber Gatewood and C. T. Fulton. Eight months before, Gothenburg had been incorporated.[104] The first county commissioner elected from Cozad came two years later in 1888, and his name was Clark Brown.[105]

Today it is a second-class city by the ranking of its population of between five hundred and eight thousand.[106]

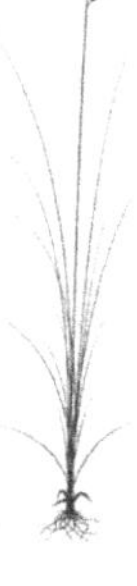

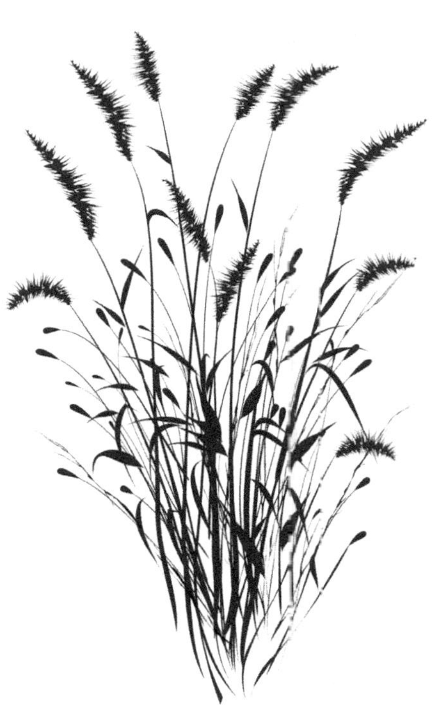

## *Chapter 5*

# Mr. Cozad's Troubles

*That trouble Mr. Cozad had in the early times of Cozad was a great misfortune.*[1]
Mary Wake,
A Family Friend Writing to a Cozad Family Member in 1909

*Pa and John Cozad never hitched it well together. Cozad was a crook and gambler and everything that was'ent (sic) on the up and up. He had sons that were as big a bulley's (sic) as he was. Whenever anyone did'ent (sic) suit their taste, the boys would hold them while old John J. bullwhipped them. You will probably remember old Jim Beardsley, he was one of the victims of their atrositys (sic).*[2]
Roy Anderson
Early Cozad Settler

WHILE IT IS CLEAR THAT JOHN JACKSON COZAD was a generous man as has been shown, and a family man, it is the other side of Cozad that is more often remembered in history. He was a man who was involved in what seemed to be a never-ending series of disputes that hovered about him throughout his life. He shot at people, was shot at by others, was jailed and forever embroiled in legal challenges. These include controversies and fights between Cozad and his neighbors and the residents of Plum Creek during the decade he was involved in his Cozad Colony. The records in the county's archives demonstrate his contentious nature.

Mari Sandoz in her book, *Son of the Gamblin' Man,* noted that there were a number of unexplained fires in the small town, including the major catastrophe in April 1876 that destroyed the town, and the burning of the depot, which was really a box car.[3] It was thought that it might have been the work of his detractors, disgruntled residents or Plum Creek villans. The work site at the Platte River bridge was vandalized although it was never determined who the culprits may have been. The Cozads were in various disputes with cattlemen.[4] Cozad was not afraid to fire his pistol at people to convince them of his rightness or seriousness in arguments and conflicts. This even included the Union Pacific Rail Road agent, Edwin Sandison.[5]

Probably the best contemporary example that reveals the violence and difficulties of the period for John Cozad was the recent airing of the program *1883* on a cable television network (2022). One can see the rawness of the Western frontier towns and how violence played an important role in them.

While most presume that Cozad's difficulties began in Nebraska, that is not the case. For example, on December 10, 1867, seven years before he came to Nebraska, John Cozad was in court because of an altercation that occurred at the Eldorado Saloon in Cincinnati. Cozad, who was also known as *Panama John,* got into a scuffle with William Adema over comments he had made about a judge whom Cozad knew and had just left their company. After Cozad hit him, yelling: *Get out you son of a bitch!* Adema began beating Cozad, who retaliated by beating Adema. At one point, as they wrestled, a pistol Adema was holding discharged passing near Cozad's head, out the window and into a neighboring house. The case then went to trial as Cozad pressed charges believing that Adema had meant to kill him. Adema was fined fifteen hundred dollars for his actions.[6]

Mari Sandoz also reported on another incident that took place in the summer of 1874 in Cincinnati when William Todd broke Cozad's jaw in an altercation. Todd had previously lost money to Cozad gambling but in this case, Cozad stated that he was trying to stop Todd from damaging the sign in front of his business. On another occasion he was mugged, and along with his father-in-law Robert Gatewood, went back to the scene, caught up with the muggers, and beat them, but they escaped. Gatewood and Cozad were arrested and thrown in jail. Traber Gatewood made arrangements for their release.[7]

Almost as soon as he began his colonization efforts in Nebraska, he found himself in trouble with some cowboys. As recounted in *The Riggs Family in America*, the following occurred:

*Mr. Cozad had a violent temper when aroused, had a haughty pride, and little tolerance for diplomatic approaches so he was constantly making enemies. That first summer (1873), he was set upon by a bunch of wild cowboys and thrown off the train five miles from Willow Creek, so he had a long hot walk home.*[8]

He argued with the Union Pacific's Cozad stationmaster and land agent, Edwin Sandison, about Sandison taking Cozad's potential real estate customers away from him. It grew so heated that Cozad pulled out his pistol and fired at Sandison.'s feet, swearing at him. Soon thereafter, Sandison was transferred to a different posting far from Cozad. Cozad had good reason to be concerned with Sandison because he was selling land at a cheaper rate than Cozad.[9]

Sandison is an interesting figure as he was considered to be a *pioneer employee* of the Union Pacific. He would later develop towns in Kansas for railroads, participated in the gold rush in Canada and died a wealthy man in California in 1918.[10]

Another example of his contentious side comes from the unverifiable and uncorroborated account of an original colonizer who was believed to be Roy Handley. His parents came to Nebraska in 1876 and Roy wrote down his recollections of those early days late in his life. They provide insights not only into John Cozad but his two sons. It needs to be remembered that parts of his manuscript contain notable errors and so may this excerpt. However, that said, Handley wrote:

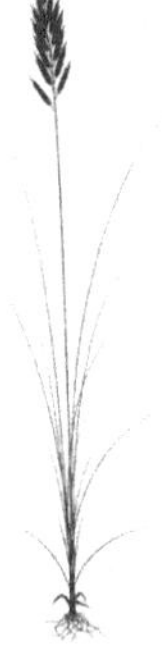

*Pa and John Cozad never hitched it well together. Cozad was a crook and gambler and everything that was'ent (sic) on the up and up. He had sons that were as big a bulley's (sic) as he was. Whenever anyone did'ent (sic) suit their taste, the boys would hold them while old John J. bullwhipped them. You will probably remember old Jim Beardsley, he was one of the victims of their atrositys (sic).*

*Pa had cut and put up some hay with Johney (sic) Stevenson down on the river between the north bank and Cozad. One day he was hauling some of it through the street. John J. and his two boys stopped him and accused him of stealing their hay. They were all set with the bullwhip to clean up on that red headed Handley (John Handley) as they called him. Pa wrapped the lines around the Jacob staff, grabbed his pitchfork and slid to the ground, old Cozad hollered run for your lives boys that damned red-head hasn't anymore sinse (sic) than to use that fork. So down the alley went the two Cozad boys with Pa at their heels.*

*The next day they had Pa arrested for stealing hay and Cozad and Pa both pleaded their cases. Pa was on the witness stand explaining the situation as to him and Stevenson putting up the hay, Cozad disputed the evidence and Pa got up and stood behind his chair and told the court that he was going repeat what he had said and it wouldn't be healthy for anyone to dispute it. He repeated and immediately (sic) Cozad disputed it and Pa swung the heavy chair, Cozad threw up his arm and the chair knocked him flat and broke his arm in two places. Jim Ware was in the courtroom and when the judge fined Pa ten dollars for contempt of court, Jim offered to pay the fine but old Dick James the sheriff come up and payed (sic) it instead.*

*Just a short time later Cozad shot Pearson down in cold blood in his own home in the presence of Pearson's two sons and then made his escape to parts unknown, he never returned to Cozad that anyone knew of unless it was some of his friends like Sam Schooley or the Gatewoods and a few other friends that he had or were relatives of his.*[11]

The errors that are included in this manuscript regarding the shooting of Alf Pearson will be discussed later. Because of Cozad's large and far-flung land holdings there were certainly some who tried to steal hay from him or use his pastures for feed, although Roy Handley was not one of them.

There were other disagreements. In the fall of 1874 Cozad, Robert and Traber Gatewood and several Cozad cousins were involved in a dispute with Lewis Gibbs. They were indicted for assault and battery, but the case was dropped. There were disputes between Cozad relatives. In 1875 Cozad was arrested for threatening to assault Henry McIntyre and was put in jail and the trial was moved to North Platte. While witnesses did show up for this case, Cozad was found guilty and assessed court costs. Another case involving the same family was also brought to court and not resolved until 1876.[12] Cozad was also sued for monetary judgments.[13]

## Disputes with a Benefactor

About five years after his arrival, John Cozad became embroiled in a complicated dispute with the Union Pacific Rail Road. Initially, the company had been an early supporter of his colonization efforts, and they had a productive and

profitable relationship.

However, sometime in late 1877 a legal dispute began between Cozad and the railroad. This dispute occurred at the same time the Union Pacific went bankrupt.[14] Only fragments of the correspondence between John Cozad and the Union Pacific remain in the archive of the Robert Henri Museum and it is difficult to ascertain with any exactness what the problems were. Part of the problem was that all of Cozad's business paperwork was destroyed in the April 1876 fire that devastated the fledging town.

The first correspondence in the archive which seems to indicate that Cozad had already tried to resolve the issues with the company was a letter written on November 2, 1877 to Silas Clark, a board member and later president of the railroad. In the letter, Cozad outlines a history of the dispute that had begun in December 1873 when he had purchased the sections and lots that formed the center of the city. Cozad had paid the company in the entirety the amount owed. The company then promised a deed by January of 1874, but this did not happen until August of 1876.[15]

The 1876 deed included a requirement that Cozad was to construct a fence along the line, one hundred feet from the center line, something not required in the original contract and an action that was actually the legal responsibility of the railroad. As a result of the delay of the company in providing title, Cozad had been unable to pass title onto those who wanted to buy property from him. This had created a crisis of confidence in Cozad as railroad employees were telling people that Cozad did not have clear title to those lands and had not kept up his end of the agreement.[16]

For his part, Cozad wanted to get the issue settled as quickly as possible because of the financial damage it was causing him. He sued the railroad for seventy thousand dollars in late 1877 or early 1878.[17]

Another piece of correspondence that the author found, dated April 30, 1878, is between Leavitt Burnham, representing the railroad's land office, and Cozad. Burnham offered a settlement of their dispute that calls for Cozad to surrender lands above and beyond what he had paid for but may not have paid taxes on. The proposed settlement required Cozad to pay off the back taxes on the land he was surrendering and whose terms he had been delinquent on. The problem for Cozad was that the titles to land that he believed he owned or was trying to sell, were now disputed. Cozad was not able to sell property with a title that was clear of any encumbrances, and he no longer had his pre-1876 paperwork that had been destroyed in the fire.[18]

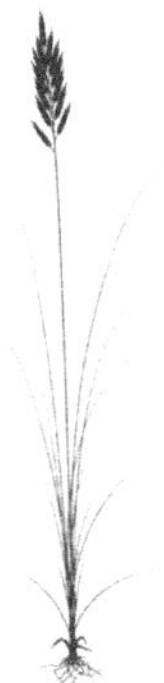

Six weeks later Cozad wrote directly to Jay Gould, the most important stockholder in the railroad, from his office in Cincinnati. He appealed to Gould for a settlement so that legal actions would not be necessary, as it would have required going to court in Omaha with the case possibly winding up in Washington.[19]

Whatever hopes Cozad had, a return letter was not forthcoming or at least a response is not in the museum's collection.

The Cozad-Gould letter does provide some insights into how Cozad had tried to work with the railroad in creating his community. He had paid seven thousand dollars, not including his time, to bring out fifteen hundred emigrants to Nebraska along with his various building projects. In total, Cozad had spent one hundred thousand dollars locating along the line of the railroad. The legal dispute had forced Cozad to stop promoting the efforts to settle Nebraska even though the future looked brighter in 1878 than it had in 1873.[20]

As important as Cozad thought he was, in the railroad's eyes he was just a minor figure in a sprawling enterprise. He had created a community that had less than one hundred people in it although there were a number of settlers in the surrounding areas. However, John Cozad and his problems were not significant to the company's higher echelon although to him he had invested a fortune in his community. He was simply a pawn in a larger financial morass.

This lack of response by Gould can probably be attributed to the larger financial crises that the company faced and how their attention was focused elsewhere at the time. One significant problem for the company was that it was taxed heavily by local, county and state entities and it had once been described as a *tax cow*. An example of this occurred in 1874 when property owned by the railroad was taken by Lincoln County in North Platte because the real estate taxes had not been paid. In addition, the company had declared bankruptcy in the summer of 1874.[21]

Another significant problem was the manipulation of the stock by its officers and owners. In 1873, the company's major stockholder became Jay Gould and he was known to be a stock manipulator. He was at the center of the company's troubles as he had actually very little care for the operation of the railroad but was more interested in financially benefitting from manipulating the company's securities. As a result, the railroad declined precipitously during his association with it.

In the end, the legal action between Cozad and the Union Pacific was settled on December 18, 1879. In the final resolution Cozad agreed to dismiss his suit against the company, pay the railroad more than two thousand dollars and release his interest in the lands that he had previously purchased, probably on option, from the railroad. Part of the settlement had included him paying back taxes owed which certainly must have given him some sense of irony since the railroad had also been delinquent in paying its taxes over the years.[22]

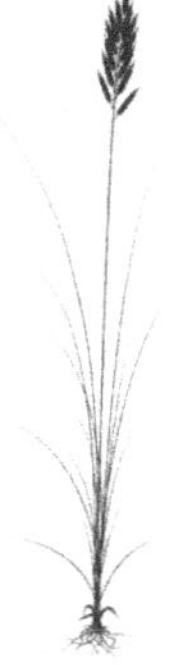

The dispute, in spite of an agreement, continued to linger through the spring of 1880 as Cozad waited for the deeds to be furnished by the company. In another letter to the company's president, Sidney Dillow, Cozad appealed for help suggesting that he would go to court if he had to.[23]

Finally, it was resolved, and as part of the settlement Cozad was given a clear title to eight sections of land and to the even-numbered blocks in Cozad as the original contract called for. Thus, the court action was not required and the entire dispute with the railroad settled. It had been a potentially ruinous dispute for Cozad, but he was able to avert disaster.[24]

## Cut From the Same Cloth

John A. Cozad, the oldest son of John J. Cozad, was in many ways cut from the same cloth and had the temperament of his father. He too found himself in legal trouble on occasion. One such occasion occurred on January 19, 1881, eight months before the family moved to Denver. A complaint was filed by Bennie Glover against the junior Cozad and Gerver Gibson. They were charged with shooting a gun into a barrel of coal oil that was owned by Mrs. Bennie Glover. Four days later they were arrested, and both pleaded not guilty. When the defendants refused to provide bail, they were jailed.[25]

A trial was convened eight days after the incident and among the witnesses called was Robert Cozad and David Claypool. After the evidence was presented, the jury found them not guilty and they were released, and the plaintiff had to pay the court charges.[26]

## Off To Denver

In the spring of 1881, John J. and Theresa Cozad made the decision to leave their settlement behind and to move on, although they continued to go back and forth to Cozad and Cincinnati.[27] There were several considerations that played into this major move. Even though he spent tens of thousands of dollars, and invested in his community heavily, all those years of effort had not been as successful as perhaps he had planned. He had tangled with area residents, politicians, businessmen, and the Union Pacific. And, as one writer later said:

> *Because of the discouragement of its citizens and the dissensions arising between them and Mr. Cozad . . . soon, Cozad, thinking he had not been fairly treated, left the town to its fate.*[28]

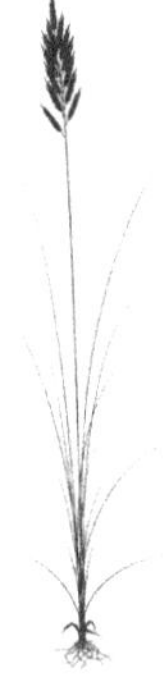

Two historians, Rex German and Russell Czaplewski, authors of *The Battle of the Bridges,* have found an additional reason for John Cozad's unpopularity. When Cozad left Dawson County in June 1881, he owed $2,000 in back taxes for the previous eight years. This was a significant issue for county residents because for most homesteaders the annual payment of taxes could be a major financial challenge and caused many a homesteading family deep anguish. The railroad, the largest taxpayer in the county, was equally delinquent in paying its taxes too. Another factor was that the cattlemen, who were called *free grazers*, did not own or did not pay taxes on the lands to the north of Lexington and Cozad, much to John Cozad's anger.[29]

Here was a wealthy man, the town's founder, owing a significant amount of back taxes, for a number of years, which in turn must have also created some financial challenges for the town and county. Once he departed, the county began to try and recover what was owed it. Equally galling must have been the fact that he had touted the fact that he was a very wealthy and prominent man to all who would listen.[30]

### The Hay Business

John Cozad's extensive and far-flung hay business took him to Denver, Colorado, which had only become a state in 1876. It had been a territory for the prior fifteen years. Denver was then a thriving and growing capital city, and it was clear it was destined to become a major Western metropolitan center. Here Cozad rented a large warehouse in 1880, and son John handled that end of the family's hay business.[31]

John J. Cozad operated a large hay business as he owned thousands of acres of grassland and rented as many as ten thousand acres of land in Nebraska at one point. The lands were regularly harvested and then the hay shipped on the railroad to distant markets like Denver and the mining camps of Leadville, Colorado. Because of the lack of pasture lands in those places the Cozads filled an important need. In the fall of 1880, more than three thousand tons of hay were sent to Leadville.[32]

The hay operations south of the town and the Platte River and extending to Willow Island were so large that Cozad brought in contractors from around the region along with local men who processed hundreds of tons of hay using a steam hay press. A hay press compacted hay from the field so that it could be stored more efficiently in bales and shipped. The baled hay was then sent westward on the Union Pacific.[33]

Another factor is that John and Theresa would get a better education for their boys in Denver than they would have received in Cozad, as they were expected to go to college. Once agreed upon, and with all the factors considered, the family made the fateful decision to move to Denver, leaving the community of Cozad behind. John Sr. apparently left first, sometime before July 1, 1881. Then, on August 24, 1881, according to Robert Cozad's diary, Johnny met the rest of the family at the train station in Colorado. Robert was sixteen and John was nineteen at the time.[34]

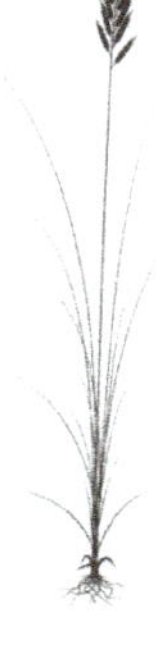

Robert Cozad would write about this major transition in his family's life just as the move to Denver was getting underway on August 15, 1881:

*We will perhaps go into the Real Estate Business – on our own capital – and partly into the Hay & probably the feed commission business. We expect to make Denver our permanent home and try to build up a fortune there.*[35]

Robert also wrote that the family wanted to divest of its Cozaddale and Cozad properties and use the proceeds to invest in Denver.[36]

The father rented a store front and opened a real estate office at 636 Larimer Street, located in the city's commercial district. The building was divided into three sections, one for John J., one for John A., and one for Robert. A sign hung on the front that said *John J. Cozad & Sons.*[37] The father was also invested in a mining operation, probably as a stockholder, in Leadville, Colorado, southwest of Denver where he also sold hay to the miners. He may have also had a hand in another business in Deadwood, South Dakota.[38] It was later speculated that he was worth three hundred thousand dollars, more than half of which was invested in Denver real estate.[39]

The family initially lived in the same building in which the family businesses were located and then moved to a boarding house at 661 Blake Street. There, Robert Cozad discovered some classmates from Chickering also living nearby.[40] After a year in the public school system in Denver, Robert returned to Cozad and worked in the family's hay business.[41]

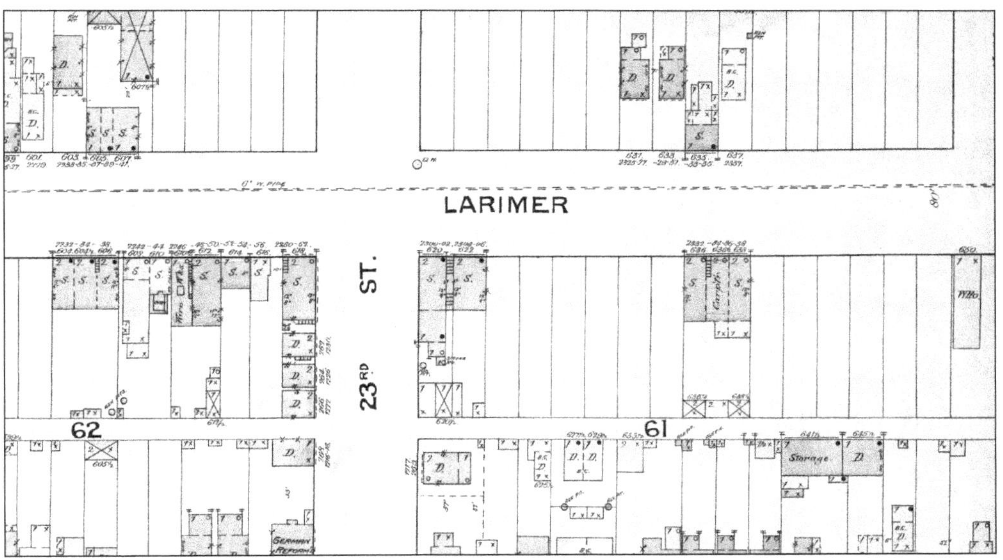


*Courtesy Library of Congress (www.loc.gov/item/sanborn05408_002/.)*

*The Cozads initially lived on 636 Larimar Street in Denver, Colorado.*

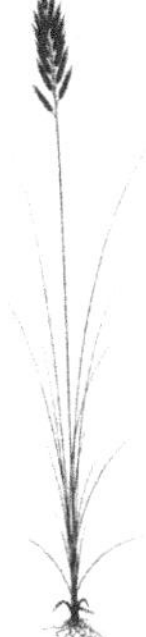

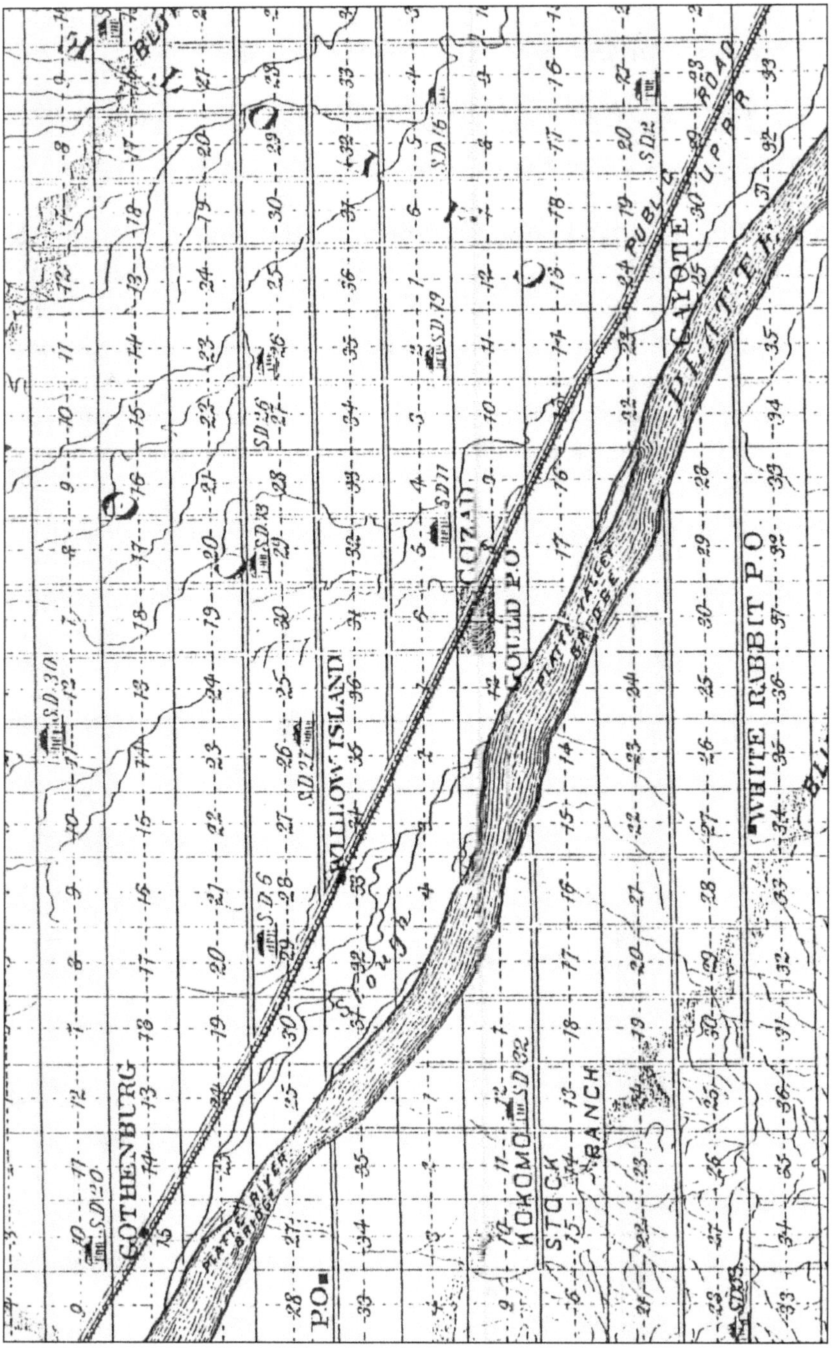

Robert Henri Museum and Art Gallery Collection

*This 1885 partial map of Dawson County shows how both Gould, then listed as the location of the post office, and Cozad, listed as a railroad stop, stood side by side from 1881 to 1885.*

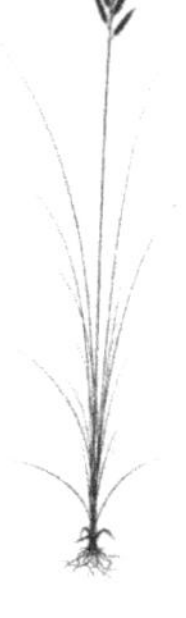

## Cozad to Gould to Cozad

Just as John Cozad was departing for Denver, the name of the community of Cozad was changed to Gould on June 15, 1881, honoring one of the important railroad moguls of the era, Jay Gould.[42] Over time, Gould had come to control the Union Pacific Railroad, and by 1882, controlled fifteen percent of the nation's railroad trackage. Gould had been associated with the New York, Lake Erie and Western Railroad in the East and was its president. It was thought that Gould might take a personal interest in the town at the 100th Meridian.

The name change reflected a strong sentiment in the community to disassociate itself from its founder and his increasing loss of influence in it. Threatening notes had been slipped under his office door, a noose found looped on the front door of the hotel and bullets found in a Bull Durham sack in his wagon. It is believed that a petition that was distributed and signed by his fellow townspeople called for the name to be changed.[43]

Surely this name change and the previously expressed feelings of dissension by his fellow townsmen, from what John Cozad must have felt was, an ungrateful community, must have been one factor in his calculations to leave. After all of the trials and tribulations and financial investment he must have been angry, disheartened and simply willing to pick up and start anew, not unlike what had

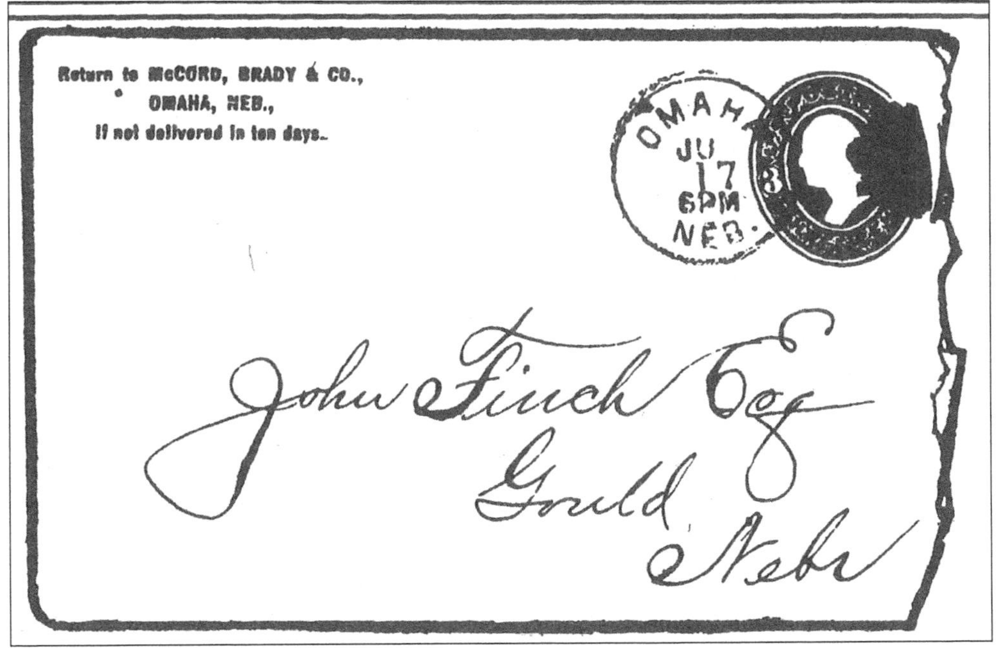


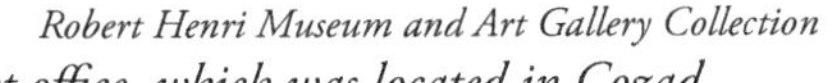
Robert Henri Museum and Art Gallery Collection

*A rare example of an envelope addressed to Gould post office, which was located in Cozad.*

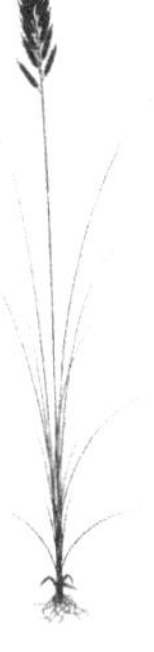

happened in Cozaddale a little less than a decade before.

This name change also reflected another loss of influence by Cozad as Traber Gatewood's tenure as the postmaster had come to an end on February 28, 1881, coinciding with the end of the presidential term of Rutherford Hayes. Gatewood had originally been appointed to the position on June 18, 1874, not long after the first colonizers had arrived. Edwin Winchell, an opponent of Cozad's and former county commissioner, was subsequently appointed to the position.[44]

The name of the post office was changed back to Cozad four years later, on October 23, 1885. By then, after two other postmasters had been appointed and left, Sam Schooley, the faithful friend of John J. Cozad, was appointed the postmaster. He was designated postmaster on July 25, 1885, and served until May 10, 1889.[45]

However, the name of the railroad stop was never changed during this time, perhaps because of Cozad's still considerable influence with the railroad or perhaps because of the inconvenience it would have caused the railroad to make changes in its timetables and promotional materials. One could get off the train at the Cozad stop, post a piece of mail at the Gould post office just a short distance away and then get back on the train at Cozad. In the early fall of 1885, the governor of Nebraska officially returned the name of Cozad to the town on the 100th Meridian and Gould faded into history.[46]

### A Shooting that Changed the World

The family had only lived in Denver for little more than a year when a tragedy that forever affected two families occurred. It is believed that Cozad family members came back occasionally to Cozad after the move to Denver, although their commitment to the community was clearly diminished. On his next to last trip back to Cozad, John Cozad and his family's life was irreparably disrupted and changed forever when he shot an area rancher, Alf Pearson (1832-1882) on October 14, 1882 after a dispute.

Most visitors to the Robert Henri Museum have a vague knowledge of the shooting of Alf Pearson, and it has been a central feature in the interpretation of the Cozad story at the museum for decades. What is particularly surprising is that many of the facts that people assume to be true about that day in the fall of 1882 are traditions handed down through the generations, hearsay, or people's modern interpretations of what might have occurred. Those stories, accepted over the last one hundred and forty years, have been piled upon one another to create a history that, in some ways, has no bearing to what is known to have happened.

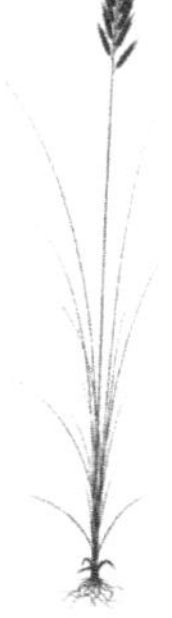

Even the terms that have described Cozad and Pearson have come to be charged in modern times. Because of his actions Cozad has been described as an assassin, a murderer, and a coward while his family and supporters have said he fired his pistol in self-defense and even suggested that Pearson received poor medical care in the aftermath causing his death. Alf Pearson has been described as a drunken rancher, a deputy sheriff, a family man and a person who came to town on that October day with a mission.

Another aspect of this story that must be remembered is that Print Olive and his gang had recently murdered two homesteaders who were suspected of stealing some of Olive's cattle in 1878 and killing Olive's brother, a deputy sheriff. They were caught by Olive and his men, hanged, and burned causing a sensation, both locally and nationally. While Olive had been found guilty and jailed, he was released in 1880 when he was acquitted in a new trial. This event was not that distant in the community's memory.

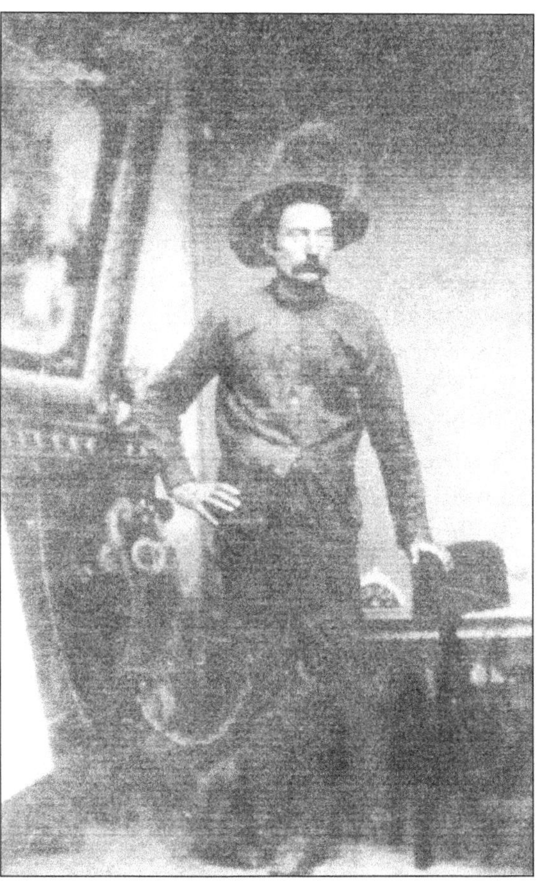

*Courtesy 100th Meridian Museum*

*Alf Pearson*

### Two Tough Men

Curiously, there are many similarities in Cozad and Pearson. They had both come west to improve their situations, both were married, had families, owned property, both had roles, albeit different ones, in the building of the bridge across the Platte River, both had harvested hay along the river, and both were hardened by the difficult experience of living on the Great Plains in the late nineteenth century. There are obvious differences also Cozad was wealthy, a professional gambler, a restless man, a visionary, possessor of a fierce temper, willing to skirt the law when necessary and also seemed to have controversies - legal or personal - in whatever endeavor he was involved with. Trouble seemed to follow him, or he created trouble.

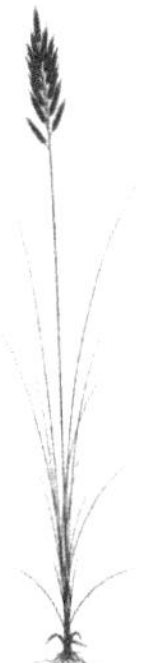

Pearson was a hard-working rancher of modest means. Originally from Union County, Indiana, and the son of a Quaker farmer, he was one of seven children. He married Rachel Harriett Agnes Leonard (1829-1894), a Presbyterian, in 1852. She was from Ohio. Since he married outside of his faith tradition, he left his Quaker faith behind. Together, they had a number of children, six of whom came to Nebraska: William, Mahlon, George, Albert, Ora, May, and Frances.

Genealogical records state that they had eleven children, some of whom stayed in Indiana. All were born in Indiana.[47]

It is believed that Alf Pearson arrived in Dawson County alone, sometime around 1874 with most of his family arriving in 1877 and 1878. Son William, who was married by this time to France Wright, arrived at the same time as the rest of the Pearson family. The remaining members of the elder Pearson's family, including his parents and siblings remained in Indiana.[48]

Because of the high price of land in Indiana, Pearson decided to homestead in Nebraska. He is believed to have initially farmed in Coyote Precinct in 1880 and then came to Cozad Precinct where he homesteaded in Township 12, Range 23 and in the southwest corner of Section 28. His wife, Harriett, homesteaded in Township 11, Range 23 and in the northwest corner of Section 4.[49]

Alfred built a three-room sod house after an earlier house had burned to the groundin 1879. Records show that he owned eighty acres, a fourteen by thirty-nine-foot sod house, a windmill and pump, a granary, hog pen, stable, and chicken coop. On his farm he planted one hundred trees in addition to fruit trees.[50]

Pearson was appointed a county Special Constable but the definition of that role today one might describe it a temporary policeman. They were appointed by a county judge or a precinct's justice of the peace. The county also had constables, who were elected just as the sheriff was. Special constables were deputized for a specific purpose, such as bringing in criminals and sometimes were part of a team of constables but once the task was accomplished their status was ended. They could be appointed for a year by a precinct's justice of the peace if they were petitioned to do so. Even John Cozad served as a special constable on at least one occasion.[51]

The first recorded action taken by Alf Pearson in the role of special constable was in July 1874 against John McIntyre who had killed a cow owned by G. A. Searight.[52] Participants in this encounter also included Traber Gatewood and Alex McIntyre who were both charged with an intent to kill the cow.[53]

In his law enforcement role Pearson would be involved with several encounters with John Cozad or members of his family. Mari Sandoz speculates that they had problems very early on.[54] There were other flash points as well. It has been suggested that there was a disagreement about the sod bridge project. Another area of disagreement was over Pearson's cattle allegedly grazing on Cozad's pastures.[55]

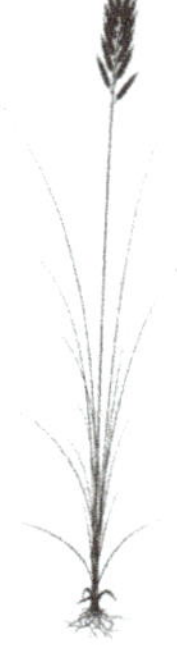

There were other episodes that may or may not have included Pearson. For example, Lewis Gibbs attempted to shoot John Cozad after the latter had assaulted Gibbs. Cozad was deputy special constable at this time. When Cozad threatened to beat one Henry McIntyre, he was arrested and placed in the Dawson County jail. The case was moved to North Platte, and Cozad was found guilty and fined for court costs. There were other disputes between Henry and John J.

even though they were related.[56]

Probably, like many area residents, Pearson, over time, tired of Cozad and his haughty manner. Mari Sandoz even relayed speculation that Alf Pearson and John Cozad had both vied for the hand of Theresa Gatewood, although that seems very unlikely given the geography of their backgrounds but also because of their social status.[57]

The names of Alf Pearson and John J. Cozad are eternally entwined in the community's history, even though it is clear that they did not like each other. Their actions led to a tragedy that followed both families decades into the future. Even today some members of the greater Pearson family remain bitter over the episode, and other sympathizers have questioned why the museum even honors John Cozad. Their family suffered the loss of the head of the family and the familial relations that could have been. To some, Cozad's actions were cowardly.

For the Cozads, their lives were also irreparably changed, first by having to leave their town that they had founded and invested so much in, disposing of their assets, probably at a reduced value, changing their identities and certainly entertaining the fear, at least for ten years after their disappearance, of being recognized and brought back to Dawson County to face the courts and justice system. For members of the Cozad family and their supporters, there was a general feeling that John's actions were justified and undertaken in self-defense. No matter what side the reader takes, it was a tragedy for everyone concerned.

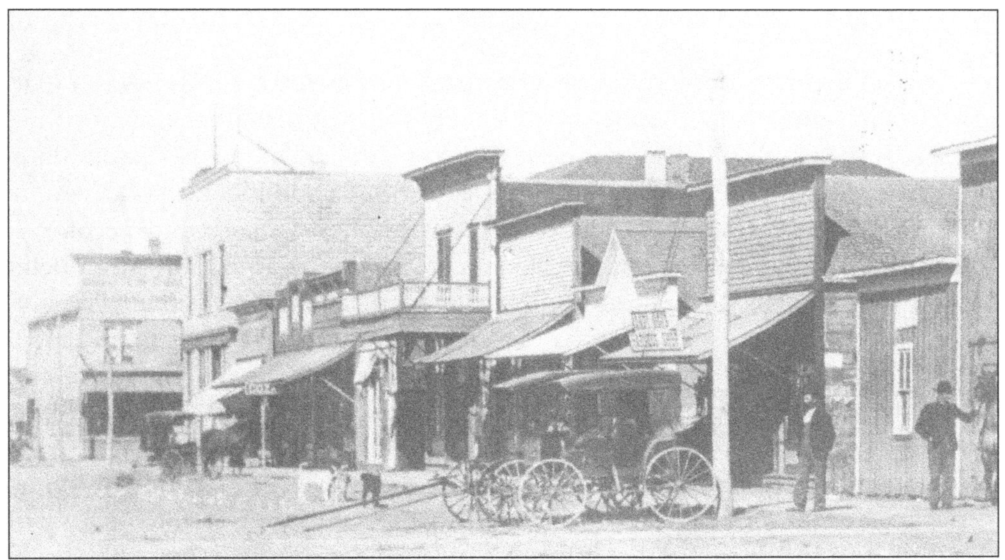

*Courtesy 100th Meridian Museum*

*On a fateful day in October 1882, John J. Cozad shot Alf Pearson on the front porch of his mother-in-law's store. The building is pictured at the far left. The building is gone, but the law firm of Berreckman, & Bazata, P.C., LLO, now stands on the site at the corner of West 8th Street and Meridian Avenue. The photograph dates to 1906 or later and is looking west on West 8th.*

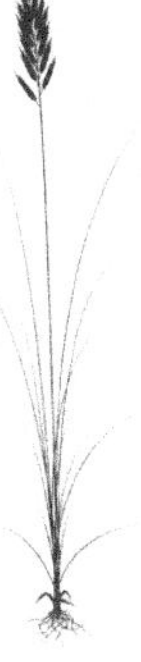

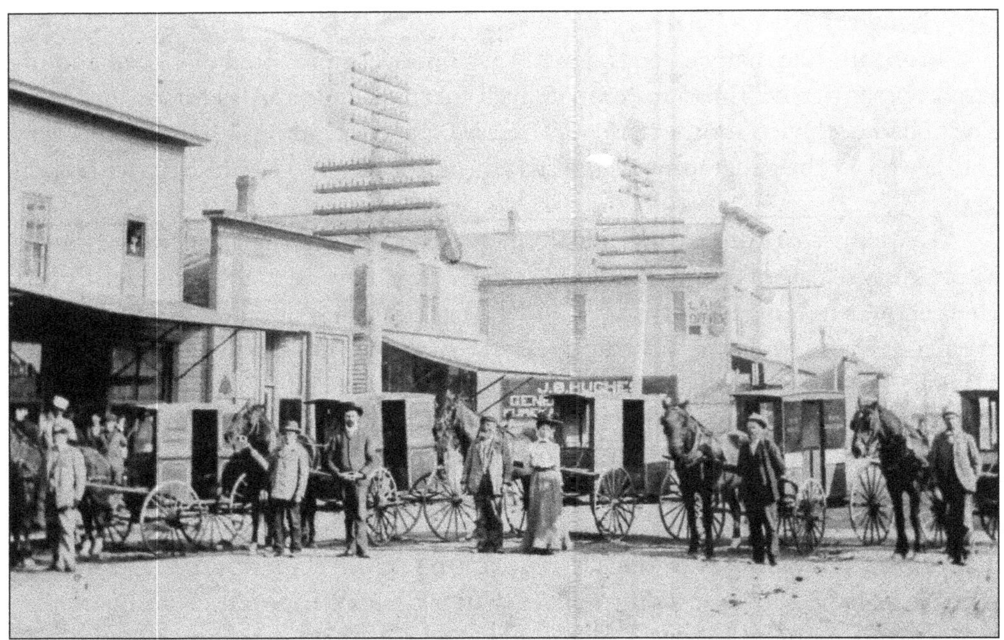

Courtesy 100th Meridian Museum

*This is another view of the Gatewood store looking north and up Meridian Avenue. The building has Land Office painted on the second floor and dates sometime before 1906.*

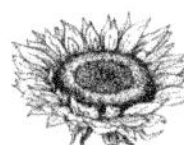

It is an event that one could say also changed the world. One question that arises is what might have happened to Robert Henri if his father had not shot Pearson. If the family's life had not been so disrupted, would they have wound up in the East and, would Robert still have gone to art school in Philadelphia? Would brother John have attended Thomas Jefferson Medical College and become a noted physician in Philadelphia? He would come to marry an equally prominent doctor, who was a member of a well-known New England family. Perhaps yes, but maybe no. In Johnny's case, Mari Sandoz argues a number of times in her book that he had shown an aptitude for a medical career. Perhaps the Cozads might have gone back East to pursue better opportunities for their sons, something we will never know.[58]

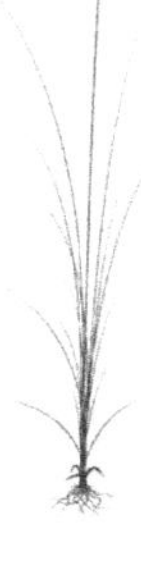

Biographers, historians, and museum staff alike have been stymied in trying to track down all the details of the story that is so central to the life of Robert Henri. In the end the complete story will probably never be known, although many fragments of the tragedy and subsequent events can be pieced together from a variety of sources that are now available. There are also contemporary documents that do provide many details and get us as close as we will ever get to the truth.

## John Cozad Perforates Alf Pearson

Newspapers are often described as *the first version of history*, and there are several accounts that provide us with the initial version of the Pearson story. There are also the inquest jury's deliberations in December 1882, and perhaps most importantly, the grand jury testimony of 1894 when John Cozad was acquitted of the murder of Alf Pearson. Much of what has been written since is often conjecture or hearsay.

On Saturday, October 14, 1882, Alf Pearson, upon hearing that John Cozad had returned from Denver, came to Cozad from his ranch north of the town, and, according to the various traditions, wanted to discuss renting pastureland along the Platte River with him. Another possible interpretation of this story is that Pearson may have wanted to rent pastureland in a section near his property that Cozad owned. This is more likely because Pearson only had three cows and it would have been a ten-mile journey to get them to the Platte from his ranch.[59]

Another version of this story states that Cozad was in a second-floor room of Julia Gatewood's store, changing his clothes in anticipation of catching a westward train. Pearson came in and told Julia Gatewood that he wanted to see Cozad and even threatened to kill him. Sandoz implies he was drunk and a later account that calls him a *drunken herder* also makes the same suggestion although that allegation does not show up in the record.[60]

The following article, appearing in the *Dawson County Pioneer* on Saturday, October 21, 1882 provides what might be the best account of what happened on that fall day:

*John J. Cozad Perforates A. Pearson: The Would-be Murderer Flees from the Scene of His Crime and Up to Date has not been Captured*

*A telegram was received by Sheriff MacLean last Saturday noon from the town of Cozad, this county, stating that A. Pearson, a farmer of the Cozad Precinct, had been shot, and requesting him to come immediately and bring a doctor with him. Owing to the west bound trains being several hours behind time the sheriff did not get to the scene of the shooting until about five o'clock. A Pioneer reporter accompanied the Sheriff and Dr. Bancroft, and the party upon arriving at Cozad found Pearson, the wounded man, very badly injured, and unable to speak, being shot in the left cheek, the ball passing through and penetrating, as Dr. Bancroft thinks, the lower lobe of the brain on the left side of the head.*

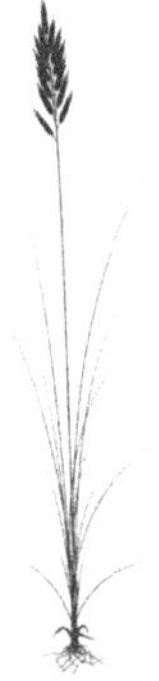

*Inquiries as to the cause of the shooting showed that Pearson came to Cozad early Saturday morning for the purpose of securing some land along the river bottom on which to pasture a bunch of cattle. He called on John J. Cozad, at the residence of the latter's father-in-law, Robert Gatewood, in order to get the land; Cozad said he would not let anybody have the land unless they rented it; Pearson replied that arrangement would suit and that he would rent the land. At this point Cozad branched off on a*

*dispute of several years standing between himself and Pearson, relative to wages for work, which Pearson has alleged that Cozad owed him, and called him a damned liar and thief if he said so, repeating the abusive language several times. Pearson informed Cozad that he did not come there to have any trouble, but to transact business, and finally losing his temper asked Cozad if he would go out of the house, the latter it is said with a pistol in hand. When a few feet from the door Pearson struck Cozad with his fist and knocked him down, and the latter immediately shot his assailant, who fell to the earth. He was picked up and carried to the store of E. Mosher, upstairs, where he has been cared for ever since.*

*Cozad started north immediately after the shooting was done, telling someone as he was leaving that when the Sheriff arrived, he would deliver himself into his custody, and that he did not propose to be taken charge of by a mob. But he has not delivered himself up yet, nor has the Sheriff been able to find him, although a diligent search has been made.*

*There are several rumors afloat, one being that he was seen going south, another that he has gone north, another that he is concealed in or near the town of Cozad, and another that a party started after him the evening of the day the shooting was done (It being reported at the time that Pearson was dead) and dealt out to him a dose of Judge Lynch. The wounded man has improved but little during the past week, but Doctor Bancroft thinks there is a possibility of recovery.*[61]

Another account, published in the Omaha *Weekly Republican* has the fight occurring in a saloon and that when they both stepped outside of the building Pearson struck Cozad with a stick after which Cozad shot Pearson. Another version, in a Cozad family history, stated that Pearson had struck Cozad with a club.[62]

Still yet another account, provided by Deline Morris Lewis in her 1972 history of the museum building in which she had lived for many years, suggested that Cozad had shot Alf Pearson in Room 4, the room at the top of the stairs coming from the western entrance. A variation of this story was repeated in a newspaper column written by Tom Allan in 1984 when he wrote that Pearson had died in that room.[63] One version of the story has Cozad going to Pearson's house and shooting him dead in front of his two sons. Another variation on this is that Cozad shot and killed Pearson's daughter.[64] As will be seen none of these accounts are believed to be true.

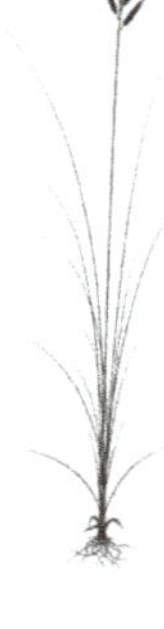

Later that October day the Dawson County sheriff arrived and began interviewing any eyewitnesses or anyone who might have known what had happened He also tried to find Cozad.

## A Different Side of the Story

Probably the account of the Pearson shooting that has been most often cited and more widely disseminated and accepted, is the one Mari Sandoz told in her *Son of the Gamblin' Man*. Her book has been, and remains, the most widely available source that interested people have had access to and so has become the primary lens through which this story has been told. Her book was published almost eighty years after the event, but she was interviewing people only fifty years after the event for her book.

Her account begins with John Cozad getting ready to depart on a westbound train to go to Denver and Alf Pearson coming into Julia Gatewood's store with a plan to talk to John Cozad. Another account has him coming to Cozad from Denver.[65]

The men began a discussion over using Cozad's pastures and after some conversation came to a financial arrangement. An argument then began over money that Pearson felt Cozad owed him. There is also a slightly different version of the story which goes that they were arguing over money Pearson believed Cozad owed him over work that had been done at the bridge. No matter, because after Cozad called him a liar, Pearson struck Cozad who fell into a shipping crate.[66]

In her account, Sandoz writes that the event happened out on the porch as the 1894 grand jury testimony suggests.[67] Then, and this is different from other accounts, Pearson pulled a knife out and at this point John Cozad, who saw it, pulled out his pistol and shot Pearson in the face. The knife dropped out of Pearson's hand and onto the floor. The appearance of the knife in the story appears in the Sandoz reporting, and an account written in 1932 by Robert Gatewood, and a family history, which is notable. Descendants of Pearson would later say that he never carried more than a bullwhip.[68] Sandoz's source of information is not noted but it may have come as a result of her research undertaken in Cozad and Lexington and Dr. Robert Gatewood, a nephew of Theresa's, which may have come directly from John Cozad whom he knew.

Traber Gatewood and others picked up Pearson and took him to an unreported destination. John Cozad, for a moment, even helped the wounded man, but soon left. He packed his bags and had a discussion with Robert and Theresa, who were also at Julia's store. Johnny was in North Platte dealing with some homesteaders and preparing to go west to Denver.[69]

It was clear to John Cozad that he could not get a fair hearing and might find himself in the same situation as Tom Hallowell who was lynched in 1876 or Ketchum and Mitchell who were murdered in 1878. This rendering of the account has the plan for the change of the family's identity happening right then on the second floor of the Gatewood store, and not as has often been recounted in Denver. The idea that the Cozads gathered again in Denver after the shooting is not part of Sandoz's recounting of the story.[70]

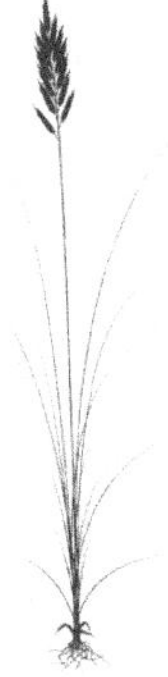

With that, Theresa and Julia Gatewood said goodbye in a very public way on the porch of the store and John rode off with Robert in a wagon to the river bridge, where John jumped down and made his way out onto the prairie and proceeded southward.[71] Perhaps someone in Cozad provided her with this accounting because it is clear that locals had their own side of the story. Yet another account states that he simply walked to the south and out of sight.[72]

Another version of the story comes from Violet Organ, a sister-in-law to Robert Henri. In late 1955 she wrote in a letter to H. B. Allen in Cozad the following:

*I do not know how much of John J. Cozad's story you are acquainted with, but here are the facts as family records reveal them. Prior to 1880 when the settlement of Cozad was beginning to reap rich harvests after a plague of grasshoppers and drouth, cattlemen from Texas began driving their huge herds to graze on the lush prairies surrounding Cozad. Time after time John Cozad was forced to drive the herds off his lands and that of the colonists. Repeated warnings were of no avail, and hostilities grew. John Cozad's life was threatened, his home burned down, and he was attacked by a drunken herder with a knife. John Cozad was dressed for a business trip to Denver when the herder leaped upon him throwing him into a packing case outside his home. In a desperate effort to save his life John Cozad got hold of his gun and shot the herder who died a few days after. To escape the vengeance of other herders who were determined to ambush and kill him – Cozad was convinced he would stand no chance of a fair trial at the time – he left secretly for Denver with his wife and two sons. He was completely cleared of guilt in the shooting a few years later.*[73]

Collectively, all these different versions of the story have provided the so-called evidence for those who have blamed Cozad for what happened but did not have a fuller or more accurate understanding of the events of the tragedy.

However, based on the contemporary evidence and sources that date from 1882 and 1894, which are closer to the actual events, and generally do agree, it can be concluded that Cozad did indeed shoot Pearson in self-defense. Even if Pearson had a knife, that does not materially change the story because Pearson, whether justified or not in attacking Cozad, instigated the physical altercation on the porch of the Gatewood store. If a knife were used, it might help to make Cozad's case more convincing. Or, if Cozad had walked out onto the porch with a gun already visible, perhaps Pearson hit him first, in a preemptive action.

It is also clear that both men were used to fighting, with Pearson especially prepared, given his tough life as a rancher and dealing with the kinds of people he had to as a special constable. Cozad might have been beaten to death if he had not fired his pistol or as is stated in the one account might have in the most generous interpretations lost his tongue which Pearson threatened to cut out according to

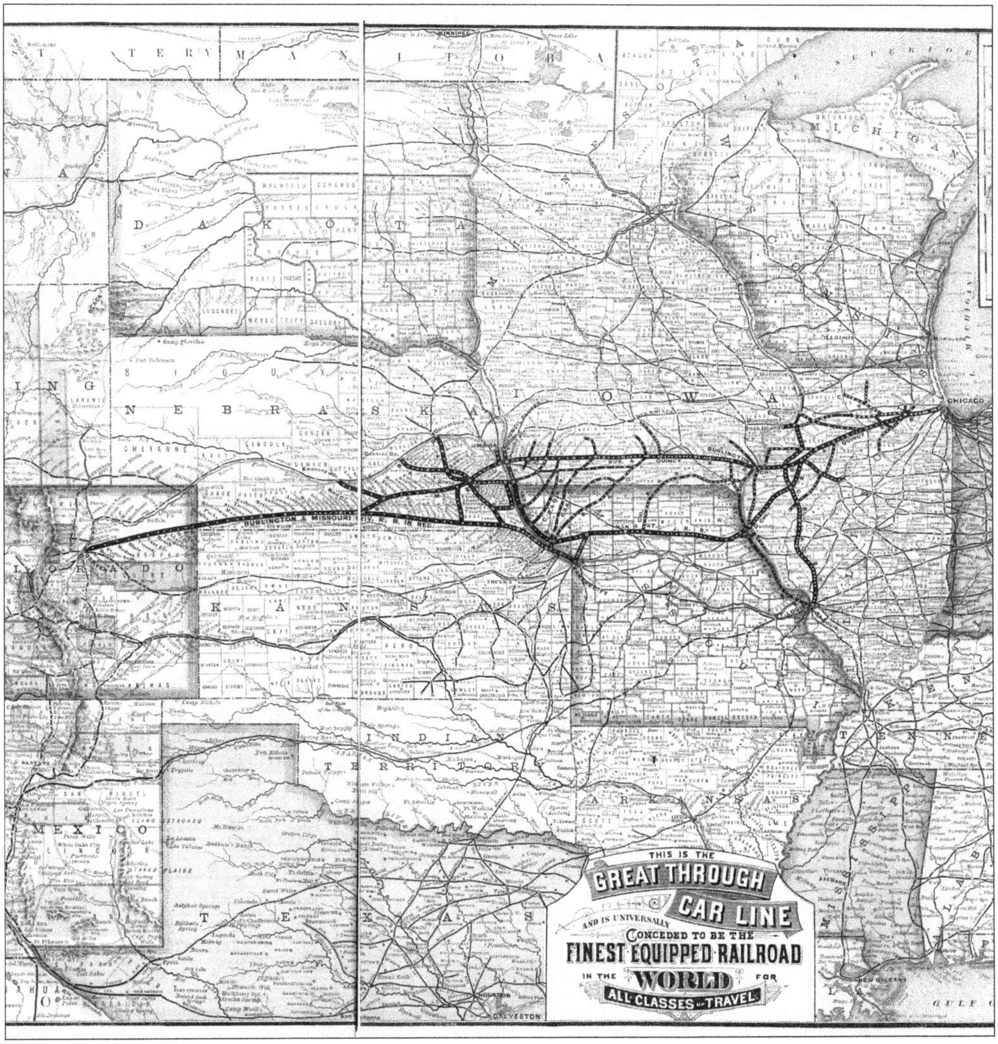

*Courtesy Library of Congress (Control Number 98688605)*

*This 1882 map of the routes of the Burlington and Missouri River Railroad demonstrates the possible routes that John Cozad could have taken to get out of Nebraska, either going to Denver or Chicago or even somewhere else.*

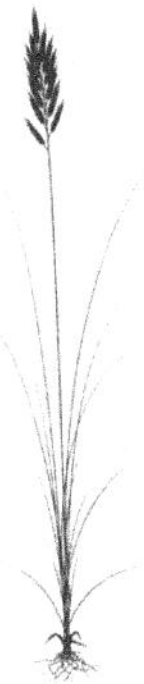

one telling of the story!

After the shooting itself, and the potential of being lynched by area ranchers and cattlemen, the next possibility that put John J. Cozad at great risk was that of arrest. Late in the day of the shooting, Dawson County Sheriff MacLean arrived in Cozad to arrest the gambling man and community founder. The next day, October 15, 1882, a warrant was issued for Cozad's arrest by R. B. Pierce, the Dawson County judge.[74]

An Abrupt Departure

It is agreed by all that John Cozad immediately left his town on the day of the shooting and disappeared. He genuinely believed he could quickly become a victim of vigilante justice, and either be hung or murdered given the feelings of many in the community and the wider region about him. While some consideration may have been given to notifying the sheriff, Cozad knew better than to stay there.[75]

Where he went remains a mystery even today because he had a number of options at the time, and he purposely did not want to leave any tracks as to where he was going. Quickly packing and making decisions about what to do, he is believed to have traveled about fifty miles southward, although as the newspaper account reports, he may have also gone northward. For the first part of the journey, he walked and then met someone traveling in a wagon along the way who took him to the nearest railway, where he boarded a train.[76] Another account has him borrowing a horse from David Claypool and riding to Kansas.[77] Yet another account states that it was his old friend Sam Schooley who got him to Kansas.[78] From there the story gets even more muddied - did he go east or west or somewhere else as he had any number of choices.

William Homer, in his book *Robert Henri and His Circle*, describes the quick departure of Cozad in *Chapter 2* and it is his belief that he returned to Denver in the immediate aftermath of the shooting. He had gone overland to catch a more southerly railroad to travel to Colorado's capital so that the likelihood of his being recognized or apprehended was reduced.

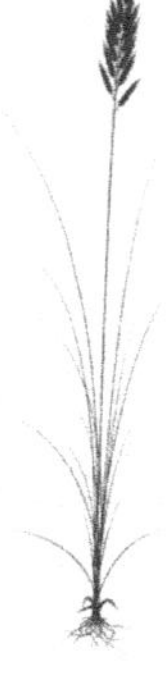

While the Union Pacific went to Denver, so did the Burlington and Missouri River Railroad, traveling along the southern tier of Nebraska. Another way he could have gotten to Denver would have been to travel much farther south to the main line of the Atchison, Topeka and Santa Fe. It is about forty-five miles from Cozad to Arapahoe, Nebraska, a station along the line of the Burlington. A Union Pacific controlled road passes halfway between the Burlington and another branch of the Union Pacific, the Kansas Division. This division passes through Ogallah, Kansas which is about one hundred forty miles from Cozad. However, all of the surviving accounts say he only traveled about fifty miles and was able to complete the journey in one day.

According to Homer, it was in Denver where he and his family reunited although it is implied that it was not a series of developments that were quickly occurring that forced the Cozad family to make immediate decisions with immediate actions and consequences. Perhaps, although it is not said by Homer, they met quickly, made plans and developed a strategy, and Cozad departed for places unknown.[79]

It is worth noting that much of Homer's second chapter was taken from Violet Organ's unpublished biography, tentatively entitled *The Life and Letters of Robert Henri*, written between 1930 and 1959, the year of her death.[80] She was a sister to Henri's second wife. While she certainly could have talked with Henri about this, and much of the material in this chapter can be verified, the question remains as to how much Henri would have revealed to her, or how much he would have even known, or remembered of his father's quick departure from Cozad in 1882.

Another perspective, however, comes from a 1996 letter that Joan Gatewood Miller wrote to the Robert Henri Museum board members. In it she recalled discussing Henri's early life with Violet Organ and it was clear to Miller that Organ knew nothing of it. Family members of Dr. Robert Gatewood had visited Organ on several occasions sharing information with her.[81]

Homer acknowledged the contribution that Dr. Robert Gatewood (1885-1966), John Cozad's nephew on his wife's side, had made to the writing of his book in 1988. Gatewood was the author of a manuscript, entitled *Who Was Robert Henri?* Written in 1932, he was someone who had direct knowledge of what had happened and surely, he and John Cozad might have discussed this in the early 1900s when Gatewood went to New York City to visit the family.[82]

Curiously, Gatewood never states in his manuscript that Cozad went to Denver, but he reveals that Cozad disappeared for seven months after the shooting and during that time only had secret communications with Traber Gatewood. This allows for the possibility that he did not go to Denver but somewhere else.[83] Perhaps Cozad went to Denver, then perhaps quickly traveled into the deeper reaches of Colorado and was able to disappear for months.

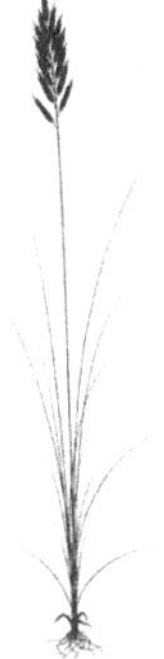

Another option, and one that this author believes is more likely, is that John Cozad turned east and went to Chicago on the Burlington and then traveled further east on its auxiliary lines to the greater New York City area. There he could disappear into one of the nation's largest population centers. Or, perhaps somewhere else altogether. Mari Sandoz also believes that Cozad turned eastward and even stopped in Iowa.[84]

Sandoz wrote that John Cozad met up with a group of men that evening from the town who were ready to lynch him, but he threatened to expose them and damage their land claims if he did not wire the code word back to the family. The gambler's bluff, as she described it, worked and he escaped being lynched.

It is curious however that this story did not come forward in time like so many others did.[85]

Robert Gatewood (1885-1966), believed that John Cozad, aside from the secret communications with Traber Gatewood, arranged to have his son, John A., meet him somewhere in the East. This could have happened in May 1883 or sometime after that. Many thought initially that he was still in hiding somewhere near Cozad because Pearson was still alive.[86]

There were alleged sightings of John Cozad in the aftermath of the shooting in several places. He was said to have been seen in Deadwood, South Dakota; Denver, and Wheeling, West Virginia. Several people reported seeing him at several cemeteries back East. At least one account said that Cozad had been lynched at the 100th Meridian sign. A Cozad historian believed he went to Europe in the aftermath of the tragic event although there is no other source that suggests that.[87]

An interesting document in the Henri Museum's collection suggests at least one other possible answer to where John Cozad went after his departure. In 1988, Jim and Leone Marshall traveled to Cozaddale, Ohio and took pictures of the Cozad home. There they met a Mr. Applegate whose father had recollections of John J. Cozad. Applegate stated that the Cozads left the Ohio town after some unknown troubles and went to Nebraska. This episode might be related to the one told in a previous chapter about his sudden departure from Cozaddale.[88]

The Cozad home, a large brick building with its three-story cupola, was said to have housed Cozad when he was trying to escape from his Nebraska troubles. He was believed to have hidden in the cupola, according to Applegate when he recalled that Nebraska lawmen came in search of Cozad, but to no avail as they could not find him. There is no corroborating evidence for this story and the account is written on a single piece of paper without attribution. But, if it is true, then the answer to what John Cozad did in those weeks and months after shooting Pearson might be partially answered.[89]

Another piece of information comes from a newspaper article that had as part of its headline *Detectives are in St. Louis Looking for John P. Cozad (sic)*. This may corroborate the previous story that in fact there was an effort made to find the senior Cozad and that it spread far and wide to bring him back to justice.[90] One final possibility is one suggested by an Ohio historian who wrote that Cozad went to Mexico and there he created another town although this seems to be the least likely of the possibilities.[91]

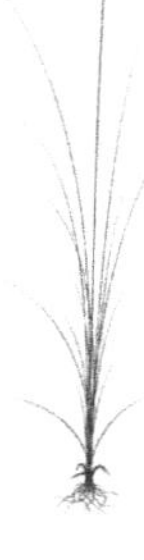

## Death of Alfred Pearson

Alf Pearson did not die immediately after he was shot; he lingered on for several weeks. However, the story took a horrible turn for the worse for the Pearson family and the Cozads when Alf Pearson died. Pearson's obituary appeared in the *Dawson County Pioneer* on December 9, 1882, and stated:

**Death of Alfred Pearson.**

Alfred Pearson the man shot by J. J. Cozad October 14th, last, died last Monday morning November 4th, between 12 and 1 o'clock, at his residence, twenty miles northwest of town. He passed away quietly and without a struggle, surrounded by his family and a circle of neighbors and friends. The coroner, H. O. Smith, was notified, who impaneled a jury and accompained by Dr. Bancroft repaired on Tuesday to the house of the deceased, where an inquest was commenced, but owing to absence of important witnesses was postponed until Wednesday the 7th. Dr. Bancroft made a post-mortem examination and found the ball imbedded in the inner bone which surrounds the left lower lobe of the brain. The ball just protruded through the bone, and the brain at that point was found covered with coagulated blood. Dr. Bancroft explained to the jury that deceased's death was due directly to the injuries inflicted by the bullet.

The jury met at the court house Wednesday morning and after examining several witnesses returned the following verdict:

State of Nebraka, } ss.
Dawson county. }

At an inquisition holden at Plum Creek, in Dawson county, on the 5th day of December, A. D. 1882, before me, H. O. Smith coroner of said county, upon the body of Alfred Pearson, lying dead, by the jurors whose names are hereto subscribed, the said juorors upon their oaths do say that the said Alfred Pearson came to his death from a pistol shot at the hands of J. J. Cozad, on the 14th day of October, A. D. 1882, in the town of Cozad, Dawson county, Nebraska; and we, the said jury, do further say that the said J. J. Cozad did fire the shot at the said Alfred Pearson with felonious intent.

Absalom Henry, E. H. Krier,
W. T. H. Tucker, J. P. Brott,
B. F. Krier, J. H. Rice.

Attest: H. O. Smith,
Coroner.

The funeral took place yesterday, Rev. C. S. Carr, of the Cozad M. E. Church officiating, the body being buried in a new burying ground just set aside for that purpose by the people of Little Buffalo Creek, the same being on the top of a commanding bluff about two miles east of Pearson's farm.

*Courtesy Dawson County Historical Museum*

*The obituary of Alf Pearson as it appeared in the Dawson County Pioneer newspaper on December 9, 1882.*

*Alfred Pearson the man shot by J. J. Cozad October 14th, last, died last Monday morning November 4th, between 12 and 1 o'clock, at his residence, twenty miles northwest of town. He passed away quietly and without a struggle, surrounded by his family and a circle of neighbors and friends. The coroner, H.O. Smith, was notified, who impaneled a jury and accompanied by Dr. Bancroft repaired on Tuesday to the house of the deceased, where an inquest was commenced, but owing to the absence of important witnesses was postponed until Wednesday the 7th. Dr. Bancroft made a post-mortem examination and found the ball imbedded in the inner bone which surrounds the left lower lobe of the brain. The ball just protruded through the bone, and the brain at that point was found covered with coagulated blood. Dr. Bancroft explained to the jury that the deceased's death was due directly to the injuries inflicted by the bullet . . .*

*The funeral took place yesterday, Rev. C. S. Carr, of the Cozad M.E. Church officiating, the body being buried in a new burying ground just set aside for that purpose by the people of Little Buffalo Creek, the same being on the top of a commanding bluff about two miles east of Pearson's farm.*[92]

However, based on a review of several sources, Pearson's death date as shown above states that *he had died last Monday on November 4th* is incorrect. The fourth of November fell on Friday. If it was the fourth of December, as is probably the case, that would have been on a Sunday. The inquisition, as reported, was held on December 7, a Wednesday. A proclamation by the Governor of Nebraska calling for the arrest of John Cozad includes a death date of December 13.

Pearson was buried in the newly established Buffalo Table Cemetery, now known as the Rhinehart Cemetery, north of Cozad.[93] The funeral, as noted, was officiated by Rev. C. S. Carr of the Cozad Methodist Episcopal Church.[94] As to his

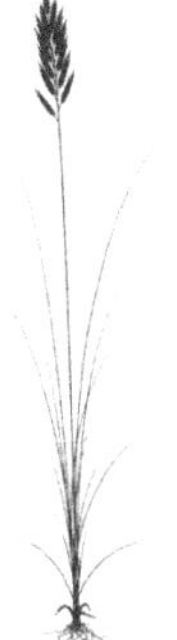

estate, it was worth $1,052.30. A farm sale was held and many of the remaining items were purchased by the children. After proving up her homestead in 1886, the property was ultimately sold by Harriett to J. T. Waller in 1888.[95]

An inquest jury was convened and met on Thursday, December 7, 1882, at the court house in Plum Creek and Dr. Bancroft reported to the group that John Cozad's shot had killed Pearson and that the bullet had lodged in the inner bone that surrounded the brain.[96] The members of the jury included Absalom Henry, E. H. Krier, W. T. H. Tucker, J. P. Brott, B. F. Krier, J. H. Rice and was attested to by H. O. Smith, the Dawson County coroner, who had called for the original inquest.[97] There were five witnesses called including Dr. W. W. Bancroft, Julia Gatewood, Henry Drew, William McLaughlin and Lew Owens.[98] The inquest, based on the testimony of the witnesses, confirmed what Dr. Bancroft had previously determined - that Cozad had fired the fateful shot. On Saturday, December 9, 1882, John Cozad was indicted for the first-degree murder of Alf Pearson and his bail was set at fifty thousand dollars.[99]

Two weeks later, on Monday, December 18, Nebraska Governor Albinus Nance offered a reward of two hundred dollars for the arrest and conviction of Cozad.[100] It seems likely that after the governor's announcement of a reward, John Cozad, if he had not already disappeared, most certainly would have had to disappear if he wanted to remain free.

If he were still in Denver, as Homer proposes, or somewhere else in the state, at least three hundred miles to the west of Cozad, he was now one step closer to the long reach of the law because he could have been arrested and then extradited from Colorado. Or, more likely, as this author believes, it did not matter at this point because Cozad was gone, perhaps already somewhere in the East. However, the indictment and offer of a reward would have mattered to Robert and Theresa, because they could have been questioned about the whole affair, and perhaps they were, but their whereabouts were known. Even if they denied knowing where John was, which they surely could, they would have been looked on with suspicious eyes, at least in Dawson County, as well as having a cloud cast over the title of the Cozad holdings when they determined to sell them.

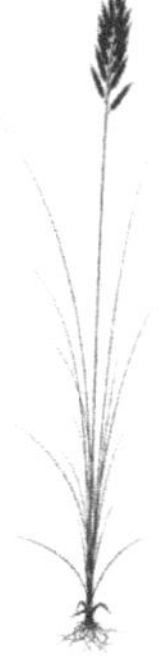

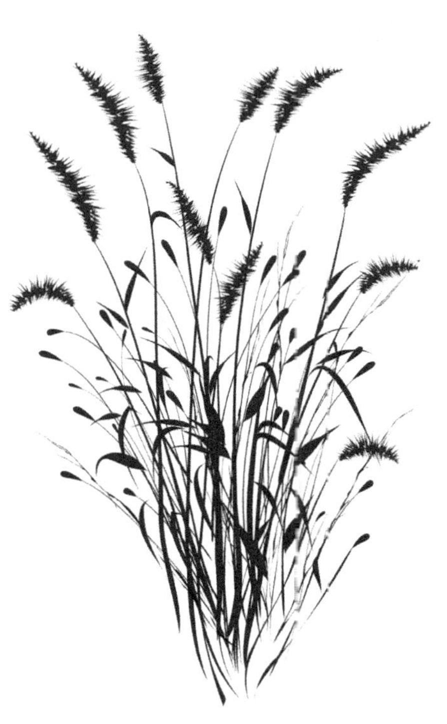

## *Chapter 6*

# The End of a Vision

*Just as he had done in every chapter of his life, controversy followed him and he seemed to revel in it. He certainly left a trail of disputes in his wake. But it also demonstrated his ability to begin anew and to start over when he had to including his efforts at Cincinnati, Cozaddale, Cozad and Denver.*[1]

Son of the Gamblin' Man

Mari Sandoz

Just six weeks after the death of Alf Pearson, another separate, but equally harrowing episode for the Cozad family occurred which also provides additional context to the disappearance of John J. after the shooting in October. Johnny Cozad, Robert's older brother, was arrested on Sunday, November 26, 1882, for allegedly trying to set fire to a room, and burning down the Johnson House in Plum Creek where he had lodged.

The various narratives surrounding this event and its aftermath, like those of the shooting of Pearson, have also figured in the telling of the Cozad story but have often been incorrect. Several accounts state that John A. was successful in burning the building down. This included the newspaper report that the owner of the Johnson House, Elijah Johnson, brought charges against the younger Cozad on the day of the incident. The charges curiously included a statement that Cozad had indeed set fire to the hotel which was valued at three thousand dollars.[2]

Another version of the story comes from a line drawing of Plum Creek that appeared in the *Dawson County Herald* which stated that Cozad had burned the building down in December 1882.[3] There is an account in which John A. committed this act of arson on the same day that Alf Pearson was shot. An account given by Mari Sandoz was that Johnny was the first person who had fled the building when the fire had started.[4] As will be seen, that is not what happened at all. In fact, two hotels in Plum Creek had perished to a fire just four weeks before, on October 20. The coals from the fire had landed near the Johnson House which was close to the two buildings but it was spared.[5]

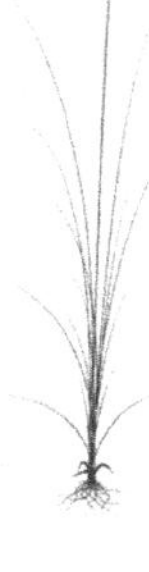

At the time of this incident there was some speculation that it was the will of the father to see the whole town burned down, which seems probable given the troubles that Cozad had previously had with the people of Plum Creek. Then, after the death of Pearson, feelings ran particularly high against John J. Cozad. But it is also believed that Johnny knew people and had acquaintances there and was not as disliked as his father.[6]

In a newspaper account it was reported that Johnny Cozad had arrived in Plum Creek and decided to stay at the Johnson House on Friday evening, November 24. This would not have attracted any attention because he knew the proprietor and had friends in town. While in his room he constructed a firebomb. His plan had been to activate the device with an extended fuse on Saturday evening, November 25, about an hour later after he had left Plum Creek, causing a catastrophic fire.[7]

Johnny Cozad departed for Denver on the Union Pacific's No. 3 train at 11:00 p.m. The incendiary device, filled with coal oil taken from hotel lamps, was timed to go off after Cozad had left. In addition, coal oil had been spread around the room. The device, however, failed to ignite the fuse, having extinguished itself, and the next morning, Sunday, November 26, was discovered under the bed by a maid. If the firebomb had worked as planned, much of Plum Creek might have burned to the ground given the weather conditions of that day.[8]

John A. Cozad stopped at Gould, (formerly Cozad), stayed overnight, and then proceeded onto Denver. An arrest warrant was issued, and Nebraska Governor Albinus Nance signed a requisition for his return from Colorado. Cozad was arrested in LaSalle Junction, Colorado, near Greeley, and taken to Denver. Cozad's lawyers tried to prevent Cozad from being brought back through a writ of habeas corpus application. (*A habeas corpus is a civil action that requires the person arrested to be brought before a judge to prevent unlawful arrest.*) That effort was successful. Then the governor's requisition arrived at the same time and the sheriff immediately rearrested the junior Cozad. He brought him back to Plum Creek and put him in the county jail on December 5. On the same day that a newspaper article relayed the story of John A. Cozad's return, another story told of the indictment of John Cozad in the murder of Alf Pearson. The feelings in Plum Creek were high, and there was a feeling that Johnny should be lynched given what he had done.[9]

**IN LIMBO.**

**John A. Cozad, the Alleged Fire-Bug, in the County Bastile.**

Young Cozad, charged with attempting to fire the Johnson House, arrived safely here Tuesday night in the custody of Sheriff MacLean and A. S. Baldwin, and was given a room—not in the Johnson House—but in the county jail. The officer and his assistant had hard work securing their prisoner, he having procured counsel who fought sturdily for their client, and succeeded in getting a writ of *habeas corpus* issued, but Sheriff MacLean at once re-arrested his man and started for Nebraska. Cozad was first arrested at Greeley, Col., and afterward taken to Denver, where the legal proceedings were had. His case will be laid before the grand jury of the present term of our District court.

*Courtesy Dawson County Historical Museum*

*A story about Johnny Cozad's attempt to burn down the Johnson Hotel appeared next to the obituary of Alf Pearson in the Dawson County Pioneer newspaper on December 9, 1882.*

At the same time, there was speculation in the *Omaha Weekly Republican* that recalled the destruction of the Cozad community in 1876 by fire when Jackson O'Neill, had perished. Another person, and one of John J. Cozad's rivals, and an enemy, was almost destroyed financially by the fire. Was Johnny Cozad the arsonist in that terrible fire, a question now raised because of the accusations that he had attempted to burn down the Johnson House?[10]

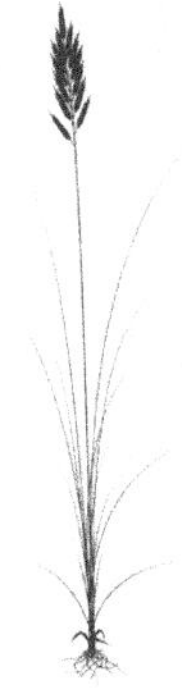

Cozad's bail was initially set at $500 but Dawson County sheriff Hugh MacLean wanted it set at $5,000, no doubt because of what had happened with the father's disappearance and his subsequent nonappearance in court. The sheriff feared that the same would happen again with the son.[11]

Even then that was a considerable amount of money and given that John J. Cozad was gone, it would have been difficult for Theresa to raise that amount of money quickly with their general financial condition probably stressed. Until the bond was raised, Johnny remained in jail. One can only wonder what the mother thought about these series of events and how they affected her family.

Theresa Cozad tried to raise the cash bail and asked family and friends to pledge property to raise bail and get her son out of jail. However, the sheriff would not change his stand of keeping Cozad in jail, even though Theresa had raised the amount in assets. Finally, Johnny Cozad's lawyer brought a case before the Nebraska Supreme Court to challenge the sheriff's refusal to release him. A ruling was made by the court on January 24, 1883, and the sheriff was commanded to release Cozad. As part of the ruling, and on the same day, Theresa Cozad, Robert Gatewood, Julia Gatewood, P.S. Gilbert and their attorney C. W. McNamar pledged assets that totaled $25,300 to cover Cozad's $5,500 bail.[12]

Still, the sheriff would not relinquish his prisoner easily and continued to confine John A. until he was released at an undetermined date.[13] In the end, the sheriff was correct, because like his father, he disappeared and did not appear before the court. In 1885, a default judgement was recorded against John A. Cozad.

Three years later, in 1888, the state of Nebraska filed a claim against John A. Cozad, Theresa Cozad, Julia Gatewood, Robert Gatewood, and their lawyer, C. W. McNamar regarding the issuance of the bail bond. McNamar claimed that Cozad was not guilty of arson, that the charges had been trumped up and that the charges were made to get him back to Nebraska given that he was a Colorado resident. Also, it was believed that the charges had not been made in good faith. The lawyer claimed that Cozad had been ill and confined to bed in Manitou, Colorado, at the time when he was supposed to appear in court. Manitou is to the northwest of Colorado Springs.[14]

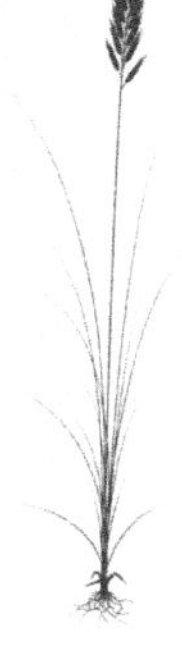

It is thought that once again Traber Gatewood was involved in a family crisis because of fears that the younger Cozad might be lynched. In the immediate aftermath of the incident, Gatewood went to Plum Creek where it was said he waited and watched.[15] It is believed that he also helped the young Cozad get his release from jail and disappear from Nebraska, never to stand charges for the attempted arson of the Johnson House. One tradition has it that Theresa received an envelope with *For Johnny* written on it that included railroad tickets that would get him out of Nebraska. Curiously, Traber's name does not appear on the list of those who pledged assets to raise bail. With that set of tickets, Johnny too disappeared into the night, believed to have been taken out of town by Sam Schooley.[16]

It is however the quickness with which Johnny was arrested and extradited which shows the real peril that would have faced the father too if he had gone to a place where he might be recognized. This demonstrates how quickly the law was able to swing into action even though the distances were great and further makes the case for the father having gone to somewhere more remote in Colorado, or back East and not to Denver after that fateful day in October 1882.

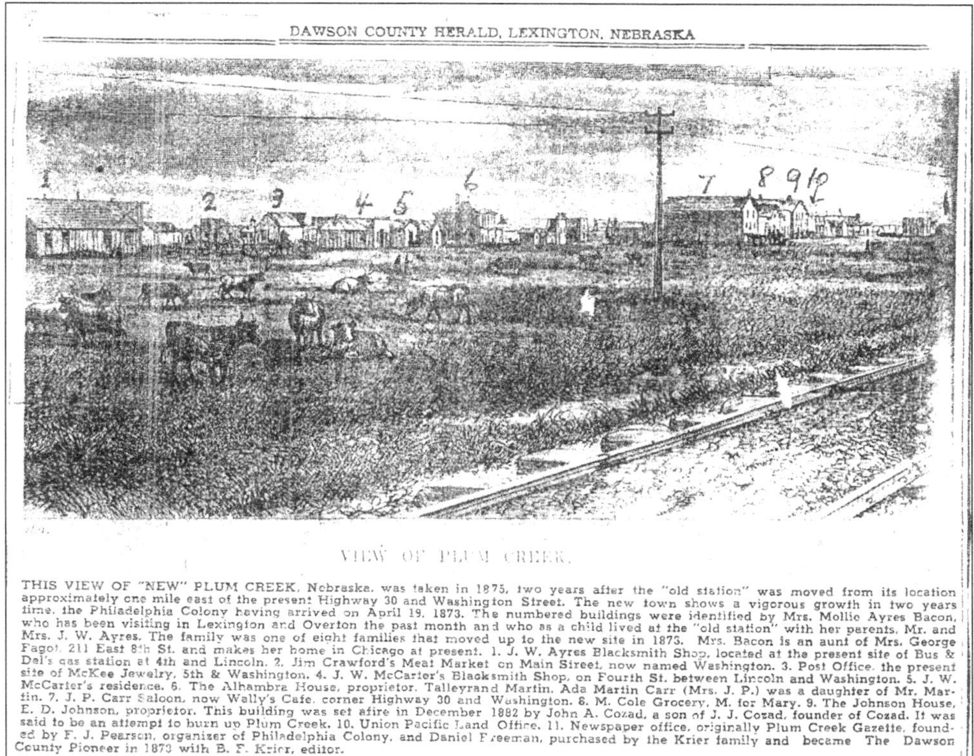

DAWSON COUNTY HERALD, LEXINGTON, NEBRASKA



VIEW OF PLUM CREEK.

THIS VIEW OF "NEW" PLUM CREEK, Nebraska, was taken in 1875, two years after the "old station" was moved from its location approximately one mile east of the present Highway 30 and Washington Street. The new town shows a vigorous growth in two years time, the Philadelphia Colony having arrived on April 19, 1873. The numbered buildings were identified by Mrs. Mollie Ayres Bacon, who has been visiting in Lexington and Overton the past month and who as a child lived at the "old station" with her parents, Mr. and Mrs. J. W. Ayres. The family was one of eight families that moved up to the new site in 1873. Mrs. Bacon is an aunt of Mrs. George Fagot, 211 East 8th St. and makes her home in Chicago at present. 1. J. W. Ayres Blacksmith Shop, located at the present site of Bus & Del's gas station at 4th and Lincoln. 2. Jim Crawford's Meat Market on Main Street, now named Washington. 3. Post Office, the present site of McKee Jewelry, 5th & Washington. 4. J. W. McCarter's Blacksmith Shop, on Fourth St. between Lincoln and Washington. 5. J. W. McCarter's residence. 6. The Alhambra House, proprietor, Talleyrand Martin. Ada Martin Carr (Mrs. J. P.) was a daughter of Mr. Martin. 7. J. P. Carr Saloon, now Wally's Cafe, corner Highway 30 and Washington. 8. M. Cole Grocery, M. for Mary. 9. The Johnson House, E. D. Johnson, proprietor. This building was set afire in December 1882 by John A. Cozad, a son of J. J. Cozad, founder of Cozad. It was said to be an attempt to burn up Plum Creek. 10. Union Pacific Land Office. 11. Newspaper office, originally Plum Creek Gazette, founded by F. J. Pearson, organizer of Philadelphia Colony, and Daniel Freeman, purchased by the Krier family and became The Dawson County Pioneer in 1873 with B. F. Krier, editor.

*Courtesy Dawson County Historical Museum*

*This view of Plum Creek, dated 1875, shows the county seat as Johnny Cozad would have known it. The Johnson House, the hotel that Cozad stayed in and allegedly attempted to destroy with a fire-bomb, is numbered 9.*

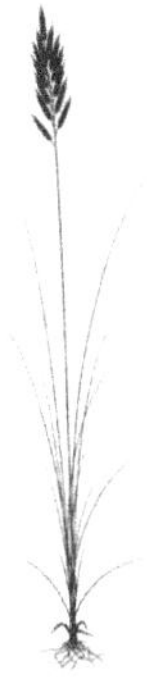

### The End of A Dream

With John J. Cozad having vanished completely, at least until the spring of 1883, it is believed that Theresa Cozad was left with the responsibility to deal with the array of properties that were still owned by them.[17] At some point he either communicated to Traber or to her directly that Theresa was to sell everything.[18] It is believed that Theresa would have had to dispose of three sets of properties – the Denver real estate and shares in the Colorado mine, the Cozaddale real estate, if it were still owned by John J., and the Nebraska real estate.

It is known that there were at least four properties sold in Denver between March and September 1883, the last being sold on September 4.[19] This may indicate that Theresa and Robert were still in Denver, at least until late that fall, given that they had established their home there in the summer of 1881. In an entry in his 1879 scrapbook Robert notes that he is at 661 Blake Street in Denver on May 13, 1883. During the summer of 1883, Robert went to Pike's Peak to visit the famed mountain and stayed with friends.[20]

With the final land transfer, the Cozads had completed the disposal of their properties in Denver. How the mine that John Cozad owned in Leadville was disposed of is not known.

In May 1883, Theresa Cozad agreed to appoint Denver lawyer George Bates as her attorney and have him sell the properties in Cozad and Dawson County for cash. Bates began the process of advertising the properties and an ad appeared in at least one Chicago newspaper, the *Chicago Tribune*. A Bushnell, Illinois businessman, Stephen A. Hendee (1830-1910), might have seen that ad or another, and soon after began to investigate purchasing property in Nebraska, and in Dawson County. There had been some Bushnell residents who had already ventured into Nebraska, Kansas and the Dakota Territory.[21]

Hendee was a successful operator of six grain elevators, a general store, and the Hendee House in Bushnell, a hotel he had originally built in 1870 and expanded. It was a much larger hotel and more substantial operation than the Cozad's hotel and residence. He was an active businessman and important leader in McDonough County, having resided in Bushnell since 1860.[22]

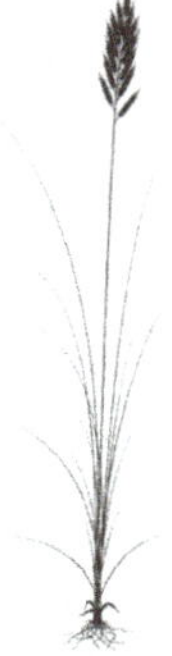

Bushnell was then a prosperous town of about two thousand three hundred people and located a little over two hundred miles southwest of Chicago. It was situated along the route of the Chicago, Burlington & Quincy and Wabash, St. Louis & Pacific railroads. It was also home to Western Normal, a college that had been organized just two years before.[23]

In the summer of 1883, Stephen Hendee came to Dawson County to investigate the Cozad lands along with others. Two other men, later to be partners in the acquisitions in the county, Isaac N. Pearson and Jesse H. Cummings, from Macomb, Illinois, went to Bushnell to visit with Hendee, presumably to discuss a potential purchase which was going to require a great deal of cash for that time.

Pearson was a vice president of the Union National Bank of Macomb as well as serving as a representative in the Illinois State Assembly. Cummings, also a banker, was married to Pearson's sister.[24]

On November 27, 1883, Stephen Hendee and Theresa Cozad, through her attorney in fact, Robert Cozad, signed a contract selling the hotel and fifty-five hundred acres of land for $20,000. Robert, now eighteen, had been given her power of attorney on February 4, 1883. However, Hendee required that the agreement protect his interests, almost certainly because of the ongoing legal troubles and uncertainties surrounding John J. Cozad.[25] Or, as the contract stated:

> *. . . to remove all incumbrances, liens and clouds on the same.*[26]

Theresa Cozad could not guarantee this part of the agreement at that time and so she asked for additional time to deal with the outstanding issues. Some of the issues included encumbrances, taxes owed, assets pledged for John A. Cozad's bail, and John J. Cozad's necessary appearance in Dawson County Court and the need for his signature on the deed. Both parties agreed that Theresa would have to deal with those issues.[27]

Another consideration was that Hendee may have been aware that properties were deeded back and forth between Cozad and Gatewood family members regularly. For example, Section Six of Cozad was turned over from John and Theresa to Robert Gatewood on August 15, 1881, just as they were leaving for Denver. This deed was not recorded in the county until December 12, 1882, eight days after Alf Pearson died. Robert and Julia Gatewood deeded the same property back to Theresa on January 14, 1884, just one month before she and John sold it to the Hendee group.[28] This was probably done to protect the assets of the Cozads from Pearson's heirs.

In January 1883, William Pearson, a son of Alf's, had filed to become the executor of his father's will and then filed attachments against all the properties that the Cozads owned in the town for damages. However, by then, Theresa Cozad had transferred all of their properties out of John's name and her name and into the names of Robert and Julia Gatewood.[29]

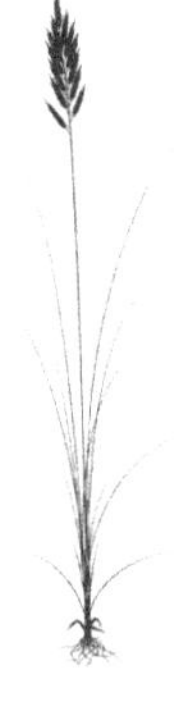

Mari Sandoz wrote that the Pearson family would ultimately get ten thousand dollars in a settlement. Dora Scrutchfield, in an account of her grandfather, Alfred Pearson, could not find any evidence of a transfer of property worth ten thousand dollars to her grandmother. She believed that if there had been that kind of settlement Harriett would not have chosen to remain in a sod house. Perhaps this traditional account began because one of Stephen Hendee's partners was Isaac Pearson and some thought they were related although they were not.[30]

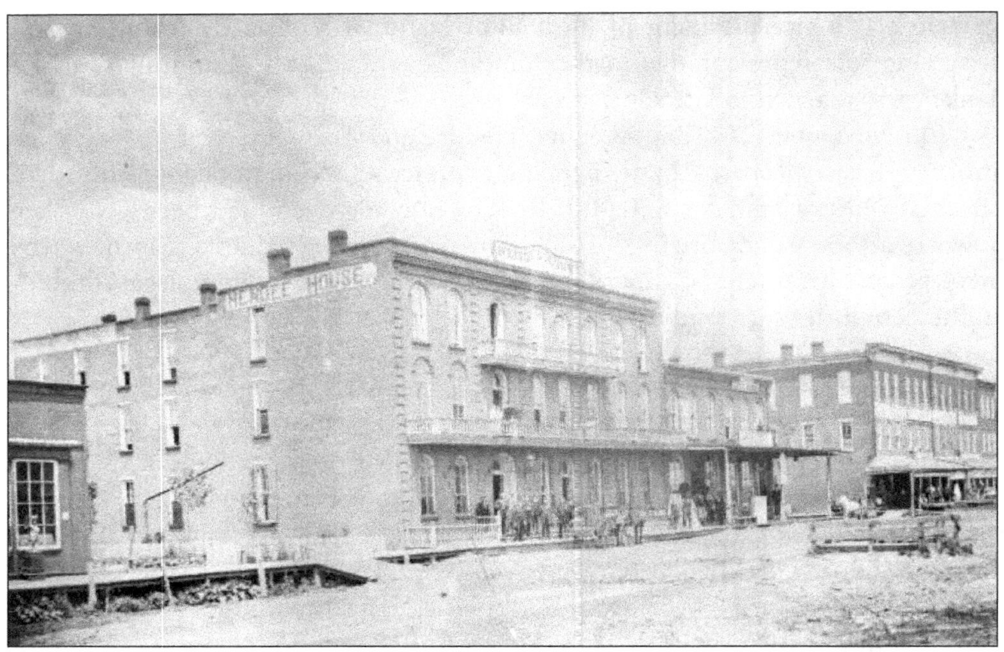

*Courtesy Western Illinois University Libraries Archives and Special Collections*

*Stephen Hendee was a successful businessman from Bushnell, Illinois. His business empire included the Hendee House in the community that was the center of his operations.*

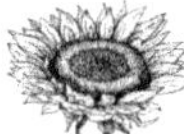

Three months later, with assurances that settled Hendee's mind, a deed for the sale of the lands in Dawson County was provided to Hendee, Pearson and Cummings on February 16, 1884. It was signed by Theresa and John J. Cozad. The Illinois group then turned over fifteen thousand dollars in gold to Theresa with five thousand dollars held aside to deal with the various challenges that might cloud the title. While Hendee had been the leader of the effort, it is thought that the two partners probably had the large amount of gold that was needed to complete the deal.[31]

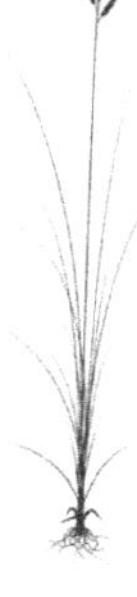

Unlike so many of the deeds that the Cozads were involved with and which were recorded often a year or two later, this one was recorded on the day the deed was signed.[32] Yet shortly after the completion of this contract, Theresa Cozad was sued by the Hendee group because she had failed to adhere to the terms which demanded that John J. Cozad be brought into court.[33] In another subsequent legal action it was agreed that Hendee would pay fifteen thousand dollars to the Cozads and that an additional five thousand dollars would be held in escrow to pay off any remaining taxes, liens or any other legal obligations. This was apparently negotiated by Robert Cozad.[34]

In hindsight, Stephen Hendee's caution, due diligence and desire to be certain he would have a clear title to the land in question was warranted because he would be drawn into John A. Cozad's bail dispute in 1885, and then twelve years later, in 1894, when he was fighting with John J. Cozad in court over the deed and the price that had originally been paid for the property.

In the decades to come, the titles passed on the Cozad/Hendee properties would create issues for future property owners, and in fact, as late as 1931, Sam Schooley had to attest that he was acquainted with John and Theresa Cozad. This affidavit was made long after both Hendee and the Cozads were dead and the legal issues between the two sides were resolved. However, some concern must have been raised about that particular title which required Schooley to testify that he had known both of the Cozads more than forty years before. Perhaps it just reflected the concerns of a cautious lawyer working on the closing.[35]

The Hendee partnership also purchased other lands including parcels in Gosper County. In total they had purchased twelve thousand acres. Another Bushnell resident, J. C. Vail, purchased more than thirty-three hundred acres, the largest single buyer. Vail would go on to plat Cayote (*Coyote or Darr*) and part of present-day Gothenburg.[36] Hendee soon began selling off parcels and would later buy out the interests of his partners in the fall of 1884.[37]

By the spring of 1884, residents from Bushnell were coming into Dawson County and in the decades to come would play a prominent role in the county's affairs.[38] The interest in Nebraska by Stephen Hendee, his partners and residents of Bushnell, Illinois was halted in the winter of 1884-85 when an important bank in the community went into receivership as two of its officers were charged with embezzlement.[39]

The bank's collapse slowed the movement of some of the community's residents to Nebraska and surely impacted Hendee's financial situation. In time, ties between the two communities faded.[40] Hendee maintained his ownership of the Hendee Hotel and his active interests in Dawson County until 1910 when he died.

## More Questions Than Answers

There are several aspects about the 1884 transaction that provide more questions than answers. The first and most intriguing is that the document is signed by both John and Theresa Cozad, who are both listed as the grantors on the warranty deed. (Curiously, John J. Cozad did not sign the original contract with the Hendee group, and this may have been one of the reasons for Hendee's concerns about the title.) This makes the effort to follow the path of the 1882 disappearance of John J. Cozad and his sudden ability to sign a deed even more puzzling.

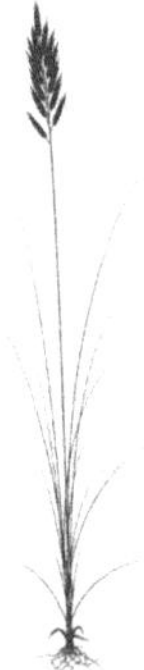

Equally interesting is that Robert Cozad attested that he had seen his father execute and sign the deed over to the Illinois group. His residence, along with his mother's, is listed as Arapahoe County in Colorado. This means that in the winter of 1884, some seventeen months after the shooting of Alf Pearson, Robert saw his father sign the required paperwork disposing of the Cozad lands and hotel, and it means presumably that they were in contact at some point. In addition, David Claypool attested that he recognized John Cozad's signature having witnessed it being written many times. Or, perhaps both attested to the correctness of the signature but never saw the elder Cozad, as it may have been done by mail.[41]

But this leads to a number of questions. Was John J. Cozad still in Colorado as evidenced by his son witnessing the document? That would confirm William Homer's belief that the family were all still in Colorado, as Bennard Perlman also believed. Or, at the minimum, did John and Robert meet secretly somewhere to coordinate the creation and signing of the document? Was this done in Colorado or somewhere else? Did this not potentially create legal jeopardy for Robert? It certainly created a conundrum for him because the witnessing of the signature meant that either he or the family may have seen or been in contact with John J. Cozad sometime after the shooting of Alf Pearson when there was a warrant for his arrest. Or perhaps John J. had simply created the document, signed it and forwarded it to Traber Gatewood and then it was given to Theresa. Perhaps Sam Schooley had acted as a go between.Why didn't Theresa use her Colorado attorney to complete the deal with Hendee, and why did she turn her legal power of attorney over to Robert? Perhaps it was to secretly handle the signing of the document by John with the lawyer not wanting to create future problems for himself. Also, how did the transfer come to be - did Robert go to Cozad and meet Stephen Hendee directly, leaving his mother behind or did she come to Cozad with him?

## Another Secret Departure

How and when Theresa and Robert left Nebraska for the last time is not entirely clear, but the deed to purchase the Cozad holdings by Stephen Hendee was signed in February 1884.[42] As has been shown, the Cozads had been living in Denver and had established a new life there. It is not clear from the historical record if they came back to Cozad after the shooting to stay there, or if perhaps they traveled to Cozad simply to execute the final paperwork to dispose of their properties and left just as quickly as they had come. As with all of the events surrounding the Cozads during this period, there remain questions. A variety of versions of what happened survive and they often present very different tellings of the story.

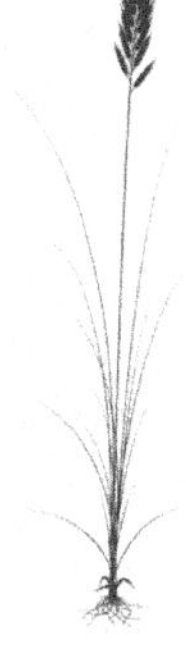

Tradition has always been that when the legal papers transferring the properties to Hendee were signed, Theresa and Robert were in Cozad. There is proof of this in Robert's 1879 scrapbook as he notes that he was in Cozad on November 16, 1883, eleven days before signing the contract with Stephen Hendee and his group. Another clue may come in the form of a sketch that Robert Cozad drew for Maggie Claypool for her autograph book on March 10, 1884. If that drawing was created in Cozad, on that date, it would mean that Robert and Theresa might have left the town later than has previously been believed.[43]

Two other factors that may have influenced the timing of their leaving were the death of Theresa's father on July 8, 1884, and brother Traber's marriage to Deborah Burgess on October 23 of the same year. Traber was thirty-two and Deborah was seventeen at the time.[44]

It must have been a difficult time for Theresa and Robert if they were in Cozad because if they ventured beyond the hotel or the Gatewood home, the whereabouts of John J. Cozad would have been the source of keen interest to those in the small community as Pearson had only died a year and a half earlier.[45] However, Julia Gatewood remained at the Hendee Hotel according to the 1885 state census record that was made on June 23, 1885. Traber, Deborah Gatewood and John Gatewood lived one block east of the former Cozad home.[46]

Another possibility is that they may have signed all the necessary legal documents in Denver and never returned to Cozad, although that contradicts most of the accounts that have come down through history.

Bennard Perlman believes that the Cozad family had already settled into their new identities in the East and that Theresa and Robert came back to Cozad, under their former names, signed the document and returned to their new home. However, that also brought the chance they would be followed back, and John Cozad discovered.[47]

When, and if, Robert and Theresa left Cozad for the final time together in 1884, tradition has it that they departed in the middle of the night, also embarking on a train from somewhere to the south. Sam Schooley, the faithful family friend, escorted them to the south in the dead of the night, in a wagon, covered with a tent, probably duplicating John J.'s escape two and a half years earlier. They carried with them about fifteen thousand dollars in gold coin that had been sewn into their clothes and possibly a couple of trunks.[48]

One remarkable artifact believed to be associated with that secret journey is a pistol that the Robert Henri Museum owns and is believed to have been carried by Schooley on the trip southward for protection.[49]

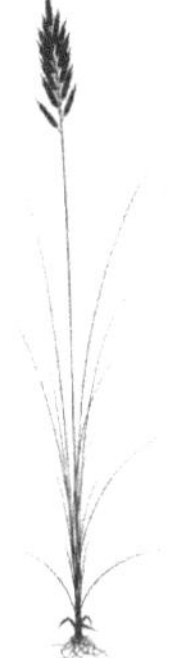

When arriving at the rail line that they left on, their choices were similar to the ones that John J. Cozad had. The mother and son could have gone in either direction. It is believed that they too did not take a Union Pacific Railway train from Cozad where they, like John J., would have been more likely to be recognized or followed. Some believe that they went to Denver to meet up with John J. and John A. although all their properties in Colorado had been sold by that time.

Based on the known evidence, Robert and Theresa probably left Cozad sometime between the middle of March and the fall of 1884. When the Cozads gathered again as a family in the East is not known. Based on the earliest sketch that the museum owns, one that was drawn on December 7, 1884, signed by *R.*

*Henri* and entitled *A Drama in Four Acts,* it can be presumed that the family had been reunited by that point.

As to all their belongings at the hotel, Dr. Robert Gatewood, Theresa Cozad's nephew would later recall that:

*After the family left, they took nothing with them so all these things were left in storage with us. As a young boy I used to get a kick reading his stories and looking at his many pictures. Mostly pen and ink. Unfortunately, all these things were destroyed in a fire.*[50]

This may answer why the museum was later able to acquire items associated with the family that were used during the hotel's management by them, including dishware.

### New Identities

After a journey that took a variety of twists and turns which are still not entirely known at this late date, the Cozads finally reunited as a family. This author believes that they initially again gathered as a family in New York City sometime in 1884.[51] Others believe that this happened in Denver in the immediate aftermath of Pearson's shooting in 1882 or even in 1883.[52]

The family concocted an elaborate scheme to hide their past and that was, for the most part, successful. Wherever it happened, either in Denver as the Henri biographers suggest, or in Cozad, as Sandoz believed, or in Atlantic City, the family eliminated its past. John J. Cozad changed his name to Richard H. Lee, the name of one of the signers of the Declaration of Independence, and an ancestor of Theresa's. Theresa Cozad's name was changed to Tessa Lee.

John A. Cozad's name was changed to the oddly spelled Frank Southrn, and Robert Henry Cozad became Robert Earle Henri, or R. Earl Henri, the name he used when entering the Philadelphia Academy of Fine Arts in 1886. His middle name was dropped by 1891. The pronunciation of his name, almost always mispronounced by visitors to the Robert Henri Museum and Art Gallery by using the French habit, *On-ree*, was actually *Hen'-ri*, or *Hen-rye* in the American fashion although he was proud of his French heritage.[53]

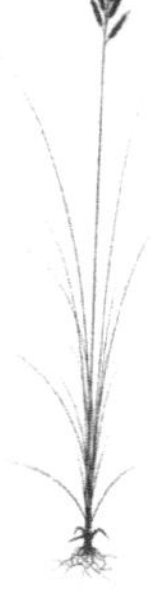

The sons and their relationship to their parents was also changed as part of this effort as they were now portrayed as adopted sons and foster brothers. Other accounts relay that Frank was said to be a brother-in-law and Robert a nephew.[54] So good was the identity change that Frank Southrn's birthplace was listed as Mexico on his 1933 death certificate. Robert Henri stayed true to his roots and listed Cincinnati as his birthplace and his parents as John and Theresa Henri, who in fact had never existed.[55]

## On the Boardwalk

The family came to settle in Atlantic City, New Jersey, a seaside community on the Atlantic Ocean. It was located on the beautiful Abescon Island that sat between two bays on the west and the Atlantic Ocean on the east. By the time the Cozads arrived, the resort was growing and hosting thousands of visitors.

The development of the area began in 1852 when construction commenced on a rail line from Camden, New Jersey, eastward to Atlantic City. With its completion two years later, an influx of tourists began to flock to the small community. At the same time the city was incorporated in 1854. A road connecting the mainland with the emerging city was finally finished in 1870 after years of construction.[56]

Within two decades it was a bustling summer resort town that was growing quickly. Atlantic City, as a resort, was officially launched in 1880. Large hotels and resorts, and boarding houses were constructed to service the many tourists, and gamblers.[57] It is not known when or how John Cozad began to focus his thoughts on Atlantic City, but he may have even come here to gamble as he had in Saratoga, New York, another resort area in upstate New York. But he also understood population trends and economic development and later invested the proceeds of the Cozad, Denver and Ohio properties into what became his Atlantic City empire.[58]

Bennard Perlman wrote that the family arrived in New York City in the fall of 1883 and stayed for a short time. He believed that Robert was placed in a boarding school in New York City and that his parents then relocated to Atlantic City. A year later Robert rejoined his parents. William Homer also believes that the Cozads arrived in New York City in late 1883 and then moved to Atlantic City.[59]

Perlman also believes that Theresa and Robert made a trip back to Cozad in November 1883 to sign the contract with the Hendee group for the Dawson County properties. Then, they returned another time to close on the property which did not happen until February 1884.[60] However, this does not answer the question of why the mother and son would have risked their new identities being exposed or someone following them back to New Jersey given their concern about John Cozad's personal safety and legal troubles at the time. Because of this question and other evidence, the author still believes that Theresa and Robert arrived in mid or late-1884.

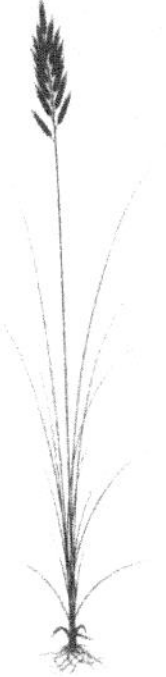

There are no listings for Robert Henri or Richard Lee in the 1882-1883 Atlantic City directories. However, an entry in the 1884 *Atlantic City Directory* lists R. H. Lee living on the *Board Walk* at Illinois Avenue. In addition, Robert Earl Henri and Frank L. Southrn are also listed as well as their business, *Southrn and Henri,* also on Illinois Avenue.[61] This may indicate that the family changed its identity and their relationships to each other sometime earlier than 1884 as

Homer and Perlman suggest, but certainly by the end of the year because Robert Cozad was identifying himself as Robert Henri. It may also account for why the names do not appear in the directories given that they were probably printed before the year they were distributed.

As in all his previous efforts, John J. Cozad used his real estate acumen to purchase prime real estate with potential. This time it was several pieces of ground that were located along the *Board Walk* as it was known. The first set of properties were at the center of the family's activities on Illinois Avenue. The second purchase would become the property that would be most well-known, and it too was on the *Board Walk* along the ocean front between Texas and Bellevue Avenues. Its ownership was registered in Robert Henri's name. Here John Cozad built breakwaters and jetties and a pier jutting into the ocean. Just as he had done in Cozaddale and Cozad, this property was only two blocks from an important rail connection, the West Jersey and Atlantic Railroad station. Today, that property is about one mile south of the numerous modern gambling resorts and a short distance from the Atlantic City Expressway and U.S. Routes 30 and 40. An irony in this turn of events is that it has been suggested that Cozad gave up gambling in 1882.[62]

The Jersey shoreline was subjected to terrible hurricanes and storms. Not long after the city was officially opened, a major storm struck the New Jersey shoreline doing extensive damage.[63] Several years later the Cozad properties were badly damaged by a storm in February 1885 as water rushed under their home and businesses including the sons' business called *Southrn and Henri's Cigar Store*. The concern was so great that the cigar store's contents were removed.[64]

John J. then purchased property on Texas Avenue, sometime after 1888, and built a complex of commercial businesses, and an amusement center and huge pavilion. The pavilion included a bar that had a one hundred and fifty-foot long front that took ten bartenders to service. This complex included a railway that used tricycles which ran on track out onto a pier into the ocean and was operated by Henri. Henri also painted houses.[65]

In 1889, another hurricane struck, and a Cozad property, *Ocean Terrace*, on Texas Avenue where he had a boarding house, was destroyed by fire.[66]

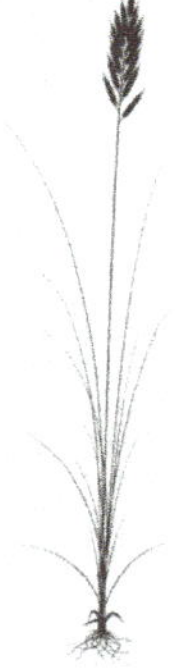

There is some dispute about this next chapter of the Atlantic City phase of the Cozad's lives. After the 1889 hurricane destroyed the boardwalk, the city rebuilt it up to Lee's property. There is a school of thought that believes when the city decided to widen it from twenty to twenty-four feet and extend the boardwalk through and beyond *Lee's Pavilion*, as it was known, after the hurricane, Richard Lee, refused to compromise and let it be constructed through his property because it would ruin the value of his complex.[67]

When he originally acquired the property, the most traveled section of the boardwalk had ended at the beginning of his pavilion. He was again involved in

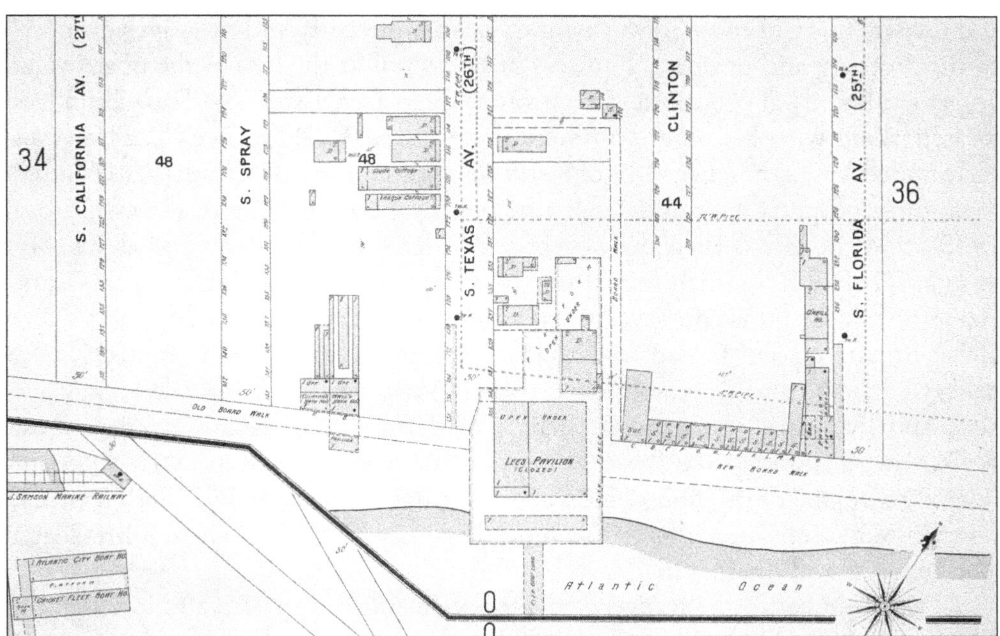


Courtesy Library of Congress (www.loc.gov/item/sanborn05408_002/.)

*When Richard and Tessa Lee, Frank Southrn and Robert Henri moved to Atlantic City in 1884, they purchased a prime piece of real estate along the Atlantic Ocean on South Texas Avenue. Initially they built several small buildings along the board walk that were destroyed in a storm. They were replaced by a large pavilion, a bar and a pier, where Robert operated a railway that extended to the ocean.*

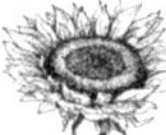

another legal battle that lasted for sixteen years and Robert was drawn into the quagmire too. At least one author believed John had simply done it for good publicity.[68]

A second view is that the city never had any intentions to widen the boardwalk past Bellevue Avenue, which was a half block east of Texas Avenue. While it wanted a forty-foot-wide boardwalk, it did not have the power to condemn property which would have been required. In 1890, the new boardwalk opened, with its twenty-four-foot width, stopping at the entrance to Lee's commercial property. However, Lee was more concerned with the future as the city was proposing a sixty-foot-wide boardwalk.[69]

His compound became known as *Fort Lee* because he constructed two fixtures made to look like artillery pieces at each end on the property.[70] He conspicuously wore two guns, dressed in a swallow-tailcoat topped off with a large western hat. He was always armed, and even when he retired for the evening, he had a pistol under his pillow.[71]

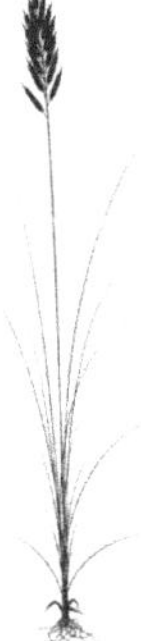

In fairness to Lee, his huge pavilion covered the boardwalk and was enclosed, and the widening of the walkway would have significantly and negatively impacted his property and business. Plus, his business was at the end of the boardwalk. Today the boardwalk continues to narrow at the place where Cozad's pavilion was located along with his other commercial ventures. By 1896, Lee's Pavilion was surrounded by a city fence although still operating. The boardwalk was rerouted around his property. Cozad did sell a strip of property in 1898 to the city. From 1908-1954 the city owned the property.[72] Elder son, then described as his *son-in-law,* Dr. Frank Southrn served on the Atlantic City Council for three years, (1895-97), just as this controversy was coming to a conclusion.

Ultimately, John Cozad sold all his holdings in Atlantic City in 1899. It is believed that he and Theresa moved to Far Rockaway, on Long Island in New York and lived in an apartment there. Curiously, one of Robert Henri's most well-known paintings, *The Beach: At Far Rockaway*, completed in 1902, and considered to be one of the finest landscape paintings in the early twentieth century, was painted there. Then, the couple moved to New York City, where John Cozad died in 1906 and Theresa in 1923.[73]

Just as he had done in every chapter of his life, controversy followed John Cozad, and he seemed to revel in it. While it is not believed that he shot anyone in Atlantic City, he certainly left a trail of disputes in his wake and for many years was remembered by the citizens of the community as the owner of *Fort Lee*. But it also demonstrated his ability to begin anew and to start over when he had to, including his efforts at Cincinnati, Cozaddale, Cozad and Denver.[74]

There is also one other account of real estate transactions that John Cozad was involved with. While in New York City, Cozad became the leader of a corporation that owned extensive tracts of land on Long Island. One of the properties the company owned was the land on the eastern shore of the East River that the Brooklyn Bridge was built on. It is important to note that this information is not found in any of the other sources that the author has seen. However, given Cozad's real estate acumen, this seems plausible or possible. However, there are other numerous mistakes in this source.[75]

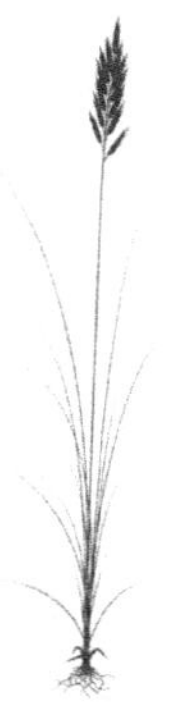

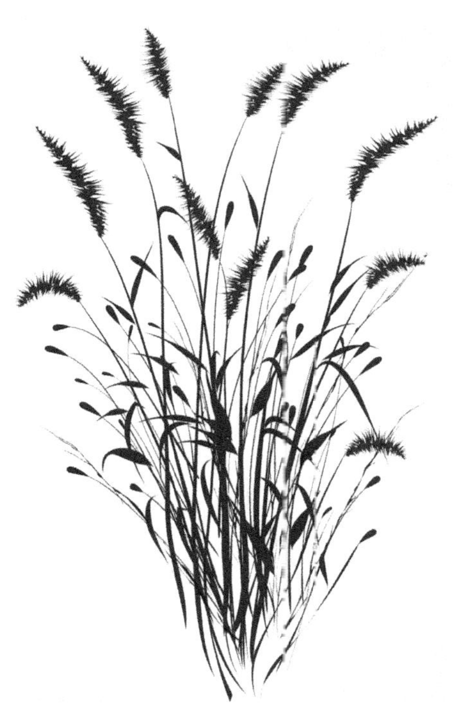

# *Chapter 7*

# Exoneration of the Cozads

*Oliver Buckley being sworn deposes and says that he has resided in Dawson County for more than 13 years last past that in 1882, and prior to that time he was acquainted with John J. Cozad and also with A. Pearson. That in the fall of 1882 said Pearson was running a threshing machine and on the morning of the shooting was threshing for Samuel Atkinson about 3 miles northwest of Cozad. That affiant was there helping thresh. That Pearson remarked that he was going to the town of Cozad as he had heard that John J. Cozad had come from Denver, and that he was going down there and do him up "the old son of a bitch if he did not make right to him," the difficulty seemed to be over the right to pasture cattle on some land claimed by Cozad. In an hour or two afterward word came back to where we were threshing that Pearson had been shot.*[1]

Deposition of Oliver Buckley

1892

Both of the Cozad indictments remained active and open cases until 1894, twelve years after the death of Alf Pearson and the alleged attempt to firebomb the Johnson Hotel in Lexington. Both men had simply vanished, at least to almost everyone in Cozad, law enforcement and the courts. Aside from Traber Gatewood and Sam Schooley, no one knew what had happened to them. It was probably through the efforts of Gatewood, that John J. and John A. ultimately were exonerated of their alleged crimes. It is not clear why or how the process of exonerating Cozad began.[2]

One curious fact that may be relevant as to what happened was that just four months before the charges against Cozad were dismissed, Alf Pearson's wife, Harriett, died on January 15, 1894. She was buried by his side in the Buffalo Table Cemetery, now known as the Rhinehart Cemetery.[3] Whether that event provided the first opportunity to begin the process of having the charges dropped is not known. However, it is a curious coincidence.

On May 9, 1894, the Dawson County Attorney E. A. Cook began proceedings to dismiss the charges against Cozad. In the case of the *State of Nebraska vs John J. Cozad,* testimony was taken from six people who had been witness to the events of that tragic day. Their testaments all mirror each other and that of the first accounts of what had happened as relayed in the newspapers. The witnesses included Julia Gatewood, Cozad's mother-in-law, Dr. William Bancroft, the physician who had attended Pearson, H. M. Sinclair, a person who had visited Pearson with Dr. Bancroft, Oliver Buckley, who had been assisting with the threshing of wheat with Pearson before he came to town, Henry Drew who had witnessed the whole event at the store, and Alex Trimble who had also seen the event.[4]

The affidavits were taken in the last weeks of April and the first week of May. Sam Schooley, the faithful friend of the Cozads, was the notary who had sworn to Gatewood's testimony and that of Oliver Buckley. The first person deposed was Julia Gatewood. Her statement of April 28, 1894 reads as follows:

*Julia Gatewood, being the first duly sworn deposes and says: That she resides at Cozad, Nebraska and has lived there for the past twenty years: that in the year 1882,*

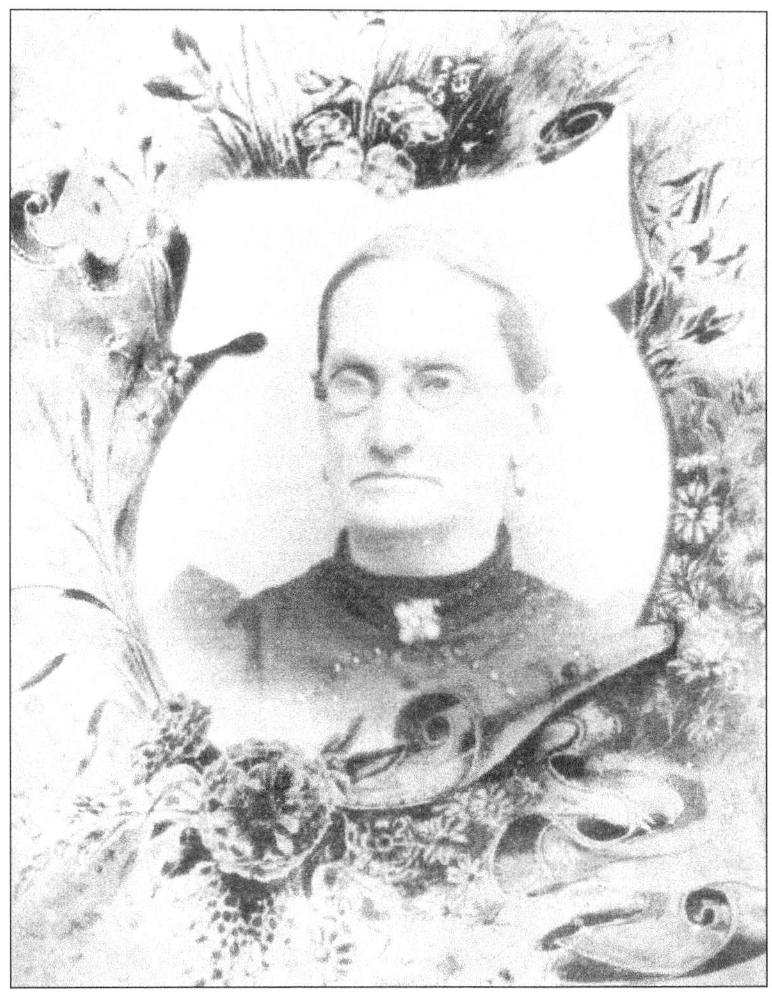

*Courtesy 100th Meridian Museum*

*Harriet Pearson*

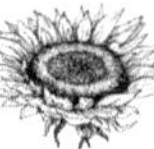

*she was acquainted with John J. Cozad who is her son-in-law and also with Mr. A. Pearson, that in the fall of 1882, she was conducting a store in the village of Cozad, that one day, the exact date the affiant has forgotten, in the fall of 1882, Cozad was sitting in her store talking with one Henry Drew, and while in conversation, Mr. Pearson came in and accosted Cozad and applied to him opprobrious epithets and seem to be very much excited and was violent and loud and vehement: Cozad who was sitting down, got up to his feet and said to Pearson: "There is a lady present" meaning this affiant and he would not stand such talk in the presence of his mother-in-law; Pearson said something about not knowing that she was present and further said to*

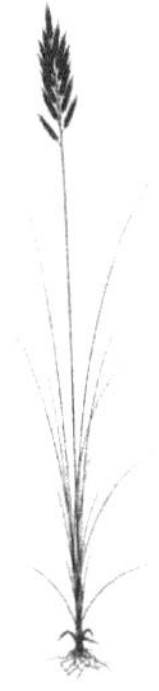

*Cozad "Come out of doors, there are no women out there." (Illegible writing) Cozad and Pearson got up and went out of doors, Drew going with them, directly after going out of doors she heard loud talking and noise as if one were scuffling or fighting; she then went to the window and looked out and saw Cozad down apparently in a dry goods box with Pearson striking him with his fists on his head; that Cozad had one hand up as to ward off the blows and was crying to Pearson to quit. That Pearson did not desist but soon after took hold of Cozad by the collar of his coat, or throat, affiant could not tell which; almost immediately after this she heard the report of a pistol and saw Pearson stagger back with Mr. Drew taking a hold of him; she then went to the door while Cozad who had regained his feet came towards her and went in the house, he was covered with blood and seemed to be bleeding about the head and the face,; she ran to him and asked him if he was shot to which he replied "No it is Pearson" and asked her to get him some water to wash himself with; she immediately got him some water and then went and found Pearson was shot; several had arrived and that they were caring for him; she next went and helped Mr. Cozad wash the blood off himself and there were at least a half a dozen cuts on his head which were bleeding and one over the right eye, one on the left cheek, and also his nose was bleeding; she wanted to go for a Doctor but Cozad told her not to do so but to get some Court plaster and assist in staunching the blood which she did, that Cozad staid (sic) at her house until he had staunched the blood and put Court plaster on his wounds perhaps half an hour in all, when he got up and left her house without saying a word to her and she has not seen or communicated with him since.*[5]

On May 1, 1894, Dr. William M. Bancroft gave testimony that was sworn to by H. O. Smith. His statement reads as follows:

*W. M. Bancroft being first duly sworn deposes that he is a physician and has lived and practiced his profession in Dawson County for the past 21 years. That he was acquainted with Mr. A. Pearson, and was called to attend him, and treat him for a gun shot wound in the face, in the latter part of the year 1882, that he found he had been shot in the cheek the ball passing in and lodging at the base of the brain, that he lived for about 12 weeks after receiving said wound and that he attended him all of said time. That he had a number of conversations with him about the occurrence in which he received the wound and that Pearson told him that Cozad shot him and when asked about the particulars told affiant, that "he was whipping the hell (sic) out Cozad and the damned Coward instead of fighting like a man hollowed (sic) like a puppy, and wouldn't fight but deserved a licking and that he made up his mind that he would lick him anyhow. That he had knocked him down in a box or behind a box affiant don't now remember which, and that he took hold of him to choke his lying tongue out of mouth (sic) when Cozad pulled a pistol from somewhere and shot him. This in substance of his story as I remember it now, we talked about it a number of*

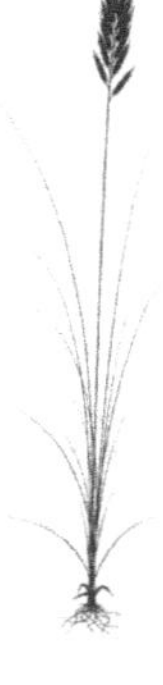

*times in the first week or two that I visited him. He stated why he was angry at Cozad, but I am not certain now what it was about except that it was about some transaction that he had with Cozad in which he claimed Cozad went back on his agreement and lied about it. W. M. Sinclair went with me on my fourth visit and the same conversation was had to him in my presence. He asked to have Sinclair to come with me and I did so.*[6]

The third witness was Oliver Buckley and his statement was also sworn to by Sam Schooley. He stated that:

*Oliver Buckley being sworn deposes and says that he has resided in Dawson County for more than 13 years last past that in 1882, and prior to that time he was acquainted with John J. Cozad and also with A. Pearson. That in the fall of 1882 said Pearson was running a threshing machine and on the morning of the shooting was threshing for Samuel Atkinson about 3 miles northwest of Cozad. That affiant was there helping thresh. That Pearson remarked that he was going to the town of Cozad as he had heard that John J. Cozad had come from Denver, and that he was going down there and do him up "the old son of a bitch if he did not make right to him" the difficulty seemed to be over the right to pasture cattle on some land claimed by Cozad. In an hour or two afterward word came back to where we were threshing that Pearson had been shot.*[7]

The fourth witness, Henry Drew, was sworn by H. W. Harldey (sic) on April 16, 1894, and he was then living in Utah. He relayed the following:

*Henry Drew being first duly sworn deposes and says that he now lives at Santa Clare in Washington County, Utah that in 1882, he resided in Dawson County, Nebraska and was acquainted with John J. Cozad and also with Mr. A. Pearson, that he was in the Village of Cozad, in the fall of 1882, and witnessed the altercation between said parties that resulted in the shooting of said Pearson by John J. Cozad, that the particulars so far as affiant said and knows are follows. Affiant was in the store kept by Mrs. Julia Gatewood the mother-in-law of Cozad and was in conversation with Cozad concerning a business matter. That Mrs. Gatewood who was sitting behind the counter and the affiant and Cozad who were sitting in front of the counter were the only ones in the Store That while the affiant and Cozad was negotiating a proposed trade Pearson came in to the store and said to Cozad, as near as I can remember now "Cozad I hear you are going to sue me" without waiting for him to reply further said "You God Damn son of a bitch if you say that my stock injured your hay ground you are a liar" Cozad who (illegible) Pearson to get out of the store as there was a woman present that he would not stand or have such talk in the presence of his mother-in-law who was a lady. Pearson then said that he did not know there was a woman in the*

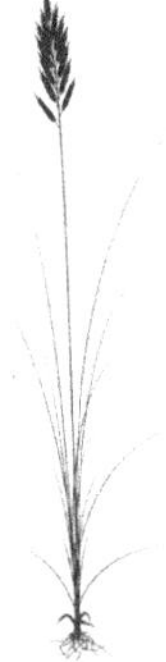

*store as he had not noticed Mrs. Gatewood until Cozad had spoken. He then said come out of doors, there are no women out there, we can talk or will talk, I can not now say positively which. That both men then went out the door. Pearson going first, when Pearson fairly got outside he again says to Cozad "I hear you are going to sue me . . ." Cozad replies "I am, if you don't keep your stock off of my land" immediately the word liar or lie, was used, I cannot tell which spoke it, but almost instantly Pearson struck Cozad and knocked him down, in falling Cozad fell into an empty dry goods box or box of some kind, and in such a way that it appeared to me that it prevented him from getting up, and the next thing I saw was Cozad in the box with his heels and head sticking up and his body down and Pearson striking him on the head and attempting to kick him. I heard Cozad hollow (sic) to Pearson to quit that he, Cozad was fast and could not get up but Pearson kept right along a striking him or at him and then I hears (sic) Cozad hollow (sic) Help! Help! I also called Pearson to stop, at least three times. When I saw he did not stop I hollowed (sic) help! Help! For the purpose of attracting attention of someone. About this time Pearson took hold of Cozad by the throat or collar. I will not say which and then I grabbed hold of Pearson and attempted to pull him away. Then I heard a report of a pistol and Pearson let go of Cozad and staggered back taking me with him. Then I saw Pearson was shot as the blood was running down his face. When I next saw Cozad he had extricated himself from the box and went into the house, he was bleeding from the nose and cuts on his face. The worst cut was close to the right temple. Pearson was very boisterous and loud when he first spoke to Cozad in the store. Seemed to be very much excited. While striking and attempting to kick Cozad he was swearing and talking vehemently, but I can not now say what he said. The reason I did not take hold of Pearson sooner to pull him off was I was afraid to do so, as soon almost as he clinched Cozad I did so. But did not attempt to when he was striking and kicking, and further affiant saith not.*[8]

An important addition to the story is Henry Drew's recollection in his deposition that he and Cozad were in conversation in the Gatewood store when Pearson walked in.

There are, however, several noteworthy discrepancies in the various accounts. In the original October and December 1882 newspaper articles, the writer states that the shooting had occurred in the home of Robert and Julia Gatewood, which was believed to be directly across the street from today's Robert Henri Museum. The house was later moved and today its original location is now a municipal parking lot.[9] However, the 1894 grand jury testimony confirmed that the shooting had occurred at the Gatewood's store which was located one block west of the Cozad's hotel, on the northwestern corner of Main Street and North Meridian streets.

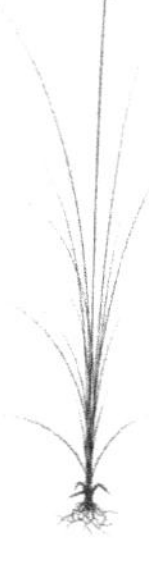

The story also confirms that John Cozad left immediately after the shooting, preventing what might possibly have been his own lynching as frontier justice was not always fair but was often quickly enacted. There is one contradiction presented in those accounts from all of the other known accounts and that is that Cozad went north and not south. Almost every account says that he went south. The basic sets of facts as presented here are in agreement even after the passage of twelve years. In addition, two of the witnesses were favorable to Cozad and three were favorable to Pearson.

Almost from the very beginning, the various accounts that were told of the shooting of Alf Pearson varied wildly with what had actually happened. One account of the Pearson shooting by an original colonizer, believed to be Roy Anderson, is quite different from those that are generally accepted. His recollections, written down many years after the event also proved his faulty memory of the incident. Anderson wrote:

*. . . Cozad shot Pearson down in cold blood in his own home in the presence of Pearson's two sons and then made his escape to parts unknown, he never returned to Cozad that anyone knew of unless it was to some of his friends like Sam Schooley or the Gatewoods and a few other friends that he had or were relatives of his.*[10]

Obviously, there are a number of errors in this account including where Cozad shot Pearson (not at Pearson's home), who witnessed it (none of the accounts have Pearson's boys at the scene) and the fact is that Cozad did in fact return albeit twelve years later. Yet it is the recollections like these that would become part of the mythology that surrounds the shooting even to this day.

There is an account relayed in the *Early Community History of Cozad* that states:

*A few days later (after the ending of the work on the bridge in 1878), following an altercation at his sister's store, Mr. Cozad shot Mr. Pearson. According to Mrs. Gatewood, lone witness to the shooting Mr. Cozad asked Mr. Pearson to take his cattle off land belonging to Cozad. In the argument that followed Mr. Pearson knocked Mr. Cozad in dry-goods box, where he was pounding him to death when Mr. Cozad shot him in the mouth.*[11]

Here we have two discrepancies, the first is the date, the shooting happened in 1882, and the second is that the store was owned by his mother-in-law and father-in-law, Julia Gatewood and not his sister.

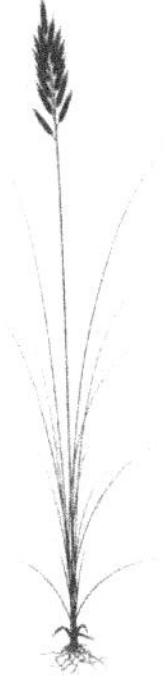

Another significant difference that has come down through time concerns a knife that was said to have been used by Alf Pearson in his attack on John Cozad. Nowhere does the mention of a knife appear in any of the contemporary accounts, although that is a common theme in the more recent retelling of that story. The use of a knife by Alf Pearson is first described in Dr. Robert Gatewood's

1932 description of the shooting included in *Who Was Robert Henri?* Gatewood, a nephew of John Cozad, would clearly lay the blame on Pearson. However, his account, which is different from the contemporary accounts, states:

*Mr. Cozad was preparing to leave for Denver on some business. He was upstairs over his mother-in-law's store dressing when a Mr. Pearson entered Mrs. Gatewood's store, drunk and demanding to see Mr. Cozad. She was very much frightened as she was alone, and he told her in his rage that he had come to kill Cozad. She ran upstairs and told Mr. Cozad what had happened. He told her to advise Pearson that he would be down presently. Pearson and Cozad had had some serious trouble a few days before when Cozad ordered him to keep his cattle off his land. He finally came down and Pearson proceeded to abuse and threaten him. Cozad ordered him out, but Pearson knocked him down among some boxes and was on him attempting to finish him, when Cozad succeeded in getting at his pistol and shot him in the mouth. Pearson died a few days later.*

*After the encounter, Cozad went upstairs, arranged his clothing left the house and instead of taking the train to Denver proceeded on foot across the country south to the Burlington railroad some fifty miles distant.*[12]

Another difference between all the accounts is that Cozad had already pulled his gun out when they walked onto the porch as was recalled in the original October 21, 1882, article. That piece of information does not appear again in the later grand jury testimony. Also, it is alledged that Alf Pearson was drunk. That too does not appear in other accounts.

Again, as with the Anderson account there are other major discrepancies. In all accounts Cozad had just come from Denver and Pearson heard he was in town. Also, Pearson, as recounted in the earlier newspaper accounts, said he did not want trouble, but just to negotiate for grazing rights. From this account we also are told that Cozad and Pearson had previously had a disagreement over Pearson's cattle on Cozad's pastures.

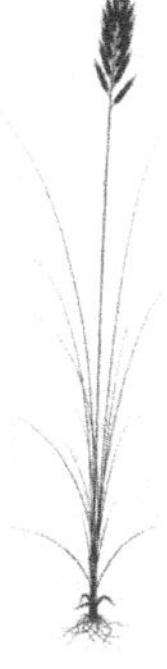

In addition, Cozad was in the store when Pearson walked in and not upstairs. With some elements of the story there are threads that match. Cozad's having been abused by Pearson, and Pearson knocking him over and into a shipping crate are events confirmed in the grand jury testimony. The recounting of Cozad going south and not to Denver confirms the author's own theory about what happened in the hours after the shooting.

A curious aspect of this recounting is that Robert Gatewood presumably discussed this with John J. Cozad in the years following the incident when they visited in New York. Could this have been Cozad's way of skirting blame for what had happened or a defense of his actions? Could Gatewood's memory have been faulty since he talked about this with Cozad years after the event? While many of the elements of the story ring true, several do not. Or is it possible that Pearson really had a knife?

One final thread in this story is that there was speculation that Alf Pearson had died because of bad medical care, and that if his treatment had been different, he might have lived. In a letter that is purported to have been written by Theresa to Johnny Cozad at the time of Johnny's incarceration, Johnny had believed that an infection had started within Pearson's body, was not treated properly and then spread throughout the rest of him. Or, one could argue that he lasted as long as he did because of good medical care.[13]

This conclusion does not eliminate the underlying issues of John Cozad having been a controversial figure that seemed to have been forever involved in some sort of trouble. And it is obvious from the grand jury accounts that Pearson came to Cozad on that morning to settle some issues that had arisen between them. Or, if one believes the newspaper account, Pearson was trying to get an agreement for pasturing his cattle on John Cozad's land.

One may also speculate that Pearson in many ways represented all those who had had their share of disputes with John Cozad during his decade in Nebraska. All those lawsuits and beatings came to be answered with that deadly altercation and the upheaval it brought to Cozad and his family.

## Nolle Prosequi

Ultimately, the 1882 indictment of Cozad for the shooting of Alf Pearson stood until May 9, 1894, when a court determined that a *Nolle Prosequi* was to be entered and the criminal case would be voluntarily ended and not pursued. Several of those 1894 witnesses had also been called during the proceedings of the original 1882 indictment, including Julia Gatewood.[14] Finally the legal challenges that had followed him for twelve years and so disrupted their lives were over. Robert Gatewood believed that his father Traber had spent a great deal of effort, money and his political connections to get the ruling.[15]

In addition, a similar *Nolle Prosequi* was also entered in the arson case of John A. Cozad and so the charges in that case, also from 1882, were dismissed. In Johnny's case there were a number of facts that could have exonerated him if there had been a fair trial. No one had seen him start any fire, he was a familiar person to the community, a number of hours had passed between when he left the hotel and the chambermaid had arrived in the room, and, finally, if guilty, why did he stop in Gould when he surely would have wanted to get out of the area as quickly as possible. The remaining question is whether it was possible that an innocent man had been wrongly charged, imprisoned, which led to him trying to evade arrest for twelve years to the point of even changing his identity?[16]

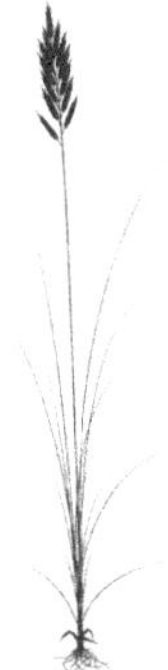

In 1888, with none of the Cozads still in Dawson County or Nebraska for that matter, Charles McNamar was forced to pay the bond himself of $5,000.

McNamar had become a Nebraska State Senator by this time, and it is not known if the Cozads ever repaid him.[17]

### The Return of John J. Cozad

While the indictment remained active against John J. Cozad, he is not believed to have returned to Cozad. He thought his life was still at risk although his brother-in-law Traber, who had so often come to the family's rescue, had believed for some time that there was no need to keep up with the mysterious lives that the Cozads lived. In fact, in about 1889, Traber had even gone to Atlantic City to visit the family although it was done with great secrecy.[18]

However, sometime after the May 1894 dismissal of the murder charges, John J. Cozad did come back to the town he had created, at least twice. There are several accounts of when these trips occurred, but a contemporary source is a newspaper account in the *Dawson County Pioneer* which reported that John Cozad had arrived on July 10, 1894, without Theresa.[19]

Another account of the visit is provided by Dr. Robert Gatewood (1885-1966), a son of Traber Gatewood. He thought he was about eight years old when he met John Cozad, his uncle, during a stay in Cozad. He does not provide an exact date in his account, but he did remember the events occurred at his grandmother's house and Cozad's elegant appearance.[20]

It has long been believed that Cozad had returned to see if he could recover some of his financial losses with regard to the property that had been so quickly disposed of in 1884, and in a manner more favorable to him.[21] Because of the need for the Cozads to be paid in gold, a necessity that placed them at great negotiating disadvantage, the price that was agreed upon was probably below what the properties were actually worth at the time. Once Cozad arrived, staying at his mother-in-law's house, he wasted little time going to work on this recovery effort.

At first, he sued Stephen Hendee over the deed that he and Theresa had originally signed over to Hendee. Cozad he claimed the properties were still rightfully his although it is not clear why he thought that was the case. One issue that he felt might have been in his favor was said to be the large number of leases he had on various properties that did not find their way into the final agreement. Their value may have been significant. These actions by Cozad were instigated during the summer of 1894 and in his suits of ejectments, he claimed that the contracts for the lands he and Theresa sold to Hendee in 1884 had in fact not been legal.[22]

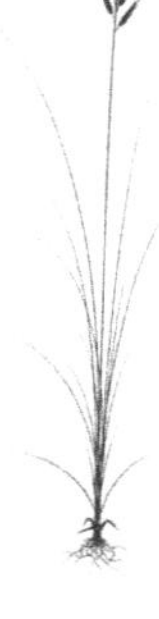

A contemporary newspaper article states that the deed that Hendee had signed had been prepared by John, deeding the properties to Theresa through Robert Gatewood and that her agents in Denver had been a facilitator of the legal transaction. Another item mentioned in the article was that the deed had not been attested. Given how careful the Hendee group had been when the original contract was created, it is hard to imagine them or their lawyer not being particularly cautious about these items.[23]

The lawsuits generated great interest because the properties in question were numerous, thousands of acres of land and parcels in the city of Cozad itself and would have impacted many people and businesses. In September, Hendee was reported to have come to Dawson County to deal with this potentially serious legal matter.[24]

Then, Cozad returned between November 21 and 23 and created at least nineteen deeds that conferred title from Cozad to the present owner although there may well be even more. Found in the collection of the Robert Henri Museum those deeds include a clause that states:

> *. . . in the event that said real estate is recovered or adjudged to John J. Cozad in the action or actions brought or to be brought for that purpose.*[25]

Each of the contracts was signed by John J. Cozad and witnessed by Sam Schooley and David Claypool. Perhaps he was goading the Hendee group into renegotiating the 1884 real estate deal or reclaiming property that had perhaps been made a part of the deal but may not have been meant to be sold.

There is additional context to this whole series of transactions because at least one of the grantees of those deeds relayed the story of what had happened decades later. The sequence of events described may have been similar in each of the other contracts that Cozad signed that November. In each situation it appears that Cozad was providing new warranty deeds on properties that the Hendee group had already sold that were part of the 1884 transaction.

On November 21, 1894, John Cozad met with Charles E. Allen regarding a piece of property in the town (*Lots 7 & 8 in Block 2 of the original town*) that Allen had owned and purchased from Stephen Hendee. Allen was summoned to Julia Gatewood's home after being told that Cozad was in town. Allen had only recently arrived in Cozad and had purchased the property along with his wife, Susan. Together they had built a small house on it. Allen surely must have been surprised when he arrived at the Gatewood family home and found the town's founder standing there.[26]

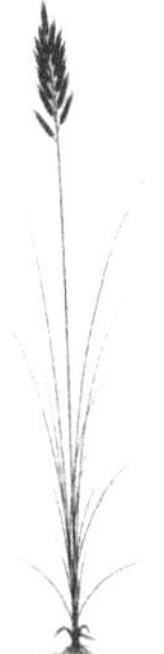

Cozad prepared a new deed giving Allen a clear title so that in the event he was successful in his legal actions against Hendee, Allen's title would not be challenged. This contract, like the others, was signed by Cozad and witnessed by Schooley and Claypool. Because of the date of the contract and its signature, the November 1894 date is probably the actual date that Cozad was in town for a second time.[27]

Once the deeds were signed, word must have quickly gotten back to the Hendee interests that Cozad was in town and was undermining their rightful ownership of the properties that had been acquired legally in 1884. The signing of those new warranty deeds came to be at the center of a larger legal fight that would find its way into the courts just two weeks later. In addition, just as quickly as John Cozad had come back to Nebraska, he was gone.[28]

On December 7, 1894, the Hendee group filed a lawsuit against John J. Cozad, Theresa Cozad, Robert H. Cozad, David Claypool, Traber Gatewood, Samuel Schooley and Julia Gatewood in the United States District Court of Nebraska in Omaha to stop them from undertaking actions against their interests. The lawsuit stated that Cozad had no remaining interest in the properties because of the 1884 deed selling the property to them. An injunction was granted by a federal judge, Elmer Dundy one week later.[29]

On December 8, 1894, a United States Marshall served a writ of injunction to John Cozad, who was then represented by Francis Hamer, and the other defendants. None of the defendants or their lawyers or representatives responded. As a result, Judge Elmer Dundy ruled in favor of the Hendee group on May 20, 1895, and wrote a judgement that stated that the deed for the properties purchased in 1884 were unencumbered by any of the legal challenges made or actions taken by John J. Cozad's actions and that the title was clear and that they could do whatever they wanted with their holdings. He dismissed the complaint against Robert Cozad and Theresa Cozad, probably because Robert and Theresa had not been involved with the new warranty deeds. He did not dismiss the complaint against the remaining defendants because they had all taken part in some of the transactions.[30]

Since John J. Cozad and his co-defendants did not respond to the action. one must wonder if Cozad's actions might have been considered a nuisance lawsuit because the judge ruled that the complainant's costs were recoverable. Also, one must wonder if Cozad had simply brought the lawsuit in hopes of a financial gain thinking that the Hendee group would quickly settle to free their own transfers of properties from any taint and remove future problems, especially given that they had been selling off parcels since 1884.

Ironically, this was a problem that Cozad had also encountered with the railroad as at least one Union Pacific land official had questioned Cozad's titles prior to the shooting of Alf Pearson. In fairness, the company had not provided Cozad with titles in a timely fashion. But if the Cozads and their allies thought that Hendee would capitulate they were wrong, as he was up to the task of challenging Cozad on his own ground. And, in the end Hendee easily prevailed, probably because he had better lawyers and because John Cozad indeed had no rights.[31]

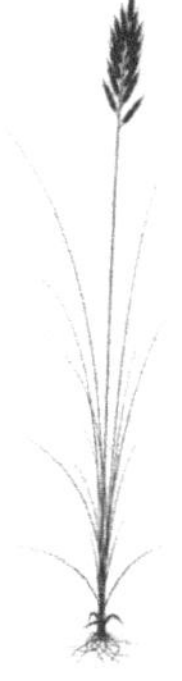

Every abstract of a title for property in Cozad or the surrounding area that was sold by the Cozads to the Hendee group in 1884 and subsequently sold after that contains the wording of that ruling by Judge Elmer Dundy to this day.[32]

There remains a letter from Traber Gatewood to Van Burke Gatewood that may provide some insight into what Traber may have thought about the proceedings with which he had been directly involved. On November 25, 1895, six months after the court case was decided in Hendee's favor, Traber wrote, perhaps about the legal action:

*They lost the suit (quit in another transcription) for the land on an account of non-appearance at U.S. Court in Omaha . . .*[33]

## Another Disappearance

It has long been believed that the visit by the town's founder was shrouded in secrecy, as it is not clear where he stayed. For example, it has been suggested that he stayed with Traber Gatewood, just a block east of today's Robert Henri Museum. Another suggestion is that he stayed at his mother-in-law's home, which was directly across the street from the museum in the present-day municipal parking lot. Other accounts have him meeting with his allies in David Claypool's kitchen.[34]

But surely word spread of his presence, and given what is known of John Cozad's personality, it seems doubtful that he would have remained in seclusion and hiding. Quickly it became known to the attorney for Stephen Hendee, along with law enforcement officials, that Cozad was back in town and tradition has it that they all wanted to meet with him.[35] And then, just as suddenly as he had come, he left. He disappeared again, presumably to return to Atlantic City. How he left town and returned back East is not known. One curious item in the article that reported about the trial was that there was great sympathy for Cozad, which was a far cry from when he had shot Alf Pearson twelve years before.[36]

By this time the Cozad family had long established themselves with their new identities in Atlantic City and presumably did not want to have their lives become even more complicated by reverting to their original identities. There were other items that may have made the real estate situation a complicated one, such as the liens placed upon Cozad's assets after the death of Alf Pearson. Or it may have been as simple as his having been gone for twelve years and his attachment to the place had also dissipated. It is believed to be the last time he was in the community but given other inconsistencies as previously noted, one must question if that conclusion is correct as well.

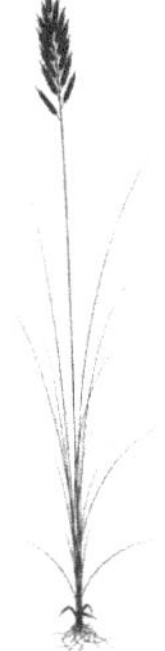

## A Different Outcome at the One Hundredth Meridian

The village of Cozad in 1894 was a different place than the one John Cozad had left in the fall of 1882. It had expanded and developed in the decade after the disappearance of the family. It was incorporated as a village in 1886.[37] While it never became the county seat or the nation's capital as John J. Cozad had once envisioned, it ultimately developed into one of the three major cities in Dawson County and a commercial center for the surrounding region.[38]

Cozad, for all his efforts, was never able to overcome Plum Creek's early advantages, in spite of the fact that the town had been moved one mile west from its original location. Along with that challenge, it always had a larger population, was a more important settlement, created more economic development for itself, and had public support to build a bridge that would allow it to remain an important commercial center. While both communities continued to grow, the county seat grew exponentially. One statistic bears this out. At the time of the April 1876 fire that destroyed much of the community, the population of Cozad was eighty (this may have included part of the Cozad Precinct), Overton - fifty, Willow Island - forty and Plum Creek - six hundred and fourteen.[39]

That discrepancy in power and population between the two towns was never overcome and remains to this day. Even the name of the town that had caused so much difficulty in the lives of the Cozad family had been changed as the city's leaders tried to erase the complicated past of the cattle town. Plum Creek's name was changed to Lexington in 1889, after residents had considered changing it to Ontario in 1882, and Corning in 1889. After a vote of the residents changed the name, shortly thereafter the railroad changed the name of its station.[40]

However, Cozad, Nebraska certainly fared better than Cozaddale, Ohio. It is now just a ghost town, although it is still shown on maps, and a small-town center of a handful of buildings still stand. One might wonder what John and Theresa Cozad would think if they visited their town on the Platte River today. While the community had struggled in the early years after its founding, in the decades after the departure of the Cozad family, important developments occurred.

### The Bridge is Finally Completed

Not long after purchasing the assets of Theresa and John Cozad, an effort was begun by Stephen Hendee to build a bridge across the Platte. The dream of building a bridge connecting his southern holdings to the village had long eluded John J. Cozad even after his personal expenditure of thousands of dollars and seven or eight years of work. The need for a new bridge had become even more acute as the area's population was growing and in fact it would more than double during the Hendee era.

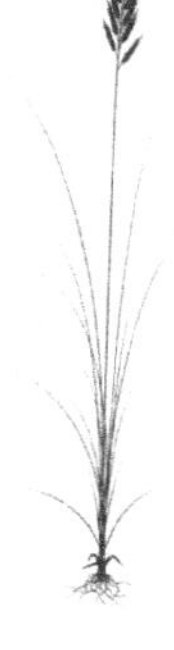

The new effort, led by Hendee, was a significant contribution that he made to the community. Hendee was described as enthusiastic about the project and a stock company was created and immediately eight thousand dollars was raised by subscription and another six thousand dollars was raised with a mortgage.[41] He was appointed the chairman of the Platte River Bridge Company, which built a new, single lane wood bridge, with three turnouts, crossing the Platte River on pilings using the design that Cozad had originally drawn up. The cost of building the new bridge, fourteen thousand dollars, was underwritten by farmers on the south side and businessmen from Cozad on the north side. The construction

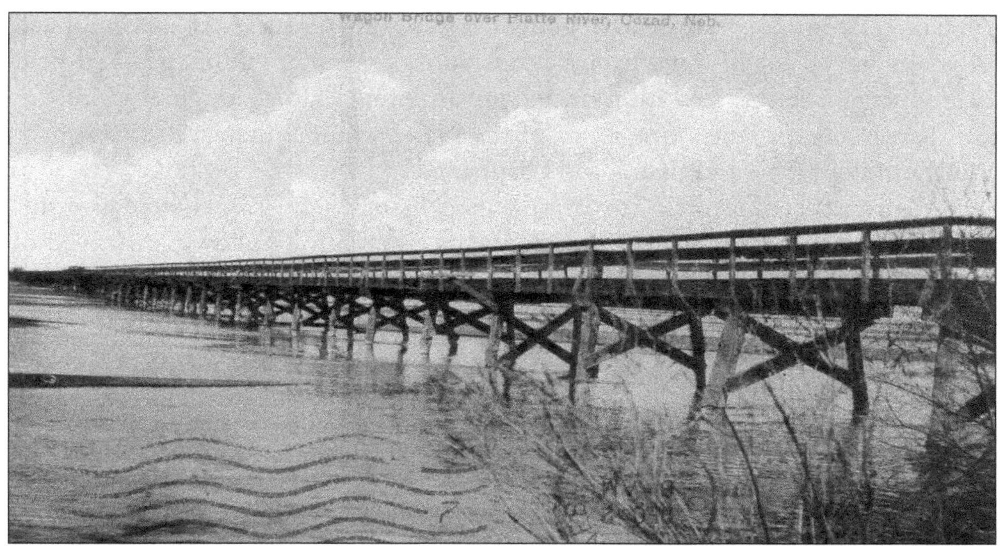


*Collection of the Robert Henri Museum and Art Gallery*

*This photograph is believed to be of the bridge that Stephen Hendee and the Platte River Bridge Company built and finished in 1885.*

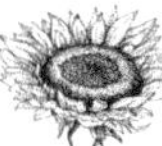

company was the Kansas City Bridge and Iron Company.[42]

But in one of those ironies, three sections of the bridge in Cozad were destroyed by an ice jam on March 14, although quickly repaired. The jam had been created by ice backing up from some of the pilings from the abandoned Cozad project. Cozad had had the last laugh.[43]

The bridge was finished on April 27, 1885. To pay for its construction it became a toll bridge with the toll collector's building at the southern end.[44] With the tolls collected, and additional subscriptions, the mortgage was paid off in addition to the stockholders on November 19, 1891. The construction of the bridge was officially paid for. Sam Schooley had even solicited owners of stock to donate their shares back so that the bridge could be given to the county.[45]

The board of the stock company then offered to give the bridge to Dawson County. Sam Schooley, David Claypool and W. H. Irwin, the original chairman of Cozad's governing body, made the presentation.

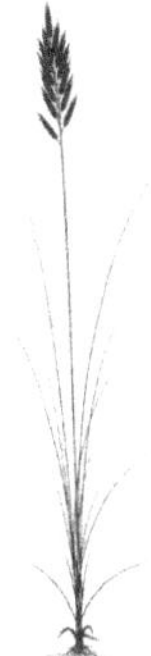

In late 1891, the bridge was given to the county and in the years following was widened to allow for the passage of two vehicles.[46] The management of the bridge then fell to the responsibility of the county and became toll-free. The community was so delighted when the news arrived of the ending of tolls that many residents marched out to the bridge and placed a free sign on the former toll keeper's building and held a community barbeque.[47]

Now, just as Cozad had planned, the residents to the south of the river could come directly into town instead of going over to Plum Creek. And, as Cozad had originally hoped for his own project, the county's taxpayers ultimately had paid for it. It might have given him satisfaction to know that his original vision for a bridge connecting the lands south of the Platte would enhance the area's economic development, and that is what happened.

At the same time the Cozad bridge was being built, efforts were also underway to build a bridge across the Platte at Gothenburg. Following the lead of Cozad, the businessmen and farmers in the Gothenburg area also clamored for a bridge which was built and eliminated those long round trips that had to be made to conduct business.

The Kansas City Bridge and Iron Company, built the Gothenburg bridge too and it was completed first, on January 13, 1885 while the Cozad bridge was finished on April 27, 1885. [48] Like the Cozad bridge, the private company that owned it turned it over to the county in 1892.[49]

As to why Hendee succeeded where Cozad had failed, one reason was that his personality was very different than Cozad's. He was cooperative when it was needed, and he quickly organized the effort and saw it through to completion. And, perhaps, he was also the better businessman and wealthier too. It is said that John J. Cozad, in 1882, was worth between two hundred and three hundred thousand dollars. One hundred and fifty thousand dollars of those assets were invested in Denver. Hendee's financial holdings included agricultural businesses counting six grain elevators, a large general store, banks, a large hotel, and other assets which were probably worth more than Cozad's business operations, even if he could make substantial profits on his gambling.[50] No matter the reason, the bridge was drawing in the population from the south of Cozad.

## Irrigation Canals Open the Spigots

Another development forever changed the course of the city and the region's history. In the summer of 1893, there was a drought of such magnitude that the community's business leaders and farmers resolved to build an irrigation system. Prior to that, irrigation had been utilized by taking water directly from the Platte and diverting it to individual farmers' properties. However, there was not yet a systematic regionwide approach to watering crops. Often times rains followed periods of drought and so the need for irrigation was given a lower priority. Finally, by that time, the theory that rain would follow the plow was totally discredited. This year also saw the beginning of the Panic of 1893, a financial collapse as bad as the one of 1873.[51]

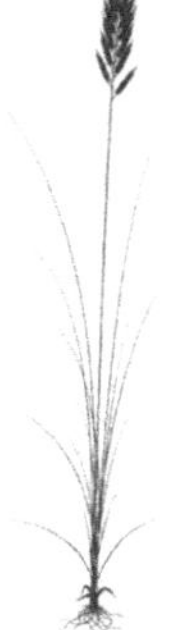

In 1889, the state legislature passed a bill that allowed for the creation of irrigation districts, although initially that authority was not widely used. The use of irrigation systems was initially condemned by many across the state. However, in 1891, a state irrigation conference was held, and the promotion of irrigation was dramatic. In fact, the use of irrigation jumped tenfold over the coming years.[52]

In 1894, the same year when John Cozad returned to Nebraska, irrigation ditches were dug by the Cozad Irrigation Company. For the first time since the original settlement in 1873, a reliable and consistent water source became widely available to farmers and thousands of acres became more productive. In 1894, there were a little more than ten miles of irrigation canals but by 1899 there were one hundred and eighty miles in place.[53]

Another result of the construction of the irrigation dams was the creation of the public power districts which used the water of the Platte for the generation of power. This, along with the creation of various lakes like Midway and Johnson, created recreation areas which later included second homes for the region's residents.[54]

But even with that significant achievement all was not bright. Statewide,

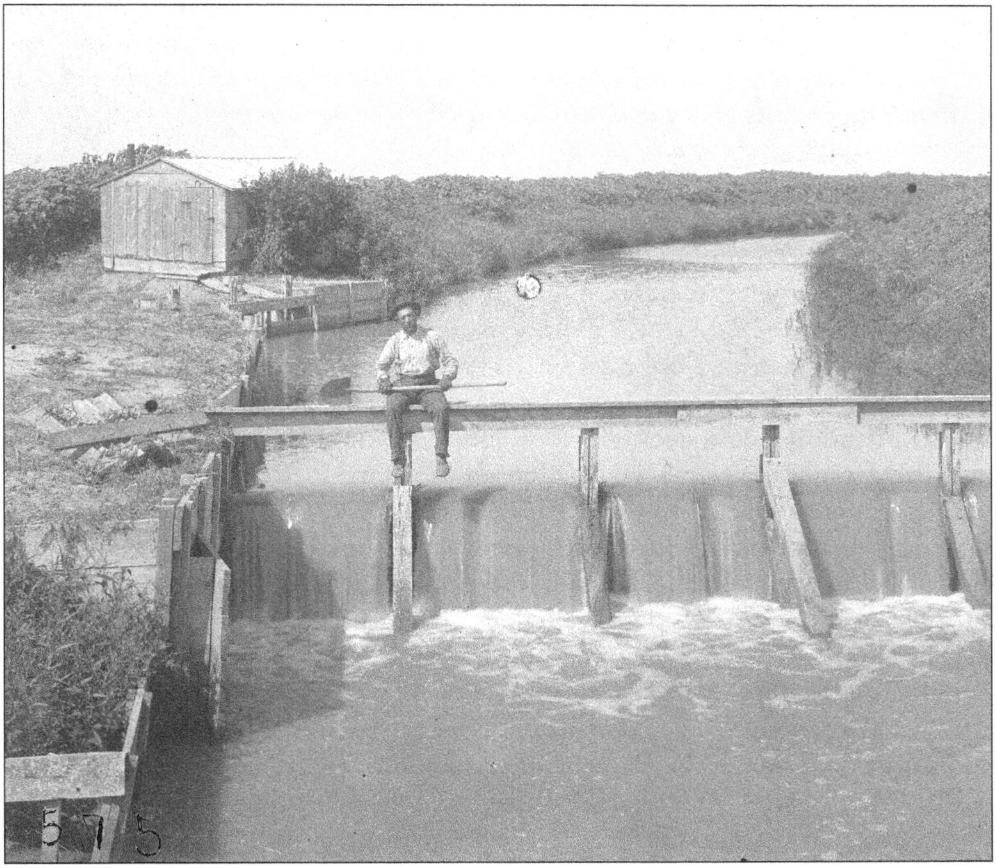

*Courtesy Library of Congress (Digital ID, nbhips 12036)*

*In 1894 the first irrigation canal was opened in Cozad to provide a steady source of water for farmers who had endured years of drought since 1873. This image by Nebraska photographer Solomon D. Butcher was taken in 1904.*

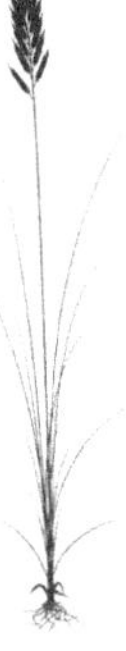

the late 1880s and 1890s were not good times as droughts swept across the state, most notably in central Nebraska. Many farmers were brought to financial ruin and unemployment rose precipitously. Things were so bad that famine threatened the state.[55]

## Destiny

For the Cozads, the dream of creating a new town that might become the county seat, and even the nation's capital at the 100th Meridian, was over. Like the efforts in Cozaddale, Denver and then Atlantic City, all had ended with disappointment and challenges. The properties that the Cozads owned in the Midwest and West were all ultimately sold along with the businesses.

Robert Gatewood wrote, perhaps reflecting on what he had heard from Cozad himself that:

*It was with genuine regret that Mr. Cozad gave up this project so dear to his heart – but his activities were so beset with difficulties and tragic interference, the final act, that of being compelled to kill a man. He was now in grave fear for the safety of his family and overwhelmed with determination to be away from it all forever, so he proceeded to change the family identity completely.*[56]

All of these developments forever changed the destiny of Cozad. When John Cozad was exonerated of murdering Alf Pearson, and returned to the city he had founded, he saw what the community might have become had fate and other factors not stepped in. Maybe it did not matter because by this time he was a successful businessman and real estate developer playing a part in the fast-growing and raucous Atlantic City. Perhaps he was satisfied that his vision had come to be, but the historical record does not reveal John Cozad's thoughts.

The community's strategic position on the Great Platte River Road and the grand corridor of America's westward expansion had, as John J. Cozad envisioned, proved to be a fortuitous one. The Union Pacific's operations, which had played such a critical role in the community's creation, continued to expand in the decades after the Cozads left. For more than three decades the railroad's main line was single track. Then in 1908, a second track was added.[57]

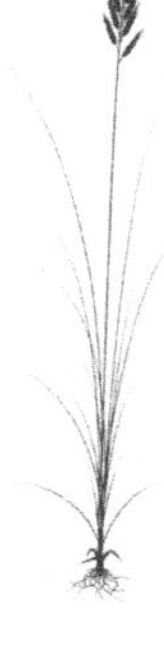

Because of the importance of the Union Pacific, three main lines running east to west were ultimately constructed to create one of the busiest railroad corridors in the nation. The largest railroad classification yard in the world lay to the west in North Platte. At one point three hundred trains passed through Cozad a day. [58] Mile long trains pass through town, day and night. This is all the more remarkable given than just one hundred and forty years ago, there was a single track stretching across the state with an occasional siding like the one in Cozad and limited service.

The access created by the railroad also allowed the diversification of the city

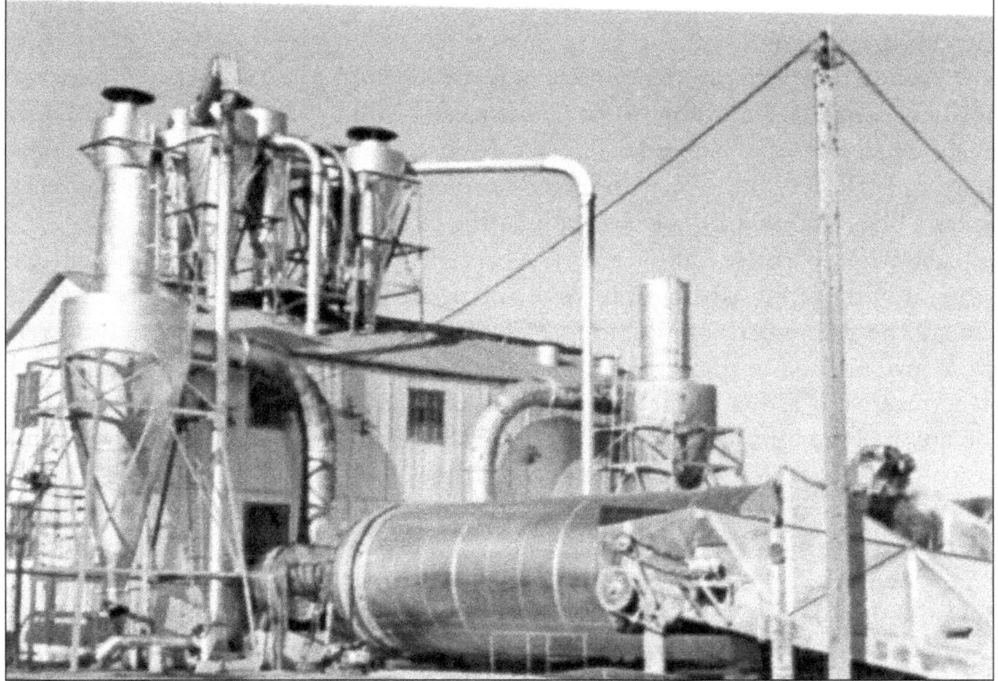


*Collection of the Robert Henri Museum and Art Gallery*

*Alfalfa Dehydration Plant, Cozad, Nebraska*

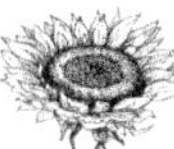

as it developed into a commercial center, whereas in its first five decades it had been primarily a small agricultural center serving farmers. With the increased and widespread use of automobiles, the business district adapted to a new customer base across a four-county region of Dawson, Lincoln, Frontier, and Gosper counties.[59] The construction of U.S. Route 30, and most importantly, Interstate 80, had a major impact on the development of the small city too.

When the Cozads arrived in 1873, 1,126,000 acres were harvested in the state and by the time Robert and Theresa left in 1884 that number had surged to 6,386,000 acres. John Cozad had been correct to invest in land and then to sell it off but also to reap the fruits of the plains in the form of his lucrative hay business. He had correctly seen the potential of Nebraska.

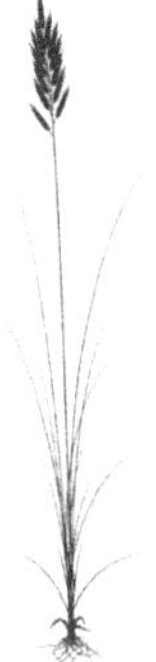

During the 1880s, Hans Anderson became one of the earliest farmers to grow alfalfa in Dawson County and he has traditionally been credited with being the first. However, at least three other farmers would claim that they had been first to grow the crop in the county.[60] Within decades it became an important crop in the region. Alfalfa, one established, could withstand droughts. After World War II, the agricultural community blossomed as four mills and dehydrating plants were built in Cozad and the community became the largest producer of alfalfa in the world.[61]

Another important development was the creation of a number of important business concerns including O. A. Cooper Feed Mills, F & S Sausage Company, Evans Frozen Foods, Nebraska Plastics, Monroe Automotive Equipment Company and Paulsen, Inc. Today, heritage tourism, and in particular, the interest in Robert Henri, plays an important role in the city's economy.[62]

As with so many towns on the Great Plains, the early twentieth century brought with it increased farm income and in the city itself a building boom that can still be seen when walking the streets. Beginning in the late 1890s, but even more pronounced in the early decades of the twentieth century, many residential structures were added to the inventory of homes. New additions were added to the north of the business district in the last years of the nineteenth century, several of which were created by the Gatewood family.

While Victorian era residences can still be found around the city today, much of the existing building inventory of houses reflects the popular Craftsman and Bungalow styles of the early twentieth century. That was brought to a halt with the agricultural depression of the 1920s in the aftermath of World War I and the Great Depression of the 1930s. In more recent decades, new houses have been built pushing the residential areas of the town to the north and beyond what John Cozad had planned.

Today, the business center is located within a district that is listed on the National Register of Historic Places. The oldest building within the district is the Atkinson Building located at 711-715 Meridian Avenue and constructed in 1890. The second oldest is the Brown and Bennison Building located at 746 Meridian Avenue. It was built in 1897. The business district entirely consisted of wood-framed structures in the Cozad era, but today's downtown is made up almost entirely of brick structures. Most of the buildings in today's historic district were built in early twentieth century. There are no commercial buildings remaining from the Cozad era aside from the Robert Henri Museum and the old Union Pacific station at 402 East 4th Street, although the date of its construction needs to be determined.[63]

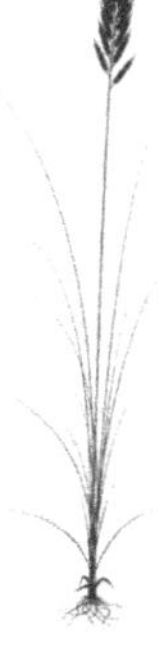

Two of the three buildings that the Cozads and Gatewoods were most associated with – the Robert and Julia Gatewood home and The Bee Hive store do not remain in their original locations. The Bee Hive was replaced by the Anderson Company's department store, which was then demolished. It was replaced by a beautiful Neo-Classical Revival styled building that still prominently stands on the corner at 801 Meridian Street. Built in 1917, it originally served as the Stockman's State Bank, and is now home to the law firm of Berreckman and Bazata, P. C. L.L.O. The Gatewood home was moved to 11th Street and still stands, although it was enlarged considerably in later years.[64]

The former Cozad home and hotel now serves as the headquarters for the Robert Henri Museum and is listed on the National Register of Historic Places. It is also occasionally referred to as the Hendee Hotel.[65]

In 1891, a handsome two-story brick school was erected that was a major enhancement to the city's educational resources. It replaced the brick building that John Cozad had originally built for the community in 1874-75.[66]

The population of the town, which had once dwindled to five families in the mid-1870s, has increased geometrically since then. *The Early History of the Cozad Community* relates that in 1876 the population of the town was five to six hundred people and that there were forty houses in the town. This information comes from files of *History Nebraska* in Lincoln, and probably actually represents a later date, perhaps the 1890s, or at the minimum may have included the larger Cozad Precinct as well.[67] In 1876, the town had just endured the plague of grasshoppers and a catastrophic fire, and many had left as a result. In the same article previously cited in *The Early History of the Cozad Community,* Sam Schooley stated that there were only ten families left in 1876.[68]

By 1881, only four men of the original group of thirty-six settlers were still there including John Cozad, C. W. Smith, A. T. Gatewood and Samuel Atkinson although one hundred and twenty-five votes had been cast in the Cozad Precincts.[69]

The figures that follow are probably more accurate, and the 1890 statistic may actually be the one cited by the community's history.

*Population of Cozad*

1876—80
1882 - 75
1890 – 542
1900 – 739
1910 – 1,096
1920 – 1,293
1930 - 1,813
1940 – 2,156
1950 - 2,910
1960 – 3,184
1970 – 4,219
1980 – 4,453
1990 – 3,823

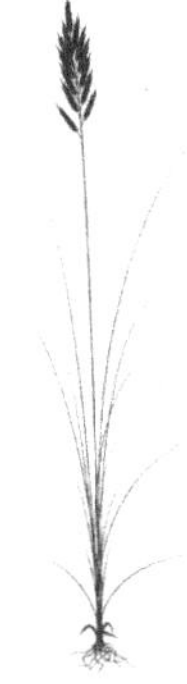

2000 – 4,163
2010 – 3,977
2019 – 3,735
2020 – 3,974 [70]

While John J. Cozad did not live to see all of these developments, by the time of his death, they were well underway. In one of those interesting coincidences, Cozad died in 1906, the same year that the Allen Opera House was built. It was erected by, and named for, the very same Charles Allen who had received a new and revised deed for his residential property from Cozad twenty-two years before. Today it is listed on the National Register of Historic Places and included within the historic district. After major renovations it is now home to a theater.[71]

Three of John Cozad's closest associates, David Claypool, Traber Gatewood and Sam Schooley all lived to see the former patch of prairie become an important commercial center for the area.

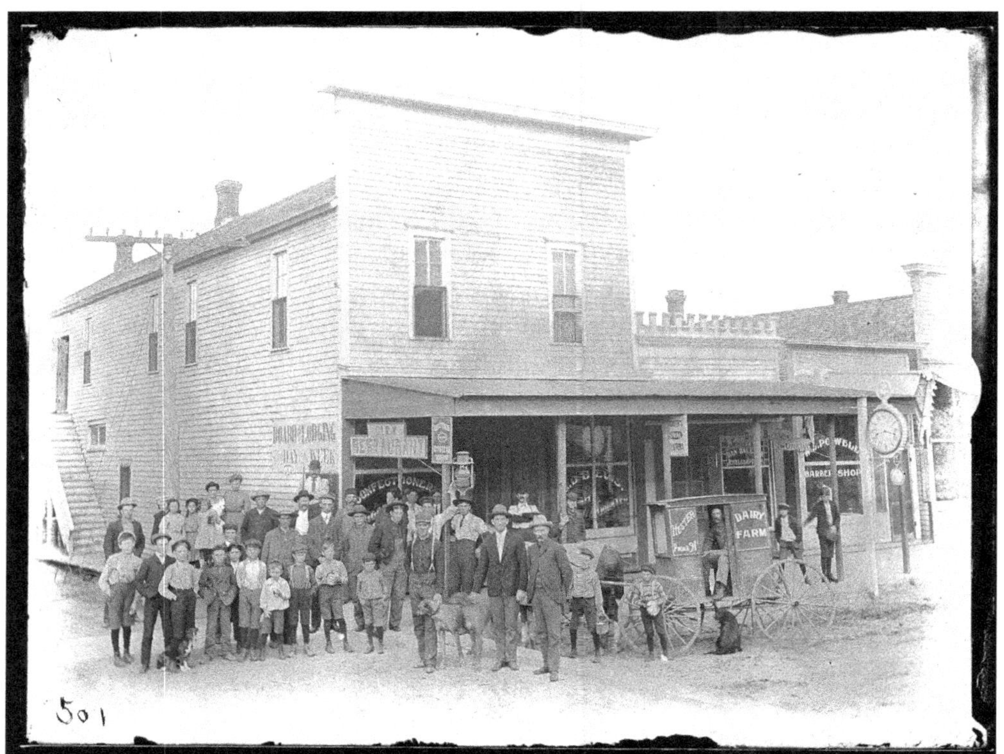


*Courtesy Library of Congress (Digital ID nbhips 13092)*

*This photograph by Nebraska photographer Solomon D. Butcher was taken in 1904 and is labeled "Oldest store building in Cozad, Nebraska, Dawson County, Nebraska." The Cozads had already been gone for more than twenty years.*

It is interesting to look back at the histories of the development of the communities of Plum Creek (now Lexington), Cozad, Willow Island and Gothenburg, all places that were created within ten years of each other. One must ask why Lexington remained the most important town in the county. Certainly, being the county seat was the critical factor, but it also had, during the early years, a bridge connecting it with the south side of the Platte River and the Republican Valley region. This remains among the most important reasons why it grew at such a rapid rate even during the same times that Cozad's settlers were facing similar difficulties and abandoning the Cozad Colony.

Another question that begs for an answer is whether it was because of John Cozad's influence, both good and bad, that the town that now bears his name, was not as important as the collective influence of the leaders of Plum Creek. Was it because as it is often described as *John Cozad's town* that others did not step into the development picture because he controlled so much of the community's destiny?

Perhaps his control of so much of the land caused that potential development to go elsewhere. Many who lived in that community were dependent on Cozad or were his family and close associates. They had a hand in numerous businesses, owned and leased properties in the town, and controlled, at least in the first few years, so much of the destiny of the Ohio Colony. Once Cozad was gone, the town's destiny moved in new directions.

That may have occurred because of land ownership. Initially, half of the land was owned by the railroad and the other was owned by the federal government, which wanted to see it be homesteaded. Maps show this checkerboard effect as the two entities owned alternate sections. In time, the homesteaders probably came to outnumber the purchasers of the railroad land, some of which had been purchased from Cozad or the railroad directly. Those who were loyal to Cozad, at least in the early years, ultimately were outnumbered by those who were not loyal to the founder or his vision and were coming out to begin creating a new home or to start new businesses.

What if he had had a different personality for example, like Stephen Hendee, who after purchasing the Cozad assets, was able to quickly bridge the Platte and have the county ultimately take over the ownership, something that Cozad tried to do and never accomplished after spending thousands of his own dollars. Hendee also remained active in the community for a much longer time and did not seem to have created the ill will that Cozad did. In the end however, the community was never able to overcome the advantages that Plum Creek had developed in those early years.

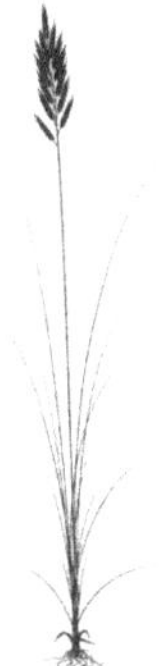

Willow Island never did develop beyond a very small hamlet, which is what Josiah Huffman wanted. He had never wanted to see settlers coming into the valley, just cattlemen. When the Cozads arrived, there was a small station, a couple of homes, a saloon, and general store.[72] It remains a modest settlement to this day. Gothenburg, formed in 1884, was built by emigrants from Sweden and others. While not as large as Cozad, it was able to develop a larger commercial district and construct its inventory of beautiful Victorian homes that reflected the growing and diversified economy. But unlike Cozad, there was not just one person who controlled so much of the community's destiny, at least in the early years.

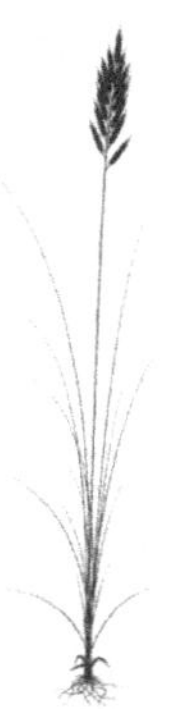

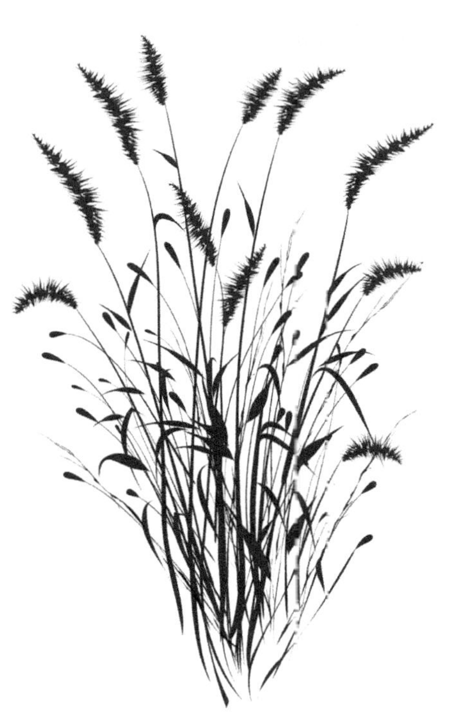

# Part II

# Unraveling the Henri Story

*We decided to respect their desire of secrecy until the last member of the family was gone. I think that now they would be happy that these things are being done.*[1]

*How satisfying it was to have the mystery solved at last.*[2]

Reveal True Story of John J. Cozad
The Cozad Local
1956

# *Chapter 1*

# Revealing The Cozad Story

*This story is . . . a most unusual one, and yearns for a Romantic Pen.*[3]
Richard Lee (John J. Cozad) to Jules Sandoz
1903

*Mr. Henri was a great teacher, a great painter, and in our opinion a great man.*[4]
Letter from Dolly Sloan to Robert Gatewood, 1931

THE REVEALING OF THE STORY OF THE DISAPPEARANCE of the Cozad family from central Nebraska and Colorado is a complicated one that took many twists and turns. It began with John J. and John A.'s abrupt departures in late 1882 and 1883 respectively, and Theresa and Robert's departure sometime in 1884. The story has traditionally been told that after the shooting of Alf Pearson, the entire family disappeared, went to Denver, and then arrived in Atlantic City in New Jersey with new identities a short time later. The museum's traditional interpretation was that they were never heard from again.

However, the shooting of the rancher in 1882 set off a complicated series of events that forced the family to take the drastic steps of settling their legal affairs quickly, divesting of their investments in Nebraska, Colorado and Ohio, probably at a loss, leaving their family and friends behind, and then reinventing themselves in the East, all while being done in secrecy. The consequences of some of those actions were still being litigated as late as the 1920s. A review of many of the documents and sources that remain also reveal conflicting stories and recollections.

### THE UNRAVELING OF THE HENRI STORY

Anyone wishing to know about Robert Henri's early biography prior to his death in 1929 would have been frustrated by the remarkable lack of any details about his boyhood and young adult years. There was nothing prior to 1884 that could be found in records or confirmed by research for example. Henri would say that he had been born to John and Theresa Henri in Cincinnati. An example of this comes from a book entitled *Robert Henri* which was included in the *Distinguished American Artists* series which stated that:

*Robert was born in Cincinnati in 1865. He comes of a family for many generations in America, the original stock being French, English and Irish. At first he thought that writing was his forte, but painting soon became the stronger attraction.*[5]

Also, he had a foster brother, Frank Southrn, and both had been adopted. Brother Frank was said to have been born in Mexico in 1858.

During his lifetime Henri would give vague accounts of his youth describing how he had traveled across the West, how he had gone to school in Cincinnati, Denver, and New York.[6] A researcher would have quickly been stymied, and in fact was, because of course he would have found nothing in the records prior to the family's sudden appearance in Atlantic City in 1884. Mari Sandoz said it best when she wrote about John Cozad:

*Unfortunately, he left his trail too shadowed and confused for the complete clarification . . .*[7]

The family's fabricated past, before their lives in Atlantic City began, disappeared from the records because there were no records. However, from that point forward there were records, and even more have come to light since.

For most residents of the small agricultural community of Cozad, the founder's whereabouts, albeit the quick reappearance in 1894, remained for the most part, although not entirely, a mystery until 1955-56. However, within the family and perhaps a close friend or two, the whereabouts of John and Theresa Cozad and their sons was known and remained a closely held secret. The family initially developed a way of communicating in which return addresses were not written on letters nor were identifying names or places used. It is not known if that tight circle of confidentiality was ever broken, although there is some evidence to suggest that it was on occasion.

This traditional account of the Cozad story states that families communicated in secret and did not leave a paper trail to be followed. According to one family member, Robert Gatewood (1885-1966), Theresa Cozad's nephew, the communications were between Robert Henri and Traber Gatewood. Letters were mailed on trains and said to be destroyed after being read.[8]

That said, the Robert Henri Museum and the Dawson County Historical Museum have in their possession transcriptions, copies or originals of some of the letters between family members during the period of the Cozad's exile which reveal that agreement appears not to have been entirely adhered to, as there are mentions of the Cozads in some of those letters. For example, at least one letter written by Traber Gatewood to his brother Van Burke in 1895 calls Robert Henri - *Bob Cozad.*[9]

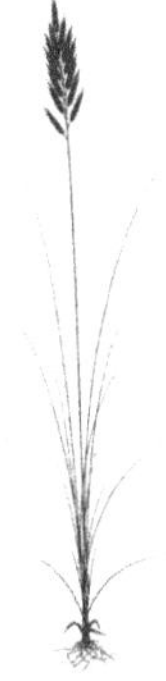

At least one correspondent, Mary Wake, a family friend, gave an accounting of how the family had hidden John Cozad's new life which she wrote in 1909, three years after his death:

*You ask if he (Traber Gatewood) knew of anything of Mrs. Cozad. He hears from them but never mentions Mr. or Mrs. Cozad to any one we know of. That trouble Mr. Cozad had in the early times of Cozad was a great misfortune, that Mr. Cozad never his whereabouts been known. When Traber and Debbie have been asked in times past anything about them they have always said they did not know. Grandma (Julia Gatewood) lived with them you know for several years, some six or seven years ago, neighbors would ask them about Grandma, how she was and where she was, but they would always say they did not know, so we quit asking. We were all surprised when Grandma came back as we supposed she would always stay with Mrs. Cozad. While I was writing letters for Grandma and reading her letters to her, she received only two or three from Mrs. Cozad, they did not come direct to her, they go to Traber and he sends them to Grandma, so the post mark is not known, there was just New York at the head of the letters. Mrs. Cozad wrote each time like she was very much distressed to have her Mother away from all her folks and living alone. She said how she wished she could come to her and how badly she felt that she couldn't. We don't see why she couldn't come there is a good deal that seem mysterious. It is supposed that Mr. C. thinks it is not safe for him to be in Cozad, on account of past threat. If he did not want to come I don't see what would hinder Mrs. C. when she wrote that she wanted to see her Mother so bad. Grandma used to go to Arapahoe occasionally then would hear if Traber had any news from them. Grandma told me before I left that Mr. Cozad was dead, but we think it is not so, I did not see any letter about it, neither did Mrs. Edwards.*[10]

## The Cozads Return

Another tradition is that the Cozads never returned to the town that had been the focus of so much of their effort. But there are several sources that have been uncovered that reveal that some of these traditions are simply incorrect and the history of the family's exile is a more complicated one than previously acknowledged.

As shown previously, John Cozad did return twice in 1894. However, he is not the only family member to have come back. Again, transcriptions of letters that are in the archives of Robert Henri Museum and the Dawson County Historical Museum demonstrate that. It is also known that Julia Gatewood, Theresa Cozad, Frank Southrn (*John A. Cozad*) and his wife Jane all came back to Cozad at least once. While there has been no evidence found to date that Robert Henri (*Robert Cozad*) ever returned, given these other visitations, one must wonder.

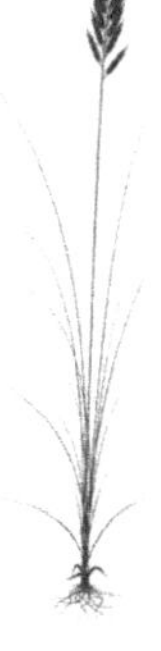

One of the traditions, for example, that has come down in time is that Theresa Gatewood Cozad and her mother Julia Gatewood never saw each other again after Theresa left Cozad. Sandoz implies that the family members never reunited and that has been the traditional interpretation that the museum has offered visitors.[11] However, that is simply not correct. It is known Julia Gatewood did indeed travel back and forth to the East from Nebraska.

On June 13, 1900, a federal census worker recorded that in the 3rd Precinct in Atlantic City there resided a Richard Henry Lee, Ress Lee (probably misspelled) and Julia Gaitwood (also probably misspelled) together. Richard Lee was recorded as being a *Retired Real Estate and Broker*. Gaitwood is recorded as the mother-in-law and is eighty-three years old although that is a different age than what is recorded elsewhere. Neither she nor her daughter have any listed occupation and she was credited with having a total of five children, three of whom were still alive.[12]

A 1905 note from Julia to Mollie Gatewood, Van Burke's wife revealed that at that time, Julia was staying in Cozad.[13] By 1908 she was in Arapahoe, Nebraska living in a new house that Traber and Debbie Gatewood had recently built.[14] As late as 1907, Julia Gatewood still owned properties in Cozad and consulted with Sam Schooley about them as he collected rents for her. Julia died in Cozad in 1909.[15]

Another family member visit to Cozad also occurred in November 1895 when Dr. Frank Southrn (*John A. Cozad*) and his wife, Dr. Jane Southrn arrived in Cozad to take Julia Gatewood back East to live with her daughter, Theresa. Dr. Jane had brought five thousand dollars of diamonds with her which was noted in a letter from Traber Gatewood to Van Burke Gatewood. While in Cozad for one week, Southrn settled his grandmother's debts and then visited Deborah and Traber Gatewood at their home south of Cozad before returning home. Interestingly, as the letter states:

*. . . they were all received out here.*[16]

Deborah in her diary stated that John J. Cozad came back to Cozad twice, although she does not provide any information as to what the dates were, but it must have been after the 1894 dropping of the charges against him and was probably the time that John J. Cozad is known to have returned to try and resolve his real estate problems to his favor.[17]

Other examples of the various family members staying in close contact include Theresa Cozad living in New York with Robert and Marjorie Henri after John J. Cozad died there in 1906.[18] She returned to Cozad on at least one occasion, in August 1910, when she stayed with the Schooleys, their old family friends and Mrs. Richard Mansfield, David Claypool's daughter. She had come back it is believed to settle her mother's estate. That visit would later be recalled in the obituary for Sam Schooley in 1941.[19] In 1916, as a stop on one of her trips that she continued to make, Theresa returned to Cozaddale as well.[20]

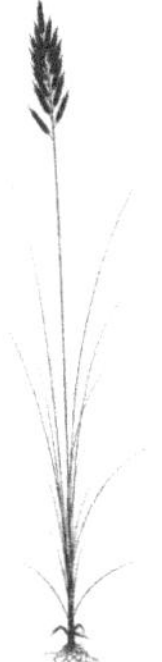

On March 30, 1911, Theresa appointed John Dryden, of Kearney with her power of attorney, to dispose of lands that she still owned in Cozad. As late as 1916, Theresa was still in possession of properties in Cozad under her mother's name, residual from Julia's estate. Prior to her death she had owned extensive property holdings.[21]

Clara Riggs, the wife of the former manager of the hotel, is said to have maintained their friendship even after the Cozads left Nebraska. Clara saw her old friend when she came back to Cozad, apparently on multiple visits long after the 1880s and gave expensive wedding gifts to the two Riggs daughters. Clara believed that she knew the assumed name of Theresa Cozad and thought that John J. Cozad had actually taken the name of Zane Grey.[22]

### Faded Memories

As the decades passed, the tragic events of the fall of 1882 faded in the memory of the town and people associated with them. Members of the various families associated with the Cozads left the area or died. By the time the first revelations about the Cozad family became widely known in 1955, the original generation of families who had settled Cozad with John and Theresa Cozad were all gone.

John Cozad (*Richard Lee*) (1830-1906) died of pneumonia in New York on December 15, 1906, at the age of seventy-six, less than a year before the Panic of 1907 began. There were some in Cozad who believed he had actually died in 1896.[23] Initially he was buried in Pleasantville, New Jersey, just west of Atlantic City. Ten years later he was cremated, and reinterred on May 17, 1916, at the Swan Point Cemetery in Providence, Rhode Island where his oldest son Frank Southrn and his wife, Jane had a family plot.[24]

Theresa Cozad (*Tessa Lee*) (1836-1923) died on February 15, 1923, in Philadelphia at the age of eighty-seven.[25] She had been living in New York City in an apartment with her husband until his death, then lived for a short time with Robert, and then went back to Atlantic City. She later returned to New York and moved into an apartment with Robert and Marjorie at 10 Gramercy Park for the last two years of her life and was where she died.[26]

She is believed to have been buried initially in Calvary Cemetery in Woodside, Queens, New York, and later moved to the Swan Point Cemetery after being cremated and placed there with her husband's cremains. Why Theresa Cozad was not buried with her husband initially is not known, perhaps it was simply a matter of practicality. Theresa and John had lived in Atlantic City until at least 1900, and then lived in several different locations after that.[27] There are no monuments or inscriptions on the Southrn monument or plot commemorating their lives in Rhode Island.

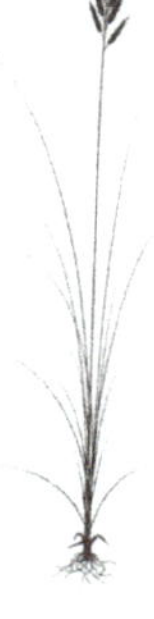

Robert Henri (1865-1929) died in New York City on July 12, 1929, was cremated, and initially placed at the New York and New Jersey Crematory the following day. One year later, on June 13, 1930, he was buried at the Swan Point Cemetery. It had long been his wish to be cremated. Even in death, his father's identity was hidden and is recorded as John Henri and having been born in Virginia.[28]

Henri married his first wife, Linda Fitzgerald Craige (1875-1905), on June 2, 1898, in Ashbourne, Pennsylvania. A former student, Linda died on December 8, 1905, in New York City and was buried in her family's plot in the prestigious Laurel Hill Cemetery in Philadelphia, Pennsylvania.[29]

Henri and his second wife, Marjorie Organ Henri (1886-1930), had married on May 5, 1908, in Elizabeth, New Jersey. She was a groundbreaking cartoonist in New York City, began taking lessons from Robert and later served as a partner in his career. Marjorie died of cancer on July 5, 1930 and was cremated. Initially her cremains were buried at the Fresh Pond Crematory in Queens, New York. It is not known if her cremains were sent to Swan Point as there are no records of her burial there.[30] There are no monuments or inscriptions on the Southrn monument or plot. [31]

Violet Organ, Robert Henri's sister-in-law, was the executor of the Henri estate from 1930 until her passing in 1959. She had been managing the estate and had even helped William Homer as he was preparing the first major biography of Robert Henri. Much of Homer's second chapter of *Robert Henri and his Circle of Friends* was taken from Violet Organ's unpublished biography of Henri written between 1930 and 1959.[32] While she certainly could have discussed with Robert Henri the family's checkered past, and much of the material in that chapter can be verified, the question remains as to how much Henri would have revealed to her, or how much he would have even known or remembered of his father's quick departure from Cozad in 1882 at least fifty years before.

Robert's older brother, John A. Cozad (*Frank Southrn)* (1863-1933), married Jane Jenks (1856-1937) on October 30, 1891. It is not known if Jane knew about John's checkered past but because she had come with him to Nebraska in 1895, she must have been given some accounting of the story, especially when people called her husband *Johnny*. Frank and his wife traveled widely during their marriage and on one of their trips even went back to Cincinnati which included a stop at Chickering, his former school which had been turned into a Jewish synagogue. In other trips he met old friends.[33]

Both were medical doctors, Southrn had graduated from the Thomas Jefferson Medical School in Philadelphia in 1889, and Jenks graduated from the Woman's Medical College of Philadelphia, then both prominent medical institutions. Southrn had specialized in gynecology and pediatrics and Jenks in pediatrics. They had met at an almshouse while doing their respective internships. Jenks was a member of the prominent Jenks family with ties to New York, New Jersey, Pennsylvania, New England and the famed Clarke Thread Company.[34]

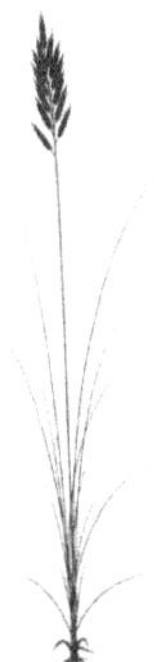

Having first resided in Atlantic City and Southrn having served on its City Council, they moved to the exclusive area called West Philadelphia for several years, and then lived at *The Normandie* in Philadelphia and finally at the *Ben-*

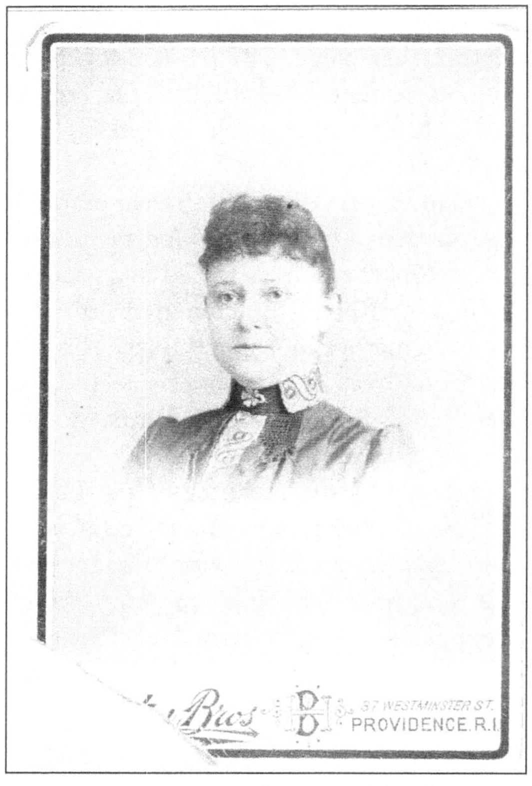


Courtesy 100th Meridian Museum
*Jane Southrn*
*March 6, 1891*

*jamin Franklin Hotel*. Frank Southrn (1858-1933), died on August 7, 1933, in Philadelphia at seventy-four years of age. Even in death his Nebraska identity was hidden as revealed by his death certificate. His birth date is listed as November 29, 1858, and birthplace was shown as Mexico. His father is listed as Frank L. Southrn.[35]

By the marriage there was a daughter, Jennie (1892-1915) who was sickly during her life and died of leukemia in Philadelphia on January 25, 1915. Both she and Frank were cremated and buried at Swan Point Cemetery in marked graves in the northeastern corner of the large cemetery.[36]

Frank's wife Jane (1856-1937) was one of the last living family members of that generation who might have had some direct knowledge of the fateful activities of the late fall of 1882 and the subsequent disappearance of the rest of the family from Nebraska. She had visited Cozad at least once in 1895. However, like most of those who surrounded the Cozad family, it is likely she had only a vague understanding of what had happened since the Cozads wanted to eliminate their past in such a thorough way. She may have never known about her husband's alleged arson charges. By the end of her life, she was blind. Jane died on July 9, 1937, at the age of eighty-one in Philadelphia and is also buried at Swan Point in a marked grave in the family plot. The bequests in her will were substantial and funded projects for children's diseases and health, the physically handicapped and the blind.[37]

As a result of these sets of circumstances, there are no Cozads (or former Cozads) buried in the town's cemetery located to the east of the town that they had created and in whose development they had so much invested in.

The connection to Rhode Island is a curious one but is a result of the fact that Jane Jenks Southrn was originally from Central Falls, Rhode Island, a small city just north of Providence, the capital of the state. Her family had long been prominent there, and in fact, Jenks Park, a beautiful and centrally located historic

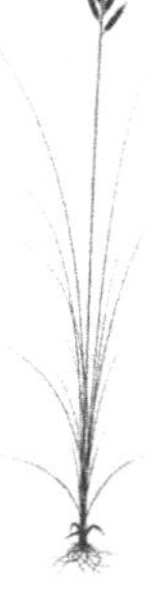

site in the community, was gifted by her father Alvin Jenks (1828-1900).[38]

As to the related families, the story is the same. Theresa Gatewood Cozad's parents remained in Cozad in the immediate aftermath of the Pearson tragedy. Robert Gatewood (1807-1884), Theresa's father, and an original settler of the Cozad Colony and a grocery business owner in the town, died in Cozad on July 8, 1884, at the age of seventy-seven.[39] The shocking events which his greater family had been a part of were still a recent memory.

Robert's wife, Julia Ann Jones Gatewood (1813-1909), who had cooked with her daughter for the guests staying in the Cozad's hotel, died on July 18, 1909, at the age of ninety-five. She had continued to travel and maintain property investments in Cozad, and late in life, had even started smoking. She was affectionately called Grandma Gatewood.[40]

There is some discrepancy as to where she died as one source says Arapahoe and another says Cozad.[41] Both spouses are buried in the northwestern corner of the Cozad Cemetery, the oldest section of the buryial ground.[42] By this marriage there were five children only three of whom survived to adulthood: Van Burke Gatewood (1836-1903), Theresa (1837-1923), and Alexander Traber (1852-1928).[43]

Van Burke Gatewood, the oldest of the three children, married twice, the first time to Rachel (1841-1871), and together they had three children: Julia, Teresa, and John. By his second marriage to Marie (1847-1910), there were three daughters, Segus, Antoinette (Nettie), Sioux and a son, Early, along with an adopted son, Frank Hudson. Van Burke was a medical doctor as was his adopted son, Frank. Early was a dentist. The father died in St. Louis, Missouri where his first wife was originally from, and he and his two wives are buried in the Reed Cemetery, in Halfway, Missouri.[44]

Alexander (A.T.)Traber Gatewood (1852-1928) was among the first group of permanent colonists to come to the Cozad Colony. He had been so close to John J. Cozad in Cincinnati that he had gambled with him and even played cards for Cozad when he was banned from an establishment. A dentist by profession, he was married in 1884 to Deborah Burgess (1867-1950). They had five children: Robert (1885-1966), Iva May (1889-1940), Theresa (1894-1966), Traber Gatewood (1898-1944), and Van Gatewood (1901-1978).

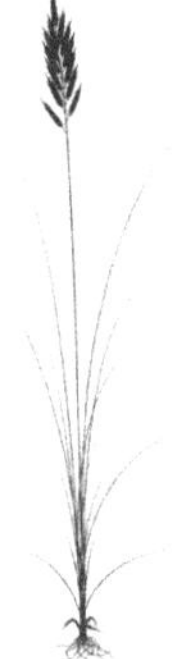

Traber and Deborah and their family left Cozad in 1889 and moved to Arapahoe, and then in 1900, went to McCook, Nebraska.[45] It is here where the parents died and are buried. With Deborah's death in 1950 the last member of that founding generation who were related to the Cozad family had died. She had been living in Denver.

Traber dealt most directly with the Cozads and was the most intimate with their various troubles, along with those of John Gatewood. However, Deborah also knew about the family's closely held secrets . She also had decided opinions

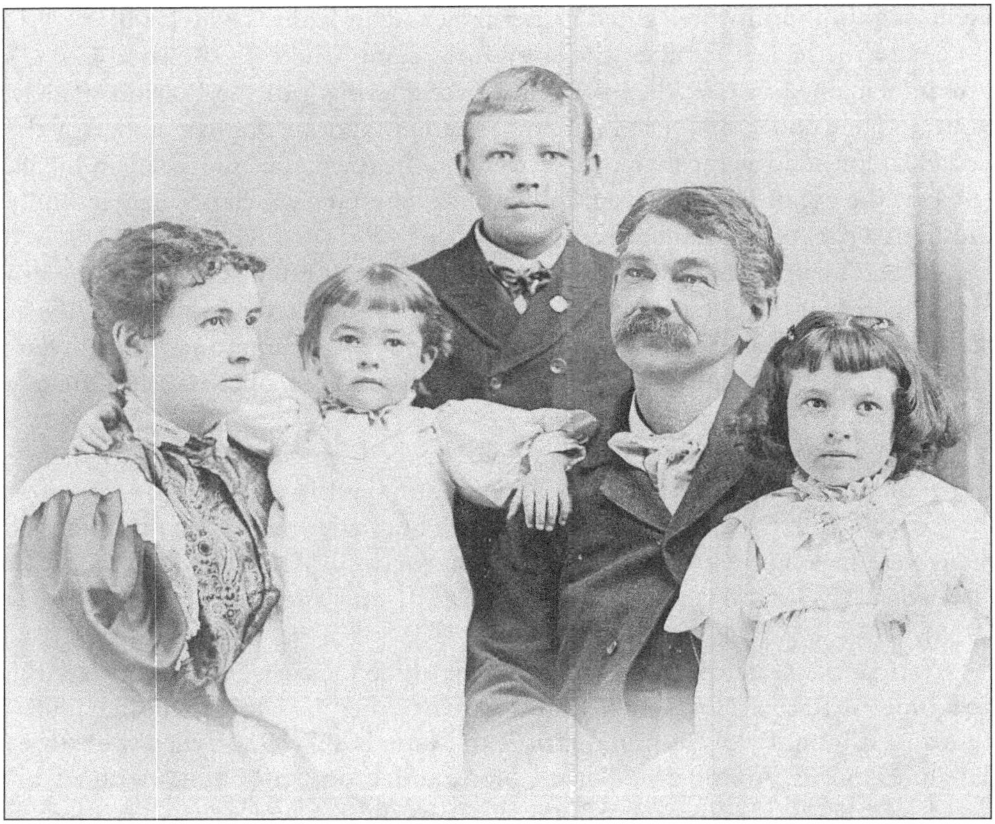

Courtesy 100th Meridian Museum

*The Traber Gatewood family in 1897. From left to right - Deborah, Iva, Robert, Traber, and Theresa. Traber was a close ally of John Cozad and one of the first settlers to arrive with the Cozad Colony in 1873. Deborah Gatewood wrote an autobiography that provides important insights into the Cozad and Gatewood families.*

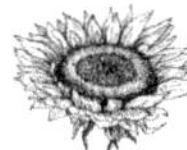

about them, as depicted in her autobiography, of which the Robert Henri Museum owns a photocopy. Her diary, as she called it, provides insights into the Cozads and their troubles but also reveals several family disputes with Julia Gatewood and John A. Cozad.[46]

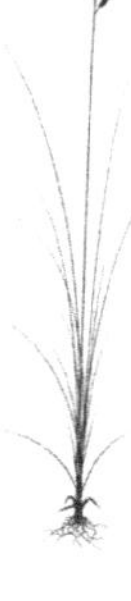

She wrote that after A.T. had helped the Cozads settle their legal challenges from 1882:

*He was all enthusiasm over his prospects. He thought the Cozads were going to offer him after he succeeded in freeing them from the legal mess they were in, Sam (Schooley) was a great help in this. His knowledge of law was at AT's command. He (Sam Schooley) told me the last time I saw him that they never paid him for his services and he had even paid his own expenses. I suppose as usual that they thought it was up to AT, the family Santa Claus, to pay their lawyers, anyway, they did not pay him. Though with his help they were finally freed and their names dropped from the criminal docket of Dawson County. The financial help and backing that AT was counting on with so much confidence was only another smoke dream. He also was out cash as well as his time. Well this is enough of the Cozads. This is not a story of their prowess . . . His generosity toward all his relatives was incredible. There was never anything left for his wife and children. It was amazing to say the least.*[47]

However, at some time after that, Traber Gatewood and John Cozad had an irreparable break that was not resolved at the time of John's death. Traber Gatewood would write to his sister Theresa:

*I loved him and was always true to him. Yet he allowed others to poison his mind against me, his best friend.*[48]

All Traber and Deborah's children ultimately moved out of Nebraska. Robert Gatewood (1885-1966), their oldest child, however, would come to play a critical role in the unveiling of the Cozad family secret to the public, just five years after his mother died.[49] Whoever was left of the succeeding generations may have heard the stories at family gatherings or in correspondence, but none of the major players of that first generation, with detailed knowledge of the entire sordid business, now survived.

The Claypool family, another of the original colonists who came to central Nebraska, and were friends of the Cozads, were also gone. David Claypool (1841-1923), a local businessman and close associate of John J., died in 1923 and is buried in the Cozad Cemetery. Mary Clark Claypool (1842-1873), his first wife, died in September 1873 as did her son, Henry E., a day after his mother. A monument for Mary is in the far northwestern corner of the Cozad Cemetery. She and her son are the earliest burials and located adjacent to the fence next to the irrigation ditch. It is believed that their remains were disturbed when the ditch was originally dug.[50]

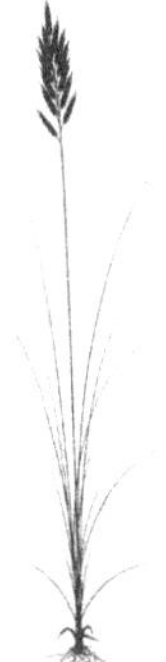

His second and third wives, Mary Hensel and Orpha Myers, were also gone, Orpha dying in 1936. His children by marriage were Mattie I. Claypool (1866-1950) and Robert Claypool (1856-1907) both died in Cozad and are buried in the Cozad Cemetery.

Samuel Schooley (1852-1941) and his wife Ella (1859-1942) both lived in Cozad and remained pillars of the community long after those events of 1882-84 and are buried in the Cozad Cemetery. They had one child who died in infancy.[51] It is believed that Schooley, a close family friend, escorted Robert and Theresa Cozad on their final journey out of Cozad in 1884 after the final legal documents turning the family's properties over to Stephen Hendee and his partners were signed. It was said that Sam Schooley knew John Cozad better than anyone else.[52] Theresa would stay at the Schooley home upon her return to Cozad in 1910.

With the passing of so many of the main figures who had been witness to the events or knew of them, involved with getting the family safely out of Cozad, assisting them afterwards or having heard the stories from those people, it now became possible for someone, like a second-generation family member, who had a detailed and intimate knowledge of what had happened, to reveal the entire story. It would be an important achievement for whomever first revealed the story given Robert Henri's international fame as an artist and art instructor.

How the saga became public is a complicated story and involved a number of well-known and important people, including Robert Henri's best friend, John Sloan; a well-known artist, Van Wyck Brooks (1886-1963), a biographer of Sloan; Mari Sandoz (1896-1966), the important Nebraska author; her father, Jules Sandoz (1858-1928), made famous by her book *Old Jules,* published in 1935. There was also Dr. Robert Gatewood (1885-1966), a member of the extended Cozad family, a son of Traber and Deborah Gatewood, a nephew to John and Theresa Cozad, and cousin to Robert Henri. He would come to be one of the most important figures in this saga.

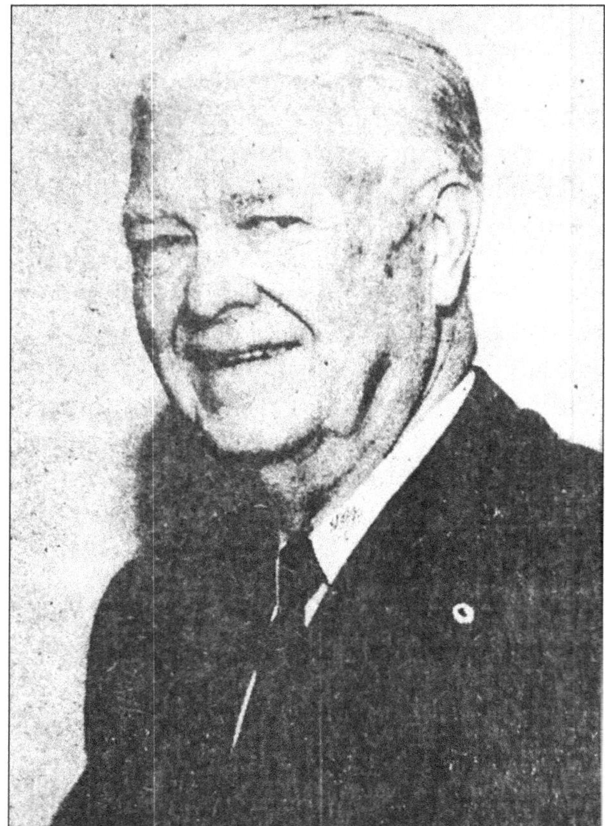

*Collection of the Robert Henri Museum and Art Gallery*
*Dr. Robert Gatewood*

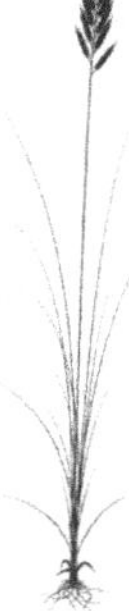

Dr. Gatewood was a well-known dentist from Las Vegas, Nevada and married to Bess Payne (1889-1969). By this marriage there were two children, a son, Robert P. and a daughter, Joan (1925-2016), who later married John Miller. Joan would also come to play an important role in revealing additional insights into the Cozad story and making a major contribution to the preservation of it.

Robert Gatewood had led an eventful life after having grown up in Cozad. He graduated from Northwestern University in 1906 and had a dental practice in McCook, Nebraska for twenty-five years along with being active in civic organizations. There he had also been the president of the city council. Then he moved to and practiced in Boulder City, Nevada, finally relocating and establishing a practice in Las Vegas. Gatewood also served in the Army in World War I.[53]

Gatewood's favorite subject was history, including that of Nebraska and Nevada, and played a considerable role in the revealing of the Cozad story. Most significantly, Gatewood had created an outline form of John J. Cozad's life and had even written two chapters for a proposed book tentatively entitled, *Who Was Robert Henri?* The manuscript was dated September 20, 1932, and provided the first Gatewood and Cozad accounts of their remarkable history. It had never been published.[54]

### The Need for a Romantic Pen

In the introduction of her book *Son of the Gamblin' Man*, Mari Sandoz (1896-1966) wrote that Richard Lee, the former John Cozad, and Jules Sandoz (1858-1928), her father, began to correspond in 1903 about a project that Lee was thinking about which included creating a new community and land development along a new rail branch line for the Short Line Railroad. The company was proposing to run track northward to the Black Hills in South Dakota through the Sand Hills and up the Survey Valley.[55]

The proposed rail line had long been the dream of many. In the late 1880s, the Burlington and Missouri River Railroad and the Atchison, Topeka Railroad and the Santa Fe Railroad had all considered connecting with the Union Pacific at Plum Creek. The Santa Fe also looked at extending its line clear north to the Black Hills. A fifth railroad also considered passing through Lexington, that would connect Duluth, Minnesota, with Pueblo, Colorado in the early 1890s.[56]

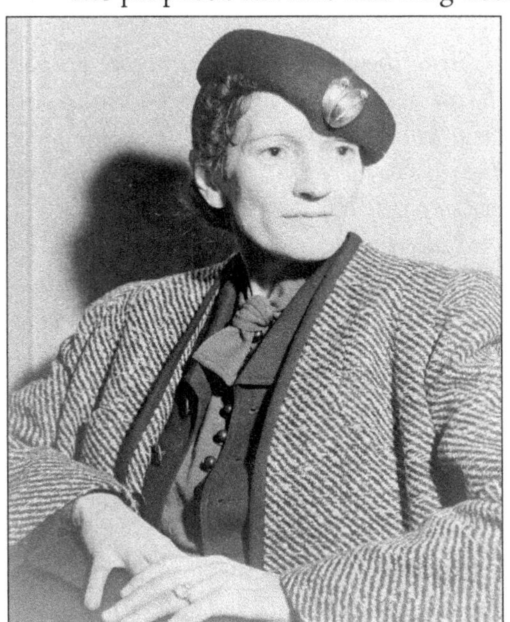

*Courtesy Library of Congress (Control Number 97502047)*
*Mari Sandoz*

During the course of this correspondence Lee proposed the need for the writing of his family's story.[57] He suggested that their family's story was a most:

> *. . . unusual one and yearns for a Romantic Pen.*[58]

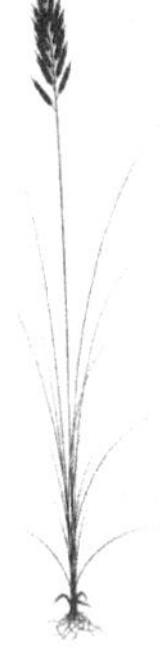

It is worth remembering that Mari Sandoz was not yet the famous author that she would become in the decades to come. In fact, her first short story was not even published until April 26, 1908, in the *Omaha Daily News* when she was twelve years old.[59]

However, in the correspondence, Lee, who was then living in New York City, relayed the fact that his son was the painter, Robert Henri. Letters between them discussed new legislation that called for six hundred-forty-acre homesteads, a bill that passed in 1904 and was called the Kinkaid Act, after its sponsor Moses Kinkaid of Nebraska.[60] It is not clear what, if anything, happened of their plans, but just three years later, John Jackson Cozad was dead. One can only wonder what Tessa Lee would have thought about starting over again in Nebraska.

Twenty-two years later, on November 13, 1928, Jules Sandoz (1858-1928) died. He is buried in the Alliance Cemetery in Alliance, Nebraska along with his fourth wife, Mary Elizabeth Fehr (1867–1938), who died on August 19, 1938.[61] The letters between Lee and Jules Sandoz presumably came into Mari's possession at some point.

## The Unraveling Begins

In a November 11, 1940, letter to Paul Hoffman, Mari Sandoz recalled how her involvement with the Cozad story began. Sandoz revealed that through a mutual artist acquaintance Dr. Robert Gatewood had learned of Sandoz's interest in the Cozad story. According to the letter she wrote that:

*Now that the family is almost gone and one of the few who remain wrote me last year (having discovered through something I said to a mutual artist friend that I had inadvertently stumbled upon part of the story) and offered me the family's complete cooperation if I would write up the story with my characteristic frankness and feeling for lusty livers coupled with my strong interest in painting.*

*While I realize that this story might go to pieces completely upon a thorough investigation, I suspect from my knowledge of the locales and the period, that it wouldn't. I could attempt this between the Indian books, or any one of half a dozen other books that have been simmering in my mind.*[62]

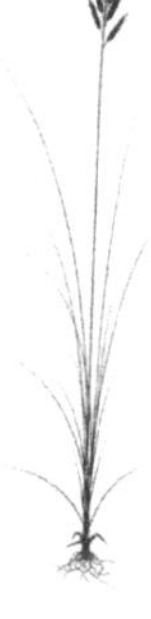

In her letter to Hoffman, she outlined what she knew of the story, although a number of details she presented were factually incorrect. For example, Sandoz in her letter had suggested that John Cozad had shot a man in Denver, returned to Cozad, and then disappeared.[63]

Apparently the first contact between Gatewood and Sandoz began with Gatewood's search for an author to write a book about the Cozad story the previous year. Sandoz wrote a letter to him on August 5, 1939, following up on a conversation she had had with a Mrs. Leary about a *Cozad mystery* as she described it.[64] Gatewood admired her work having read *Slogum House* and *Old Jules* and her description of early Nebraska.[65] Gatewood had been looking for a writer who could relay the remarkable story to the public. He was then living in Las Vegas, Nevada.[66]

Ms. Sandoz suggested that a different author would better be able to tell the story than herself. But she wrote, she could not recommend one. She suggested that if Gatewood was still looking for an author in 1942, by the time she would be done with several books that she was working on, she would be willing to discuss it again with him. She wrote that:

*Nothing of this story will get out through me. I realize how important secrecy in this matter is – in addition to the ethical compunctions I would naturally feel.*[67]

Unfortunately, they never corresponded again and in fact, almost got into a legal dispute over the information that had been shared when her book came out twenty-one years later.[68] It is not known why they did not continue to communicate because as Robert Gatewood's daughter, Joan Gatewood Miller, would relate three decades after the Sandoz book was published, the information that her father had was much more exciting than what was included in *The Son of the Gamblin' Man*.[69]

Robert Gatewood felt that Sandoz had in fact stolen his information or at least did not feel that Sandoz had shown enough interest in what he had revealed to her, or perhaps some other event intervened. Joan Miller clearly believed that Sandoz had plagiarized her father's work. There was a belief in the family that Gatewood would hold off publishing a book he was writing until a later time.[70] For her part, Sandoz may have felt at some point that she had enough material to work with based on her own extensive research that she had completed and her own knowledge of Nebraska history.

By 1942 she had finished *Crazy Horse: The Strange Man of the Oglala's*, and then began preliminary work on a potential book about the Cozad mystery. Between 1942-43 Mari Sandoz came to Cozad and Lexington to do research. She undertook an investigation into archival materials, legal records, letters and interviewed people including those who knew the Cozads. During her interviews, she felt a reluctance on the part of those she was talking with to reveal the story.[71]

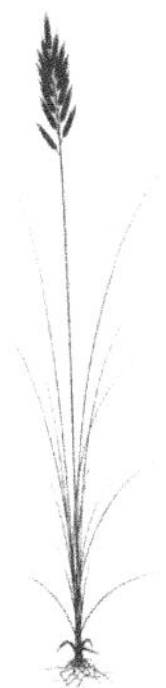

In the years that followed she finished a number of articles, short stories, and books including *The Tom-Walker*, *Miss Morissa: Doctor of the Gold Trail*, *The Buffalo Hunters: the Story of the Hide Men*, *The Cattlemen: From the Rio Grande*, *The Horsecatcher*, and worked on *Love Song to the Plains* and *The Story Catcher*.[72] Even as she completed those projects, she worked on and off on the Cozad book between 1942-1960.

## The Tipping Point

The mid-1950s proved to be the tipping point for the revelation of the Cozad story to the public. The first significant development occurred when a biography of John Sloan (1871-1951) was published in February 1955. Entitled *John Sloan: A Painter's Life,* it was written by Van Wyck Brooks (1886-1963), a well-regarded American author. Among Brooks' previous books were, *The Ordeal of Mark Twain* (1920), *The Flowering of New England, 1815-1865* (1936) for which he won the Pulitzer Prize and *Makers and Finders: A History of the Writer in America, 1800-1915* (1952).

Sloan had been Robert Henri's oldest and dearest friend, a fellow artist and to whom Henri had entrusted the family's most guarded secrets although he was vague about the details. This may have been a function of poor memory or purposeful blurring. Dolly (1876-1943), Sloan's first wife, wrote after Henri's death, that Theresa Cozad, who was a close friend of the Sloans, had told her the entire story about the Nebraska chapter of their lives when Henri married Marjorie Organ.[73]

In the Sloan biography, written after his death in 1951, Robert Henri's ties to Nebraska and the Cozad story were revealed to a national audience for the first time. There was only one paragraph in Chapter II of the Van Wyck Brooks book entitled *Henri and His Circle*, but it laid out, in a very general way, along with a minor error, what had happened to the Cozad family.[74] Because of the book's initial popularity, a second printing was undertaken just one month later in March 1955.

There is some dispute about how Brooks obtained the information about Henri's connection to Nebraska which was included in his book. Joan Gatewood Miller, a grandniece of Theresa Gatewood Cozad, wrote a letter to Rex German and Elma Johnson, two members of the Robert Henri Museum, in 1996, and offered one possibility. She wrote that her father, Dr. Robert Gatewood (1885-1966), had written an outline form of John Cozad's life and two chapters for a future book entitled, *Who Was Robert Henri?*. It was dated September 20, 1932 and had never been published.[75]

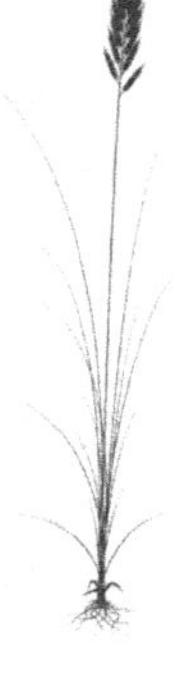

At the suggestion of Dolly Sloan, Gatewood sent his manuscript to a New York City publisher for review. Miller suggested that Sloan's wife had kept a copy of the manuscript. Perhaps this was the source of Brooks' information for the biography.[76] There are other Gatewood items in the John Sloan Manuscript Collection at the Delaware Art Museum, but the dentist's manuscript is not listed among them.[77] (*A copy of Dr. Gatewood's manuscript is however, located in the papers of William Homer, Robert Henri's biographer, also at Delaware Art Museum.*[78]) Dolly Sloan would later claim that Theresa Gatewood Cozad had told her the entire story of the Cozad family drama which Joan Gatewood Miller disregarded entirely.[79]

The information that Brooks had used may have also come from Helen Sloan (1911-2005), John Sloan's second wife, whom he married in 1944. Or, perhaps it had come from other information contained within Sloan's papers that were presumably in her possession. (*The John Sloan Manuscript Collection at the Delaware Art Museum in Wilmington, Delaware was not donated until 1978.*) Near the end of his life, John Sloan (1871-1951) deposited a three-hundred-fifty-page unpublished manuscript, now entitled *John Sloan Notes*, at the Delaware Art Museum reminiscing about the famous people he had known during his lifetime, including Henri. He had done this at the urging of his wife Helen. The Sloan biographer would have found that manuscript in the museum's archives during his research.[80]

Another possibility is that Eulabee Dix Becker, an American miniaturist painter, who in writing her memoir, described literary and cultural gatherings at *Petitpas*, a New York City restaurant. Those included Robert Henri, John Sloan, John B. Yeats and Van Wyck Brooks. Some of that information might have been gathered at one of those meetings, perhaps after Henri had died.[81] No matter how Brooks came by the information, and in fact all of the accounts may be correct in some form, the story was now public.

Finally, there is a curious reference in the Sloan biography that Henri made no secret of the family's problems and that he was proud of his past. Perhaps this happened after John Cozad died in 1906, when there were no more potential ramifications to the story getting out. On this count, more research needs to be done.

## The True Story

The next important development occurred in late 1955 and proved to be most fortuitous to the telling of the Cozad story. In this case, it occurred in the community that John Cozad had founded. *The Early History of the Cozad Community and Surrounding Communities,* edited and compiled by Charles E. Allen and Frank Johnson, was printed in serial form in *The Cozad Local*, the community's newspaper in 1953-1954.[82] It was later compiled into a soft-cover book format and printed in the same year. Allen was the same person who had met John Cozad in 1894 when the town's founder had signed a deed for him which was said to clear a contested title. Charles Allen was a prominent member of the Cozad community as he was a founder of the Presbyterian Church, owner of a general store, builder of the Opera House building on 8th Street, founded the Cozad State Bank and perhaps most importantly to the area's farmers, helped with the first irrigation ditches in Gothenburg and Cozad. He later served as the president of the Nebraska State Irrigation Association. Allen was also elected to public office, serving as a councilman and mayor of Cozad.[83]

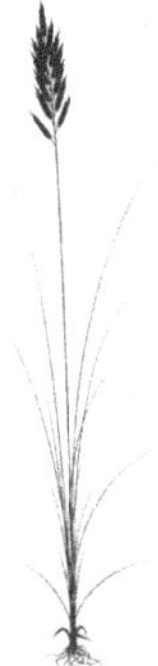

The book is an important local history resource because the compilers interviewed original settlers, or knew them, or their descendants. The mystery of the disappearance of the Cozads, while not revealed in the newspaper articles or the booklet, was addressed by at least one source, long dead, who suggested that he knew more about the story and what had happened to the family, and in particular to both sons. The source was none other than Sam Schooley.[84] He certainly would have known what had happened to the family in 1882-84, given his assistance to get Theresa and Robert Cozad to Kansas so that they could assume their new lives and some legal work he did for John Cozad later.[85] The local history book helped to further the interest in the Cozad story and provided some tantalizing hints about it.

While the Brooks book lacked the details of the tragedy, and the *Early History* included teasers, these two sources were followed by a special newspaper section of the *Cozad Local* in 1956 that described in much more detail what had happened to the Cozads and revealed Robert Henri's true identity. It included an essay that was copyrighted by Robert Gatewood. For the first time since the Cozad family's disappearance more than seventy years before, a curtain had been pulled back from the story that had been kept from the community and the public.

On November 27, 1956, a special edition of *The Cozad Local* was published with the title *Reveal True Story of John J. Cozad*. The edition was produced by Harry B. Allen, who had spent more than a year preparing for its publication after traveling extensively across the country tracking down information. This special edition of the newspaper was reproduced years later by the Robert Henri Museum and given to visitors.[86]

One of readers of *The Early History of the Cozad Community* was Dr. Robert Gatewood and for the special newspaper section, Gatewood produced his account of the Cozad story, revealing what he knew of the story from his personal experience and recollections. For the first time since 1882, a family member spoke publicly about what had happened seven decades before. Not only had Gatewood met John Cozad in 1894 as a boy in Cozad, he also wrote that:

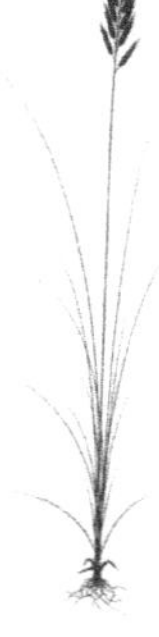

> *. . . many years later he (A.T. Gatewood, his father) gave me the story when I visited the Cozads in New York. We decided to respect their desire of secrecy until the last member of the family was gone. I think that now they would be happy that these things are being done.*[87]

Those recollections, along with others from O. O. McIntyre, were included in the *Cozad Local* special section. McIntyre was a grandson of Joan Jones, the sister of Julia Jones Gatewood, and a second cousin to Robert Gatewood (1885-1966). He was a nationally known columnist for *The Cosmopolitan* magazine.[88]

As it turned out, the contacts between the Lees, Robert Henri and Robert

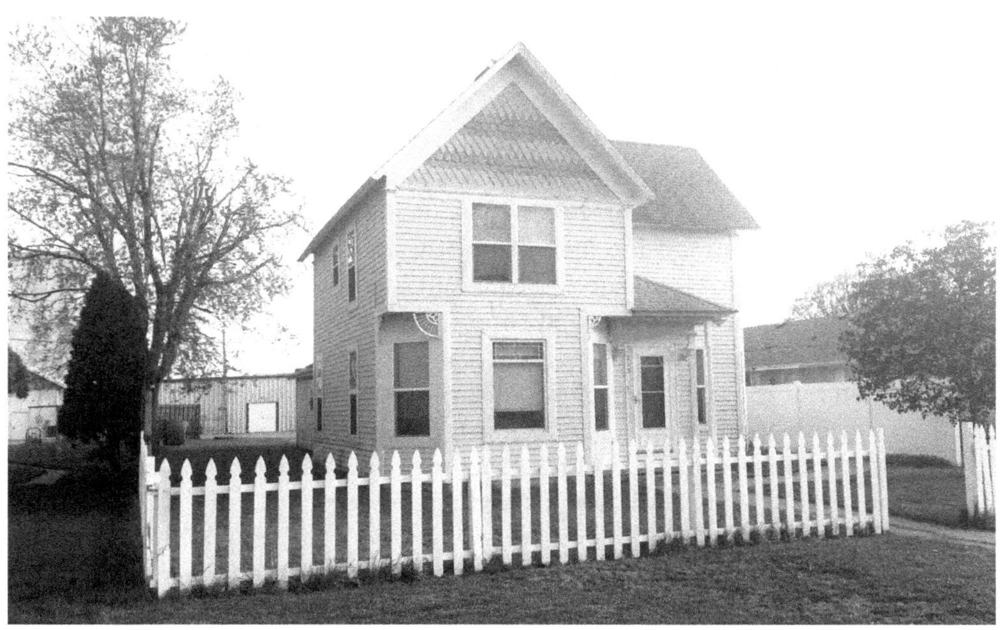

Courtesy Peter Osborne

*The home of Ella and Sam Schooley played host to the visit of Theresa Cozad when she returned to Cozad along with other family members. The house has been moved to its present location but it originally sat two blocks to the west of City Park, a parcel of ground the Schooleys sold to the City of Cozad.*

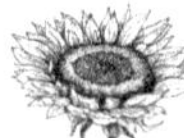

Gatewood were more numerous than the article revealed. There is a photocopy of a letter from Robert Henri to Robert Gatewood in the museum archives discussing a visit in the winter of 1914 and signed by Robert Henri.[89] Robert Henri would continue to write Gatewood until as late as 1928.[90] When in New York City, Dr. Gatewood was introduced as Robert Lee and as a nephew of Richard Lee.[91]

Many Cozad residents must have read the 1956 edition of the paper with amazement and surprise or as one writer said:

*How satisfying it was to have the mystery solved at last.*[92]

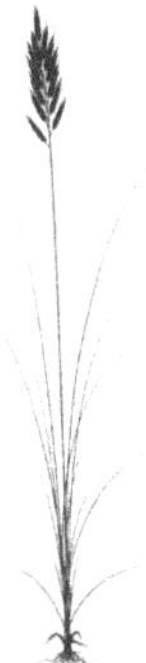

But there were some who did not. The oldest of the area's residents might have heard of the 1894 visit of John J. Cozad, or the visit of John A. Cozad in 1895 or the visits of Julia Gatewood or Theresa Gatewood Cozad's various trips back. Older residents might have vaguely remembered that Sam and Ella Schooley had hosted Theresa Cozad at their home and visited with other Cozad family members. In fact, those visits were remembered in Sam Schooley's obituary in 1941, just fifteen years before the publication of the special section.[93] But for most it would have been a surprise.

Another important development that also occurred in 1955 after the local history booklet's publication, was the culmination of the effort by Harry B. Allen, an area farmer and dogged researcher, to track down a photograph of John Cozad and to see if Robert Henri had ever painted a portrait of his father. A May 1955 edition of *Time* magazine included a story about a Henri exhibition that had taken place at the Montclair Art Museum in Montclair, New Jersey. Allen followed up on that information and soon he was trying to find Violet Organ, who had been mentioned.[94]

As a result of the story, he contacted the New York Chamber of Commerce and then was able to track down and contact Violet Organ, Robert Henri's sister-in-law, and they began corresponding. She provided two photographs of John J. Cozad, one of which may have been his wedding photograph and the other which was taken by famed Civil War photographer Mathew Brady in Washington, D.C. in the 1870s. Both images are the only known photographs of Cozad to exist and both appeared in the 1956 *Cozad Local* special section.[95]

He also contacted the estate's agent for Henri's paintings, Hirschl and Adler Galleries in New York City. The gallery made arrangements to send a copy of a picture of the 1903 painting of John Cozad by Henri with an offer also to sell it.[96]

In addition, Organ provided a photograph of the painting by Henri of his father which was also used on the back side of the *Cozad Telephone Directory* that year. Henri had created the portrait in 1903, just three years before his father's death, and it was on display in Montclair.[97] Ultimately the paintings of John Cozad, Theresa Cozad, John A. Cozad and Robert Henry Cozad were acquired by the Sheldon Art Museum in Lincoln, Nebraska. In 2016, they were displayed at the Robert Henri Art Gallery as part of a loan with the Sheldon, the first time they had ever been or seen in Cozad.[98]

## Son Of the Gamblin' Man

When the 1956 special edition *Reveal True Story of John J. Cozad* was published, it was noted that a famous author was at work on a book, although the author's identity was not revealed, and that a movie producer was also interested.[99] That author was Mari Sandoz. Sandoz certainly would have read the section along with the 1880 diary of Robert Henry Cozad (*Robert Henri*) that Gatewood had in his possession and had been reproduced in the newspaper. She apparently had been in contact with Harold B. Allen and Dr. Gatewood in 1955 and 1956 respectively as the work on her book continued.[100]

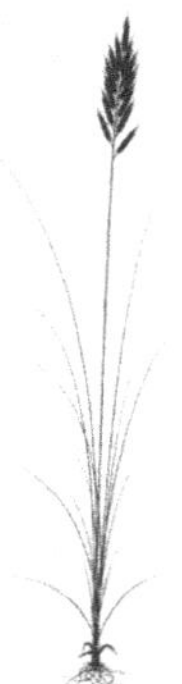

Sandoz had believed that her book would be published in the fall of 1959 but it was not until January 1960 when she submitted the galleys to the publisher.[101]

In 1960, the Sandhills writer's *Son of the Gamblin' Man: The Youth of an*

*Artist*, a fictional account of the Nebraska chapter of Robert Henri's life, was released.[102] While she had been offered the opportunity to present the story as non-fiction, she had refused because there were too many problems filling in many of the blank parts of the story, a problem that this author encountered as well.[103]

The book is still considered to be the most accurate historical account of those remarkable days in central Nebraska's early settlement history. Her exceptional research skills led her through archives, interviews, and reams of historical data. Aside from the dialogue between the characters, which is contrived, but probably accurate given her own roots in the Sandhills country, the book describes the community as it was.

She disliked the original cover as it used a very old design of playing cards; her picture on the back cover of the book did not reflect well on her, as it showed her blind eye, and it was of a poor quality.[104]

One of the curious coincidences is that Sandoz admired Henri's work even before she knew anything of the story. In fact, in writing to someone in 1959, not long before the publication date, she said of the book:

> *I wanted the form to be a written approximation of a Henri painting.*[105]

She was even familiar with the building in which Henri had painted his father's portrait, the Allen Williams Studio in New York City. Sandoz had been in the building many times. And, as it turns out, she was familiar with the Cozad story long before she wrote about it. After the publication of the book, she was interviewed by Robert Perkin, a reporter with the *Rocky Mountain News*. She remembered that:

> *I knew the story from my childhood, grew up with it . . . My father knew Cozad and corresponded with him. It wasn't until I grew up that I realized other people didn't know the story.*[106]

Sandoz wrote her publisher Clarkson Potter that she hoped that in future editions, there might even be color photographs of some of Henri's paintings included.[107] In another letter that she wrote to Mary Abbot, also in 1959, she reflected that:

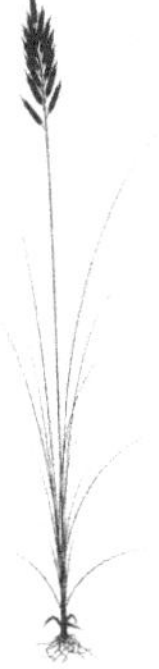

> *This book of mine is a step by step development of the painter Henri in a family and a locale where such talent had never shown itself. I was interested in his techniques and also in the great qualities of leadership that helped limit Henri as a painter but help make a greater contribution to American art than if he developed the painting potentials of an angel.*[108]

One outcome of the publication of the Sandoz book was it was presumed by some, wrongly in fact, that Mari Sandoz had been the first to break the Cozad-Henri story which was of course incorrect. Sandoz gave a brief overview in her *Preface* of how the unveiling of the Cozad story had happened. She wrote:

*I put the book aside until the story began to leak out. Van Wyck Brooks revealed the gist of it in his John Sloan in 1955 and the next year Harry B. Allen gave a brief account of it to the Cozad Local. So I felt free to tell the story that John Cozad, in letters to my father in 1903, characterized as a most unusual one, and yearns for a Romantic Pen. Unfortunately, he left his trail too shadowed and confused for the complete clarification demanded by non-fiction.*[109]

While Sandoz acknowledged having been in correspondence with Dr. Gatewood more than twenty years earlier, she did not acknowledge his copyrighted work. Dr. Gatewood had published six articles about Robert Henri in the *Cozad Local* (1954, 1956, 1958, 1959), two pieces in the *Omaha World Herald* (1956, 1959) and two in the Lincoln papers, the *Journal* and the *Star* (1957) along with the *Kansas City Star* (1957). Articles also appeared in the *Cozad Local, Lincoln Journal, Lincoln Star* in 1965 although that was after the publication of her book. Because the story appeared on the news wires of the time, it was printed in many other newspapers as well.[110]

Because Sandoz never acknowledged any of those articles, Gatewood was upset and disappointed, according to his daughter Joan Gatewood Miller. Gatewood's lawyer believed that there was potential for legal action. In the end, none was taken. Robert Gatewood also believed that the Sandoz book was not as good as it could have been and that there was so much more information available, presumably from him, than some of the hearsay that she had used.[111]

With the publication of the book in 1960, Mari Sandoz began the efforts to promote it. At an event in Denver on May 17 of that year three of Traber Gatewood's granddaughters came to visit with her. In addition, she began to receive letters from various Gatewood and Cozad family members from around the country.[112] Another interesting encounter took place in 1964 when Sandoz met with Joan Gatewood Miller in Portland, Oregon for a luncheon. The author offered, as Miller described it, *words of regret* that she had not been in contact with Robert Gatewood during her writing of the *Son of the Gamblin' Man.*[113] In fact, Robert Gatewood later relayed to his daughter that the story could have been an even better one because the historical facts were even more remarkable than the fictional account.[114] Dr. Gatewood later wrote to William Homer, the Henri biographer that:

*Mari Sandoz's book is of course partly fiction as I did not collaborate with her. In fact it might have hindered her in her effort when writing the story.*[115]

However, in the end, the book was not as successful as Sandoz thought it would be because of poor advertising and promotion. She even suggested that some might think the book had been *a real stinker.*[116] In the case of Clarkson Potter, the publisher, it was in the view of Sandoz, the worst of any of her relationships she had with a publisher.[117]

In spite of the intrigue and disappointment that had come with the revealing of the story, since the Robert Henri Museum's creation in the early 1980s the book has been an important resource for tour guides, volunteers and visitors in understanding the Cozad legacy. It is still sold in the museum's gift shop and is regularly the focus of regional book clubs to analyze.

### Robert Henri and His Circle

While the events from 1955-1960 revealed much of the story of the Cozads, there was still more information that would become public in the next several decades that expanded the knowledge of the Nebraska legacy of Robert Henri and Cozad history. There were contacts, for example between the Gatewoods and Violet Organ over the years. In 1944, Robert and Bess Gatewood along with Joan Gatewood Miller visited Violet in New York City at Henri's former residence. It had been kept in the same appearance as it had been when he died. She in turn visited the Gatewoods in Las Vegas, Nevada, and the families maintained a cordial relationship until she died in 1959. In fact, Violet took Joan Gatewood Miller to visit some of the subjects that Henri had painted.[118]

An important aspect of this relationship is that when Violet Organ was working on her own book on Robert Henri, with a working title of *The Life and Letters of Robert Henri*, she received information from the Gatewoods that proved to be helpful.[119] The book was never finished because of her death and the work that she did complete on the manuscript was incorporated into William Homer's *Robert Henri and His Circle*, originally published in 1969 and revised in 1988. Homer acknowledged her contribution. In addition to Organ's contributions, Robert Gatewood sent a series of letters to Homer revealing what he knew of the Cozad story.[120]

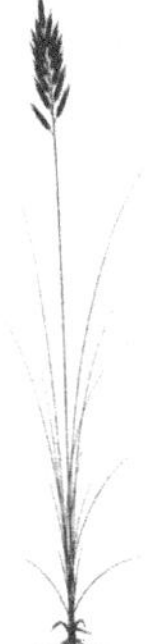

### Return of a Gatewood Family Member

In the early 1960s, Dr. Robert Gatewood returned to his hometown, the first time he had been there in decades. As he said that day, Cozad was *sure different than it had been in 1900* when he left. He had come to Nebraska from Nevada in 1965 to see a premier of a centennial memorial art exhibit of the work of Robert Henri at the Sheldon Art Gallery (now Sheldon Museum of Art) in Lincoln.[121]

It had been almost ten years since he had helped Harry Allen with the *Cozad*

*Local* special edition that revealed the family's story and several years since Mari Sandoz had published her book. His long involvement with the revealing of the Cozad story ended on November 20, 1966, with his death in Las Vegas, Nevada. Curiously, there is no mention in his obituary of his critical role in revealing the history of one of America's greatest artists.[122] His children donated the 1880 diary of Robert Cozad to the Sheldon Art Museum in 2000.[123]

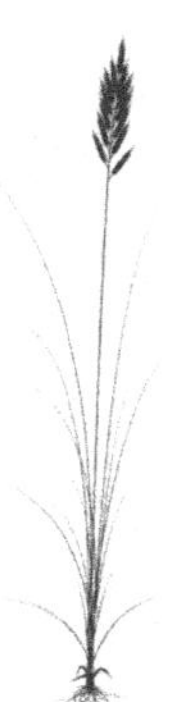

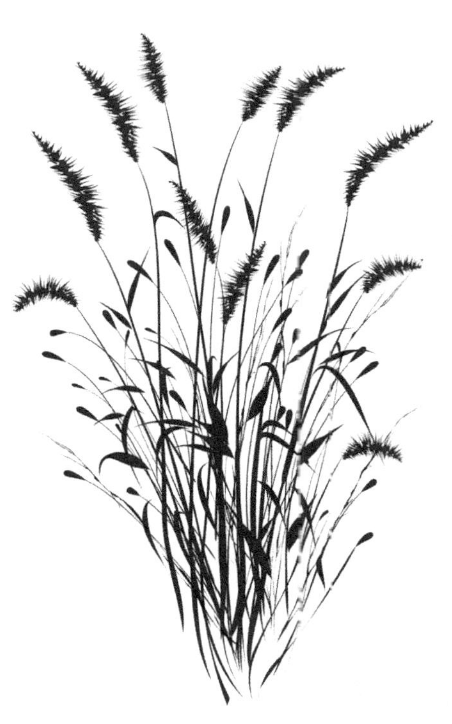

## *Chapter 2*

# The Origins of the Art Spirit

*The effect of this environment – both parental and geographical – on the formation of Henri's personality was undoubtedly considerable.*[1]

*The stimulating influences of my mother who had a natural love for books and painting and the constructive enthusiasms of my father counted favorably against the environment – the far West, cowboys, etc., etc., in which there was no association with artists. . . I am rather glad it happened as it did for that boy's life is part of my experience – my storehouse – and it does not matter to me at all that I didn't paint a picture when I was in the cradle.*[2]

Robert Henri and His Circle
William Homer

It is believed that Robert Cozad first came to Nebraska with his parents in the summer of 1873 as his father was exploring the area and beginning the establishment of the colony. If not, he probably came in the late fall of 1873 when the first group of colonizers arrived. He attended the Chickering Classical and Scientific Institute in Cincinnati in 1875, 1877, and 1878, graduating in 1879.[3] While he may have wanted to attend the new schoolhouse that was built in Cozad in 1874-75, his mother had other ideas. It is believed he came out to Nebraska during school breaks.

He, like many boys his age, was fascinated with the sights and sounds of the Great Plains and the West which were so unlike anything he had been exposed to in the East. His Nebraska experience would have far-reaching effects on his life as is apparent from pieces that he wrote while in the state and later recollections.[4]

In the November 20, 1876, edition of *The Hundredth Meridian* newspaper, one of the few editions of that newspaper that still exists, *A Letter from A Young American* appears and was written by Robert. At the time he was eleven years old, and it may be his first published piece.[5] His letter to the editor provides an insightful look into life on the Great Plains and also served as a promotional piece to encourage others to come to Nebraska:

*As so many settlers are writing letters to the Meridian, I thought I would write one too, to interest the boys. I have spent three summers here and now spending my first winter and have never seen a Buffalo or Indian, but I have seen droves of deer, elk, antelope, wild horses, jack rabbits, gophers, pole cats, and grasshoppers. I have a horse and saddle, and have a good time riding over the prairie. . . We see many beautiful ponies.*

*Some of the hunters wear pretty suits of buckskin with fringe all around. I saw one who had rows of gold dollars on his suit for buttons. They wear their hair very long and a belt around the waist filled with pistols and great spurs on their boots. They raise fine crops here, but the hoppers mostly do the harvesting. It's thought they will not be here next year.*

*The air is very pure and it's very healthy. Nobody ever gets sick, but sick folks*

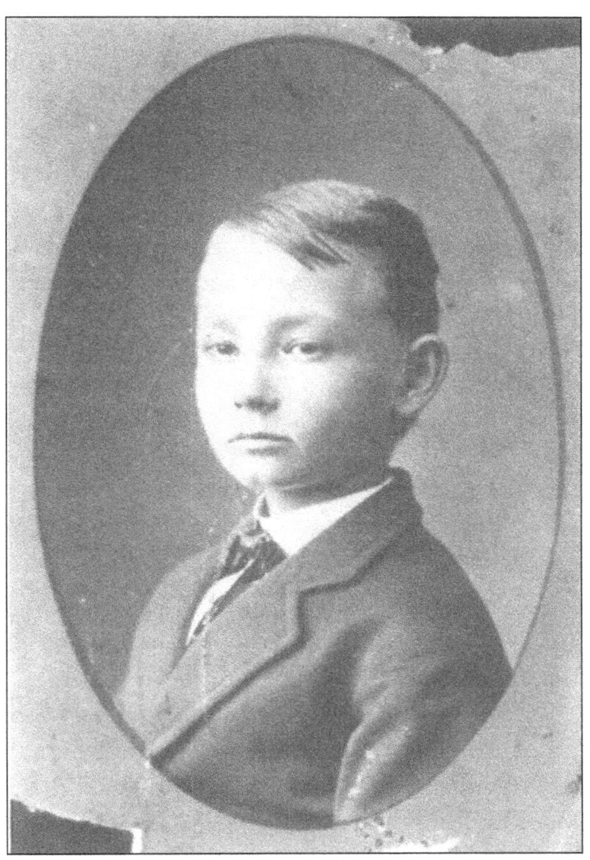

*Collection of the Estate of Robert Henri*

*Robert Henry Cozad about the time the family came to Nebraska in 1873*

*who come here get well. The winter is mild, only once in a while the wind blows a little hard.*

*We have a nice two story school house furnished with Excelsior seats, desks, large globe, maps all around and a large black board in the wall at each end. Our teacher is a pretty little lady, and wears a gold watch, a fine ring, and a little bit of a fool and we love her dearly.*

*I have nothing more to say now except that I want all the boys who read this to come out west and we will grow up with the country. Bob* [6]

Cozad, at an early age, became a lifelong diarist and a writer. For example, when he was ten, he began writing a book and two years later wrote a play in Cincinnati entitled *The Bloody Villain* that was performed by students at Chickering. He created a small paper called *The Runty Papers* that included his own illustrations. This work of fiction was about a minstrel group. Henri also wrote *Dan Dover, Abe, Boy Detective* and *Irish, the Boy Inventor.*[7] In later recollections, he said that his initial choice for a vocation had been to become a writer.

Robert spent part of his time in his office regularly maintaining scrapbooks and diaries. An active journalist, he kept a diary from his teenage years, beginning on September 23, 1879, until the year before his death in 1929. His 1880 diary or *notebook*, as he called it, and which still survives, has been transcribed in its entirety and has been placed in the archive of the Robert Henri Museum.[8] The original diary is at the Sheldon Museum of Art in Lincoln. The manuscript provides important information about his life in the Platte River valley along with details about the present museum building. Some of his sketches that go along with his entries can also be found in that diary.

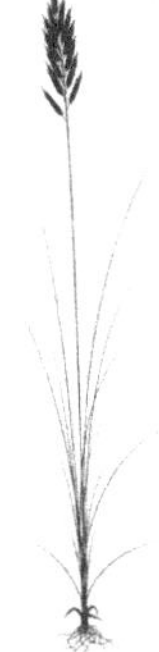

Robert's life, and his brother's activities are recounted in the handwritten diary that is more than two hundred pages long. Detailed insights can be had into the family's daily life. His time in Nebraska, as recounted in the diary, was not all about writing and work. Cozad's diary reveals other aspects of his life including regularly swimming and fishing in the Platte River, riding his horse Darby, driving cattle, weather conditions, following the political developments of the day, local clubs, business activities in town, deaths of area residents, fairs and community events, county happenings, social activities, and his reading habits. There is also an accounting of his finances including cash on hand and money owed him, participation in sporting activities and his bouts with poison ivy.[9]

In addition, the 1880 Federal Census entries for Dawson County, another important primary source, list the Cozad family as living in Nebraska. The entry records John as being a farmer, Theresa as keeping house, and John and Robert attending college.[10]

### Robert The Scrapbooker

It was also during this time that Theresa Cozad began giving scrapbooks to the boys for their birthdays. Henri's mother encouraged reading and the seeking of knowledge as evidenced by the clippings in his scrapbooks. They are filled with clippings of current events, news, poetry, and cultural events of the time, stories about famous people, young ladies, women, and miscellaneous information. The scrapbooks include spiritual writings, illustrations, excerpts, and family items, such as a poem that was pasted into the book after the death of an infant brother.

Included in one of the scrapbooks is a lithograph of *Gipsy Musicians of Spain.* Who knows if that might have been the roots of his love for Spanish culture and his numerous visits there later as an artist. Or, if *Gipsy Girl*, a painting (with its title also misspelled) on display in the museum's gallery had its inspiration beginning with this scrapbook clipping. There are articles about the places where he lived, including Cozaddale along with the report card from his school in Cincinnati.[11] Three of his scrapbooks are owned by the Robert Henri Museum.

Articles from *Harper's Weekly* and *Appleton's Magazine* found their way into his scrapbooks as well as some of his own personal activities. The range of his interests was quite wide including biblical stories, accounts about the West and famous American figures. There are clippings reporting on the death of William Bryant, the assassination of James Garfield and other historical events. From the scrapbooks we also find that in the early 1880s his favorite writers were Charles Dickens, Sylvanus Cobb, Jules Verne, Mary J. Holmes and Mark Twain. Included between the covers are also wood engravings including one of Gypsie Musicians.[12]

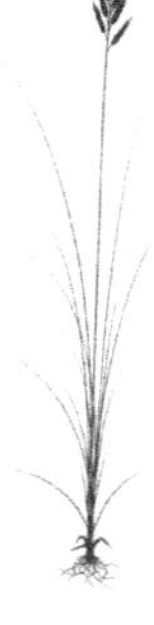

At one point, Henri went to the Spillses Dancing School and illustrations about dancing found their way into the scrapbooks along with cartoons that he would copy. He also meticulously indexed each book.[13]

Occasionally items related to Cozaddale and Nebraska can be found glued

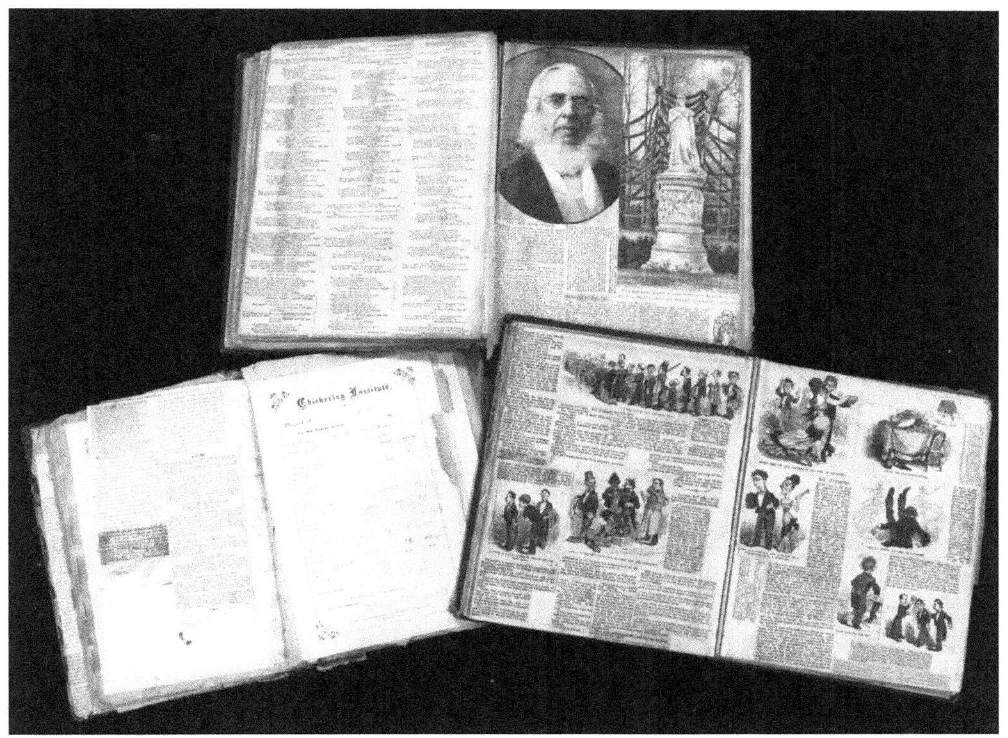

*Robert Henri Museum and Art Gallery Collection*

*Robert Cozad's Scrapbooks*

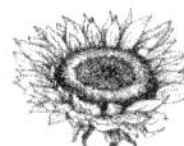

onto their pages and occasionally insights into their lives can be found. In 1876, Henri wrote on the inside cover of his scrapbook:

*I am eleven years old. I leave my ma tomorrow to go alone for the first time to school in Cincinnati.*[14]

From another scrapbook, one used for the year 1878, it is clear that the Cozads had retained their ties to Cincinnati until at least 1879, and probably even longer. On June 24, Robert Cozad made an annotation in his scrapbook referencing Cincinnati and indicating that he was there on that day and had been born there.[15]

In another entry in what is believed to be an 1879 scrapbook, a fourteen-year-old Robert Cozad wrote that:

*I am in better health than I ever was now and am a great boy for hearty playing as well as a great story reader. I love to write and draw. I am left handed.*[16]

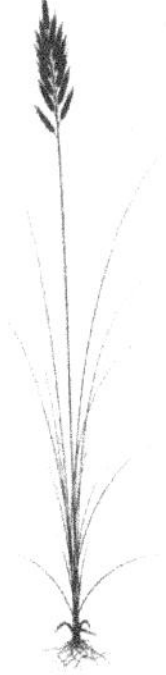

Both of Henri's biographers, William Homer and Bennard Perlman, believe that Theresa may have pasted at least some of the articles that can be found in them. Henri may have colored the illustrated pieces himself, making his initial forays into the artistic career that would define his life.[17]

Robert's relationship with his father has been described as:

*Deep and enduring, seasoned by parental firmness.*[18]

Another description comes from William Homer who wrote:

*(John J.) Cozad was a model of independent action, fighting fairly but vigorously for his beliefs against seemingly insurmountable obstacles. Young Henri doubtless also inherited his father's visual acuity and deft hand.*[19]

### In my office is my desk and printing press

As Robert Cozad got older, he took on more responsibilities as he got involved with one of his father's most important business activities, the cutting and shipping of hay. When he was fifteen, in 1880, he took charge of the hay operations on the Cozad family's sprawling acreage. In that position he had employees to oversee and did the accounting. The haying operation was a large one with considerable responsibility and a number of hired men to oversee at what he called the *hay camp*.[20]

On September 4, 1880 Robert described the hay operations:

*The amount of labor that is now going on in this immediate vicinity is wonderful. John J. Cozad is now furnishing employment to scores of people, many of whom would be compelled to leave their claims, to hunt employment to get a means of support, during the coming winter; besides the bridge work, he is letting out hay contracts; so all that will work, may, and at a fair price; a ride over the hay fields, would satisfy any one that there are a great many manifesting their willingness to work. Mr. Goodyear from Custer county, has the largest contract and is now running for mowers and expects to add two more in a few days he is stacking from thirty to thirty five tons a day; and will be kept busy on his job about three weeks; he finds employment for about fifteen hands; and is doing work with a vim, that few will surpass. Mr. Stonecipher, is working on a 150 ton contract. Whipple & Chapin, have a 200 ton contract; several others have contracts but we have failed to learn their names. A hay press is being run day and night to prepare the hay for the western market; the press occupies the attention of 16 to 18 hands and bales from ten to twelve tons in ten hours; the press is run by steam power. Will Claypool is Capt. of the "little Injun" which runs as steady as a top. Will knows just how to make the little fellow get up and clatter, as if it was the little folks at home.* [21]

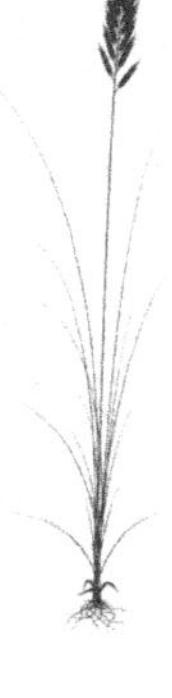

He wrote in another diary entry:

*It revives me up and makes me feel like I am some body to have a responsible position and be depended on . . . No one knows how much good this does me. It makes me want to do something.*[22]

Another entry in his diary reveals that the men who were working at the hay camp respected him. He wrote:

*I stay with the press all the time. See that everything is right. The men have grown to consider me to be one of the bosses . . . The men I have often hears say, when they did not know I was in hearing: If Boby keeps the accounts it will be correct. He never neglects his business.*[23]

At one point John Cozad had suggested that he might station Robert at his Leadville operations but that did not come to be.[24] His management of the effort created a family confrontation at one point when Robert ordered the hay press to be continued to be used even though it was not functioning properly, according to Traber Gatewood. Traber had argued publicly in front of all of the hired men with Robert to no avail. There would continue to be some animosity between the younger man with his uncle for a time to come.[25]

John J. Cozad gave his son a small printing press. Perlman writes that it was installed on the second floor of the brick hotel that had been built and now serves as the Robert Henri Museum. He also believes that Robert Cozad's office was located there as well, mimicking the office of his father in the adjoining room. The historic record of this arrangement is quite different, however. An 1880 floor plan of the building, drawn by Robert, shows his office on the first floor, adjacent to his father's and Johnny's office. In an entry dated June 1880, Robert writes:

*In my office is my desk and printing press.*[26]

The room is actually smaller than shown and not as large as his father's office and it would have been cramped quarters to have a printing press there along with all the supplies, and the typical office equipment that would have been needed at the time. This room was probably the center of his various projects including the writing of his diary and creation of such works as his *Runty Papers*.[27]

With his printing press, Robert turned out custom orders including eleven hundred election tickets for Dawson County. He also printed greeting cards.[28] It is thought that one of the most widely distributed examples of his work of the period was a poster entitled *Ho! For the Great Platte Valley*. The poster was printed and placed in railroad stations and other public places in Cincinnati and probably

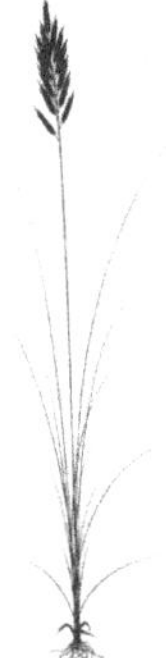

all across Ohio, Indiana and Pennsylvania. However, more likely it was printed by the *100th Meridian* newspaper in Cozad.[29]

Robert sold chromolithographs and holiday cards in his grandmother's store. At one point he gave one thousand of the cards to his grandmother to sell. Later, he began painting them himself.[30] He also produced fliers and advertisements and also included possible items to purchase in his diary.[31] Not only was Robert an author, journalist, and budding artist but also a printer and entrepreneur, business manager and a young man of many talents.

He was also involved with the effort to bridge the Platte River. His diary has multiple entries about the construction efforts and the progress being made. In late June 1880, he witnessed what could have been a fatal accident when Johnny tried to make a repair to a part of the bridge's structure but fell into the river and after being pinned against timbers finally was able to pull himself out of the swirling river.[32]

### THE CREATIVE INSTINCT

The origins of Robert Henri's artistic skills came at an early age. On August 1, 1964, Robert Gatewood wrote to William Homer, Henri's biographer about Henri's artistic and literary skills. He was one of the few people outside of his immediate family who had not only known about him as a young man but as an adult. He said in his letter to the writer:

*As a boy Henri displayed a marked talent as an artist also as a writer. He wrote many stories long hand and illustrated them with his drawings which were really very fine. . . However, I happen to have one of his diaries (1880) which the paper (Cozad Local) published. I have kept this one thinking it might be quite interesting sometime in the future. . . He showed great talent in those days and we thought that probably he would turn out to be a writer. However he has shown genius both as a writer and a painter and teacher. His life in the early West was typical and he experienced the things that the early pioneers went there.*[33]

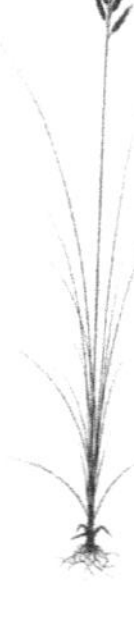

In a letter written later in life, Henri recalled when he first began to draw. He wrote:

*As far back as I can remember.*[34]

As to when he wanted to become an artist, he wrote to Thelma Anthony in 1926:

*I never had any other idea, but for a time it was mixed up with writing . . . I thought it would be great to be a picture painter, but as practically all the accounts I read or heard were to the effect that artists surprised their parents and the neighbors by doing masterpieces in infancy, I was not in that class.*[35]

Of his upbringing, in which he did not identify Nebraska as part of his heritage, he wrote:

*The stimulating influences of my mother who had a natural love for books and painting and the constructive enthusiasms of my father counted favorably against the environment – the far West, cowboys, etc., etc., in which there was no association with artists. . . I am rather glad it happened as it did for that boy's life is part of my experience – my storehouse – and it does not matter to me at all that I didn't paint a picture when I was in the cradle.*[36]

As to the date of his earliest pictures he wrote to George Zug in 1919:

*I remember doing what was considered a good deal of damage, by my teachers to the books I was supposed to study and which I so hated to study. The fly leaves and the margins were very inviting when pencils were at hand.*[37]

During his Cincinnati years and time in Nebraska, Robert Cozad began creating drawings, and as previously noted, some of those images appeared in his diaries and scrapbooks. At a young age he is believed to have also developed a talent for drawing and is said to have carried a sketch pad.[38] Mari Sandoz relays that he was drawing, albeit primitively, when he first arrived in Nebraska and some of those early drawings were hung in the telegrapher's office in Willow Island.[39] One can see examples of his early sketches on the pages of his 1880 diary which the Robert Henri Museum has copies of and which the Sheldon Art Museum owns.[40] He also illustrated his *Runty Papers* and copied other illustrations from *Punch's Almanac 1847-1851* and painted greeting cards.[41]

The museum has a photocopy of at least one sketch that is believed to have been created while he was in Cozad. It was drawn for Maggie Claypool's autograph book. She was a relative, and perhaps even a love interest, and was two years younger than Robert. Curiously, the sketch is signed *"Col." R. H. Cozad,* and is dated March 10, 1884, when he was almost nineteen years old. It may be the earliest existing sketch of Robert Cozad's that has been found to date. The drawing is of a swan in a body of water and is very beautifully done, indicating that he had achieved proficiency in his drawing and obviously had artistic talent by then. He autographed the sketch with the following:

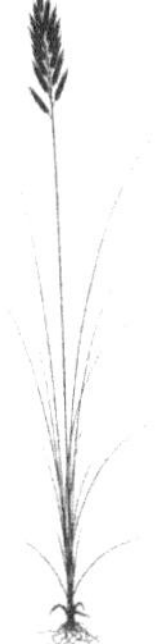

*To Maggie:*
*Words are like sky rockets. They go fizzing, and banging about, making a brite*

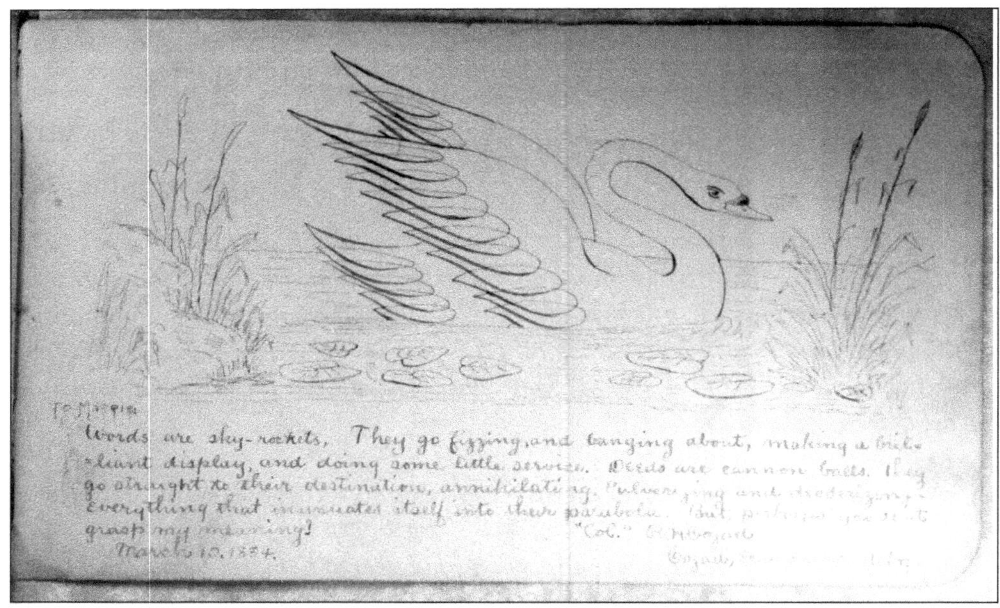


*Robert Henri Museum and Art Gallery Collection*

*An early Robert Cozad sketch drawn for Maggie Claypool's autograph book.*

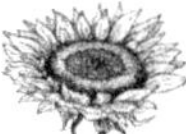

*(sic) giant display, and doing some little service. Deeds are cannon balls. They go straight to their destination, annihilating, pulverizing and deodorizing everything that insinuates itself into their parabola. But, perhaps you don't grasp my meaning!* [42]

When William Homer was writing his biography of Robert Henri, he and Mari Sandoz discussed Cozad's earliest artworks. She told him that some of Robert Cozad's early drawings had been saved by a cowboy who had worked for John J. Cozad. The cowboy left the Cozad area, relocated to the Sand Hills and that she had seen them there. [43]

In *Son of the Gamblin' Man*, she describes a sketch that Robert had drawn when seven years old of John Cozad's father sticking his head out of a train watching a herd of bison. She also described other sketches, including one of soldiers shooting civilians, a fire sweeping through a town, Custer's last stand in Montana, and Daniel Freeman on the Platte River. Whether these descriptions are of the sketches that Sandoz saw is unknown or was just a literary guess is unknown. However, the location of those drawings was then, at the time of their discussions, not known.[44]

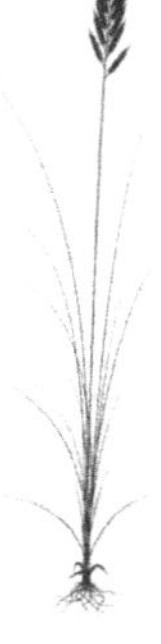

Mari Sandoz wrote that Robert met a photographer, who was also an artist, perhaps in 1880, whose name was Joseph Brander. Photographing portraits of people all over the country, he painted on the side. It has been suggested that

Robert helped to drum up business and several family members were photographed by Brander. The photographer also shared some insights about painting with the young Cozad. However, he turned out to be a huckster, at least when it came to his photographs, which were often labeled with different captions but of the same subject.[45]

Additionally, when Robert Cozad left town with his mother in 1884 it is believed that some of his drawings, illustrations and stories were given to members of Theresa Cozad's family. These items, according to Dr. Robert Gatewood, a nephew to Theresa, were believed to have been lost in a fire.[46] Unfortunately, we know nothing, at this late date, of his artistic production in Denver.

The earliest original sketch that the museum owns was drawn on December 7, 1884, signed by *R. Henri,* and entitled *An American Drama in Four Acts.* It was presumably created in Atlantic City. The inspiration was probably from one of the popular magazines of the time - *Puck, Judge or Harper's Weekly.*[47] This image is significant because it demonstrates the level of his skills before his entrance into the Pennsylvania Academy of Fine Arts in Philadelphia in 1886. His scrapbooks of this time also included cartoons of the period.

By the time he reached Atlantic City he was such a talented artist that he attracted the attention of another artist, James Alberts Cathcard. A story written by Preston Wright appeared in the *Lincoln Star* on October 18, 1925, that provides additional context to Henri's earliest creative talents.

*Robert Henri was the son of John and Theresa Henri. From his childhood they had discerned in him the creative instinct. But whether he was to be a writing man or a painter they did not know. They allowed him to write or to draw as the mood suited with his own inclination seeming to lean toward authorship. It was their conclusion that to press him in any definite direction would be unwise. The saner course was to let matters drift until events should serve to crystallize his ambitions.*

*Nevertheless, when possible, his mother took him to exhibitions of pictures.*

*When Robert Henri was nineteen years old repairs had to be made to the rear of the Henri home which temporarily left a considerable wall surface in an unfinished condition. It was an ideal place for a young artist to practice and Robert did several sketches in colors, knowing that they would be obliterated when the repairs were completed . . . By chance James Alberts Cathcard happened on the scene before this could be done . . . his eyes fell upon the sketches so casually placed by Robert Henri upon the wall.*

*"Who was the artist?" he asked . . . Mrs. Henri told him. To her surprise, he examined the sketches closely, showing much interest. "Your son ought surely to go to the Academy of Fine Arts in Philadelphia and study painting."*[48]

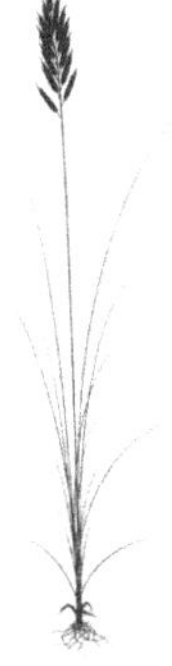

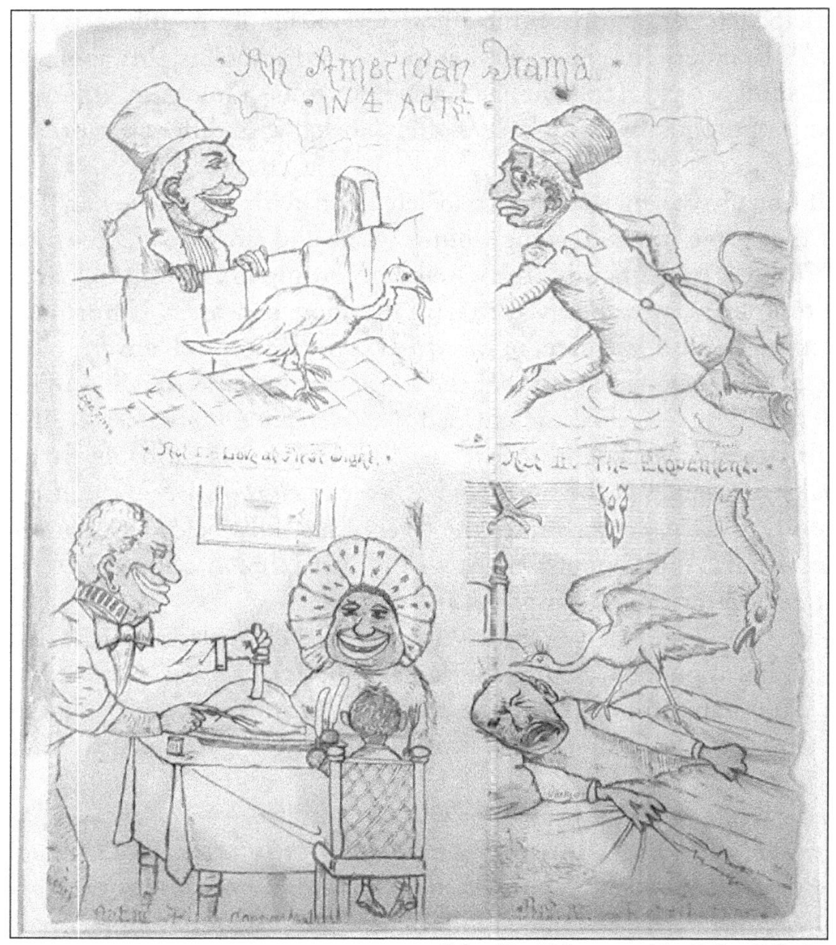


*Robert Henri Museum and Art Gallery Collection*

*An American Drama in 4 Acts, December 7, 1884*
*The oldest original Robert Henri sketch in the Robert Henri'Museum and Art Gallery collection (2023)*

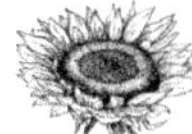

From that chance encounter in late 1884, just after having arrived in Atlantic City from either New York or Nebraska, would come a major turning point in Henri's life. We can surmise that he was, to use a cliché, getting better with age. It is also the commencement of his eastward focus that Henry David Thoreau wrote about:

*We go eastward to realize history and study the works of art and literature. Retracing the steps of the race. We go westward as into the future, with a spirit of enterprise and adventure.*[49]

By the time he entered the Philadelphia Academy of Fine Arts, in 1886, it was the oldest art organization in the country and he was on the road to the greatness that he would later achieve.[50] The museum owns a portrait that is attributed to Robert Henri, believed to be painted in 1886, and may have been completed while he was at the Philadelphia Academy although that attribution has been questioned.[51]

## The Nebraska Legacy of Robert Henri

When one assesses the life and upbringing of Robert Cozad, there are some themes that are apparent. Robert's young life was one that was peripatetic, as was his family's. He moved five times between the age of eight and nineteen. While this book has focused mainly on his Nebraska legacy, his time in Ohio, which includes a great deal of his youth, and his time in Colorado, while not as long, but in some ways as consequential, given what had happened with John Cozad in 1882, are all tied together. Robert Cozad was deeply affected by his time living on the frontier, the wild West and extensive traveling but because of the circumstances that occurred ten years after he arrived, he was never able to tell the world of his Nebraska experience.

Robert Cozad was regularly going back and forth from Ohio to Nebraska and then from Nebraska to Colorado. Curiously he was following the present routes of Interstate Highways 80 and 76 as he traveled along the Union Pacific, and perhaps the Burlington Northern, and Atchison and Topeka railroads. His 1878 scrapbook lists all three states and the addresses that he was living in during that year. Robert was then thirteen years old.

Surely that regular traveling to what must have been far off places to him impacted him for the rest of this life. It exposed him to such geographically different places such as Ohio, and one of the mightiest and most strategic of American rivers, the Ohio River. The Great Platte River Road was a major thoroughfare into the West with the river and its two branches then leading into Colorado and Wyoming along with the Colorado River which flowed to the Baja. The landscape across those hundreds of miles surely would have fascinated him.

He would have witnessed the rolling landscape of Ohio with its rich agricultural lands, then farther to the west, the productive farms of Iowa, and finally the amazing landscapes of Nebraska, with its flat valley of the Platte River, and the rolling hills off to the south and north, the prairies, and the tough landscape of the ranchlands and the Sandhills to the west. The open skies of Nebraska and the surrounding states would certainly remain burned in his memory along with the dependence on and the effect of weather in one's daily living.[52] The Great Plains were a far cry from the crowded environs of Cincinnati with a vastness not found anywhere else in the country. Surely the Rocky Mountains of Colorado would have impressed him, particularly as a young man. They would have been within

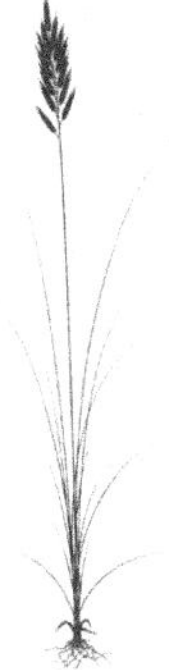

sight of his residences in Denver and Leadville where his father had a mine.

Henri had long held a sympathetic view of the native peoples which might well have been born during the time he was in Nebraska. While he would not have seen many Native Americans during his time there, he certainly would have heard the stories about them that were told as several confrontations between the settlers, railroad men and native peoples that had occurred just to the east of Cozad in the decade before his family had arrived in Nebraska.

While Robert Cozad reported in 1876, just three years after arriving, that he had not seen a buffalo or Native American, Mari Sandoz tells the story of Johnny and Robert coming across a badly wounded Pawnee after an attack by the Sioux on the Pawnees not far from where the boys were staying. Perhaps that was just a piece of fiction to fit into her novel.[53]

During his lifetime he would hear about the Battle at the Little Big Horn in Montana in the summer 1876 and is said to have sketched scenes of it, and the tragedy at Wounded Knee Creek in South Dakota in the winter of 1890. He witnessed the closing of the West and the removal of Native Americans across the country to reservations and the destruction of so much of their culture.

He admired Red Cloud, the famous Lakota chief, for whom the Nebraska town was named, and which was established two years before Cozad. He had even read one of his speeches.[54] Henri painted Southwestern Indians during stays in Santa Fe and today they are some of his most prized paintings.

He once said, later in life:

*I am with the Indians.*[55]

His feeling about anarchy, and he was described as a *philosophical anarchist* by Mari Sandoz, and his *creative independence* may have some of their roots in Nebraska.

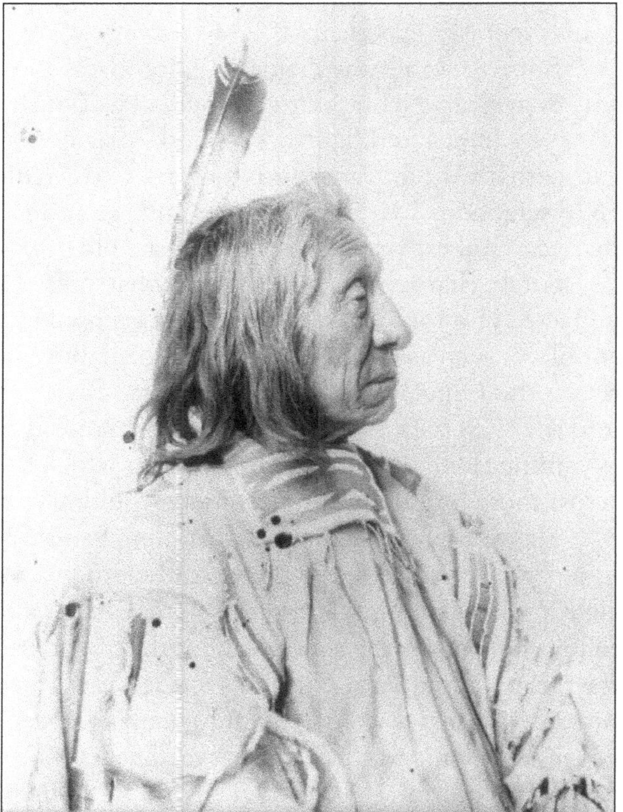

*Courtesy Library of Congress (Control Number 2004674599)*
*Red Cloud*

Emma Goldman, the leading anarchist of her day, and a friend of Henri wrote:

*He was an anarchist in his conception of art and its relation to art.*[56]

The definition of anarchy by the Merriam-Webster dictionary is broadly defined:

*1a: absence of government*
*b: a state of lawlessness or political disorder due to the absence of governmental authority*
*c: a utopian society of individuals who enjoy complete freedom without government*
*2a: absence or denial of any authority or established order*
*b: absence of order*

Later in his life he railed against state power and the institution of religion as features of oppression. Surely, he would have seen examples of that with his father's various battles against the Plum Creek forces including those in government positions. He would watch his father's troubles unfold with the Union Pacific Rail Road, a major corporation of the era led by Jay Gould. His disagreements with organized religion would come later in life, after leaving Nebraska as was his feelings that the institutions at this time had failed during the lead up to and the fighting of World War I, prior to America's entry.[57]

The museum owns a sketch that is attributed to Robert Henri that is entitled *Coxey's Army* and named for the large group of men that came from various parts of the country, and even through Cozad in 1894, to protest the financial Panic of 1893 and its effects upon the country.[58]

He had witnessed first-hand what one might argue were the benefits of anarchy, the free and voluntary associations of individuals, and the rule of direct democracy, during his early years on the Great Plains. Henri had also watched the rugged individualism that was so common in the frontier communities with its struggles against the environment and in the early years the lawlessness of the West. His opposition to World War I, and violence in general, may have some of their roots in Nebraska as he witnessed firsthand how violence often settled scores.[59]

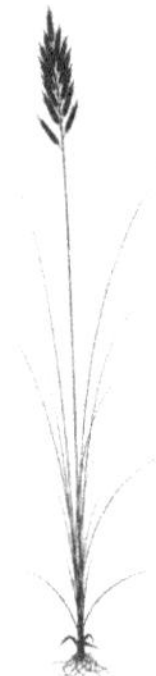

### Traveling Around the World

In his life after leaving the West and Midwest, he would travel to Philadelphia, a place that was worlds from where he had come, to New York where he would come to reside, and one of the greatest cities in the world even at that time. In addition, his travels took him far beyond the East Coast, across the country and around the world. He would go to France, Ireland, Holland, Spain and other far-flung places. The traveling of those early years would certainly have inspired him in his adult years.

In the decades after 1882, the Cozad story would continue to unfold as Frank Southrn went to Thomas Jefferson Medical College in Philadelphia. On several occasions in her book Mari Sandoz suggests that Johnny had been thinking about a medical career long before he came to Atlantic City. She cites occasions when medical issues arose and Johnny played a part in the resolving of them.[60] Southrn would have a remarkable career along with his wife. Robert Henri went on to the Pennsylvania Academy of Fine Art, also in Philadelphia. He then went to France to obtain additional artistic training. Both men would become accomplished in their fields and widely recognized.

The Nebraska experience for the entire family was a transformative one but it would also haunt them until the ends of their lives, both in a positive and negative way. The father's problems and scandals would cast a long shadow over the family for the rest of their lives. Mari Sandoz wrote:

*(He) lived to see one of sons grow into greatness as an artist and a teacher and leader of artists, a son he condemned to live and die under a fictitious name and biography.*[61]

There had been legal troubles almost from the very beginning of the settlement of Cozad, and on occasion both sons were drawn into confrontations with the law. However, Frank Southrn, even with his legal challenges that had occurred in Plum Creek in 1882, returned to Cozad without any reported problems in 1895, and the remaining family and friends welcomed him back. By this time, he was a well-known doctor in Philadelphia. The surviving contemporary documents of family members continue to refer to him as Johnny and not Frank.

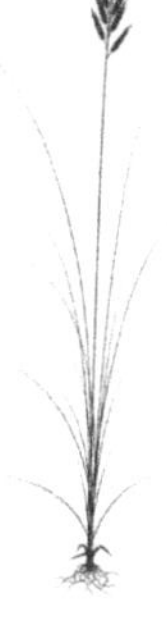

Robert had been involved with these legal scuffles as well, having been arrested for minor crimes that he was later exonerated of. However, the 1894 legal problems that his father created with the reselling of the property he had already sold to Stephen Hendee had presented problems for Robert. He was named as a defendant in the legal case against John J. Cozad in Federal court although ultimately the son's name was removed from the case. He did not appear, nor did his father, or the others, who were subpoenaed.

By 1894-95, at the time of the federal court case, Henri was on his way to becoming the well-known artist and teacher. He had already attended the Pennsylvania Academy of Fine Arts in Philadelphia, and the Académie Julian and Ecole des Beaux Arts in Paris. Returning to the United States in 1891, he taught at the School of Design for Women and two of his paintings were exhibited at the Chicago World's Fair in 1893.[62] Had he appeared in court it might have created a serious scandal for him just as he was achieving wider fame. And an inquiring journalist who dug deeper might have found other stories as well, especially if he had spoken to Stephen Hendee and his associates, who probably knew where some of those skeletons were buried.

### Did Henri Return to Nebraska?

While three of the family members returned to Cozad as has been seen, Robert Henri did not, or at least is not believed to have returned at this time. Perhaps it was his fear of his past being exposed and the scandal that would have created or perhaps there was an uneasiness about what had transpired here more than a decade before. Perhaps there was no desire to return at all. But because three of his family members did so with no repercussions, there remains a possibility he did come back to the place of his youth. Henri made a number of cross-country trips including one to Pike's Peak in Colorado in 1893 and may have passed through Nebraska and maybe even Cozad on the railroad.[63] He also traveled to the Southwest and California traveling by rail, so there are other possible times he came back or through the Platte River valley depending on the route he traveled.

It has long been believed, and the Henri museum staff presented this view to visitors, that he did not paint any landscapes of Nebraska, or at least none that have come to light at this date. Until now it was also believed that he had never exhibited his work in Nebraska while he was alive. Recent discoveries prove otherwise. In 1895, 1908, 1914, 1916, 1919, 1920 and 1925 works of his were exhibited in Nebraska. All but the 1895 show were part of annual exhibitions sponsored by groups like the Nebraska Art Association, the Omaha Society of Fine Arts, and the University Library and in Omaha. He is not believed to have come to any of the shows or receptions, as the media accounts do not mention him attending.[64]

His work was well received, including this 1919 article about a show that elicited the following comments:

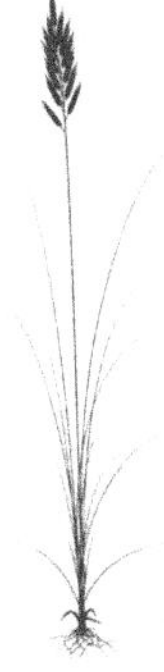

*Robert Henri, instructor at the Art League in New York and one of the most popular of our teachers, especially among the new cult that believes in finishing a six foot canvas in one day, is also well represented by two, for him, very small portraits, also his transitional style . . . He is one of the most interesting characters in New York art circles. Intensely sincere and independent, he has more than once created a sensation on New York exhibition juries.*[65]

## Art In Omaha Is Attracting Crowds to Fontenelle Gal

By MRS. LETA MOORE MEYER

THE sixty oil paintings which the Omaha Society of Fine Arts exhibits for ten days at the Fontenelle, are mostly of a very serious and sincere nature.

The nine Monticellis afford the student an unusually good opportunity for study. All done in his distinctive manner of poetic beauty and mystery, they show two distinct phases of his work and the transition between them. He was a contemporary of the Barbizon school in France about the time when it was considered an iron bound rule that all landscapes must be first scumbled in brown, raw umber, and the lights only thickly painted in, the explosion of which theory gained Constable his fame. The two pictures, "The Peacock Garden" and "The Pet Dove," show a half-hearted conformity to the rule and were evidently done in his earlier years. He gets away from it in "Star of Bethlehem," and in the somewhat stilted and timid "The Lark," and still farther in "Feeding the Chickens," when he was beginning to use the thick impasto characteristic of most of his work. The other four pictures are done in the usual style of his maturity.

The two styles of George Inness can also be studied. The "Roman Campagna," is done in the stilted photographic style of the days when he was a soldier in the civil war and when he was considered hopeless as an artist. "Moonrise" is Inness at his best and is done in the scumbled brown method above mentioned, with the lights painted in heavily and gives a beautiful effect of night and its beauty.

Robert Henri, instructor at the Art league in New York and one of the most popular of our teachers, especially among the new cult that believes in finishing a six-foot canvass in one day, is also well represented by two, for him, very small portraits, also his transitional style. The large, breezy pictures of his earlier years, disregarding drawing and structure and which expressed his inspiring enthusiastic personality, have now given place to those painted mostly of the Indians of the southwest, accurate and right in structure and drawing and technique but rather lifeless and wooden. The two here shown are evidently between the two and possess the virtues of both. "Irish Girl," particularly has a fine feeling of the bony structure of the head and of the body and he has very successfully made use of the old method of scraping out the dress entirely. These two pictures are unfortunately hung in the hall where one cannot get much distance on them. Some years ago the French government bought one of Mr. Henri's pictures for the Luxembourg and it is said the price was $40,000. He is one of the most interesting characters in New York art circles. Intensely sincere and independent, he has more than once created a sensation on New York exhibition juries.

work until he signed a co
produce so many pictures
at a stated price and could
longer. There is a fine A
Ryder, "The Tempest," whi
apt to be liked in a tempor
bition, as one must live with
to love it. A fine memoria
tion of this, one of the gr
our artists, was held at th
politan museum in New Y
winter.

An excellent example of
fortunate Blakelock, who p
last years in an insane as
shown. There is a very f
bigny, especially interesti
new from the subject, "La
noon on the Oise." There i
nfe Charles H. Davis, bu

### Y. W. (

The vesper hour on Sun
o'clock will be in charge
"Z. Z. class" of girls from
Methodist church. Mrs. J
Wilson will speak and Mis
M. Wyatt will sing at th
service. The program of m
reading which follows du
social hour in the club roo
will be given by the "Z. Z.

This is the friendliest ho
week and every girl in tow
come. Come and meet ol
and make new ones, and le
clubs and classes and soci
which will turn a listless wi
a wide-awake happy one fo

The Students' club Bibl
will meet on Monday afte
3:30 for a lesson, and to
plans for a special progra
given at the end of the
course.

The business women's Bi
meets on Thursday night
o'clock for supper, imm
after which its lesson will
sented. This plan makes
ble for the members to ke
engagements. Register e
January for this course.

**Girls' Department.**

The Girls Reserve com
the High School of Comm
which Miss Mildreth Gre
president, will hold its
meeting in the club room
afternoon at 4 o'clock. Mr
Harris Redgley, club lead
present the plans for the fu
the meeting of the Centr
Freshman club Wednesday
noon Miss Evelyn Lane, c
of the program committee,
a short talk on the custom
Japanese people preparator
Japanese play to be given
Student club in February.
cial hour will be in charge
Beatrice Rosenthal. Miss
Eads has been secured as l
this club.

The present committees
dent club will join in an in
nic supper in the gy
Thursday afternoon.

*Robert Henri Museum and Art Gallery Collection*

*A newspaper article in the Omaha Daily Bee reporting on a Robert Henri painting in an art exhibition and his career on January 12, 1919*

It is the 1895 show in Lincoln that is of particular interest. In January, Henri displayed his work *Wet Day, Atlantic City* at a show sponsored by the Hayden Art Club in Lincoln. This was at the same time that the court battle between John Cozad and Stephen Hendee was taking place in the federal court in Omaha. Six months after the art show, John Cozad lost his legal battle. Henri, like his father had not attended the proceedings.

What might Robert Henri have thought about all of this - his artwork being displayed in the state that he had left just ten years before, under a cloud. Perhaps someday documents will surface that will tell us more about a possible return.

Henri's path crossed those of fellow Nebraskans during the course of his life as a painter. For example, Henri painted Eulabee Dix, a prominent socialite in New York and a fellow artist, twice. The paintings are both well-known. One is entitled *Portrait of Miss Eulabee Dix (Becker) in Wedding Gown* (1910), and the other *Lady in a Black Gown* (1911). The former is a significant painting that resides in the collection of the Museum of Nebraska Art in Kearney, Nebraska, and considered to be one of Henri's finest. The latter is in the collection of the High Museum in Atlanta, Georgia.[66]

Dix had spent part of her early life, about five years, in Beatrice, Nebraska, about two hundred miles from Cozad. Her family's residency was during a time after the Cozads had left. One can only wonder if they ever talked about their Nebraska experiences during those painting sessions or during other times when they saw each other socially. Dix's biographer thinks that they did not. Another curious connection is that Eulabee Dix Becker knew Van Wyck Brooks, the author of the biography on John Sloan. It was Brooks who had revealed for the first time, in a nationally read and distributed book in 1955, that Robert Henri had Nebraska roots.[67]

It is also possible that he may have met one of Nebraska's most famous daughters, Willa Cather (1873-1947), the great author of the early twentieth century. Edith Lewis (1882-1972), later Cather's long-time partner, had been the roommate of Achsah Barlow (1879-1945) beginning in 1899 at Smith College. Barlow had taken art lessons at the Art Students League and New York School of Art where Henri had taught. In addition, Lewis, Cather and Barlow, and her husband, Earl Brewster, kept in regular contact over the years. The world in which Cather and Henri traveled was a small one and it is quite possible they knew each other and perhaps had even socialized.[68]

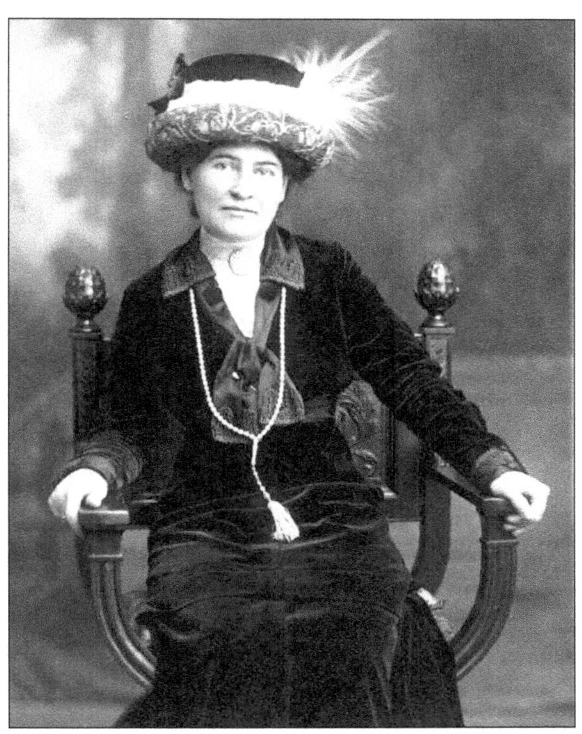

*Courtesy Aime Dupont Studio, New York, Public Domain*

*Willa Cather*

Robert Henri was a cousin of Mary Cassatt (1844-1926), both being sixth-great-grandchildren of Jacque Cossart, who came to New Amsterdam (New York City) in 1662.[69] But again, he probably could not have spoken to her of his own true family history because of what had happened in 1882. In fact, they both could have traced their heritage back to the sixteenth century and another common ancestor.[70]

His ancestry included a member of the Constitutional Convention in 1787, which created the first governing document of the United States. Another ancestor, for whom he was named, was Henry Cozad, who served in the War of 1812. By the nineteenth century the various branches of the family were spelling their last name very differently.[71]

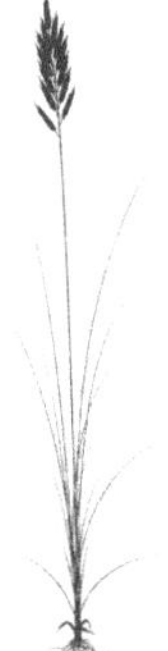

By the time Robert left Nebraska for the final time in 1884, at the age of nineteen, he had what might be described as a *Western swagger* which can be seen in an 1897 photograph taken of him in a studio, perhaps in Philadelphia or New York. Henri aficionados and students of his art and biographers have speculated about how his Nebraska experience affected his future career. There is no doubt that his personality, values and career were guided in part by his having spent some of his most formative years on the frontier exposed to the rawness of the environment, the vast array of interesting characters and a myriad of experiences.

It was in Atlantic City where William Homer believes that Henri painted his first painting in 1885, copied from an 1884 *Harper's Weekly* illustration. The scene was of the Hudson River in New York State from the historic Fort Putnam. The painting is believed to have been destroyed by a fire in 1888 or 1889. A framed print of the illustration with a notation of its history is included in the collection of the Robert Henri Museum. It was also in 1884 that Henri obtained his first art book, entitled *Art Recreations: A Guide to Decorative Art.*[72] In September 1886 Robert Henri left Atlantic City to attend the Pennsylvania Academy of Fine Arts in Philadelphia. As he left to begin a new chapter of his life he wrote:

*I am well pleased with my situation and expect to do well.*[73]

One of the most fascinating pieces of the Cozad and Henri story is that his real identity is not believed to have been discovered, especially given his fame and wide travels. One only need to recall his experience as a young man that upon moving to Denver he remade his acquaintance with fellow Chickering classmates, just several years removed from attending the Cincinnati school. The chances of not meeting someone from his past seem small, especially in his years immediately after leaving Nebraska, although that is what is generally believed. He had connections to so many localities – Cincinnati, Cozaddale, Cozad, Denver and later New York and Atlantic City that it seems so unlikely. At least four of those cities were centers of much activity. Perhaps someday more evidence will come forth that will cast more light on the subject.

### A Transforming Experience

For Robert Henri, his time in Nebraska, when he arrived at the age of eight in 1873 until his final departure in 1884, at nineteen, was a transforming experience as they are the formative years for most people. One only need to look at the life of Nebraska's most famous writer, Willa Cather, who had a similar background to see how much her experience on the Great Plains impacted her writing some of the greatest books on pioneering experiences.

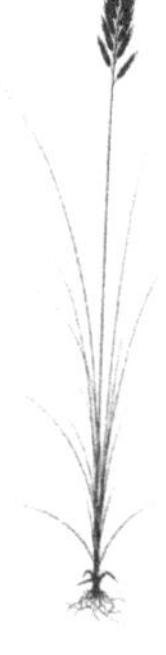

His lifelong habit of journal keeping along with detailed records, and writing short stories, and the first chapters of his artistic career - as evidenced by the sketches found in the Robert Henri Museum collection and elsewhere - all have ties to the state. He certainly would have experienced the brilliant light of Nebraska, the extremes of weather and the remarkable landscape. Henri worked hard on building the bridge crossing the Platte, helped managed the family's hay

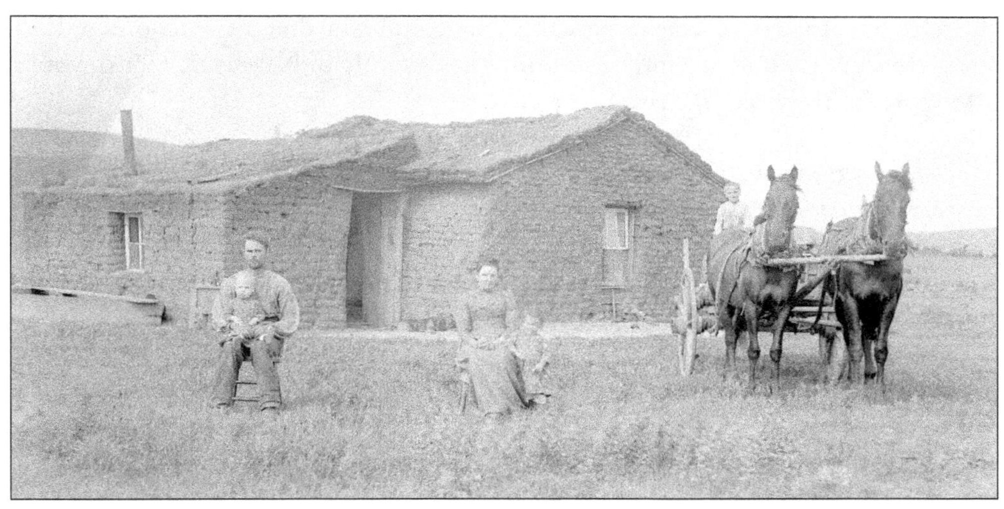

*Courtesy Library of Congress (Digital ID nbhips 10752)*
*Homestead in East Custer County, Nebraska*

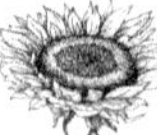

operations including machinery, tended to horses, and dealt with tough cattlemen, helping his father prevent theft of their hay.

William Homer, one of the important biographers of Henri wrote what is the most insightful piece on the Nebraska experience:

*The effect of this environment – both parental and geographical – on the formation of Henri's personality was undoubtedly considerable. Although we cannot prove conclusively that his Western environment decisively shaped the young man's character, everything points to its making a strong impression that was never eradicated. For a period of ten years 1872-1883, he was intermittently exposed to the rigors of frontier life in Nebraska, far from the sophisticated, cosmopolitan atmosphere of the large Eastern cities. And as a boy, he often traveled through the West and Middle West, where he could witness first hand the life and landscape of the growing nation.*

*At an early age he was thrust into contact with vast expanses of raw, unspoiled nature; to escape it on the frontier was impossible. This experience undoubtedly helped him to conceive of nature as an insistent viral force which man should seek to embrace for his own betterment. . . It may seem cliché to attribute his democratic spirit, his individualism and his suspicion of external controls to an upbringing in a pioneering community . . . much of Henri's personality can be explained by the fact that he spent his formative years in the West.*[74]

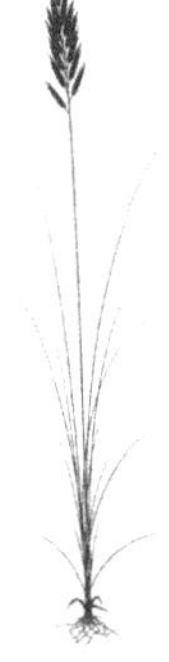

On the impact of the remarkable environments that he encountered all across the country and around the world, but certainly in Nebraska, Henri would later write in his book, *The Art Spirit*, that:

*I find nature "as is" a very wonderful romance and no man-made concoctions have ever beaten it either romance or sweetness.* [75]

Homer also wrote, and again, his time in Nebraska would have certainly impacted his feelings about freedom:

*The key to Henri's personality is his belief in the freedom and inherent dignity of the individual. The conviction did not stem from any religious dogma but a deep humanistic faith in the innate value of man as a unique being. Henri's ideal was the self-reliant individual who searched honest within himself for the answers to the central questions of art and life.*[76]

When reading Henri's book, *The Art Spirit*, one can see, as did Homer, that there remained in him a part of this Nebraska legacy – the notions of freedom and self-reliance. When Henri speaks of the freedom of the individual to create what he wanted, that would have been a common sentiment held by many of the homesteaders and settlers that he knew on the Great Plains from 1873-1884 or had watched go by on the Mormon, Oregon and California trails.

Robert Henri is often described as a pioneer, a term he would have been very familiar with and had various meanings for him. In 1931, two years after his death, the *Robert Henri Memorial Exhibition* was held and coordinated by John Sloan and Eugene Speicher. Sloan was Henri's best friend and one of the few people, other than family, who knew about his Nebraska roots. Fifty-four paintings were in the show, many of which were loaned from the Henri estate.

The show was first displayed in New York City where it was exhibited at The Metropolitan Museum of Art from March 9 to April 19, 1931. The show then traveled to the Baltimore Museum of Art in May. The museum's director, R. J. McKinney, not knowing of Henri's Nebraska roots or his association with the early pioneers of the Great Plains, wrote the following in the exhibition catalog:

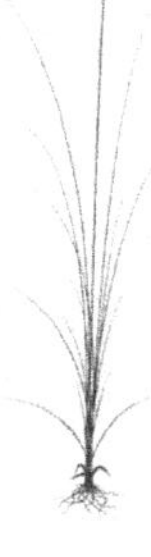

*It is the museum's privilege at this time to present in retrospect the work of Robert Henri, whose deep and guiding influence has left an indelible impression upon the painting craft and whose kindly character and vigorous personality have stimulated all who came in contact with him. A pioneer, ever ready to explore, making use of material at hand, and like a pioneer, building constructively, untrammeled by the faddisms of the day, he has achieved greatness.*[77]

In the end, Nebraska was one of those sign-posts that he referred to in his book, *The Art Spirit - a place on the way to be -* as he might have said. He wrote in 1923:

*There are moments in our lives, there are moments in a day, when we seem to see beyond the usual. Such are the moments of our greatest happiness. Such are the moments of our greatest wisdom. If one could but recall his vision by some sort of sign. It was in this hope that the arts were invented. Sign-posts on the way to what may be. Sign-posts toward greater knowledge.*[78]

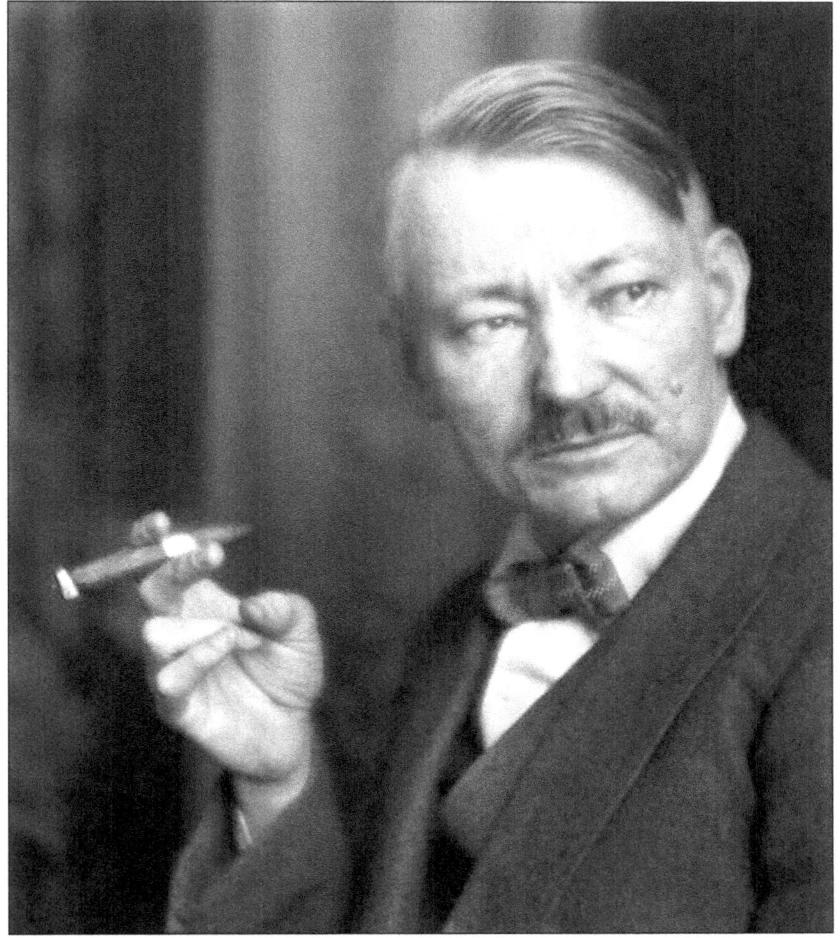

*Courtesy Andrew Cozad*

*Robert Henri*

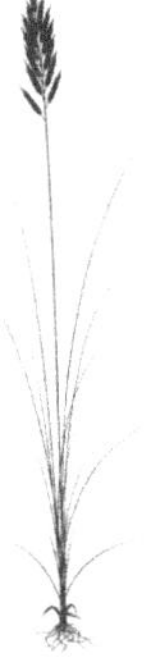

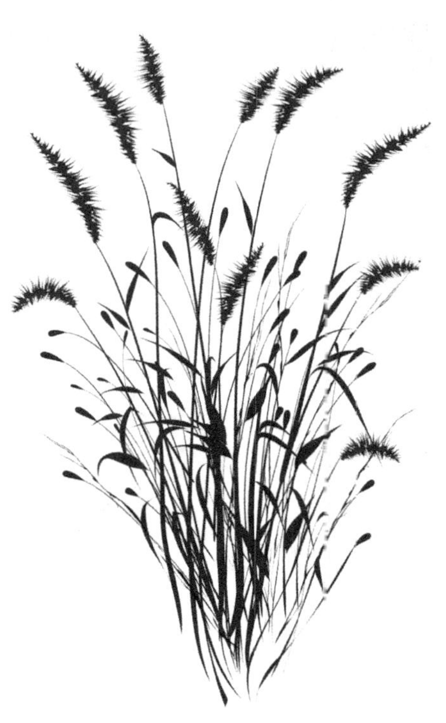

# Part III

# The Hendee

PLAN OF THE HOUSE

*The Rooms colored yellow in the above plat are used by us. The other parts of the house-on the first floor—are used as storeing [sic] rooms.*

*Upstairs in the house—Over the parlor is ma's & pas room. Over the office of pa & Johnnie is Johnnie's and my room. Over my office is a spare room for Johnnie & I. One small room over the dining room is our washroom. The other parts of the upstairs are store rooms.*

*In my office is my desk & printing press. In Pas and Johnnies office they have their desk and other things in the business line. Otherwise the rooms are furnished neatly.*[1]

Robert Cozad
1880 Diary

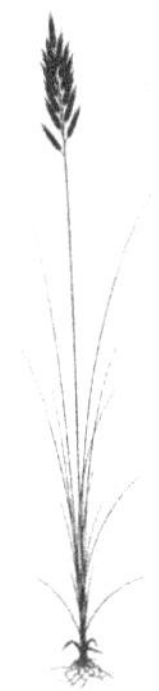

# *Chapter 1*

## The Emigrant Hotel
## 1879-1884

*During the 1870s when the first towns of Dawson County, Nebraska were being established it was considered essential that some buildings be of brick to show the world they were towns of permanence and substance. Of these brick buildings, only the Hendee Hotel survives in Dawson County.*[2]

National Register of Historic Places Inventory
Nomination Form for The Hendee Hotel
1979

*The last few days we have been arranging the house. We are now occupying the whole east part of the house.*[3]

Robert Henry Cozad
1880 Diary

The telling of the Cozad story must also include one of the few but significant remaining artifacts in the town with which the family was associated from 1873-1884. Today it is the home of the Robert Henri Museum. While the town retains the family's name, there are very few places where one can stand on a location and know for certain that John, for example, stood or stayed there. But just as the Cozad story is an enigma, so is the history of the building.

Trying to uncover the Robert Henri Museum building's architectural past and its history is a complicated task because of the numerous renovations that have been completed during the course of its one-hundred-and-forty-year history. As each project was undertaken, more and more of the original construction materials, particularly on the exterior, were replaced or changed.

There are several significant dates in the building's history including its initial construction (1878-1879)[4], the first major renovations (c. 1890s), the construction of an attached kitchen with a small addition (unknown dates), the moving of a small wood framed building onto the site (c. 1909-1929)[5], a second major renovation when the building was stuccoed (c. 1910-1913)[6], renovations to convert the building into multiple residential units (c. late 1930s-1940s)[7], the construction of a new block addition on the northeast corner of the structure (1940)[8], the building of a brick addition on the northwestern side of the building (1958)[9], the renovations that were completed to convert the building into a museum (1980s), the rebuilding of the south and west walls of the building (2006) and more recently with major upgrades to the building's various infrastructure systems (2016-2023).

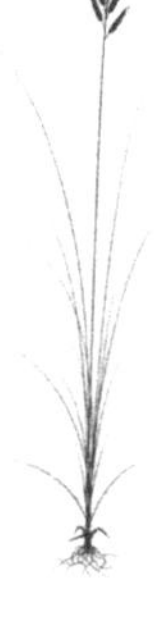

On the exterior, aside from the brickwork, most of the architectural features are not from the Cozad era (1878-1884). Most of those architectural elements have been replaced at one time or another including window frames, casings, sash, doors, soffits and fascia. The interior of the building has also seen many changes including door openings, divisions of rooms, and changes in use. There are also other projects that have been completed that have not been documented in the building's recorded history.

Trying to track down the history of the building's occupants and its uses can also be a challenging task and the facts that have been uncovered so far are revealed here. However, it is believed that there still is more information to be found.

### The Emigrant Hotel

The first building that the Cozads used as a residence when they arrived, on a part-time basis, was also the town's hotel. It was probably constructed in late 1873 or early 1874 and formed a part of that small cluster of buildings near the original railroad station. Local historian Kieth Buss located it at 540 Meridian Avenue at its junction with U.S. Highway 30.[10]

This lodging place, known as either the *Emigrant Hotel or Emigrant House*, has been described as a wood-framed building, two stories high, with its dimensions being thirty feet by eighty feet. It housed, at times, up to six families and was managed by Julia Gatewood.[11]

There is also a surviving account by at least one lodger, A.T. Griffith, whose description was included in a 1926 eighth grade Cozad school class history of the community. His account follows:

*The day after his arrival (1874), he, with fourteen other land seekers, accompanied by J. J. Cozad and David Claypool, the two promoters of the town, and real estate agents, started out to look for land claims. They returned in time for supper at the hotel. Upon inquiring what his bill for lodging, breakfast and supper was, he was informed that $5 would be about right. Mr. Griffith just had two $5 bills and a $2 bill, besides a railroad ticket to Cincinnati, Ohio. He gave the landlady $5.00, packed up his chest of carpenter tools and his trunks and went to the station to wait for a train to take him back east. While waiting, a man who lived here, asked him to stay longer, telling Mr. Griffith that he could stay with him for $3 a week. This he decided to do. Later he took up a homestead a few miles east of Cozad.*[12]

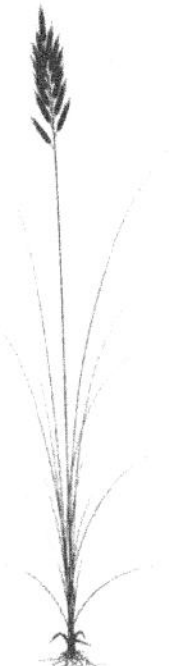

In late 1878 or early 1879, according to most accounts, John Cozad began the construction of what was then the largest brick building in the fledgling community.[13] At least one contemporary account about Cozad, an article in the *Omaha Weekly Bee,* dated September 10, 1879, includes a reference to a brick hotel measuring sixty-four feet in length.[14] The length of the present museum building is sixty-five feet.

However, there remains some questions about the hotel's construction date. Correspondence by Jan Patterson, a previous museum director, suggests an earlier date, although not a definitive one. She does not cite any source. There are also several other sources that raise the question. A hotel in Cozad was described in the journal of an Army officer in 1874 as the following:

*Their) Hotel Building is really one of the best-looking structures that I have seen west of Omaha.*[15]

When the building, along with so many others was destroyed by the 1876 fire, it was valued at fifteen thousand dollars, a significant amount for the time and place according to a North Platte newspaper account. This would seem to confirm the account of Lt. James E. H. Foster.[16] It seems curious that a wood-framed building could possibly have been the best-looking structure between Omaha and Cozad given that Kearney and Grand Island were established by that point and probably had any number of wood framed buildings.

A September 5, 1874, article in the *North Platte Enterprise* states that Cozad was going to build a brick house in the fall. Then, in June of 1875, a North Platte newspaper reported that brick making was about to begin and that Cozad would be erecting a brick residence that would need five thousand bricks.[17]

Others have speculated that Cozad already had plans to build a substantial brick house and that after the fire occurred, he decided to enlarge the building

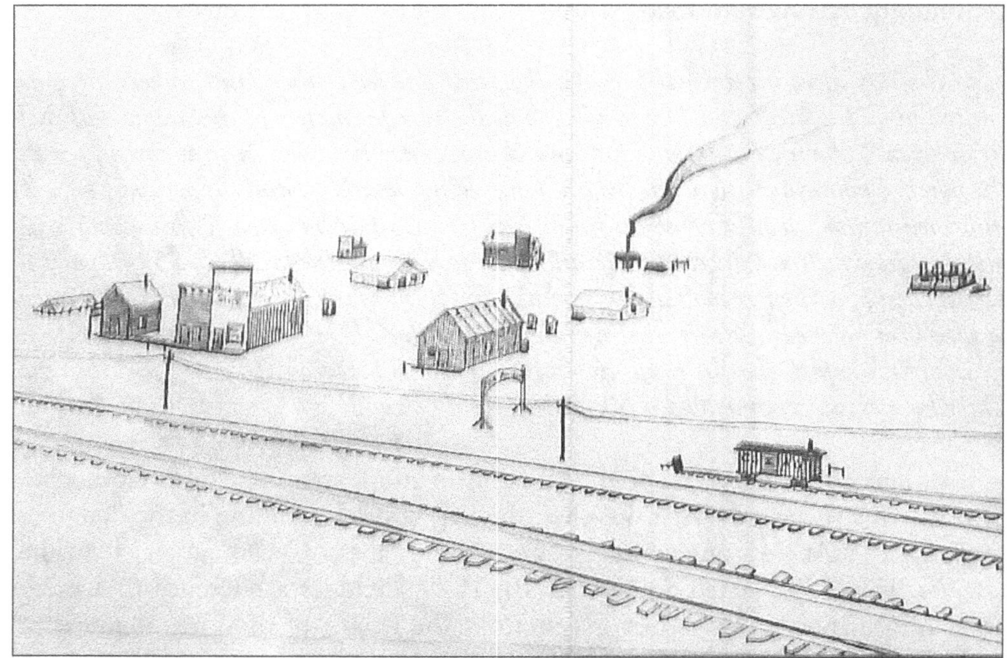

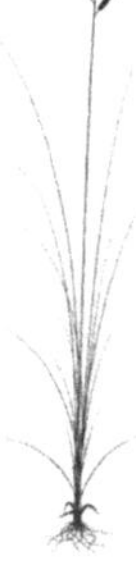

*Collection of the Robert Henri Museum and Art Gallery*

*This grainy photograph of a drawing of the early settlement at Cozad shows the collection of buildings near the Union Pacific's tracks. While the artist is unknown, the illustration shows what the Emigrant Hotel may have looked like. It is believed to be the third building from the left with the false front.*

to include both a hotel and residence, but there is no surviving documentation or contemporary sources at this time that confirms this. Yet with these newspaper accounts that possibility seems more plausible.[18]

## THE BRICK HOTEL

The most notable feature of the current museum building is its brick construction. This was distinctive because most of the buildings built in Cozad in those early decades were wood-framed. Communities encouraged the construction of brick structures because it lent an air of permanence to those newly settled areas and there was less fire risk, although one remained. It has been suggested that it cost five thousand dollars to build.[19]

The building was constructed using brick molded and fired in Traber Gatewood's brickyard, which was located east of the town near present day U.S. Route 30 near the Strever property (1971).[20] The actual location was north and west of the northwest corner of the Cozad Cemetery. Betty Menke, in her important monograph, entitled *Robert Henri Museum and Historical Walkway*, relates that the brick used measured one foot long, but repair work undertaken in the museum (2020) confirmed that the brick was a typical size and not the length she proposed. Perhaps what she meant to say was that the building's walls were one foot deep.[21]

However, the kind of adobe brick that was used, while considered adequate to serve the purposes at the time, has led to major structural problems in the one hundred and forty years since its construction. In 2004, an engineering firm provided the following analysis of the brick that had been used for construction:

*These exterior brick walls contain two layers (wythes) interconnected by header courses. Typically, the best brick is placed in the exterior layer and the interior layer consists of a lesser quality. This interior brick layer usually consists of an adobe brick. This adobe brick was usually under burned, and thus tended to be quite soft and extremely absorbent. Based on the observations, it appears as though the exterior and interior layers are composed of this adobe brick. The brick deterioration is probably caused by moisture buildup under an impermeable coating and delaminating from freeze-thaw damage. Both the concrete stucco and interior plaster trapped the moisture behind the wall.*[22]

The foundation was:

*. . . made of brick wall, which splayed outward at the bottom to help form a solid bearing foundation. The actual footing was usually made of local limestone slabs placed directly on the earth. The foundation wall is made of brick masonry made of brick from a local brickyard.*[23]

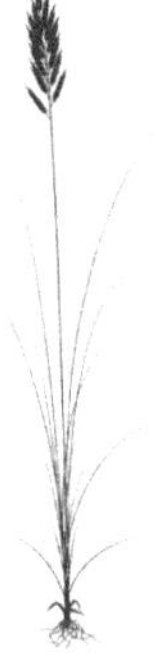

Today it is said to be the oldest brick structure in Dawson County and is generally accepted to have been completed in 1879. If it is not the oldest, it is certainly one of the oldest.[24] The side-gabled building was constructed in the Italianate style that was popular from 1840-1885. The style was very common across America and particularly in the Northeast and in the new towns that were being established in the Midwest. It began to be used in the 1830s.[25] Italianate buildings constructed near the end of the style's popularity were much more elaborate, such as the Cozad home in Cozaddale, with more detailing and *decorative exuberance* as it was called. [26]

Rural styles were often less exuberant and simpler, and that is the case with the museum building. Also, their popularity remained long after urban areas had begun to use newer styles.[27] The large brick structure on Eighth Street in Cozad was evocative in its basic design, and size, to the home John J. Cozad had built in Cozaddale, Ohio, although not nearly as ornate. It is curious that style began to decline after the financial crisis of 1873, the same time that John Cozad was establishing his community in Nebraska. This simpler design may also reflect John J. Cozad's feelings about the town compared to Cozaddale, the difficulty in getting materials shipped, or may have been an indication of his financial situation.

Other features of the house included wood floor joists with wood flooring, and some of those original floors remain, although others have been replaced. The plaster walls and ceilings that remain in much of the building are original as is the tin ceiling in the current lobby and gift shop area. Today there are twenty-six double hung windows although some were added after the building's construction.[28]

The original roof, laid on top of wood framing with wood lap siding, was sheathed with wood shakes. Late nineteenth century photographs confirm this. However, there is an entry in Robert Cozad's 1880 diary that mentions that a portion of the tin roof had blown off and that he and Johnny had spent some time rolling up tin that had been torn off. This may have only been a portion of the roof, for example, the front porch or the kitchen wing. A shake roof remained on the building until the twenty-first century.[29]

The original building was almost four thousand square feet with later additions adding almost one thousand more square feet.

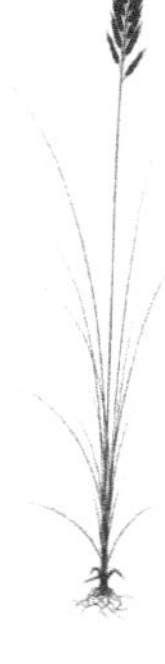

### Opening the Riggs Hotel and Cozad Residence

When the construction of the large brick building was finished, John J. Cozad sold the building to Joseph (1815-1898) and Clara (1854-1921) Riggs along with five hundred acres of land to the north and east of the community in April 1879. Another version of this story, by a Riggs family historian, believes that they only rented it from Cozad.[30]

Joseph Riggs was born in Hubbard, Ohio in 1815. He was married twice; his first wife had died, and he married his second wife, Clara, in 1871. She was thirty-seven years his junior and by this marriage there were four children. Riggs had lived just a few miles south of Cozaddale in Goshen and he and Cozad were large landowners. Another source suggests that the Riggs family were from Cincinnati. Either way, the Cozads and Riggs probably had known each other before they came to Nebraska.[31]

According to a family history, Riggs had arrived in Nebraska in 1876, initially renting the *Emigrant Hotel* from the Cozads or Gatewoods. This arrangement would be short-lived because of the building's destruction during the fire in April of that year. Riggs lost all of his family's furniture in that conflagration. The rest of the Riggs family came west from Ohio in either late 1878 or early 1879 and initially settled in at Plum Creek because there was adequate housing there. One of the four children of Joseph and Clara, Amanda, was born there in 1879.[32]

It is believed that as part of the April 1879 agreement with Riggs, Cozad's mortgage included a provision that allowed the Cozad family to live in the brick hotel and have their meals there.[33] There are no contemporary accounts of how the building was furnished during the Riggs era or how the building's rooms were arranged. A Riggs family member believed it was the Riggs who originally furnished the hotel.[34]

Both Clara and Joseph ran the hotel for about one year, along with two servants, Sally Hendrick and Elias Waldron. In addition, the Riggs children lived there too. During this time Clara and Theresa became good friends and continued to see each other in the years to come.[35]

In the first year after the hotel opened, it went through the cycles of occupancy and there are several sources that provide insights. For example, just after the building opened, Eugene Young (1851-1935) and his new bride, Nettie Ball (1851-1914) came back to Cozad from California after their nuptials and honeymooned at what was called the *Riggs Hotel*.[36] The Youngs became boarders after their honeymoon until more permanent quarters were found. He later became the county superintendent of schools.[37]

At Christmas in 1879, there were only a few people in Cozad, all of them the original colonizers, and so the hotel was probably not fully occupied. But, in March 1880, the hotel was full, as between twenty-five and thirty people were staying there, probably filling all the building's rooms completely.[38]

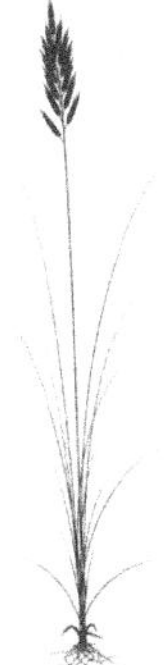

Robert Cozad portrays the relationship between the Riggs and his family in a negative light in his 1880 diary, and it is those impressions, one of a fifteen-year-old boy, that found their way into Mari Sandoz's book, *Son of the Gamblin' Man*. One story is that the quality of the meals dropped when John Cozad was away on business, and Robert became so dissatisfied that he decided to go to his grandmother's for his meals and board. His mother told him he would have to pay his grandmother out of his own pocket. He apparently did.[39]

The agreement between Riggs and Cozad did not work out and was short-lived.[40] In late June 1880, a little more than one year after Clara and Joseph Riggs had taken ownership, Robert Cozad noted in his diary that:

*Pa had Mr. Riggs to leave the house. He is now keeping Hotel on the opposite side of the street of us in the old Goodyear House.*[41]

Riggs had fallen behind on the mortgage payments, and as reported by Robert, moved across the street to manage another hotel that was also called the *Riggs House* in direct competition to the Cozads. Joseph Riggs was then sixty-six and perhaps did not want to run such a busy hotel operation, service the needs of the Cozads, and on top of that, manage the farm that he had acquired from Cozad. Or perhaps he and Cozad did not get along particularly well.[42]

Another possibility is that there was simply not enough revenue generating rooms for the Riggs. Either late in 1880 or 1881 the Riggs family left Cozad altogether and moved to Arnold, Nebraska. The Riggs House was subsequently moved to a lot across from the northeast corner of what is today, City Park or Veterans Park.[43]

Two years later, in 1882, Cozad obtained a court order, and the properties that had been sold to the Riggs were put up for auction at a sheriff's sale. Cozad was the high bidder and became the owner again.[44]

The Riggs family would come back to Cozad a few years later when Joseph operated a furniture store along with an undertaking business, a common business combination of the time. Clara became an important medical assistant to the townspeople during a time when there were no hospitals. They both remained active in the community until their deaths.[45]

## The Cozads Take Over

Beginning in the summer of 1880, the Cozad family resided in the town of their creation for the longest, most continuous and significant period since their arrival in 1873. Robert had finished his schooling at Chickering in June 1879, and with the Riggs family gone, the Cozads began to establish a different kind of footprint in the building. Now, the large brick building became their permanent residence.

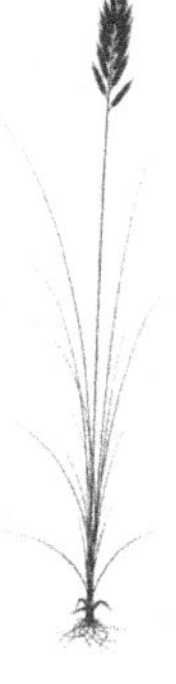

There are no known surviving sources that describe how the hotel was laid out prior to the summer of 1880 so it is not known what rooms the Cozads had previously occupied. From an interpretive point of view, the museum has always told visitors that the floor plan described in the Sandoz book is what was used.[46] However, there are no other records that confirm that.

With the Riggs family living across the street, the Cozads rearranged the house to better suit their needs. They certainly wanted more room than they had been previously using, along with perhaps gaining more privacy. They may have even made some renovations, although that is not known or references to it are not found in any sources. Perhaps items were brought out from Cozaddale.[47]

During that summer it is believed that the Cozads divided the large brick building into two sections, a private residence that was used by them and the other, a smaller percentage than previously used by the traveling public. The private sections were spread across two floors. Two bedrooms, one for the parents and one for the boys, occupied the second floor along with storage areas. An office for Robert and John J. was on the first floor and a parlor for the family's private use was created along with a separate entrance to the exterior. Much of the eastern half of the building was reserved for their personal use.[48]

It is during this summer, that Robert Cozad's journaling skills provide the most complete and detailed contemporary source of information about the building.[49] It is in the pages of his 1880 diary that Robert Cozad drew a plan of the first floor of the building, described the purposes of its rooms and provided written descriptions of the second floor. Unfortunately, the second-floor descriptions do not include a floor plan and so the purpose of several of the rooms remain

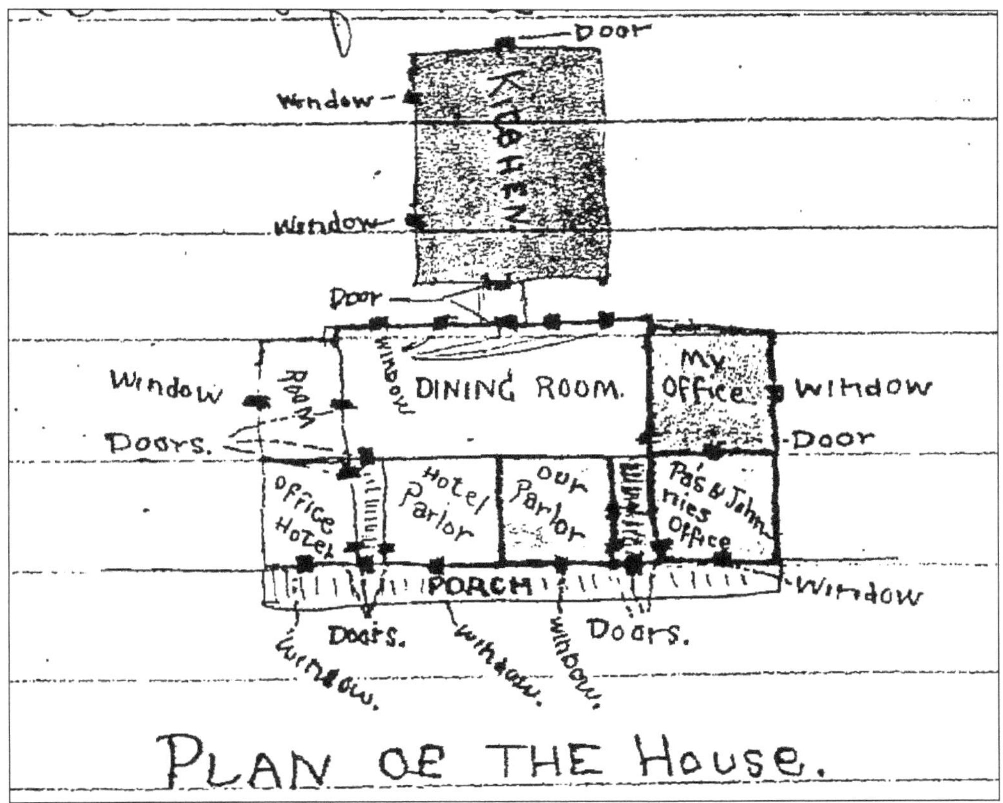


*Collection of the Robert Henri Museum and Art Gallery*

*Robert Cozad drew a plan of the first floor of the house in his 1880 diary. The museum's current layout reflects Henri's drawing.*

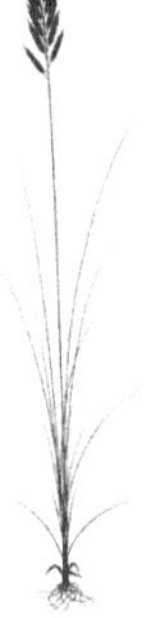

unclear, although Robert did write about some of them. His diary describes how it probably remained until the family moved to Denver in the summer of 1881. His descriptions follow:

*The last few days we have been arranging the House. We are now occupying the whole ~~west~~ east part of the house.*

*PLAN OF THE HOUSE*

*The Rooms colored yellow in the above plat are used by us. The other parts of the house-on the first floor—are used as storeing [sic] rooms.*

*Upstairs in the house—Over the parlor is ma's & pas (sic) room. Over the office of pa & Johnnie is Johnnie's and my room. Over my office is a spare room for Johnnie & I. One small room over the dining room is our washroom. The other parts of the upstairs are store rooms.*

*In my office is my desk & printing press. In Pas and Johnnies office they have their desk and other things in the business line. Otherwise the rooms are furnished neatly.*[50]

The diary entry does, however, leave us with questions. Robert accounts for three of the rooms on the second floor and describes specific uses for them. Then, he points out that several rooms were used for storage, but they remain unidentified. Curiously, he does not mention specifically any of the rooms being used for hotel purposes, except for the parlor on the first floor, nor does he describe any of the hotel's operation. Because his diary is filled with so many descriptions of his various activities it is a curious omission, if it is that.[51]

However, his designation on his floor plan of a parlor room for hotel guests, along with an office for the hotel, would seem to indicate that some portion of the building, even if it was a couple of rooms, were still being used for the traveling public or lodgers. Mari Sandoz wrote that the building returned to being a hotel after the Riggs' departure and that Theresa cooked meals while the boys helped with serving and cleaning up.[52]

The following sections describe what is known about the building. The information is gleaned from photographs, contemporary paperwork and current analyses of the historic fabric of the building.

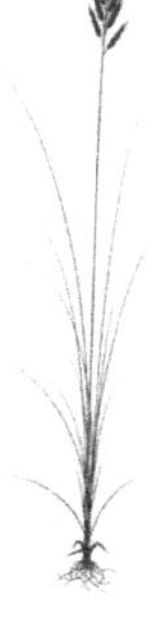

*Exterior*

The original structure was two and a half stories, rectangular in shape, and measured sixty-five feet by twenty-seven feet. Two extensions on the north side were added later. The building had a gabled roof that was sheathed with wood shake shingles at the time of construction. There were at one time five chimneys,

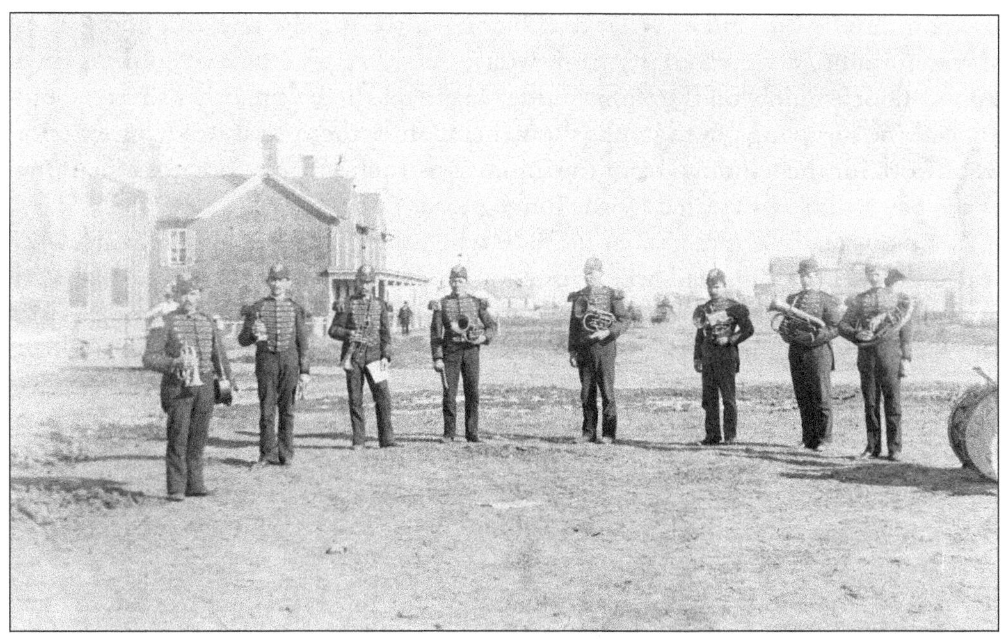

*Courtesy 100th Meridian Museum*

*This may be the oldest known picture of the present-day museum, believed to have been taken in 1890. The Cozad Coronet Band is standing on East 8th Street, and the view is looking toward the east.*

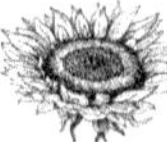

although only three remain today, two having been covered during a reroofing project in the twentieth century. The interior walls of the building were also constructed of brick, which created its footprint. A wooden extension that measures twenty-six by thirteen feet was built on the backside of the building but was not attached originally.[53]

A large wrap-around porch, typical of period structures, extended from one end of the building to the other. There were, it is known, in later times, captain's chairs placed on the front porch for hotel guests and lodgers to sit in. [54] There are two hitching rings in a cement block at the eastern end of the building that may date to the original Cozad era.[55]

There were bracketed cornices on the front porch, and those that remain may be the originals saved from various renovations or at least are from a much earlier time. From the earliest photographs, there appears to have been no decorative cornices elsewhere on the building.[56]

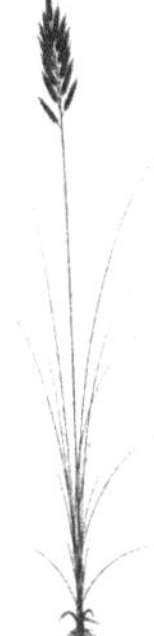

Large, rectangular floor to ceiling windows originally were on the porch (south) side of the first floor and were similar to ones in the family home in Cozaddale, Ohio and typical of the Italianate style. The segmented, arched two-over-two windows, found on the rest of the first floor, and on the second floor, were also common in that time. What may be one of the earliest known photographs of the building, a view looking from west to east, shows a pair of shutters on a second-floor window on the western side.[57] Perhaps there were other shutters, but none of the surviving photographs show them. Since there is no surviving exterior woodwork for the windows from the initial construction, any evidence remaining of the paint shadows created by the hinge pins is gone.

A paint analysis undertaken in 2020 when the trim was being repainted revealed that the building had been painted at least five different colors. An oil-based primer was put on the bare wood when original construction was completed in 1879, and the building's trim was painted a buff-ivory color. In the years following, several other combinations were used, including green-gray, ochre-maroon, light gray and white.[58]

There was, at least in the 1890s, a windmill in what is now the back yard, along with an outhouse, although it was probably erected earlier, given the needs of the hotel and its visitors and the Cozads. By the early twentieth century, there were at least seventy-five windmills located in the town.[59]

Three small outbuildings were added after 1900 on the north side of the property. A wooden boardwalk ran in front of the building, typical of nineteenth century rural towns. The level of the street was considerably lower than the walkway and it is only in the twentieth century that the street has come to the same level as the current sidewalk.[60]

*Entranceways*

At the time of the Cozad's ownership, there were three doors on the south side of the building, all having transoms. The doorways are less decorative, unlike many of those in Italianate houses, which often had elaborate entranceways.[61] The door on the far western end led into the hotel office (today it is a floor to ceiling window), the next door to the east accessed the rooms on the second floor that were used by the public via a staircase, and the hotel parlor used by guests. On the eastern end of the building was another door that led into the Cozad's private parlor, John J.'s office and to a stairway to the second-floor suite of bedrooms of the Cozad boys and parents. There was no exterior doorway leading out of John J.'s office as there is today. It was a later addition.

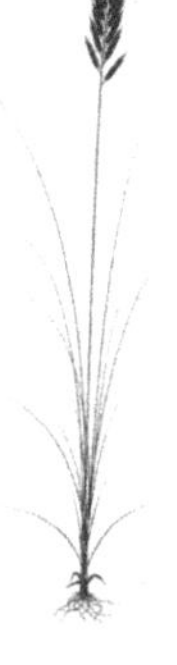

*First Floor*

Robert Cozad's floor plan shows the original layout of the first-floor. Because of the various changes that have been made to the building over the last one hundred and forty years, it would be difficult without his drawing to determine the various functions of the individual rooms in 1880.[62]

### *Visitor Lobby*

This room served as the hotel's office, and it was here visitors that would sign the guest register and pay for their meals and lodging. At the time of the hotel's opening Clara and Joseph Riggs would presumably have met their guests in this room as did the Cozads. This room served this purpose until well into the twentieth century. The tin ceiling is believed to be original to the building.[63]

Just beyond the lobby on the curved part of a dividing wall can be found the initials *RHC* placed there by Robert Henry Cozad, perhaps in 1879, when the building's construction was being completed. The style of the signature is very similar to what is found in the September 21, 1880, entry in his diary.[64]

The initials were discovered when the building was being restored and wallpaper being removed in the mid-1980s.[65] It was a major find, especially given all the renovation work. It is very faint and written directly on the plaster which 0was a common tradition for wallpaper hangers to pencil their names and the date on the bare plaster walls before they  hung the wallpaper.

### *Storage Room*

A room adjacent to the hotel office, where the gift shop is now located, is what Robert simply described on his floor plan as a *Room.* A wall separated it from the hotel office, so there was no access to it from the office, unlike today, where an archway that was later cut leads into the gift shop. It may have been used for storage or some other purpose related to the hotel's operations.

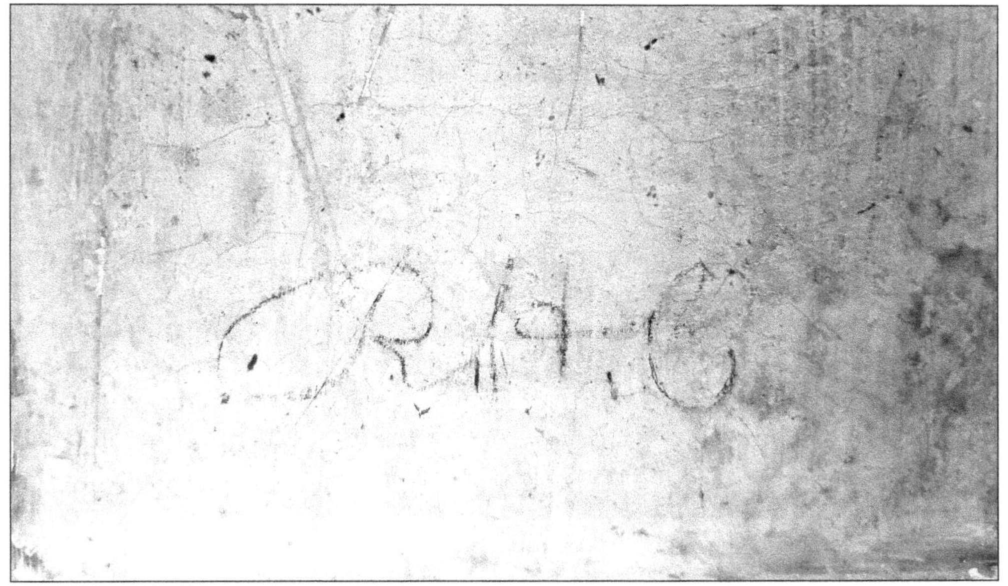


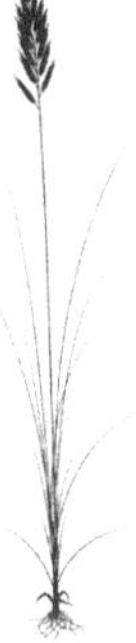

*Robert Henri Museum and Art Gallery Collection*

*Robert Henry Cozad's initials on the original plaster can still be seen just beyond the lobby on the column. They may have dated from 1878 or 1879, when the building's construction was being completed.*

*Hotel Parlor*

As part of the Cozad's effort to maintain separate public and private living space, a room was set aside for use by hotel guests. Here, guests could spend their time relaxing, talking, reading the papers, and resting after a day of traveling or before they went out to establish their land claims. In many hotels, gambling would have been a staple of the times, but it is believed that John J. Cozad did not initially allow gambling in the town or in this building. Gambling was done in secrecy in several buildings in the town, according to Mari Sandoz's book.

The room had a coal stove on its west wall, along with a floor to ceiling window so that visitors could see out onto the street. There was only one way to access this room and that was from a front entrance on the southwest corner. The room was restored in the 1980s to appear as it did in the Cozad era, and the wallpaper is a period reproduction along with the floor and trim colors. Today it is furnished with artifacts from the 1880s.

*Cozad Family Parlor*

The Cozads maintained a separate parlor that was accessible only from a door on the southeastern corner of the room and from the family's private entrance from the front of the building. As a lover of music, Mrs. Cozad encouraged the appreciation of music in her sons as well. She is said to have brought the first piano to Cozad, although a Riggs family history suggested that James Riggs had brought the first piano to the community when he moved into the Emigrant Hotel and it was destroyed in the 1876 fire. It is also known that there were parties in the hotel with music played by Traber Gatewood.[66]

Today it is furnished with artifacts dating from the 1880s, and the wallpaper and paint in the room are period reproductions. It too was heated by a coal stove located on the western wall.

*Dining Room*

The dining room was, and remains, the largest room in the house. The room was eleven feet wide and forty feet long and is believed to retain some of its original wainscoting.[67] The room served both the traveling public, homesteaders, and the Cozads who had their meals there. The main feature in the room was a large table where the diners ate. The Cozads sat at one end and used fine china, fine utensils, and napkins. Guests sat at the other end on benches and ate off lesser quality tinware.[68]

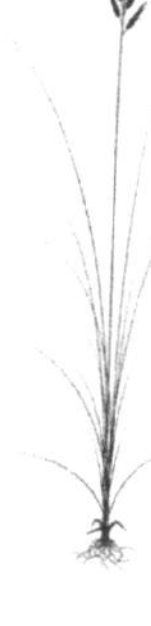

A surviving contemporary description of the room was given by L.P. Owens, whose family arrived in Cozad in March 1880. He wrote:

*There were twenty-five to thirty people who got off the train that morning and the old hotel was sure full. The kitchen and dining room were in a 16 x 40 building built on the north end of the brick hotel. The huge table, about four feet wide and twenty-five feet long was made of stock boards and there were large chairs and benches around it. And the table was really filled that first morning we ate there. The Cozad family were seated at the head of the table, there were the father, mother and two sons. My brother introduced all of us to the big "owner" of Cozad, (that was John J. Cozad himself.) I can recall that he wore a big gold chain around his neck, and this chain fell across his chest to his gold pocket watch. I thought it was really great to know the "king of faro and poker games."* [69]

Owens' description may be a result of faulty memory or subsequent mistakes in relaying the story. There may have been so many people in the building that the dining area was extended into the kitchen. The dining room and kitchen are clearly shown on Cozad's floor plan as separate.

The dimensions were changed in the mid-1900s when a bathroom was installed at the western end and the dining room shortened in length. Today the small room is used for storage. Another room was created at the eastern end with a false wall and was removed during the renovations in the 1980s.

*Kitchen*

The kitchen in the original hotel was a separate building connected by a breezeway as can be seen on Cozad's 1880 floor plan.[70] The room did not look as it does today as the present structure was constructed as an addition, attached to the building at a later date. It was smaller than the current room, and there were no windows on the east side of the room and a doorway led to the back yard on the north side. Two windows were located on the west side.

Today there is a sink in the room that is said to be from the original kitchen and was purchased at an auction in the late 1970s when the contents of the building were sold. Some of the dishware that is included in the museum's collection, and on display, is believed to have come from the Cozad era.[71]

One possible explanation for the different dimension is that there may have been a fire after 1880 that either destroyed the original kitchen or damaged it badly. Or, the kitchen wing may have deteriorated since it had been constructed and was simply taken down. Perhaps it was simply enlarged and attached to the main building during one of several renovations that were undertaken, eliminating the breezeway.

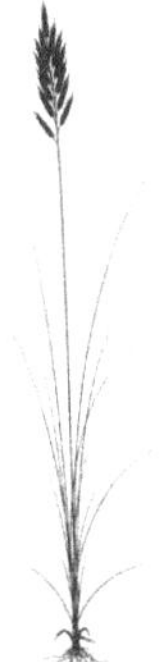

*Robert Cozad's Office*

Robert Cozad used this room for his office and his printing business. Here he worked on his diaries, journals and scrapbooks and he drew sketches that would ultimately lead him to a career as an artist.

*John and Johnny's Office*

This room housed the office of John J. and Johnny Cozad. One of the unique architectural features in this room is the archway leading into Robert's office. The exterior entrance and window on the eastern side of the room did not exist in the Cozad period, they were added later.

John J. conducted his real estate business in this room, and many land transactions took place or were planned out here. Also, Cozad's hay business was headquartered here and coordinated by Johnny. This corner of the building was reserved for the family as can be seen on Robert's floorplan.[72]

*Second Floor*

Just as with the first floor, the second-floor rooms were clearly delineated between guests and the Cozad's private living quarters.

*Johnny and Robert's Bedroom, Johnny and Robert's Storeroom and Washroom*

A large bedroom on the southeast corner of the building was used by both Johnny and Robert Cozad. It would have had a panoramic view to the east and south as one would have been able to see the railroad line, the Platte River and the hill country to the south. It is not known if they had just a single bed, but presumably there were two beds as the boys got older.[73]

Next to this room, in the northeast corner of the building, was a storeroom for both boys. A small adjacent room, off the hall, to the west was used as a washroom for them.[74]

*John and Theresa Cozad's Bedroom*

Like their son's bedroom, their room also faced to the south, toward the Platte River. There was one closet tucked into the southeast corner. An interesting feature that was found during the restoration were the initials *RH* written on the western wall of the room.

Today they are preserved behind glass and while it is presumed that they are Robert's, the style is noticeably different from the initials found on the first floor. These could be the initials of someone else entirely different perhaps, even the wallpaper installer. One piece of evidence to suggest it is the latter possibility comes from a September 21, 1880, entry in Robert's diary which states:

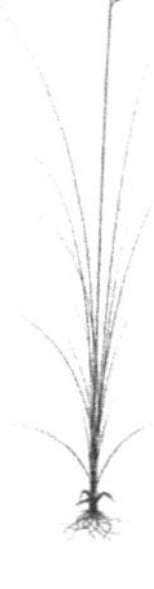

*A Note—Lately I have been signing papers where only initials were needed, and always before on all little occasions where I had any signing to do—school papers, etc. I have signed R.H.C. three initials joined together. Many a person would know this to be my signature even if it were seen in California or some other distant place—all on account of my always signing it in that special way.*[75]

Until more evidence comes to light, the origin of the signature will remain a mystery.

### *Hotel Rooms*

There are five rooms on the north side of the second floor that were probably used for hotel rooms. They were small, including just a bed, quilt spread, chair, dresser, bowl and pitcher, and a chamber pot for toilet needs. Clothes could be hung on pegs that were on the wall, and a braided rug probably covered the floor.[76]

### *Unidentified Rooms*

There are two large rooms located on the southwestern side of the building, and their role in the first years of the hotel's history is not clear. Perhaps they were initially used by the Riggs family, as they had a family and servants or were used as boarding rooms, or even storage for the Cozads. There has also been some speculation that the room on the eastern side of the main staircase may have been a sitting room for the Cozads.

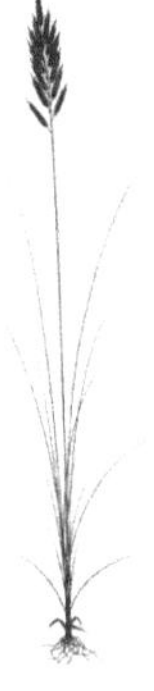

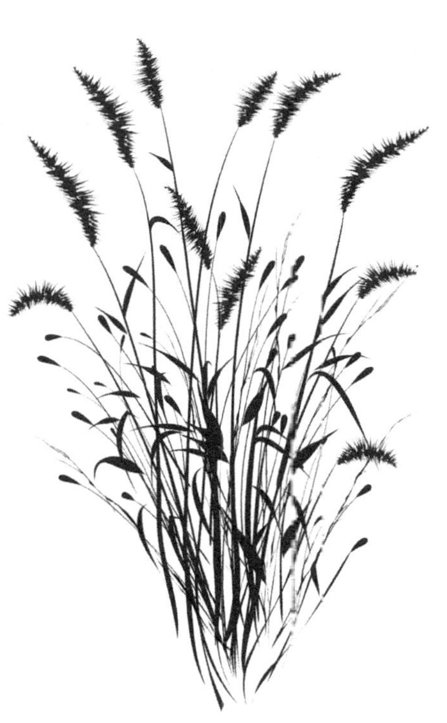

# *Chapter 2*

# The Hendee Hotel
## 1884-1920

*It was during this period 1883 to 1910 that the Hendee Hotel played an important part in the affairs of Cozad, a developing frontier community. In the hotel the early settlers stayed until they could move into their own homes. Train passengers, traveling salesmen, and the town bachelors also stayed in the hotel. Traveling doctors had their offices in the hotel before they moved onto the next town. Even traveling fortune tellers offered their services at the hotel. The local lodges also had their banquets in the hotel dining room.*[1]

National Register of Historic Places Inventory
Nomination Form for The Hendee Hotel
1979

While the Robert Henri Museum has long honored the Cozad family with its preservation and interpretation of their former home and hotel, the building has a much fuller history. In fact, the Cozads only owned the building for a relatively short period of time, from its construction in 1878-79 until 1884, when the last of the family members departed after its sale to Stephen Hendee and his partners.

When the last of the Cozad family members left, the building then passed through the hands of five owners who sometimes hired people to manage it. Those owners included Hendee (1884-1910), John C. Simonson (1910-1920), William Foster and the William Lewis families (1920-1979), Wayman May (1980-1983) and lastly the Robert Henri Foundation, and now known as the Robert Henri Museum and Historical Walkway (1983-present).[2]

The Cozads sold the hotel and five thousand acres to Stephen Hendee in 1884 for twenty thousand dollars.. Hendee then transferred the hotel to his daughter Luem on September 18, 1885, but it reverted back to the father when she got married to Clarence Clark.[3] The elder Hendee died on June 20, 1910, and the hotel, without the vast acreage, was sold several months later by his estate. At the time, the transfer included the brick hotel building and two hundred and fifty feet of street frontage. The property was purchased by John C. Simonson (1867-1929) for two thousand dollars.[4] It had been part of the property designation described as the *Gatewood Addition* which was created on July 29, 1892.[5]

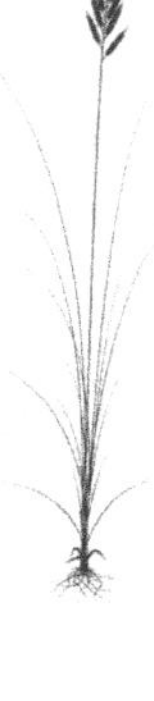

Simonson was also from Bushnell, Illinois and he had moved to Dawson County to take up farming sometime before 1900 as he is listed in the 1900 U.S. Census as living in Nebraska. Married to Olive Edie (1867-1959), they may have known Stephen Hendee because of their connections to Bushnell and because the sale of the hotel occurred very quickly after Hendee's death. Simonson sold ninety feet of the street frontage to Fred Anderson. Previously, a building built by Henry Nielsen had stood on the site, but a movie theater was later built on the land. Simonson sold the hotel in 1920, and he died nine years later and buried in Bushnell.[6]

It has been suggested that in 1910, Mary Edwards, a friend of Theresa Cozad, wanted to buy the building but was dissuaded by family because of the responsibility that the large operation entailed.[7]

During the various ownerships from 1884-1983 the building came to have several names. The various names included *The Hendee House, The Hendee, The Hendee Hotel, The Foster House* and, today, the *Robert Henri Museum* or *The Boyhood Home of Robert Henri*. The most used name, and the one still used today locally is the *Hendee Hotel.* It is this name which has long remained attached to the building. Until 2020, the original hotel sign still hung on the front porch. It was taken down in 2021 and placed on display in the museum, given the historical value of it. Curiously, mail still occasionally comes to the museum, addressed to the Hendee Hotel.

## The Hendee Hotel

Stephen Hendee hired managers who either leased the hotel and operated it or worked there including Asahel Keith Maryott (1836-1907) and Emily Herrick Maryott (1842-1931) as their family are believed to have succeeded the Cozads and Gatewoods.[8] As the Riggs family had done before, it is presumed they leased or rented the hotel from Stephen Hendee. They had come to the Cozad area to farm in 1876 after having arrived in Burt County, Nebraska to homestead in 1865.[9] The family moved to Cozad in 1883 and were managing it in 1885 according to a Nebraska State Census. A. K., as the senior Maryott was known, was the town constable in 1888.[10]

There were nine children born to the parents Alice, Elnora (1861-1940), Clara, Viola, Frank, Miles (1873-1939) and Fred (1876-1951), Merton, and Herbert. Of the nine, Miles went on to fame as he became become one of Nebraska most famous regional painters in the early twentieth century. His earliest sketches were made of the Cozad area and along the Platte River. Maryott's paintings are valued possessions today by their owners.

He was also a taxidermist, an award-winning marksman, and a professional baseball player. However, it was his murder of Sheriff George Albee in 1926 in Oshkosh, Nebraska, where he lived at the time, that he gained a terrible notoriety. After a trial he was sentenced to prison for the rest of his life.[11]

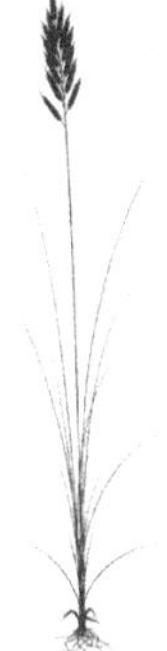

It is possible that Robert Cozad and Miles Maryott (1873-1939) may have known each other? It remains an open question and one that has never been suggested by Maryott researchers.

Other managers included B. F. Lindsey (1891), M. H. Deems (1896), E. W. Morris, and H. M. Edie. In his obituary, David Claypool, one of the original founders of Cozad, was remembered as having run the Hendee Hotel for many years. Martha Trent Durland was the cook at the hotel from 1891-93 and Miss Maggie Smith succeeded her in 1893. Hannah Nichols was a waitress in 1883.[12]

During the various ownerships from 1884-1910 the building came to have several names including: *The Hendee House, The Hendee*, and *The Hendee Hotel.*

At the time of the 1885 Nebraska State Census, it is shown that, curiously, Julia Gatewood was living at The Hendee and Traber Gatewood and his wife

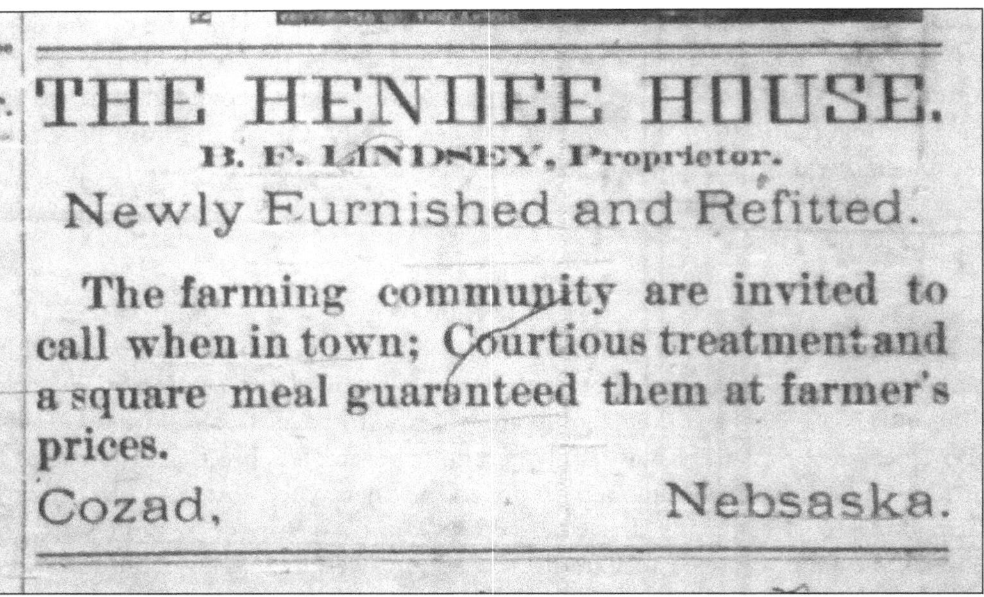

THE HENDEE HOUSE.

B. F. LINDSEY, Proprietor.

Newly Furnished and Refitted.

The farming community are invited to call when in town; Courtious treatment and a square meal guaranteed them at farmer's prices.

Cozad, Nebsaska.

*Courtesy Dawson County Historical Museum*

*In 1892, B.F. Lindsey operated The Hendee House, and it had been refurnished.*

THE HENDEE

M. H. DEEMS, Prop.

This hotel has been thoroughly renovated and refitted. The patronage of the public is solicited. Commercial trade a specialty.

Bus to and from all trains.

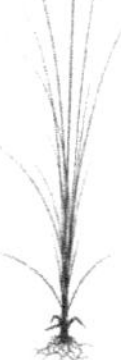

*Courtesy Dawson County Historical Museum*

*In the fall of 1896, as shown in this newspaper ad, The Hendee was renovated. It is not known what work was completed or undertaken.*

Deborah, lived on the next block to the east.[13]

At least twice during his ownership Hendee made substantial improvements to the hotel building. In 1892, an ad in a local newspaper said the hotel had been newly refurbished and refitted. Then, another ad in the *Cozad Tribune* in 1896, indicated that the hotel had recently had additional renovations made and that it had been retrofitted. Those improvements are not described in any sources but probably included replacing furniture and floor coverings, repainting and perhaps new wallpaper, new steam heating fixtures, and electricity or gas lamps for lighting.

The hotel building's original layout of its rooms was probably preserved during this time. Sometime in the 1890s the porch was extended to wrap around the east side of the building, and a door and window were added to provide a new entrance and exit.[14] A small one-story building, to the north of the hotel building is shown on the insurance map in 1909 and is probably an outhouse.[15]

A major change that occurred during this period was that the Cozad-era extension on the back of the building was either removed, rebuilt or perhaps even destroyed because of some kind of an incident. It is not clear what happened at this late date. The current kitchen addition on the north side of the building was probably erected during the Hendee ownership based on an 1890s photograph in

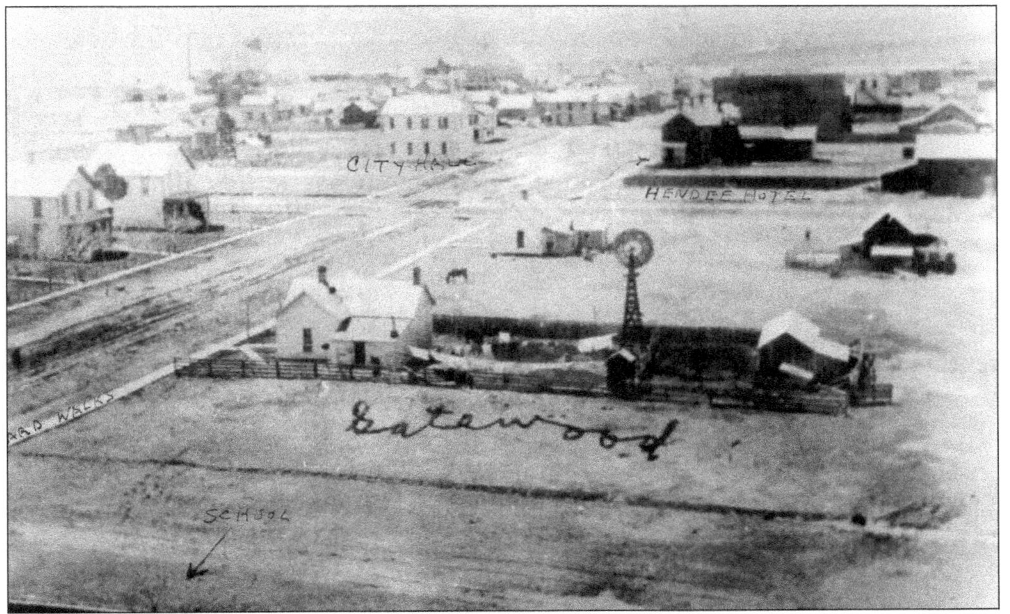


*Robert Henri Museum and Art Gallery Collection*

*This undated photograph shows the Hendee Hotel at the top right. This view, looking toward the west, was taken from the bell tower of the Cozad school, which was two blocks to the east of the Hendee Hotel. It is one of the oldest images in the museum's collection and shows the emerging community of Cozad, probably in the 1890s.*

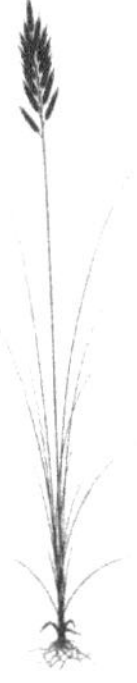

the Robert Henri Museum's collection and data found on the 1909 Sanborn Fire Insurance Company map of Cozad.

The former kitchen wing is considerably different than it was during the Cozad era as it has more windows and doors. It is attached to the building unlike the first extension which had a breezeway that connected the two structures. In addition, at an undetermined time an addition was placed off the north end along with a shed addition on the east side. This new addition must have had a utilitarian purpose because no effort was made to cover over the exterior siding of the kitchen section on the south wall.[16] The kitchen retained its functions in the Hendee-Simonson era, although none of the original utilities or equipment remain, except for a sink that may have been in the hotel originally.[17]

Hendee's improvements and changes reflected a developing business for the hotel and a growing local economy in Cozad, as its population doubled from five hundred to one thousand during the almost thirty years he owned the hotel.

While there were managers for the hotel during Hendee's ownership, he must have returned to Cozad to check on his investments and deal with legal documents when he sold properties. He appears to have had more success in his commercial real estate ventures, both in Nebraska and Illinois, than John J. Cozad ever did and fewer legal troubles too. Hendee even purchased additional property in Cozad.

There are occasional newspaper stories that offer glimpses into the hotel, its history and operations. One such account appeared in the March 13, 1877 edition of the local newspaper and reported that Jerome Whaley, who was described as a firebug, almost was burned to death. He was boarding in several rooms at the Hendee when he lit a match to see what time it was and then fell asleep. In doing so the bed clothes he was wearing caught fire and he awoke to find himself in flames. Just a few seconds more and he would have died.[18]

Stephen Hendee died on June 20, 1910 and was buried in Bushnell, Illinois. He had created a business empire in two states and had been successful in his ventures. It is also curious the building has retained his name, and not with any association with Cozad. Hendee was essentially able to carry out John J. Cozad's dream of building a permanent and successful community, constructing a bridge across the Platte River and having the county accept its ownership, and casting off what in some ways was Cozad's dark cloud over the community as local residents were elected and appointed to serve in county positions in the Hendee era. Even with his death his name has continued to live on in Cozad because the name of his hotel would survive long afterwards, and in fact, the museum is still occasionally called *The Hendee.*

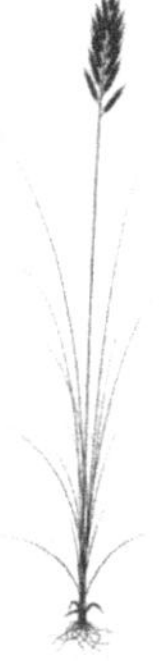

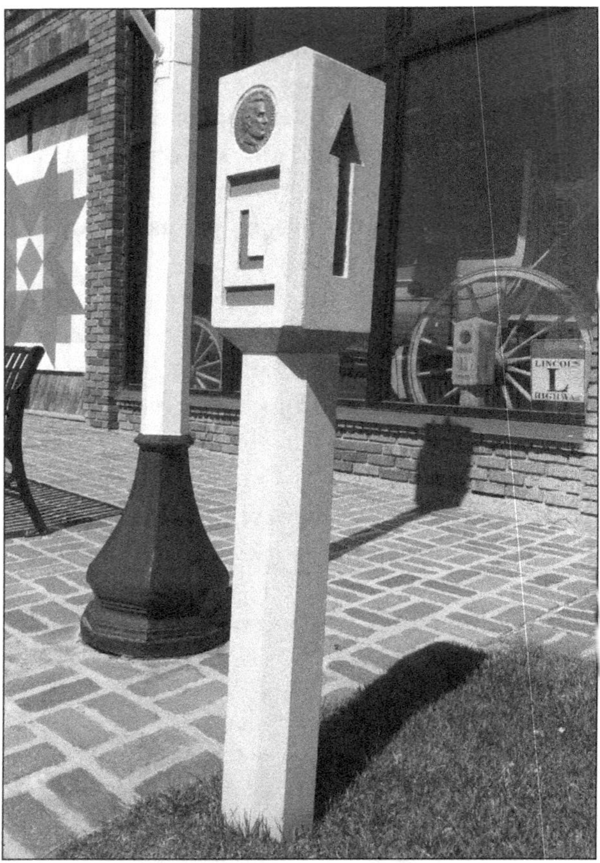


Courtesy Peter Osborne

*Concrete markers were placed along the entire length of the Lincoln Highway. The monument shown, standing in front of the 100th Meridian Museum, is a reproduction. An original monument can be seen inside the museum behind it.*

Cozad setting building, sellin and staying the men were charge week for use of th during William Fo ership of the buildi previously used as a shop. The building standing as late as 197 poor condition. It was quently demolished.[23]

### THE LINCOLN HIGH

In the late summer 1913, a caravan includi seventeen cars and two truck drove past the Hendee Hotel on a newly designated transcontinental roadway known as the *Lincoln Highway.* The *Trailblazer Tour,* sponsored by the Lincoln Highway Association, was the first group of automobiles to traverse its length beginning in Indianapolis, Indiana, and ending in San Francisco, California. It is not known if any of the travelers in 1913 stayed in the hotel on that auspicious day, but they certainly saw the building as they drove through.[24]

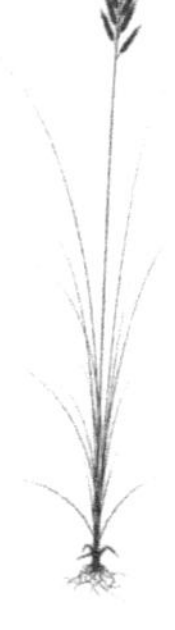

The Lincoln Highway, also known as the *Gateway to the West,* was part of a national effort to improve the roadways of the United States as the use of automobiles was becoming more popular in the opening decade of the 1900s. In 1904, for example, Nebraska had about eighty-nine thousand miles of public roads but most of those were simply dirt trails. In the entire state there were only seventeen miles covered with stone and only six miles covered with a sand and clay mixture. Most of those roads were maintained by local municipalities. Beginning in 1911, Nebraska legislators passed a law giving county commissioners greater authority to improve the roads within their jurisdiction. The situation in the state was similar to many other states in the union, particularly the agricultural ones. At the same time the number of automobiles in Nebraska exploded. In 1906, there were just over one thousand vehicles registered, and by 1910 there were more than eleven thousand.[25]

The idea of creating a transcontinental highway to promote automobile usage, better roads, and economic development was the idea of Indiana businessman, Carl Fisher, whose group of allies decided to honor the memory of President Abraham Lincoln. This national effort began with the creation of the Lincoln Highway Association (LHA) in the summer of 1913. The group then laid out a designated route, and finally, dedicated it on October 31 of the same year.[26]

As part of its overall strategy, the LHA promoted the construction of sections of paved roads that were one mile long and called *Seedling Miles.* These would demonstrate the importance of good roads to various constituents including businesses, individuals, government officials and tourist related agencies. The only *Seedling Mile* that still exists in Nebraska is located in Grand Island and is listed on the National Register of Historic Places. It was built in 1915. There were two others, one in Kearney and one in Fremont and both have long disappeared to progress.[27]

The roadway had an important impact on the development of a national road network and provided a significant economic stimulus to all of the towns that it passed through. Cozad, like hundreds of rural towns from Indianapolis to San Francisco, California, all benefitted from its designation. For example, the highway's designation may well have been one of the reasons John Simonson had the Hotel Hendee building stuccoed to upgrade its appearance to meet what he expected would be a growing business for himself.[28]

The actual route of the Lincoln Highway in Nebraska has changed over the decades. Today it passes through Cozad, as it once did, however, it does so two blocks south of the museum.[29] The original roadway, designated as the *Historic Lincoln Highway 1913 Route*, came into Cozad from Lexington on Road 761, and then passed along Eighth Street. Following Eighth Street west, it turns onto Avenue O and proceeds north where at the junction with Road 766 it bears west, proceeding to Gothenburg. South and west of Gothenburg one can still follow the original 1913 *stair-step route*, a pattern that it followed throughout the region along what were once dirt country roads all the way to North Platte along section lines.

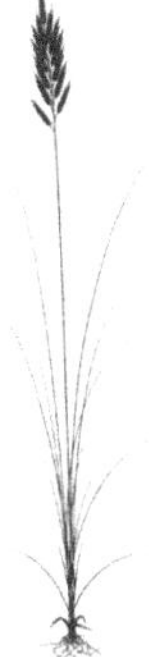

A major promotional effort undertaken by the LHA was the Transcontinental Military Convoy which in 1919 began in Washington D.C. and included a caravan of military vehicles following the Lincoln Highway across the country. Serendipitously, one of the participants was a future U.S. President, Dwight Eisenhower, then a second lieutenant. He would later sign the legislation creating the Interstate Highway system.[30]

Then, in 1921, U.S. Route 30, was designated as a *post road* and part of a developing federal interstate highway system. In Nebraska, Route 30 began in Omaha and continued to the western boundary of the state, closely following or paralleling the route of the Lincoln Highway.[31] In the decades that have followed, the federal highway has been widened, straightened, and relocated and is now the Lincoln Highway.

The historic Lincoln Highway is commemorated in Dawson County at several sites. Another original highway marker is preserved at its original location in Lexington, and one of the few surviving era highway bridges has been preserved in Overton between Route 30 and the railroad's main line. The Dawson County Historical Museum has an exhibition about the highway. In front of the Robert Henri Museum today there is a reproduction of an original Lincoln Highway marker. Next door, in the 100th Meridian Museum, an original concrete marker is displayed in its front window.

### Buster Brown and Tige Come to Town

The late nineteenth and early twentieth century proved to be a prosperous and important time in the hotel's history. It hosted a number of fascinating guests and became a local institution. Typical ads for the period promoted that it:

> *. . . seeks commercial trade which was a specialty and public patronage was sought.*[32]

Other ads reflected on its importance to the local community and that:

> *Our table is furnished with the best the market affords*
> *Come have Christmas dinner at the Hendee House*
> *Treat the family to a bountiful Thanksgiving dinner and attend the Thanksgiving Ball at the Hendee House*
> *Cigars for sale at the Hendee House:*
> *20 cents, 10 cents, 5 cents, Montez, Peerless, Rosedall, all excellent* [33]

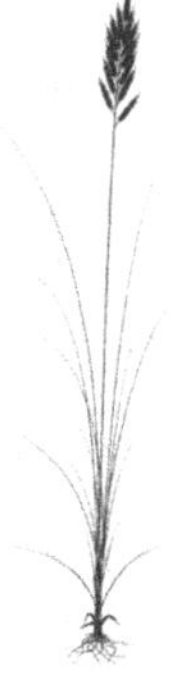

The building long served as a hotel and center of activity, but it became a community center as well serving as a public dining place, a location where traveling salesmen could set up shop, and even, it is said, a place where ladies of the night plied their trade. The hotel has also been used as a millinery shop, a photography shop and there were music teachers who gave lessons. A man was injured in front of the building and brought inside and treated for his wounds. Traveling doctors stayed at the hotel while practicing before moving on.[34]

There were a number of memorable events at the hotel over the decades. Traveling salesmen used the small building next to the hotel as a place to display their wares. The Buster Brown Shoe Company's representative came to Cozad

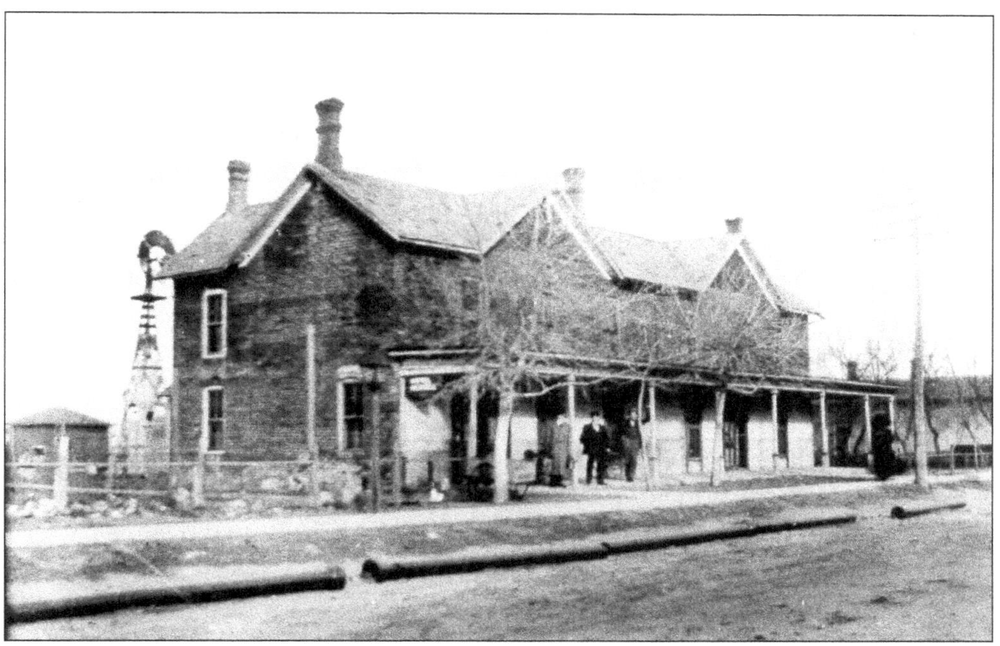

*Collection of the Robert Henri Museum and Art Gallery*

*This image of the Hendee Hotel shows what it looked like before it was completely stuccoed. From the porch floor halfway up the exterior wall is wood siding. From there to the ceiling, stucco has been laid on the brick to protect it. A windmill can be seen in the backyard, where the art gallery is today.*

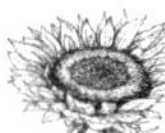

with samples for area stores to see as well as potential customers. As part of the company's effort to promote its products it hired dwarfs and used a bulldog, called Tige, as part of the company's marketing strategy. The traveling shows, which were used from 1904-30, came to the Hendee Hotel at least once.[35]

During the visit, which was still remembered in the 1980s, children snuck into the show room adjacent to the hotel and teased the dog. The dwarf, portraying Buster Brown, chased them out, but the children looked in through the building's windows to watch anyway.[36] The arrival of the traveling show would have been of great interest because of the ongoing advertising campaigns but also because Buster Brown and Tige were featured in comic books, films and even a Broadway show.

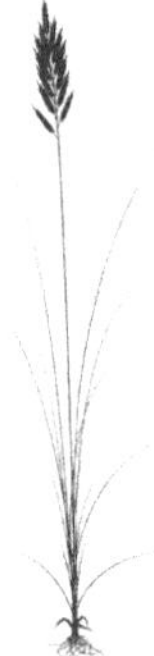

The Phillip Morris dwarf also visited the Hendee. Johnny Roventini, known popularly as Johnny Philip Morris, was known for his issuing a *Call for Philip Morris,* then a popular brand of cigarettes. He traveled the country doing advertisements for the company and serving as its spokesman on the radio, television and print. He was also well acquainted with some of the most famous actors and actresses of his day. Another person who came to the Hendee was a man described as *Hollywood's Tallest Man in the World*.[37]

One of the incidents that particularly stands out occurred in December 1903. Although not from Cozad, but needing employment, Sam Burgess had taken the marshal's job. In that position he had tangled with Mike O'Brien and Miles Maryott. He served as a town marshal for six weeks but resigned after a series of controversies that were the result of his strong law and order feelings.

After his resignation, he started a new job as a night porter at the Hendee. While on duty, he was in the visitor lobby reviewing the register to see who might be staying in the hotel. Just as he leaned over to read it a shotgun blast blew out the window across from him. O'Brien and Maryott were accused of firing the shotgun although they were not formally charged for lack of evidence. As for Miles Maryott, he complained that if he had fired the shot as Burgess alleged, the marshal would have been dead because he was an excellent marksman. Burgess wound up in a hospital in Grand Island as his wounds healed and then returned to Cozad. Later he served in the military in the Philippines and did come back to Cozad on occasion.[38]

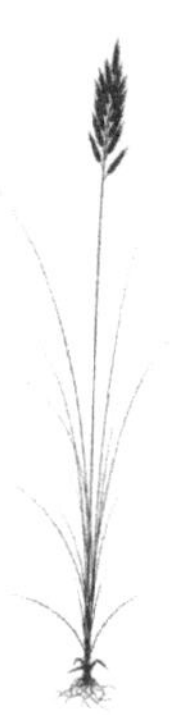

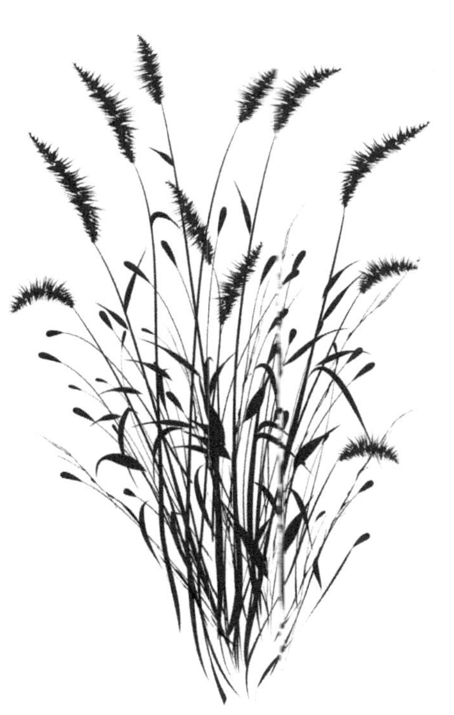

*Chapter 3*

# The Foster-Lewis Era
## 1920-1980

*In 1910 John C. Simonson purchased the hotel from the Hendee estate and in 1920 he sold it to William J. Foster. It continued in use as a hotel during this time and managed to survive the transition from train to automobile travel because the Lincoln Highway went by it on 8th Street. After William J. Foster's death in 1936 the hotel was used by the Foster family as a private residence and today the hotel is owned by a granddaughter, Mrs. William Lewis.*[1]

National Register of Historic Places Inventory
Nomination Form for The Hendee Hotel
1979

On November 6, 1920, William Foster (1851-1936) and his wife Sarah Brock (1864-1938) purchased the Hotel Hendee along with one hundred and fifty feet of street frontage, from John Simonson for four thousand five hundred dollars. Earlier in the year, they sold ninety feet of street frontage on the western side of the property to Fred Anderson. Previously the home of Henry Nielsen had stood on the corner lot.[2]

Initially the building continued to serve as a hotel and community center but it was converted into small apartments and suites of private residences for members of the Foster and Lewis families and other renters sometime after the death of William Foster in 1936.[3] One factor that may have played a role in the change of use was the Great Depression which began during the 1920s in rural America and culminated with national economic collapse of the 1930s.

It is not clear when or how that conversion happened because two additions were built, one in circa 1940, and the other in circa 1958, which would seem to indicate that the changes in occupancy were made over time. In the 1920 Federal Census, William and Sarah Foster were living in the building along with their daughter, Audrey, and son, Leland and several lodgers, L.G. and Theresa Crownover and Harvey Davis and his wife.

The 1930 Federal Census shows William and Sarah Foster were living in the building along with their daughter, Audrey, and two lodgers, William and Anita Thurman. The 1940 Federal Census lists the William and Deline Lewis family, Radie Morris and Audrey Foster living in the hotel.[4]

Other accounts report that each of the suites was taken by family members at various times. Deline Morris Lewis (1903-1980) and William Lewis (1896-1973) lived in a suite in the central part of the building along with their children, Sally (1932–2019) and William (1936–2012), Deline's parents, Jessie Morris (1878-?) and Radie Foster Morris(1883-?) lived in a suite, Deline's Aunt Gay had a suite on the east end of the building, and Audrey Foster (1887-?) lived in the western section of the building, in what is now the lobby, gift shop and bathrooms. The Thurmonds lived in the east apartment for a time. In addition, the remaining rooms were rented to other lodgers, or as family members passed away, other ten-

ants were found.[5]

Foster and Lewis family members would live in the building until the late 1970s, making themthe owners with the longest tenure of ownership in the hotel's history. Deline Lewis (1903-1980), a granddaughter of William Foster, was the last family member to own the hotel until she died on November 24, 1980.[6] After almost sixty years of ownership, the Foster-Lewis families no longer had an association with the building, and it went up for public auction. In 1980, it was sold to Cozad realtor and community booster, Wayman May.[7]

May, fearing the Cozad homestead might be demolished, purchased the building with the intention of turning it into a series of apartments, similar to what the Foster and Lewis families had done. Finding that it would be a an expensive task and daunted by the significant amount of work that needed to be done, it was sold to Cozad Historical Society for five thousand dollars. It was then purchased by the Robert Henri Museum and Historical Walkway Foundation in 1983.[8]

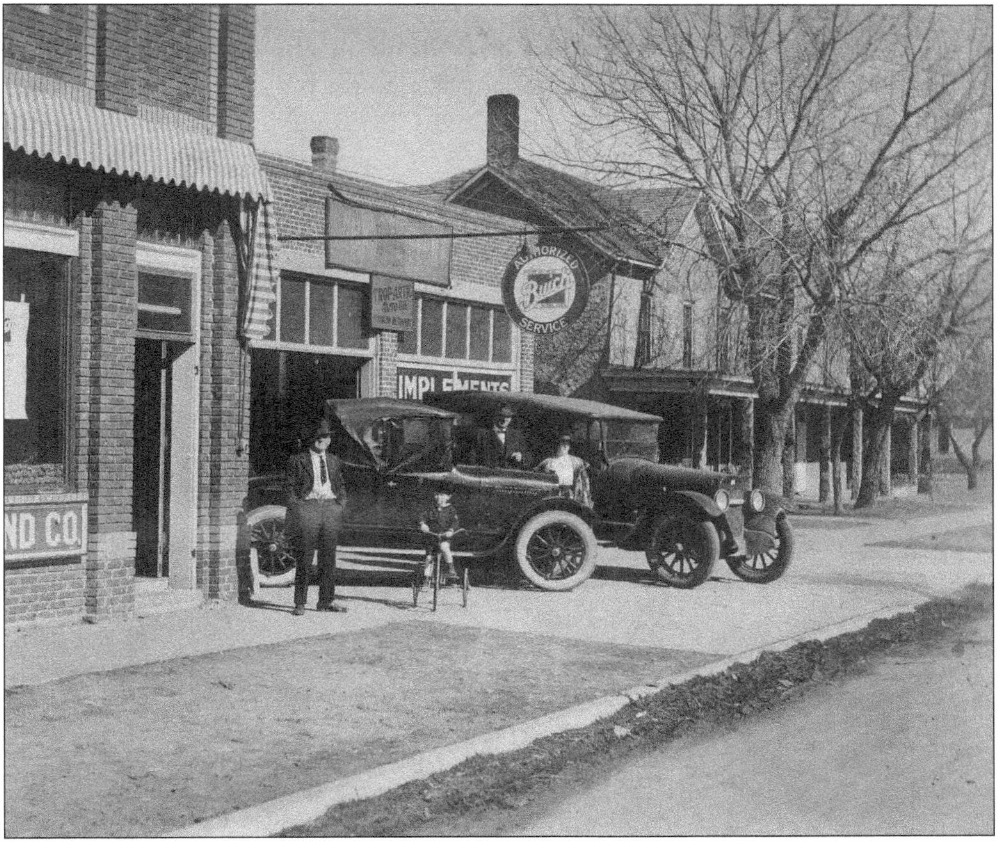

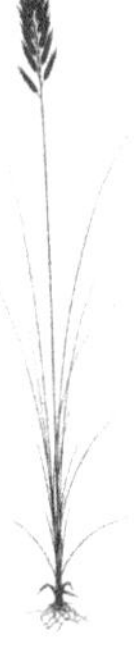

*Courtesy 100th Meridian Museum*

*In the early years of the twentieth century, new buildings were constructed on all three sides of the Hendee Hotel, which can be seen in the background.*

## More Change Comes To The Hendee

The Hendee-Simonson-Foster-Lewis eras of the building's architectural history is one of regular change but also presents the greatest of puzzles. All three sets of owners made improvements and updates to the building to reflect their needs, plans and different visions. However, it was during the Foster-Lewis era that most of the significant changes were made that came to substantially alter the building's interior appearance from its original design and functionality.

## The Foster-Lewis Era

Changes also came as the original property platted and owned by John J. Cozad was decreased in size. Buildings went up on all three sides of the property in the early twentieth century as the City of Cozad grew, and brick buildings replaced the old wood framed buildings that had been constructed between 1874 and 1900. An alley developed that connected East 8th Street with East 9th Street and would ultimately become the Robert Henri Museum's Historical Walkway. This probably came into regular use when a building was constructed at 242 East 8th Street. Two large trees, which had been visible in photographs in the early 1900s, had grown much larger and partially shaded the building from the street.[9]

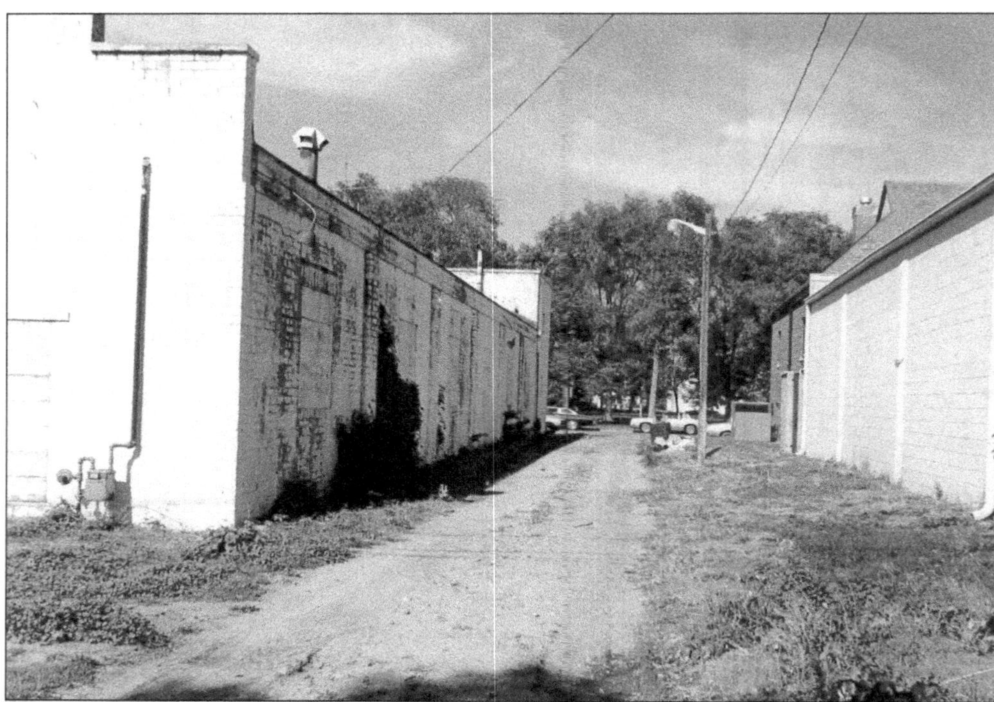

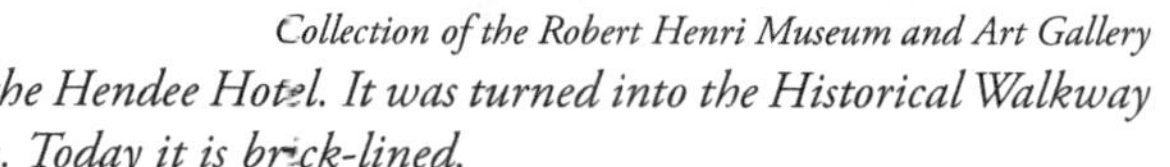

*Collection of the Robert Henri Museum and Art Gallery*

*An alley ran along the east property line of the Hendee Hotel. It was turned into the Historical Walkway in the 1980s by the Robert Henri Museum. Today it is brick-lined.*

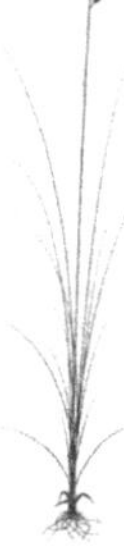

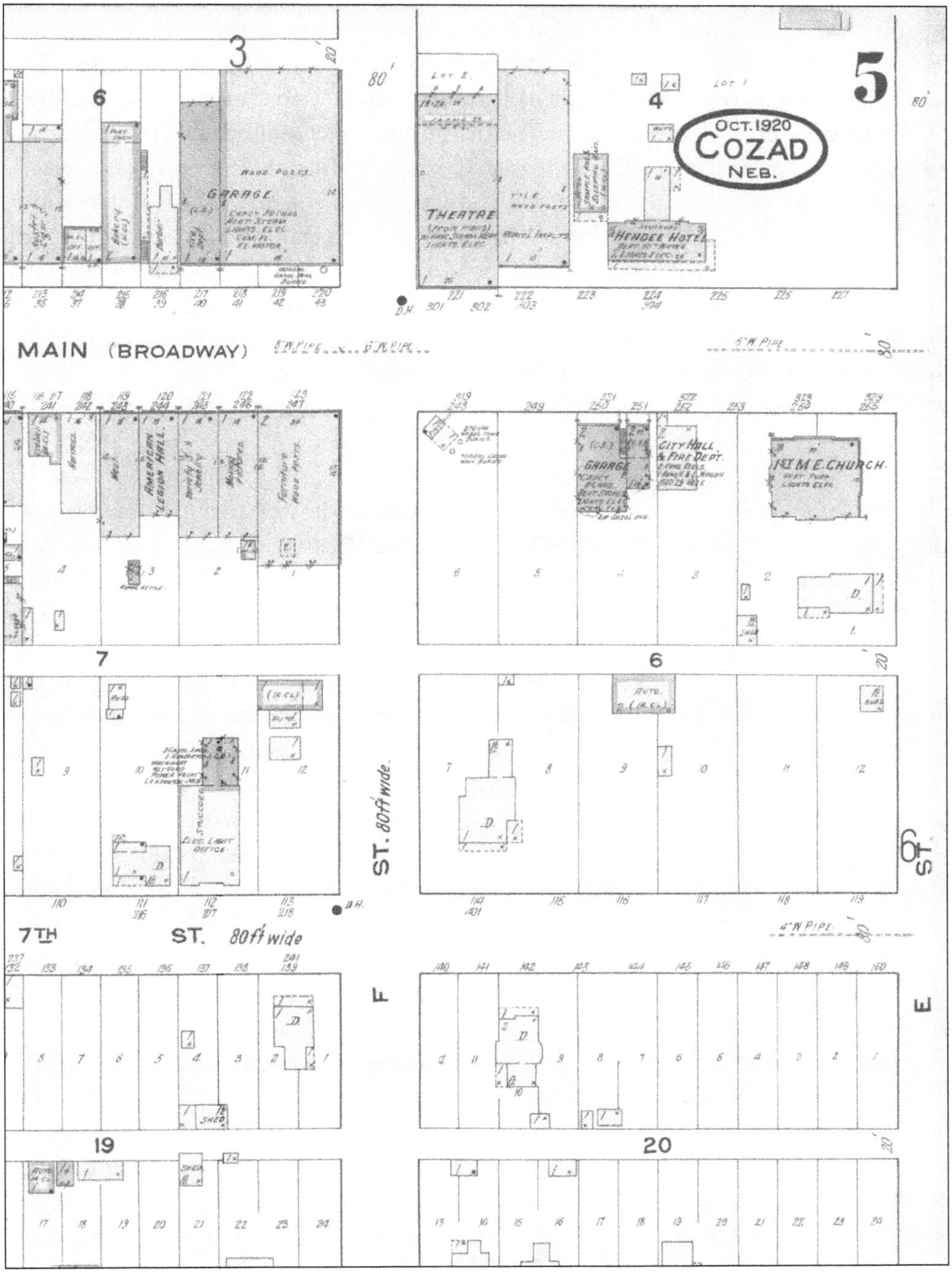

Courtesy Library of Congress (www.loc.gov/item/sanborn05408_002/.)

*By 1920 new buildings were being built around the Hotel Hendee as shown on this Sanborn Insurance Company map.*

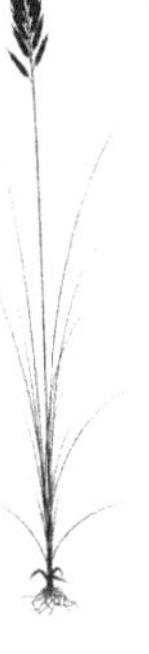

Since Robert Cozad had not created a floor plan for the second floor, there is a gap in the knowledge of its uses and function. The first time a detailed plan of the second floor was created was not until after 1958, and by then the building was being used in very different ways. It is not known who created those drawings of both floors or when. As a result, assumptions have been made by the author based on comparing the 1958 drawing, Cozad's 1880 drawing and other pieces of information found in the museum's archive. While a great deal is known about the history of the building, there remain important gaps in the knowledge of the building's past, particularly of the second floor. Robert Cozad only described briefly how the rooms were used but that does not help to better understand how the second floor appeared leaving those interested in the building's architectural history to take educated guesses at what might have been.

The following sections describe what is known about the building:

*Exterior*

At some point during the Hendee-Simonson-Foster ownership, parts of the porch roof structure may have been replaced because of water damage. It is known that the original porch posts were replaced but at an undetermined time. By the 1920s new porch posts can be seen in photographs and were stuccoed to match the building.[10]

The ornamental bracketing, which may be original to the building, is believed to have been saved during various roof and porch renovation and repair projects. They were reinstalled because as was seen in a paint analysis, the paint colors of the brackets do match the earliest colors that the building's trim was painted. The overall shape of the large wrap around porch that extended to the eastern side of the building was maintained. The deck of the porch must have been replaced several times, based on photographic evidence with the last installation prior to the museum's renovations in the 1980s being of plywood.

The building's trim paint colors during this time were ivory (?), green-gray, ivory, ochre-maroon, and light gray. The trim was painted white when the museum renovated the building.[11]

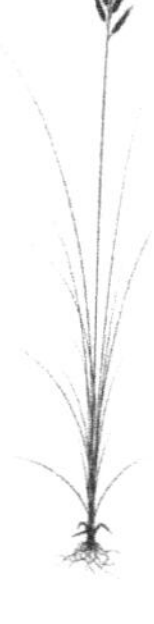

The large floor to ceiling windows on the first floor remained until renovations were undertaken during the museum's ownership after 1983. Several new windows were added, including one at the far western end of the building on the second floor in what was a large room in the southeast corner, one directly below it on the western end in the office and a third on the first floor adjacent to the original front door used by hotel patrons. It was removed during museum renovations. Another was added in John J.'s former office and on the second floor directly above it.

Also, at the east end of the building, the two hitching rings embedded in cement block remain.[12] At some undetermined date, the windmill in the back yard, shown in an 1890s picture, was removed, probably when the public water system in Cozad became available. Two wood-framed garages were built, one circa 1915 and another circa 1946 on the northern half of the property. They are both gone today, removed during the restoration in the 1980s, although their footprints remain in the ground.[13]

The wooden boardwalk which ran in front of the building was replaced with a new sidewalk and as time went by the level of the street was raised to its current level, based on a review of historic photographs.

*Entranceways*

At the time of Cozad's ownership, and based on Robert Cozad's 1880 floor plan, it is believed that there were only two doors with transoms on the south side of the building. The door on the western end led into the hotel office and accessed the stairway up to the rooms on the second floor that were used by the traveling public. It also led to the hotel parlor used by guests.

Sometime after the Cozads left, but before the building was stuccoed in the early 1910s, a new entrance was opened into the office on the far western end of the building. Prior to that it was a window according to Cozad's floor plan.[14] Today, that former door opening has been altered and is once again a window.

At some time, again after the Cozads left, and perhaps during the Foster-Lewis era, a wall was erected that created a hall between the staircase and the office and led into the dining room. This allowed for various residents to access the dining room directly without having to go through the former office, which became part of an apartment suite. Also, a small window was installed that would have provided some light in the newly created narrow hallway that had been created and can be seen on 1970s photographs. It was removed during subsequent renovation work.

*First Floor*

While it is known what the first floor looked like during the Cozad era because of Robert Cozad's 1880 floor plan, the changes that followed were not documented but made to suit the various managers and owners. It is believed that during the Hendee-Simonson-Foster eras, probably until 1936, the functions of the rooms probably remained as they had been during the Cozad years. After Foster's death, major changes were made to the building that give it its current appearance. New door openings were cut, new rooms created with different functions, and two additions were constructed on the north side of the building. A number of new floors were installed, probably after the removal of older floor boards. All of the current door trims are believed to have been installed at this time. It is also believed that new plumbing was added to the building in the 1950s.[15]

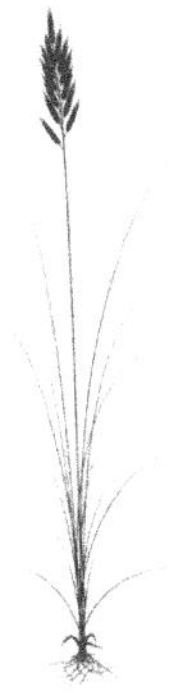

In the decades between 1884 and 1980 a variety of fashions influenced the different owner's tastes. For example, there were at least five layers of wallpaper applied on the plaster walls that were uncovered during renovations in the 1980s.[16] There are relatively few layers of paint on the woodwork. Doors and window trims were changed as the new openings were made. This indicates that they were installed in the mid-twentieth century.

### *Visitor Lobby, Adjacent Room and a New Addition*

The front lobby continued to serve as the hotel's office during the Hendee-Simonson-Foster eras, until at least 1936, or perhaps even later. On the 1958 floor plan, the room is still described as an office. A window was installed on the south wall between the two entrances on the western end of the building, probably to provide light for the hall.

The room adjacent to the former hotel lobby, on the north, was opened up with the removal of a section of the brick wall, creating a large suite of rooms, according to the 1958 floor plan.[17] What was once described as a *Room* in the 1880 drawing by Robert Cozad now became a kitchen.

In 1958, a cement brick addition, measuring twenty-two by fifteen feet, was built on the northwest corner of the building. It butted up against the former kitchen section and allowed for the creation of two new bedrooms and a bath.[18] The floors of the former Hendee kitchen, bathrooms, annex and modern kitchen are all identical and may have been installed at the same time.

### *Old Kitchen*

The kitchen retained its functions in the Foster-Lewis era, although none of the original utilities or equipment remain except for a sink, which is believed to have been in the hotel originally.[19] The kitchen that was used in the Hendee era did not change until the Robert Henri Museum came into existence. A new floor was laid during the renovations of the 1980s.

### *Former Hotel Parlor*

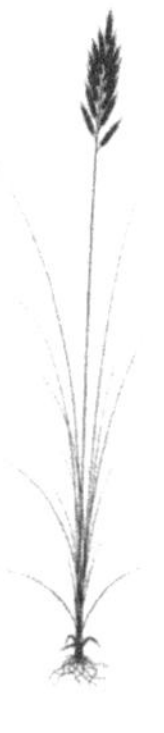

During the Cozad era, there was only one entrance into this room, the one at the southwestern corner, near today's main front entrance. It is presumed that its function, used for guests to gather and relax in, remained the same during the Hendee-Simonson-Foster eras. After William Foster died, this room was converted into a bedroom. The other two sets of doors into this room were added later, probably after 1936 when the transition into a series of apartments took place. When the hotel was turned into apartments for members of the Foster-Lewis families, this room was part of a suite of rooms, serving as a bedroom with the doorway on the east providing access to the adjacent living room.

*Former Cozad Parlor*

The former Cozad parlor became a living room. This room became part of a suite of rooms, serving as a living room, with the doorway on the west providing access to the adjacent bedroom when the transformation was undertaken. Another doorway was added to access the dining room. During the Cozad era, there was only one entrance into this room, the one at the southeastern corner of the room, near today's main front entrance.

*Dining Room*

The dining room remained the largest room in the house and retained its purpose through the Foster-Lewis era. It was originally eleven feet wide and forty feet long, but during the Foster renovations it was shortened with a shared bathroom added at the western end, and a bedroom that measured eleven by eight and a half feet, at the eastern end. The bathroom remains, although it is used for storage today, but the bedroom wall was removed during the renovations undertaken by the museum. With the new arrangement, the dining room continued to serve its original purpose for the family members living there.

*Robert Cozad's Office, John and Johnny's Office,*
*New Room and addition*

The room that had once been used by Robert Cozad for his office, along with the room that had been used by John J. as an office, were believed to have been converted sometime after 1936. A new bedroom that was partitioned off from the dining room and an addition, on the northeast corner of the building and measuring fifteen by twelve feet, was built in 1940.[20] Combined, these rooms created a whole new suite. Robert's former office was converted to a kitchen. The small brick addition, measuring fifteen by twelve feet, and which is stuccoed on the exterior, included a bathroom. The addition was used until the 2010s as an office for the museum's director.[21]

*Second Floor*

As with the first floor, rooms on the second floor were also renovated to suit the needs of the Lewis and Foster family members. In some ways the functions of the rooms remained as they had been, in other cases changes were made. Much of the woodwork dates from this era.

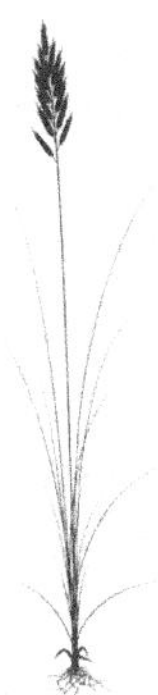

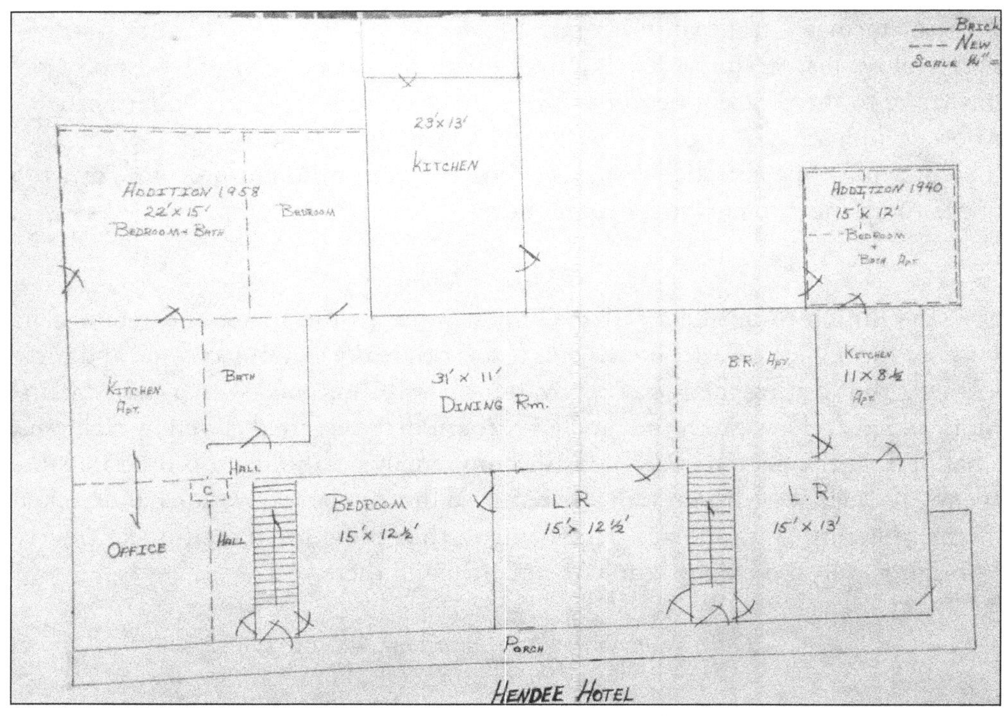


Collection of the Robert Henri Museum and Art Gallery

*This floor plan of the of the first floor of the Hendee Hotel was created after 1958 and illustrates how the rooms were utilized during the Foster-Lewis era, when the building served as a residence for members of the two families.*

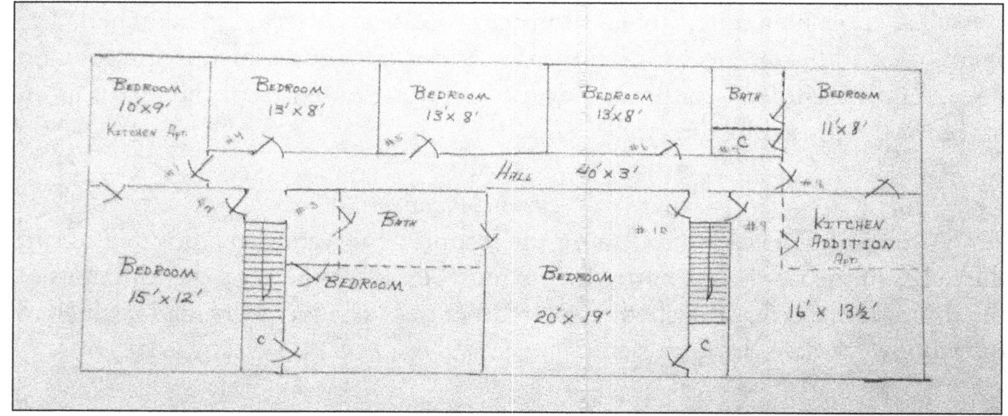


Collection of the Robert Henri Museum and Art Gallery

*This floor plan shows the layout of the second floor of the Hendee Hotel and was also created after 1958.*

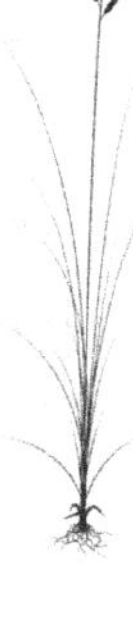

*Johnny and Robert Cozad's Bedroom, John and Robert's Storeroom and Washroom*

It is presumed that during the Hendee-Simonson era the original room configuration and usage as hotel rooms remained for the Cozad boys' bedroom, storage room and adjacent smaller room to the west. The adjacent room had been used as a washroom during the Cozad era and may have served the same purpose from 1884-1920. During the Foster-Lewis era, this collection of rooms was transformed into a suite that included a new bathroom, new closet, bedroom, kitchen and living room. The 1958 floor plan of the building shows them as rooms 7, 8 and 9.[22]

*John and Theresa Cozad's Bedroom*

It is believed that the Cozads' former bedroom was continued to be used as a hotel room in the Hendee-Simonson era and then became a bedroom in the Foster-Lewis era. An opening was cut into the adjacent room on the west, and the family members shared a joint bathroom. It is numbered as room 10 in the 1958 floor plan.[23]

*Hotel Rooms*

The four remaining small rooms on the second floor are believed to have been used as hotel rooms through the Hendee and Simonson eras. During the Foster-Lewis era, those rooms, numbered 1, 4, 5 and 6 in the 1958 floor plan, were used as bedrooms, and it is remembered that at least some of them were used by high school students who lived in the country but stayed in town during the week.[24] Room 1 at the far northwestern corner later became a kitchen that was part of the suite along with the room at the far southwestern corner of the building.[25]

*Unidentified Rooms*

The two large bedrooms on the southwestern side of the second floor were presumably used for boarding rooms during the Hendee-Simonson era. In the Foster-Lewis era, the room next to the former bedroom of the Cozad parents was divided into a bedroom and bathroom and connected to what had been their bedroom. The second large room, at the southwestern corner, along with the smaller room to the north, were connected and served as a suite. A door connects the two rooms, an addition from the Lewis-Foster era.[26]

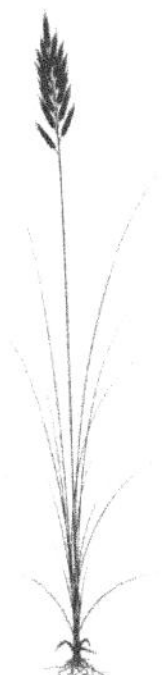

The Passing of An Era

The final connection of the Foster-Lewis family's ownership of the Hendee Hotel, and its use as a hotel and residential complex, came to an end on November 24, 1980, with the passing of Deline Lewis (1903-1980), the former kindergarten schoolteacher in Cozad.

The building's ownership then passed to Wayman May (1919-2010), a Cozad businessman and active participant in the community's affairs. He served on a variety of community boards including the Cozad Industrial Development Corporation, Dawson County Board of Realtors and was one of the founders of Camp Comeca. During May's ownership he rented rooms to tenants including Zoey Miller, a former Cozad resident, whose father worked for May in his insurance business.[27]

May owned the building until its purchase by the Cozad Historical Society in 1983 and then the Robert Henri Museum and Historical Walkway. A new chapter was about to begin in the life of the building.

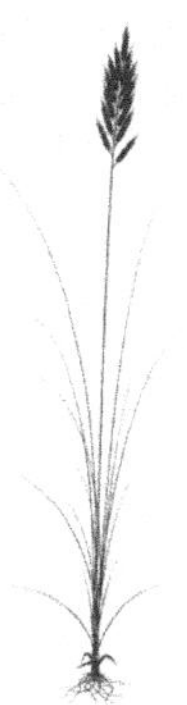

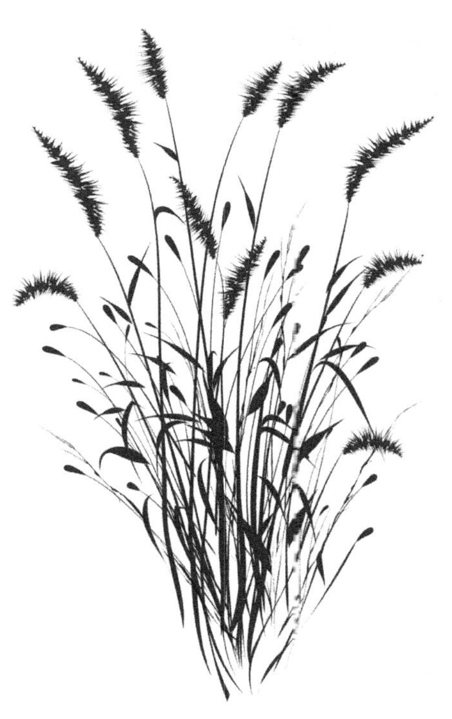

## *Chapter 4*

# Saving the Cozad and Henri Legacy

*The Robert Henri Museum and Historical Walkway Foundation hopes to take this important first step in the preservation of history. It does need help.*

Museum Flyer, circa 1984

*Never underestimate the power of women, especially Cozad, Nebraska, grandmothers.*[1]

Tom Allen

Omaha World Herald, October 7, 1984

*(The museum) will eventually have a collection of Henri paintings, sketches and some writings on display. It will be furnished with furniture from the founder's era. It will be more of an art gallery than a museum.*[2]

Shirley Paulsen

Leader of the effort to restore the Robert Henri boyhood home

While some Cozad residents had a knowledge of the importance of the Hendee Hotel and its relationship to the Cozads and Robert Henri after the 1956 special edition of the *Cozad Local*, the building was still in private hands. It was used as a residence by members of the Foster-Lewis's family and other tenants. Deline Lewis, a granddaughter of William Foster, and who still lived in the building, understood its significance to the community and to the larger art world.

An important historical designation was made near the end of the Foster-Lewis family's ownership of the former hotel on March 30, 1979. With Mrs. William (Deline) Lewis' approval, Kieth Buss, the president of the Cozad Historical Society prepared the National Register of Historic Places Inventory Nomination Form. This application, which was approved on January 26, 1979, placed the building on the United States Department of Interior's National Register of Historic Places. This was an important tool if federal or state funding was to be obtained in preserving the site.[3]

From the records, it appears that Mrs. Lewis assisted Buss in his efforts by providing information on the history of the house. She had written a short history of the building in 1972.[4] The document is noteworthy for several reasons but one of the most important is that it was the first known detailed effort made to document the history of the structure and remains one of the most important resources for researchers today. Using *The Cozad Tribune*, the *Early History of Cozad and the Surrounding Community (edited by Charles Allen)*, and *Son of the Gamblin' Man* by Mari Sandoz as historical resources, Kieth Buss undertook considerable effort to research the building's past.[5]

The listing on the National Register brought prestige and attention to the building's important history and its unique architectural legacy. It would also initiate efforts that began a long journey to see the building become a museum to honor the legacy of Robert Henri. It would be ten more years until another building, the Allen Opera House, would be listed on the National Register in Cozad, and almost forty years until the business district was nominated to be on the Register as the Cozad Downtown Historic District.[6]

Another development that portended well for the future was the construction of Interstate Route 80, which curiously followed much of the same route that John Cozad had predicted would be the main pathway to the west. When the surveyors were laying out the proposed Interstate Route 80 in the 1950s and 1960s, they followed the exact same route as the Union Pacific surveyors had followed a century before. For its entire route through Nebraska, Interstate Route 80 parallels the main line of the Union Pacific Railroad.[7] Since its construction, most of today's visitors to the museum come after seeing the highway signage on the roadway.

Today, the Robert Henri Museum and Art Gallery is a national treasure that is the result of the work of many volunteers, board members and professional staff that have toiled away for almost forty years. Visitors come from all over the world to see the museum and gallery.

But it is also the story of what might have happened if the local community had not stepped up at a critical moment. As the 1980s began, with the Foster and Lewis families no longer living in the building, the City of Cozad had called for the building's demolition, given its deteriorating condition.

Wayman May, a realtor in Cozad, believed it would be a major mistake and tragedy to demolish the building, because it was the home of the city's founder and the boyhood home of his son, Robert, the internationally known painter. May purchased the building, believing he could convert it into apartments, using it in a way similar to what the Fosters and Lewis's had done. But he found that the building would require a tremendous investment, beyond what he may have wanted to spend. Soon May discarded his ambitious plan, and he sold the building to the Cozad Historical Society for five thousand dollars.

The community, then worried that the building might be demolished, began a remarkable effort to preserve Robert Henri's boyhood home and his Nebraska legacy. It started with a small group of people who saw the opportunity to honor a forgotten founder and to bring recognition to the town that was once home to a world-renowned artist.

On April 19, 1983, this small group of community leaders met to become the organization that came to be called the Robert Henri Museum and Historical Walkway.[8] The original board members were Shirley Paulsen, Chairman, Willard Bellamy, Bruce Hart, Marvel Brunk, Mildred Umshler, Betty McKeone, Biggi Young and Barbara Landerscasper.[9]

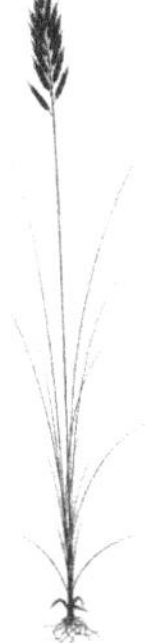

After a series of meetings over six months, an official proposal was publicly unveiled on September 13, 1983, to undertake such an effort. It was presented by the Robert Henri Museum and Historical Walkway Foundation, the official legal name of the entity that would move the effort forward.[10] The group was legally incorporated on November 21, 1983.

Fundraising efforts began, and the first major effort was started on December 8, 1983. The foundation began an extensive effort in the community to raise money and raising tens of thousands of dollars to undertake the project, including a fifty-thousand-dollar grant from the Peter Kiewit Foundation.[11] The organization also solicited the help of numerous organizations like the Union Pacific Foundation. In addition, they campaigned locally and in two days raised $68,000.

Once the plans were formulated, agreed to, and announced, the museum's foundation purchased the museum building on January 24, 1984. The property was later surveyed on July 31, 1984 by Dawson County Surveyor Gary Donelson, and then in August 1984, Wayman May sold the former Hotel Hendee to the Cozad Historical Society for five thousand dollars. The Robert Henri Museum and Historical Walkway Foundation then took title. With that purchase, the core group started the ambitious undertaking of converting the abandoned and severely deteriorated structure into a historic site along with three other buildings.

Things moved quickly as work began on restoring and renovating the old Hendee Hotel. Led by Shirley Paulsen, a group of committed volunteers worked day and night to get the building ready for an art show on October 10, 1984. The work was made difficult by the fact that very little was known about its history even though the goal was to restore the building to the period when the Cozads lived in the building. [12] The museum officially opened on May 24, 1986, after an extensive renovation effort.[13]

Since that time, thousands of visitors have come to the museum for tours and to experience its history. Countless programs have been sponsored for area citizens, including civic groups and school groups along with various artists programs and exhibits.

### Country School, New Hope Evangelical Country Church and Pony Express Station

It is significant that the Robert Henri Museum's destiny fits into a larger narrative and context of the many historic preservation activities that were accomplished in the 1970s and 1980s. New historic sites across the country were being created with various organizations acquiring old buildings that were threatened with demolition and moving them to a new site and creating faux villages or collections of historic buildings.[14] Many of those are still operating and, in fact, there are several located in the region, including the Stuhr Museum in Grand Island, the Buffalo County Historical Society and Trails and Rails Museum in Kearney, Pioneer Village in Minden, the Prairie Museum in Holdrege and the Dawson County Historical Museum in Lexington.

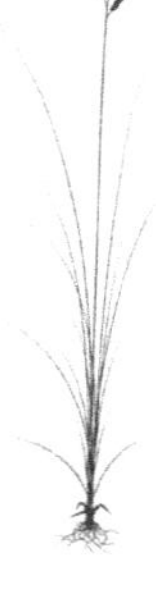

The new organization laid out plans in 1983 that called for the acquisition and preservation of four buildings that were a century old, and then renovating and refurbishing them. The group proposed that it would cost $100,000 to undertake the effort. The buildings included the present-day Robert Henri

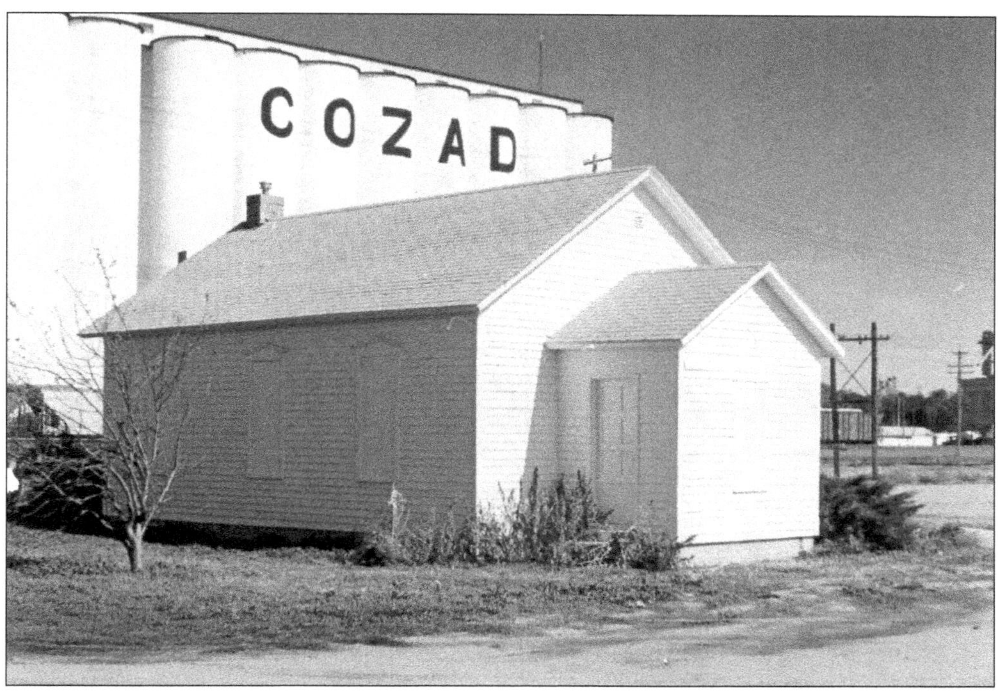


*Courtesy 100th Meridian Museum*

*The Country School, District No. 86, Cozad, was located about nine miles north of the city and moved to Bellamy Field, pictured here, in Cozad after it was given to the Cozad Historical Society in 1960. In 1985 the school was moved to its present location on East Street.*

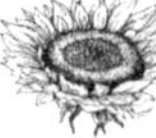

Museum, the Pony Express Station located in City Park (now Veterans Park), the Christian Science Church (formerly the New Hope Evangelical Church) and the District 86 Schoolhouse.[15]

At the same time the Hendee Hotel was being purchased, the Country School and New Hope Evangelical Country Church were also acquired. The Country Schoolhouse was given by Dorothy and Archie Smith to the Cozad Historical Society in 1960. It had been built around 1880. It had been situated south of Cozad for a number of years in Bellamy Park as it awaited removal to a more permanent location.[16]

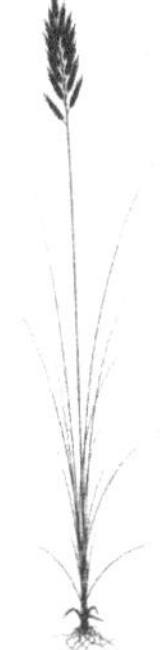

The historic schoolhouse was acquired by the Robert Henri Museum and Historical Walkway Foundation on July 26, 1984. In the spring of 1985, it was moved by the Robert Henri Museum and Historical Walkway Foundation to its current location across the street from the City Park (now Veterans Park) on E Street. It was repaired and restored as nearly to its original state as possible. The schoolhouse was then used by various school groups wanting to experience the life of country school children in the late nineteenth and twentieth centuries. This

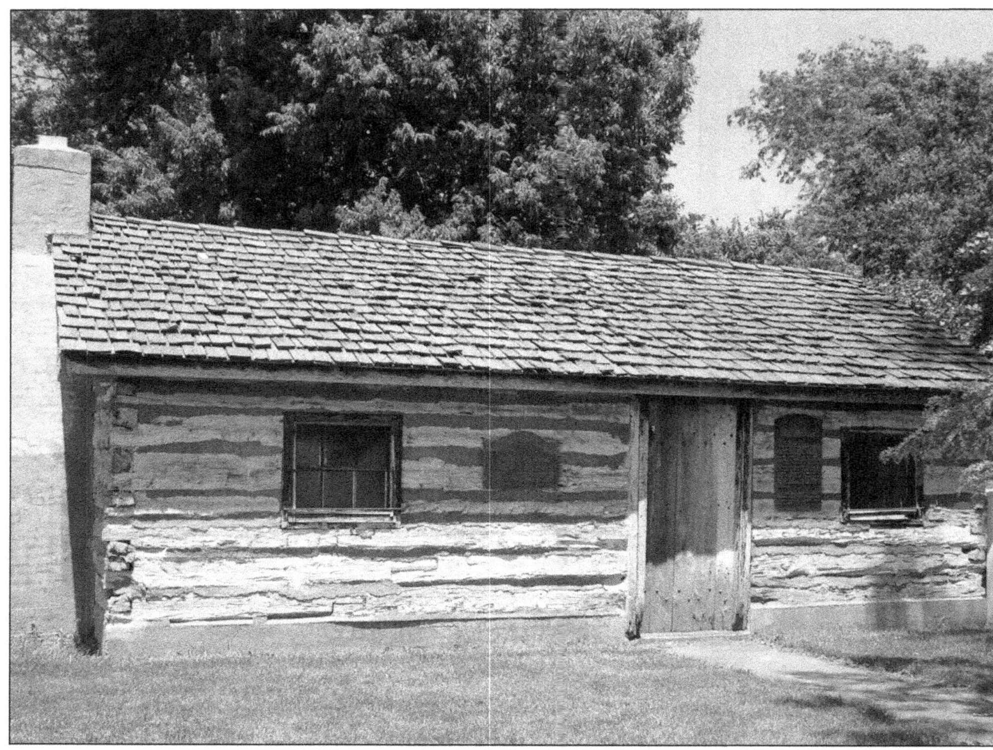

*Robert Henri Museum and Art Gallery Collection*

*The former Willow Island Pony Express Station was moved and is now located in City Park in Cozad on East 9th Street.*

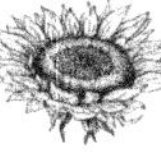

was done for many years.[17]

The New Hope Evangelical Country Church was built in 1909. In 1921, it was sold to the Christian Science Society Church, and moved into Cozad and located on East 10th Street. Its congregation declined in membership over time and closed in 1981. There had been an active congregation in the building for over sixty years. The building was purchased in 1983 from the First Church of Christ, Scientist in Boston, Massachusetts, by the Robert Henri Museum and Historical Walkway Foundation so that it might be preserved as typical of the early country churches in the area. It came to be known as *The Little Church by the Park* and was used for meetings, ceremonial rites for various community organization, the activities of the Cozad Arts Council, a children's theater, and small weddings.[18]

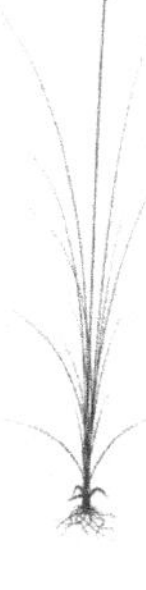

A third building that was also included in the collection was the Willow Island Pony Express Relay Station, formerly located in Darr, but then moved to City Park (now Veterans Park) in 1936. While not owned by the museum, it was included in the historical walkway and opened for tours.[19]

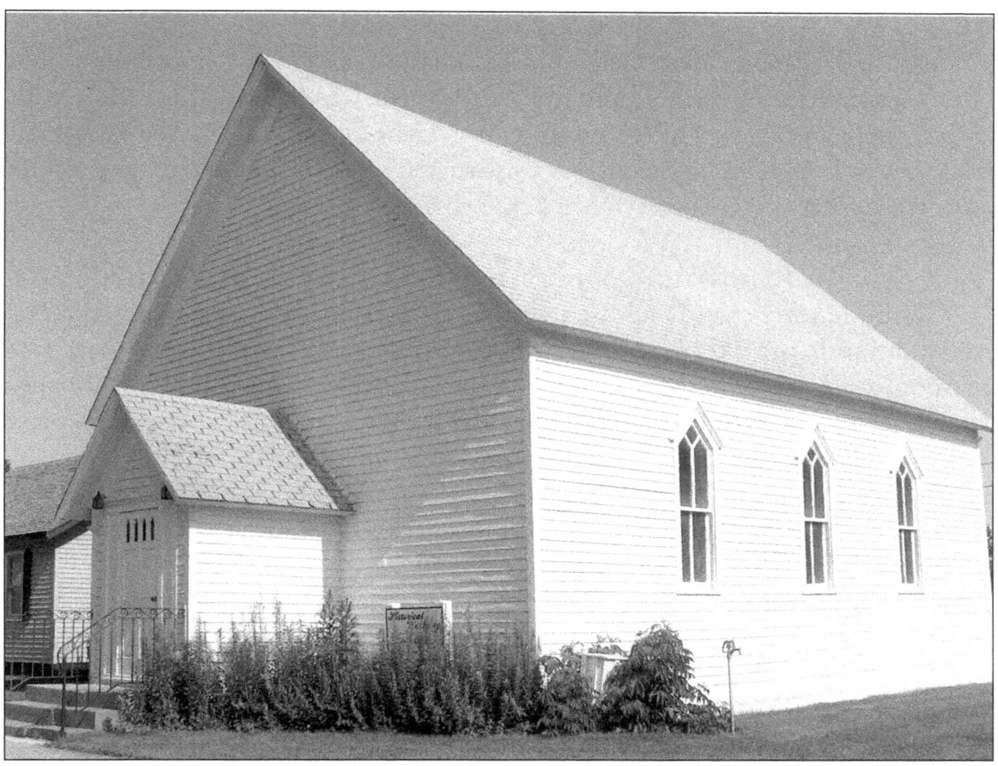

*Courtesy 100th Meridian Museum*

*The Little Church By The Park, formerly known as the New Hope Evangelical Country Church, and later the Christian Science Society Church was purchased by the Robert Henri Museum and Historical Walkway Foundation in 1983. It was moved to its present location on East 10th Street by The Christian Science Society.*

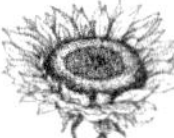

As all of the activity was going on with creating a complex of the four buildings, the Nebraska Humanities Council awarded a grant (*The Rebirth of the Cozad Revelation, Grant 84-04*) to conduct research and write histories about all four buildings.[20] This effort was undertaken by Betty Menke, and in 1985, all four of the research projects were completed and published. One of the results of this grant was a booklet, entitled *Robert Henri: Museum and Historical Walkway*. It was the most extensive history of the Cozad experience written since the publication of Mari Sandoz's book in 1960. For many years it was sold in the museum's gift shop.

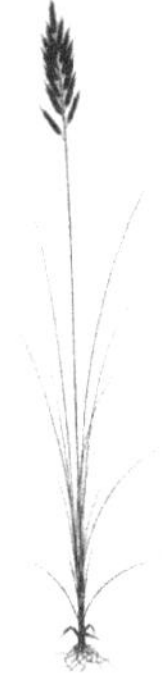

### The Historical Walkway

Part of the Robert Henri Museum Foundation's original vision was to create a brick walkway from the museum to East 9th Street. This allowed for a short walk to the other three sites, which were all within sight of each other. The Historical Walkway, as it came to be called, was constructed of old bricks taken up from the streets of Lexington when they were being paved.[21]

### The Renovation and Restoration of the Hendee Hotel

With money in hand and the research having been done, the effort to renovate and restore the old hotel began and continues to this day. The museum was in a poor state at the time the restoration efforts began. The building had badly deteriorated and needed extensive work as layers of wallpaper were removed, plaster walls repaired, new ceilings, floors and windows installed. Additional major updates were made including the installation of a new electrical system and a fire, smoke, and security alarm systems. Linoleum was removed from some of the original wooden floors and samples were retained.

From this late date, now almost forty years later, and reviewing the photographs in the museum's collection, it is almost impossible to describe all the work that was done by dedicated volunteers. An amazing array of projects was completed that Wayman May had correctly believed would require a major investment of time and money.

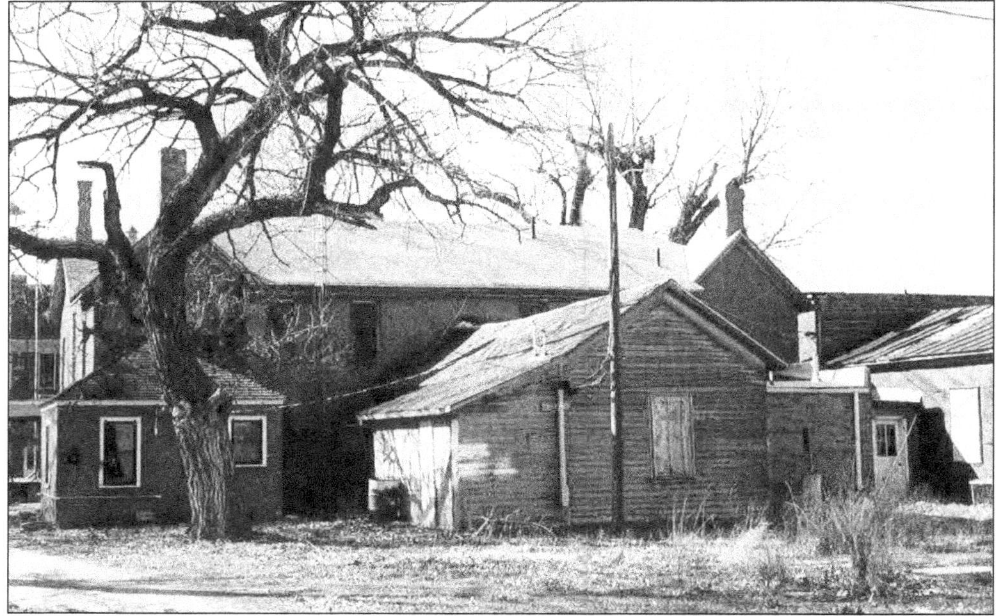

*Robert Henri Museum and Art Gallery Collection*

*The condition of the future Robert Henri Museum was poor, as so many issues needed to be addressed to get it open to the public.*

The following sections describes what was done to the building during its renovation.

*Exterior*

When the 1980s restoration began, the porch was badly deteriorated. The original porch posts had been replaced by two 2" x 6" planks nailed together and stuccoed.[22]

Two large and rotting trees that stood in front of the building were removed before they could have caused catastrophic damage to the building if they had blown over.[23] All the windows in the building were replaced with new ones as the original windows, and later replacements were all deteriorated. The building was restuccoed in 1982, almost eighty years after the original stucco had been placed on the brick.[24]

*First Floor*

*Visitor's Lobby*

The former front door at the western end of the building that had been used for access into the hotel lobby was closed and converted to a window. The window that had been between the two entrance doors was removed and the wall that had divided the former lobby into two smaller rooms was eliminated. The flooring was replaced although the original tin ceiling was preserved and repaired where necessary. Today the room continues to serve as a place to greet visitors just as it was for decades.

*Former Storage Room*

The former *Room,* as described by Robert Cozad, and which had been used as a kitchen during the Foster-Lewis era, was converted into the museum's gift shop in more recent years. New restrooms and a modern kitchen were built in the wing of the building that had been constructed in 1958. They had formally been two bedrooms and a bathroom.

*Former Hotel Parlor*

The room was refurbished, repainted and repapered. The wallpaper used was a type of reproduction for the period that the Cozads were here. Since the 1980s it has served as an example of what a typical parlor room for the guests of the 1880s might have looked like. The floor, although painted, is original.

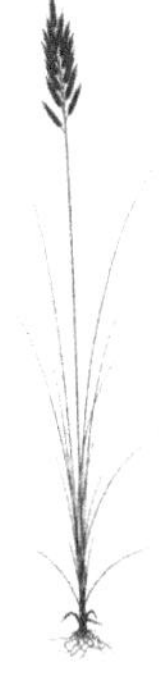

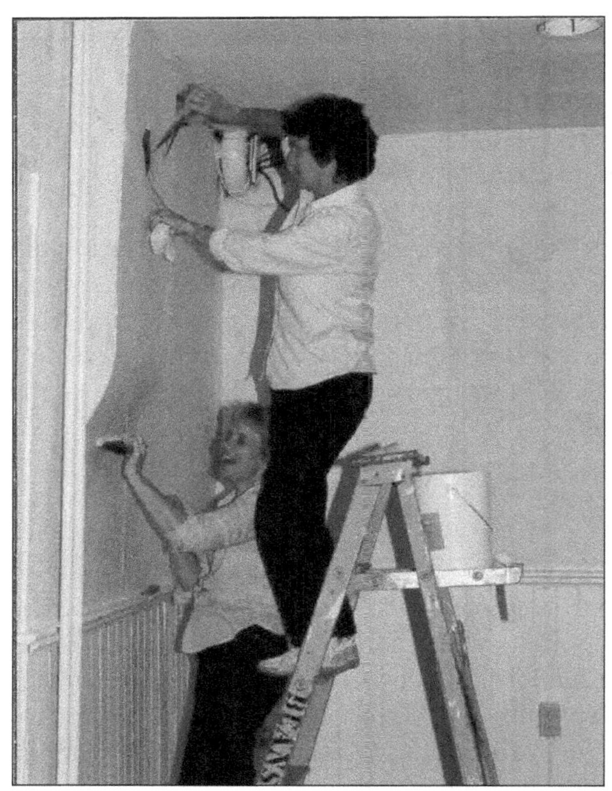

*Robert Henri Museum and Art Gallery Collection*

*Volunteers from the Cozad community worked countless hours renovating and restoring the museum building over a period of several years.*

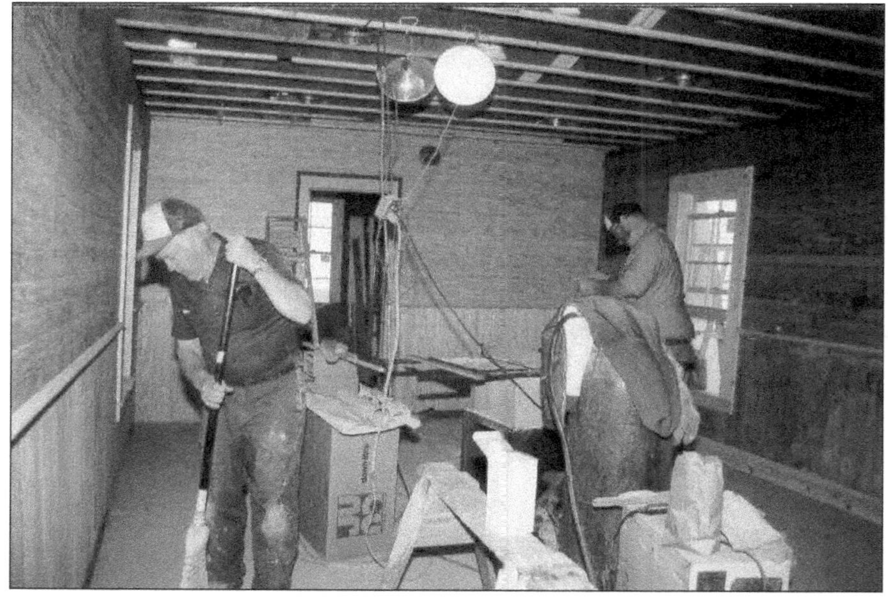

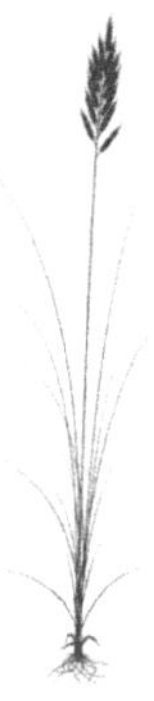

exhibits that related to the Cozad family and displayed memorabilia.[26] In 2022, a new exhibit was installed that interpreted the significance of the former office in the life of Robert Cozad.

*John and Johnny Cozad's Office*

The former office of John and Johnny was turned into a gift shop during the museum era and in the early years of the museum's existence was used as the main access into the building.[27] In more recent times it has been restored to portray John's office and in 2022 became home to an interpretive exhibit of both John and Johnny's business interests in Cozad.

*Second Floor*

After the purchase of the building and renovations by the Robert Henri Museum Foundation, many of the second floor rooms were used for exhibits or storage. In recent years UV film has been placed on all of the windows on the first and second floor.

*Director's Office*

This room was originally for hotel guests, but in the Foster-Lewis era it served as part of a two-room suite, attached to the room directly to the south. A small door leading into the current library was added during the Foster-Lewis era. The flooring in this room was replaced and the wainscoting was also added along with new lighting. This room has been used as the director's office since the 2010s.

*Museum Library*

This room was originally a room for guests, but in the Foster-Lewis era it served as a single bedroom. A small door leading from the director's office was added during the Foster-Lewis era. The floor in this room is covered with linoleum, which probably covers over the original flooring. New lighting was installed, and this room has been used as the museum's library and photocopy room since the 2010s.

*Homestead Room*

This room was originally a room for guests during the Hendee era, but in the Foster-Lewis era it served as a bedroom for short term tenants. The floor in this room is covered with linoleum and covered with carpet, and new lighting was added. This room has been used for interpretive functions since the 2010s.

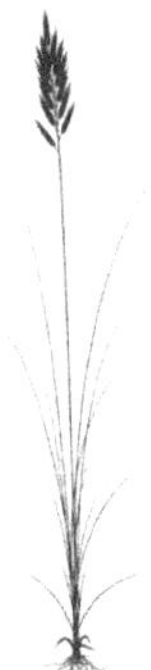

*Johnny and Robert's Bedroom*

This room has retained many of its original features after the kitchen addition was removed during the 1980s renovations. The window in the southeastern corner of the building was probably not extant at the time of the building's construction because it is smaller than other windows in the building. Or, its dimensions may have been changed. There are no photographs of this side of the building before the 1980s in the museum's collection. New electrical fixtures were installed and the flooring, while painted, is original. The kitchen, which was a small room that was enclosed in this room was removed during the renovation work. In 2010s, it was arranged as it might have been when Johnny and Robert used it.

*Storage room for Johnny and Robert Cozad*

This room has been used for exhibits and at least one artist in residence has stayed in it in 1988. Today it is closed off to the public. The suite also includes a functioning bathroom and closet.

*John and Theresa's Bedroom*

One of the most extraordinary efforts that the museum undertook in restoring the building was to have the original wallpaper in Theresa and John Cozad's bedroom duplicated. Another feature of the room are the initials *RH* that are written in pencil directly on the plaster of the western wall. They are very different than the penciled initials of Robert Cozad's in the hall on the first floor. Those initials are closer in appearance to those that he used in his 1880 diary.

The initials could be the wallpaper installer's initials. They could have also been from an earlier time, perhaps in the mid-1870s when some have suggested the building may have been built. Until more information is found it will not be known from whom they might have come.

There is also a doorway that leads into what was once a bathroom in the adjacent room that was probably created during the Foster-Lewis era. A closet is in the southeast corner.

*Unidentified Large Rooms*

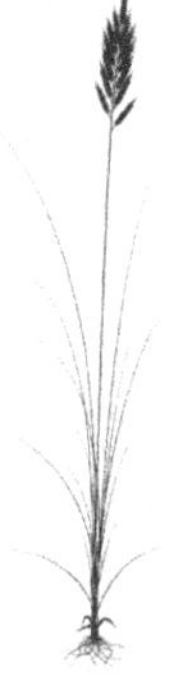

The first room to the west of the original Cozad parents' bedroom was connected to the bedroom and also included a bathroom and served as a suite during the Foster-Lewis era. It is believed that this room may have been used for long term boarders because of its size from the very beginning or even for servants and employees. Most of the flooring is original, but a section where the bathroom once was has been replaced with slightly wider boards.

After the museum began its restoration, false plywood panels were installed over the original plastered walls, and various art exhibits were hung in this room. Until the construction of the Robert Henri Art Gallery in 2014, it was where the Robert Henri painting *Queen Mariana* had hung. Today it remains an exhibit room for the museum.

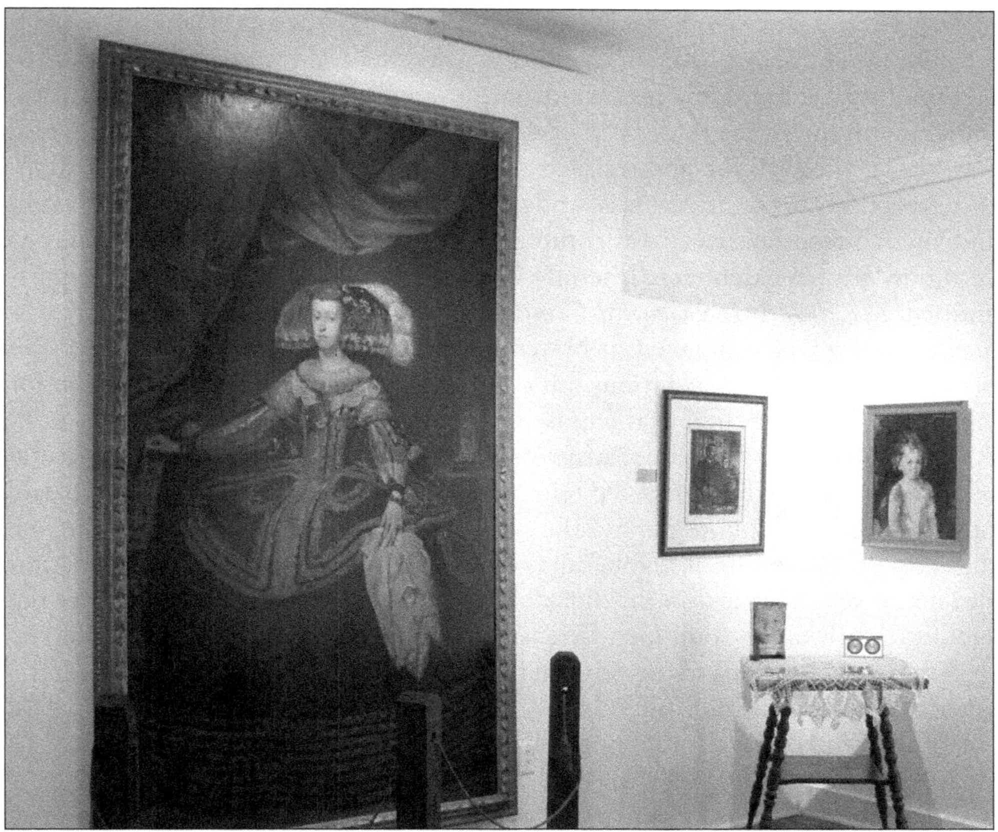

*Robert Henri Museum and Art Gallery Collection*

*Queen Mariana, the largest painting that Robert Henri ever painted, was donated by Janet LeClair, the executor of the Henri estate, in 1988. It was the museum's first Henri painting and hung in one of the large rooms in the southwest end of the building, which was used for exhibits for many years.*

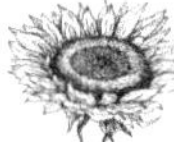

A second large room, in the southwestern corner of the building, had probably been used for long-term boarders because of its size as well. It was connected to the current director's office as part of a suite during the Foster-Lewis era. After the museum began its restoration, false walls were installed here too, and various art exhibits were hung in this room for many years. Today it remains an exhibit room.

While the extensive renovation and restoration work took some time to complete, the museum officially opened in 1986. With that has come a steady stream of thousands of visitors including area senior groups, school classes, individuals, artists, historic preservationists, art connoisseurs and travelers ever since.[28]

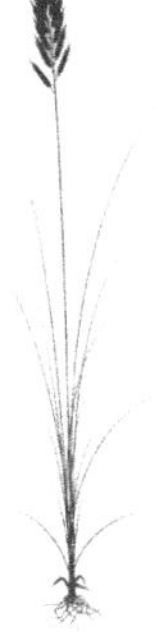

## Structural challenges and infrastructure projects

In the summer of 2002, in an effort to assess the condition of the historic hotel building, the museum's general operations, and to suggest recommendations, the museum under the leadership of then President Tom Gozinski, and Director Kay Lhotak, applied for, and received a Conservation Assessment Program grant.

A conservation survey was undertaken by Jeanne Brako, a Conservator, and an architectural survey was completed by James Pettijohn and Ed Kinney of Pettijohn*Kinney Architects/Interiors from Overland Park, Kansas. The report, entitled *The 2002 IMLS General Conservation Survey Report: Conservation Assessment Program* was completed in November 2002 and laid out a comprehensive plan for the museum's operations but especially important, a course of action for repairs that were required to the museum structure.[29]

Ever since the hotel's construction in 1878-79, there had been structural problems with the building. Deterioration of the brick is evident even in late nineteenth century photographs. The condition of the exterior of the building by the early 2000s was troubling because there were problems with the foundation and major vertical cracks in the outside walls, particularly at the corner where the southern and western walls met. Extensive repairs were also needed, including the replacement of sections of the original foundation, first floor joists along with the deteriorating stucco and roof.[30]

The architectural firm reported that:

> *The foundations on the original hotel are in very poor or in bad condition. There is a serious question whether the building will be operational for very long unless remedial work is performed on the foundations. The high porosity of the brick, the high water table and a general breakdown of the plaster protection coating has led to a deterioration of the bearing capacity of the brick foundation. There is one area in the southwest corner of the basement where a large amount of brick dust has filtered down through the walls and has deposited a large pile on the floor. The moisture present in the brick has also led to wood rot where the floor joists bear on the wall. There are several areas in the hotel where the floor joists have rotted to the point that the floors are sloping towards the exterior.*[31]

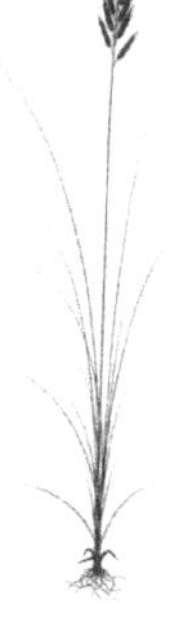

The stucco on the building, particularly on the west and south sides, which was only twenty years old, was in poor condition as it was delaminating from the brick and causing the windows to be pulled out of their casings. The firm recommended taking the stucco down on the whole building and that a lightweight synthetic stucco be reinstalled.[32]

Less than two years later, Paul Brungardt of Brungardt Engineering in Kearney prepared a detailed report that again studied the seriousness of the structural problems and outlined a course of action.[33] Over time the structure had settled and sagged to a point where by 2003, walls were separating, there were gaps in the second-floor windows and the floor of the lobby was decidedly drooping at one end. [34]

The firm recommended taking down the western and southern walls. Bracing was recommended along with the installation of new gutters. Steel rods and plates were recommended to reduce the rotation of the exterior walls. Brungardt relayed that if the work was not undertaken to correct the situation, the building would continue to deteriorate and collapse in the future.[35]

The result of both of these reports would require a major fundraising effort to address the challenges that had been identified. Finally in 2004, the museum began the complicated effort to make the necessary structural repairs but to also remain open to the public at another location. The museum's collection was moved temporarily to 112 East 8th Street, now the home of The Cut Barn (2023) in downtown Cozad. The museum's collection of artwork was relocated to the Museum of Nebraska Art in Kearney which developed a separate *Robert Henri Room*. Work commenced the same year, and one of the first projects was the leveling of the first floor on the western end of the building.

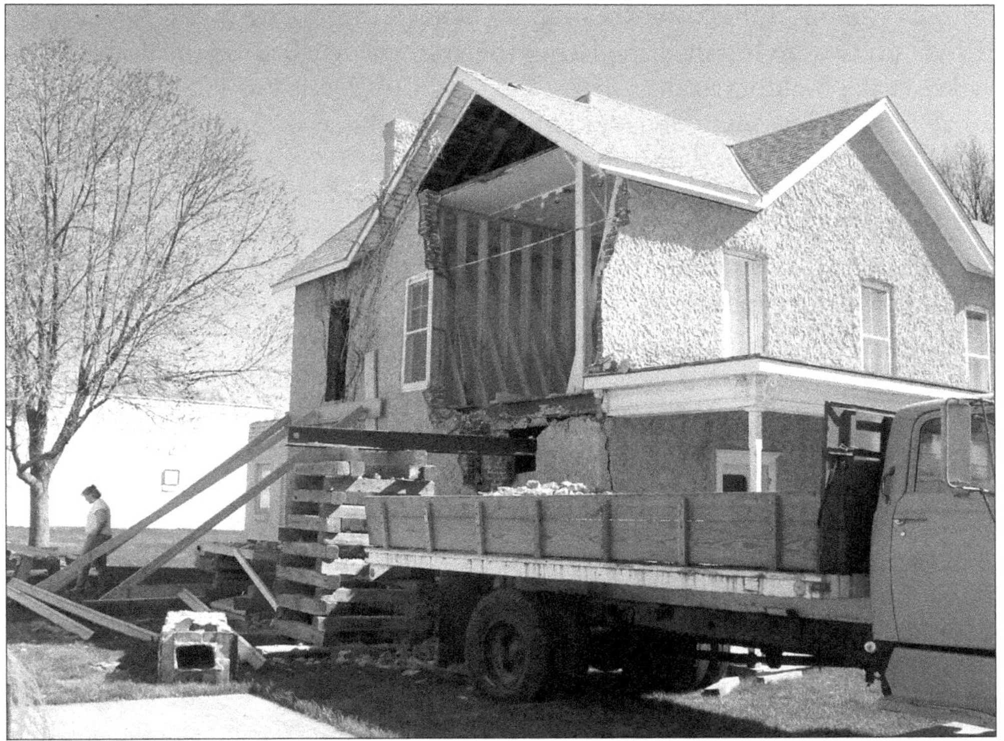

*Robert Henri Museum and Art Gallery Collection*

*In 2004 the museum began to undertake a major construction project to completely replace the west and south walls of the building and to shore up the foundation. Both walls were in danger of collapse after years of neglect.*

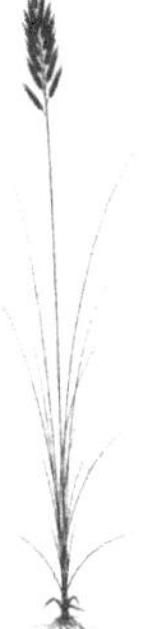

The most difficult and challenging project undertaken was to rebuild the western and southern walls of the museum and build new supports in the foundation to stabilize it. The south and west sides of the building were then restuccoed with a lightweight material.

After the major project was completed, and an expenditure of almost one half million dollars, the museum reopened. It had been the most extensive work done on the building since the restoration in the 1980s. Not only did it include the exterior work but, windows and flooring replaced, interior walls and ceilings repaired, wallpaper was redone and rooms repainted.[36] The museum building's roof was covered with asphalt composition shingles at that time and then in 2014, a new roof was installed on the museum building. All of the soffits were replaced too.[37]

Over the decades there have been many projects, not listed here, that were undertaken that were not well documented and further research needs to be accomplished in that part of the building's history.

For the last decade the museum has been upgrading its infrastructure. Many projects have been completed as the institution has looked to the future and the preservation of the historic Cozad homestead. Beginning in 2018, four new HVAC units were installed, replacing the systems that had originally been installed in the building in the 1980s. The last HVAC unit was installed in 2022. Installation of new plumbing and hot water heaters was completed in the building in 2021 along with numerous electrical updates.[38]

In 2020, the building was repainted in the colors that had been used when it was stuccoed in the 1910s after a paint bullet analysis was done. Repair work at the time included repairing or replacing some of the sills and discarding the storm windows which in many cases had deteriorated to the point where they could not be repaired.

In 2021, new gutters were installed on both its main building and the art gallery as a result of recommendations made by a conservation expert. There was concern that the water was not being directed away from the building and was damaging the foundation and stucco. In 2022, new storm windows were installed in an effort to protect the museum building and to save money on utilities.

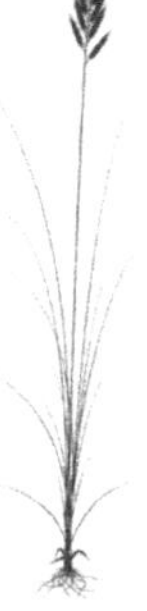

The building's interior has been painted several times and various exhibitions have been installed over the years in the former dining room, Robert and John's office and the addition to the back of the former kitchen as the museum updates it interpretation of the Cozad time in the community and the impact that Nebraska had on Robert Henri's life.

### The Robert Henri Art Gallery

Through the efforts of the executor of the Robert Henri estate, Janet LeClair, Henri's *Queen Mariana* was gifted to the museum in 1988. It is the jewel in the crown of the museum's collection, and was hung on the second floor of the museum in an area that was not climate controlled.

In 2012 the museum sent its most important painting, *Queen Mariana*, to the Gerald Ford Conservation Center in Omaha for conservation treatment. This was completed as part of a loan with the Mississippi Art Museum when the painting was sent to Jackson, Mississippi, for an exhibition.

This effort galvanized the museum and its membership to build a new gallery that would be climate controlled and secure. There was also a concern by the museum's board and director that the large rooms at the southwestern end of the second floor of the south side of the building, which included the galleries of Henri sketches and other original artwork, were not handicapped accessible.[39]

After raising the required funds, and, again, with a major community commitment, a new gallery was erected and officially opened on August 25, 2015. The gallery has since become home to the museum's growing collection of paintings and sketches and is the most visited aspect of its operations.

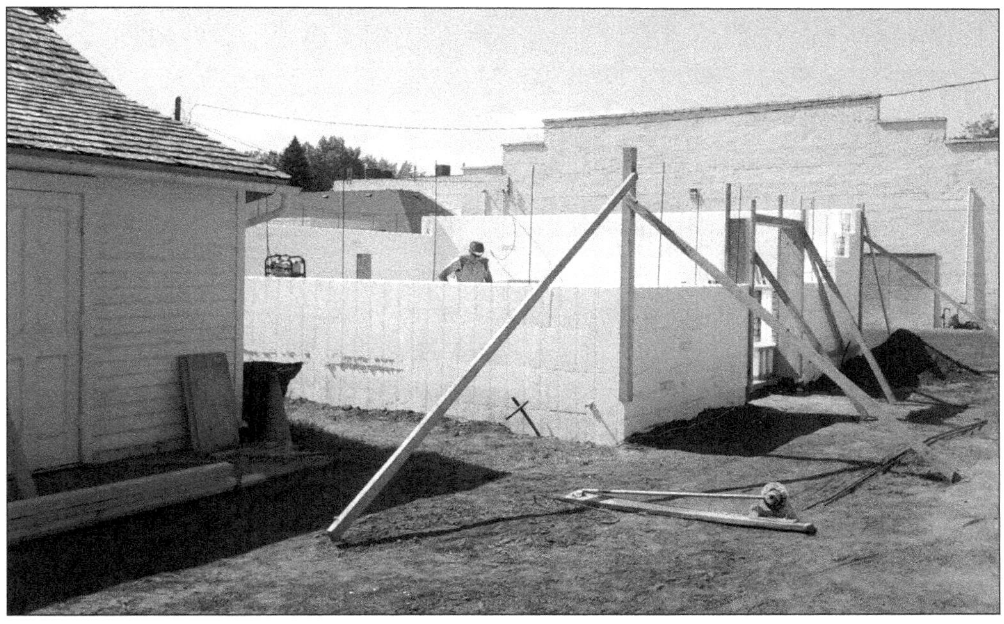

*Robert Henri Museum and Art Gallery Collection*

*After raising a considerable amount of money and drawing from community support, the museum built a new gallery directly to the north of the museum building. The building's plans included radiant heat, a security system, lighting and an excellent place to display a growing number of Henri paintings and sketches.*

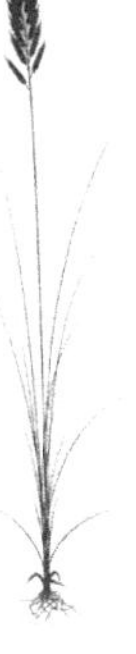

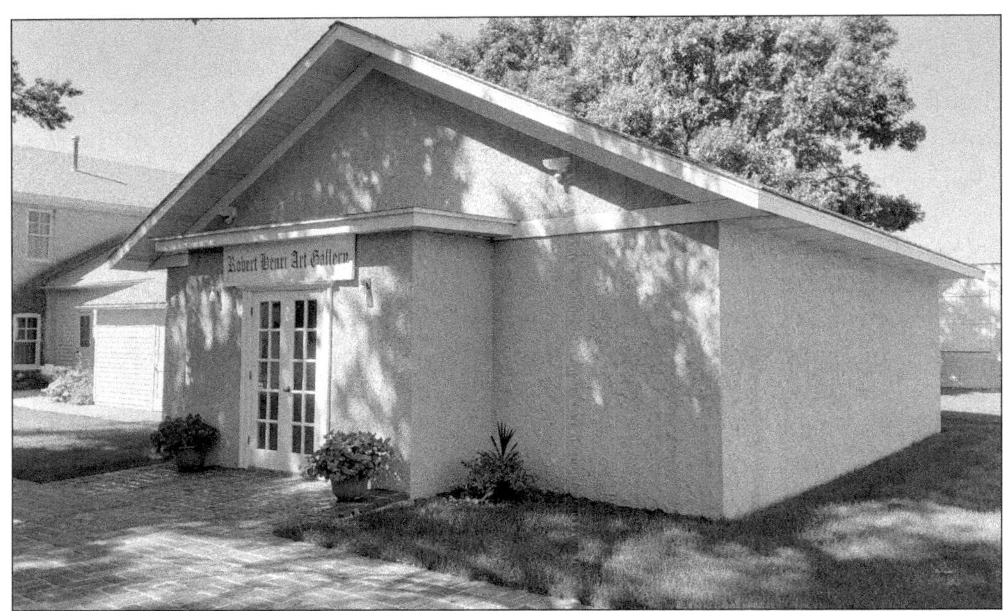


*Robert Henri Museum and Art Gallery Collection*

*The Robert Henri Art Gallery*
*2022*

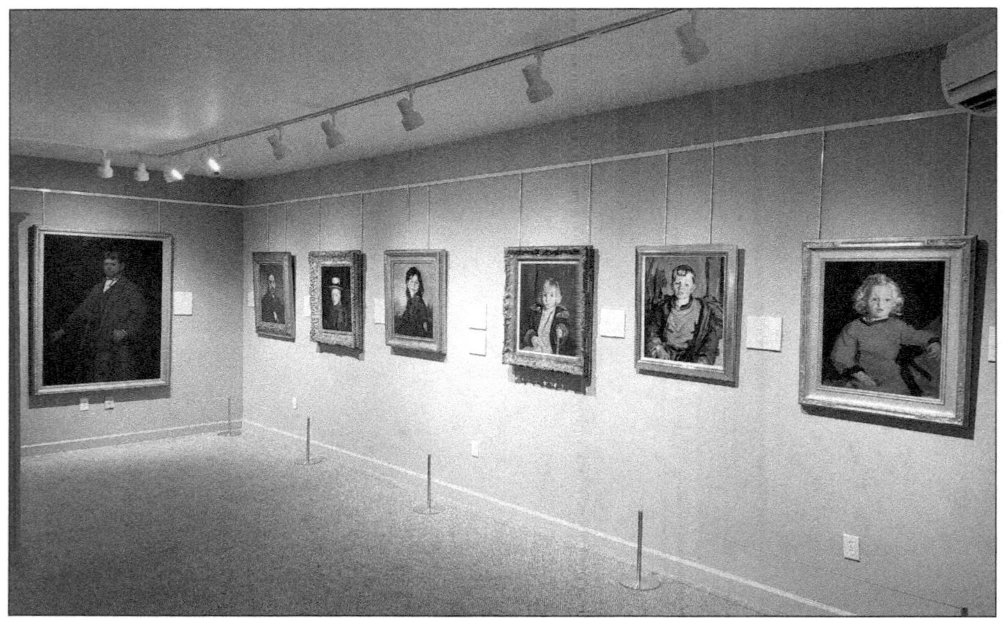

*Robert Henri Museum and Art Gallery Collection*

*The Robert Henri Art Gallery*
*Through My Own Language: Robert Henri and His Portraits, Paintings and Sketches*
*2022*

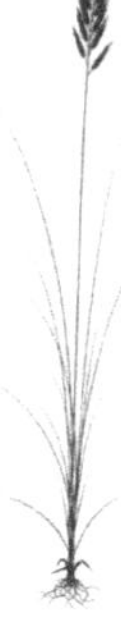

## Ghost Stories: Is the Museum Haunted?

Finally, one of the most commonly asked questions by visitors and residents alike is whether the Henri Museum is haunted. It certainly makes sense that it is a possibility, for it has stood for more than one hundred and forty years, and there have been many people who have stayed here as they traveled, others were lodgers, or others did business. It was for many years a center of activity in town. It is known that at least one person died in the building, and there were probably others whose names are lost to history. Perhaps even a marriage or two may have happened there. A baby was born to Ora Ashley Nunn, perhaps in 1915.[40] It is a place that holds many secrets.

Seances have been held in the building and were said to have been done in rooms with the shades drawn so that onlookers could not see. Paranormal investigations have also been undertaken at the museum and there are at least three You Tube videos that were done. Noises can be heard in them although it is not clear what the noise is.[41] As has been attested by the museum's various directors over the decades, and others, it is almost certainly haunted. Some have suggested that the spirits began to become active again because of all the work that was being done in the building in the 1980s.[42]

Each museum director has had their share of stories including the author. One of the most interesting and unusual of the stories comes from Susan Brasch, the Artist in Residence for the museum in 1988. She stayed in the room, at the far northeastern corner of the museum that Robert and Johnny Cozad used for storage adjacent to their bedroom. Thirteen years later she relayed to Jan Patterson, then the museum's director the following:

*I was in the hotel for nine weeks during my residency with the Nebraska Arts Council and did experience some odd happenings but nothing really major. I would hear glass breaking in the night, voices, and what sounded like a stack of books dropping. At the top of the stairs is that motion sensitive light with the alarm system and (my) first thought was it just moths flitting in front of it and who knows what the imagination does to one when you are the only one and there are creepy mannequins down the hall from my room. Consequently, I would get to my room by eight pm and not leave until morning because whether or not it was my imagination playing tricks on me or something actual, larger shadows moving in the hallway and a rustle (sic) of material and the occasional smell of tobacco. I don't smoke and have never been around smokers, but it smelled like a pipe for some reason.*

*While there, I mentioned some of the activity and they mentioned that while they were renovating the hotel that folks had had many incidents including where someone felt that they had been literally pushed off the ladder that they were on by an unseen force.*

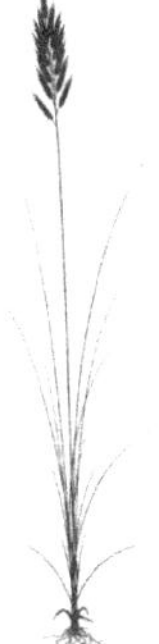

*I would be interested in knowing if actual ghosts have ever been seen and what*

*other activities others have experienced. What fun for you to make contact with paranormal investigators. It will be interesting to see what they come up with in regards to the energy that resides in that place.*[43]

The late Jan Patterson, a long-time director, had *The Art Spirit* book fall on her head from a bookshelf. She ultimately thought that maybe the spirits needed some soothing music upstairs. She and Caroline Gaudreault, her successor as the director, also had experiences with some of the paintings and mannequins.[44]

The author has his own stories during his time as director. On one occasion, in the morning, during the fall of 2019, as he was walking along the second-floor hallway, he smelled the distinctive odor of pipe smoke. It only lasted for perhaps fifteen minutes and then it was gone.

On another occasion he smelled, in the second-floor room that Robert and John Cozad had used for storage, a very strong smell of vanilla extract. At first, he thought that perhaps it might have been spilled on the floor in the distant past. In discussing this with Karmen Morse, then the executive director of the Cozad Chamber of Commerce, she suggested that perfumes used vanilla extract as part of their formulas in an earlier time. The smell lasted about an hour and then was gone. Perhaps it was from one of the former prostitutes who are said to have lived in the building and who were once again wandering the halls.[45]

However, it is important to note that the use of the building for those activities has never been documented, although they might be a difficult task to prove because of the illegality of the activities. The tradition is that while the first floor was used for private living quarters, the second floor was used by the ladies of the night. The story held such sway with some people that they refused to participate in fundraising efforts in the 1980s to restore the building.[46]

Very few visitors have ever made observations but service dogs have on occasion refused to go up the stairs to the second floor. They obviously know something more than we do.

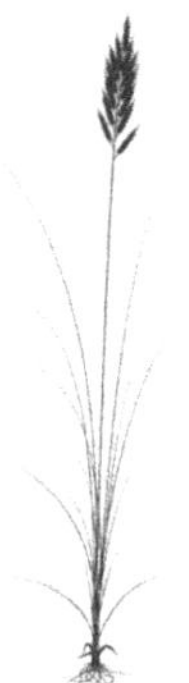

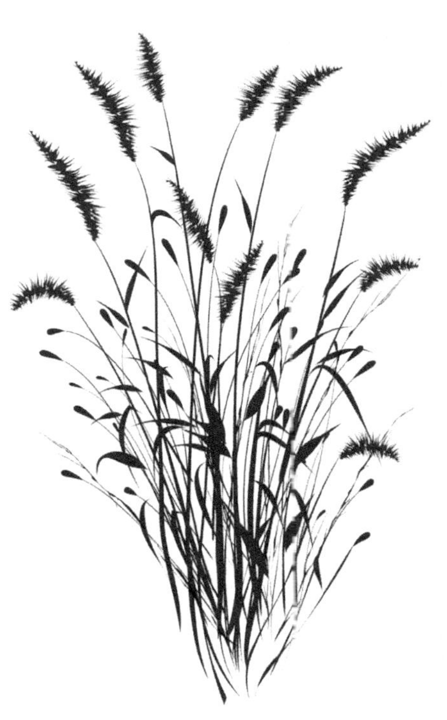

# Part IV

# Epilogue

*The essence of history is remembering.*
Unknown

# Epilogue

*I want to write the book I want to read.*[1]
David McCullough

One of my most important goals as a writer and historian over the years has been to honor the dreams of the people who have created our country's museums, art galleries, historic sites, state and national parks, state and national forests, and natural preserves. It takes someone special, or an inspired group, to have a vision, such as preserving a significant cultural or natural resource, and then moving a complicated process along until there is a dedication ceremony, signs are unveiled, and people begin visiting. These are the people who have given us many of the places that we now prize.

There are special characteristics shown by these visionaries, such as Carolyn Pitts who led the effort to save the historic architecture of Cape May, New Jersey, a late nineteenth century seaside resort. Her determined efforts, during the 1960s, which were controversial at the outset, resulted in the creation of a National Historic Landmark District and a state treasure. In spite of those who opposed her, and various lawsuits brought against the city, she prevailed. The community is a beautiful place to visit and very few of its current residents who benefit from the beautifully restored buildings even remember who she was.[2]

Or perhaps it was the Mount Vernon Ladies Association who saved George Washington's home along the Potomac River in Virginia in the 1850s. The house sat in a state of disrepair until Ann Pamela Cunningham viewed the venerated founder's home from a riverboat and determined that it needed to be saved. At the time, there were no mechanisms to save historic sites such as the preservation organizations or historical societies that are now so common across the country. We enjoy the benefits of their hard work more than one hundred and fifty years later. The Association has managed the site through good times and bad including the Civil War from 1861-65.[3]

At Washington's Crossing, about eight miles north of Trenton, New Jersey, Philadelphia surgeon Isidor Strittmatter purchased almost three hundred acres of land on both sides of the Delaware River in the early twentieth century. Strittmatter, a student of the American War for Independence, had saved what was believed to be the most significant tracts of land where the famed 1776

Christmas Crossing of the Delaware had taken place. Most of those land acquisitions would ultimately come to be established as two historic sites - Washington Crossing State Park (New Jersey) and Washington Crossing Historic Park (Pennsylvania). They are among the most historically significant state parks in the nation, and curiously, the only noteworthy Revolutionary War sites not owned and managed by the National Park Service.[4]

Another example is the Bowman's Hill Wildflower Preserve (BHWP). This unique area, about one hundred acres in size, was set aside within Washington Crossing Historic Park. It was one of the early leaders in the native wildflower preserve movement in the United States. Those lovers of wildflowers and native plants created an institution that would become a model for the creation of other preserves across the country. The BHWP remains a dynamic organization today and a leader in the nature preserve movement.[5]

Like all of these previously successful efforts, which admittedly were accomplished back East, and some of which were documented in books written by the author, the endeavor to save the Robert Henri boyhood home is similar to those previously mentioned struggles. In the early 1980s, the dedicated and driven *Grandmothers of Cozad* took on what seemed to be an impossible task, saving the old Hendee Hotel from demolition. It was a race against time as the building had deteriorated and been left vacant. Little could they have known that their remarkable effort would lead to an even grander dream in the decades to come in the creation of a significant national resource dedicated to preserving the work of Robert Henri.

All of these examples demonstrate that these visionaries are often single-minded in their focus. They looked for, and found, creative, proactive strategies to implement their goals that often straddled the political divide. They found the money, volunteers and community support to carry on. Our national, state, and local treasures have been saved by such people. For their hard work and devotion, we are grateful, even if we do not always know who they are today.

## Starting With An Agenda

While the author does not normally begin a book with an agenda in mind, there is one theme that is consistent in all my books about parks, historic sites, museums and institutions. They specifically honor the founders and the visionaries who carried those efforts forward. Often, the founders have long ago passed from the scene, moved from the area, or pursued other interests. Their names are forgotten and the current beneficiaries of their hard work and dedication often just assume that the site, building or institution that they are enjoying was always there. Perhaps there is a dusty old picture hanging somewhere of the founder but his or her contemporaries are usually gone and there is no direct connection to that person or the group of people who worked so hard years ago to establish a

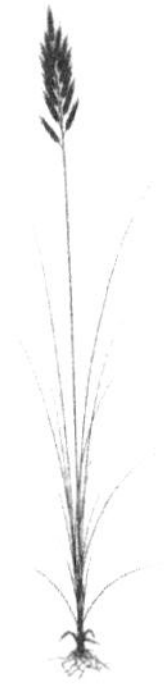

treasure that is beloved today. The old scrapbooks that record those heady days when the institution was created are stuffed in a closet in a dark corner of the organization's office.

Sometimes the founders still live in the communities they galvanized, or perhaps their children have continued the work on pushing the mission forward, and that is the case with the Robert Henri Museum and Art Gallery. In this case, some of those founders continued to maintain an interest in their pet project. In discussing the effort to save the Henri boyhood home, I did meet one of the founders and some of the early supporters who still remember the complicated effort and hard work that it took to create this special place and see it shared by future generations. To meet with them during the writing of this book and to discuss the history of the institution along with their memories was a great pleasure. We are appreciative of their hard work in the decades gone by.

Then there are the next generation of visionaries who have carried that mission forward by sacrificing their time, donating money, dealing with challenges and urging others to do the same. They might give tours, make the repairs, build the exhibits, keep the books, clean the bathrooms, cut the grass, or serve in public office to protect the public's investment. While their vision for the institution may be different from the founders, they remain committed to that original mission. To those folks we offer our collective thanks as well.

## Robert Henri and Me

Robert Henri and this author have a history that goes back to 2015 when I wrote a biography of one of the artist's students entitled *Elizabeth Grandin: A Clinton Treasure.*[6] Henri had a charismatic personality who taught many women during the course of his career. Grandin was single and from a wealthy family who were among the earliest settlers in Hunterdon County, New Jersey. At the time, my focus was on her and the connection she had to the community of Clinton, New Jersey.

My professional career had taken me to the Red Mill Museum Village in Clinton as the Curator of Education and Special Events. During my time working there the museum's director, Amy Hollander, and curator of exhibits, Elizabeth Cole, created a retrospective of her work. The museum owned a collection of Grandin's paintings including a full-length portrait of her mother that is very evocative of Henri's larger portraits. Her works reflect her training by Henri and are prized possessions for those who own them. The local library, which her family had founded, also owned a collection of her paintings and personal items that were willed to them after her passing in 1970.[7]

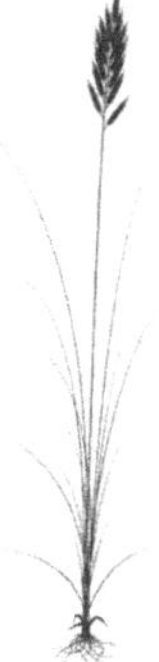

Miss Grandin had been taught by some of the most important teachers of that era including William Merritt Chase, Robert Henri, Charles Guerin, Othon Friesz and another of Henri's students, Rockwell Kent. In her written recollec-

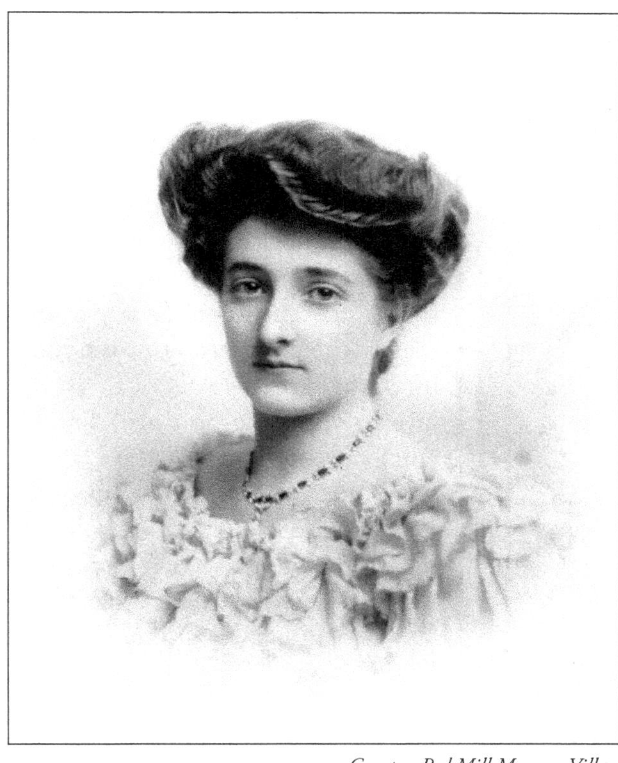

*Courtesy Red Mill Museum Village*

*Elizabeth Grandin*

tions created later in life, she recalled two trips she took to Spain with Henri and his wife, Marjorie.

My project concluded with the publication of a book, and presentation of my research in the back yard of her former home in Clinton for the Red Mill Museum Village's *Splashes of History* program. On that summer evening I thought that was the end of my passing connection to Robert Henri. Several times over the next few years on my way to Denver I tried to donate a copy to the Henri museum only to find it closed. During my job interview for the position of executive director in the late fall of 2018, Marlene Geiger finally received the much-traveled copy of the book.

Little could I have known that just three years after that lecture in Clinton, I would wind up being the director of the museum that honors Henri's legacy and by extension, Elizabeth Grandin's. This remains one of the most serendipitous moments of my forty-three year professional career.

It was not until research began for this book that other connections to my professional past were made. Job Cozad, Robert Henri's (*Robert Cozad*) great-great grandfather, had lived about twenty miles south of Port Jervis, New York, where I was the Executive Director of the Minisink Valley Historical Society. In addition, he was a real estate promoter and sold lands in Sussex and Morris counties in northwestern New Jersey. A book I wrote, entitled *Images of America: Hacklebarney and Voorhees State Parks*, tells the story of that park, which is in Morris County and not far from Job's land.[8]

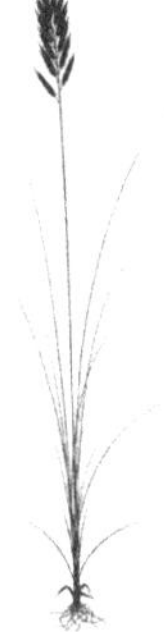

Another fascinating connection comes from my books on the state parks at Washington Crossing along the Delaware River in New Jersey and Pennsylvania which featured Dr. Isidor Strittmatter, the man whose strategic purchase of land allowed for the two parks to be created. He was a surgeon and gynecologist of some fame and like Frank Southrn (*Johnny Cozad*), he graduated from

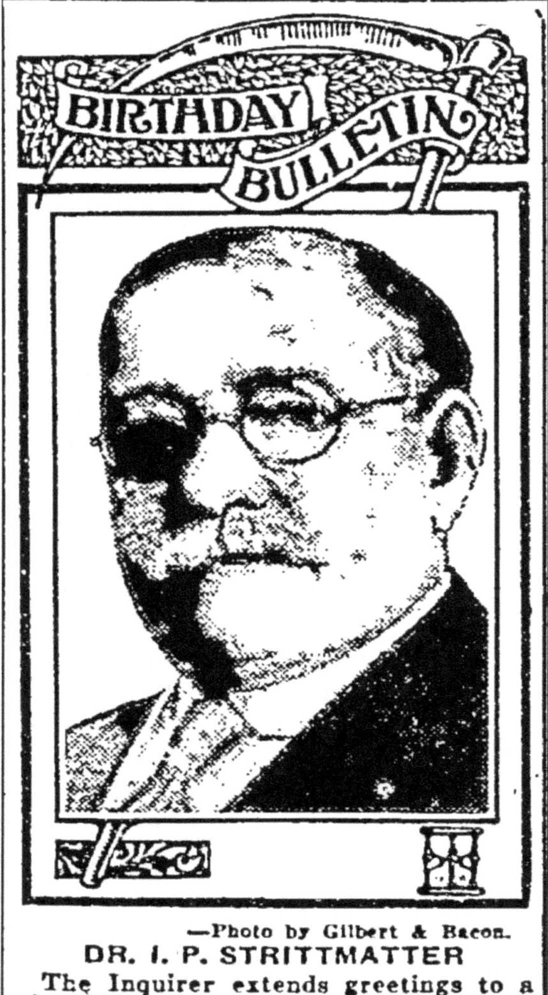


—Photo by Gilbert & Bacon.
DR. I. P. STRITTMATTER
The Inquirer extends greetings to a widely-known physician.

*Courtesy Peter Osborne*

*I. P. Strittmatter*
*The visionary whose donations and sales helped to create the parks where General George Washington crossed the Delaware on Christmas 1776.*

Thomas Jefferson Medical College in Philadelphia in 1881. Southrn graduated in 1889, so it is possible they may have known each other. Perhaps Strittmatter even taught Southrn and even more conceivable is the notion that they perhaps were both on the teaching staff at the same time since Southrn also taught there. Strittmatter was very interested in the American Revolution, and Jane Southrn, Frank's wife, was a member of the Daughters of the American Revolution.[9]

My mother was a great fan of the Impressionists, and her home was lined with prints of those famed painters, including those of Mary Cassatt's. She regularly went into New York City and visited the Metropolitan Museum of Art with its amazing collection including several Robert Henri paintings in the American wing. She died a little less than a year before I came to the Henri Museum but I have to think she would have been pleased and so proud of her son's job posting, and that some of our paintings very much reflect the era of the Impressionists.

Finally, there is also a Nebraska connection with Henri and me other than my job at the Robert Henri Museum and Art Gallery. It is that I live in Red Cloud, Nebraska, named for the famed chief of the Lakota. While he is not believed to have ever visited the town that was named for him, in 1871 a small group of settlers who admired him named what became the Webster County seat to honor him. It is just a few miles north of the Kansas border and is the only town in America named for him. Robert Henri was very sympathetic to America's original peoples, including Red Cloud.

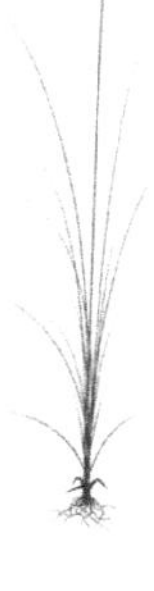

When one considers all the serendipitous events surrounding this book it is clearly destiny that it should be written.

## A Book is Born

In the spring of 2019, the idea of writing a book about Robert Henri's Nebraska legacy and the architectural legacy of the Hendee Hotel began to coalesce in my mind. Having just finished a run of writing ten books in ten years, there was a hesitancy to commit to another book project and the necessary deadlines, dedication of time, and the sheer amount of work it takes to write and design a book.

My early books were all written in the early hours of each morning when I was a historic site administrator in Port Jervis. Then, after moving on professionally, I was commissioned to write five more books by patrons of state parks, a museum and a nature preserve. In those projects I was able to devote my efforts full-time, which was a much easier task given that I was committed to those projects alone. When this project began in earnest, there was a return to that setting aside of an hour or two a day for researching and writing. This effort also fits into another pattern, as almost all my book projects have been on topics that have not been written about before.

The idea to write this book originated when I read the *Cozad Local* special section, published in 1956 that revealed what had happened to the Cozad family after their early 1880s disappearance from the community. There were questions about some of the information revealed in that remarkable piece of local history which ultimately brought me to the realization that we were only telling part of the story at the museum of that stunning revelation and that there was a much richer history as to how the family's secret came to be made public. The effort to untangle that complicated story became *Part 2, Chapter 1* in this book. Who could have known that a couple of questions raised from reading that special section would lead to a journey that took almost four years to complete?

Other discoveries along the way pushed the effort farther along and included a paint analysis that was required when the museum's exterior trim was repainted, repair work done on soffits and fascia boards on the second floor, two bricks uncovered during a plumbing project, and old photographs and documents discovered in boxes and files. As each discovery came to light it became clearer that a book was needed and that the knowledge gleaned from those activities, along with other sources that were being discovered, had to be documented, not only for those of us who tell that story today at the museum but also for posterity. So, it went from being *a project,* as I initially called my research and note taking, into this book of more than four hundred pages. And, as the late David McCullough, the famed American historian and writer, often said in lectures it was clear that: *I wanted to write the book I wanted to read.*

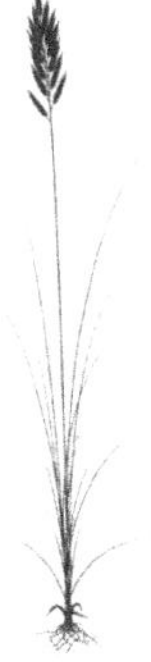

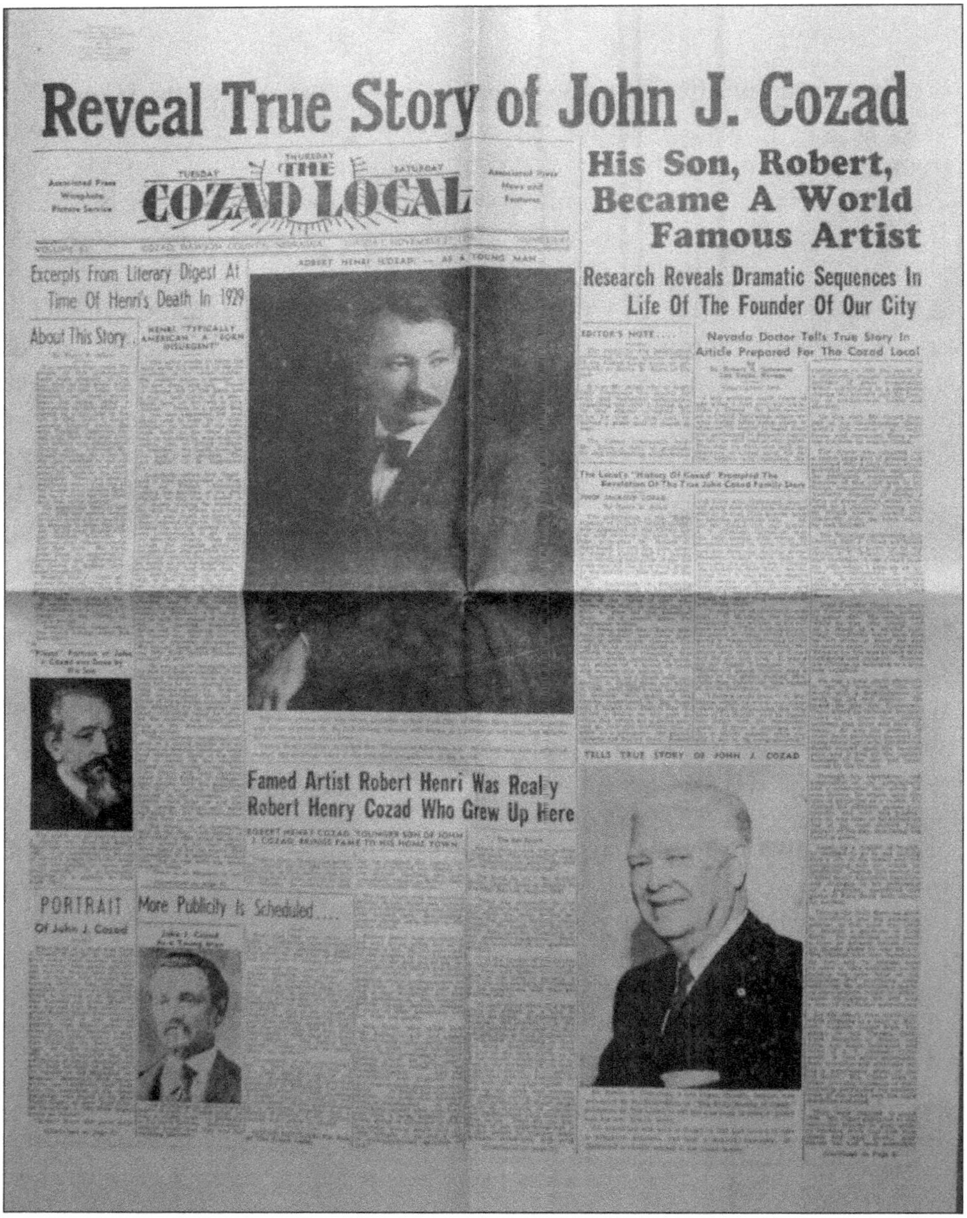

# Reveal True Story of John J. Cozad

THE COZAD LOCAL

## His Son, Robert, Became A World Famous Artist

### Research Reveals Dramatic Sequences In Life Of The Founder Of Our City

Nevada Doctor Tells True Story In Article Prepared For The Cozad Local

Excerpts From Literary Digest At Time Of Henri's Death In 1929

About This Story

ROBERT HENRI COZAD — AS A YOUNG MAN

### Famed Artist Robert Henri Was Really Robert Henry Cozad Who Grew Up Here

TELLS TRUE STORY OF JOHN J. COZAD

PORTRAIT Of John J. Cozad

More Publicity Is Scheduled....

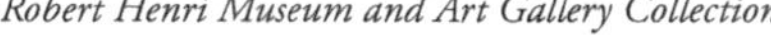

*Robert Henri Museum and Art Gallery Collection*

*The Cozad Local edition that revealed what had happened to the Cozad family for the first time. When it was published in 1956, readers saw how the family had reinvented themselves in Atlantic City, New Jersey and New York City.*

## Just One More Question

Habits of the last twenty years as an author got dusted off and questions were posed to everyone who had some tie to the museum's past. I am sure that our volunteers, friends, benefactors, visitors and fellow researchers all felt like I was a new version of *Columbo*, the 1970s television detective played by Peter Falk. He would wear his suspects down with an unending number of questions. And then, if one remembers the television series, Columbo would get his answers with that final question, and announce that the person was under arrest.

As I met with all of them, I found myself often saying, near closing time or in the middle of an event or project:

*Just one more question . . .*

They were all forever patient and gracious, probably wanting to hide when they saw me coming. Once again, the author found himself traipsing across the countryside taking pictures, visiting cemeteries, going to art museums, working in various archives, and finding that the conventional wisdom on various subjects was not quite so accurate.

It was resolved early on to start with an empty page of white paper much as Robert Henri would have started a painting without any preconceived notions and a blank canvas. This was necessitated because so many of the sources contradicted each other and, in some cases, were simply incorrect. With that approach came new information and different interpretations of the data and traditional accounts. Where possible the author tried to use primary sources but in many parts of the book that was simply not possible

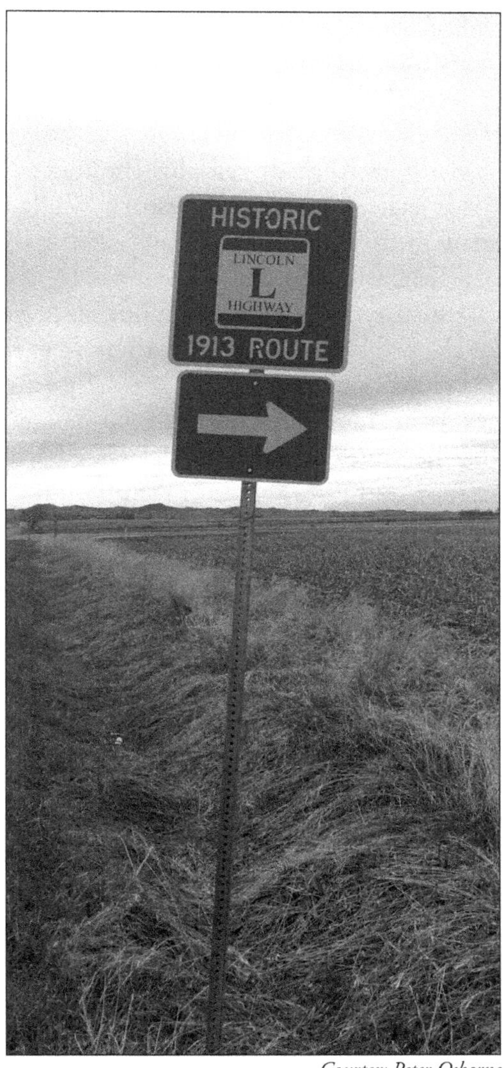


*Courtesy Peter Osborne*

*The writing of this book found the author traveling around the region gathering information and taking pictures. For example, the 1913 historic route of the Lincoln Highway is marked with commemorative markers like this one south and west of Gothenburg, Nebraska.*

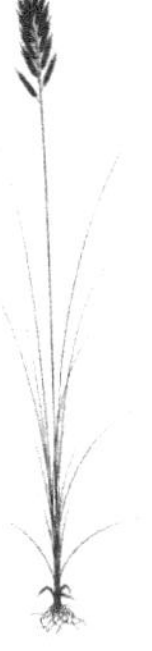

or practical. In fact, the primary sources were often at odds with themselves and so the author has attempted to tell the story as completely as possible while also letting the reader know of problems with the various sources.

This book is no different from the author's previous books in that readers will be surprised by some of the information that has been found which contradicts what has previously been said. Some of it will be altogether new, and some of it will provide a greater context to the traditional presentations that have been made to visitors, and members, and by researchers and authors.

In 2007 the author wrote a book called *Vigilance & Perseverance: The History of the Old Decker Stone House* for the Minisink Valley Historical Society in Port Jervis, New York. It remains the most comprehensive book ever written on the Fort Decker Museum of History. While the people who had lived in the building knew more about the building during their residency than the author could ever hope to know, the author's knowledge spanned the entire two-hundred-and sixty-year history of the old stone house. A wealth of new information was uncovered for the project. For example, there were the seances held in the building, a portion of a child's skull was found in the basement from an accidental shooting, and stories from elderly neighbors about a baby alligator kept in a barrel in the backyard and then released into the Delaware River. There were an array of interesting characters who lived there, not to mention a fascinating Revolutionary War history.

That does not even include the fact that the building was haunted and that our high-tech lighting system was regularly set off by the long-gone Mrs. Sarah Campfield, when she went to bed at 9:15 p.m. every night. She had lived there for fifty years, longer than anyone else, until her death in 1956. The stories could go on and on.

This project is no different except that there were no alligators kept in a barrel in the backyard here or released into the Platte River. However, a gun wrapped in wallpaper, and buried in a tin can, was found in the backyard when some work was being done. Some have suggested that it was the gun that John Cozad used to shoot Alf Pearson but that is not the case. A second gun that escorted Theresa Cozad and Robert Cozad out of the town in 1884 under the watchful eye of Sam Schooley also resides in the museum's collection.

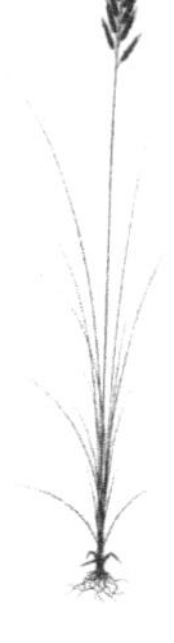

During the research, there was no mention of portions of skulls being found or Native American raids on the building. However, the old Hendee Hotel is haunted by most accounts, and there are stories recounted earlier that have come down from previous directors and others who have had an association with the building of strange things happening.

Just two years after writing that book on Fort Decker, I was on to new professional endeavors and left Port Jervis. In reflecting upon that book all these years later, it is important to remember that the information that was gathered would have been lost if it had not been written down at the time or if an archive of documents and photographs had not been saved. That is why it was so important to get this book on Henri's Nebraska legacy written now, as well as establishing an archive at the museum.

## The Promised Land

Ever since the day that Marlene Geiger, our president, interviewed and then hired me, I have been honored to be the leader of this fine organization. Every morning when I walk through both buildings for my daily rounds, I reflect upon the fact that I am walking in the steps of so many people who have come before me and who have given of themselves to save and promote Henri's legacy. There is this need to occasionally pinch myself when I open the doors to the gallery and see our collection of Robert Henri's paintings and think about how I got to Cozad. I often reflect on the fact I have an important responsibility to take this effort into the next chapter of our future.

Those footsteps include those of the *Grandmothers of Cozad* who saved the museum building from demolition in the 1980s. There are pictures of them in our archives removing plaster, scraping off wallpaper, painting and cleaning the museum building in those early years. There are the many members of the board of directors who have struggled through times of funding shortages and then at one point had to move the museum's collection out of the building when the western and southern exterior walls of the building had to be reconstructed. Then there are the museum's previous directors or coordinators as they were sometimes called. All served the museum ably, under difficult financial times. The author is part of an amazing forty-year-old legacy that began in the early 1980s when the museum was formally incorporated.

There have been some remarkable contributions made to the museum over the years, including Janet LeClair's 1988 donation of *Queen Mariana*, the jewel in the crown of our collection. Patrons and members Tammy and Larry Paulsen have purchased paintings for the museum, donated others and have loaned yet more for the museum. Their contributions took us from the realm of having just a few sketches and *Marianna* to becoming an important center for Henri's work. They have built on the legacy of Larry's parents, Ike and Shirley Paulsen, important figures in the museum's founding. At critical moments their generosity has taken us forward. There are many other donors to be sure and collectively they have made the museum what it is today. To them we also offer our collective thanks.

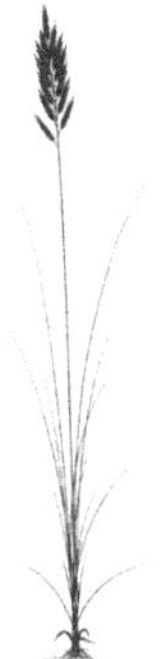

And then there is the community at large which has supported the efforts to create and build a museum and finance it. Local businesses have donated funding, services, art displays, food, and their time over the decades to help our organization. Another important source of funding has come through the generosity of the Dawson County Commissioners, the Dawson County Visitors Commit-

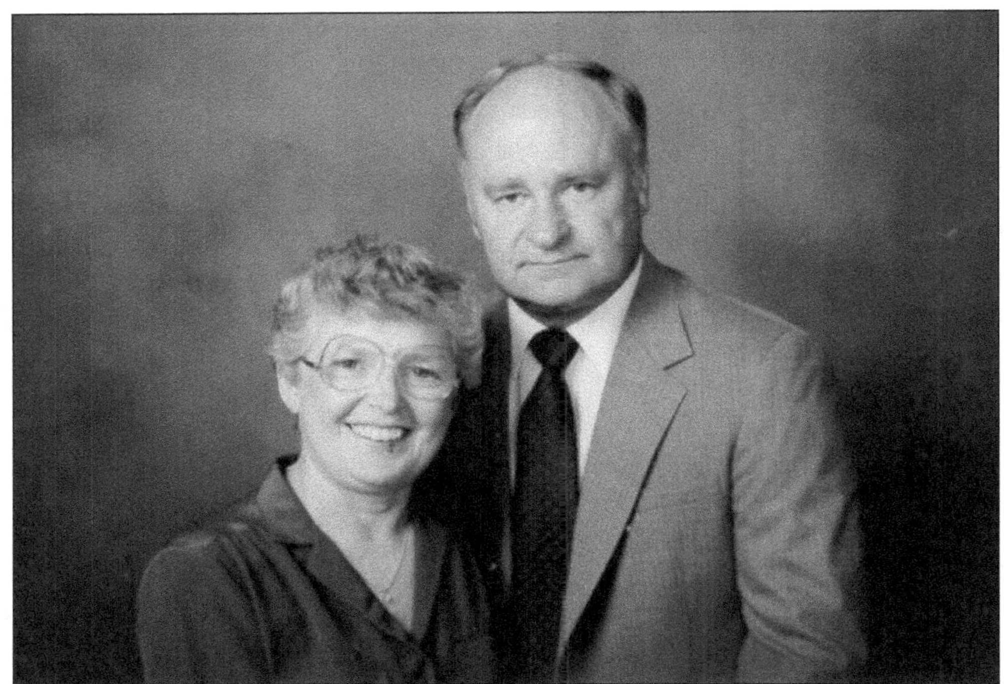

*Collection of the Robert Henri Museum and Art Gallery*

*Shirley and Ike Paulsen*

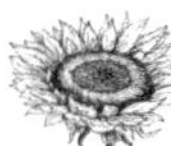

tee and the Cozad Tourism Committee which have provided substantial funding through the Lodging Tax over the decades to undertake major infrastructure projects and promotional efforts.

That community includes our volunteers who often live in Cozad or nearby and have given thousands of hours toward running of the museum. There are also our visitors who have offered ideas of how we might build on the legacy. When we contemplated creating a new exhibit in the Art Gallery in 2019 we met regularly with visitors to discuss how we might create a new show, building upon what had been done in the past. Today's positive reviews are partially a result of having met with them.

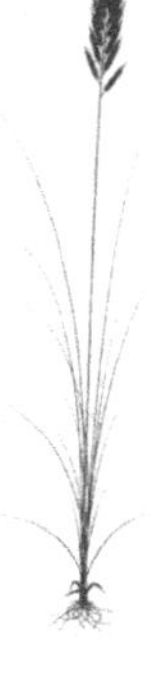

Finally, there has been a major shift in emphasis that has taken place in the interpretation of the site and the artist Robert Henri over the years. While the founders and their successors have always promoted both, there is a reality, as is said in the newspaper business, that *if it bleeds it leads*. And so, the shooting of Alf Pearson by John Cozad remains clearly at the top of many people's minds and their interests when they visit. However, we are making a determined effort to put more focus on Henri's art and his Nebraska legacy, which is so much more.

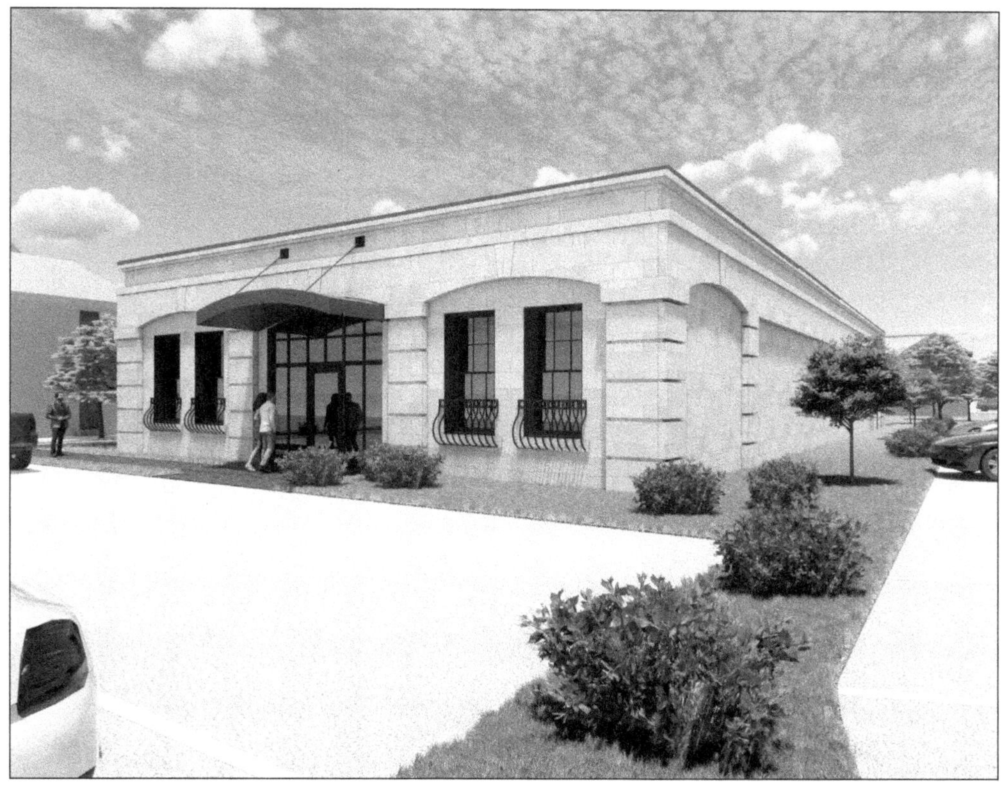

Courtesy WILKINS A | D | P

*The New Robert Henri Gallery*

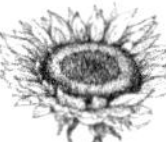

While the Pearson story is a tragic one, and is so recognized, it is but one historic moment in one hundred and forty years of the community's history.

As this book project came to a close the museum is beginning its next chapter with the construction of a new gallery to the rear of the present one. The new building will allow the museum to significantly increase the number of paintings it has on display. The new gallery will allow the institution to become a national center of Robert Henri's work. Once again, the Paulsen family is stepping forward to create this new asset for the community. Tammy and Larry Paulsen will be making a major donation that will allow for the construction of the modern facility by Paulsen, Inc.

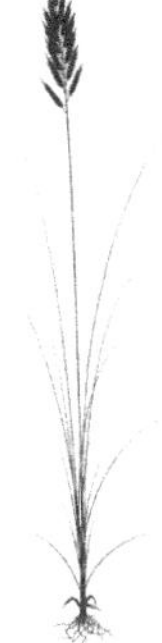

As each new project gets finished, a new water heater here, an exhibit built there, the archive gets better organized, new paintings are donated to our collection, or a new gallery rises up, our organization moves toward what I like to call the *Promised Land.* That journey will not be finished when I leave at some point in the future or the next director leaves because it is a continuous process, there will always be something to do - more funding to be raised or a new project completed. But collectively, after almost four decades, we as an institution keep getting closer to the *Promised Land.*

Peter Osborne
Executive Director
Robert Henri Museum and Art Gallery

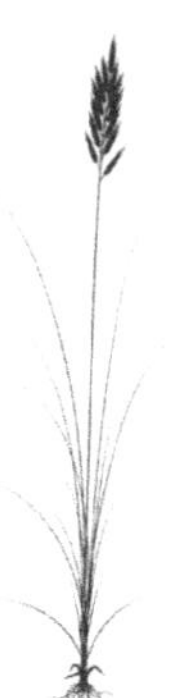

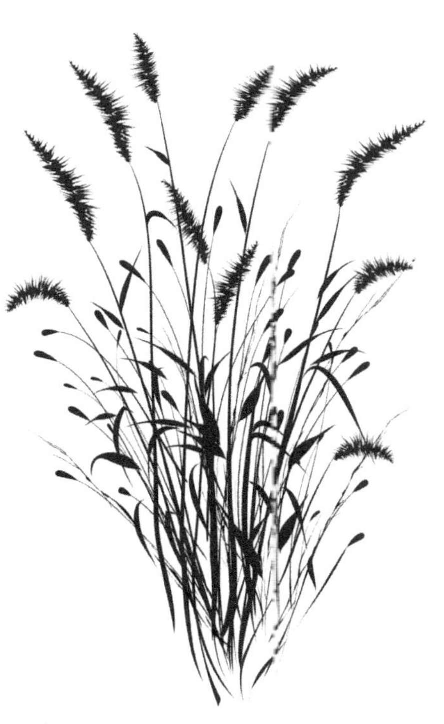

# Appendix

## Robert Henri Timeline

- June 24, 1865: Robert Cozad born in Spence's Station, Ohio to John J. and Theresa Cozad.
- 1868-1872: Cozad family lives in Cozaddale, Ohio, a town founded by John J. Cozad.
- 1872: John Cozad first is attracted to central Nebraska and visits what is now Cozad
- 1873: John Cozad buys 40,000 acres of ground from the Union Pacific Railroad
- 1873 and 1874: First contingent of homesteaders and emigrants arrive.
- 1877: Dawson County turns over management of the small settlement to Cozad residents.
- 1873-1879: Robert Cozad attends school in Cincinnati, Ohio and spends summers in Cozad, Nebraska.
- John Cozad attempts to build bridge across the Platte River but fails.
- 1879: The Cozad family moves to Cozad after Robert graduates from Chickering Institute in Ohio.
- 1878-1879 Emigrant Hotel, future home of Cozad family (and now the museum) is built.
- 1880 Cozad family moves into Emigrant Hotel full time.

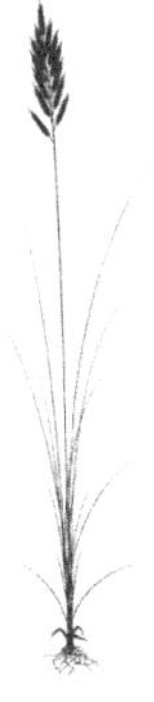

- 1879-1881: Robert Cozad spends time sketching, writing, fishing and helping to run his father's hay business on the Platte River.
- 1881: The Cozad family leaves Cozad and moves to Denver Colorado.
- 1882: John J. Cozad shoots and kills local rancher and special constable, Alf Pearson, during an argument in Cozad. John disappears. Johnny Cozad is charged with attempted arson in Lexington a short time later.
- 1884: John and Theresa Cozad sell their hotel, businesses and remaining land in Cozad to Stephen Hendee and his partners from Illinois.
- 1884: The entire Cozad family reunites in New York City and settle in Atlantic City, New Jersey under assumed names. John Cozad becomes Richard Lee, Theresa Cozad becomes Tess Lee, Johnny Cozad becomes Frank Southrn and Robert Cozad becomes Robert Henri.
- 1885: Robert Henri completes his first painting.
- 1886 Cozad is officially incorporated as a village.
- Three of the four Cozad family members return to Cozad for visits at different dates - John, Theresa and Johnny – but it is unknown if Robert returned. He participated in art shows in Omaha and Lincoln but did not come back to Nebraska for them.

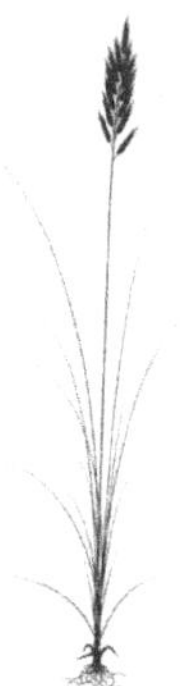

# DIRECT LINE
# OF
# ROBERT HENRI

| | | |
|---|---|---|
| JACQUES COSSART<br>( 1595 - 1681 ) | - | RACHEL GELTON<br>( CA 1600 - ???? ) |
| JACQUES COSSART<br>( Bpt 1639 - ca 1685 ) | - | LYDIA WELLEMS<br>( ca 1640 - ca 1688 ) |
| ANTHONY COSSART<br>( 1673 - 1756 ) | - | ELIZABETH VALENTINE<br>( 1674 - ca 1721 ) |
| JACOB COZAD<br>( Bpt 1701 - 1772 ) | - | ANNAH COX<br>( 1701 - 1785) |
| JOB COZAD<br>( 1731 - 1815 ) | - | ABIGAIL CLARK (1ST WIFE )<br>( ???? - 1776) |
| JOB COZAD<br>( 1769 - 1820 ) | - | CATHERINE FINK<br>( 1770 - 1830 ) |
| HENRY COZAD<br>( 1792 - 1861 ) | - | MARGARET CLARK (2ND WIFE)<br>( 1802 - 1834 ) |
| JOHN JACKSON COZAD<br>( 1830 - 1906 ) | - | THERESA GATEWOOD<br>( 1837 - 1923 ) |

**ROBERT HENRI**
(1865-1929)

*Collection of the Robert Henri Museum and Art Gallery*

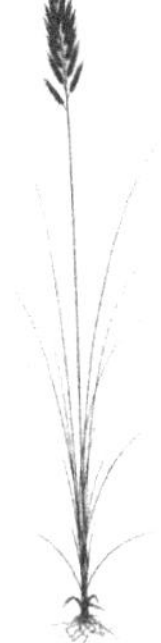

## Ownership Through The Years

There have been seven sets of owners of the Hotel Hendee including:

John and Theresa Cozad
(Construction 1878-1879)
V
James and Clara Riggs
(1879-1880)
V
John and Theresa Cozad
(1880-1884)
V
Stephen Hendee
(1884-1910)
V
John Simonson
(1910-1920)
V
William Foster and the Lewis family, and lastly Deline Lewis
(1920-1980)
V
Wayman May
(1980-1983)
V
The Robert Henri Foundation
and later
The Robert Henri Museum and Historical Walkway
(1983-Present)

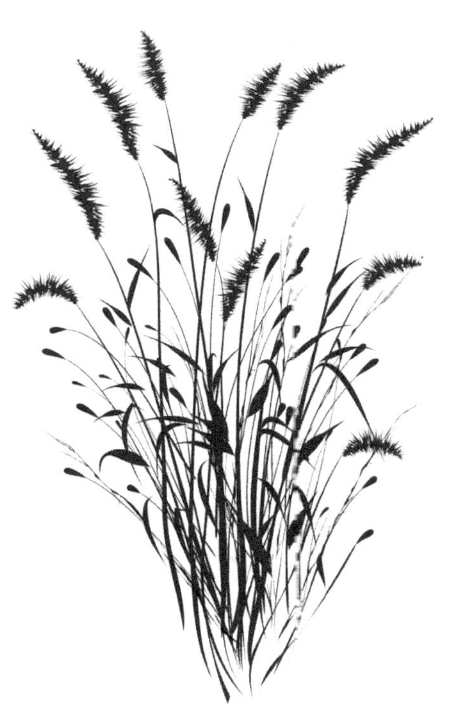

# Endnotes

The following abbreviations are used to identify where specific reference sources can be found. In some cases, they cannot be found elsewhere.
RHM – Robert Henri Museum and Art Gallery
MONA – Museum of Nebraska Art
DPL – Denver Public Library
DCHM – Dawson County Historical Museum
MS – Mari Sandoz papers

FRONT MATTER
1 (Richardson 1986, 288)

FOREWORD
1 (Henri 1923 (2007))

INTRODUCTION
1 (Bargman, It Will Be Down to the Wire (RHM) 1984, 15)
2 The Union Pacific has had a number of corporate names over the last one hundred and eighty years. This is the name that was in use at the time of the founding of Cozad, Nebraska.
3 (Homer 1969, revised 1988, 272, 8n) (Sandoz 1960, x)

PART 1
1 (Sandoz 1960, x)
2 (Nelson 1983, 101)

PART 1, CHAPTER 1
3 (Ho! For the Great Platte Valley (Poster - RHM) 1879)
4 (Taylor 2015)
5 (Mattes 1987, 6)
6 (The Otoe-Missouria Tribe 2023)
7 (Charles E. Allen, Frank Johnson, Glenda France 1998, 64) (Rex German and Russ Czaplewski 1992, ii)
8 (Foresman n.d., 17) (Homer 1969, revised 1988, 19)

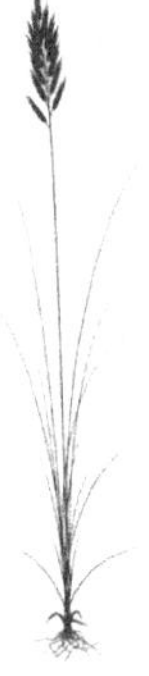

9 (James Olson and Ronald Naugle 1997, 13-14) (Holen 2022) (Bozell 1994)(Bozell 1994)
10 (S. R. Holen and K Holen 2014, 433-434)
11 (James Olson and Ronald Naugle 1997, 13-14)
12 (James Olson and Ronald Naugle 1997, 15-16)
13 (James Olson and Ronald Naugle 1997, 17-18))
14 (James Olson and Ronald Naugle 1997, 19)
15 (James Olson and Ronald Naugle 1997, 19-22, 32)
16 (James Olson and Ronald Naugle 1997, 19-22, 32) (The Otoe-Missouria Tribe 2023)
17 (James Olson and Ronald Naugle 1997, 22) (Marker Monday: Pawnee Villages 2023)
18 (Charles E. Allen, Frank Johnson, Glenda France 1998, 73-74) (C. Anderson 1938, 4) (Werger 2019)
19 (James Olson and Ronald Naugle 1997, 27)
20 (James Olson and Ronald Naugle 1997, 54)
21 (James Olson and Ronald Naugle 1997, 47, 53) (Leroy Hafen and Carl Rister 1950, 215-216)
22 (Leroy Hafen and Carl Rister 1950, 222) (James Olson and Ronald Naugle 1997, 53)
23 (Leroy Hafen and Carl Rister 1950, 238)
24 (James Olson and Ronald Naugle 1997, 55)
25 (James Olson and Ronald Naugle 1997, 66) (Oregon Trail: National Historic Trail Map)
26 (James Olson and Ronald Naugle 1997, 57)
27 (Rex German and Russ Czaplewski 1992, 2)
28 (James Olson and Ronald Naugle 1997, 58-59)
29 (Nebraska's Mormon Trail: A 19th Century Exodus)
30 (James Olson and Ronald Naugle 1997, 59, 63)
31 (James Olson and Ronald Naugle 1997, 64)
32 Susan's last name has also been spelled Hale and Haile.
33 (James Olson and Ronald Naugle 1997, 66)
34 (Nelson 1983, 91) (Charles E. Allen, Frank Johnson, Glenda France 1998, 3)
35 (Map of Township No. 10 North, Range No 23 West of the Sixth Principal Meridian 1868)
36 (Map of Township No. 10 North, Range No 24 West of the Sixth Principal Meridian 1869)
37 (Charles E. Allen, Frank Johnson, Glenda France 1998, 56) (Framnzwa 1990, 81) This discrepancy can be explained by realizing that the trail was always in a state of flux, moving as the conditions dictated like flooding, streams or other natural challenges.
38 (Penry 2016) (Shumway 1918)
39 (Leroy Hafen and Carl Rister 1950, 460)
40 (The History of the Willow Island Pony Express Station Located in the City Park of Cozad, Nebraska (RHM)) (Leroy Hafen and Carl Rister 1950, 461-464)
41 (National Park Service - Pony Express National Historic Trail 2020)
42 (James Olson and Ronald Naugle 1997, 109)
43 (Leroy Hafen and Carl Rister 1950, 461-464)
44 (National Archives - Homestead Act of 1862 2016)
45 (National Archives - Homestead Act of 1862 2016)
46 (National Archives - Homestead Act of 1862 2016)
47 (Rex German and Russ Czaplewski 1992, 3)
48 (Hendee 2016) (Fitzpatrick 1925, 50-51) (Charles E. Allen, Frank Johnson, Glenda France 1998, 2, 77) (Nebraska State Historical Society 2006)
49 (James Olson and Ronald Naugle 1997, 67-77)

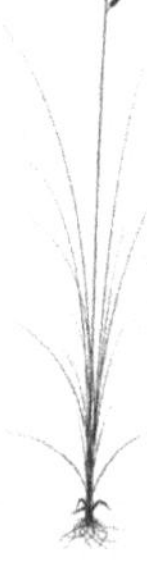

50 (James Olson and Ronald Naugle 1997, 67-77)
51 (Excursion to 100th Meridian, 1866 (RHM)) (General Land Office November 29, 1862) (Seymor 1969, 27) (Brey 1980) (Rody, Notes and Corrections to Book Manuscript, Vol 1 (RHM) 2023, 1)
52 (James Olson and Ronald Naugle 1997, 113-114) (Excursion to 100th Meridian, 1866 (RHM))
53 (Cozad Chamber of Commerce and Historical Land Mark Council)
54 (Penry 2016) (Jerry Penry to Peter Osborne (RHM) 2022) (Charles Allen 1973, 3)
55 (Cozad Chamber of Commerce and Historical Land Mark Council)
56 (Ambrose 2000, 180-181)
57 (Excursion to 100th Meridian, 1866 (RHM)) (Cozad Chamber of Commerce and Historical Land Mark Council)
58 (Charles E. Allen, Frank Johnson, Glenda France 1998, 3-4)
59 (Charles E. Allen, Frank Johnson, Glenda France 1998, 3) (Charles Allen 1973, 4)
60 (Cozad Chamber of Commerce and Historical Land Mark Council) (Charles Allen 1973, 3)
61 (Brey 1980) (Charles E. Allen, Frank Johnson, Glenda France 1998, 4)
62 (E. C. Schafer to Harry B. Allen, May 8, 1963 (RHM))
63 (The Texas General Land Office 2022)
64 (Correspondence between Peter Osborne and Jerry Penry (RHM) 4.28.2022 - 5.2.2022) (Barry Combs and James Wigton 2012, 5)
65 (Powell 1878, 3)
66 (Cozad Chamber of Commerce and Historical Land Mark Council) (Powell 1878)
67 (Charles E. Allen, Frank Johnson, Glenda France 1998, 78) (Rex German and Russ Czaplewski 1992, 22) (Jerry Penry to Peter Osborne (RHM) 2022) For many years the geographical center of the lower forty-eight states was actually to the south and east of Cozad, near present day Lebanon, Kansas. As a result, a park was created, and a robust tourism site was established. That is until 1959 when Alaska and Hawaii were admitted to the Union and the center of the United States moved north and east to Belle Fouche, South Dakota, where a monument presently marks the location.
68 (Vaughan Winter 2021) (James Olson and Ronald Naugle 1997, 2-4)
69 (Charles E. Allen, Frank Johnson, Glenda France 1998, 4-5)
70 (James Olson and Ronald Naugle 1997, 163-164)
71 (James Olson and Ronald Naugle 1997, 163-164)
72 (James Olson and Ronald Naugle 1997, 158, 166-167) (Sandoz 1960, 15)
73 (James Olson and Ronald Naugle 1997, 165) (Rex German and Russ Czaplewski 1992, 22)
74 (James Olson and Ronald Naugle 1997, 165-166)

PART 1, CHAPTER 2
1 (History of Warren County 1882, 618)
2 (Ambrose 2000, 169)
3 (B. Perlman, Robert Henri: His Life and Art 1991, 1)
4 (Marilyn Cozad and Marsha Pilger 2003, 86-87, 169) There are discrepancies with the death dates for both Job and Daniel. (R. Gatewood, Cozad Family Genealogy (RHM))
5 (Descendants of Jacques Cossart and his wife, Lydia (RHM), 169) (Marilyn Cozad and Marsha Pilger 2003, 170) (Sandoz 1960, 6) (Homer 1969, revised 1988, 7-8) (R. Gatewood, Cozad Family Genealogy (RHM))
6 (Eugene Willard, editor 1916, 582) (History of Hocking Valley, Ohio 1883, 1337)

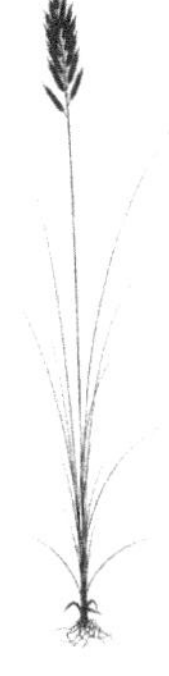

7 (Dr. Robert Gatewood to William Homer (RHM) August 1, 1964) (Homer 1969, revised 1988, 8)
8 (Perlman 1991, 1) (Marilyn Cozad and Marsha Pilger 2003, 170-171) (Sandoz 1960, 6, 324)
9 (James, 4)
10 (Henry and Kate Ford 1881, 102-103) (McCullough 2019, 195) (Perlman 1991, 1) (Homer 1969, revised 1988, 8) (Sandoz 1960, 4) (Gatewood, John J. Cozad, Alfred Pearson, Robert Henri: trio of early years (RHM) 1998, 1D) (Dr. Robert Gatewood to William Homer (RHM) August 1, 1964)
11 (Sandoz 1960, 4, 324)(Phillips 1970) (R. Gatewood, Cozad Mystery Cleared: Town Founder Used a New Name Became Successful Promoter in the East 1956) Where Hazel Phillips got some of her information for her short pamphlet is unknown and unsourced so this biographical insight into South America may be suspect. (Gatewood, John J. Cozad, Alfred Pearson, Robert Henri: trio of early years (RHM) 1998, 1D) (D. R. Gatewood September 20, 1932, 2) (Homer 1969, revised 1988, 8)
12 (Perlman 1991, 1) (Phillips 1970, 2) (D. R. Gatewood September 20, 1932, 2) (R. Gatewood, Cozad Mystery Cleared: Town Founder Used a New Name Became Successful Promoter in the East 1956) (Rody, Notes and Corrections to Book Manuscript, Vol 1 (RHM) 2023, 42)
13 (Sandoz 1960, 4) (D. R. Gatewood September 20, 1932, 2-3) (R. Gatewood, Cozad Mystery Cleared: Town Founder Used a New Name Became Successful Promoter in the East 1956) (B. Perlman, Robert Henri: His Life and Art 1991, 1)
14 (Mari Sandoz Collection (MS), Card 6525A)
15 (Homer 1969, revised 1988, 8)
16 (Homer 1969, revised 1988, 8)
17 (Homer 1969, revised 1988, 8)
18 (Sandoz 1960, 96) (D. R. Gatewood September 20, 1932, 3) (Homer 1969, revised 1988, 10)
19 (West Virginia, U.S., Marriages Index, 1785-1971 2008) (Homer 1969, revised 1988, 10)
20 (Homer 1969, revised 1988, 8, 10) (Perlman 1991, 1) (Phillips 1970, 3) (Marilyn Cozad and Marsha Pilger 2003, 98) (Sandoz 1960, 61) (D. R. Gatewood September 20, 1932, 4)
21 (McCullough 2019, 11)
22 (Henry and Kate Ford 1881, 102-103) (McCullough 2019, 195, 228) (Historical Census Statistics on Population Totals by Race, 1790 to 1990, and by Hispanic origin, 1970 to 1990, for the United States, Regions, Divisions, and States 2002)
23 (Henry and Kate Ford 1881, 102-103)
24 (Henry and Kate Ford 1881, 120)
25 (Henry and Kate Ford 1881, 104-112)
26 (Henry and Kate Ford 1881, 104-112)
27 (U.S., Civil War Draft Registrations Records, 1863-1865 for Ohio, 11th Congressional District, Vol I of Vol 4 n.d., 93)
28 (A. Cozad 2023)
29 (Henry and Kate Ford 1881, 104-105, 119, 121)
30 (Rody, Notes and Corrections to Book Manuscript, Vol 2 (RHM) 2023, 45)
31 Today the intersection is at the center of commercial district which includes the Duke Energy Convention Center.
32 (Robert Cozad Scrapbook - 1878 (RHM) 1878) (Perlman 1991, 4)
33 (Cincinnati Directory 1868, 145, 614, 211) (Rody, Notes and Corrections to Book Manuscript, Vol 1 (RHM) 2023, 2)

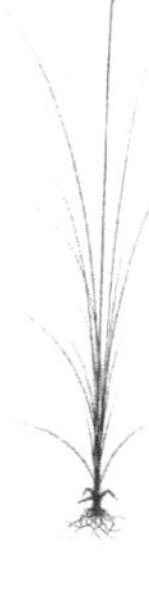

34 (Dr. Robert Gatewood to William Homer (RHM) August 1, 1964) (R. Gatewood, Cozad Family Genealogy (RHM) n.d.) (Rody, Notes and Corrections to Book Manuscript, Vol 1 (RHM) 2023, 2)
35 (Cincinnati Directory 1868, 145, 614, 211) (D. Gatewood c. 1940) (D. R. Gatewood September 20, 1932, 5)
36 (Cincinnati Directory 1868, 145, 614, 211) (D. Gatewood c. 1940) (D. R. Gatewood September 20, 1932, 5) (McCullough 2019, 254, 242)
37 (Cincinnati Directory 1868, 145, 614, 211) (Go West Young Man! 1876)
38 (Bill of Fare - Central Dining Saloon (RHM) n.d.) (D. Gatewood c. 1940)
39 (Homer 1969, revised 1988, 10) (Perlman 1991, 1, 2)
40 (Homer 1969, revised 1988, 10)
41 (Henry and Kate Ford 1881, 178) (Find-A-Grave - William Venable 2022) (Foresman, 3)
42 (Henry and Kate Ford 1881, 178)
43 (Homer 1969, revised 1988, 10) (Robert Cozad Scrapbook - 1878 (RHM) 1878) (Perlman 1991, 3)
44 (B. Perlman, Robert Henri: His Life and Art 1991, 3)
45 (B. Perlman, Robert Henri: His Life and Art 1991, 3)
46 (Tess Lee to Frank Southrn (RHM) 1891)
47 (Homer 1969, revised 1988, 10) (Henry and Kate Ford 1881, 212) (Perlman 1991, 3) (Dr. Robert Gatewood to William Homer (RHM) August 1, 1964)The Cincinnati Art Museum would not be built until after the Cozads were gone although today they own several Robert Henri paintings.
48 (Google Arts and Culture - The Whistling Boy 2022), (Sandoz 1960, 55) (Frank Duvenek 2022) (Cincinnati Art Museum - Museum History 2022)
49 (Goss 1912, 319, 456)
50 (Cincinnati Directory 1868, 145, 614, 211)
51 (Perlman 1991, 2) (Cincinnati Directory 1868, 145, 614, 211) (Cozaddale, Ohio (RHM) n.d.) (Bogan 2004, 1)
52 (Nelson 1983, 93) (Perlman 1991, 2) (Phillips 1970, 1) (Sandoz 1960, 6) (Marilyn Cozad and Marsha Pilger 2003, 98)
53 (Bogan 2004, 1) (B. Perlman, Robert Henri: His Life and Art 1991, 2)
54 (Homer 1969, revised 1988, 10)
55 (Federal Census, Hamilton Township, Warren County, Ohio 1870, 29)
56 (Bogan 2004, 1) (B. Perlman, Robert Henri: His Life and Art 1991, 2)
57 (U.S., Register of Civil, Military, and Naval Service, 1863-1959, 1873, Vol. No. 1 1959, 839) (Bogan 2004, 1)
58 (M. Cozad n.d.) (Marilyn Cozad and Marsha Pilger 2003, 98) (Bogan 2004, 1) (History of Warren County 1882, 293, 608, 618) (Henry and Kate Ford 1881, 101)
59 (Bogan 2004, 1) (Federal Census, Hamilton Township, Warren County, Ohio 1870, 29) (Marilyn Cozad and Marsha Pilger 2003, 98)
60 (Bogan 2004, 1) (Federal Census, Hamilton Township, Warren County, Ohio 1870, 29) (Marilyn Cozad and Marsha Pilger 2003, 98)
61 (Sandoz 1960, 132)
62 (Perlman 1991, 2)
63 (Perlman 1991, 2)
64 (Virginia and Lee McAlester 1984, 211-229)
65 (Virginia and Lee McAlester 1984, 211-229) The home survives and was recently restored.

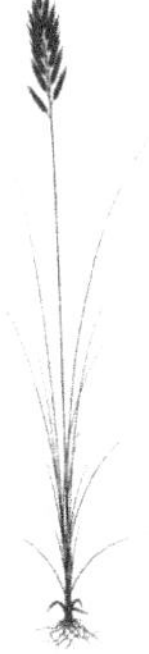

In 2019 it was slated to become a bed and breakfast. Unfortunately, the tower could not be saved when th renovation work was undertaken.
66 (Marilyn Cozad and Marsha Pilger 2003, 100)
67 (Marilyn Cozad and Marsha Pilger 2003, 329) (Rody, Notes and Corrections to Book Manuscript, Vol (RHM) 2023, 2) Another source has him dying in Cincinnati.
68 (Marilyn Cozad and Marsha Pilger 2003, 329) (Rody, Notes and Corrections to Book Manuscript, Vol (RHM) 2023, 2)
69 (Marilyn Cozad and Marsha Pilger 2003, 329)
70 (Certificate of Ownership, Cemetery of Spring Grove (RHM) 1867)
71 (Homer 1969, revised 1988, 271) (Find-A-Grave - William Cozad 2022) (Perlman 1991, 2) (Marilyn and Marsha Pilger 2003, 98, 328-329) On the matter of the children the sources differ as Perlman, Home Hazel Phillips have different dates and information regarding the births of the children. Phillips, for exam has two of the children buried in Maineville, not far from Cozaddale, and the Spring Valley Cemetery recc as shown in Find-a-Grave.com, have all four children buried in Cincinnati. Mari Sandoz in her book state the Cozads only had five children and not the six that Marilyn Cozad's research recorded.
72 (Homer 1969, revised 1988, 10)
73 (Sandoz 1960, 6) (D. Anderson)
74 (Perlman 1991, 2) (Bogan 2004)
75 (Nelson 1983, 93) (Phillips 1970, 3) (Perlman 1991, 2) (Sandoz 1960, 280)
76 (Sandoz 1960, 6) (Mari Sandoz to Jacques Chambrun (RHM) 1945)
77 (Phillips 1970, 1-3) (History of Warren County 1882, 618) (Bogan 2004, 1) (Bogan 2004, 1)
78 (Phillips 1970, 1-3) (History of Warren County 1882, 293, 331, 618)
79 (B. Perlman, Robert Henri: His Life and Art 1991, 4)

PART 1, CHAPTER 3
1 (Charles E. Allen, Frank Johnson, Glenda France 1998, 4)
2 (Rex German and Russ Czaplewski 1992, 20)
3 (Rex German and Russ Czaplewski 1992, 21)
4 (Charles E. Allen, Frank Johnson, Glenda France 1998, 4) (Nelson 1983, 92) (Menke, The Rebirth of tl Cozad Revelation - (RHM) 1985, 1-2)
5 (Charles E. Allen, Frank Johnson, Glenda France 1998, 11) (Nelson 1983, 92)
6 (Nelson 1983, 92) (Sandoz 1960, 21-22) (Charles E. Allen, Frank Johnson, Glenda France 1998, 5, 11) (Moseley 1998, 25g) (Rody, Notes and Corrections to Book Manuscript, Vol 2 (RHM) 2023, 56)It was tl Costin family who greeted the Cozad family upon their arrival according to Mari Sandoz.
7 (Rex German and Russ Czaplewski 1992, 20)
8 (Rody, Notes and Corrections to Book Manuscript, Vol 1 (RHM) 2023, 2-3) (Rody, Notes and Correcti to Book Manuscript, Vol 2 (RHM) 2023, 56)
9 (Gatewood, John J. Cozad, Alfred Pearson, Robert Henri: trio of early years (RHM) 1998, 1D) (Robert Gatewood to H. B. Allen (RHM) 1956) (Dr. Robert Gatewood to William Homer (RHM) August 1, 19 (R. Gatewood, Cozad Mystery Cleared: Town Founder Used a New Name Became Successful Promoter in East 1956)
10 (James, 2)
11 (James Olson and Ronald Naugle 1997, 44-46, 67)
12 (James Olson and Ronald Naugle 1997, 156-158)
13 (James Olson and Ronald Naugle 1997, 94-97)
14 (Ambrose 2000, 169)
15 (James Olson and Ronald Naugle 1997, 112)

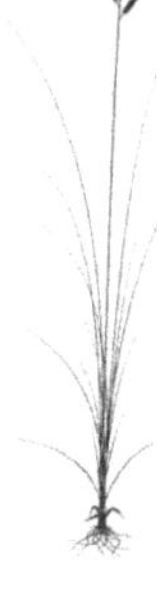

16 (Sandoz 1960, 7)
17 (Rex German and Russ Czaplewski 1992, 72)
18 (Rex German and Russ Czaplewski 1992, 20)
19 (Rex German and Russ Czaplewski 1992, 20)
20 (Sandoz 1960, 11-12) The former geographic center of the United States is located in Lebanon, Kansas, just south of Red Cloud, Nebraska. For many years, until 1959, it was a tourist site as people stood at the marker to have their picture taken. Then with the addition of Hawaii and Alaska into the Union the center was moved northward and westward to Belle Fouche, South Dakota where it remains to this day.
21 Unfortunately, to correct a longstanding historical error, he never said it, just had quoted it. ("Go West, Young Man: The Mystery Behind the Famous Phrase 2015)
22 (James Olson and Ronald Naugle 1997, 176)
23 (Charles E. Allen, Frank Johnson, Glenda France 1998, 3) (Joan Gatewood Miller to Elma Johnson and Rex German (RHM) July 12, 1996) Laura Rody, a staff member of the Wilson Public Library has undertaken a major research effort to uncover the complicated land records regarding the early settlement of Cozad. At the time the author and she discussed some of the results of her findings she was preparing a new history of Cozad for the 150th celebration of the city's founding.
24 (Henry and Kate Ford 1881, 121)
25 (Penry 2016)
26 (Map of Township No. 10 North, Range No 23 West of the Sixth Principal Meridian 1868) (Map of Township No. 10 North, Range No 24 West of the Sixth Principal Meridian 1869)
27 (Map of Township No. 10 North, Range No 23 West of the Sixth Principal Meridian 1868) (Map of Township No. 10 North, Range No 24 West of the Sixth Principal Meridian 1869)
28 (Charles E. Allen, Frank Johnson, Glenda France 1998, 78) (Penry 2016) (Map of Township No. 10 North, Range No 23 West of the Sixth Principal Meridian 1868) (Map of Township No. 10 North, Range No 24 West of the Sixth Principal Meridian 1869)
29 (Sandoz 1960, 38-39)
30 (Rody, Notes and Corrections to Book Manuscript, Vol 2 (RHM) 2023, 62-63)
31 (Horn 2018)
32 While the Early history of Cozad account is considered definitive, Francis Moore actually filed the first claim on September 30, 1873 and Richard May placed his claim in April, probably in the Grand Island land office. (Charles E. Allen, Frank Johnson, Glenda France 1998, 3) (Rody, Notes and Corrections to Book Manuscript, Vol 1 (RHM) 2023, 4, 6)
33 (Rody, Notes and Corrections to Book Manuscript, Vol 1 (RHM) 2023, 6)
34 (Charles E. Allen, Frank Johnson, Glenda France 1998, 5) (Nelson 1983, 93) This deed, according to Nelson, was not recorded until six years later. When calculated the purchase averaged out to $4.59 per acre.
35 (Charles E. Allen, Frank Johnson, Glenda France 1998, 5)
36 (Charles E. Allen, Frank Johnson, Glenda France 1998, 5) (Huey 1884) It was not until the construction of Interstate Route 80 that the flooding was not as severe because the highway acted a levee stopping the flooding.
37 (Charles E. Allen, Frank Johnson, Glenda France 1998, 5) (Lewis, Hendee Hotel (RHM) 1972, 1) Marcus Long's name is spelled two ways – Marcus and Marquis – in various histories.
38 (Nelson 1983, 93) (Sandoz 1960, 61-62)
39 (Sandoz 1960, 7)
40 (Rex German and Russ Czaplewski 1992, 20)

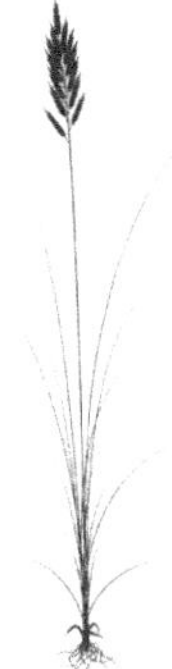

41 (D. R. Gatewood September 20, 1932, 13)
42 (Rex German and Russ Czaplewski 1992, 21)
43 (Rex German and Russ Czaplewski 1992, 21) (Rody, Notes and Corrections to Book Manuscript, Vol 1 (RHM) 2023, 5)
44 (Rex German and Russ Czaplewski 1992, 21)
45 (Perlman 1991, 3)
46 (Sandoz 1960, 45)
47 (Mari Sandoz Collection (MS), Card 653A)
48 (T. G. Cozad 1923) In another entry on the adjacent page Cozad wrote: Owned in 1900 20 thousand acres.
49 (Dr. Robert Gatewood to William Homer (RHM) August 1, 1964)
50 (Rody, Notes and Corrections to Book Manuscript, Vol 1 (RHM) 2023, 5)
5151 (Rody, Notes and Corrections to Book Manuscript, Vol 1 (RHM) 2023, 15-16)
52 (Nelson 1983, 93) (Menke, The Rebirth of the Cozad Revelation - (RHM) 1985, 3) (Rex German and Russ Czaplewski 1992, 22) (Rody, Notes and Corrections to Book Manuscript, Vol 2 (RHM) 2023, 66) (Go West Young Man! 1876) (Rody, Notes and Corrections to Book Manuscript, Vol 1 (RHM) 2023, 5)
53 (Nelson 1983, 94)
54 (Nelson 1983, 93)
55 (Nelson 1983, 93) (Menke, The Rebirth of the Cozad Revelation - (RHM) 1985, 3) (Sandoz 1960, 19)
56 (Sandoz 1960, 6-13)
57 (Sandoz 1960, 35) (Nelson 1983, 93)
58 (Nelson 1983, 94) (Menke, The Rebirth of the Cozad Revelation - (RHM) 1985, 3) (Charles E. Allen, Frank Johnson, Glenda France 1998, 3) (Perlman 1991, 3) (Sandoz 1960, vii, 47)
59 (Nelson 1983, 94)
60 (Nelson 1983, 94) (Kinnan 2019) (B. Perlman, Robert Henri: His Life and Art 1991, 3)
61 (Charles E. Allen, Frank Johnson, Glenda France 1998, 29) (Rex German and Russ Czaplewski 1992, 23) (McCullough 2019, 42) (Rody, Notes and Corrections to Book Manuscript, Vol 2 (RHM) 2023, 68)
62 (Ho! For the Great Platte Valley (Poster - RHM) 1879)
63 (Charles E. Allen, Frank Johnson, Glenda France 1998, 28)
64 (Alverson n.d.) (The Cossart Family Association 1939, No. 936)
65 (Rex German and Russ Czaplewski 1992, 77)
66 (N (Rex German and Russ Czaplewski 1992, 20) elson 1983, 93) (Nelson 1983, 93) (Menke, The Rebirth of the Cozad Revelation - (RHM) 1985, 5) (Sandoz 1960)
67 (Rex German and Russ Czaplewski 1992, 20) (Phillips 1970, 2) (Trifling Case Entertained in Court - It Proves Neither a Mountain Nor a Mole-Hill 1867) (Sandoz 1960, ix, 324) (Rody, Notes and Corrections to Book Manuscript, Vol 2 (RHM) 2023, 42)
68 (Menke, Robert Henri: Museum and Historical Walkway (RHM) 1985, 2) (Menke, The Rebirth of the Cozad Revelation - (RHM) 1985, 3-4) (Sandoz 1960, 5) (Nelson 1983, 95) (Charles E. Allen, Frank Johnson, Glenda France 1998, 11) (Mari Sandoz Collection (MS), 6537A)
69 (Russell Czaplewski to Smithsonian Magazine (DCHM) 1985) (Rex German and Russ Czaplewski 1992, 100)
70 (Homer 1969, revised 1988, 10) (D. Anderson n.d.)
71 (Rex German and Russ Czaplewski 1992, 20)

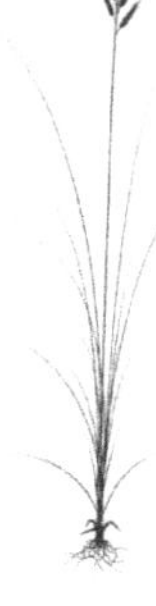

72 (Sandoz 1960, 99-100)
73 (Nelson 1983, 95) (Charles E. Allen, Frank Johnson, Glenda France 1998, 7)
74 (Sandoz 1960, 45)
75 (Charles E. Allen, Frank Johnson, Glenda France 1998, 7) (Nelson 1983, 92)
76 (Nelson 1983, 92-93) (Charles E. Allen, Frank Johnson, Glenda France 1998, 7) (Menke, The Rebirth of the Cozad Revelation - (RHM) 1985, 2)
77 (Homer 1969, revised 1988, 18)
78 (Traber Gatewood to Theresa Gatewood (RMH) 1907)
79 (Nelson 1983, 93)
80 (Menke, Robert Henri: Museum and Historical Walkway (RHM) 1985, 3)
81 (Julia Ann 'Grandma" Gatewood (Mrs. Robert) 1909) (Homer 1969, revised 1988, 8) ((US Census, 1900, 3rd District, Atlantic City, New Jersey, Enumeration District 17, Sheet 14) Julia Gatewood stated that she had five children in this census count although she may have purposely given a miscount. (Homer 1969, revised 1988, 8) (Family Genealogy Files of the Gatewood, Cozad, Henri Families (RHM))
82 (Perlman 1991, 1) (Homer 1969, revised 1988, 8) (D. Gatewood c. 1940) (R. Cozad n.d., 54/238) (Joan Miller to William Homer (RHM) April 28, 1969) (D. R. Gatewood September 20, 1932, 3) (Joan Gatewood Miller to Elma Johnson and Rex German (RHM) July 12, 1996, 2)
83 (Perlman 1991, 1) (1860 United States Federal Census, Year: 1860; Census Place: Kanawha, Virginia; Roll: M653_1356; Page: 291; Family History Library Film: 805356 1860) (Sandoz 1960, 179) (D. Gatewood c. 1940) (Joan Miller to William Homer (RHM) April 28, 1969) (D. R. Gatewood September 20, 1932, 4-5) (Washington 1901, Chapter 2, p. 4) While Booker Washington writes about his time working in the salt mines and learning to read and write he never mentions the Gatewood salt facility specifically.
84 (Charles E. Allen, Frank Johnson, Glenda France 1998, 29)
85 (Menke, The Rebirth of the Cozad Revelation - (RHM) 1985, 5) (Charles E. Allen, Frank Johnson, Glenda France 1998, 23)
86 (Charles E. Allen, Frank Johnson, Glenda France 1998, 14) (Buss, Flour mill, Gatewoods, Fultons, opera house in Cozad annals (RHM) 1998, 1f)
87 (Death Notice - A.T. Gatewood 1928) This death notice also has the change of the name of the town from Cozad to Gould during his time as postmaster a fact not confirmed by the postal records. (Charles E. Allen, Frank Johnson, Glenda France 1998, 10)
88 (Charles E. Allen, Frank Johnson, Glenda France 1998, 29)
89 (Charles E. Allen, Frank Johnson, Glenda France 1998, 29)
90 ( (Record of Appointment of Postmasters, 1832-1971, Records of the Post Office Department, Adams to Douglas Counties, Nebraska (NARA) 1832-1971, 497) (Charles E. Allen, Frank Johnson, Glenda France 1998, 29, 38) (D. Gatewood c. 1940) (Mari Sandoz Papers (MS), Card 3786)
91 ( (Record of Appointment of Postmasters, 1832-1971, Records of the Post Office Department, Adams to Douglas Counties, Nebraska (NARA) 1832-1971, 497) (Charles E. Allen, Frank Johnson, Glenda France 1998, 29, 38) (D. Gatewood c. 1940)
92 (Dr. A. T. Gatewood, A Bryan Democrat of the Old Guard of 1896 (RHM))
93 (Record of Appointment of Postmasters, 1832-1971, Records of the Post Office Department, Adams to Douglas Counties, Nebraska (NARA) 1832-1971, 497) (Charles E. Allen, Frank Johnson, Glenda France 1998, 29, 38) (D. Gatewood c. 1940)
94 (Buss, Flour mill, Gatewoods, Fultons, opera house in Cozad annals (RHM) 1998, 1f)

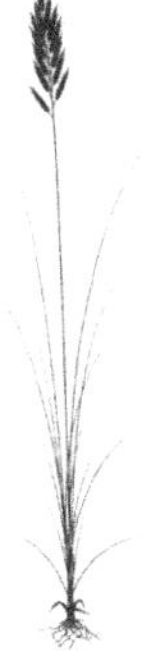

95 (David Claypool (RHM) 1923) (Charles E. Allen, Frank Johnson, Glenda France 1998, 96) (History of Warren County 1882, 613) One source says they arrived in April, another in May.
96 (Perlman 1991, 3) (David Claypool) (Rody, Notes and Corrections to Book Manuscript, Vol 1 (RHM) 2023, 5)
97 (Charles E. Allen, Frank Johnson, Glenda France 1998, 96) (David Claypool (RHM) 1923)
98 (Charles E. Allen, Frank Johnson, Glenda France 1998, 64)
99 (Charles E. Allen, Frank Johnson, Glenda France 1998, 28, 96) (Buss, Flour mill, Gatewoods, Fultons, opera house in Cozad annals (RHM) 1998, 1f) (Rody, Notes and Corrections to Book Manuscript, Vol 2 (RHM) 2023, 76)
100 (Charles E. Allen, Frank Johnson, Glenda France 1998, 28, 96)
101 (Charles E. Allen, Frank Johnson, Glenda France 1998, 96) (Sandoz 1960, 163)
102 (Charles E. Allen, Frank Johnson, Glenda France 1998, 96)
103 (Rex German and Russ Czaplewski 1992, 99) (Sandoz 1960, 133) (Rody, Notes and Corrections to Book Manuscript, Vol 2 (RHM) 2023, 76)
104 (Cozad's Oldest Citizen Passes Away 1941) (Handley, 4) (Charles E. Allen, Frank Johnson, Glenda France 1998, 60) (C. Anderson 1938, 9)
105 (Cozad's Oldest Pioneer Passes Away 1941) (Charles E. Allen, Frank Johnson, Glenda France 1998, 23, 60) (Sandoz 1960, 200)
106 (Cozad's Oldest Pioneer Passes Away 1941) (Charles E. Allen, Frank Johnson, Glenda France 1998, 60)
107 (Charles E. Allen, Frank Johnson, Glenda France 1998, 96)
108 (Sandoz 1960, 50) (Charles E. Allen, Frank Johnson, Glenda France 1998, 29)
109 (Menke, The Rebirth of the Cozad Revelation - (RHM) 1985, 4) (Charles E. Allen, Frank Johnson, Glenda France 1998, 6, 10) (Rex German and Russ Czaplewski 1992, 23)
110 (Charles E. Allen, Frank Johnson, Glenda France 1998, 29) (Rex German and Russ Czaplewski 1992, 23) (Rody, Notes and Corrections to Book Manuscript, Vol 1 (RHM) 2023, 7)
111 (Nelson 1983, 94) (North Platte Enterprise 1874)
112 (Go West Young Man! 1876)
113 (Ho! For the Great Platte Valley (Poster - RHM) 1879)
114 (Ho! For the Great Platte Valley (Poster - RHM) 1879)
115 (Ho! For the Great Platte Valley (Poster - RHM) 1879) (Charles E. Allen, Frank Johnson, Glenda France 1998, 29) (Go West Young Man! 1876)
116 (Rex German and Russ Czaplewski 1992, 21)

PART 1, CHAPTER 4
1 (Charles E. Allen, Frank Johnson, Glenda France 1998, 63)
2 (Rex German and Russ Czaplewski 1992, 25)
3 (Menke, The Rebirth of the Cozad Revelation - (RHM) 1985, 2) (Sandoz 1960, 11-12)
4 (Sandoz 1960, 50)
5 (Menke, The Rebirth of the Cozad Revelation - (RHM) 1985, 2) (Sandoz 1960, 11)
6 (R. H. Cozad 1880, 47/231) (Sandoz 1960, 279)
7 (Rex German and Russ Czaplewski 1992, 123)
8 (Rex German and Russ Czaplewski 1992, 85) (Sandoz 1960, 235)
9 (Menke, Robert Henri: Museum and Historical Walkway (RHM) 1985, 3) (Nelson 1983, 94)
10 (Menke, Robert Henri: Museum and Historical Walkway (RHM) 1985, 3)
11 (Rex German and Russ Czaplewski 1992, 23)

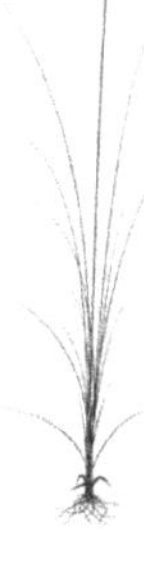

12 (John J. Cozad had a great vision for township location (RHM) 1988, 10C) (Menke, The Rebirth of the Cozad Revelation - (RHM) 1985, 3, 5) (Menke, Robert Henri: Museum and Historical Walkway (RHM) 1985, 3) (Nelson 1983, 94)
13 (Record of Appointment of Postmasters, 1832-1971, Records of the Post Office Department, Adams to Douglas Counties, Nebraska (NARA) 1832-1971) (Charles E. Allen, Frank Johnson, Glenda France 1998, 79) (Perlman 1991, 3)
14 (Nelson 1983, 91-92)
15 (Rex German and Russ Czaplewski 1992, 25)
(John J. Cozad had a great vision for township location (RHM) 1988, 10C) (Menke, Robert Henri: Museum and Historical Walkway (RHM) 1985, 3) (Nelson 1983, 94-95) (Rex German and Russ Czaplewski 1992, 35) (Sandoz 1960, 141-142) (Mari Sandoz Papers (MS) n.d.)
17 (Charles E. Allen, Frank Johnson, Glenda France 1998, 10) (Nelson 1983, 95) (Rody, Notes and Corrections to Book Manuscript, Vol 2 (RHM) 2023, 82)
18 (John J. Cozad had a great vision for township location (RHM) 1988, 10C) (Menke, Robert Henri: Museum and Historical Walkway (RHM) 1985, 3) (Nelson 1983, 94-95) (Rex German and Russ Czaplewski 1992, 75)
19 (Nelson 1983, 95) (Menke, Robert Henri: Museum and Historical Walkway (RHM) 1985, 3)
20 (Nelson 1983, 95) (Menke, The Rebirth of the Cozad Revelation - (RHM) 1985, 3)
21 (Menke, The Rebirth of the Cozad Revelation - (RHM) 1985, 3)
22 (Union Pacific Depot at the 100th Meridian, Cozad Nebraska 1998, 23g)
23 (Waymarking 2022)
24 (Rex German and Russ Czaplewski 1992, 70)
25 (Charles E. Allen, Frank Johnson, Glenda France 1998, 11)
26 (Charles E. Allen, Frank Johnson, Glenda France 1998, 69)
27 (The Writers Almanac 2020) (Charles E. Allen, Frank Johnson, Glenda France 1998, 3) (Rex German and Russ Czaplewski 1992, 28) (Sandoz 1960, 72-75) (James Olson and Ronald Naugle 1997, 95) (Nelson 1983, 94) (Homer 1969, revised 1988, 12)
28 (The Writers Almanac 2020) (Nelson 1983, 94) (Menke, The Rebirth of the Cozad Revelation - (RHM) 1985, 3) (Rex German and Russ Czaplewski 1992, 148)
29 (The Writers Almanac 2020) (Rex German and Russ Czaplewski 1992, 147)
30 (Charles E. Allen, Frank Johnson, Glenda France 1998, 19)
31 (Henshaw 1957) (Sandoz 1960, 164) (Gatewood, John J. Cozad, Alfred Pearson, Robert Henri: trio of early years (RHM) 1998, 1D) (R. Gatewood, Cozad Mystery Cleared: Town Founder Used a New Name Became Successful Promoter in the East 1956)
32 (Charles E. Allen, Frank Johnson, Glenda France 1998, 29) (Sandoz 1960, 264-265) (Rex German and Russ Czaplewski 1992, 82) (Nelson 1983, 101)
33 (Rody, Notes and Corrections to Book Manuscript, Vol 1 (RHM) 2023, 7)
34 (Rex German and Russ Czaplewski 1992, 44-45, 64)
35 (Potter 2012)
36 (Sandoz 1960, 127-128, 147)
37 (Sandoz 1960, 147)
38 (Charles E. Allen, Frank Johnson, Glenda France 1998, 9) (Rex German and Russ Czaplewski 1992, 48-49)
39 (Mari Sandoz to Jacques Chambrun (RHM) 1945)
40 (Rex German and Russ Czaplewski 1992, 50) (Sandoz 1960, 144)
41 (Rody, Notes and Corrections to Book Manuscript, Vol 1 (RHM) 2023, 7) (Menke, The

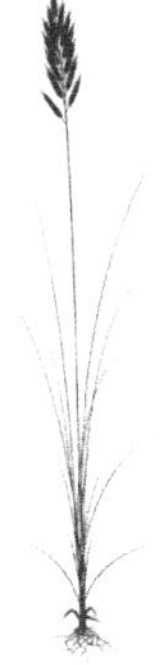

Rebirth of the Cozad Revelation - (RHM) 1985, 10) (Charles E. Allen, Frank Johnson, Glenda France 1998, 48) (Susan Brasch to Jan Patterson (RHM) 2011 n.d.)
42 (Rex German and Russ Czaplewski 1992, 67) (James Olson and Ronald Naugle 1997, 168)
43 (Rex German and Russ Czaplewski 1992, 43)
44 (Rody, Notes and Corrections to Book Manuscript, Vol 1 (RHM) 2023, 7)
45 (Sandoz 1960, 189)
46 (Nebraska Historical Marker: Mitchell and Ketchum Homesteads 2015) (Myers 2002) (Rex German and Russ Czaplewski 1992, 51-52, 54)
47 (Sandoz 1960, 174, 190)
48 (Nebraska Historical Marker: Mitchell and Ketchum Homesteads 2015) (Menke, The Rebirth of the Cozad Revelation - (RHM) 1985, 5, 10) (Myers 2002) (Sandoz 1960, 268)
49 (Menke, The Rebirth of the Cozad Revelation - (RHM) 1985, 10) (Perlman 1991, 4)
50 (Ho! For the Great Platte Valley (Poster - RHM) 1879)
51 (Sandoz 1960, 167)
52 (Charles E. Allen, Frank Johnson, Glenda France 1998, 29, 40) (Sandoz 1960, 85, 209-210) (Rody, Notes and Corrections to Book Manuscript, Vol 1 (RHM) 2023, 8)
53 (Charles E. Allen, Frank Johnson, Glenda France 1998, 63)
54 (Nelson 1983, 95) (Charles E. Allen, Frank Johnson, Glenda France 1998, 6, 12, 15, 57) (C. Anderson 1938, 6-7) (Rex German and Russ Czaplewski 1992, 72) (Perlman 1991, 3) (Sandoz 1960, 85) (Class of 1925 - Eight Graders 1925)The school's construction date has been said to be 1874 and it was located on the same place as the larger and impressive brick school that was subsequently built in 1891. In an 1876 letter to the newspaper Robert Cozad describes the school as already standing although he does not say if it was brick or not.
55 (Nelson 1983, 95) (Charles E. Allen, Frank Johnson, Glenda France 1998, 6, 12, 15, 57) (C. Anderson 1938, 6-7) (Rex German and Russ Czaplewski 1992, 72) (Perlman 1991, 3) (Sandoz 1960, 85) (Class of 1925 - Eight Graders 1925).
56 (Rex German and Russ Czaplewski 1992, 77) (Sandoz 1960, 115)
57 (Testimonial of Appreciation to John Cozad from Presbyterian Church of the United States (RHM) 1875) (First Presbyterian Church of Cozad, Nebraska 2020)
58 (Testimonial of Appreciation to John Cozad from Presbyterian Church of the United States (RHM) 1875)
59 (Rex German and Russ Czaplewski 1992, 32)
60 (Charles E. Allen, Frank Johnson, Glenda France 1998, 11, 64) (Rex German and Russ Czaplewski 1992, 11, 32-34)
61 (Rex German and Russ Czaplewski 1992, 38)
62 (Rex German and Russ Czaplewski 1992, 40) (Rody, Notes and Corrections to Book Manuscript, Vol 1 (RHM) 2023, 8)
63 (Rex German and Russ Czaplewski 1992, 40)
64 (Charles E. Allen, Frank Johnson, Glenda France 1998, 65)
65 (Charles E. Allen, Frank Johnson, Glenda France 1998, 65) (D. R. Gatewood September 20, 1932, 13)
66 (Charles E. Allen, Frank Johnson, Glenda France 1998, 65) (D. R. Gatewood September 20, 1932, 13) (Rody, Notes and Corrections to Book Manuscript, Vol 1 (RHM) 2023, 5)
67 (German, Paper on Alf Pearson's Shooting 2019)
68 (Rex German and Russ Czaplewski 1992, 36)
69 (Charles E. Allen, Frank Johnson, Glenda France 1998, 64-65) (Rex German and Russ Czaplewski 1992, 80)

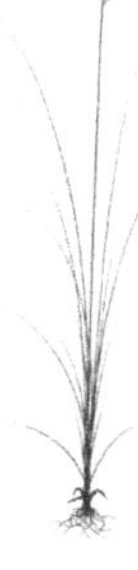

70 (Rex German and Russ Czaplewski 1992, 35-37)
71 (Charles E. Allen, Frank Johnson, Glenda France 1998, 11) (D. R. Gatewood September 20, 1932, 14)
72 (Rex German and Russ Czaplewski 1992, 75) (Sandoz 1960, 233-234)
73 (Handley, 5)
74 (Charles E. Allen, Frank Johnson, Glenda France 1998, 64-65) (Rex German and Russ Czaplewski 1992, 38) (Sandoz 1960, 241)
75 (Rex German and Russ Czaplewski 1992, 74-75) (Charles E. Allen, Frank Johnson, Glenda France 1998, 65) (Sandoz 1960, 224-226) (D. R. Gatewood September 20, 1932, 14)
76 (Charles E. Allen, Frank Johnson, Glenda France 1998, 65) (B. Perlman, Robert Henri: His Life and Art 1991, 5)
77 (Rex German and Russ Czaplewski 1992, 75)
78 (Charles E. Allen, Frank Johnson, Glenda France 1998, 11, 60, 63-65) (Rex German and Russ Czaplewski 1992, 80) (Gatewood, John J. Cozad, Alfred Pearson, Robert Henri: trio of early years (RHM) 1998, 2D) (D. R. Gatewood September 20, 1932, 13) (R. Gatewood, Cozad Mystery Cleared: Town Founder Used a New Name Became Successful Promoter in the East 1956) (Schooley 1912)
79 (Rex German and Russ Czaplewski 1992, 20-21) (Rody, Notes and Corrections to Book Manuscript, Vol 1 (RHM) 2023, 7)
80 (Charles E. Allen, Frank Johnson, Glenda France 1998, 65) (Gatewood, John J. Cozad, Alfred Pearson, Robert Henri: trio of early years (RHM) 1998, 2D) (D. R. Gatewood September 20, 1932, 6)
81 (Record of Appointment of Postmasters, 1832-1971, Records of the Post Office Department, Adams to Douglas Counties, Nebraska (NARA) 1832-1971) (Charles E. Allen, Frank Johnson, Glenda France 1998, 79)
82 (Rex German and Russ Czaplewski 1992, 3-4)
83 (Rex German and Russ Czaplewski 1992, 4-6, 18)
84 (Rex German and Russ Czaplewski 1992, 51)
85 (Rex German and Russ Czaplewski 1992, 4, 31, 42, 51)
86 (F. E. Shearer 1879, 34)
87 (Rex German and Russ Czaplewski 1992, 68)
88 (Foster 2013, 32)
89 (Rex German and Russ Czaplewski 1992, 68)
90 (F. E. Shearer 1879, 38)
91 (Rex German and Russ Czaplewski 1992, 70)
92 (Robert Cozad Scrapbook - 1878 (RHM) 1878)
93 (F. E. Shearer 1879, 38)
94 (Rex German and Russ Czaplewski 1992, 24)
95 (Rex German and Russ Czaplewski 1992, 27)
96 (Rex German and Russ Czaplewski 1992, 27)
97 (Rex German and Russ Czaplewski 1992, 8)
98 (James Olson and Ronald Naugle 1997, 147-150)
99 (Rex German and Russ Czaplewski 1992, 31) (James Olson and Ronald Naugle 1997, 184) (Rody, Notes and Corrections to Book Manuscript, Vol 1 (RHM) 2023, 8)
100 (Rex German and Russ Czaplewski 1992, 31-32, 80) (Sandoz 1960, 153) (Rody, Notes and Corrections to Book Manuscript, Vol 1 (RHM) 2023, 8)
101 (C. Anderson 1938, 2) (Rex German and Russ Czaplewski 1992, 78)

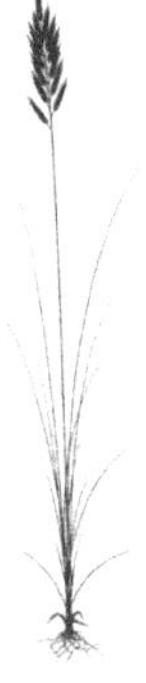

102 (C. Anderson 1938, 2) (Sandoz 1960, 160-161)
103 (Ho! For the Great Platte Valley (Poster - RHM) 1879) (Sandoz 1960, 158-159)
104 (Rex German and Russ Czaplewski 1992, 122)
105 (Rex German and Russ Czaplewski 1992, 143)
106 (Nebraska Incorporation Places by Legal Classification 2014)

PART 1, CHAPTER 5
1 (Mary Wake to Mrs. Gatewood (RHM) February 22, 1909)
2 (Handley, 1)
3 (Sandoz 1960, 57-58, 241)
4 (Rex German and Russ Czaplewski 1992, 75) (Rody, Notes and Corrections to Book Manuscript, Vol 1 (RHM) 2023, 3, Rody, Notes and Corrections to Book Manuscript, Vol 2 (RHM) 2023, 104)
5 (Sandoz 1960, 163)
6 (Trifling Case Entertained in Court - It Proves Neither a Mountain Nor a Mole-Hill 1867)
7 (Sandoz 1960, 64-66, 202) (D. R. Gatewood September 20, 1932, 5) (Cincinnati Enquirer 1874)
8 (Sandoz 1960, 35-36) (Nelson 1983, 93)
9 (Sandoz 1960, 151-153) (Rody, Notes and Corrections to Book Manuscript, Vol 2 (RHM) 2023, 56)
10 (Rody, Notes and Corrections to Book Manuscript, Vol 1 (RHM) 2023, 3)
11 (Handley n.d., 1-2) (Sandoz 1960, 200-201, 207)
12 (Rex German and Russ Czaplewski 1992, 79-81)
13 (Rex German and Russ Czaplewski 1992, 89)
14 (Cincinatti Daily Gazette 1874)
15 (John Cozad to S.H.H. Clark (MONA) 1877)
16 (John Cozad to S.H.H. Clark (MONA) 1877) (Rody, Notes and Corrections to Book Manuscript, Vol 2 (RHM) 2023, 108)
17 (Rody, Notes and Corrections to Book Manuscript Vol 2 (RHM) 2023, 108)
18 (Leavitt Burnham to John Cozad) April 30, 1878)
19 (John Cozad to Jay Gould (RHM) June 14, 1878)
20 (John Cozad to Jay Gould (RHM) June 14, 1878)
21 (Rex German and Russ Czaplewski 1992, 27-28) (Union Pacific Files for Bankruptcy 1874)
22 (Sandoz 1960, 116)
23 (John Cozad to Sidney Dillow (MONA) 1880?)
24 (Rex German and Russ Czaplewski 1992, 78-79)
25 (Legal Paperwork for John A. Cozad (RHM) n.d.) (Cozad Family Papers, Legal Transactions and Deeds (RHM) )
26 (Legal Paperwork for John A. Cozad (RHM) n.d.) (Cozad Family Papers, Legal Transactions and Deeds (RHM) )
27 (Homer 1969, revised 1988, 16)
28 (C. Anderson 1938, 3)
29 (Russell Czaplewski to Smithsonian Magazine (DCHM) 1985) (Russell Czaplewski to Smithsonian Magazine (DCHM) 1985) (Rex German and Russ Czaplewski 1992, 76) (Sandoz 1960, 158-159) (German 2019, 1)
30 (Russell Czaplewski to Smithsonian Magazine (DCHM) 1985) (Russell Czaplewski to Smithsonian Magazine (DCHM) 1985) (Rex German and Russ Czaplewski 1992, 76)

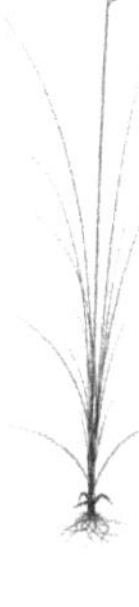

31 (Sandoz 1960, 248) (Homer 1969, revised 1988, 16)
32 (R. Cozad n.d., 98/282) (Rody, Notes and Corrections to Book Manuscript, Vol 1 (RHM) 2023, 12)
33 (Rex German and Russ Czaplewski 1992, 77) (Homer 1969, revised 1988, 16) (Sandoz 1960, 246-247) (R. Cozad n.d., 297/95, 200/117)
34 (Homer 1969, revised 1988, 16) (Jane Scholl to Russ Czaplewski (DCHM) 1985) (Jane Scholl to Russell Czaplewski (DCHM) March 11, 1985) (Rex German and Russ Czaplewski 1992, 76) (D. Anderson n.d.)
35 (Henri) 1881) (R. Henri, Diary, 1881) (R. Cozad n.d.) (Homer 1969, revised 1988, 16)
36 (Perlman 1991, 5) (Perlman 1991, 5)
37 (Perlman 1991, 5) (Perlman 1991, 5) The building is no longer there, the site is occupied by a parking lot. (Homer 1969, revised 1988, 16)
38 (Homer 1969, revised 1988, 16) (Sandoz 1960, 145, 202)
39 (Mari Sandoz Collection (MS), Card 6592)
40 (B. Perlman, Robert Henri: His Life and Art 1991, 5)
41 (Homer 1969, revised 1988, 16)
42 (Record of Appointment of Postmasters, 1832-1971, Records of the Post Office Department, Adams to Douglas Counties, Nebraska (NARA) 1832-1971, 568) (Record of Appointment of Postmasters, 1832-1971, Records of the Post Office Department, Adams to Douglas Counties, Nebraska (NARA) 1832-1971, 568)
43 (Nelson 1983, 101) (Sandoz 1960, 219, 288)
44 (Record of Appointment of Postmasters, 1832-1971, Records of the Post Office Department, Adams to Douglas Counties, Nebraska (NARA) 1832-1971, 497) (Record of Appointment of Postmasters, 1832-1971, Records of the Post Office Department, Adams to Douglas Counties, Nebraska (NARA) 1832-1971, 497) (Sandoz 1960, 273)
45 (Record of Appointment of Postmasters, 1832-1971, Records of the Post Office Department, Adams to Douglas Counties, Nebraska (NARA) 1832-1971, 497) (Record of Appointment of Postmasters, 1832-1971, Records of the Post Office Department, Adams to Douglas Counties, Nebraska (NARA) 1832-1971, 497)
46 (Rex German and Russ Czaplewski 1992, 141-142)
47 (Diefenderfer 1998, 1) (Charles E. Allen, Frank Johnson, Glenda France 1998, 128) (Scrutchfield 1998, 5D)
48 (Diefenderfer 1998, 1) (Charles E. Allen, Frank Johnson, Glenda France 1998, 128)
49 (Scrutchfield 1998, 5D)
50 (Diefenderfer 1998, 2) (Charles E. Allen, Frank Johnson, Glenda France 1998, 128) (Rody, Notes and Corrections to Book Manuscript, Vol 2 (RHM) 2023, 116)
51 (Rody, Notes and Corrections to Book Manuscript, Vol 1 (RHM) 2023, 9-10)
52 (Scrutchfield 1998, 5D)
53 (Diefenderfer 1998, 1) (Charles E. Allen, Frank Johnson, Glenda France 1998, 128) (Rex German and Russ Czaplewski 1992, 78)
54 (Sandoz 1960, 75)
55 (Sandoz 1960, 288)
56 (Rex German and Russ Czaplewski 1992, 79)
57 (Sandoz 1960, 299)
58 (Sandoz 1960, 171-172)
59 (Rody, Notes and Corrections to Book Manuscript, Vol 1 (RHM) 2023, 1) (Charles E. Allen, Frank Johnson, Glenda France 1998, 128) (Rex German and Russ Czaplewski 1992, 90)

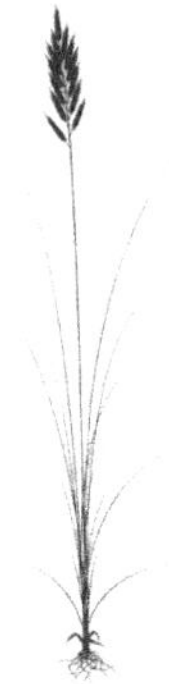

(Sandoz 1960, 290) (Violet Organ to H. B. Allen (RHM) 1955) (D. Anderson n.d.) (R. Gatewood, Cozad Mystery Cleared: Town Founder Used a New Name Became Successful Promoter in the East 1956)

60 (Charles E. Allen, Frank Johnson, Glenda France 1998, 128) (Rex German and Russ Czaplewski 1992, 90) (Sandoz 1960, 290) (Violet Organ to H. B. Allen (RHM) 1955) (D. Anderson n.d.) (R. Gatewood, Cozad Mystery Cleared: Town Founder Used a New Name Became Successful Promoter in the East 1956)

61 (John J. Cozad Perforates A. Pearson (RHM) 1882)

62 (Rex German and Russ Czaplewski 1992, 100) (James, 4)

63 (Lewis, Hendee Hotel (RHM) 1972, 3) (Allan, Nebraska Byways: Grandmothers Revitalize Cozad 1984)

64 (Mari Sandoz Collection (MS), Card 3442)

65 (Sandoz 1960, 290-291) (D. R. Gatewood September 20, 1932, 14) (Charles E. Allen, Frank Johnson, Glenda France 1998, 128) (R. Gatewood, Cozad Mystery Cleared: Town Founder Used a New Name Became Successful Promoter in the East 1956)

66 (Sandoz 1960, 290-291) (Scrutchfield 1998, 5D)

67 (Sandoz 1960, 290-291)

68 (Sandoz 1960, 290-291) (D. R. Gatewood September 20, 1932, 14) (R. Gatewood, Cozad Mystery Cleared: Town Founder Used a New Name Became Successful Promoter in the East 1956) (James, 3) (Rody, Notes and Corrections to Book Manuscript, Vol 2 (RHM) 2023, 121)

69 (Sandoz 1960, 292-295)

70 (Sandoz 1960, 294, 299-301)

71 (Sandoz 1960, 296)

72 (D. R. Gatewood September 20, 1932, 14)

73 (Violet Organ to H. B. Allen (RHM) 1955)

74 (Charles E. Allen, Frank Johnson, Glenda France 1998, 128) (Charles E. Allen, Frank Johnson, Glenda France 1998, 128) (Death of Alfred Pearson 1882) (Death of Alfred Pearson (RHM) 1882) (Sandoz 1960, 299-300)

75 (Sandoz 1960, 294-295)

76 (Gatewood, Cozad Mystery Revealed 1956) (R. Gatewood, Cozad Mystery Cleared: Town Founder Used a New Name Became Successful Promoter in the East 1956)(Gatewood, Who Was Robert Henri? September 20, 1932, 14) (D. R. Gatewood September 20, 1932, 14) (Sandoz 1960, 321) Gatewood in his manuscripts says that he boarded a Burlington-Missouri train.

77 (Menke, The Rebirth of the Cozad Revelation - (RHM) 1985, 5-6)

78 (Rex German and Russ Czaplewski 1992, 99)

(Homer 1969, revised 1988, 17)

80 (Homer 1969, revised 1988, x)

81 (Joan Gatewood Miller to Elma Johnson and Rex German (RHM) July 12, 1996, 4)

82 (Homer 1969, revised 1988, x) (A copy of the manuscript is found in Homer's papers at the Delaware Art Museum. More about this manuscript comes later in a future chapter.)

83 (Gatewood, Who Was Robert Henri? September 20, 1932, 15) (D. R. Gatewood September 20, 1932, 15) (Joan Gatewood Miller to Elma Johnson and Rex German (RHM) July 12, 1996, 3)

84 (R. Gatewood, Cozad Mystery Cleared: Town Founder Used a New Name Became Successful Promoter in the East 1956) (Sandoz 1960, 301, 321)

85 (Sandoz 1960, 321-322)

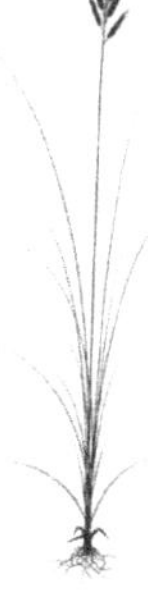

86 (R. Gatewood, Cozad Mystery Cleared: Town Founder Used a New Name Became Success-

ful Promoter in the East 1956) (Sandoz 1960, 301)
87 (Sandoz 1960, 299-301,321) (James, 4)
88 (Marshall 1988)
89 (Marshall 1988) (Marshall 1988)
90 (Rex German and Russ Czaplewski 1992, 100)
91 (Phillips 1970, 4)
92 (Death of Alfred Pearson (RHM) 1882) It is important to note that Pearson died three weeks after being shot by Cozad. This is relevant because some sources state that he died seven weeks after. That assumption was probably made because it was not reported until December 9, 1882, nine weeks after the shooting.
93 (Scrutchfield 1998, 5D)
94 (Death of Alfred Pearson (RHM) 1882)
95 ( (Diefender 1998, 3) (Charles E. Allen, Frank Johnson, Glenda France 1998, 129) (Rody, Notes and Corrections to Book Manuscript, Vol 1 (RHM) 2023, 11)
96 (Death of Alfred Pearson (RHM) 1882)
97 (Death of Alfred Pearson (RHM) 1882)
98 (This Is A Report of Some of the Events and Testimony Relating to Alf Pearson's Death (RHM) n.d., 2) (Charles E. Allen, Frank Johnson, Glenda France 1998, 45)
99 (Rex German and Russ Czaplewski 1992, 99)
100 (Messages and Proclamations, 1862-1892, Governors of Nebraska 1892, 270)

PART 1, CHAPTER 6
1 (Sandoz 1960, 322)
2 (Rex German and Russ Czaplewski 1992, 93)
3 (View of Plum Creek, Undated) (View of Plum Creek Undated)
4 (Sandoz 1960, 306)
5 (Rex German and Russ Czaplewski 1992, 91)
6 (Lex Turns Up Story Accusing John A. Cozad of Trying to Burn Their Town n.d. (Lex Turns Up Story Accusing John A. Cozad of Trying to Burn Their Town (RHM) Undated, taken from December 2, 1882 edition of Lexington newspaper) (Rex German and Russ Czaplewski 1992, 93, 103)) (Sandoz 1960, 304, 310)
7 (Rex German and Russ Czaplewski 1992, 93, 96) (Lex Turns Up Story Accusing John A. Cozad of Trying to Burn Their Town (RHM) Undated, taken from December 2, 1882 edition of Lexington newspaper)
8 (Rex German and Russ Czaplewski 1992, 95) (Lex Turns Up Story Accusing John A. Cozad of Trying to Burn Their Town (RHM) Undated, taken from December 2, 1882 edition of Lexington newspaper)
9 (Lex Turns Up Story Accusing John A. Cozad of Trying to Burn Their Town (RHM) Undated, taken from December 2, 1882 edition of Lexington newspaper) (Rex German and Russ Czaplewski 1992, 95, 99) (Rody, Notes and Corrections to Book Manuscript, Vol 1 (RHM) 2023, 12)(Rody, Notes and Corrections to Book Manuscript, Vol 2 (RHM) 2023, 131)
10 (Rex German and Russ Czaplewski 1992, 100)
11 (Rex German and Russ Czaplewski 1992, 100) (Sandoz 1960, 311)
12 (Rex German and Russ Czaplewski 1992, 101-102)
13 (Rex German and Russ Czaplewski 1992, 102-103)
14 (Cozad Family Papers, Legal Transactions and Deeds (RHM) )
15 (Sandoz 1960, 308)

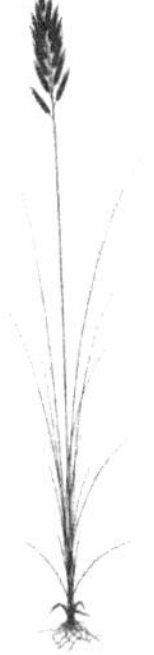

16 (Nelson 1983, 101) (Sandoz 1960, 313)
17 (D. R. Gatewood September 20, 1932, 15) (D. R. Gatewood September 20, 1932, 15) (R. Gatewood, Cozad Mystery Cleared: Town Founder Used a New Name Became Successful Promoter in the East 1956)
18 (D. R. Gatewood September 20, 1932, 15)
19 (Real Estate Transfers 1883) (Real Estate Transfers, 8.24.1883 (DPL) n.d., 7) (Real Estate Transfers, 9.4.1883 (DPL), 2) (Real Estate Transfers, 3.17.1883 (DPL), 3) (Real Estate Transfers, 8.2.1883 (DPL), 7)
20 (B. Perlman, Robert Henri: His Life and Art 1991, 6) (Robert Cozad Scrapbook - 1878 (RHM) 1878)
21 (Buss, Bushnell, Illinois: Its Investment and Settlement in Dawson County, Nebraska (RHM), 1, 4)(Rex German and Russ Czaplewski 1992, 103-104)
22 (Newton Bateman and Paul Selby 1907, 903-904)
23 (K. Buss, Bushnell, Illinois: Its Investment and Settlement in Dawson County, Nebraska (RHM), 1, 4)
24 (Rex German and Russ Czaplewski 1992, 104) (Buss, Bushnell, Illinois: Its Investment and Settlement in Dawson County, Nebraska (RHM), 4)
25 (K. Buss, Bushnell, Illinois: Its Investment and Settlement in Dawson County, Nebraska (RHM), 2) (Rex German and Russ Czaplewski 1992, 104-105) (Lewis, Hendee Hotel (RHM) 1972, 1)
26 (Land Transactions 1875-1937 (RHM))
27 (Rex German and Russ Czaplewski 1992, 106)
28 (Abstract of Title of Southeast Quarter of Section 6, Township 10, North of Range 23 W, Dawson County, Nebraska, Warranty Deed of James and Arlene McAdams (RHM) 1954)
29 (Sandoz 1960, 314) (Dawson County Pioneer 1883)
30 (Sandoz 1960, 320) (Scrutchfield 1998, 5D)
31 (Land Transactions 1875-1937 (RHM)) (Abstract of Title of Southeast Quarter of Section 6, Township 10, North of Range 23 W, Dawson County Nebraska, Warranty Deed of James and Arlene McAdams (RHM) 1954)
32 (Abstract of Title of Southeast Quarter of Section 6, Township 10, North of Range 23 W, Dawson County, Nebraska, Warranty Deed of James and Arlene McAdams (RHM) 1954)
33 On the same day as the signing of the contract Theresa Cozad was in court, perhaps related to this sale.
34 (Rex German and Russ Czaplewski 1992, 105-106)
35 (Abstract of Title of Southeast Quarter of Section 6, Township 10, North of Range 23 W, Dawson County, Nebraska, Warranty Deed of James and Arlene McAdams (RHM) 1954)
36 (K. Buss, Bushnell, Illinois: Its Investment and Settlement in Dawson County, Nebraska (RHM), 2) (Rex German and Russ Czaplewski 1992, 104-105)
37 (Abstract of Title of Southeast Quarter of Section 6, Township 10, North of Range 23 W, Dawson County, Nebraska, Warranty Deed of James and Arlene McAdams (RHM) 1954) (Lewis, Hendee Hotel (RHM) 1972, 1)
38 (Rex German and Russ Czaplewski 1992, 105)
39 (K. Buss, Bushnell, Illinois: Its Investment and Settlement in Dawson County, Nebraska (RHM), 3) (Rex German and Russ Czaplewski 1992, 113)
40 (Buss, Bushnell, Illinois: Its Investment and Settlement in Dawson County, Nebraska (RHM) n.d., 2, 3)
41 (Land Transactions 1875-1937 (RHM)) (Abstract of Title of Southeast Quarter of Section 6,

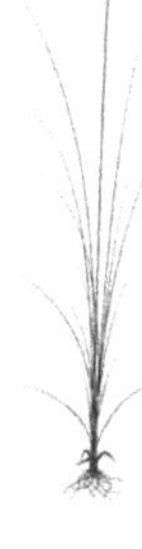

Township 10, North of Range 23 W, Dawson County, Nebraska, Warranty Deed of James and Arlene McAdams (RHM) 1954)
42 (Land Transactions 1875-1937 (RHM)) (Abstract of Title of Southeast Quarter of Section 6, Township 10, North of Range 23 W, Dawson County, Nebraska, Warranty Deed of James and Arlene McAdams (RHM) 1954)
43 (Maggie Claypool's Autograph Book (RHM) 1884)
44 (D. Gatewood c. 1940) (Robert Gatewood - Cozad 1884)
45 (Death of Alfred Pearson 1882) (Death of Alfred Pearson (RHM) 1882)
46 (Nebraska, State Census Collection, 1860-1885 1885, 11)
47 (B. Perlman, Robert Henri: His Life and Art 1991, 6)
48 (Nelson 1983, 101) (Menke, The Rebirth of the Cozad Revelation - (RHM) 1985, 6) (Rex German and Russ Czaplewski 1992, 106) (Sandoz 1960, 314) (D. R. Gatewood September 20, 1932, 15)
49 (Rex German and Russ Czaplewski 1992, 106) See museum's accession records on the pistol that is currently (2023) on display.
50 (Dr. Robert Gatewood to William Homer (RHM) August 1, 1964)
51 (R. Gatewood, Cozad Mystery Cleared: Town Founder Used a New Name Became Successful Promoter in the East 1956)
52 (Homer 1969, revised 1988, 19)
53 (Homer 1969, revised 1988, 17, 272)
54 (R. Gatewood, Cozad Mystery Cleared: Town Founder Used a New Name Became Successful Promoter in the East 1956) (B. Perlman, Robert Henri: His Life and Art 1991, 5) (Homer 1969, revised 1988, 17) (Mari Sandoz Papers (MS) n.d.)
55 (Homer 1969, revised 1988, 7, 17) (Man Behind the Name: Mystery of Cozad is Finally Broken)
56 (Atlantic City, New Jersey 2022)
57 (Atlantic City, New Jersey 2022)
58 (Atlantic City, New Jersey 2022) (Sandoz 1960, 324)
59 (Homer 1969, revised 1988, 17-18) (B. Perlman, Chronology of Robert Henri, 1) (B. Perlman, Robert Henri: His Life and Art 1991, 6)
60 (B. Perlman, Robert Henri: His Life and Art 1991, 6)
61 (Atlantic City, New Jersey Directory 1884, 34, 40, 54) (Sandoz 1960, 325) (Jacqueline Silver-Morillo, Atlantic City Free Public Library to Peter Osborne 2022)
62 (What Happened to John Cozad: Story from Atlantic City Reveals Final Story in the Life of John J. Cozad (RHM) 1957, 2) (Atlantic City, New Jersey Directory 1884, 34, 40, 54) (Homer 1969, revised 1988, 18-19) (Mari Sandoz Collection (MS), Card 6602)
63 (Atlantic City, New Jersey 2022)
64 (B. Perlman, Robert Henri: His Life and Art 1991, 6)
65 (What Happened to John Cozad: Story from Atlantic City Reveals Final Story in the Life of John J. Cozad (RHM))
66 (Rody, Notes and Corrections to Book Manuscript, Vol 2 (RHM) 2023, 144)(What Happened to John Cozad: Story from Atlantic City Reveals Final Story in the Life of John J. Cozad (RHM) 1957) (Certificate of Ownership, Cemetery of Spring Grove (RHM) 1867)
67 (Sandoz 1960, 325) (What Happened to John Cozad: Story from Atlantic City Reveals Final Story in the Life of John J. Cozad (RHM) 1957, 2)
68 (Rody, Notes and Corrections to Book Manuscript, Vol 1 (RHM) 2023, 12)(What Happened to John Cozad: Story from Atlantic City Reveals Final Story in the Life of John J. Cozad

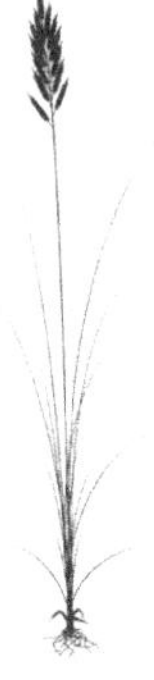

(RHM) 1957, 5) (Rody, Notes and Corrections to Book Manuscript, Vol 2 (RHM) 2023, 145)
69 (What Happened to John Cozad: Story from Atlantic City Reveals Final Story in the Life of John J. Cozad (RHM) 1957, 5)
70 (Sandoz 1960, 325) (What Happened to John Cozad: Story from Atlantic City Reveals Final Story in the Life of John J. Cozad (RHM) 1957, 2)
71 (Gatewood, John J. Cozad, Alfred Pearson, Robert Henri: trio of early years (RHM) 1998, 3D) (D. R. Gatewood September 20, 1932, 16) (R. Gatewood, Cozad Mystery Cleared: Town Founder Used a New Name Became Successful Promoter in the East 1956) (What Happened to John Cozad: Story from Atlantic City Reveals Final Story in the Life of John J. Cozad (RHM) 1957)
72 (Atlantic City, New Jersey 1894) (What Happened to John Cozad: Story from Atlantic City Reveals Final Story in the Life of John J. Cozad (RHM) 1957, 2, 7) (Rody, Notes and Corrections to Book Manuscript, Vol 2 (RHM) 2023, 145)
73 (Rody, Notes and Corrections to Book Manuscript, Vol 1 (RHM) 2023, 12) (R. Gatewood, John J. Cozad, Alfred Pearson, Robert Henri: trio of early years (RHM) 1998) (Marilyn Cozad and Marsha Pilger 2003, 104) (Rody, Notes and Corrections to Book Manuscript, Vol 2 (RHM) 2023, 145)
74 (Sandoz 1960, 322)
75 (James, 3)

PART 1, CHAPTER 7
1 (This Is A Report of Some of the Events and Testimony Relating to Alf Pearson's Death (RHM) n.d., 4-5)
2 (Menke, The Rebirth of the Cozad Revelation - (RHM) 1985, 6)
3 (Charles Allen 1973, 129) (Charles E. Allen, Frank Johnson, Glenda France 1998, 129)
4 (This Is A Report of Some of the Events and Testimony Relating to Alf Pearson's Death (RHM) n.d., 3)
5 (This Is A Report of Some of the Events and Testimony Relating to Alf Pearson's Death (RHM), 3)
6 (This Is A Report of Some of the Events and Testimony Relating to Alf Pearson's Death (RHM), 4)
7 (This Is A Report of Some of the Events and Testimony Relating to Alf Pearson's Death (RHM), 4-5)
8 (This Is A Report of Some of the Events and Testimony Relating to Alf Pearson's Death (RHM), 5-6)
9 (Flour Mill, Gatewoods, Fultons, opera house in Cozad annals n.d.) This map of the historic structures speculates that the Julia and Robert Gatewood home was actually located at 807 Meridian Avenue. This would have been next to the Gatewood's store.
10 (Anderson n.d., 1) (Handley, 1)
11 (Charles E. Allen, Frank Johnson, Glenda France 1998, 65)
12 (D. R. Gatewood September 20, 1932, 14)
13 (Sandoz 1960, 310) (Sandoz 1960, 312) (Rody, Notes and Corrections to Book Manuscript, Vol 2 (RHM) 2023, 154)
14 (Rex German and Russ Czaplewski 1992, 149) (Rex German and Russ Czaplewski 1992, 149)
15 (Gatewood, John J. Cozad, Alfred Pearson, Robert Henri: trio of early years (RHM) 1998, 2D)

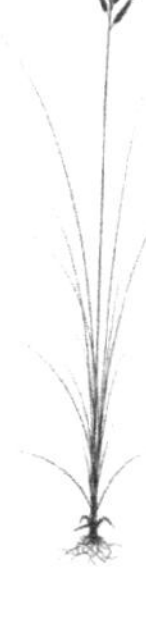

16 (Rex German and Russ Czaplewski 1992, 149) (Rex German and Russ Czaplewski 1992, 103, 149)
17 (Rex German and Russ Czaplewski 1992, 101-102, 138-139)
18 (D. Gatewood c. 1940)
19 (Genealogica Data in Family Genealogy Files (RHM) 1980) (Rex German and Russ Czaplewski 1992, 148-149)
20 (The Cozad Local (RHM) 1956, 1) (Gatewood, John J. Cozad, Alfred Pearson, Robert Henri: trio of early years (RHM) 1998, 1-2) (D. R. Gatewood September 20, 1932, 1) (R. Gatewood, Cozad Mystery Cleared: Town Founder Used a New Name Became Successful Promoter in the East 1956) This confirmed by Joan Gatewood Miller in a 1996 letter as she states it was 1894 too.
21 (Gatewood, John J. Cozad, Alfred Pearson, Robert Henri: trio of early years (RHM) 1998, 1-2D) (D. R. Gatewood September 20, 1932, 1)
22 (Rex German and Russ Czaplewski 1992, 149)
23 (Rex German and Russ Czaplewski 1992, 149)
24 (Rex German and Russ Czaplewski 1992, 149)
25 (Cozad Family Papers, Legal Transactions and Deeds (RHM) )
26 (Charles E. Allen, Frank Johnson, Glenda France 1998, 6) (Cozad Family Papers, Legal Transactions and Deeds (RHM) ) (D. R. Gatewood September 20, 1932, 1)
27 (Charles E. Allen, Frank Johnson, Glenda France 1998, 6) (Cozad Family Papers, Legal Transactions and Deeds (RHM) ) (What Happened to John Cozad: Story from Atlantic City Reveals Final Story in the Life of John J. Cozad (RHM) 1957, 8)
28 (Abstract of Title of Southeast Quarter of Section 6, Township 10, North of Range 23 W, Dawson County, Nebraska, Warranty Deed of James and Arlene McAdams (RHM) 1954) (Charles E. Allen, Frank Johnson, Glenda France 1998, 6)
29 (Abstract of Title of Southeast Quarter of Section 6, Township 10, North of Range 23 W, Dawson County, Nebraska, Warranty Deed of James and Arlene McAdams (RHM) 1954) (Rex German and Russ Czaplewski 1992, 149)
30 (Abstract of Title of Southeast Quarter of Section 6, Township 10, North of Range 23 W, Dawson County, Nebraska, Warranty Deed of James and Arlene McAdams (RHM) 1954)
31 (Abstract of Title of Southeast Quarter of Section 6, Township 10, North of Range 23 W, Dawson County, Nebraska, Warranty Deed of James and Arlene McAdams (RHM) 1954)
32 (Abstract of Title of Southeast Quarter of Section 6, Township 10, North of Range 23 W, Dawson County, Nebraska, Warranty Deed of James and Arlene McAdams (RHM) 1954)
33 (Traber Gatewood to Van Burke Gatewood (RHM) )
34 (Menke, The Rebirth of the Cozad Revelation - (RHM) 1985, 6) (D. R. Gatewood September 20, 1932) (Gatewood, John J. Cozad, Alfred Pearson, Robert Henri: trio of early years (RHM) 1998, 1D) (R. Gatewood, John J. Cozad, Alfred Pearson, Robert Henri: trio of early years (RHM) 1998, 1D)
35 (Charles Allen 1973, 6) (Charles E. Allen, Frank Johnson, Glenda France 1998, 6)
36 (Charles Allen 1973, 6) (Charles E. Allen, Frank Johnson, Glenda France 1998, 6) (Rex German and Russ Czaplewski 1992, 150)
37 (Nebraska Incorporation Places by Legal Classification 2014)
38 (Charles E. Allen, Frank Johnson, Glenda France 1998, 48)
39 (Rex German and Russ Czaplewski 1992, 37)
40 (Charles E. Allen, Frank Johnson, Glenda France 1998, 48) (Rex German and Russ Czaplewski 1992, 142-143)

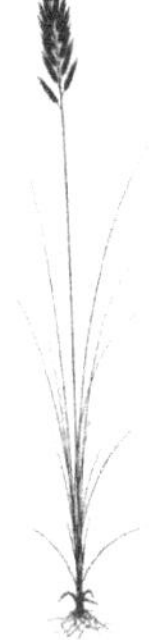

41 (Charles E. Allen, Frank Johnson, Glenda France 1998, 65-66)
42 (Rex German and Russ Czaplewski 1992, 110-111)
43 (Rex German and Russ Czaplewski 1992, 110-111)
44 (Charles E. Allen, Frank Johnson, Glenda France 1998, 52, 64-66) (Rex German and Russ Czaplewski 1992, 108, 111)
45 (Charles E. Allen, Frank Johnson, Glenda France 1998, 65-66)
46 (Charles E. Allen, Frank Johnson, Glenda France 1998, 65-66)
47 (Charles E. Allen, Frank Johnson, Glenda France 1998, 52, 64-66) (Rex German and Russ Czaplewski 1992, 145-146)
48 (Rex German and Russ Czaplewski 1992, 110-111)
49 (Rex German and Russ Czaplewski 1992, 146)
50 (Rex German and Russ Czaplewski 1992, 100) (Newton Bateman and Paul Selby 1907, 768, 903) (Rody, Notes and Corrections to Book Manuscript, Vol 2 (RHM) 2023, 163)
51 (Charles E. Allen, Frank Johnson, Glenda France 1998, 96,44) (Rex German and Russ Czaplewski 1992, 147)
52 (James Olson and Ronald Naugle 1997, 339-341)
53 (Charles E. Allen, Frank Johnson, Glenda France 1998, 12, 96,44, 151)
54 (Charles E. Allen, Frank Johnson, Glenda France 1998, 66)
55 (James Olson and Ronald Naugle 1997, 262-263)
56 (Gatewood, John J. Cozad, Alfred Pearson, Robert Henri: trio of early years (RHM) 1998, 2D)
57 (Charles E. Allen, Frank Johnson, Glenda France 1998, 40)
58 (Paulsen 2020)
59 (Menke, The Rebirth of the Cozad Revelation - (RHM) 1985, 9) (National Register of Historic Places Registration Form - Cozad Downtown Historic District (RHM) 2018, 31)
60 (Czaplewski 1988 (?), 3-4)
61 (National Register of Historic Places Registration Form - Cozad Downtown Historic District (RHM) 2018, 30) (Rody, Notes and Corrections to Book Manuscript, Vol 2 (RHM) 2023, 166)(Charles E. Allen, Frank Johnson, Glenda France 1998, 27, 28)
62 (Menke, The Rebirth of the Cozad Revelation - (RHM) 1985, 9)
63 (National Register of Historic Places Registration Form - Cozad Downtown Historic District (RHM) 2018, 3)
64 (National Register of Historic Places Registration Form - Cozad Downtown Historic District (RHM) 2018, 6) (Charles E. Allen, Frank Johnson, Glenda France 1998, 12)
65 (K. Buss, National Register of Historic Places Inventory - Nomination Form - The Hendee Hotel (RHM) 1979)
66 (Charles E. Allen, Frank Johnson, Glenda France 1998, 12)
67 (Charles E. Allen, Frank Johnson, Glenda France 1998, 6)
68 (Charles E. Allen, Frank Johnson, Glenda France 1998, 6)
69 (Meridian Star . . . first Cozad paper 1998, 18c)
70 (Menke, The Rebirth of the Cozad Revelation - (RHM) 1985, 9) (Rody, Notes and Corrections to Book Manuscript, Vol 2 (RHM) 2023, 168-169)(US Census Records - 1890 - 2019 n.d.) (Hewitt 1876) (Andreas 1882)
71 (National Register of Historic Places Registration Form - Cozad Downtown Historic District (RHM) 2018, 4)
72 (Sandoz 1960, 32-33)

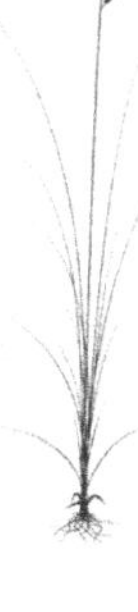

PART II
1 (The Cozad Local (RHM) 1956) (Reveal True Story of John J. Cozad 1956, 1)
2 (Nelson 1983, 101)

PART II, CHAPTER 1
3 (Sandoz 1960, x)
4 (Dolly Sloan to Robert Gatewood (RHM) August 23, 1931)
5 (Pousett-Dart 1922, ix)
6 (Homer 1969, revised 1988, 6)
7 (Sandoz 1960, x)
8 (Gatewood, Who Was Robert Henri? September 20, 1932, 16) (Gatewood, John J. Cozad, Alfred Pearson, Robert Henri: trio of early years (RHM) 1998, 3D)
9 (Traber Gatewood to Van Burke Gatewood (RHM) November 20, 1895)
10 (Mary Wake to Mrs. Gatewood (RHM) February 22, 1909)
11 (Sandoz 1960, 326)
12 (US Census, 1900, 3rd District, Atlantic City, New Jersey, Enumeration District 17, Sheet 14 ) (US Census, 1900, 3rd District, Atlantic City, New Jersey, Enumeration District 17, Sheet 14 1900) (Federal Census, Dawson County, Nebraska, Enumeration District 167 1880)
13 (Julia Gatewood to Mollie Gatewood (RHM) May 12, 1905)
14 (Julia Gatewood to Mollie Gatewood (RHM) April 6, 1908)
15 (Julia Ann 'Grandma" Gatewood (Mrs. Robert) 1909)
16 (Traber Gatewood to Van Burke Gatewood (RHM) November 20, 1895)
17 (D. Gatewood c. 1940)
18 (Theresa Cozad to Julia Gatewood (RHM) April 10, 1906) (Homer 1969, revised 1988, 126)
19 (Theresa Cozad to Nettie Gatewood (RHM) October 24, 1910) (Rody, Notes and Corrections to Book Manuscript, Vol 2 (RHM) 2023, 176)
20 (J. W. Montgomery to Theresa Cozad (RHM), October 29, 1916)
21 (Theresa Cozad to Nettie Gatewood (RHM) October 24, 1910) (Cozad Family Papers, Legal Transactions and Deeds (RHM)) (Julia Ann 'Grandma" Gatewood (Mrs. Robert) 1909)
22 (Nelson 1983, 101) (Menke, The Rebirth of the Cozad Revelation - (RHM) 1985, 4) (Betty and Roger Menke 1985, 62)
23 (Marilyn Cozad and Marsha Pilger 2003, 107, 328) (Homer 1969, revised 1988, 126) (Genealogica Data in Family Genealogy Files (RHM) 1980) (Mari Sandoz Collection (MS) n.d.) Homer states that he died in New York while Cozad and Pilger say that he died in Philadelphia as does the research of Kieth Buss.
24 (Marilyn Cozad and Marsha Pilger 2003, 328) (Genealogica Data in Family Genealogy Files (RHM) 1980) (Dolly Sloan to Robert Gatewood (RHM) August 23, 1931) (Henshaw 1957)
25 (Marilyn Cozad and Marsha Pilger 2003, 107) (Genealogica Data in Family Genealogy Files (RHM) 1980)
26 (Genealogica Data in Family Genealogy Files (RHM) 1980) (Robert Henri to Robert Gatewood (RHM) August 12, 1928) (Marilyn Cozad and Marsha Pilger 2003, 107, 328) (Homer 1969, revised 1988, 126) As with all things about the Cozads there are contradictory pieces of evidence as to what happened to John and Theresa after they left Atlantic City.
27 (Robert Henri to Robert Gatewood (RHM) August 12, 1928) (Marilyn Cozad and Marsha Pilger 2003, 328, 107) (Genealogica Data in Family Genealogy Files (RHM) 1980) As with all things about the Cozads there are contradictory pieces of evidence as to what happened to John

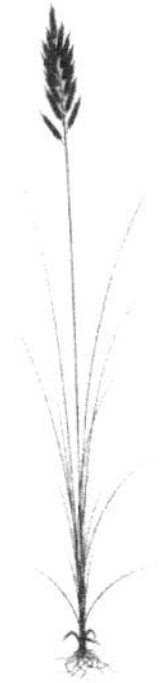

and Theresa after they left Atlantic City.
28 (Dolly Sloan to Robert Gatewood (RHM) August 23, 1931) (Death Ceritificate of Robert Henri 1929)
29 (Descendants of Jacques Cossart and his wife, Lydia (RHM), 329) (Genealogical Data in Family Genealogy Files 1980) (Family Genealogy Files of the Gatewood, Cozad, Henri Families (RHM)) (Genealogica Data in Family Genealogy Files (RHM) 1980) (Marilyn Cozad and Marsha Pilger 2003, 108, 329)
30 (Marilyn Cozad and Marsha Pilger 2003, 329) (Descendants of Jacques Cossart and his wife, Lydia (RHM), 329) (Family Genealogy Files of the Gatewood, Cozad, Henri Families (RHM)) (Genealogica Data in Family Genealogy Files (RHM) 1980) (Death Ceritificate of Marjorie Henri 1930)There is some discrepancy about the date of Marjorie's birth, it has been shown as 1887 or 1886.
31 (Map of Internments of the Southrn, Lee and Henri family members (Location: Group 355, Location L, Lot 33) (RHM))
32 (Homer 1969, revised 1988, x)
33 (Marilyn Cozad and Marsha Pilger 2003, 519) (Foresman n.d., 18-20) Foresman believes that they were married on February 23, 1891. (Frank Southrn to Robert Henri (RHM) 1891)
34 (Foresman n.d., 18-20, 23)
35 (Genealogical Data in Family Genealogy Files 1980) (Family Genealogy Files of the Gatewood, Cozad, Henri Families (RHM)) (Genealogica Data in Family Genealogy Files (RHM) 1980) (Death Certificate of Jane J. Southrn (RHM) January 25, 1915) (Death Certificate of Jane Southrn (RHM) July 9, 1937) (Death Certificate of Frank Southrn (RHM) August 7, 1933) (Marilyn Cozad and Marsha Pilger 2003, 519)
36 (Family Genealogy Files of the Gatewood, Cozad, Henri Families (RHM)) (Genealogica Data in Family Genealogy Files (RHM) 1980) (Death Certificate of Jane J. Southrn (RHM) January 25, 1915)(Death of Jane M. Southrn 1937) (Death Certificate of Jane Southrn (RHM) July 9, 1937) (Death Certificate of Frank Southrn (RHM) August 7, 1933) (Marilyn Cozad and Marsha Pilger 2003, 519) Cozad and Pilger have Southrn as having died and buried in Cozaddale which is a mistake.
37 (Foresman, 26) (Death Certificate of Jane Southrn (RHM) July 9, 1937)
38 (Kennedy 1978)
39 (Robert Gatewood - Cozad 1884)
40 (Julia Gatewood to Mollie Gatewood (RHM) April 5, 1908)
41 (Joan Gatewood Miller to Elma Johnson and Rex German (RHM) July 12, 1996, 1) (Family Genealogy Files of the Gatewood, Cozad, Henri Families (RHM)) There is a discrepancy with regards to Julia Gatewood's death. The Miller letter states that Julia Gatewood died in Arapahoe at Traber Gatewood's home and Miller's knowledge is very definitive. Another unsourced genealogical file says that she died in Cozad.
42 (Cozad Cemetery, Cozad Nebraska 2019)
43 (US Census, 1900, 3rd District, Atlantic City, New Jersey, Enumeration District 17, Sheet 14 1900) Julia Gatewood stated that she had five children.
44 (Family Genealogy Files of the Gatewood, Cozad, Henri Families (RHM))
45 (Charles E. Allen, Frank Johnson, Glenda France 1998, 29)
46 (D. Gatewood c. 1940)
47 (D. Gatewood c. 1940)
48 (Traber Gatewood to Theresa Gatewood (RMH) 1907)
49 (Family Genealogy Files of the Gatewood, Cozad, Henri Families (RHM)) (The Cozad Local

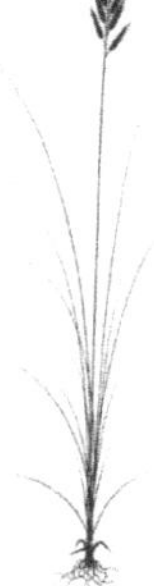

(RHM) 1956, 1) (D. R. Gatewood September 20, 1932)
50 (Family Genealogy Files of the Gatewood, Cozad, Henri Families (RHM)) (Cozad Cemetery, Cozad Nebraska 2019)(Charles E. Allen, Frank Johnson, Glenda France 1998, 96)
51(Mrs. Ella Schooley 1942) (Cozad Cemetery, Cozad Nebraska 2019)
52 (Cozad's Oldest Citizen Passes Away 1941)
53 (Services Set for LV Dentist 1966)
54 (Joan Gatewood Miller to Elma Johnson and Rex German (RHM) July 12, 1996, 2-3) (D. R. Gatewood September 20, 1932) (Homer 1969, revised 1988, 271n)(Services Set for LV Dentist 1966)
55 (Rex German and Russ Czaplewski 1992, 142) (Sandoz 1960, 327-328)(Helen Stauffer 1992, 352)
56 (Rex German and Russ Czaplewski 1992, 142-143)
57 (Sandoz 1960, x) Joan Gatewood Miller believed that John Cozad would have never identified himself by his real name but rather his assumed name.
58 (Sandoz 1960, x)
59 (Helen Stauffer 1992, 463)
60 (Sandoz 1960, 327-328)
61 (Findagrave.com (Mary Sandoz) 2019 ) (Findagrave (Jules Sandoz) 2019)(Alliance Cemetery, Alliance, Nebraska 2019)
62 (Helen Stauffer 1992, 177)
63 (Helen Stauffer 1992, 177) Sandoz in her letter had suggested for example that John Cozad had shot a man in Denver, returned to Cozad and then disappeared. This letter was probably written before she had begun her extensive investigations into the Pearson murder and the Cozad story.
64 ((Helen Stauffer 1992, 156-157) (Joan Gatewood Miller to Elma Johnson and Rex German (RHM) July 12, 1996, 3)
65 (Joan Gatewood Miller to Elma Johnson and Rex German (RHM) July 12, 1996, 3) (Mari Sandoz to Jacques Chambrun (RHM) 1945)
66 (Family Genealogy Files of the Gatewood, Cozad, Henri Families (RHM))
67 (Helen Stauffer 1992, 157)
68 (Joan Gatewood Miller to Elma Johnson and Rex German (RHM) July 12, 1996, 3)
69 (Joan Gatewood Miller to Elma Johnson and Rex German (RHM) July 12, 1996, 3)
70 (Joan Gatewood Miller to Elma Johnson and Rex German (RHM) July 12, 1996, 3) (Marilyn Cozad to Jan Patterson (RHM) 2013)
71 (Sandoz 1960, ix-x) (Helen Stauffer 1992, 352) (Perkin 1960)
72 (Helen Stauffer 1992, 464-465)
73 (Dolly Sloan to Robert Gatewood (RHM) August 23, 1931)
74 (Brooks 1955, 17)
75 (Joan Gatewood Miller to Elma Johnson and Rex German (RHM) July 12, 1996, 2-3) (Gatewood, Who Was Robert Henri? September 20, 1932) (D. R. Gatewood September 20, 1932) (Homer 1969, revised 1988, 271n)
76 (Joan Gatewood Miller to Elma Johnson and Rex German (RHM) July 12, 1996, 2-3)
77 (Sarena Deglin and Eileen Myer Sklar 2002, 24)
78 (Wolfrom 2008, 11) A copy was recently given to the Robert Henri Museum by the Delaware Art Museum and is now in its archives.
79 (Joan Gatewood Miller to Elma Johnson and Rex German (RHM) July 12, 1996, 4)
80 (Homer 1969, revised 1988, 271n) (Lougherly 1995, 373)(Sarena Deglin and Eileen Myer

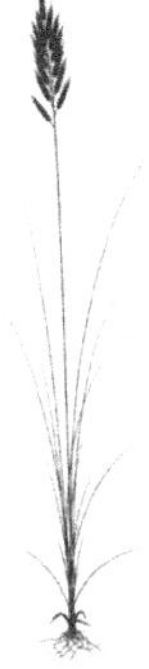

Sklar 2002, 7) John Sloan may have even consulted Robert Gatewood's notes to refresh his own memory as Henri had died a number of years before.
81 (Ridley 1997, 119)
82 (Charles E. Allen, Frank Johnson, Glenda France 1998, 83) (The Cozad Local (RHM) 1956, 1)
83 (Bergman, Charles Edgar Allen and Family 2020) (Bergman 2020)
84 (Charles E. Allen, Frank Johnson, Glenda France 1998, 7)
85 (R. Gatewood, Cozad Mystery Cleared: Town Founder Used a New Name Became Successful Promoter in the East 1956, 3, 19)
86 (The Cozad Local (RHM) 1956) (Reveal True Story of John J. Cozad 1956) (Rowley 1956)
87 (The Cozad Local (RHM) 1956) (Reveal True Story of John J. Cozad 1956, 1))
88 (Reveal True Story of John J. Cozad 1956, 1) (The Cozad Local (RHM) 1956)
89 (Robert Henri to Robert Gatewood (RHM) February 6, 1914)
90 (Robert Henri to Robert Gatewood (RHM) August 12, 1928)
91 (Joan Gatewood Miller to Elma Johnson and Rex German (RHM) July 12, 1996, 3)
92 (Nelson 1983, 101)
93 (Cozad's Oldest Pioneer Passes Away 1941)
94 (The Cozad Local 1956, 1, 3) (Reveal True Story of John J. Cozad 1956, 1, 3) (Montclair Art Museum to H.B. Allen 1955, 1,3)
95 (Reveal True Story of John J. Cozad 1956, 1, 3)
96 (Norman Hirschl to H. B. Allen (RHM) 1955)
97 (Reveal True Story of John J. Cozad 1956, 1, 3)
98 In 2019 an opera called The Gambler's Son was performed in both Cozad and Lincoln and was centered on Henri painting his father in 1903. The loan paperwork between the Sheldon and Henri is located in the Accession files.
99 (The Cozad Local 1956, 1) (Reveal True Story of John J. Cozad 1956, 1, 3)
100 (Helen Stauffer 1992, 178n) (Helen Stauffer 1992, 178n)
101 (Helen Stauffer 1992, 306, 350)
102 (Sandoz 1960, iv)
103 (Helen Stauffer 1992, 338)
104 (Helen Stauffer 1992, 350)
105 (Helen Stauffer 1992, 338)
106 (Perkin 1960)
107 (Helen Stauffer 1992, 341-342)
108 (Helen Stauffer 1992, 337)
109 (Sandoz 1960, x) It is curious that Sandoz only gave Harry B. Allen an acknowledgment for his article in the Cozad Local entitled About This Story and neglected to mention Robert Gatewood's article, which was much longer, entitled Nevada Doctor Tells True Story in article prepared for the Cozad Local.
110 (Joan Gatewood Miller to Elma Johnson and Rex German (RHM) July 12, 1996, 2)
111 (Joan Gatewood Miller to Elma Johnson and Rex German (RHM) July 12, 1996, 2) (Robert Gatewood to H. B. Allen (RHM) 1961)
112 (Helen Stauffer 1992, 357-358) (Mari Sandoz Collection (MS), Box 10, Folder 22)
113 (Joan Gatewood Miller to Elma Johnson and Rex German (RHM) July 12, 1996, 3)
114 (Joan Gatewood Miller to Elma Johnson and Rex German (RHM) July 12, 1996, 3)
115 (Dr. Robert Gatewood to William Homer (RHM) August 1, 1964)
116 (Helen Stauffer 1992, 354)

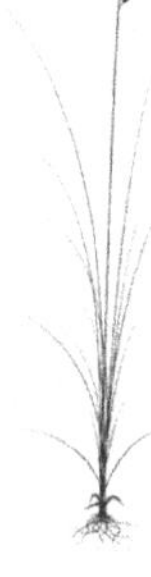

117 (Helen Stauffer 1992, xxix)
118 (Joan Gatewood Miller to Elma Johnson and Rex German (RHM) July 12, 1996, 4) (Joan Miller to William Homer (RHM) April 28, 1969) The date of the visitr may have been 1946.
119 (Joan Gatewood Miller to Elma Johnson and Rex German (RHM) July 12, 1996, 4)
120 (Homer 1969, revised 1988, x)
121 (Cozad Sure is Somewhat Different Than in 1900 1965) (Joan Miller to William Homer (RHM) April 28, 1969)
122 (Services Set for LV Dentist 1966)
123 (R. Cozad)

PART II, CHAPTER 2
1 (Homer 1969, revised 1988, 17-18)
2 (Homer 1969, revised 1988, 13)
3 (Homer 1969, revised 1988, 12)
4 (Homer 1969, revised 1988, 12) (B. Perlman, Robert Henri: His Life and Art 1991, 3)
5 (B. Perlman, Robert Henri: His Life and Art 1991, 4)
6 (Homer 1969, revised 1988, 12) (Perlman 1991, 3) There are questions about this date because in a 1998 commemorative edition of The Tri-City Trib a short article entitled Meridian Star: first Cozad paper, p 18c states that the first newspaper was not published until December 11, 1879, although Robert Cozad's recollections would appear to be correct that he had spent three summers to date in Cozad.
7 (R. H. Cozad 1880) (Menke, The Rebirth of the Cozad Revelation - (RHM) 1985, 5) (Perlman 1991, 3) (Homer 1969, revised 1988, 10, 15)
8 (R. Cozad, 198/115)
9 (R. Cozad)
10 (Federal Census, Dawson County, Nebraska, Enumeration District 167 1880, 5)
11 (Homer 1969, revised 1988, 15)
12 (Homer 1969, revised 1988, 15)
13 (Homer 1969, revised 1988, 10) (Perlman 1991, 3-4) (Robert Cozad Scrapbook - 1878 (RHM))
14 (Perlman 1991, 3)
15 (Robert Cozad Scrapbook - 1878 (RHM)) The Robert Henri Museum and Art Gallery owns three of the bound books.
16 (Homer 1969, revised 1988, 13)
17 (Homer 1969, revised 1988, 10) (Perlman 1991, 3-4)
18 (Homer 1969, revised 1988, 13)
19 (Homer 1969, revised 1988, 18)
20 (Homer 1969, revised 1988, 16) (Sandoz 1960, 202, 249) (R. Cozad, 92/276, 94/278)
21 (R. Cozad, 95/297)
22 (R. Cozad, 289/105) (Homer 1969, revised 1988, 16)
23 (R. Cozad, 289/105)
24 (R. Cozad, 90/274)
25 (Sandoz 1960, 304) (R. Cozad, 92/276, 285/101)
26 (R. Cozad n.d., 22/206)
27 (Perlman 1991, 4) (R. Cozad, 205/21, 201/17, 26/210) On at least one occasion he speaks of writing in his mother's room which may have been the Cozad family parlor.
28 (R. Cozad, 134/217)

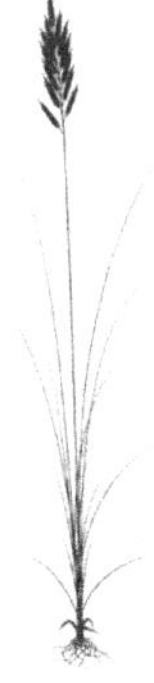

29 There is some question about the source of this poster as it may have been printed in Cincinnati or by the newspaper in Cozad although it is not known and there is no supporting documentation. (Ho! For the Great Platte Valley (Poster - RHM) 1879) (Homer 1969, revised 1988, 16) (B. Perlman 1991, 4)
30 (Sandoz 1960, 271) (R. Cozad, 283/99)
31 (R. Cozad, 42/226)
32 (R. Cozad, 29/213)
33 (Dr. Robert Gatewood to William Homer (RHM) August 1, 1964)
34 (Homer 1969, revised 1988, 12)
35 (Homer 1969, revised 1988, 13) (B. Perlman, Robert Henri: His Life and Art 1991, 6)
36 (Homer 1969, revised 1988, 13)
37 (Homer 1969, revised 1988, 13)
38 (Bargman, An Introduction: A Museum to honor a famous Cozad Native Son (RHM) 1984, 3) This information is not sourced from a primary source.
39 (Sandoz 1960, 32)
40 The Sheldon Art Museum in Lincoln, Nebraska owns the original copy of the diary.
41 (Perlman 1991, 4) (Homer 1969, revised 1988, 13) Unfortunately, Homer does not cite the source of this data.
42 (Maggie Claypool's Autograph Book (RHM) 1884) (Sandoz 1960, 202)
43 (Homer 1969, revised 1988, 272n) (Sandoz 1960, 14, 162-163)
44 (Homer 1969, revised 1988, 272n) (Sandoz 1960, 14, 162-163)
45 (Sandoz 1960, 215-217)
46 (Homer 1969, revised 1988, 272n) (Robert Gatewood to H. B. Allen (RHM) 1956)
47 (Deeds n.d.)
48 (Wright 1925)
49 (Richardson 1986, 288)
50 (Homer 1969, revised 1988, 19)
51 It has not been determined with a definitive judgment as there is some controversy around the painting.
52 (Sandoz 1960, 32)
53 (Sandoz 1960, 42-43)
54 (Antliff 2018)
55 (Antliff 2018)
56 (Goldman 1982, 529)
57 (Antliff 2018) (R. Henri, An Appreciation by an Artist 1915, 415)
58 (Antliff 2018)
59 (Antliff 2018)
60 (Sandoz 1960, 272)
61 (Sandoz 1960, ix)
62 (Robert Henri: Selected Chronology (RHM) 1990?, 1)
63 (Stafford 2019, 32) (Rody, Notes and Corrections to Book Manuscript, Vol 2 (RHM) 2023, 214)
64 (Omaha Exhibitions of Robert Henri - 1895-1925 (RHM))
65 (Meyer 1919, 18)
66 (Ridley 1997, 127,140,141, 144,145,162)
67 (Ridley 1997, 32-33) (Brooks 1955)
68 (Willa Cather Archives 1923) (Homestead 2019)

69 (R. Gatewood, Cozad Family Genealogy (RHM))
70 (Perlman 1991, 1)
71 (Perlman 1991, 1)
72 (Homer 1969, revised 1988, 19) (Atlantic City, New Jersey Directory 1884, 34, 40, 54) (Marilyn Cozad and Marsha Pilger 2003, 104) (Atlantic City, New Jersey 2022) (B. Perlman, Robert Henri: His Life and Art 1991, 6) (Robert Henri Collection, Robert Henri Museum and Art Gallery, Cozad, Nebraska)
73 (Homer 1969, revised 1988, 20)
74 (Homer 1969, revised 1988, 17-18)
75 (R. Henri 1923 (2007), 239)
76 (Homer 1969, revised 1988, 5)
77 (Baltimore Museum of Art 1931, 7)
78 (Henri 1923 (2007), 9)

PART III
1 (R. Cozad n.d., 22)

PART III, CHAPTER 1
2 (K. Buss, National Register of Historic Places Inventory - Nomination Form - The Hendee Hotel (RHM) 1979, 3)
3 (R. Cozad, 205/21)
4 (Menke 1985, 6) (Menke, Robert Henri: Museum and Historical Walkway (RHM) 1985, 3-4)
5 (K. Buss, National Register of Historic Places Inventory - Nomination Form - The Hendee Hotel (RHM) 1979, 2)
6 (Menke 1985, 15) (Menke, Robert Henri: Museum and Historical Walkway (RHM) 1985, 8)
7 (K. Buss, National Register of Historic Places Inventory - Nomination Form - The Hendee Hotel (RHM) 1979, 2)
8 (K. Buss, National Register of Historic Places Inventory - Nomination Form - The Hendee Hotel (RHM) 1979, 2)
9 (K. Buss, National Register of Historic Places Inventory - Nomination Form - The Hendee Hotel (RHM) 1979, 2)
10 (Buss, Flour mill, Gatewoods, Fultons, opera house in Cozad annals (RHM) 1998, 1f)
11 (John J. Cozad had a great vision for township location (RHM) 1988, 10C) (Menki 1985, 3) (Menke, Robert Henri: Museum and Historical Walkway (RHM) 1985, 3) (Nelson 1983, 94-95) (Charles E. Allen, Frank Johnson, Glenda France 1998, 62)
12 (Charles E. Allen, Frank Johnson, Glenda France 1998, 62) (Sandoz 1960, 93-94)
13 (K. Buss, National Register of Historic Places Inventory - Nomination Form - The Hendee Hotel (RHM) 1979, 3) (Menke, Robert Henri: Museum and Historical Walkway (RHM) 1985, 3)
14 (Rex German and Russ Czaplewski 1992, 72) (K. Buss, National Register of Historic Places Inventory - Nomination Form - The Hendee Hotel (RHM) 1979, 2)
15 (Foster 2013, 32)
16 (North Platte Republican 1876)
17 (North Platte Republic 1875) (North Platte Enterprise 1874)
18 (Buss, Hotel is Almost as Old as Cozad (RHM) 1984, 5) (Perlman 1991, 3) (Sandoz 1960,

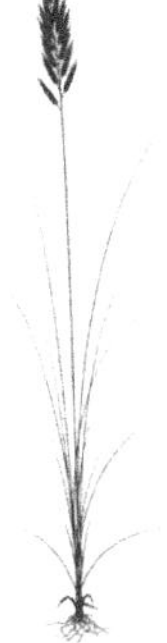

51, 144)The date of the beginning of the construction has often been speculated about as can be seen in correspondence in the RHM collection written by Jan Patterson bubeen substantiated.
19 (K. Buss, National Register of Historic Places Inventory - Nomination Form - The Hendee Hotel (RHM) 1979, 3) (Sandoz 1960, 115)
20 (Menke, The Rebirth of the Cozad Revelation - (RHM) 1985, 3) (Charles E. Allen, Frank Johnson, Glenda France 1998, 29, 38) (Homer 1969, revised 1988, 12) (Lewis, Hendee Hotel (RHM) 1972, 1) Mari Sandoz places the brickyard to the north of original settlement. (Sandoz 1960, 51) Another recollection, in Allen's book, is that the brickyard was located where the Anderson store stood. The National Register nomination states that it was produced at the local kiln that was owned by John Cozad.
21 (Nelson 1983, 98) (Menke, The Rebirth of the Cozad Revelation - (RHM) 1985, 3) (Lewis, Hendee Hotel (RHM) 1972, 2)
22 (Paul Brungardt, Brungardt Engineering 2004, 2) (Paul Brungardt, Brungardt Engineering April 29, 2004, 2)
23 (James Pettijohn*Ed Kinney 2002, 4)
24 (K. Buss, National Register of Historic Places Inventory - Nomination Form - The Hendee Hotel (RHM) 1979, 3)
25 (Virginia and Lee McAlester 1984, 212)
26 (Virginia and Lee McAlester 1984, 212)
27 (Virginia and Lee McAlester 1984, 212)
28 (James Pettijohn*Ed Kinney 2002, 3, 5)
29 (R. Cozad n.d., 221/37) (James Pettijohn*Ed Kinney 2002, 3)
30 (K. Buss, Hotel is Almost as Old as Cozad 1984, 5) (Buss, Hotel is Almost as Old as Cozad (RHM) 1984, 5) (Nelson 1983, 98) (Charles E. Allen, Frank Johnson, Glenda France 1998, 137) (Betty and Roger Menke 1985, 61)
31 (Nelson 1983, 97-98)(Buss, Hotel is Almost as Old as Cozad (RHM) 1984, 5) (Menke, The Rebirth of the Cozad Revelation - (RHM) 1985, 4) (Charles E. Allen, Frank Johnson, Glenda France 1998, 23) (Betty and Roger Menke 1985, 61)
32 (Nelson 1983, 97-98) (Buss, Hotel is Almost as Old as Cozad (RHM) 1984, 5) (Menke, The Rebirth of the Cozad Revelation - (RHM) 1985, 4)
33 (Buss, Hotel is Almost as Old as Cozad (RHM) 1984, 5) (Nelson 1983, 98) (Nelson 1983, 98)
34 (Nelson 1983, 98) (Betty and Roger Menke 1985, 51)
35 (R. H. Cozad 1880) (R. H. Cozad 1880) (Nelson 1983, 98) (Charles E. Allen, Frank Johnson, Glenda France 1998, 137-138)
36 (Lewis, Hendee Hotel (RHM) 1972, 2) (Charles E. Allen, Frank Johnson, Glenda France 1998, 15-16)
37 (Charles E. Allen, Frank Johnson, Glenda France 1998, 16) (Lewis, Hendee Hotel (RHM) 1972, 2)
38 (Nelson 1983, 98)
39 (Nelson 1983, 98) (Sandoz 1960, 221-222)
40 (Sandoz 1960, 222-223)
41 (R. Cozad n.d., 205/21)
42 (Nelson 1983, 99)
43 (Nelson 1983, 99)
44 (Buss, Hotel is Almost as Old as Cozad (RHM) 1984, 5)
45 (Charles E. Allen, Frank Johnson, Glenda France 1998, 137) (Betty and Roger Menke 1985,

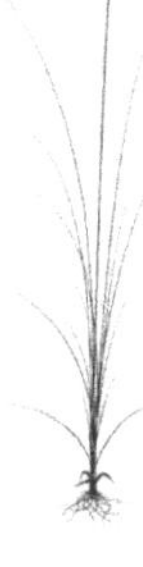

62)
46 (Sandoz 1960, 223)
47 (Nelson 1983, 99)
48 (Buss, Hotel is Almost as Old as Cozad (RHM) 1984, 5)
49 (R. Cozad)
50 (R. Cozad, 22)
51 (R. Cozad)
52 (Sandoz 1960, 234)
53 (K. Buss, National Register of Historic Places Inventory - Nomination Form - The Hendee Hotel (RHM) 1979, 2) (James Pettijohn*Ed Kinney 2002, 6)
54 (Menke, Robert Henri: Museum and Historical Walkway (RHM) 1985, 4)
55 (Menke, Robert Henri: Museum and Historical Walkway (RHM) 1985, 4)
56 (Osborne, Paint Analysis of the Robert Henri Museum (RHM) 2020, 5)
62 (Collection of Photographs of the Hendee Hotel (RHM) n.d.) In this picture, the building's brick is exposed.
58 (Osborne, Paint Analysis of the Robert Henri Museum (RHM) 2020)
59 (Charles E. Allen, Frank Johnson, Glenda France 1998, 50)
60 (Bargman, It Will Be Down to the Wire (RHM) 1984, 15) (Collection of Photographs of the Hendee Hotel (RHM)) (Lewis, Hendee Hotel (RHM) 1972, 3)
61 (Virginia and Lee McAlester 1984, 226-228)
62 (Menke, Robert Henri: Museum and Historical Walkway (RHM) 1985, 9) (R. Cozad n.d.)
63 (Menke, Robert Henri: Museum and Historical Walkway (RHM) 1985, 9) (K. Buss, National Register of Historic Places Inventory - Nomination Form - The Hendee Hotel (RHM) 1979, 2)
64 (R. Cozad n.d., 112/95)
65 (Menke, The Rebirth of the Cozad Revelation - (RHM) 1985, 5)
66 (Nelson 1983, 97) (Sandoz 1960, 235)
67 (Menke, The Rebirth of the Cozad Revelation - (RHM) 1985, 4) (K. Buss, National Register of Historic Places Inventory - Nomination Form - The Hendee Hotel (RHM) 1979, 2)
68 (Menke, The Rebirth of the Cozad Revelation - (RHM) 1985, 4) (Buss, Hotel is Almost as Old as Cozad (RHM) 1984, 5) (Betty and Roger Menke 1985, 61)
69 (Charles E. Allen, Frank Johnson, Glenda France 1998, 23)
70 (R. H. Cozad 1880, 22/206)
71 (Menke, Robert Henri: Museum and Historical Walkway (RHM) 1985, 9) (Lewis, Hendee Hotel (RHM) 1972, 3)
72 (R. H. Cozad 1880, 206)
73 (R. H. Cozad 1880, 206)
74 (R. H. Cozad 1880, 206)
75 (R. Cozad n.d., 112/195)
76 (Menke, Robert Henri: Museum and Historical Walkway (RHM) 1985, 4)

PART III, CHAPTER 2
1 (K. Buss, National Register of Historic Places Inventory - Nomination Form - The Hendee Hotel (RHM) 1979, 3)
2 (K. Buss, National Register of Historic Places Inventory - Nomination Form - The Hendee Hotel (RHM) 1979, 3-4) (Menke, The Rebirth of the Cozad Revelation - (RHM) 1985, 7-9)
3 (Lewis, Hendee Hotel (RHM) 1972, 1) (Newton Bateman and Paul Selby 1907, 903)

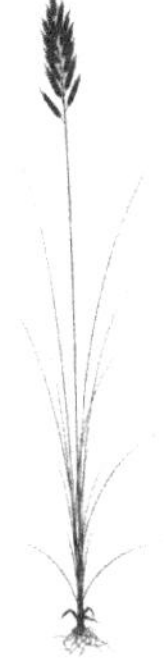

4 (Lewis, Hendee Hotel (RHM) 1972, 1)
5 (Lewis, Hendee Hotel (RHM) 1972, 1)
6 (We Relate 2020) (US Census Records - 1890 - 2019, 1900, 1910) (Lewis, Hendee Hotel (RHM) 1972, 1)
7 (Menke, Robert Henri: Museum and Historical Walkway (RHM) 1985, 8)
8 (Buss, Hotel is Almost as Old as Cozad (RHM) 1984, 5)
9 (Buss, Hotel is Almost as Old as Cozad (RHM) 1984, 5) (Sullivan 1996, 7) (Charles E. Allen, Frank Johnson, Glenda France 1998, 24) Allen's book states that they began to operate the hotel in 1883 which would predate the Hendee ownership. Unfortunately there are no surviving records that confirm this or to correct it.
10 (Charles E. Allen, Frank Johnson, Glenda France 1998, 82) (Osborne, From Cozad to State Prison: The Colorful Character of Miles Maryott (RHM) 2022) (Nebraska, State Census Collection, 1860-1885 1885)
11 (Buss, Hotel is Almost as Old as Cozad (RHM) 1984, 5) (Sullivan 1996, 7-9)
12 (Buss, Hotel is Almost as Old as Cozad (RHM) 1984, 5) (Menke, Robert Henri: Museum and Historical Walkway (RHM) 1985, 7-8) (David Claypool)
13 (Charles E. Allen, Frank Johnson, Glenda France 1998, 82)
14 (Map of Cozad 1910, Section 1)
15 (K. Buss, National Register of Historic Places Inventory - Nomination Form - The Hendee Hotel (RHM) 1979, 2, 9) (Map of Cozad 1910, Section 1)
16 (Map of Cozad , Section 1)
17 (Lewis, Hendee Hotel (RHM) 1972, 3)
18 (Cozad, Nebraska, March 13, 1897)
19 (Menke, Robert Henri: Museum and Historical Walkway (RHM) 1985, 8) (James Pettijohn*Ed Kinney 2002, 4)
20 (Osborne, Paint Analysis of the Robert Henri Museum (RHM) 2020)
21 (Menke, Robert Henri: Museum and Historical Walkway (RHM) 1985, 8) (K. Buss, National Register of Historic Places Inventory - Nomination Form - The Hendee Hotel (RHM) 1979, 2, 9)
22 (K. Buss, National Register of Historic Places Inventory - Nomination Form - The Hendee Hotel (RHM) 1979, 2, 9) (Map of Cozad 1920 1920) (Lewis, Hendee Hotel (RHM) 1972, 2) The nomination form suggests that the building was built in 1903 but it does not appear on the 1909 Sanborn Insurance Map and so was not on the site then.
23 (K. Buss, National Register of Historic Places Inventory - Nomination Form - The Hendee Hotel (RHM) 1979, 2, 9) (Map of Cozad , 1) (Lewis, Hendee Hotel (RHM) 1972, 2)
24 (Nebraska Lincoln Highway Scenic and Historic Byway Corridor Management Plan Undated, 4) (Weingroff 2017, 2)
25 (James Olson and Ronald Naugle 1997, 298-299) (Nebraska Lincoln Highway Scenic and Historic Byway Corridor Management Plan Undated, 4) (National Register of Historic Places Registration Form - Cozad Downtown Historic District (RHM) 2018, 28)
26 (Weingroff 2017, 2)
27 (Pushendorf 2013) (Weingroff 2017, 4)
28 (Osborne, The Trains of Our Memory: A History of the Railroad Museum of Pennsylvania 2016, 37)
29 (Osborne, The Five Mile Woods: A History 2017, 111)
30 (Weingroff 2017, 4)
31 (James Olson and Ronald Naugle 1997, 300)

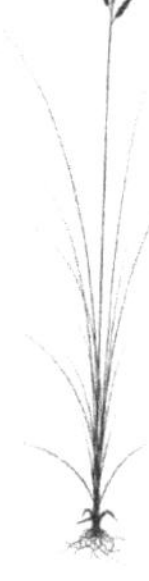

32 (The Hendee - Advertisement (RHM) 1896)
33 (Menke, The Rebirth of the Cozad Revelation - (RHM) 1985, 8)
34 (K. Buss, National Register of Historic Places Inventory - Nomination Form - The Hendee Hotel (RHM) 1979, 4)
35 (Menke, The Rebirth of the Cozad Revelation - (RHM) 1985, 7-8)
36 (Menke, The Rebirth of the Cozad Revelation - (RHM) 1985, 7-8)
37 (Menke, The Rebirth of the Cozad Revelation - (RHM) 1985, 8)
38 (Buss, Hotel is Almost as Old as Cozad (RHM) 1984, 5) (Burgess 2020) (K. Buss, National Register of Historic Places Inventory - Nomination Form - The Hendee Hotel (RHM) 1979, 4) (Rody, Notes and Corrections to Book Manuscript, Vol 1 (RHM) 2023, 13)

PART III, CHAPTER 3
1 (K. Buss, National Register of Historic Places Inventory - Nomination Form - The Hendee Hotel (RHM) 1979, 4)
2 (Menke, Robert Henri: Museum and Historical Walkway (RHM) 1985, 8) (Lewis, Hendee Hotel (RHM) 1972, 1)
3 (Menke, Robert Henri: Museum and Historical Walkway (RHM) 1985, 8) (K. Buss, National Register of Historic Places Inventory - Nomination Form - The Hendee Hotel (RHM) 1979, 4) (Lewis, Hendee Hotel (RHM) 1972, 3)
4 (Menke, Robert Henri: Museum and Historical Walkway (RHM) 1985, 8) (K. Buss, National Register of Historic Places Inventory - Nomination Form - The Hendee Hotel (RHM) 1979, 4) (Lewis, Hendee Hotel (RHM) 1972, 3) (US Census, Cozad, Enumeration District 26-6, Sheet 81 B 1940)
5 (Lewis, Hendee Hotel (RHM) 1972, 3) (Zoey Miller to Peter Osborne 2022)
6 (Osborne, Foster-Lewis Genealogy 2021) (Lewis, Hendee Hotel (RHM) 1972, 1)
7 (Menke, Robert Henri: Museum and Historical Walkway (RHM) 1985, 8)
8 (Menke, Robert Henri: Museum and Historical Walkway (RHM) 1985, 9)
9 (K. Buss, National Register of Historic Places Inventory - Nomination Form - The Hendee Hotel (RHM) 1979, 2)
10 (Collection of Photographs of the Hendee Hotel (RHM) n.d.)
11 (Osborne, Paint Analysis of the Robert Henri Museum (RHM) 2020)
12 (Menke, Robert Henri: Museum and Historical Walkway (RHM) 1985, 4)
13 (K. Buss, National Register of Historic Places Inventory - Nomination Form - The Hendee Hotel (RHM) 1979, 4) (Map of Cozad 1920 1920, Section 5) There was a small structure behind the Hendee Hotel on the 1909 Sanborn Insurance Map which be one of the garages.
14 (R. H. Cozad 1880)
15 (Bargman, It Will Be Down to the Wire (RHM) 1984, 15)
16 (Bargman, It Will Be Down to the Wire (RHM) 1984, 15) (Bargman, It Will Be Down to the Wire (RHM) 1984, 15)
17 (1958 Floor Plan of the Hendee Hotel (RHM))
18 (K. Buss, National Register of Historic Places Inventory - Nomination Form - The Hendee Hotel (RHM) 1979, 2)
19 (Lewis, Hendee Hotel (RHM) 1972, 3)
20 (K. Buss, National Register of Historic Places Inventory - Nomination Form - The Hendee Hotel (RHM) 1979, 2) (1958 Floor Plan of the Hendee Hotel (RHM))
21 (1958 Floor Plan of the Hendee Hotel (RHM))
22 (1958 Floor Plan of the Hendee Hotel (RHM))

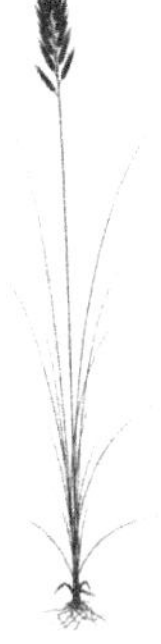

23 (1958 Floor Plan of the Hendee Hotel (RHM))
24 (Geiger 2021)
25 (1958 Floor Plan of the Hendee Hotel (RHM))
26 (1958 Floor Plan of the Hendee Hotel (RHM))
27 (Zoey Miller to Peter Osborne 2022) (Wayman May June 9, 2010)

PART III, CHAPTER 4
1 (Allan, 1984) (Allan, Nebraska Byways: Grandmothers Revitalize Cozad 1984)
2 (Ellis 1984)
3 (K. Buss, National Register of Historic Places Inventory - Nomination Form - The Hendee Hotel (RHM) 1979)
4 (Lewis, Hendee Hotel (RHM) 1972, 3)
5 (K. Buss, National Register of Historic Places Inventory - Nomination Form - The Hendee Hotel (RHM) 1979)
6 (City of Cozad, Nebraska 2018) (National Register of Historic Places Registration Form - Cozad Downtown Historic District (RHM) 2018)
7 (Ambrose 2000, 127) (James Olson and Ronald Naugle 1997, 357-358)
8 (Bargman, An Introduction: A Museum to honor a famous Cozad Native Son (RHM) 1984) (Bargman, An Introduction: A Museum to honor a famous Cozad Native Son (RHM) 1984, 3)
9 (Drive Started in September 1983 1984, 3)
10 (Drive Started in September 1983 1984, 3)
11 (Allan, Nebraska Byways: Grandmothers Revitalize Cozad 1984)
12 (Bargman, It Will Be Down to the Wire (RHM) 1984, 15)
13 (Geiger, Preservation of Cozad and Robert Henri legacies vital (RHM) 1998, 16c-17c)
14 (Osborne, Where Washington Once Led: A History of New Jersey's Washington Crossing State Park 2012, 21, 247, 308)
15 (Brako 2002, 1-2)
16 (Menke, The History of the Country School District No. 86 (RHM) 1985) (Brako 2002) Jeanne Brako suggests in her report that the building was constructed in 1875. (James Pettijohn*Ed Kinney 2002, 1)Petti*Kenny believe that the building was built in 1889
17 (Menke, The History of the Country School District No. 86 (RHM) 1985)
18 (Menke, The History of the Little Church by the Park (RHM) 1985)
19 (Menke, The History of the Willow Island Pony Express Express Station located in the City Park of Cozad, Nebraska (RHM) 1985)
20 (Menke, The Rebirth of the Cozad Revelation - (RHM) 1985) (Menke, Robert Henri: Museum and Historical Walkway (RHM) 1985) (Menke, The History of the Country School District No. 86 (RHM) 1985) (Menke, The History of the Little Church by the Park (RHM) 1985) (Menke, The History of the Willow Island Pony Express Express Station located in the City Park of Cozad, Nebraska (RHM) 1985)
21 (Bargman, It Will Be Down to the Wire (RHM) 1984, 15) (Allan, Nebraska Byways: Grandmothers Revitalize Cozad 1984)
22 (Bargman, An Introduction: A Museum to honor a famous Cozad Native Son (RHM) 1984) (Bargman, It Will Be Down to the Wire (RHM) 1984, 15)
23 (An Album (RHM) 1984)
24 (James Pettijohn*Ed Kinney 2002, 4)
25 (Brako 2002, 3)
26 (Brako 2002, 6)

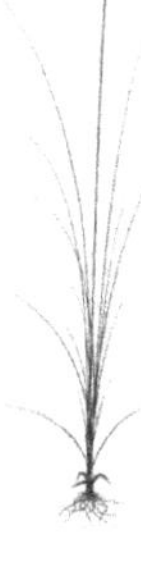

27 (Brako 2002, 3)
28 (Menke, Robert Henri: Museum and Historical Walkway (RHM) 1985, 9) (Geiger, Preservation of Cozad and Robert Henri legacies vital (RHM) 1998)
29 (James Pettijohn*Ed Kinney 2002) (Brako 2002)
30 (Dorsey 2003)
31 (James Pettijohn*Ed Kinney 2002, 4)
32 (James Pettijohn*Ed Kinney 2002, 4-5)
33 (Paul Brungardt, Brungardt Engineering April 29, 2004)
34 (Dorsey 2003)
35 (Paul Brungardt, Brungardt Engineering April 29, 2004)
36 (Solicitation to Raise Funds for Renovation Work 2006)
37 (James Pettijohn*Ed Kinney 2002, 5) (Karre 2022)
38 (James Pettijohn*Ed Kinney 2002, 7)
39 (Patterson 2014 (?))
40 (Betty and Roger Menke 1985, 6)
41 (Menke, The Rebirth of the Cozad Revelation - (RHM) 1985, 8)
42 (Stacy Easterday to Jan Patterson (RHM) 2011)
43 (Susan Brasch to Jan Patterson (RHM) 2011)
44 (Jan Patterson to Stacy Easterday (RHM) 2011)
45 (Kinnan 2019)
46 (Kinnan 2019)

PART IV, EPILOGUE
1 David McCullough gave many presentations where in reflecting on his career he used this quote.
2 (Osborne, The Five Mile Woods: A History 2017, 22)
3 (Osborne, Where Washington Once Led: A History of New Jersey's Washington Crossing State Park 2012, 18-19)
4 (Osborne, Where Washington Once Led: A History of New Jersey's Washington Crossing State Park 2012, 74-111)
5 (Osborne, The Five Mile Woods: A History 2017, 22-23)
6 (Osborne, Elizabeth Grandin: A Clinton Treasure 2015)
7 (Osborne, Elizabeth Grandin: A Clinton Treasure 2015)
8 (Descendants of Jacques Cossart and his wife, Lydia (RHM), 51) (Osborne, Images of America: Hacklebarney and Voorhees State Park 2004, 7-13)
9 (Foresman, 18, 22) (Osborne 2014, 130)

BIBLIOGRAPHIC ESSAY
1 (Sandoz 1960, x)
2 (The Cozad Local (RHM) 1956)
3 (Cozad Historical Society 1979) (Buss, National Register of Historic Places Registration Form 1979)
4 (Bergman, Charles Edgar Allen and Family 2020) (Bergman 2020) (National Register of Historic Places Registration Form - Cozad Downtown Historic District (RHM) 2018) (National Register of Historic Places Registration Form - Cozad Downtown Historic District (RHM) 2018)
5 (Charles E. Allen, Frank Johnson, Glenda France 1998, 1)

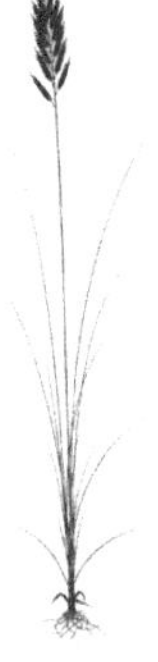

6 (National Park Service 2008) (Scotts Bluff Area Visitors Bureau)
7 (Smith 1997)
8 (Wolfrom 2008)
9 Laura Rody believes that perhaps Theresa meant parcels and not sections as this would have meant that Cozad owne twelve percent of Dawson County and if it included the homesteaded land that he would have owned twenty-five percent of the county. (Rody, Notes and Corrections to Book Manuscript, Vol 2 (RHM) 2023, 312)
10 (Foresman)

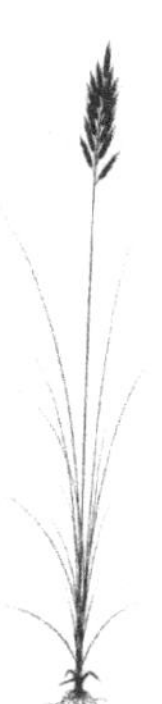

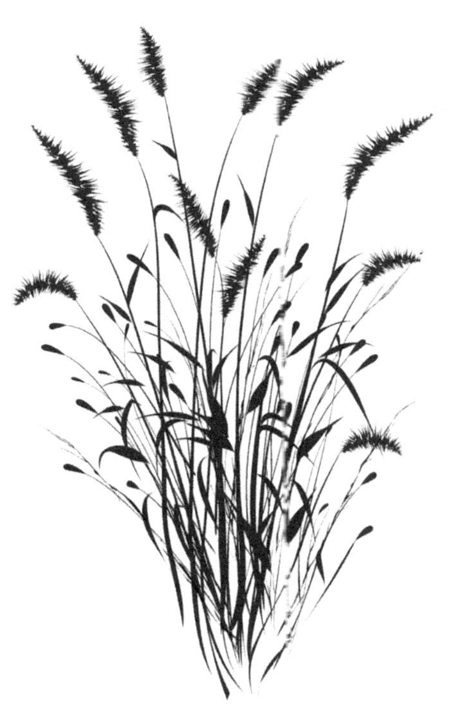

# Bibliography

*"Go West, Young Man: The Mystery Behind the Famous Phrase.* July 9, 2015. https://blog.newspapers.library.in.gov/go-west-young-man-the-mystery-behind-the-famous-phrase/ (accessed June 16, 2023).

"1860 United States Federal Census, Year: 1860; Census Place: Kanawha, Virginia; Roll: M653_1356; Page: 291; Family History Library Film: 805356." 1860.

"1958 Floor Plan of the Hendee Hotel (RHM)." 1958.

*Abstract of Title of Southeast Quarter of Section 6, Township 10, North of Range 23 W, Dawson County, Nebraska, Warranty Deed of James and Arlene McAdams (RHM).* R. E. Bannister and S.G Deines, Bonded Abstrators, 1954.

Allan, Tom. "Nebraska Byways: Grandmothers Revitalize Cozad." *Omaha Sunday World-Herald,* October 7, 1984.

"Alliance Cemetery, Alliance, Nebraska." 2019.

Alverson, Joe. "Marilyn Cozad: Not Just Another Cozad." *Tri-City Trib*, n.d.

Ambrose, Stephen. *Nothing Like It In The World.* New York: Simon and Shuster, 2000.

Anderson, Cora. "History of Cozad, Nebraska (DCHM)." Cozad, Nebraska, 1938.

Anderson, Daphne. "Robert Henri: Nebraska's Favrorite Son." Lincoln: Sheldon Memorial Art Gallery & Smith Kramer Fine Art Services, n.d.

Andreas, A. T. *History of the State of Nebraska.* Chicago: The Western Historical Company, 1882.

Antliff, Allan. "Decolonizing Modernism: Robert Henri's portraits of the Tewa Pueblo Peoples." *The Art Bulletin,* 2018: 106-132.

*Atlantic City, New Jersey.* 6 21, 2022. https://www.acnj.gov/page/history-of-atlantic-city (accessed 6 21, 2022).

"Atlantic City, New Jersey." *Sanborn Insurance Map.* 1894.

*Atlantic City, New Jersey Directory.* Atlantic City, New Jersey: Holdzcom and Company, 1884.

Baltimore Museum of Art. *Catalogue of a Memorial Exhibition of the Work of Robert Henri.* Baltimore: Baltimore Museum of Art, 1931.

Bargman, Mary. "An Introduction: A Museum to honor a famous Cozad Native Son (RHM)." *Scope: Tri-City Trib*, September 25, 1984.

—. "It Will Be Down to the Wire (RHM)." *Tribscope*, September 25, 1984.

—. "Our Historical Buildings: The Little White Church and the Pony Express Station." *Tribscope*, September 25, 1984.

—. "Our Historical Buildings: The Old Schoolhouse (RHM)." *Tribscope*, September 25, 1984.

Barry Combs and James Wigton. *Central High School Timeline.* Omaha: Omaha High School, 2012.

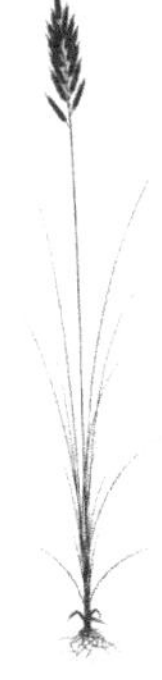

Bell, Bob Boze. "Son of A Gunfighter: John J. Cozad vs Alfred Pearson, A Lifetime of Aliases." *True West*, October 2013.

Bergman, C. "Charles Edgar Allen and Family." *Banner*, March 2020.

Betty and Roger Menke. *The Rebirth of the Cozad Revelation - Interview.* Cozad: Robert Henri Museum and Historical Walkway, 1985.

"Bill of Fare - Central Dining Saloon (RHM)." n.d.

Bogan, Dallas. *Warren County Local History: Remembering the Forgotten Local Town of Cozaddale.* 2004.

Bozell, John. "Big Game Hunters: The Ice Age and the First Immigrants." *Nebraska History 75*, 1994.

Brako, Jeanne. "2002 IMLS General Conservation Survey Report: Conservation Assessment Program for the Robert Henri Museum and Historical Walkway (RHM)." Washington, D.C., 2002.

Brey, William. "Carbutt and the Union Pacific's Grand Excursion to the 100th Meridian." *Stereo World*, May-June 1980: Pages 4-9.

Brooks, Van Wyck. *John Sloan: A Painter's Life.* New York: E.P. Dutton, 1955.

Burgess, Don, interview by Peter Osbonre. (2020).

Buss, Kieth. "Bushnell, Illinois: Its Investment and Settlement in Dawson County, Nebraska (RHM)." n.d.

Buss, Kieth. "Bushnell, Illinois: Its Investment and Settlement in Dawson County, Nebraska (RHM)." n.d.

Buss, Kieth. "Genealogica Data in Family Genealogy Files (RHM)." 1980.

Buss, Kieth. *National Register of Historic Places Inventory - Nomination Form - The Hendee Hotel (RHM).* Cozad, Nebraska: Cozad Historical Society, 1979.

Buss, Kieth. "National Register of Historic Places Registration Form." Cozad, Nebraska, 1979.

—. "Hotel is Almost as Old as Cozad (RHM)." *Scope: Tri-City Trib*, September 25, 1984.

—. "Flour mill, Gatewoods, Fultons, opera house in Cozad annals (RHM)." *Tri-City Trib*, September 10, 1998.

"Certificate of Ownership, Cemetery of Spring Grove (RHM)." 1867.

Charles Allen, Editor. *Early History of the Cozad Community: Pioneer Families 1873-1973.* Cozad, Nebraska: Tri-City Printers, 1973.

Charles E. Allen, Frank Johnson, Glenda France. *Early History of the Cozad Community and Pioneer Families, 1873-1998 (RHM).* Cozad, Nebraska: The Cozad Local, 1998.

*Cincinatti Daily Gazette.*July 9, 1874.

*Cincinnati Art Museum - Museum History.* 2022. https://www.cincinnatiartmuseum.org/about/museum-history/ (accessed July 20, 2022).

*Cincinnati Daily Gazette.* "Union Pacific Files for Bankruptcy." July 9, 1874.

*Cincinnati Directory.* Cincinnati, 1868.

*Cincinnati Enquirer.* June 26, 1874.

*Cincinnati Enquirer.* "Trifling Case Entertained in Court - It Proves Neither a Mountain Nor a Mole-Hill." December 11, 1867.

Class of 1925 - Eight Graders. "History of Cozad." Cozad Schools, 1925.

"Collection of Photographs of the Hendee Hotel (RHM)." n.d.

"Correspondence between Peter Osborne and Jerry Penry (RHM)." 4.28.2022 - 5.2.2022.

"Cozad Cemetery, Cozad Nebraska ." 2019.

Cozad Chamber of Commerce and Historical Land Mark Council. "The 100th Meridian Nebraska Historic Marker." Cozad, Nebraska, n.d.


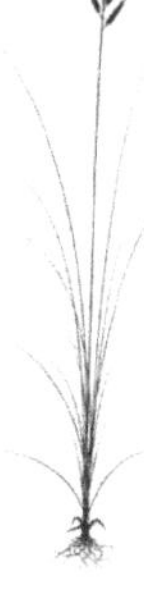

"Cozad Family Papers, Legal Transactions and Deeds (RHM)."
*Cozad Local (?).* "Cozad, Nebraska, March 13, 1897." March 13, 1897.
*Cozad Local.* "Cozad Sure is Somewhat Different Than in 1900." November 4, 1965.
*Cozad Local.* "Lex Turns Up Story Accusing John A. Cozad of Trying to Burn Their Town (RHM)." Undated, taken from December 2, 1882 edition of Lexington newspaper.
*Cozad Tribune.* "The Hendee - Advertisement (RHM)." July 17, 1896.
Cozad, Andy. "Genealogy of General Thomas J. Stonewall Jackson in relation to John J. Cozad." 2023.
"Cozad, Dawson County, Nebraska." *Sanborn Map Company.* New York City, New York: Sanborn Map Company, December 1909.
Cozad, Marilyn. "Descendants of Jacque Cossart and his wife, Lydia." n.d.
Cozad, Robert. *Diary, 1880, 2022 Transcript (RHM).* n.d.
Cozad, Robert Henri. *Diary 1880 (RHM) Whitney version.* 1880.
Cozad, Theresa Gatewood. "Lee February 17, 1923 - Accounts, Names of Friends, Dates of Family history, History, Deaths and Notes (RHM)." New York, 1923.
"Cozaddale, Ohio (RHM)." n.d.
*Cozad's Oldest Citizen Passes Away.* 1941.
"Cozad's Oldest Pioneer Passes Away." April 28, 1941.
Czaplewski, Russell. "Where Alfalfa Was Queen: Alfalfa Production in Dawson County, Nebraska 1884-1987." 1988 (?).
"David Claypool (RHM)." 1923.
"David Claypool." n.d.
*Dawson County Herald.* "View of Plum Creek." Undated. (RHM)
*Dawson County Pioneer.*January 20, 1883.
*Dawson County Pioneer.* "Death of Alfred Pearson (RHM)." December 9, 1882.
*Dawson County Pioneer.* "John J. Cozad Perforates A. Pearson (RHM)." October 21, 1882.
"Death Ceritificate of Marjorie Henri." July 6, 1930.
"Death Ceritificate of Robert Henri." July 13, 1929.
"Death Certificate of Frank Southrn (RHM)." Philadelphia, August 7, 1933.
"Death Certificate of Jane J. Southrn (RHM)." Philadelphia, January 25, 1915.
"Death Certificate of Jane Southrn (RHM)." Philadalphia, July 9, 1937.
"Death Notice - A.T. Gatewood." *Unknown.* September 27, 1928.
Deeds, Daphne Anderson. "Robert Henri: Nebraska's Favorite Son." n.d.
"Descendants of Jacques Cossart and his wife, Lydia (RHM)." n.d.
Diefender, B. S. *US GenWeb.* 1998. http//files.usarchives.org/ne/dawson/biography/pears/001.txt (accessed 2022).
Diefenderfer, Beverly Scrutchfeid. *US Gen Web.* August 1998. http://files.usgwarchives.org/ne/dawosn/biography/pears001.txt.
"Dolly Sloan to Robert Gatewood (RHM)." August 23, 1931.
Dorsey, Dean. "Henri Museum restore project." *Tri-City Tribune,* October 30, 2003: 2.
"Dr. A. T. Gatewood, A Bryan Democrat of the Old Guard of 1896 (RHM)." n.d.
"Dr. Robert Gatewood to William Homer (RHM)." August 1, 1964.
"E. C. Schafer to Harry B. Allen, May 8, 1963 (RHM)." May 8, 1963.
Ellis, Karen Kuhns. "Century Old Cozad Hotel to Get Facelife." *North Platte Telegraph,* June 6, 1984.
Eugene Willard, editor. *A Standard History of the Hanging Rock Region of Ohio.* Lewis Publishing Company, 1916.

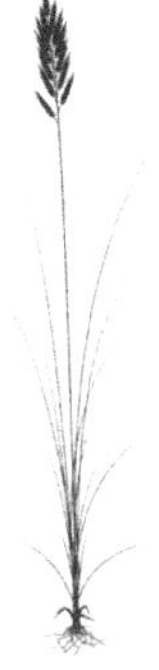

"Excursion to 100th Meridian, 1866 (RHM)." n.d.
F. E. Shearer, Editor. *The Pacific Tourist: An Illustrated Guide.* New York: J. R. Bowman, 1879.
"Family Genealogy Files of the Gatewood, Cozad, Henri Families (RHM)." n.d.
"Federal Census, Dawson County, Nebraska, Enumeration District 167." 1880.
"Federal Census, Hamilton Township, Warren County, Ohio." 1870.
*FindA Grave.* 2020. https://www.findagrave.com/memorial/155331789/stephen-a.-hendee#view-photo=132326162 (accessed 12 17, 2020).
*Find-A-Grave - William Cozad.* 2022. https://www.findagrave.com/memorial/78913191/william-e-cozad (accessed 3 12, 2022).
*Find-A-Grave - William Venable.* 2022. https://www.findagrave.com/memorial/8649041/william-henry-venable (accessed 3 4, 2022).
*Findagrave (Jules Sandoz).* 2019. https://www.findagrave.com/memorial/79637002/jules-ami-sandoz (accessed February 6, 2022).
*Findagrave.com (Mary Sandoz).* 2019 . https://www.findagrave.com/memorial/79637019/mary-elizabeth-sandoz (accessed February 6, 2022).
*Findagrave.com (Shirley Paulsen).* 8 23, 2019. https://www.findagrave.com/memorial/107741884/shirley-a-paulsen#view-photo=77615672 (accessed 8 23, 2019).
*First Presbyterian Church of Cozad, Nebraska.* 2020. https://cozadpresbyterian.com/About-Us/index.html (accessed May 24, 2020).
Fitzpatrick, Lillian Linder. *Nebraska Place-Names.* Lincoln, Nebraska: University of Nebraska, 1925.
"Flour Mill, Gatewoods, Fultons, opera house in Cozad annals." n.d.
Foresman, Robert. "The Other Son of the Gamblin' Man (RHM)." n.d.
Foster, Lt. James E. H. *A Brave Soldier and Honest Gentleman: Lt. James E. H. Foster in the West, 1873-1881.* Lincoln, Nebraska: University of Nebraska Press, 2013.
Framnzwa, Gregory. *Maps of the Oregon Trail.* St. Louis, Missouri: The Patrice Press, 1990.
*Frank Duvenek.* 2022. https://americanart.si.edu/artist/frank-duveneck-1371 (accessed July 22, 2022).
"Frank Southrn to Robert Henri (RHM)." March 15, 1891.
Gatewood, Deborah. "Personal Diary of Deborah Gatewood (RHM)." c. 1940.
Gatewood, Dr. Robert. *Who Was Robert Henri? (RHM).* September 20, 1932.
Gatewood, Robert. "Cozad Family Genealogy (RHM) " n.d.
—. "Cozad Mystery Cleared: Town Founder Used a New Name Became Successful Promoter in the East." *Omaha World Herald,* December 16, 1956.
—. "John J. Cozad, Alfred Pearson, Robert Henri: trio of early years (RHM)." *Tri City Trib,* September 10, 1998.
Geiger, Marlene, interview by Peter Osborne. (January 15, 2021).
—. "Preservation of Cozad and Robert Henri legacies vital (RHM)." *Tri-City Trib,* September 1998, 1998.
General Land Office. *Report of the Commissioner of the General Land Office made to the Secretary of the Interior relating to Land Grants made for the Pacific Railway under the Pacific Railway Act of 1862, and to the management and increased value of the retained mineral.* Washington D., November 29, 1862.
German, Rex. "Alf Pearson ." 2019.
German, Rex. "Paper on Alf Pearson's Shooting." 2019.
"Go West Young Man!" *Highland Weekly News.* Hillsboro, Ohio, February 24, 1876.
Goldman, Emma. *Living My Live.* Salt Lake City: Peregrine Smith Books, 1982.

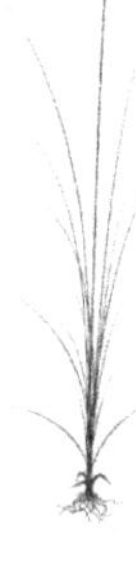

*Google Arts and Culture - The Whistling Boy.* 2022. https://artsandculture.google.com/asset/the-whistling-boy-frank-duveneck-american-b-1848-d-1919/gQGJgu9rrvUWhA?hl=en (accessed July 19, 2022).

Goss, Charles. *Cincinnati: The Queen City.* Cincinnati, Ohio: S. J. Clarke Publishing, 1912.

Handley, Roy. "Recollections (RHM)." n.d.

Helen Stauffer. *Letters by Mari Sandoz.* Lincoln: Univeristy of Nebraska Press, 1992.

Hendee, David. *Nebraska: 150 Years Told Through 93 Counties.* Omaha, Nebraska: Omaha World-Herald, 2016.

Henri, Robert. *Diary, 1881.* 1881.

—. "An Appreciation by an Artist." *Mother Earth. Vol 10, No. 1,* 1915.

Henri, Robet. *The Art Spirit.* Philadelphia: J.B. Lippincott (Basic Books Edition 2007), 1923 (2007).

Henry and Kate Ford. *History of Cincinnati, Ohio.* Cleveland, Ohio: W. W. Williams, 1881.

Henshaw, Tom. "Nebraska Town Finally Discovers Its Founder." *Panama City News,* April 29, 1957.

Hewitt, Lucy. *Early Days in Dawson County.* 1876.

*Historical Census Statistics on Population Totals by Race, 1790 to 1990, and by Hispanic origin, 1970 to 1990, for the United States, Regions, Divisions, and States.* September 13, 2002. https://www.census.gov/library/working-papers/2002/demo/POP-twps0056.html (accessed July 17, 2023).

*History of Hocking Valley, Ohio.* Chicago: Interstate Publishing Compay, 1883.

*History of Warren County.* Chicago: W, H Beers, 1882.

*Ho! For the Great Platte Valley (Poster - RHM).* Cincinnatti, Ohio: John Cozad, 1879.

Holen, Steve. "The Search for the Earliest Americas: An Old Archaelogical Controversy (Lecture)." October 29, 2022.

Homer, William. *Robert Henri and His Circle.* New York: Hacker Art Books, 1969, revised 1988.

Homestead, Melissa, interview by Peter Osborne. (2019).

Horn, Johnathan. "Homestead." *Colorado Encyclopedia.* November 24, 2018. www.coloradoencyclopedia.org/article/homestead (accessed 10 15, 2022).

Huey, W. T. "Dawson County Map." 1884.

"In Remembrance: Ivan (Ike) and Shirley Paulsen." 1985, October 18, 1985.

"J. W. Montgomery to Theresa Cozad (RHM), October 29, 1916." n.d.

"Jacqueline Silver-Morillo, Atlantic City Free Public Library to Peter Osborne." December 12, 2022.

James Olson and Ronald Naugle. *History of Nebraska.* Lincoln, Nebraska: University of Nebraska Press, 1997.

James Pettijohn*Ed Kinney, Architects/Interiors. "Conservation Assessment Report for Robert Henri Museum and Historical Walkway (RHM)." Overland Park, Kansas, 2002.

James, Edward. "John Jackson Cozad (RHM)." n.d.

"Jan Patterson to Stacy Easterday (RHM) 2011." n.d.

"Jane Scholl to Russell Czaplewski (DCHM)." March 11, 1985.

"Jerry Penry to Peter Osborne (RHM)." May 2, 2022.

"Joan Gatewood Miller to Elma Johnson and Rex German (RHM)." July 12, 1996.

"Joan Miller to William Homer (RHM)." April 28, 1969.

"John Cozad to Jay Gould (RHM) June 14, 1878." n.d.

"John Cozad to S.H.H. Clark (MONA)." November 2, 1877.

"John Cozad to Sidney Dillow (MONA)." 1880?

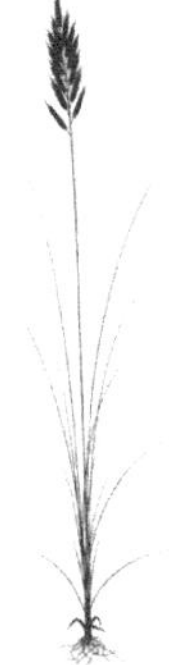

"Julia Gatewood to Mollie Gatewood (RHM)." May 12, 1905.
"Julia Gatewood to Mollie Gatewood (RHM)." April 5, 1908.
Karre, Larry, interview by Peter Osborne. (September 15, 2022).
Kennedy, Patricia. *National Register of Historic Places Nomination Form - Central Falls, Rhode Island.* Providence, Rhode Island: Rhode Island Historic Preservation Commission, 1978.
Kinnan, Jane, interview by Peter Osborne. (February 8, 2019).
"Land Transactions 1875-1937 (RHM)." n.d.
"Leavitt Burnham to John Cozad) April 30, 1878." n.d.
"Legal Transactions of the Cozads (RHM)." n.d.
Leroy Hafen and Carl Rister. *Western America: The Exploration, Settlement and Development of the Region Beyond the Mississippi.* New York: Prentice-Hall, 1950.
Lewis, Deline. "Hendee Hotel (RHM)." 1972.
Lewis, Deline. "Hendee Hotel (RHM)." 1972.
*Lexington Clipper.* "Mrs. Ella Schooley." July 9, 1942.
Lougherly, J. *John Sloan: Painter and Rebel.* New York: Henry Holt, Co., 1995.
"Maggie Claypool's Autograph Book (RHM)." 1884.
"Man Behind the Name: Mystery of Cozad is Finally Broken." n.d.
"Map of Cozad ." *Sanborn Fire Insurance Maps.* New York City: Sanborn Map Company, 1910.
"Map of Cozad 1920." *Sanborn Fire Insurance Map.* New York City: Sanborn Map Companyt, 1920.
"Map of Internments of the Southrn, Lee and Henri family members (Location: Group 355, Location L, Lot 33) (RHM)." n.d.
*Map of Township No. 10 North, Range No 23 West of the Sixth Principal Meridian.* State of Nebraska, State Surveyors Office, 1868.
*Map of Township No. 10 North, Range No 24 West of the Sixth Principal Meridian.* State of Nebraska, State Surveyors Office, 1869.
"Mari Sandoz Collection (MS)." n.d.
"Mari Sandoz Papers (MS)." n.d.
"Mari Sandoz to Jacques Chambrun (RHM)." September 7, 1945.
Marilyn Cozad and Marsha Pilger. *Cozad Connections: Twenty-Eight Thousand Descendants of Jacque and Lydia (Willems) Cossart (RHM).* Self published, 2003.
"Marilyn Cozad to Jan Patterson (RHM)." February 14 2013.
*Marker Monday: Pawnee Villages.* June 30, 2023. https://history.nebraska.gov/marker-monday-pawnee-villages/ (accessed Jume 30, 2023).
Marshall, Jim and Leone. "Recollections - 1988 (RHM)." 1988.
"Mary Wake to Mrs. Gatewood (RHM) ." February 22, 1909.
Mattes, M. *The Great Platte River Road.* Lincoln, Nebraska: University of Nebraska Press, 1987.
McCullough, David. *The Pioneers: The Heroic Story of the Settlers Who Brought the American Ideal West.* New York: Simon and Schuster, 2019.
Menke, Betty. *Robert Henri: Museum and Historical Walkway (RHM).* Cozad, Nebraska: Robert Henri Museum and Historical Walkway, 1985.
Menke, Betty. "The History of the Country School District No. 86 (RHM)." 1985.
Menke, Betty. "The History of the Little Church by the Park (RHM)." 1985.
Menke, Betty. "The History of the Willow Island Pony Express Express Station located in the City Park of Cozad, Nebraska (RHM)." 1985.
—. *The Rebirth of the Cozad Revelation - (RHM).* Cozad, Nebraska: Nebraska Committee for the Humanities, 1985.

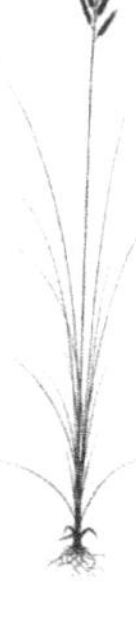

*Messages and Proclamations, 1862-1892, Governors of Nebraska.* Lincoln, Nebraska, 1892.

Meyer, Leta Moore. "Art in Omaha is Attracting Crowds." *Omaha Daily Bee*, January 12, 1919.

"Montclair Art Museum to H.B. Allen." November 30, 1955.

Moseley, Steve. "Cozad neighbor Willow Island traces its roots to delivery of mail in 1894." *Tri-City Trib*, September 10, 1998.

Myers, Roger. *Roots Web.* 2002. https://sites.rootsweb.com/~txmdhms/wanted_legends_print_olive_1.htm (accessed 12 26, 2020).

*National Archives - Homestead Act of 1862.* October 3, 2016. https://www.archives.gov/education/lessons/homestead-act (accessed August 27, 2019).

*National Park Service - Pony Express National Historic Trail.* 2020. https://www.nps.gov/poex/learn/historyculture/index.htm (accessed March 26, 2023).

National Park Service. "Scotts Bluff National Park Brochure." 2008.

*National Register of Historic Places Registration Form - Cozad Downtown Historic District (RHM).* Middletown, Wisconsin: Mead & Hunt, 2018.

*Nebraska Historical Marker: Mitchell and Ketchum Homesteads.* 2015. http://www.e-nebraskahistory.org/index.php?title=Nebraska_Historical_Marker:_Mitchell_and_Ketchum_Homesteads (accessed November 30, 2020).

*Nebraska Incorporation Places by Legal Classification.* 2014. https://neded.org/files/research/stathand/asect7.htm (accessed 3 19, 2021).

"Nebraska Lincoln Highway Scenic and Historic Byway Corridor Management Plan." Undated.

*Nebraska State Historical Society* . January 10, 2006. https://www.nebraskahistory.org/publish/publicat/timeline/dawson-john-l.htm (accessed November 15, 2021).

"Nebraska, State Census Collection, 1860-1885." *Cozad Precinct, Enumeration District 199.* 1885.

*Nebraska's Mormon Trail: A 19th Century Exodus.* Trail guide, Lincoln, Nebraska: Nebraska Travel and Tourism, Department of Economic Development, n.d.

Nelson, Marjorie. "The Riggs Family in America (RHM)." 1983.

Newton Bateman and Paul Selby. *Historical Encyclopedia of Illinois and History of McDonough County.* Chicago: Munsell Publishing Company, 1907.

"Norman Hirschl to H. B. Allen (RHM)." December 5, 1955.

*North Platte Enterprise.*April 4, 1874.

*North Platte Enterprise.*September 5, 1874.

*North Platte Republic.*June 19, 1875.

*North Platte Republican.*May 6, 1876.

"Omaha Exhibitions of Robert Henri - 1895-1925 (RHM)." n.d.

"Oregon Trail: National Historic Trail Map." n.d.

Osborne, Peter. *Elizabeth Grandin: A Clinton Treasure.* Clinton, New Jersey: Red Mill Museum Village, 2015.

Osborne, Peter. "Foster-Lewis Genealogy." 2021.

—. "From Cozad to State Prison: The Colorful Character of Miles Maryott (RHM)." Robert Henri Museum and Art Gallery, 2022.

—. *Images of America: Hacklebarney and Voorhees State Park.* Portsmouth, New Hampshire: Arcadia Publshing, 2004.

—. *No Spot in This Far Land Is More Immortalized: A History of Pennsylvania's Washington Crossing Historic Park.* Yardley, Pennsylvania: Yardley Press, 2014.

Osborne, Peter. *Paint Analysis of the Robert Henri Museum (RHM).* Cozad, Nebraska: Robert Henri Museum and Art Gallery, 2020.

—. *The Five Mile Woods: A History.* Doylestown, Pennsylvania: Heritage Conservancy, 2017.

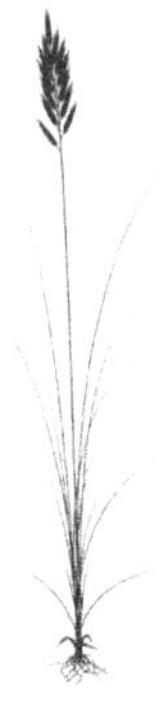

—. *The Trains of Our Memory: A History of the Railroad Museum of Pennsylvania.* Yardley, Pennsylvania: Yardley Press, 2016.

Osborne, Peter. *Through My Own Language: Robert Henri and His Portraits, Paintings and Sketches.* Robert Henri Museum and Art Gallery, 2019.

—. *Where Washington Once Led: A History of New Jersey's Washington Crossing State Park.* Yardley, Pennsylvania: Yardley Press, 2012.

Patterson, Jan. "Grant Application to Sunderland Foundation (RHM)." 2014 (?).

Paul Brungardt, Brungardt Engineering. "Structural Inspection of Robert Henri Museum - Hendee Hotel (RHM)." Kearney, April 29, 2004.

Paulsen, Larry, interview by Peter Osborne. (November 1, 2020).

Penry, Jerry. "The Short Cut Method." *The American Surveyor*, 2016.

Perkin, Robert. "Western Author Knocks U.S. Fiction." *Rocky Mountain News*, May 18, 1960.

Perlman, Bennard. "Chronology of Robert Henri." n.d.

—. *Robert Henri: His Life and Art.* Mineloa, New York: Dover Publications, 1991.

Perlman, Bennear. *Painters of the Ashcan School: The Immortal Eight.* Mineola, New York: Dover Books, 1979.

Phillips, Hazel. *Invincible Gambler, Folklore Series No. 9.* Lebanon, Ohio: Warren County Historical Society, 1970.

Potter, James. "Wearing the Hempen Neck-Tie: Lynching in Nebraska, 1858-1919." *Nebraska History, 93*, 2012.

Pousett-Dart, Nathaniel. *Distinguised American Artists: Robert Henri.* New York: Frederick A. Stokes Company, 1922.

Powell, John Wesley. *Report on the Lands of the Arid Region of the United States with a More Detailed Account of the Lands of Utah.* Washington, D.C. : US Government Printing Office, 1878.

Pushendorf, Bob. *National Register of Historic Places Nomination Fort - Lincoln Highway - Grand Island Seedling Mile.* Washington, DC: U.S. Department of Interior, 2013.

"Real Estate Transfers, 3.17.1883 (DPL)." *Rocky Mountain News.* 1883.

"Real Estate Transfers, 8.2.1883 (DPL)." *Rocky Mountain News.* 1883.

"Real Estate Transfers, 8.24.1883 (DPL)." *Rocky Mountain News.* n.d.

"Real Estate Transfers, 9.4.1883 (DPL)." *Rocky Mountain News.* 1883.

"Record of Appointment of Postmasters, 1832-1971, Records of the Post Office Department, Adams to Douglas Counties, Nebraska (NARA)." 1832-1971.

Rex German and Russ Czaplewski. *Battle of the Bridges.* Kearney, Nebraska: Morris Publishing, 1992.

Richardson, Robert, ed. *Henry Thoreau: A Life of the Mind.* Berkeley, California: University of California Press, 1986.

Ridley, Jo Ann. *Looking for Eulabee Dix.* Washington, DC: The National Museum of Women in Arts, 1997.

"Robert Cozad Scrapbook - 1878 (RHM)." 1878.

"Robert Gatewood to H. B. Allen (RHM)." December 10, 1956.

"Robert Gatewood to H. B. Allen (RHM)." June 20, 1961.

"Robert Gatewood to H. B. Allen (RHM)." January 10, 1956.

"Robert Henri Collection, Robert Henri Museum and Art Gallery, Cozad, Nebraska." n.d.

"Robert Henri to Robert Gatewood (RHM)." February 6, 1914.

"Robert Henri to Robert Gatewood (RHM)." August 12, 1928.

"Robert Henri: Selected Chronology (RHM)." 1990?

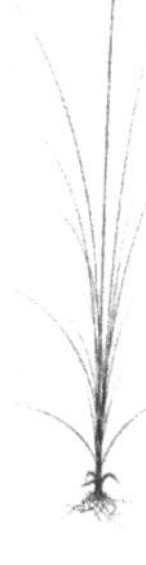

Rody, Laura. "Notes and Corrections to Book Manuscript, Vol 1 (RHM)." 2023.

Rody, Laura. "Notes and Corrections to Book Manuscript, Vol 2 (RHM)." 2023.

Rowley, Walter. "Farmer Turned Detective to Solve Case." *Omaha World Herald*, December 16, 1956.

"Russell Czaplewski to Smithsonian Magazine (DCHM)." *Smithsonian Magazine.* February 20, 1985.

S. R. Holen and K Holen. "The Mammoth Hypothesis: The Middle Wisconsin (Oxygen Isotype Stage 3) Peopling of North." In *Paleoamerican Odyssey (2nd Edition).* Texas A&M University Press, 2014.

Sandoz, Mari. *Son of the Gamblin' Man.* Lincoln: University of Nebraska Press, 1960.

Sarena Deglin and Eileen Myer Sklar. *John Sloan Manuscript Collection: A Finding Aid to the Collection in the Helen Farr Sloan Library & Archives.* Wilmington, Delaware: Delaware Art Museum, 2002.

Schooley, Sam. "Sketch of John J. Cozad (MS)." 1912.

*Scope: Feature Magazine of Tri-City Trib.* "Drive Started in September 1983." October 1984.

*Scope: TriCity Trib.* "An Album (RHM)." October 1984.

Scotts Bluff Area Visitors Bureau. *Western Nebraska: Scotts Bluff and Gering.* n.d.

Scrutchfield, Dora. "Alternative point of view for incident in Cozad's early years (RHM)." *Tri-City Trib*, September 10, 1998.

"Services Set for LV Dentist." 1966.

Seymor, Silas. "The Great Union Pacific Excursion, 1866." *Nebraska History 50*, 1969: 27-53.

Shumway, Grant Lee. "A Tribute to Robert Harvey." *NE History & Record of Pioneer Days, Vol VI, No 3 (part 1)* , 1918.

Smith, Diane. "Guide to the Robert Henri Papers (YCAL MSS 100)." 1997.

"Solicitation to Raise Funds for Renovation Work." September 2006.

"Stacy Easterday to Jan Patterson (RHM) 2011." n.d.

Stafford, Ron. *Robert Henri Archives Inventory.* 2019.

Sullivan, Shirley. *Miles Maryott: His Life and Times* . Kearney, Nebraska: Morris Publishing, 1996.

"Susan Brasch to Jan Patterson (RHM) 2011." n.d.

Taylor, Stephen. *"Go West, Young Man": The Mystery Behind the Famous Phrase - Hoosier State Chronicles.* July 9, 2015. https://blog.newspapers.library.in.gov/go-west-young-man-the-mystery-behind-the-famous-phrase/ (accessed June 27, 2022).

"Tess Lee to Frank Southrn (RHM)." June 17, 1891.

"Testimonial of Appreciation to John Cozad from Presbyterian Church of the United States (RHM)." June 19, 1875.

The Cossart Family Association. *The Cossart Family History (RHM).* 1939.

*The Cozad Local (RHM)* .November 27, 1956.

*The Cozad Local.* "Reveal True Story of John J. Cozad." November 27, 1956.

*The Cozad Republic.* "Julia Ann 'Grandma" Gatewood (Mrs. Robert)." July 23, 1909.

*The Gazette.* "Robert Gatewood - Cozad." July 16, 1884.

"The History of the Willow Island Pony Express Station Located in the City Park of Cozad, Nebraska (RHM)." n.d.

*The Otoe-Missouria Tribe.* 2023. https://www.omtribe.org/who-we-are/history/ (accessed June 16, 2023).

*The Texas General Land Office.* 2022. https://s3.glo.texas.gov/glo/history/archives/map-store/index.cfm#item/3091 (accessed 5 11, 2022).

*The Writers Almanac.* July 21, 2020. www.writersalmanac.com (accessed July 21, 2020).

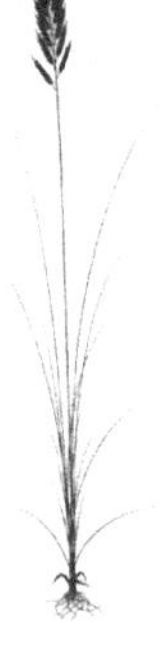

"Theresa Cozad to Julia Gatewood (RHM)." April 10, 1906.
"Theresa Cozad to Nettie Gatewood (RHM)." October 24, 1910.
*This Is A Report of Some of the Events and Testimony Relating to Alf Pearson's Death (RHM).* n.d.
"Traber Gatewood to Theresa Gatewood (RMH)." January 30, 1907.
"Traber Gatewood to Van Burke Gatewood (RHM) ." November 20, 1895.
*Tri-City Trib - Celebrate 88.* "John J. Cozad had a great vision for township location (RHM)." June 27, 1988.
*Tri-City Trib.* "Meridian Star . . . first Cozad paper." September 10, 1998.
*Tri-City Trib.* "Union Pacific Depot at the 100th Meridian, Cozad Nebraska." September 10, 1998.
*U.S., Civil War Draft Registrations Records, 1863-1865 for Ohio, 11th Congressional District, Vol I of Vol 4.* n.d.
*U.S., Register of Civil, Military, and Naval Service, 1863-1959, 1873, Vol. No. 1.* 1959.
"US Census Records - 1890 - 2019." n.d.
"US Census, 1900, 3rd District, Atlantic City, New Jersey, Enumeration District 17, Sheet 14." 1900.
"US Census, Cozad, Enumeration District 26-6, Sheet 81 B." 1940.
Vaughan, Carson. "The Meridian Chaser: Ricocheting between Climate Divides Old and New." *The Sierra Club Magazine*, Winter 2021.
"Violet Organ to H. B. Allen (RHM)." December 17, 1955.
Virginia and Lee McAlester. *A Field Guide to American Houses.* New York: A. Knopf, 1984.
Washington, Booker T. *Up From Slavery: An Autobiography.* 1901.
"Wayman May June 9, 2010." *North Platte Telegraph.* 2010.
*Waymarking.* 2022. https://www.waymarking.com/waymarks/WMK49Q_Former_Union_Pacific_Depot_Cozad_NE.
*We Relate.* December 29, 2020. https://www.werelate.org/wiki/Person:John_Simonson_(2).
Weingroff, Richard. *Highway History, The Lincoln Highway.* 2017. https://www.fhwa.dot.gov/infrastructure/lincoln.cfm (accessed March 28, 2020).
Werger, Crystal. "Railroad Comes to Plum Creek and Changes Life in Dawson County ." *Banner - Dawson County Historical Society Museum*, September 2019.
*West Virginia, U.S., Marriages Index, 1785-1971.* 2008.
"What Happened to John Cozad: Story from Atlantic City Reveals Final Story in the Life of John J. Cozad (RHM)." 1957.
"Willa Cather Archives." *Willa Cather to Earl Brewster and Achsah Barlow Brewster, February 21, 1923, Letter 2000.* 1923.
Wolfrom, Katelyn. *William Innes Homer – Robert Henri Papers: A Finding Aid to the Collection in the Helen Farr Sloan Library & Archives, Delaware Art Museum.* Wilmington, Delaware: Delaware Art Museum, 2008.
Wright, Preston. "Discoveries in Humans: Milkman Perceived Artist in Robert Henri and Gave Genius His Very First Criticsms." *The Lincoln Star*, October 18, 1925.
"Zoey Miller to Peter Osborne." September 13, 2022.

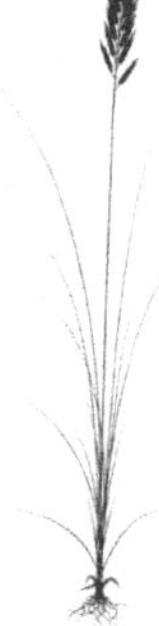

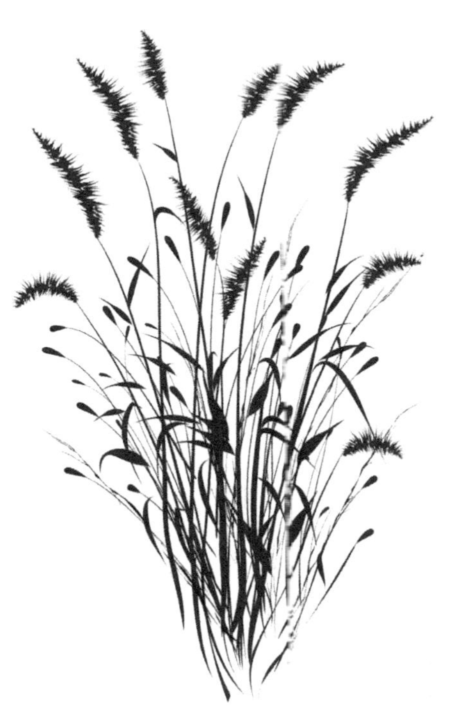

# Bibliography Essay

*Unfortunately, he (John Cozad) left his trail too shadowed and confused for the complete clarification demanded by non-fiction. I have kept to the facts available and only filled in the few holes necessary to reconstruct something of the crucible in which the dross of the son's (Robert Cozad) was burned away and the gold of freed to find itself.* [1]

Mari Sandoz
Son of The Gamblin' Man

One of the interesting ironies about Robert Henri is that even though he revealed his Nebraska roots to very few people, mainly family and his closest friend, John Sloan, there are four museums in the state that own his works today. Also, that since the opening decades of the twentieth century, his work has been on display here, even as he was at the height of his career. What would he think now that he is honored in a state that he and his family chose to disassociate from?

The state's three most important art museums – the Joslyn Art Museum in Omaha, the Sheldon Art Museum in Lincoln, and the Museum of Nebraska Art (MONA) in Kearney, all own works by Henri and archival materials too.

The Josyln currently owns two Henri paintings and they have been on permanent display as part of the larger American Collection exhibition. The Sheldon owns what is believed to be the most comprehensive collection of Henri's paintings and sketches in Nebraska. The museum owns seventeen paintings, and sixteen sketches. Over the years it has regularly featured Henri's paintings at the museum and has loaned them out for exhibitions.

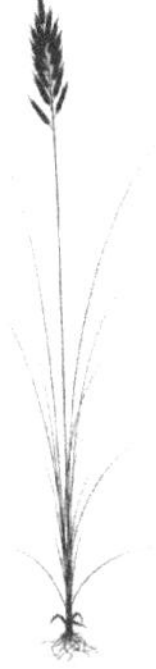

MONA is the owner of six of Henri's paintings including its most well-known *Portrait of Miss Eulabee Dix (Becker) in Wedding Gown* (1910). It is a remarkable full-length portrait of a woman who also lived in Nebraska. They also own three sketches and additional manuscripts. In addition, the museum has a remarkable collection of three thousand works of various artists in diverse media ranging from nineteenth century pieces to contemporary art.

Finally, there is the Robert Henri Museum and Art Gallery, which owns or manages an amazing collection of Robert Henri's paintings and sketches either painted by him, or attributed to him or his students, and is said to be the largest on display in the country. It also owns the works of three of his students. While there are museums that own collections of Henri's works, the Robert Henri Museum and Art Gallery has more on exhibition

### THE ROBERT HENRI ARCHIVE AT THE MUSEUM

The Robert Henri Museum maintains a large collection of resources related to Henri's life, career, his colleagues and exhibitions undertaken before and after his death. A research library is available to scholars and the visiting public alike. However, no systematic effort was made to compile and organize the large volume of materials that the museum had collected until recently.

The museum also owns an important collection of materials related to the Cozad family, Robert Henri and the history of the community. While most of its collection is made up of secondary sources, there are some original family documents, including letters, scrapbooks, and family photographs in addition to personal items from various donors over the last four decades. There are also copies of primary sources, various research papers, newspaper clippings, exhibition booklets, and the definitive genealogical materials created by Marilyn Cozad and Martha Pilger.

A significant collection of transcriptions of documents relate to John Cozad's real estate transactions and his various legal problems. Because of various lawsuits, the issues of the titles related to some of the Cozad properties were not resolved until, at least in one case, the 1920s. These materials provide new insights into the family's troubles in Cozad and reveal the legal aspects of those troubles.

In 2019 a new archive room was created at the museum and a number of primary, and secondary sources that had previously been stored in boxes and old file cabinets were rediscovered. They were invaluable to the creation of this book. This effort is a major contribution to the body of work about the Cozads and the Nebraska experience. In addition, the author has been acquiring new research materials to enhance the collection and to widen the scope of what has been collected previously. All these documents were placed into acid-free files and boxes as they were found.

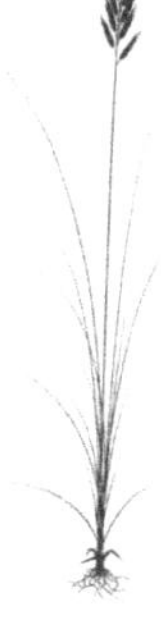

A question that remains is what happened to the voluminous collection of paperwork that John J. Cozad must have maintained for all of his real estate transactions. While we know all of his paperwork prior to 1876 was destroyed in the fire that consumed the small town, there must have been many files created after that. It would include all of his bookkeeping paperwork and personal records of which he surely kept along with remaining items from Theresa, John A. or Robert. Were all of those records left with the Gatewoods when he disappeared from Cozad? Did he take them with him, or have them sent to him? Was it presumed that he would be able to reclaim the materials at some future date when his legal challenges were resolved? When did the fire occur that destroyed the family's records that the Gatewoods had? And, finally, were the records destroyed by family members at a later date, perhaps after John and Theresa died? All these questions may never be resolved.

### The 1880 Cozad Diary and Scrapbooks

The 1880 diary of Robert Cozad is a remarkable primary source, and in fact may be the most valuable of all of the resources that the Robert Henri Museum has had access to since its creation in the 1980s. The journal is also a state treasure. If all Robert Henri's journals were transcribed collectively, they would match the treasure the journals of Captains Meriwether Lewis and William Clark. The entries provide a fascinating glimpse into the fledgling community's life, the agricultural economy, the bridge that John Cozad attempted to build across the Platte River and the personalities of the Cozad community. One of its most significant aspects is that it provides insights into the hotel and private residence of the Cozads after they committed to living in Nebraska full time. They are the only contemporary description of the building and its uses known to exist until the 1930s.

It is believed that Robert Cozad began keeping a journal, or a notebook as he called it, on September 23, 1879, the same year that he graduated from Chickering Institute in Cincinnati Ohio. He would have been fourteen at the time. He kept journaling for the rest of his life and the following journals still survive elsewhere including the following:

1881, 1883, 1886, 1887, 1888, 1889, 1890, 1891, 1896-1901, 1902, 1903, 1904, 1906, 1908, 1909, 1910, 1911, 1912, 1913, 1914, 1915, 1919, 1922, 1924, 1926, and 1928

One mystery is regarding the location of the 1879, 1882 and 1884 diaries, which would prove to be as valuable as the 1880 diary. We know the first one exists because of a note in the 1880 diary. The 1882 diary may have been lost to the upheaval in the lives of the family in the aftermath of the shooting of Alf Pearson by John Cozad.

The 1884 diary may have met a similar fate because that was the year that Robert left Nebraska after the hotel and other properties were sold to Stephen Hendee and his family changed their identity. Yet, the 1883 diary survives, so that only makes the story more confusing. Some items, including the 1880 diary, came into the possession of the Gatewoods after the Cozads left but most were destroyed in a fire. But, what those items were, is unknown. It is remarkable that

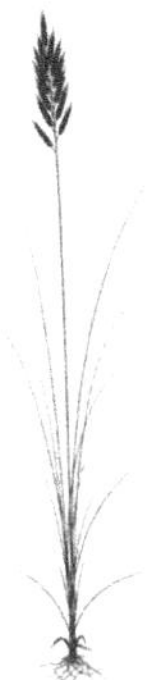

the diaries from the Nebraska years have survived despite several near calamities.

Today, the original copy of the 1880 diary resides in the collection of the Sheldon Museum of Art in Lincoln, Nebraska. It contains entries from May to November of that year and is one hundred and twenty-two pages long. Since the Cozads lived in the hotel from 1880 until 1881, it is an important primary source. The Robert Henri Museum's intern Jake Whitney created an annotated version of the diary in 2022.

It has been digitized and the Sheldon staff was kind enough to let the Robert Henri Museum have access to it. The museum also has had copies of pages of the diary that came from an unknown source, created perhaps in 2016, and that are much clearer to read than the Sheldon copy. Robert Gatewood did loan the diary to the Archives of American Art at the Smithsonian Institution and they microfilmed the manuscript. Perhaps the museum's copies of pages and illustrations came from that film.

Another important piece of the Nebraska legacy of Robert Henri are his boyhood scrapbooks. Robert Cozad was a keeper of scrapbooks as his mother gave him a new one every year for his birthday. The museum owns three of Robert Cozad's scrapbooks thanks to the Robert Henri estate and the family of Janet LeClair who gave them to the museum many years ago. They provide part of the framework for the telling the story of an artist whose young life was filled with travel and various adventures. They also provided critical historical information about the family's homes in Cincinnati, Cozaddale, Cozad and Denver.

## Revealing The Cozad Story

A significant, but small collection, that the museum owns are the letters of friends, and Cozad and Gatewood family members. The Dawson County Historical Museum and the Henri Museum both own transcriptions of some of the letters. The transcriptions were made by Marilyn Cozad. Marilyn was a great supporter of the museum and contributed a definitive family genealogy to the archive along with many letters that discussed her research findings.

These letters provide fascinating insights into the Cozad and Gatewood families. Most importantly they reveal that while the family did maintain their secrecy about the disappearance of the Cozads to the outside world, there were conversations going on within the family, which is very different from the story that was told at the museum to visitors in previous decades.

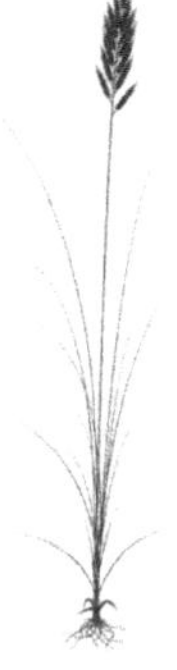

Another important source is the diary of Deborah Burgess Gatewood, wife of Traber Gatewood. The museum has a photocopy of the original. It provides a wealth of information about the difficulty of the early lives of the homesteaders, along with firsthand accounts of the family dynamics not only with her husband but his relatives, and, the Cozads. It is one of the few contemporary family accounts that is known to exist and confirms much of what has been said about the

Cozads.

The most significant primary source regarding the Cozad's disappearance and their new life in the East that survives is Robert Gatewood's *Who Was Robert Henri?* This unpublished 1932 manuscript, prepared by Dr. Gatewood, was created just three years after Robert Henri had died and one year before Frank Southrn, his brother, died. It is the only known document that survives that provides many of the details about the disappearance of the Cozads from Nebraska. It also discusses the visits of Gatewood to the Cozads in New York, along with other interesting facts.

A copy of the original manuscript is deposited at the Delaware Art Museum in Wilmington, Delaware, and the Henri Museum also has a photocopy. There are some errors in the manuscript, but given that there may have been some faulty memories, or intentional misleading memories on John Cozad's behalf, it still remains an important resource.

The second most significant source that reveals the uncovering of the Cozad story is the special edition of *The Cozad Local* that was headlined *Reveal True Story of John J. Cozad.* This section provided an article written by Dr. Gatewood along with a transcript of Robert Cozad's 1880 diary and additional family material.[2]

The museum also acquired a collection of letters between Harry Allen, Robert Gatewood and Violet Organ which were written during the most critical moments in 1955-1956 when the entire Henri story was being revealed to the world and, in large part, because of the efforts of these three indviduals.

A number of visitors to the museum are Cozad descendants and while most think that they are directly related to John J. Cozad, they are actually related to one of John's brothers as his only children to live to adulthood, Robert and Johnny, each had no children that survived to produce offspring. For many years the late Marilyn Cozad and Marsha Pilger worked on and produced an extensive seven volume genealogy entitled *Cozad Connections: Twenty-Eight Thousand Descendants of Jacque and Lydia (Willems) Cossart.* It is a remarkable work of research on the family. Through this effort one can see what the familial relationships were between those early colonists of Cozad, Nebraska, and how their relationships, which began back in Ohio and elsewhere, continued here.

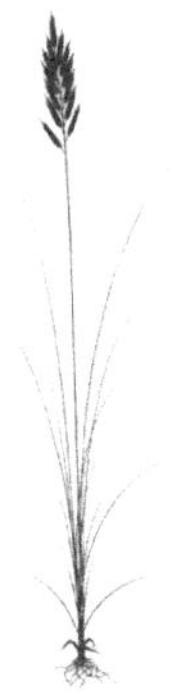

Local English teacher, Betty Menke, wrote an excellent synopsis of the complicated Cozad story. Menke's *The Rebirth of the Cozad Revelation*, was written in 1985, and funded by the Nebraska Committee for Humanties (now Humanities Nebraska). It was the first locally written manuscript to comprehensively tell the story of the Nebraska legacy of Robert Henri and provide a history of the museum building in some detail. Others had written brief histories on specific topics, and the museum did have a docent notebook that volunteers used for giving tours, but nothing like Betty's work had ever been undertaken or sold in the museum's gift shop. It is an important resource and provided many insights to the author.

Betty also wrote the histories of the Pony Express Station, the Country School, District No. 86 and the New Hope Evangelical Country Church, or the Christian Science Society Church, which are the only attempts to document those buildings distant pasts. They, like *The Rebirth of the Cozad Revelation*, were funded by the Nebraska Committee for Humanities. She and her husband Roger, as part of *The Rebirth of the Cozad Revelation* effort, interviewed a number of area residents which reveals information about the Cozads.

The author has continued to collect resources related to the history of the building including consultant's and engineering reports that examine the building's architecural challenges that various museum boards have faced over the years.

Many files and scrapbooks also relate to the institutional history of the museum. Members, for most of the museum's existence, have been diligent in keeping a record of the major developments that have occurred, along with photographing the operations of the museum.

### Other Local Resources

The Wilson Public Library owns a large collection of local history materials which were consulted for this project. They have obituaries, genealogical files along with files about Robert Henri and the Cozad family and land records of the early settlement. It was there, for example, that the author began to first see the results of the national attention that Dr. Robert Gatewood received when he began writing about the Cozad family, their removal from the community and their altered identity. The story was published by the Associated Press and picked up by countless newspapers and media outlets.

The 100$^{th}$ Meridian Museum has an impressive collection of local history materials, including materials on Robert Henri and the Cozad family. They are the successor organization to the Cozad Historical Society and are located in the building next to the Robert Henri Museum.

The Dawson County Historical Museum owns an extensive collection of county-related materials, including microfilmed copies of period newspapers. Unfortunately, the newspaper collection does not include any of the early Cozad papers. If those are ever found, they would prove to be a gold mine of contemporary information. However, the newspapers they do own provided a wealth of information from the 1890s forward along with a collection of materials related to Cozad.

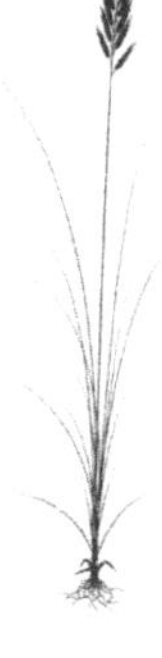

One of the best accounts of the shooting of Alf Pearson by John Cozad appeared in the October 2013 issue of the *True West* magazine. It is beautifully illustrated and written by Bob Boze Bell, one of the West's great writers and artists. the late Jan Patterson, then the Robert Henri Museum's director contributed research to the article.

## HISTORY OF THE HENDEE HOTEL AND COZAD

In researching the book, the author found that there were six sources that were critical to the telling of the story of the Cozads residency in the community that was named for them including the history of the Hendee Hotel, and the larger community. They include the *National Register of Historic Places Registration Form for the Hendee Hotel, The Riggs Family in America 1632-1982, The Early History of the Cozad Community and Pioneer Families: 1873-1998, The Rebirth of the Cozad Revelation, The Battle of the Bridges* and *Son of the Gamblin' Man.*

Several of these resources provide detailed information about the history of the former Hendee Hotel, now known as the Robert Henri Museum. In 1979, one hundred years after it had been constructed, a nomination to place the Hendee Hotel on the United States Department of the Interior's National Register of Historic Places was researched, prepared, reviewed and approved. Kieth Buss, then the president of the Cozad Historical Society, prepared and signed the final nomination form. Some of the information for the nomination may have come from Deline Lewis, then the owner of the building. Buss also prepared a number of other research papers about Cozad history that remain important sources.[3]

The nomination provided the most detailed architectural history of the building that existed until this book was published. Buss was an excellent researcher and prepared several papers on the Cozad story, all of which are impeccably sourced, well-written, and provide accurate interpretations.

Another important source that provides some of the more detailed accounts of the museum building and its earliest history is included in a chapter of Marjorie Nelson's *The Riggs Family in America 1632-1982* and published in 1983. The chapter discusses Joseph and Clara Riggs, who ran the hotel in its first year of operation. This book provides several recollections from contemporaries on the founding of Cozad. It also includes a description of the hotel and its operations.

It is worth observing that there are some notable mistakes in some of the information that has been previously presented. As with so much of the telling of the Cozad story, there are differing versions. For example, there are major differences regarding the burning of the Johnson House in Plum Creek, the shooting of Alf Pearson and the departure of the Cozads which appear to have come from various traditions that were passed down. In addition, there was often no attribution of sources included.

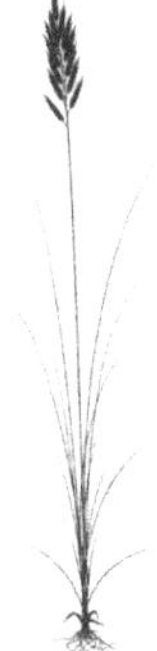

An interesting, but questionable source of information was that 1925 history in booklet form that was created by the eighth grade students in the Cozad school system. While it makes for fascinating reading, too many of the facts as presented turn out to be incorrect. It has been of such interest because the writers were only forty years beyond the original settlement of the community.

*The Early History of the Cozad Community and Pioneer Families: 1873-1998* remains an invaluable source of material about the formation of the community and compiles an encyclopedia of information about the early decades of the community and its significant participants. The original edition, published in 1955, was compiled by Charles E. Allen. Allen was an important figure in Cozad serving as the mayor, a member of the town council as well as being the president of the Cozad State Bank and active in community organizations. He also built the Allen Opera House in the downtown.[4] And, curiously, Allen was a witness to John J. Cozad's last return to the community in 1894 and was an accidental participant in his controversial land dealings during that visit.[5]

The booklet was reproduced for the 1973 centennial of the community. In 1998, the one hundred and twenty-fifth anniversary of the creation of the community, the booklet was enhanced considerably with a new section on Cozad families, agriculture and businesses.

The best researched non-fictional work on the Cozad family's time in Nebraska is the book written by Rex German and Russ Czaplewski. First published in 1988, and reprinted a number of times, *The Battle of the Bridges*, is a historian's dream. Well written, and well sourced, its focus is on the various efforts to bridge the Platte River in Dawson County. It recounts John Cozad's expensive attempt to build a sod bridge but it also describes the major challenges that the Cozads faced or problems that were created by their own actions. Aside from the information found in the primary sources themselves, this is the best book written about the history of Cozad.

### MARI SANDOZ

The most important book that tells the story of Robert Henri's boyhood in Nebraska is Mari Sandoz's *Son of the Gamblin' Man*. Published in 1960, it is an excellent fictional account of Robert Henri's life on the Great Plains and the challenges that those early settlers faced. Sandoz's book is the result of extensive research, for which she was well known, and is considered to be an accurate portrayal of the times when John and Theresa Cozad were living in Cozad with their sons, John A. and Robert. As the author points out, the dialogue between the characters is contrived.

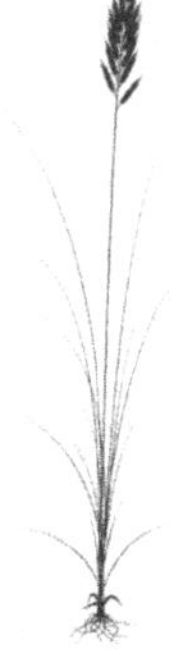

The author reviewed the research materials found in Sandoz's collection of notes that she used for her book. During the course of his research the author was able to confirm her research with other sources that he was using. In looking at her records, one can see the basis for her effort, and follow her research trail which included interviews, letters, newspaper articles and her own knowledge of Nebraska history. She also relied heavily on the 1880 diary of Robert Cozad.

Her notes, created while compiling her novel, *Son of the Gamblin' Man*, are an important resource because she was then just fifty years removed from the series of events that led the Cozads to leave their town but also their story of the creation of Cozad. She was also able to interview people who knew the Cozads or had been early settlers in the region and also track down other threads in the story.

Aside from Sandoz, very few people have ever explored the complicated story in depth or tried to make some sense of its many twists and turns. Her book played a significant part in the complicated revealing of the Cozad story to the general public and the residents of the town as recounted earlier in this book. Sandoz's correspondence provides contemporary accounts of how that revelation ultimately came to happen because of a series of chance encounters. Many of those letters are found in *Letters of Mari Sandoz: Edited and With an Introduction by Helen Winter Stauffer.*

One of the questions that remains regarding the *Son of the Gamblin' Man* is what happened to the relationship between Sandoz and Dr. Robert Gatewood. After their initial contacts they did not correspond again. Perhaps Sandoz had done enough of her own research and did not feel that she needed or perhaps even trusted his information, which is speculation on the author's part. As can be seen in her notes she relied heavily on the materials that he had written and provided for the 1956 edition of the *Cozad Local.*

He would later reflect that Sandoz had not included what he felt might have been the more interesting or amazing parts of the story. Gatewood may have also felt that Sandoz had used his story and knowledge for her own benefit because he did consider legal action against her after the publication of the book.

Today there are several institutions dedicated to the preservation of the legacy of Sandoz. The Mari Sandoz High Plains Heritage Center located in Chadron, Nebraska, celebrates the life of the writer, her literature and the culture of the High Plains.

The Center features exhibits, a preservation and preparation workroom equipped with a digital imaging laboratory, and an archival library. The Center also serves as the repository for the Mari Sandoz Heritage Society, which has loaned its expansive collection of Sandoz materials for the exhibits and archives. The Society assists in educational programming and encourages research and publishing about the High Plains region.

The University of Nebraska-Lincoln's Love Library in Lincoln, Nebraska, houses the Sandoz Collection, which is composed of manuscripts, correspondence, research files, notes, maps, and Sandoz's personal library. In addition to her own work the collection also contains books, articles and taped interviews about Sandoz. This collection is also an important source for history and literature of Nebraska and the Great Plains region.

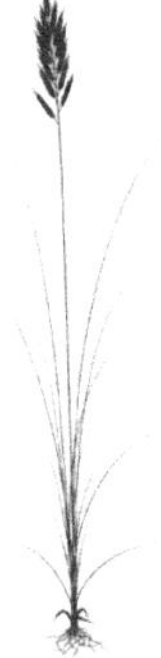

## NEBRASKA HISTORY

For the sections of the book on the larger state of Nebraska history, the author relied primarily on the *History of Nebraska* (3rd edition) by James Olson and Ronald Naugle. The authors did an excellent job trying to encapsulate so much history into a readable volume on the state's fascinating past. This book was particularly helpful in writing the first two chapters.

### The Overland Trails

The Overland Trails have been explored in numerous works over the decades in addition to many monuments and several interpretive centers. There are at least five historic sites in Nebraska where one can experience the trials and travails of those weary travelers including The Archway in Kearney, the Mormon Trail Interpretive Center in Omaha, Rock Creek State Park in Fairbury, Scotts Bluff National Monument in Scottsbluff and Chimney Rock Historic Site near Bayard. Historic Nebraska maintains a beautiful interpretive center there. All are worth visiting.[6]

### The Union Pacific Railroad

The sprawling history of the Union Pacific Railroad is a fascinating one and is also a national story that continues to this day. For the purposes of this work, the most important source were *Nothing Like It in the World* by Stephen Ambrose and the Olsen and Naugle book. While the UP history is complex, this book only deals with its part in the Cozad story and the 100th Meridian.

### Miles Maryott

The most important resource available on Miles Maryott is *Miles Maryott: His Life and Times* by Shirley Sullivan. While it discusses Maryott and his family's ties to Cozad, the book does not mention the family's tie to the Hotel Hendee. It does however provide important insights into Maryott's career and the paintings that the museum owns.

### Robert Henri Biographers

Robert Henri's two biographers, William Homer, author of *Robert Henri and His Circle*, and Bennard Perlman, author of *Robert Henri: His Art and Life*, both wrote briefly about the Cozads' time in Nebraska, although their main focus was on Henri's remarkable artistic and teaching career. Homer's work was the first to explore Henri's life and remains one of two definitive works. He devoted one chapter of his groundbreaking book to Henri's Ohio, Nebraska and Colorado legacy. The book was written with the assistance of Violet Organ. She was the sister of Marjorie, Robert's second wife, and the subject of some of his paintings.

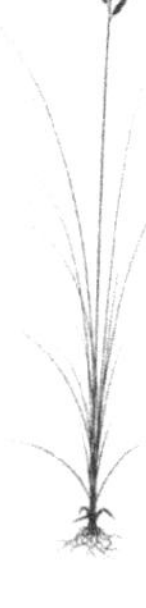

It is also worth remembering that the first edition of Homer's book was written in 1969, and then revised in 1988, just four years after the Robert Henri Museum had been founded. The 1988 edition is the one that this author used because it included corrected and new information. Homer interviewed Harry B. Allen, who was the author and compiler for the *Cozad Local* special section revealing the story about the disappearance of the family in 1882-84. Also, he spoke to Robert Gatewood, Betty Menke, an important member of the Robert Henri Museum, and of course Janet LeClair, executor of the Henri estate.

Bennard Perlman, an important Baltimore artist and author of a number of art books, provides excellent insights into Henri's life in his book *Robert Henri: His Life and Art.* Perlman's book, published in 1991, is considered by some to be the best Henri biography. He spent a great deal of time in primary sources related to the Ohio, Nebraska and Colorado chapters of Henri's life. Perlman also created a valuable timeline of the artist's life which was very helpful in completing the story and played an important part in the research undertaken for the Henri Museum's exhibit *Through My Own Language: Robert Henri and His Portraits, Paintings and Sketches* in 2019-2020. Perlman also wrote *The Immortal Eight,* which is still considered one of the most important histories of the Ashcan School or Movement, of which Henri is described as the founder.

Violet Organ had intended to write a full-length biography of Robert Henri but died before it was completed, which is unfortunate given her proximity to Henri's life. In the letters that the Robert Henri Museum owns, she speaks of the book being almost completed.

While Homer used parts of her manuscript in his work, he must have been in a difficult position because, for example, Organ did not believe that the Cozads had ever gone to Denver according to a letter in the Robert Henri archives. That is clearly incorrect. She relayed an incorrect date as to when John Cozad was exonerated. These insights come from Gatewood family members who met with her. While this author has never seen her manuscript, the letters that the museum owns offer one perspective of what she knew.

A final significant writer who knew the family well was Dr. Robert Gatewood. His earliest manuscript is *Who Was Robert Henri?* was prepared in 1932 and is a fascinating document given that he knew all the principals. He would write other pieces in the future, particularly after 1956, but the manuscript was closer to the actual events and in fact written three years after Henri's death.

Another source concerning the life of Robert Henri is a DVD entitled *Robert Henri and the Art Spirit* that was produced in 1990 by Spence Film Productions in Lincoln, Nebraska. Even though it is more than twenty years old it still is a very good documentary of the life of Henri.

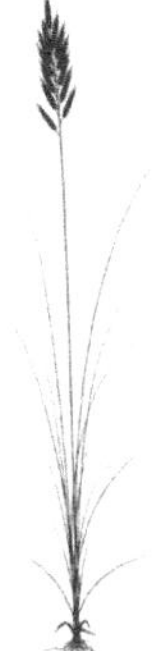

## Robert Henri Collections

Collections of Robert Henri archival materials are scattered across America. The largest collection is the one still owned by the Robert Henri estate (2022). It is remarkably intact and encyclopedic. The collection contains materials from his early life right up until his death. It includes his inventory of paintings, correspondence, diaries, letters and a myriad of publications with topics that would be fascinating to a biographer, and have been in the past. At present it is maintained in a private and secure location.

One of the most interesting aspects of Henri's career and life is how much of the primary source materials associated with him are scattered in such a variety of collections, never mind his artwork which are in musuems around the world. It can be presumed that some of the items wound up in private collections because of a friendship or relationship with Henri. In other cases, perhaps his wife Marjorie or executors of his estate, gave things away or sold them. Items continue to surface at auctions and in private collections and sometimes are donated to the Henri museum.

Several notable repositories contain Henri materials. A substantial collection of Robert Henri's papers resides at Yale University's Beinecke Library. They were a gift from Violet Organ's estate which she had inherited from Robert Henri's estate. The donation made by John C. LeClair in 1963 includes correspondence, writings, photographs, color investigations and various printed materials.[7]

The Yale collection was microfilmed and now is also included in the collection of the Archives of American Art at the Smithsonian Institution in Washington, D.C. The collections include additional material lent by the late Janet LeClair, the executor of the Henri estate, and then donated to Yale University. Included are his diaries (including the 1880 manuscript), and other items of interest.

There is also the William Innes Homer - Robert Henri Papers collection in the Delaware Art Museum which includes copies of all the references Homer used when writing his biography, *Robert Henri and His Circle*.[8] Also located there is the John Sloan Manuscript Collection which contains Robert Gatewood's revealing manuscript about the Cozad family's past and their flight from Nebraska. It is also worth noting that the Delaware museum hosted what may have been the largest collection of Henri paintings in a retrospective in 1984 that traveled to several other major institutions. The Robert Henri Museum has copies of all the slides that were created of the paintings and has produced a Powerpoint program for its gallery.

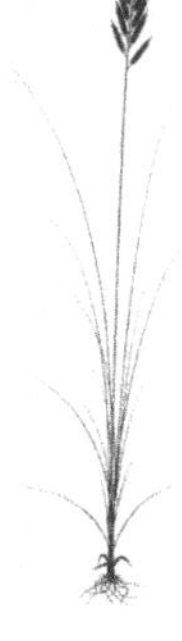

The Mari Sandoz Collection located at the Love Library in Lincoln includes manuscripts, correspondence, research files, notes, and maps, of this famed Nebraska writer. Most important are her notes that were the basis of her research for *Son of the Gamblin' Man*, her fictional account of Robert Henri's boyhood in Nebraska. The collection is also microfilmed and available for use by researchers.

A number of archival items can be found at the Sheldon Art Museum in Lincoln, Nebraska and the Museum of Nebraska Art (MONA) in Kearney, Nebraska. MONA for example owns an eclectic collection that includes pages from Robert Cozad's scrapbooks, envelopes, and letters related to John Cozad's railroad transactions. They were given by an anonymous donor from Cozad. One must wonder how those items got to the donor.

## Remaining Mysteries

### The Ohio Chapter

The Ohio chapter deserves more research than has been given not only here, but in the major biographies. It is where John Jackson Cozad was born, but also where he spent a considerable number of years living in Allensville, Cincinnati and Cozaddale. The article entitled *Invincible Gambler, Folklore Series No. 9* by Hazel Phillips provides some interesting tidbits about the Cozads but this author found it often to be unreliable as he knew the Cozad story in much more detail. But she must have found her information from somewhere unless it was speculation. Another publication entitled *Warren County Local History: Remembering the Forgotten Local Town of Cozaddale* was also helpful as it provided more insights into the community that Cozad created. *The History of Warren County* provided additional information about the creation of Cozaddale and what subsequently happened to it.

*The History of Cincinnati, Ohio,* and *Cincinnati: The Queen City 1788-1912* provided information about what the city would have looked like when the Cozads were living there and also about the institutions that they went to like the Opera House or the manufacturing expositions.

This book and Perlman's book contain material about the land transactions of John Cozad in Ohio, but this topic needs additional research. Not only would it reveal the nature of his holdings there, but it might also provide more insights as to why he left so quickly.

Another line of inquiry is the positions that John and Theresa took with regard to loyalties during the Civil War. Were they Southern sympathizers or Unionists? And, did John serve in the Union Army?

Was it possible that Theresa Gatewood Cozad, may have been a Southern sympathizer although there is no evidence of that? The Gatewoods had been in Virginia for more than two centuries and the pull of that state may have been a strong one for her when she was in Ohio. More research will need to be done on this subject.

### The Colorado Chapter

While the Colorado chapter appears to be short lived, there is still much to be found about it too. For example, the Cozads owned several parcels in Denver, along with a mine in Leadville. The hay business operations predated their move to Denver, Where the family lived from 1881-83 there is probably not as much material, as compared to Cozaddale or Cozad, it was as Robert Cozad noted, the family's hope was to make their fortunes there. Sadly, other influences prevailed.

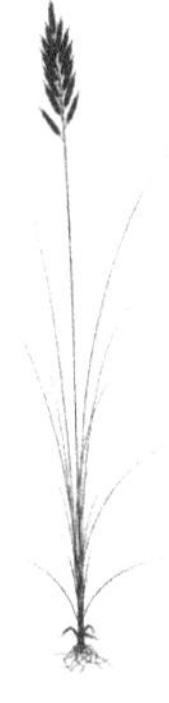

### THE NEW JERSEY CHAPTER

While the New Jersey chapter of the Cozad's lives goes beyond the scope of this book, more research needs to be done in the first year or two that the Cozads, with their new identities, transitioned to a new life in Atlantic City. Research might uncover exactly when the Cozads all regrouped at the oceanfront city and if John had been there prior to moving in 1882 or 1883. In addition, Cozad's time on the boardwalk was filled with controversy and legal fights, all of which deserve further investigation.

### WARRANTING FURTHER EXPLORATION

The Cozad story is a complicated one, and a number of avenues warrant further exploration. The Cozads were great documentarians and were the *keepers of paper* so to speak. While a large body of materials remain in various archives including the Archives of American Art, Yale's Beinecke Library, the Robert Henri estate, the Delaware Art Museum, and a smattering of smaller collections at the Museum of Nebraska Art and the Sheldon Art Museum, this author believes that that there are other materials still to be discovered in smaller archives. Perhaps they are gone, destroyed perhaps at the time of Theresa's death or even Robert's death, but with all the discoveries revealed in this book, it seems likely that there is still more to find.

For example, there are the numerous real estate transactions of John J. Cozad in Ohio, Nebraska, Colorado and New Jersey. While the museum owns a small collection of personal family papers including some legal documents, the author believes that there is a much larger story that surrounds the various land transactions. Theresa Cozad's correspondence to the Union Pacific states that John Cozad had sold about one hundred and twenty-five sections of land, or eighty thousand acres.[9] Cozad's legal transactions provided for controversy and troubles between him and other landowners, especially Stephen Hendee. There must have been voluminous files on all those transactions that began in the 1860s and continued until his death in 1906. Were they disposed of when he died, or Theresa died? Perhaps they were discarded when Henri died or sometime after that.

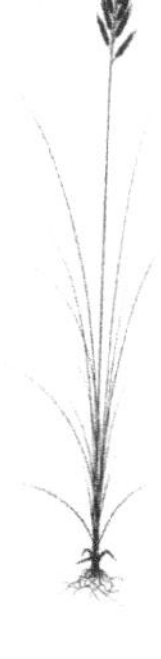

The whole relationship between the Union Pacific Railroad and John Cozad is worth further exploration, especially the initial purchase of what has been believed to be forty thousand acres. To track down all of the property transfers would be a herculean task but one that would certainly provide more insights into the real estate dealings of Cozad. The author suspects that the relationship with the railroad was a more complicated one than has often been portrayed by others, and some evidence of the issues that created challenges in that relationship were discussed earlier in the book. Some of the evidence, at least from the Cozad side, can be found in the museum's archives.

John Cozad, along with his sons, regularly had legal troubles beginning in

Ohio and continuing with residents in Dawson County and then Atlantic City. He was almost like *Pig Pen*, a character from the *Peanuts* comic strip by Charles Schulz, who always had a cloud of dust swirling around him. Further research would probably turn up more legal troubles to be sure.

The life of Frank Southrn, formerly John A. Cozad, who became a prominent physician in Philadelphia would certainly provide insights into the Cozad family's time in Nebraska, especially since he returned to Nebraska at least once, in 1895, after his exoneration the year before from the charges of alleged arson in Lexington. Robert Foresman wrote a fascinating paper called *The Other Son of the Gamblin' Man* that provides insights into Southrn's life but in particular speculates about Johnny's troubles in Cozad before his disappearance.[10] Surely there must be more about Robert's life in the telling of Johnny's life.

Much, much more could be written about the Cozad community and its life. Sandoz's notes contain lots of information about various citizens as well as in the surviving newspapers. The land records would also provide insights as to where they were coming from and who they were.

The author sees the Cozaddale-Cozad-Denver-Atlantic City, or Ohio-Nebraska-Colorado-New Jersey connection as a continuous thread. They are all tied together because of property and investments, and they are co-mingled by chronology. Much more research needs to be done in the Cozaddale, Denver and Atlantic City historical records. Perhaps items would be found there that would better explain what happened with the properties and investments, particularly in the immediate aftermath of the Pearson tragedy and clarify the chronology of the Cozad's lives.

### The Robert Henri Museum and Art Gallery

A detailed look is needed at the institutional history of the Robert Henri Museum. This book has only looked at the Cozad family history and that of the Hendee Hotel and just touched only lightly on the museum's creation and development. It is, however, a remarkable story. While the author had wanted to include that story in this book, it proved to be a project that required its own book because of the many twists and turns that it took. It would have also added a significant number of pages to this book which is much longer than originally planned.

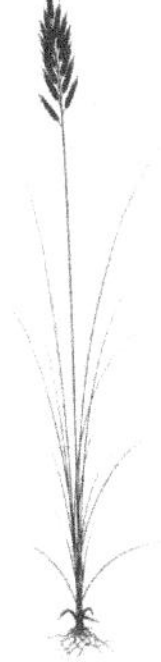

Also, over the decades there have been many projects, not listed here, that were undertaken that were not well documented, and further research needs to be accomplished in telling that part of the building's history.

Even with this four-hundred-plus page book and Mari Sandoz's three-hundred-and-thirty-page book, *Son of the Gamblin' Man*, there is still so much more to discover. As in so much of the Robert Henri story, there are still gaps in our knowledge that need to be tracked down.

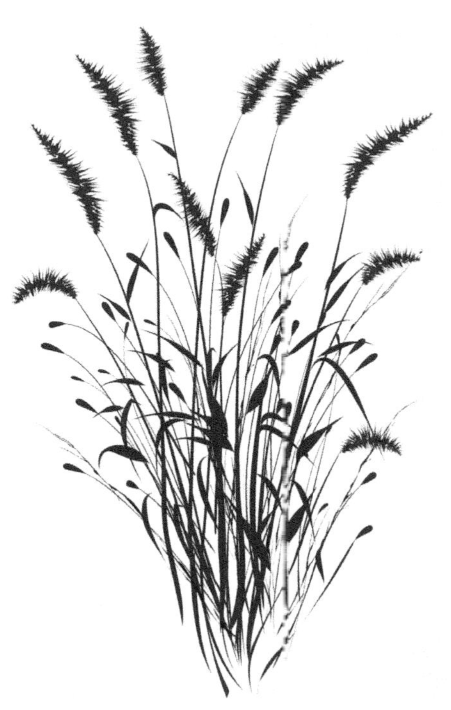

# Index

## A



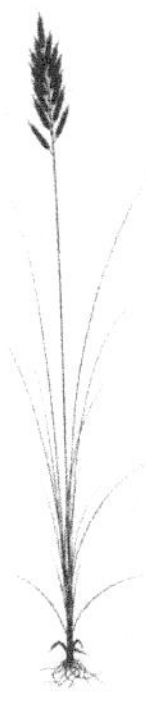

**B**



**C**



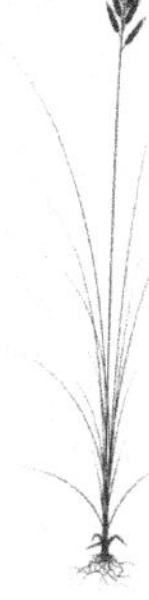

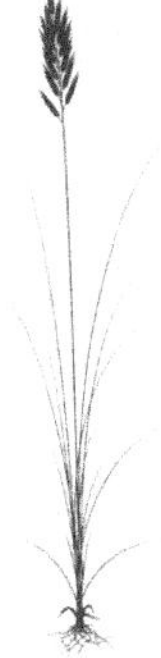

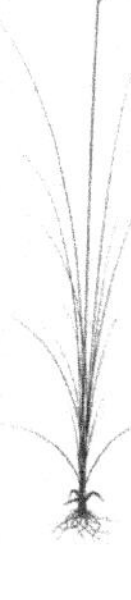

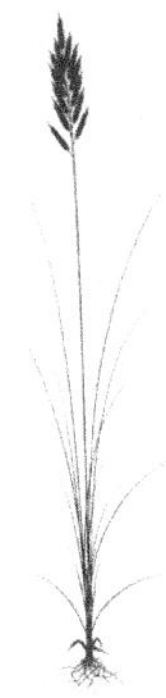

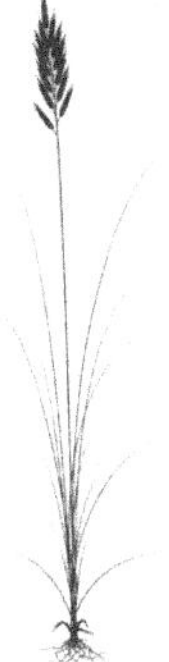

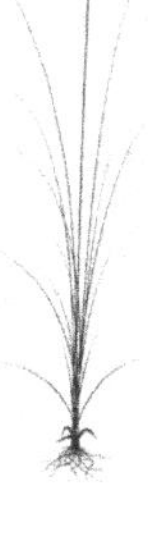

**K**



**L**



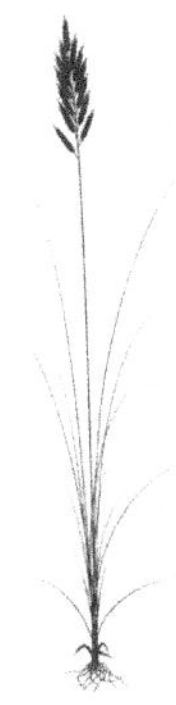

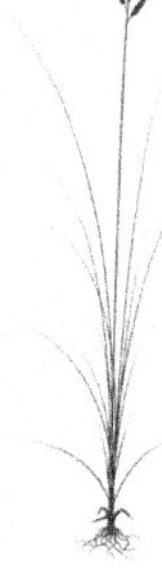

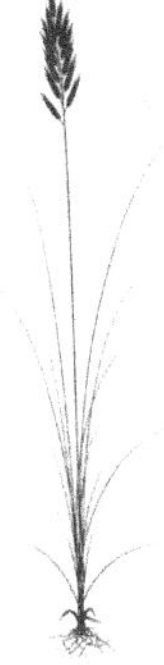

## Q



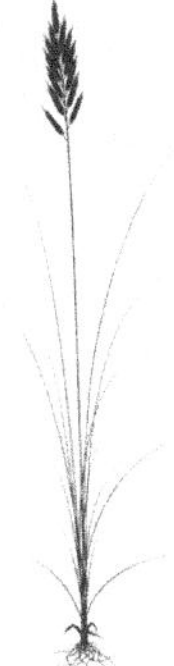

## R



## S



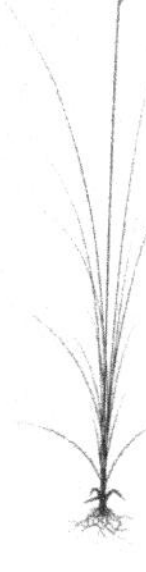

**T**



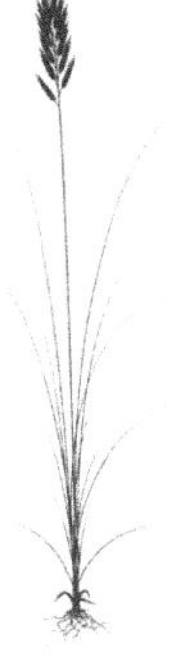

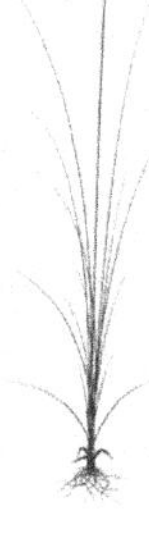

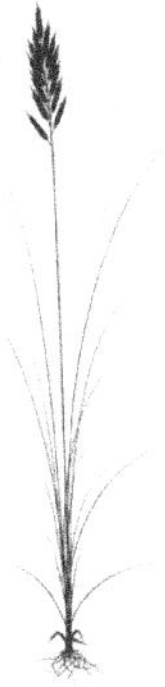

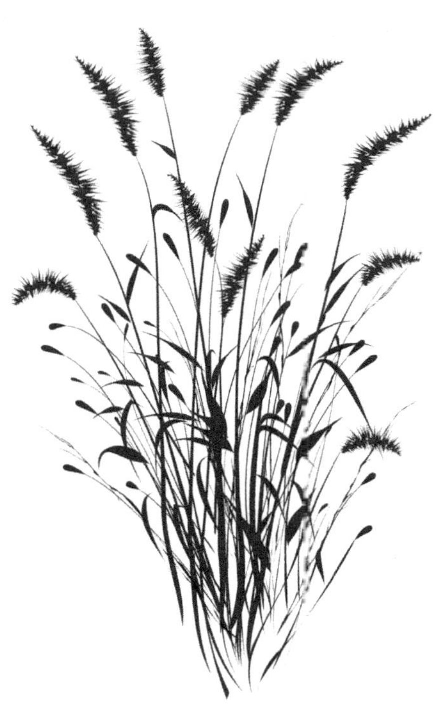

# Acknowledgements

Without the following people, institutions, and agencies this book could not have been completed. It is a project that has consumed a great deal of time over the last four years, not only for the author, but also for the many supporters who made it possible. First and foremost, I want to thank the Board of Directors, volunteers and supporters of the Robert Henri Museum and Art Gallery. Without their assistance this book would never have been written. They have supported me in so many ways with opinions, ideas, insights, and criticisms where necessary. They should celebrate the publication of this book as much as I do.

Marlene Geiger, the museum's president, read the many versions of the book over the last four years offering her commentary, asking questions and wanting to know the answers to the many questions I had raised. I have often thought of her as in some sense or another as the corporate memory of our museum since she has been involved with the institution almost since the beginning. She was kind enough to write the *Preface.*

Chuck Birgen, also a reader of many versions, and I had many conversations about the activities of John Cozad and his legal and financial affairs and controversies during his time in Nebraska. Those conversations led to important conclusions that have been made in this book. He read the book many times and regularly offered his views on various themes in the book.

Jan Anderson was a reader and editor and offered many suggestions during the project that make this a better book. Jan is one of our faithful volunteers and often gives tours to visitors, her dedication to the museum made me want to write this book so that our guides would have the most accurate information possible when they were giving tours. We are also grateful to Doris Hupf, who often volunteers with Jan and was also a reader of various versions of the manuscript and offered her views of the information presented. Our regular conversations about some aspect of the Cozad story always inspired me to continue forward. Both were named Heritage Heroes by History Nebraska in 2023.

The late Dr. Marilyn Peterson, a writer and published author herself, and exemplary teacher, read every version of the manuscript while she was alive and

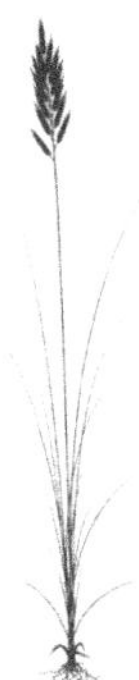

offered wonderful advice and exceptional encouragement because she understood the challenges of writing a book, trying to gather all the information together and attempting to make sure it is accurate. It was with sorrow as the book was coming to an end that she died and did not live to see the final product.

The late Jan Patterson and Caroline Gaudreault Valenzuela, both former directors of the Robert Henri Museum, compiled various materials over the years, many of which were used in this book. Jan knew many of the various Cozad and Henri researchers and kept copies of her letters and notes which proved to be very useful and, in some cases, allowed for eye-opening discoveries.

The work of the late Betty Menke, whose pioneering work in writing the first substantive history of the building and the Cozad family's time in Nebraska helped immeasurably in this effort. Her histories of the Pony Express Station, the Country School, District No. 86 and the New Hope Evangelical Country Church or the Christian Science Society Church are the only one of their kind. Karmen Morse, the former director the Cozad Chamber of Commerce, tracked down relevant materials relating to the incorporation of the city of Cozad. Marcus Kloepping, the mayor of Cozad also helped with finding information about the creation of Cozad.

Crystal Werger, Executive Director, Dawson County Historical Society Museum provided materials from the museum's files and insights as we met over the last three years and discussed what I was finding. I am grateful for her professional assistance and that of the members of her museum. Her quote graces the back cover of the book.

Laurie Yocom, the Director of the Wilson Public Library in Cozad pointed my way towards resources in her collection and elsewhere which was particularly helpful in the early months of the project. Coco Canas scanned many of the photographs of the restoration work at the museum that were used in the book and also photographed the old Robert and Julia Gatewood house. Jerry Penry, a surveyor and historian from Denton, Nebraska and the Deputy State Surveyor at the Nebraska State Surveyor's Office was kind enough to discuss with the author the 100th Meridian and the details of its importance and saved me much embarrassment with his insights.

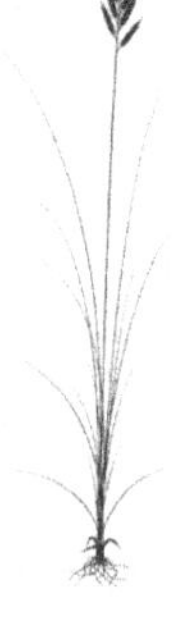

Dan and Kathy Sullivan researched newspaper archives online and made so many additions to this book project. They uncovered some of the most startling discoveries about Robert Henri and his connection to Nebraska even long after he left. They found articles about John Cozad during his time in Cincinnati. Most importantly, they gave me critical insights that encouraged me to change the basic layout of the book which now reads much better than it did when they first read it. The project had stalled when we first met to discuss it and their thoughts and insights are what brought the final product to fruition. They are the official muses of this book.

We are grateful to Jean Jacobson from the Museum of Nebraska Art in Kearney who provided important resources related to the Cozads and Robert Henri, along with Karissa Johnson, the Curator at MONA. Rachel DiEleuterio, the librarian and archivist of the Delaware Art Museum in Wilmington, Delaware provided a copy of Robert Gatewood's 1932 manuscript which proved to be so helpful. The Sheldon Museum of Art allowed access to the 1880 diary of Robert Cozad. Also, the Dawson County Clerk of the District Court and staff, Gayla Koerting, Curator of Government Records, History Nebraska gave the project assistance. The research of Bennard Perlman and William Homer proved to be invaluable and their books remain the standard for Henri research.

We are grateful to History Nebraska for allowing publication of photographs in their collection, Mormon Trail Center at Winter Quarters, and the Denver Public Library staff which provided insights into their collection and guidance to specific sources related to the Cozad real estate transactions. Mike Marshall and Judy Andres of the 100th Meridian Museum in Cozad searched for and provided photographs for the book along with historical information. Rex German wrote an article that discusses the shooting of Alf Pearson that provided insights into that tragic event that he shared with the author. The late Jane Kinnan provided information on the Riggs family and their involvement with the Emigrant Hotel. She was the great granddaughter of Joseph Riggs. Jake Whitney reviewed the 1880 diary transcription during his internship here in 2022. Jessica Sharkey, our museum's 2023 curator, offered words of encouragement

Andrew Cozad provided rare photographs of the Cozad family along with other genealogical materials. They are an important contribution to the larger history of the Cozad family and we are grateful for his assistance. Steve Holen provided important insights and research materials about the arrival of the early Indigenous peoples.

Laura Rody shared her extensive Cozad land records research with the author and those records laid out the details of John Cozad's land acquisitions in the Cozad area. My own research in the land records was made immeasurably easier because of her work and we are so grateful for her willingness to share her knowledge and her help in so many other ways. Her effort is a significant contribution to the early history of Cozad.

Others include my old friend Bob Beardslee from Red Cloud who offered me many insights during the writing of the book. I am still grateful to an old colleague, Rick Hibbard, who taught me how to design books, to lay them out and get them printed so many years ago.

The following readers of the final manuscript offered their corrections, insights, questions and opinions on a variety of topics. I am so grateful for their patience and hard work. They include Marlene Geiger, Chuck Birgen, Jan Anderson, Doris Hupf, Dan and Kathy Sullivan, Judith and Rick Reeve, William Lord,

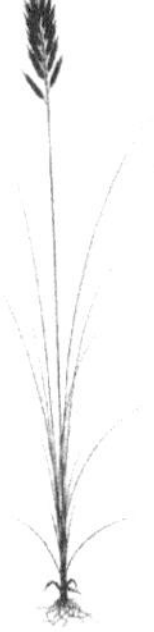

Sydney Green, Julie Geiger, Crystal Werger, Laura Rody, Jean Jacobson, Melanie Nutt, Craige LeClair and Janet LeClair. Thank you. Whatever editorial mistakes or errors of fact that remain are mine and mine alone!

The final legal paperwork and costs for the publication of the book was made possible because of the financial generosity of the following institutions and individuals:

The *Give Big Cozad* 2022 event sponsored by the Cozad Community Foundation, Tim and Laurie Yocom, Randy and Cindy Schneider, Tim Hansen, Mark and Jen McKeone, Waypoint Bank (Cozad), Marlene Geiger, Chuck Birgen, Cal Berreckman, Coco Canas, Robert and Melanie Nutt, Scott and Roz Trusdale, Claude and Karen Berreckman, the Cozad Ambassadors, Charlie and Suzie Block, Dan and Cindy Finnegan, Kevin and Vicki Gilbert, Security First Bank (Cozad), Brian Davis, Judy Eggleston, and Doug Keller. David Burkholder and the Kosman Foundation also made major financial contributions to the cause.

And finally, to those who remain unnamed or were mistakenly omitted from the acknowledgements, we thank you for your help in making this project possible.



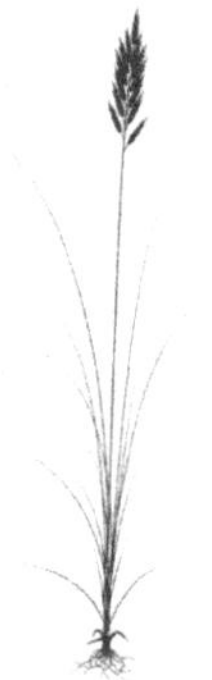

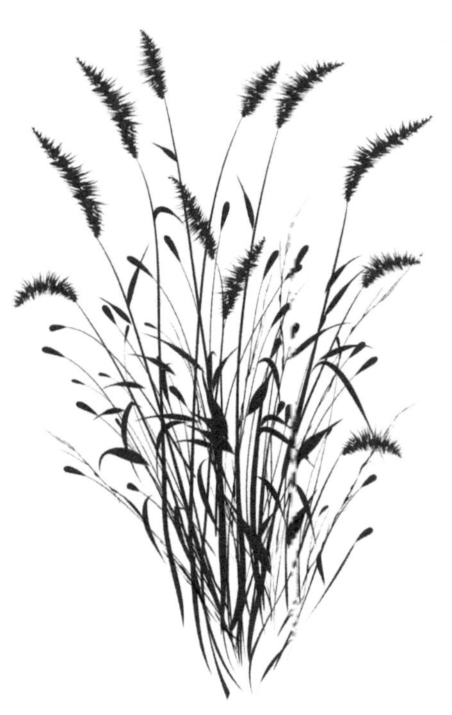

# About the Author

Peter Osborne is an independent historian, historic site administrator, writer and lecturer who has worked in the public history field for almost forty years. Born in Paterson, New Jersey, he holds a Bachelor of Arts degree from Rutgers, the State University of New Jersey. Osborne's professional interests include Theodore Roosevelt, Franklin and Eleanor Roosevelt, the state and national park systems, the Civilian Conservation Corps and the famed Corps of Discovery Expedition led by Captains Meriwether Lewis and William Clark.

Osborne has been published widely over the last two decades. He has written four books on the Depression era and and state parks - *We Can Take It! The Roosevelt Tree Army at High Point State Park 1933-1941, Images of America Series: High Point State Park and the Civilian Conservation Corps, Images of America: Hacklebarney and Voorhees State Parks (New Jersey)* and *Images of America: Promised Land State Park (Pennsylvania).*

Osborne co-authored with Mark Hendrickson and Jon Inners, *So Many Brave Men: A History of the Battle at Minisink Ford* which was considered for the George Washington Book Prize in 2011. Between 2012 and 2014 he wrote a comprehensive two-volume, twelve-hundred-page history of the state parks at Washington Crossing along the Delaware River. They were commissioned by William Farkas, president of Yardley Press of Yardley, Pennsylvania and entitled *Where Washington Once Led: A History of New Jersey's Washington Crossing State Park* and *No Spot in This Far Land Is More Immortalized: A History of Pennsylvania's Washington Crossing Historic Park.* They will be an important resource for park historians and students of the famed Christmas Crossing of 1776 for many years to come. In 2017 they were the recipient of the *Ann Hawkes Hutton Park Ambassador Award.*

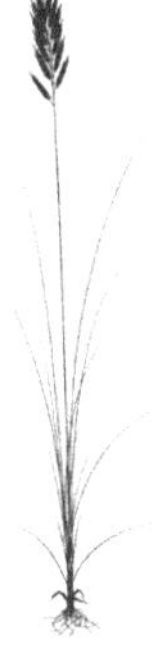

In early 2016, he finished writing the first institutional history of the Commonwealth of Pennsylvania's official railroad museum. The book is entitled *The Trains of Our Memory: A History of the Railroad Museum of Pennsylvania 1965-2015.* Osborne then completed a two-volume history of the Five Mile Woods Preserve in Lower Makefield Township, Pennsylvania in 2017. The books are en-

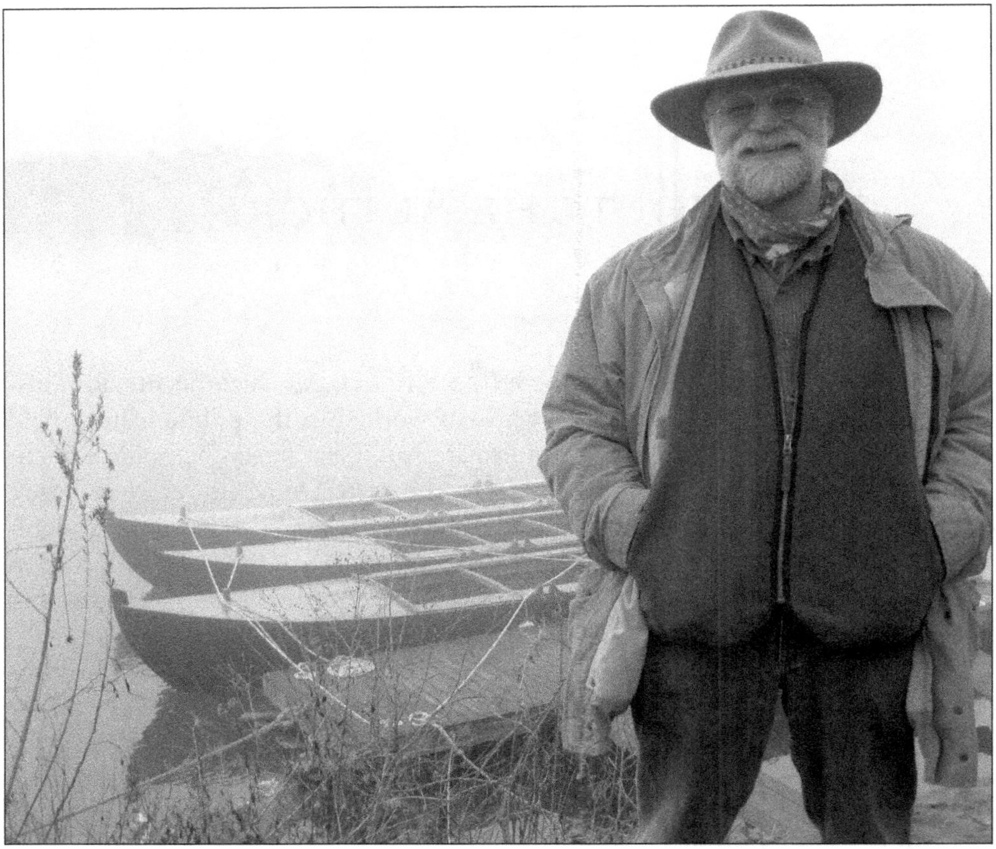

*Contributed Photograph*

*The author at the McKonkey's Ferry landing at Washington Crossing Historic Park at Washington Crossing, Pennsylvania.*

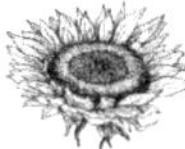

titled *The Five Mile Woods Preserve: A History* and *Images of the Five Mile Woods Preserve* and were commissioned by Preserve founder Donald Formigli.

Osborne was the Executive Director of the Minisink Valley Historical Society in Port Jervis, New York, from 1981-2009 and the Port Jervis City Historian from 1989-2003. During his directorship at the Society, he was responsible for the Society's Fort Decker Museum of History, and the interpretation of its long and eventful history which included the fort's destruction during British Indian Department Captain Joseph Brant's raid into the Minisink region in 1779. Osborne then served as the Curator of Education and Special Events at the Red Mill Museum Village in Clinton, New Jersey from 2010-11. In 2011 he began a six-year stint as a full-time writer and independent historian. Since 2018 he has served as the Executive Director of the Robert Henri Museum and Art Gallery in

Cozad, Nebraska and is particularly interested in the Nebraska legacy of Henri. The museum owns the largest collection of Henri's paintings and sketches or those attributed to him on display in the country.

During his long career, he served on the board of directors of the Depot Preservation Society, Port Jervis Centennial Committee, Orange County Historical Society as its Recording Secretary, the Grey Towers Heritage Association as Treasurer, the Delaware and Hudson Transportation Heritage Council as Treasurer, the Upper Delaware Scenic Byway's original incorporator and Treasurer, and as the Unitarian-Universalist Fellowship of Sussex County, New Jersey's webmaster. More recently he has served on the Cozad 150 committee that celebrated the Sesquicentennial of the community's founding.

He lives in Red Cloud, Nebraska and owns the Wild Horse Creek Company. The mission of his company is to provide exciting journeys of discovery into our nation's history through presentations, lectures, demonstrations, motor coach tours and publications. The Wild Horse Creek Company (formerly the Pienpack Company) has been providing programs to civic, historical, fraternal, church groups, seminars, meetings, Elderhostel, and Road Scholar programs for forty years.

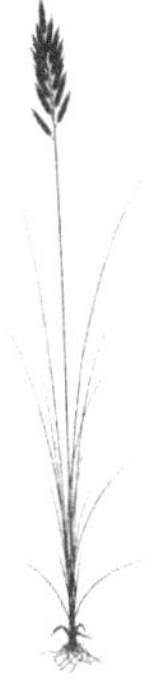

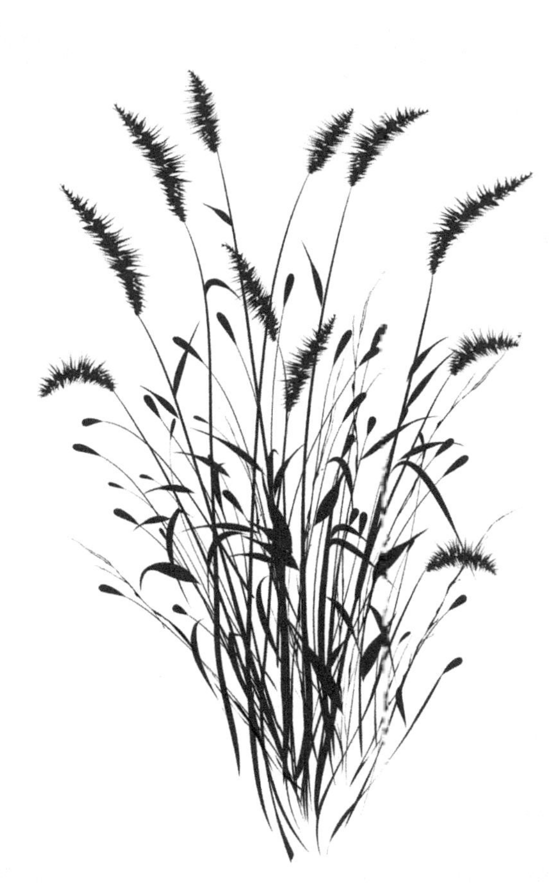

# Colophon

The manuscript was prepared in Microsoft Word and transferred into Adobe InDesign CS4 for production. The book block was typeset in Adobe Garamond Pro. The cover was set in Trajan Pro and Adobe Garamond Pro. The paper is White 50lb. The paperback cover is four-color with a gloss film lamination, and perfect-bound. The cover and the book's interior design were created by Peter Osborne and the Wild Horse Creek Company. The book was then converted into a PDF and printed in the United States by Lightning Source, Inc. located in La Vergne, Tennessee. It was originally published by the Robert Henri Museum and Art Gallery in Cozad, Nebraska. The book is available for purchase from the Robert Henri Museum and Art Gallery, local and regional bookstores, and major online retailers including Barnes and Noble and Amazon.

The picture used for the front cover was taken of Cozad, Nebraska in 1904 by the well-known Custer County photographer Solomon Butcher. It was taken long after the Cozads left the town they had established. At the center of the picture is the former Bee Hive General Store, which was owned by Julia Gatewood. It was here on the front porch where John Cozad shot Alf Pearson during their argument in 1882. There are few, if any, surviving photographs of Cozad when the Cozad family lived there from 1873-1884. The photograph is from the collection of History Nebraska in Lincoln, Nebraska (*Catalog No. nbhips 13091*) but accessed from the Library of Congress collection.

The photograph of Robert Henri on the back cover was taken circa 1900 and comes the Library of Congress in Washington, D.C. (*Control Number 2006676256*). The photograph of the author is a contributed image taken at the Willa Cather Memorial Prairie in Red Cloud, Nebraska.

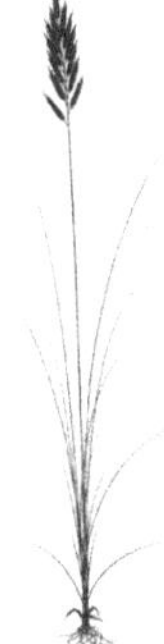

# Contact Information

If the reader has additional historical materials or items of interest related to the history of the John J. Cozad family, the Hendee Hotel or Robert Henry Cozad's (Robert Henri) time in Ohio, Nebraska, and Colorado, please feel free to contact the museum at:


Robert Henri Museum and Art Gallery
218 East 8th Street, PO Box 355, Cozad, Nebraska 69130
*Phone:* 308-784-4154, *E-mail:* rhenri@cozadtel.net
*Web Page:* www.roberthenrimuseum.org


*All the proceeds from the sales of this book go towards furthering the mission and programs of the Robert Henri Museum and Art Gallery.*

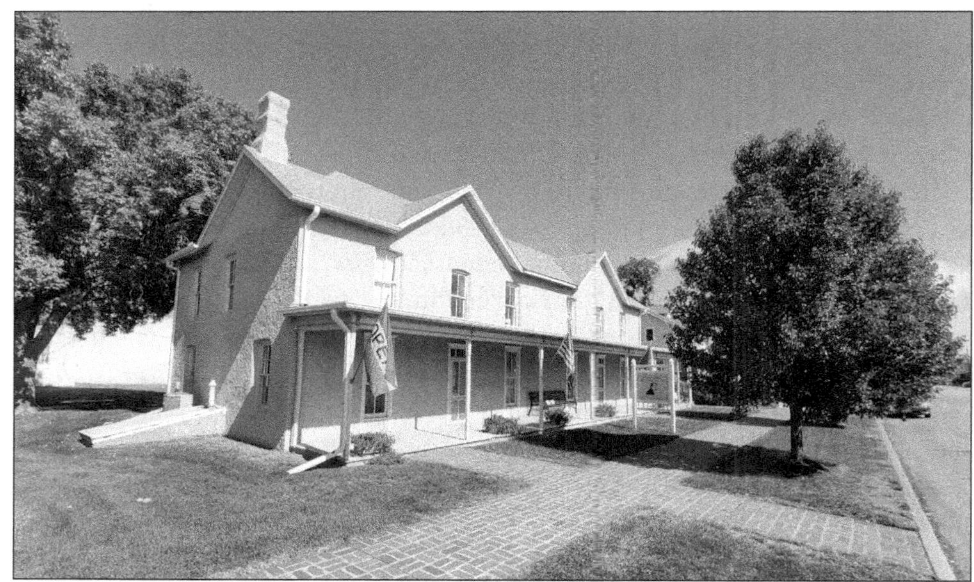

*Courtesy Chuck Birgen*

*Robert Henri Museum and Art Gallery*
*2023*

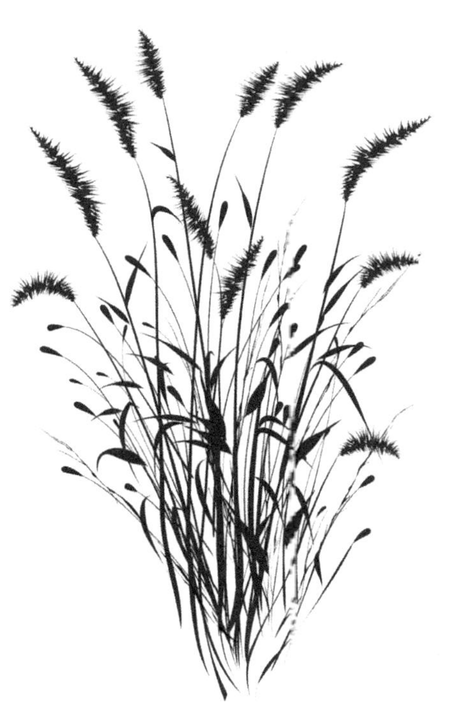

# What Others Have Written About Peter Osborne's Books

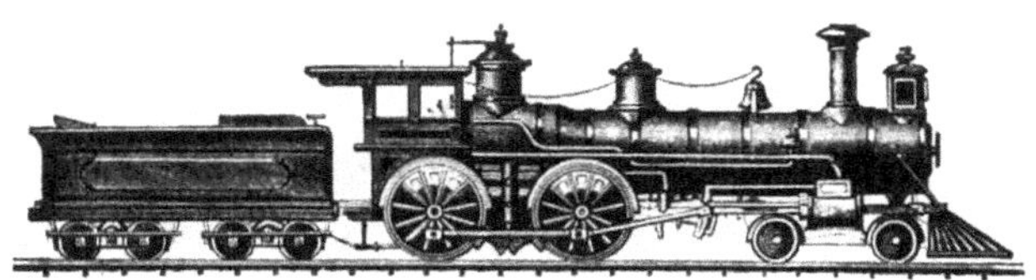

The Trains of Our Memory:
A History of the Railroad Museum of Pennsylvania 1965-2015

An institutional history might seem like dull reading, but Peter Osborne has written an easy-to-digest account of the first 50 years of the Railroad Museum of Pennsylvania . . . Perhaps the best way to convey the scope of the book is to put it in terms of page counts: 16 pages of front matter, nearly 400 pages of history, 82 pages of essays by principals in the story, 39 pages of endnotes, 18 pages of index listings, and 16 pages of bibliography . . . This book is a magnum opus. All museums, especially railroad museums, should be so fortunate to have such an encyclopedic and exhaustive record of their mission and work.

*Dan Cupper*
*Deputy Editor, Railroad History magazine*

---

Where Washington Once Led:
A History of New Jersey's Washington Crossing State Park

The Committee was certainly impressed with the scholarship and exhaustive effort that went into *Where Washington Once Led.* One of our Committee members commented that this was indeed the 'Bible of Washington Crossing Park' and we all agreed. The topographical nature of the history was outstanding and the detail was immense, which will be a huge boon for future researchers. The maps and illustrations are wonderful and many Committee members commented that other state parks cry out for such professional and similar coverage.

*New Jersey Studies Academic Alliance - Author Awards Committee*

Sometimes people get the impression of history being stagnant and dull. Washington Crossing State Park, however, is a dynamic place, with a dynamic history reflecting changes in how we relate to our past that can be just as instructive and entertaining as the events it memorializes. It was especially interesting to read the personal accounts of some of the superintendents as well as Osborne's own observations in a chapter called *A Year in the Life of the Park*. Osborne has done a wonderful job bringing that long story to life with this comprehensive history.

*GSL Reviews, GardenStateLegacy.com, Issue 21, September 2013 (New Jersey)*

I think most people would readily agree that setting aside areas of natural beauty such as the National Parks so that we as well as future generations may enjoy them is a national priority. Far fewer, unfortunately, would agree that historical areas and buildings should be preserved and honored. These places are our *landmarks* where we tell our American story to our own generation and preserve it for generations to come. This book is about the Washington Crossing Park in New Jersey which honors one of the pivotal points in the American Revolution - Washington's surprise attack on the Hessians at Trenton on December 26, 1776. This book is not about the attack itself. You can read about that in one of my all-time favorite history books - *Washington's Crossing* by David Hackett Fischer.

This book is about how the park came to be. The story is full of quirks, characters and odd turns-of-events. It has been superbly researched and written by Peter Osborne who has a number of other historical publications to his credit. It is a lesson for all of us about how to guard the places and buildings which earlier generations have made historic by their actions. For this reason alone, the book is worth the time to read.

Perhaps, more importantly, it is also the story about how the park evolved and was shaped by succeeding generations. A historical park is nothing if it does not tell its story afresh and invite people to share its story while enjoying the site which has been set aside. Peter captures the ongoing history of this park which continues to tell its story and involve people from far and near. *Where Washington Once Led*, we must now lead. This book will help us do it.

*Dogearred Bookmarker*
*Review on Amazon.com*

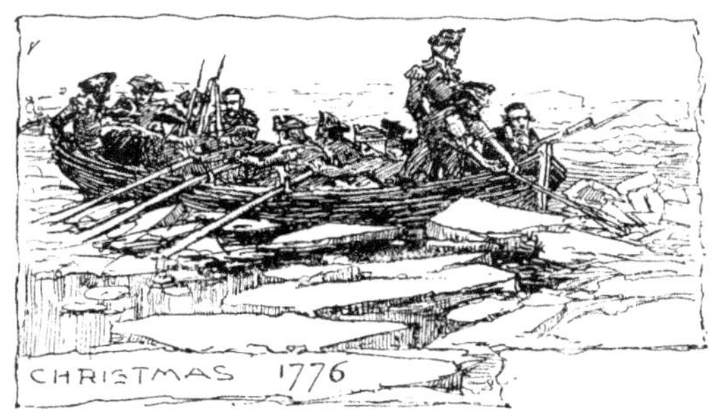


No Spot in this Far Land is More Immortalized
A History of Pennsylvania's Washington Crossing Historic Park

On Christmas night in 1776, George Washington and 2,400 men crossed the icy Delaware River into Trenton and then later Princeton, where they went on to win decisive victories that changed the course of the Revolutionary War. But it wasn't until 1895 that efforts to memorialize the event and place began. Twenty-two years later, in 1917, a park commission was created, and in 1921 the group formally dedicated Washington Crossing Park to pay tribute to the famed crossing.

Yet in the nearly one hundred years that (the) Washington Crossing (parks), both in New Jersey and in Pennsylvania, existed, perhaps no in-depth research has been done on the scale of what writer and historian Peter Osborne has accomplished. Osborne, who has a degree in American history, this past July published *No Spot In This Far Land Is More Immortalized: A History of Washington Crossing Historic Park,* which focuses on Pennsylvania's park, after publishing *Where Washington Once Led: A History of New Jersey's Washington Crossing State Park*, which focuses on New Jersey, in December 2012. Both books were sponsored by Yardley Press.

Combined, the books total more than twelve hundred pages and reveal how park administrators overcame many challenges to organize ideas, raise funds and develop the public areas.

*Times of Trenton (New Jersey)*

I bought this book for my son-in-law's birthday . . . he and my daughter just love the Washington Crossing area . . . so much so they were married there and every year they go to dinner at the Washington Crossing Inn . . . and delight in every minute of it . . . So, I held my breath . . . but Chuck's smile says it all!

*TS*
*Review on Amazon.com*

www.ingramcontent.com/pod-product-compliance
Lightning Source LLC
LaVergne TN
LVHW061218100826
845148LV00004B/787

*9798218100193*